Movement Behavior
and
Motor Learning

Health Education,
Physical Education,
and Recreation Series

Ruth Abernathy, Ph.D., Editorial Adviser

Chairman, Department for Women,
School of Physical and Health Education
University of Washington, Seattle, Washington 98105

Movement Behavior and Motor Learning

Third Edition

Bryant J. Cratty, Ed.D.

Professor and Director,
Perceptual-Motor Learning Laboratory
Department of Kinesiology
University of California
Los Angeles, California

Lea & Febiger • 1973 • Philadelphia

Library of Congress Cataloging in Publication Data

Cratty, Bryant J
    Movement behavior and motor learning.

    (Health education, physical education, and recrea-
tion series)
    Bibliography: p.
    1. Movement, Psychology of. 2. Motor learning.
I. Title.

BF295.C7 1973   152.3   73-1938

    ISBN 0-8121-0425-0

Library of Congress Catalog Card Number: 73-1938

Published in Great Britain by Henry Kimpton Publishers, London

Printed in the United States of America

This book is
dedicated to DARREN

PREFACE

Since the writing of the second edition in 1967, the number of courses dealing with motor learning and associated subjects have continued to proliferate on the campuses of American universities and colleges. Most departments of physical education presently have at least one course dealing with the type of subject matter contained in this text; numerous curricula have more than one offering, including courses such as Motor Learning, Psychology of Physical Activity, and Motor Development, in their catalogues.

Also during the past five years, many younger scholars in this country, in Canada, and in other parts of the world have increased their research activity. This interest has often resulted in conferences. The one at Iowa in 1969 is only one example. The Canadians have had "motor learning" conferences yearly. This same trend is evidenced at the international level. A conference on the psychology of sport was held in Washington in 1968; and a second was held in Madrid in 1973. Their competencies have produced new information of both a theoretical and an applied nature.

It is for these reasons that the third edition was written. New chapters dealing with perceptual-motor activities, with retention, and with individual differences appear in the present text, and the other chapters have undergone considerable revision. I have attempted to write in smoother, clearer language than that found in the earlier editions.

An enormous amount of available information was screened prior to this revision, and for this reason the content of this third edition is selective, rather than being an exhaustive summary of all available data. Although the total number of references contained in the bibliography have proliferated, some of the previous references were eliminated. In an effort to make it more lucid a considerable number of illustrations have been added to the text. The chapter on motor development was eliminated, primarily because of the increasing availability of other texts dealing more thoroughly with this aspect of human motor behavior.

The information in this edition has been arranged within the following format. The second chapter in the introductory section deals with a historical description of attempts to evaluate movement attributes. Section II contains five chapters exploring the manner in which perceptual processes interact with, and at times influence, movement attributes and motor learning. The chapters include perceptual-motor relationships, kinesthesis, visual-space perception, and the influence of instructions upon motor performance and learning.

Section III covers data concerned with motor performance and learning. Following Chapter 8, an overview of the neurological foundations of voluntary movement, other chapters cover "personal equations" in movement, ability traits, as well as the manner in which movement behaviors contribute to human communication.

Performance modifiers of various types are covered in Section IV. The chapters in this section include "motivation," "anxiety, stress, and tension," as well as "social motives" and "individual differences." In the latter chapter is information concerning how body-build, maturation, intelligence and personality traits interact with movement capacities of various kinds.

Motor learning is given extensive treatment in Section V. Information dealing with the neurological and biochemical bases of motor learning and retention and the influence of various practice factors are contained in this section. Other chapters cover subjects such as retention and transfer of training. The text concludes with a summarizing chapter.

I hope that the content serves both undergraduate and graduate students, for ideas are offered which, it is hoped, will not always placate, but will at times even stimulate them. For the fledgling researcher, numerous questions are posed, which hopefully will lead him to the discovery of valid answers.

An industrious office staff has worked many hours on the manuscript. Thus, I would like to thank Brian Tash and Donna Hokoda for their efforts. I hope that the readers will find their efforts, as well as mine, worthwhile.

BRYANT J. CRATTY

Los Angeles, California

CONTENTS

Section II. Perception

CHAPTER

CHAPTER

I
INTRODUCTION

1
INTRODUCTION

Movement is a fundamental dimension of human behavior. Man manipulates his environment through contractions of large muscles, as internal smooth muscle acts to integrate and nourish these observable movements. Primitive man survived through the appropriate application of strong, forceful acts, whereas modern man has molded fine movements into vehicles for oral and written expression. Manual skill enables some to earn their livelihoods, and accurate movements of large muscles allow others to express themselves in sports and games. The analysis of movement characteristics is a means of assessing maturation and is an important method of studying the total personality.

Early theorists postulated that all human behavior involves movement. It was contended that immobile thought is accompanied by unobservable but measurable movements of the vocal apparatus and that these small movements are chained together as we think, remember, and learn. Although later writers seemed to place "thinking" and "moving" into two behavioral niches, more recent scientific findings tend to make it difficult to isolate human functions into two discrete categories: one characterized by motionless thought, the other by observable movement. Instead, human behavior appears to lie on a continuum from functions that seem largely "motor" to those that involve no observable movements.

In the past century, growing scientific interest has been evidenced by an increasing number of studies devoted to behavior located near the "movement" end of this continuum. Contemporary research has often focused on man's capacity to move with force, speed, and accuracy and the methods by which complex skills are learned. Some investigations have been concerned with athletic performance or with the re-education of the handicapped in the basic functions of walking and talking. Other research has dealt with proficiency in industrial skills or with the integration of man and machine. Whatever the purposes of these investigations, however, knowledge about purposeful human movement more and more has come to occupy the time and thought of the anthropologist, the physiologist, the psychologist, the engineer, and the educator.

Motor Behavior as Viewed
by the Anatomist-Physiologist

The physiologist considers man as an interrelated group of functioning anatomical systems. Behavior is integrated by the nervous system nourished by the digestive system, while growth is controlled and regulated by the endocrine glands. Observable movement is viewed as a function of muscle contraction acting as a system of levers and pulleys formed by bone, tendon, and ligament. Efficient motor functioning is usually said to depend on tissue adaptations based on use and the body's ability to utilize nutrients and to dispel the waste products of muscular work.

A molecular rather than a molar approach is taken by the physiologist. Man is assumed to react to discrete kinds of internal and external stimuli as they affect specialized sensory end-organs. Explanation of the many behavioral variations of persons possessing relatively similar anatomical equipment is left to the psychologist.

While the physiologist studies human performance rather mechanistically, the learning process is virtually ignored. Neurophysiologists are only beginning to identify changes taking place within the nervous system during the learning process. Nerve impulses have been traced as they are received from the environment by the sense organs, areas of the brain receiving these impulses have been mapped, and the pathways carrying messages to the muscles have been isolated. Anatomical changes accompanying modifications of behavior brought about through practice, however, have yet to be clearly identified.

The Psychologist Studies Motor
Learning and Motor Performance

The psychologists regard their discipline as the science of behavior. Controlled experiments are carried out, theories are formed, and an attempt is made to control or predict total action patterns. Throughout the history of experimental psychology, there has been extensive study of the motor behavior of animal subjects. Human skill has come in for somewhat less examination, but studies in this more limited area are becoming more prevalent.

During the past 20 years, in particular, there has been renewed interest in the performance of humans in various movement tasks. Impetus has been given to the study of skill by several conditions: the performance requirements of pilots during World War II, the need to understand the functioning of complex man-machine systems in industry and in the military, and the evolvement of theoretical statements that purport to account for the complexity and variability of the perceptual-motor behavior of humans.

The movements of animals have been studied for several reasons, among them: (1) the inheritance and environmental influences on animal behavior are easily controlled, and (2) their nervous systems are simpler than man's, thus animal reactions are generally more predictable in the experimental situation. Men engage in complex verbal symbolism to form internal thoughts, whereas mice seem merely to move through the maze to food.

Progressive changes of behavior brought about through practice, termed "learning," have been the subject for extensive experimentation. Learning has been studied as a function of the type of sensory stimuli available or the meanings individuals attach to their learning situation. Learning concepts are usually illustrated with fluctuations in measures of performance, which take the form of "learning curves." Psychologists differ on two main points when discussing the learning process: (1) the nature of sensory factors that influence an organism's response, and (2) rewards (reinforcements) in a situation that cause some patterns of behavior to become stereotyped and others to be discarded.

Earlier investigators concluded that learning and human performance are based on reactions to discrete sensory stimuli and that learning takes place as bonds are strengthened between stimuli and the organism's responses. Other theorists contended that environmental stimuli are organized into patterns and that subsequent performance is based on the meaning or the significance attached to the total field of experience.

One school of thought holds that, in order for an act to be learned, some type of reward has to be present in the learning situation, although this may be only relief of an individual's "tension-level." Others feel that learning may occur merely because stimuli and response occur at the same time.

Some learning theories deal extensively with the *motor performance* of various organisms, indeed, many are based on research involving movement behavior. Other theories merely make reference to the "type" of learning called "motor learning," and still others virtually ignore the means by which skilled movements are acquired and focus primarily on intellectual-perceptual behavior.

More recent learning theories compare man's performance to that of the electronic computer. Whereas several years ago computers were considered so complex as to be almost human, several contemporary theories imply that man is so complex that he is nearly machine-like! Thus, computer terms such as "memory drum," "input-output," "channel capacity," and the like are used within some contemporary theoretical frameworks.

Learning theories are concerned with the explanation of several levels of behavior. Some attempt to elucidate all the possible modifications of human functioning, others outline the general nature of the acquisition of complex tasks, and others are concerned with specific types of learning: "reasoning," "motor learning," "verbal learning," and the like.

The psychologist has not ignored the motor performance and learning of healthy human beings, despite the many animal experiments reported in the literature. Generally utilizing fine motor skills, he has studied the influence of various types of practice and the role of differing sensory stimulation on the learning process. In an effort to clarify concepts pertinent to the central focus of the text, extensive reference has been made to psychological research in motor skills and motor learning, to investigations concerned with the perceptual process, and to those elucidating various learning theories in the chapters that follow.

The Engineer
Studies Motor Performance

In the past 50 years, the engineer has begun to study the capacities of men to learn and perform motor skills. Studies have usually been of an applied rather than of a basic nature and have involved manual-manipulative skills needed to perform various industrial tasks effectively.

The industrial engineer has often filmed time-motion studies by which components of manipulative performance have been categorized. This scientist has generally been concerned with practical problems and has studied movements requiring a relatively small amount of space and minimal amounts of force.

More recently a "new breed" of engineer has come to the forefront to study man's capacity to learn complex movements. The human factors specialist, part life scientist and part engineer, has begun to explore human performance in complex man-machine systems. The human factors specialist generally studies perceptual-motor performance, reactions under various conditions of stress, and the influence of types of sensory stimuli on decision-making. The integration of man to "machines" as simple as the hammer and the screwdriver has been reported in articles next to those that treat human functioning in complex air-defense warning systems. The human factors engineer utilizes traditional psychological and physiological research, while devising unique evaluative techniques to solve new problems.

Others Consider Motor Behavior

Man's capacity to move with accuracy has not been the exclusive concern of the engineer, psychologist, physiologist, and anthropologist. Numerous other disciplines have been interested in the movement behavior of human beings.

The writings of historians often relate to the influence of historical trends on the work and play movements of people. The emphasis on vigorous developmental activities to harden the male youth of the European nations during the past 300 years probably resulted from the pressures of war, rather than from more subtle factors. The dictator's use of massed physical activities to mold the minds of men into united action has been documented in historical works.

The medical profession has also been concerned with the gross movements involved in locomotion, as well as with manual skills. Psychiatrists, physical therapists, and prosthetics specialists are constantly studying methods of improving the movement capacities of the atypical. Re-education of the handicapped and the influence of movement therapy on the mentally retarded and emotionally disturbed have been the subjects of their investigations.

The psychologist has helped the musician to explore the nature of skills necessary to play various instruments. The serial-like buildup of responses, from note-to-chord-to-phrase, has been investigated.

Other members of the performing arts have also evidenced interest in specific aspects of motor performance. Dance specialists have studied the nature of creative movements. Actors have spent a considerable amount of time attempting to understand the manner by which one may best express meaning and emotions through facial and bodily movements.

The Educator and Motor Skill

Although the educator would seem to be mainly concerned with behavior of an intellectual nature, many have been interested in various aspects of motor learning. Many of these skills involve men's attempts to communicate with one another. The transmission of information verbally, through writing, and with various devices such as the typewriter involves motor performance. The influence of various methods of teaching handwriting has also been studied.

During recent years, educators have become interested in what might be termed "the clumsy child syndrome," wherein a child is marked by a group of symptoms that make it difficult for him to achieve even moderate status at play. Throughout the country many schools have instituted programs to correct motor problems in elementary and secondary school-age children.

Child development specialists in education have studied various motor indices of human maturation. Longitudinal studies have attempted to categorize the progressive acquisition of learned movements noted as children mature and to identify normal stages in motor development.

The educational psychologist has spent a considerable amount of time investigating the learning process as it takes place in the classroom. Much of his work has been concerned with various motor tasks. One of the principles underlying some of the recently developed teaching-learning machines involves a motor act, pressing the correct button.

Thus educators have been concerned with small as well as large movements. The child's facility in learning to walk, to talk, to write, and to move efficiently has been the subject of extensive educational research.

And What then of
the Physical Educator?

The questions then arise: With what body of knowledge should the physical educator be concerned? What should be the subject of his basic research? What kinds of understandings should prospective teachers gain? The therapist studies gross human movement; the engineer, manual skill; the physiologist, functions underlying motor performance; while the psychologist studies motor performance and learning from several standpoints. What, then, is the physical educator's unique area of concentration?

Should man's movement behavior be viewed microscopically, as by the anatomist, or should a macroscopic or molar approach be taken? Should prospective physical education teachers be interested in the teaching of sports, dance, and individual activities as ends in themselves, or should they take a more basic approach? And if so, where shall one look for knowledge—to the psychologist, the physiologist, or the therapist? Or should principles that are unique to the field of physical education be derived?

Although helpful in the past, the traditional approach of the kinesiologist no longer seems to offer a complete explanation of variations in human movement. Describing man as a system of bony levers moved by muscles and undergirded by various physiological systems seems to place little emphasis on individual performance differences.

School administrators want to know *what* the physical educators are doing and *why* and *how* they propose to do it. Members of academic disciplines on the university campus attempt to ascertain whether research being performed by physical education faculties can be conducted better by some other life scientist. Researchers from other fields sometimes wonder aloud whether physical educators are producing *basic* research, and if so, within what areas of human behavior?

The physical educator has often been hard pressed to provide meaningful responses to these queries. However, it appears that his professional respectability may be based on the adequacy of his answers and on the quality of the subsequent performance to which his responses will hopefully commit him. It is thus hoped that the statements that follow will help to clarify the central focus of the text, and may also provide some basic operating principles for the professional worker in the school and for the researcher in the laboratory.

1. Physical educators should be concerned mainly with that aspect of

human behavior characterized by observable, purposeful, voluntary movement, movements that are task-centered and those that are reasonably complex.

2. Physical educators generally are called on to teach healthy human beings, and thus should be familiar with all aspects of movement behavior that these individuals evidence. However, of main concern should be movements that need relatively large amounts of space and involve large skeletal muscles.

3. Movement behavior is worthy of investigation as a unit in itself and does not necessarily need to be related to various physiological-anatomical processes which may accompany it. A comprehensive approach should be taken to the study of motor performance and learning. Study should be made of motor tasks measurable not solely in units of strength but also in terms of spatial accuracy.

4. Concern should be directed toward the rather permanent change of movement behavior brought about through practice, *"motor learning."* Interest should be generated in variations of practice and the influence of various factors on learning proficiency.

5. One should not ignore but, on the contrary, utilize to best advantage research in psychology, medicine, physiology, and other disciplines to aid in gaining a thorough understanding of gross motor performance and learning.

Words and Definitions

In the previous pages numerous terms that need defining have been presented. Such terms as *motor behavior, movement behavior, motor learning, motor skill, movement skill,* and *motor performance* require reasonably precise explanations to provide a common basis of understanding of the concepts that follow. Many of the terms defy simple definition; clarification depends on critical examination of the experimental evidence and of various theoretical assumptions underlying learning. Words, however, stand for ideas. We are able to think with more clarity as our grasp of terms is expanded. It is thus one of the purposes of this book to expand the reader's vocabulary by presenting words that represent concepts, verbal tools with which more thorough understandings may be possible.

Movement Behavior. Movement behavior refers to overt movements of the skeletal muscles. The term *behavior* places the definition more specifically than does the word *movement;* thus movement behavior is *observable* movement of the body, excluding such functions as visceral changes, conduction of nerve impulses, and circulation of body fluids. Movement behavior is *observable* and not simply *recordable* movement, for most internal fluctuations are measurable by various devices.

Movement behavior is a general term and refers to movements that may be termed "skilled performance," those that indicate emotion or tension and others that seem purposeless and random. Reflex actions, movements that are elicited in reaction to some stimuli without conscious volition on the part of the individual, may also be considered a facet of movement behavior.

Although acts that involve the execution and completion of an identifiable task may be considered a form of movement behavior, it is believed that these require a more precise definition. The terms *movement behavior* and *motor behavior* are used interchangeably throughout the text.

Motor Performance. Motor performance is a relatively short-term aspect of movement behavior marked by movement oriented toward the execution of an identifiable task. Inherent in the definition is the assumption that an observer can detect, identify, or otherwise discover the goal or purpose of another's movement. Motor performance is thus considered to be goal-centered, purposeful, measurable, observable movement behavior of relatively short duration.

Although it might be argued that all movement involves some physiological goal, that an individual needs to move to live or that perhaps the psychiatrist or psychologist is able to give meaning to the most random of movements, it is believed that the definition presented is valid.

Motor performance has numerous dimensions usually identified through statistical analysis, as well as through subjective observation. Studies reported in the physical education literature have generally regarded motor performance as manifestation of the contractile strength of muscle tissue. A more comprehensive approach to the study of motor performance will be taken in these pages. Perception, motivation, and maturation, as well as other behavioral and environment factors, will be analyzed in an attempt to gain deeper understanding.

Motor Skill. Motor skill may be termed' "reasonably complex motor performance." While the phrase "reasonably complex" is of course subjective and somewhat vague, in the definition reference must usually be made to the nature of the task and the status of the learner. For example, an adult can hardly be said to be skilled because he is able to walk or to run; whereas walking is an extremely skilled act to an eight-month-old child.

The term *skill* denotes that some learning has taken place and that a smoothing or an integration of behavior has resulted. Extraneous movements have been omitted, and the performance is executed with increasing speed and accuracy, a decrease in errors, or perhaps the ability to apply greater force. A skilled act has to be learned. It is not one that can be termed *instinctive* or *reflexive* or one in which successful performance is achieved in a single trial.

Motor Learning. Motor learning may be thought of as the rather *per-*

manent change in motor performance brought about through practice and excludes changes due to maturation, drugs, or nutrients. The concept of learning involves two main inferences: (1) that a rather permanent change in behavior, verifiable by comparing performance trials separated in time, has occurred, and (2) that the change has been caused by practice.

"That learning takes place through practice" on the first inspection appears to be a simple concept. However, members of the psychological community have been occupied for the past 100 years examining the nature and conditions of practice and precisely how practice produces permanent behavioral changes.

At times the terms *learning* and *performance* have been used interchangeably in the literature. *Performance,* however, is immediate and short-term in nature and subject to certain factors that fail to influence the long-term changes that take place during the learning process. Learning, however, must often be studied indirectly by inspecting measures of performance.

Studies investigating the effects of massing and distributing motor practice on learning help to clarify the distinction between learning and performance. With the massing of performance trials, little improvement often results; however, with the introduction of rest periods a marked increase in performance often is elicited. This further illustrates the rather temporary state suggested by the term "performance," implying that "learning" is a more subtle concept that, at times, may best be facilitated when there is no performance!

Motor learning, therefore, may also be thought of as the *potential* to engage in an efficient movement, rather than solely as a measure of performance fluctuations recorded. The complexities of various learning concepts as they apply to the acquisition of motor skills are dealt with in Chapters 17, 18, and 19.

Motor Fitness. Motor fitness refers to individual *capacity* to perform a motor task. It is the potential one has to perform a motor skill and, as we shall see later, may be somewhat specific. An individual must be declared fit to perform a particular task measured by certain kinds of units in a defined situation.

Whereas most research in motor fitness has been based on measures of strength and endurance, the concept as defined here includes other performance dimensions: capacity to utilize space effectively in the accurate performance of a task, the application of speed, and the effective combination of various factors when performing a skilled act.

Motor Educability. While *motor fitness* refers to capacity to *perform, motor educability* may be defined as the capacity to *learn.* Generally, the research has attempted to identify a general educability factor based on the relationship between amounts of improvement evidenced as an individual attempts to learn several tasks. The term implies that individuals may be found whose performance may be easily molded and who may easily learn (be taught) several kinds of motor skills. The term *motor educability* is related to such concepts as "coordination" and "general athletic ability."

Fine Motor Skill and Gross Motor Skill. Dichotomous classification of these terms has been inferred by much of the previous discussion. However, a rigid categorization of skills as either "fine" or "gross" is difficult to make. Rather, it is believed that skills may be placed on a continuum, from those that may be considered "gross" to those that may be termed "fine." To those movement performances near the "fine" end of the continuum the term *manual* (or *manipulative*) *skill* has usually been applied.

Classification of motor tasks into various portions of this continuum may be made with reference to the size of muscle involved, the amount of force applied, or the magnitude of space in which the movement is carried out. Physical educators generally refer to "big" muscle activity, indicating a preference for a cataloging system based on the muscle or force concept. Industrial psychologists, on the other hand, have devised various classifications based on function, the spatial dimensions of the task, and/or the part of the body involved in the movement.

Although a more detailed discussion of the relationship between various fine and gross motor skills is presented in Chapter 11, it should be emphasized that the main concern in this text is with performance classified near the "gross" end of the continuum. Generalizations from studies of fine motor skills are identified.

Sensory-Motor Skill and Perceptual-Motor Skill. In recent years researchers have been increasingly concerned with a more comprehensive approach to understanding motor performance. Whereas the motor "output" seemed to be the first aspect of performance to draw the attention of researchers, in the past several years the types of sensory cues influencing performance and the formation of meanings from sensory experience (the process of perception) have been studied in greater detail. Thus the terms *sensory-motor* and *perceptual-motor* performance have been coined, indicating the important influences the sensory cues and the perceptual process have on the motor act.

Evolution of the Human Action System

The study of the evolution of movement capacities may be made only from indirect evidence. Function may be deduced only from structure and from the bone and stone implements that primitive men made with their hands. Problems arise when attempting to differentiate structurally a man from a preman, a preman from an ape, and so on. Are the differences based on cranial capacity as it increased from 750 to 1500 cc.? Was the opposability of the thumb to the hand or the ability to remain upright for a period of time the important criterion? The development of dentition and of facial characteristics that permitted speech, the ability to use tools, the ability to make them—what were the keys to the human evolution?

What are the interrelationships between such apparently diverse findings and functions as the size of the animal bones adjacent to primitive human-like skeletons and the development of speech? Chimpanzees can thread needles. Is finger opposability crucial when one identifies an early man? Inspection of the arm-hand-shoulder region of the ape and of man reveals few significant differences; the brain of the ape and of man do not differ so much as do those of the zebra and the horse.

If *toolmaking* is the crucial test of humanness, and many anthropologists subscribe to this, what then of the primates who have been found using sticks to entice ants from their mounds? Does breaking off a stick constitute making a tool? Were the first toolmakers the pebble people of antiquity who chipped off one or two flakes from one end of an oval stone, held the other end, and then proceeded to knock the brains out of small game? Or was the first man the bone-age Australopithecine who placed an antelope jaw on the end of an antelope leg bone and attempted to perform a frontal lobotomy on his fellows and on the hapless baboon? Some discoveries of our ancestor's bony remains do not clarify these questions, but only add to them. Instead of looking for the missing link, by the 1930's the anthropologists became acutely aware of the innumerable missing *links* they still had to find.

Of primary importance is consideration of the interrelationships between the time taken by various portions of the action systems to evolve. Did the body system, the face, and brain capacity evolve at reasonably even rates? Until the 1940's this was believed to be so. And yet with the Java skull were found lower limb bones that resembled those of modern man. In Africa Dart and Broom[279] uncovered advanced primates who possessed ape-like brain cases, carried over man-like pelvises.

And what of the relationships between erect posture, toolmaking and dentition changes? Do sharp canine-shaped teeth in a wedge-shaped protruding mouth hinder speech? Does the formation of words require a flattened molar? Was the ability to speak hastened by some change in face and dentition? Or were words developed simply because, to catch larger game, men needed to communicate in more sophisticated ways with each other?

The answers to some of these questions have been made only tentatively, but in the past 15 years anthropology together with many other disciplines has sprinted ahead. With the help of carbon and argon dating techniques some of the answers to these questions are beginning to become clear.

It is apparent that one of the early changes in the primates that produced structures similar to those of modern man was their grasping ability. This change enabled the early primates to move to the trees, and brachiation began producing a visceral system that became relatively well adapted to upright locomotion. This mammalian development has been dated as occurring about 10,000,000 years ago.

The second major change in the structure and function of man was the assumption of upright posture, evidenced by the evolvement of a rounder pelvis different from the wedge-shaped bony girdle possessed by the tailless apes. Two theories attempt to account for this. It is believed by some that the more successful of the great apes stood upright for increasing periods of time to see over the tall grass and to sight their prey and enemies better. Others suggest that these premen were already upright as they moved through the trees and thus simply alighted on the ground and began to move using the lower part rather than the upper part of their bodies. The rough date for the assumption of an upright posture, based upon the C-14 content of fossil remains, has been placed at 1,000,000 to 2,000,000 years ago.

Finally brain changes began to appear, the head moved directly above the spinal column, marked by the gradual relocation of the foramen magnum to the center rather than to the rear of the skull. Cranial capacity increased from 750 to 1500 cc. Speech and association areas appeared and the cerebellar cortex began to expand and to grow as man began to utilize his hand-eye action system and became able to view his world for increasing periods of time from an upright posture. These latter developments and the emergence of man possessing modern cranial characteristics have been recently dated at only 50,000 years ago!

The discovery of the order in which these changes occurred, however, presented additional problems. For example, as the great apes began to move on their rear feet, their viscera became more vulnerable to attack. Thus, those early apes who began to protect themselves best with small rocks fashioned into implements for defense were the most successful and survived. However, upright posture placed the eyes in better position for use, and thus more successful anthropoids began to gain increased head mobility. They became able to move their upper limbs 180 degrees instead of in the narrowly restrictive space field of their immediate ancestors whose hands rested on the ground. Thus, verticality promoted the use of the hands not only for defense, but also for more extensive exploratory-manipulatory tasks. The changing visual field encouraged greater head mobility and the neck became free from the bands of the restrictive musculature possessed by the earlier primates.

Evolution and Modern Man

Structurally and functionally the unique features of the modern human action system include eyes that can scan and deal with a complex three-dimensional and moving space field, a pelvis that together with locked knees affords a stable base and permits freedom of the upper limbs to deal with the environment for extended periods of time, a mobile neck and upper trunk area that permits flexibility of action, coordination of the eye-hand action system, a brain and facial characteristics that facilitate symbolic speech behavior, and development of the associative areas of the brain that mediate abstract thoughts relatively independent of direct action.

A critical question remains, however. Is man a successful animal? There is no doubt that he seems to have modified his environment to his needs (or possibly to his destruction). Upright posture has given man certain intellectual and functional advantages; structurally and functionally, however, he still seems to be thousands of years away from an efficient accommodation to verticality. Innumerable functional problems are believed to arise from the relatively recent assumption of an upright stance. Adults are plagued by varicose veins and hernias. An infant's large head does not seem to fit easily through a woman's narrow birth channel. Back pains, flatfeet, and other conditions stemming from the evolutionary struggle to stand up are a constant plague.

Physiologically man still seems to be a poorly adapted organism. In addition to the rudimentary remains of apparently useless organs which frequently become infected or dysfunction to plague him, physiological systems are not adapting as rapidly as the environment requires. The frequency of stomach ulcers and other conditions attests to this. Are the relatively stable constitutions of the astronauts indicative of an evolutionary trend, as opposed to that of the businessman with ulcers?

And most important, what are the future directions of human evolution and structural change? Will the emphases placed on creative thought, automation, and cognition result in a reduction of muscle size and of gross action capacities and the expansion of our brain case? Is the larger child being produced in recent generations indicative of a trend to gigantism which led to the disappearance of other mammals? These and other questions are important, but the primary questions remaining and of importance to those interested in the action patterns of men is how much of an *animal* is man today? What percentage of his time should be devoted toward meeting his action needs versus intellectual contemplation? Should programs of equal vigor be developed for *all* men to drain excess animal energies which "kick back" into the constitution and destroy it? The answers to these and other questions will be found only after a thorough consideration of available anthropological evidence, together with an interdisciplinary study of the human behavior including its psychological, sociological, and physiological underpinnings.

Action and Evolution

The carbon dating techniques contributed by Libby and his colleagues raised some difficult questions for the anthropologist, paleontologist, and geologist. For example, it became apparent that man's time on earth had been badly overestimated. He was found to be a much newer creature than imagined, posing the question of how such marked structural changes in the face region, the lower limbs, and pelvic areas could have taken place in the brief million years allotted to modern man on the C-14 scale. Darwin suggested that evolution was a more gradual process than was revealed by the carbon dating methods. The problem then became how to reconstruct evolution to answer these questions. Man moves with muscles, but these had long disappeared from the skeletal remains of the man-like creatures. Could one experimentally produce and investigate evolution on organisms now living? The anthropologist Washburn[1149] attempted this very thing. During the last decade and basing his research on the assumption that muscle changes may have influenced bony structure more rapidly than was formerly believed, he performed some unique and exciting experiments. First utilizing rats and later chimpanzees, he found that, by surgically altering the jaw muscles of the face, marked and immediate changes in the bony ridges around the jaw and over the eyes could be induced. In this way, Washburn began to demonstrate that *actions* were vital to the evolution of man—as the muscles functioned so did the skeleton form itself. And most important, this formation probably took place rather rapidly.

The questions and answers that these findings raise are thought-provoking and hold most important implications for those interested in the actions of modern man. Exercises for adult males could include provision for counteracting some of the effects of his incomplete and somewhat unsuccessful efforts to stand upright, and, rather than concentrating on limb strength, the body builder might well concentrate on developing musculature in the back and in the abdominal region. Programs should provide for the fact that man remains more animal-like in some of his physical and visceral makeup than he would perhaps like to believe. Furthermore, the mounting scientific evidence concerning the anthropological underpinnings of man's action system suggests that, at the graduate levels, specific courses might be instituted. These offerings, taught with the help of anthropologists, should begin to explore some of these problem areas.

1. How did man evolve to function in the way in which he does at the present time?

2. What functional imperfections present in the physiological and structural makeup of man should be taken into consideration by program planners?

3. What are the interdependencies of the portions of the action system that may have important implications for the learning of skill and for more efficient strength-endurance programs? What primitive reflexive patterns remain, sometimes aiding and sometimes inhibiting traditional components of sports activities?

4. What are the implications for program and for teaching of the most recent neurological developments in man, i.e., do verbalization and "over-intellectualization" inhibit the "animal-like" output of his action system?

Thus these recent anthropological writings suggest several areas for scholarly consideration. The beginnings of the scientific movement in physical education were spearheaded by physicians who felt that vigorous action was synonymous with freedom from disease. Recent scientific excursions have had the backing of literature written by the psychologist and sociologist. Therefore it seems reasonable that a more penetrating look at the evolutionary beginnings of the structural interrelationships underlying man's action systems, aided by the physical anthropologist, may reveal new and exciting dimensions to the quest for knowledge about human movement.

Summary

The study of motor skills and learning is the concern of many academic disciplines. The medical profession is concerned with the motor performance of atypical individuals; the anthropologist studies motor performance within a culture or as a function of evolution; the anatomist-physiologist studies motor performance as a function of structure; the psychologist uses animal subjects or employs the fine motor skills of men to investigate many basic problems; and the human factors engineer studies manual skills in industry or in man-machine systems. The physical educator, on the other hand, has the study of factors accompanying the gross motor performance and learning of healthy human beings as his unique area.

Motor behavior is a general term for observable movement. *Motor performance* is observable, voluntary, goal-centered movement. *Motor learning* is the rather permanent change in motor performance brought about through practice. *Motor fitness* refers to capacity to perform, whereas *motor educability* is capacity to learn. *Motor skill* is performance involving reasonably complex adjustments acquired through the learning process. *Fine* motor skills and *gross* motor skills are considered as opposite ends of a continuum on which all movements may be placed. The terms *sensory-motor* skill and *perceptual-motor* skill emphasize the sensory and perceptual determiners of the motor act.

A behavioral rather than an anatomical approach is taken to the study of motor performance and learning in this text. "Flexibility" is the goal: plasticity in teacher behavior should result in the ability to modify the motor performance of students. Throughout the book, the teacher-reader is encouraged to assess the learner, the situation, and himself accurately prior to forming a plan of action.

Student Reading

Berelson, B., and Steiner, G. A.: *Human Behavior.* New York, Harcourt, Brace & World, Inc., 1964.

Bilodeau, E. A.: *Acquisition of Skill.* New York, Academic Press, 1966.

Brace, D. L., and Montagu, M. R.: *Man's Evolution.* New York, The Macmillan Company, 1965.

Cratty, B. J.: *Teaching Motor Skills.* Englewood Cliffs, N.J., Prentice-Hall, Inc., 1972.

Dart, R. A.: *Adventures With the Missing Link.* New York, Viking Press, 1959.

Fitts, P. M., and Posner, M. I.: *Human Performance.* Belmont, Calif., Brooks/Cole Publishing, 1967.

Gagne, R. M., and Fleischman, E. F.: *Psychology and Human Performance.* New York, Henry Holt & Co., 1959.

Hill, W. C. O.: *Man As An Animal.* London, Hutchinson and Company, 1957.

La Barre, W.: *The Human Animal.* Chicago, The University of Chicago Press, 1965.

Welford, A. T.: *Aging and Human Skill.* New York, The Oxford University Press, 1958.

Welford, A. T.: *Fundamentals of Skill.* London, Methuen & Co., Ltd., 1968.

Woodworth, R. S.: *Dynamics of Behavior.* New York, Henry Holt & Co., 1958.

various ages also appeared. Bryan[146] published results of an extensive study in 1892 in which he explored the speed and accuracy of voluntary movements of children, of both sexes and of different ages, using various limbs and noted the changes that occurred. Investigators also began to explore the manner in which movement accuracy was molded by vision,[123] as well as by "the movement sense,"[1220] and another researcher[1111] in the 1890's published a report of study of the manner in which spectator-observers influenced motor skill and physical endurance. By 1903, according to Buchner's[148] tabulation, about 16 reports of studies dealing with motor activity and human movement had appeared in various journals sponsored by the American Psychological Association.

Between the turn of the century and World War II, there was a glimmering of interest in what might be termed "the psychology of athletics." Even before World War I, a smattering of reports of studies that explored basic psychological dimensions of athletics appeared in American journals, although some were more philosophical than scientific.[874] Cummins,[275] for example, in 1914 studied simple motor reactions (tapping speed) as well as attention and suggestibility in a small group of basketball players. In 1922 Noble[851] measured the acquisition of throwing skill in athletes participating in the same sport. By the 1920's a sport psychology laboratory had been established in which the temperament, as well as the motor abilities, of athletes was studied.[465] During the 1920's and 1930's there was a sporadic scientific interest in motor ability testing and in studies of motor learning. Also during these decades the pioneer investigative work of Gilbreth[432] on industrial skills began to spawn studies of the dexterities needed on the production line. Thus, during this period one is able to find studies, both practical and theoretical, that deal with fine motor skills—physical activities in which primarily the hands and fingers are involved. The scientists of that time were held back somewhat by a lack of knowledge about and sophistication in the use of statistics and by the absence of helpful electronic equipment, which came into use following World War II. During the 1930's and 1940's, certain motor tests tended to persist in measuring adult and childhood intelligence, although for the most part the subtests of the Binet and Wechsler contained measures intended to tap verbal and cognitive functions. During these same years, however, Florence Goodenough,[450] formulating the "Draw a Person Test of Intelligence," and Stanley Porteus,[901] with his maze drawing tests, kept alive "performance-type" intelligence tests, whose scores were based primarily on motor responses. (A more extensive review of the development of intelligence tests and the motor components they contained may be found in Cratty.[257])

Toward the end of the 1940's and during the 1950's there was an expansion of scientific interest in motor skills. The term "perceptual-motor" was coined, indicative of the observations made by several researchers that voluntary movements of any magnitude or duration generally are controlled by some kind of perceptual processes, visual and/or kinesthetic.

It was during the 1950's and early 1960's that Edwin Fleishman[358–373] conducted his relatively sophisticated work. Using a large number of air-force trainees as subjects, Dr. Fleishman carried out numerous investigations of manual skills, of the complex hand-eye-foot coordinations needed when flying, and even studies of fitness and of large muscle control. His factor analyses have resulted in the formulation of valid tests to ascertain the fitness and motor efficiency of children and youth, and his research on manual skills has been employed in studies of work efficiency in education, the military, and industry.

The 1950's and 1960's have also brought to the forefront more sophisticated measurement techniques. Perhaps the most elaborately equipped program during these decades was that initiated by Karl U. Smith[1025–1027] at the University of Wisconsin. Apparatus that induce various kinds of visual-motor distortions both of time and of space are still employed in this rather monumental research program. Some of the studies from this laboratory are reviewed in Chapter 4.

Several trends are represented in contemporary research efforts about motor ability and motor learning. Although some of these categories will be drawn from more than will others during the course of this text, all have meaning for workers interested in the applied and theoretical aspects of human movement.

1. Research about psychology of sport has begun to expand primarily owing to the impetus given the subject in this country by the formation of the North American Society for Psychology in Sport and Physical Activity.

2. Physical educators have become highly interested in the psychological bases of sport and physical skills. Virtually all teacher training institutions in this country now have at least one course in this general subject area.

3. During the middle and late 1960's many general educators and special educators became literally transfixed by the various hypotheses that suggested that refining a child's movement skills would result in direct transfer to his intellectual and perceptual functioning. This movement has at times resulted in meaningless movement cures being applied to the wrong children for extended periods of time, but at the same time the educator of the 1970's is more likely to observe the obvious things a child can or cannot do with his body and will strive to give him some form of meaningful physical education during his formative elementary school years.

4. A general interest in motor learning has resulted in the production of numerous studies. An active and scholarly society was formed in

Canada in the late 1960's and has since produced excellent conferences and papers, as did the Symposium on Motor Learning held at the University of Iowa in 1969. The North American Society for Psychology in Sport and Physical Activity, holding meetings independently and jointly with the National Association for Health, Recreation, and Physical Education, continues to expand its membership and its functions, one of which is to explore the basic parameters of motor learning and performance.

5. There has also been an increased interest in the nature of the basic motor unit and the manner in which it may modify itself during the learning of motor skills. The classic work by Basmajian, briefly reviewed in the following pages, is among the most provocative research of this type.

Early Devices

Mosso,[817] in an article appearing in 1890, described an "ergograph" with which strength and fatigue studies could be conducted. This device (Fig. 2–1) could record a series of repetitive movements rather than a single maximum effort as was the case previously. This equipment was the forerunner of a host of similar devices which appeared in the following decades.

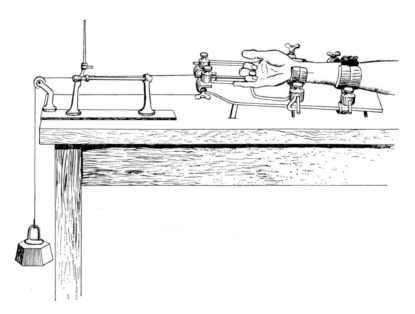

FIGURE 2–1. Mosso ergograph used to measure strength. (Redrawn from Hunsicker, P. A., and Donelly, R. J.: Instruments to measure strength. Res. Quart., *26*, 414-419, 1956.)

Static strength (the ability to apply pressure without movement) is often evaluated with a cable-tension device as shown in Figure 2–2. With various arrangements, one of which is also depicted, the experimenter can evaluate the strength of various muscle groups by determining how much static force they can apply on a cable passing through the tensiometer and over the riser, which records tension in pounds. This device was

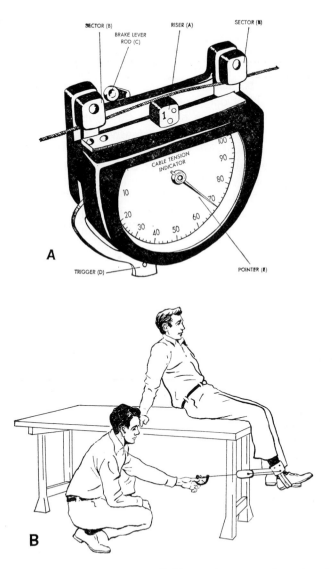

FIGURE 2–2. A, Tensiometer. B, Cable tension strength-testing technique to measure static strength. (Redrawn from Hunsicker, P. A., and Donelly, R. J.: Instruments to measure strength. Res. Quart., *26*, 414-19, 1956.)

originally developed to determine optimum cable tensions on the early airplanes.

Reaction Time and Movement Speed

Simple reaction time is usually measured with a device similar to that illustrated in Figure 2–3. With his hand on the switch at left, the subject must move the switch from the center to one side as the light flashes or changes from one bulb to the other. Reaction time is measured by finding the duration of elapsed time from the onset of the stimulus light to the *beginning* of the movement of the switch. This is a measure of simple reaction time because the movement made is relatively direct and simple, since the subject does not have to form any complex judgments about when or how to move as he views the lights.

Complex reaction time was studied extensively in the 1950's by Franklin Henry and his students.[520] One device for evaluating this is shown in Figure 2–4. The subject sits facing the apparatus with the middle finger of his right hand resting on the hand-reaction key. With the onset of the stimulus light, he lifts his hand as quickly as possible from the key, moving it about 6 inches to grab the first tennis ball, then back to the switch, and then to the second ball which, when touched, disconnects the

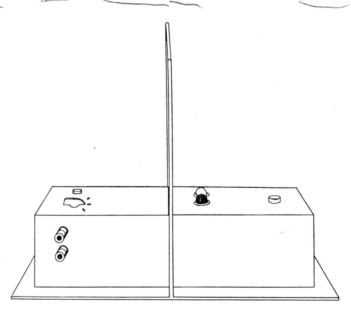

FIGURE 2–3.   Device to measure simple reaction time. (Courtesy of Carron, A. V.: *Laboratory Experiments in Motor Learning.* Englewood Cliffs, N.J., Prentice-Hall, Inc., 1971.)

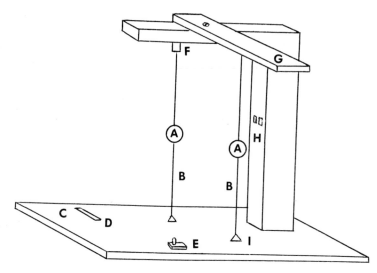

**FIGURE 2–4.   Speed of movement apparatus. A, Tennis ball; B, 48-lb. nylon
cord; C, baseboard; D, reaction key; E, push button; F, friction contacts; G,
side arm; H, signal lights; I, cord holder. (Redrawn from Howell, M. L.: Influence of emotional tension on speed of reaction and movement. Res. Quart.,
1, 22-32, 1953.)**

circuit. With this and similar devices a number of measures are obtain-
able: reaction time, the time taken for the hand to leave the reaction
key; total response time, the time from start of the stimulus until the
subject seized the last ball; and movement time, calculated by subtracting reaction time from total response time.

Reaction time tests, both simple and complex, have been employed on
occasion to evaluate the ability of athletes to respond quickly in large
muscle skills. For example, several researchers have evaluated the quickness of the sprinting start and the reaction time of football players off
their mark. The athletes in these studies are usually placed so that their
hands and/or feet are on switches, and, at a given sound or light signal,
they are required to move off the blocks, or, in the case of the football,
players, hit a nearby object with their shoulders.

Complex reaction time tests have been employed with European athletes, and, when experimental conditions are similar to those they encounter in their sport, the results are moderately predictable of athletic
success. In the test shown in Figure 2–5, the slalom skier is required to
respond to light cues indicating whether he is to move straight ahead or
through a gate to the right or to the left. Thus, the experiment requires
discrimination among three stimuli and complex choice reactions by
having to go through one of three gates. Under these conditions it is
as he breaks thru electronic eye

FIGURE 2–5. Various field tests of complex reaction time were devised after it was found that laboratory data evaluating both simple and complex reactions times were not predictive of athletes' success in sports. In the experiment illustrated, the skier is required to quickly pass through one of the gates in response to light cues that are flashed as he breaks the electronic eye. The accuracy of his decision and the speed with which he makes it are determined by filming the experiment with a high-speed camera. (Courtesy of Vanek, M., and Cratty, B. J.: *Psychology and the Superior Athlete.* New York, The Macmillan Company, 1970.)

assumed that reaction time would be significantly slower than under simpler conditions in the laboratory.[1130]

Manual Dexterity:
Tapping and Steadiness

Tapping tests were included in early batteries of motor coordination tests and are still employed in research. At times, the subject has to tap for speed, whereas in other research he may have to tap alternately from one contact plate to a second. In the task depicted in Figure 2–6, the score is derived by determining how quickly the subject can place a mark (or several marks), usually using a pencil, in all the circles shown. Tapping skills are usually found to be relatively independent of manual skills in which finger dexterity or accurate writing and printing behaviors

FIGURE 2–6. Section from tapping test. Examinee is required to make three pencil dots in each of a series of 1/2-inch diameter circles working as rapidly as possible. Score is the number of circles completed in the time limit. (Courtesy of Fleishman, E. A.: *The Structure and Measurement of Physical Fitness.* Englewood Cliffs, N.J., Prentice-Hall, Inc., 1964.)

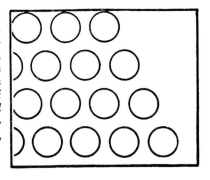

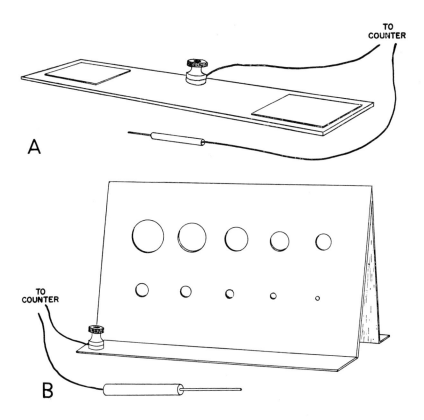

FIGURE 2–7. Electronic apparatus to test manual dexterity. (Courtesy of Carron, A. V.: *Laboratory Experiments in Motor Learning.* Englewood Cliffs, N.J., Prentice-Hall, Inc., 1971.)

are required. Fleishman has named the factor that contributes to a tapping score "aiming."

In more recent years, electronic counters have resulted in more reliable scoring based on the number of contacts made alternately on each square plate by the subject as he holds the stylus, as shown in Figure 2–7A. Simple steadiness apparatus have also been used extensively to study the amplitude of the oscillation rate of the various limbs (Fig. 2–7B). The subject attempts to hold the cursor in holes of decreasing size for a specified time. The score is the number of times the stylus touches the edge of the holes. The touches may be electronically counted. The manner in which the stylus is held and whether the arm is straight or bent will significantly alter this type of score, as will instructions (when the subject is told to remain steady it generally detracts from the steadiness score).

Dynamic arm-hand steadiness is evaluated by asking the subject to hold a small stylus as steadily as possible in a task such as that pictured in Figure 2–8 in which the object is to move with precision along a complex pathway. Scores on this task are computed by counting the number of times the stylus touches the sides of the pathway and the traversal speed.

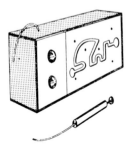

FIGURE 2–8.   Track tracing test. The subject inserts the stylus in the slot and then moves it slowly and steadily at arm's length, trying not to hit the sides or back of the slot. Score is the number of errors (contacts) for the total trials. (Courtesy of Fleishman, E. A.: *The Structure and Measurement of Physical Fitness.* Englewood Cliffs, N.J., Prentice-Hall, Inc., 1964.)

During the early 1960's I evaluated the agility of blindfolded subjects to move their total bodies through similar mazes, constructed of plastic tubing that formed long circuitous pathways from 50 to 60 feet long. Using this device we investigated a variety of factors, including the influence of spacing and massing practice, the transfer of training from learning the smaller mazes to learning and performance in the larger mazes, and the relationships of various personality variables to success in maze traversals* (Fig. 2–9).

---

* This general line of investigation to studies exploring the travel abilities of the blind, to investigations of kinesthesis and kinesthetic aftereffects, and to studies of the total body in action may be used to teach academic skills. Some of the work on kinesthesis is reviewed in Chapter 5.

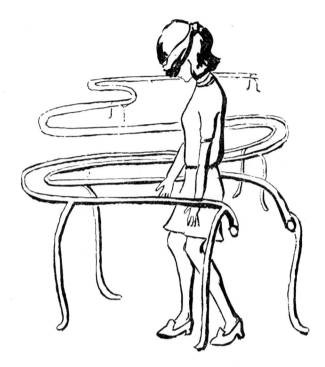

FIGURE 2–9. The type of maze task used over the years in our laboratory, employing blindfolded sighted college subjects. (Courtesy of Cratty, B. J.: *Movement and Spatial Awareness in Blind Children and Youth.* Springfield, Ill., Charles C Thomas, 1971.)

Complex Dexterity and Manual Abilities

Fine finger dexterity is evaluated by tasks that require finger-to-thumb oppositions, such as the selection, picking up, transporting, and fixing of objects. An example is shown in Figure 2–10, the "Purdue Peg Board Test." The ability to assemble small parts, such as in wiring electrical circuits, watchmaking, and similar tasks involving skillful finger manipulations, is evaluated in this manner.

FIGURE 2–10. Purdue peg board test. The examinee is required to place pegs in holes or to complete as many peg-washer-collar-washer assemblies as possible in the time allowed. Score is the number of pegs placed or the number of assemblies completed in the time period. (Courtesy of Fleishman, E. A.: *The Structure and Measurement of Physical Fitness.* Englewood Cliffs, N.J., Prentice-Hall, Inc., 1964.)

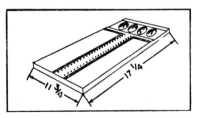

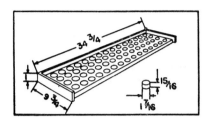

FIGURE 2–11. Minnesota rate of manipulation test. The subject fills the board with blocks, using one hand, as rapidly as possible; or he may be required to turn the blocks over in the holes as rapidly as possible. Score is the time needed to complete the task. (Courtsy of Fleishman, E. A.: *The Structure and Measurement of Physical Fitness.* Englewood Cliffs, N.J., Prentice-Hall, Inc., 1964.)

A skill that reflects an individual's ability to assemble larger components on an assembly line is evaluated by the "Minnesota Rate of Manipulation Test" (Fig. 2–11). The subject fills the board with blocks as rapidly as possible using one hand. In other uses of the test, the blocks must be turned over in their holes as rapidly as possible, using alternate hands on each row.

Classifications of Manual Skills

Gilbreth's[432] classification of working tasks into components he termed "therbligs" (Gilbreth spelled backwards) during the early part of this century formed the basis for the numerous time-motion studies that followed. Although there was little scientific verification of the components, shown in Figure 2–12, intuitively these subskills provided helpful starting points for those interested in the manner in which people function in assembly tasks and in similar operations in factory situations. One might question this classification from several standpoints, e.g., how can one tell whether a performer is "searching" or "planning," or what is the difference between "grasp" and "use"? At the same time it might be advantageous for the reader interested in large muscle skills to apply the "therbligs" concept to various sports skills, although it may be necessary to make up new "therbligs."

A more contemporary classification of manual skills based on detailed factor analysis is outlined in Chapter 10.

The development and use of more sophisticated electronic devices resulted in increasingly detailed analysis of manual skill operations. For example, in the task shown in Figure 2–13 the time needed to grasp pins, to carry them from place to place (transport time), and reaction time could be carefully measured. In general, in this type of task, speed of transport time is not as modifiable by practice as are manipulative components of the task (time needed to grasp and release objects).

Visual-Motor Coordinations

By the 1930's a number of control precision devices with which to evaluate complex motor coordinations found their way into extensive

FIGURE 2–12.   "Therbligs," components of work tasks, classified by Gilbreth. The signs under each task are often substituted for each of the operations shown. (Courtesy of Smith, K. U., and Smith, W. M.: *Perception and Motion.* Philadelphia, W. B. Saunders Co., 1962.)

use in psychological research laboratories. The most popular, and one that seems still to occupy "center stage," is the pursuit rotor, shown in Figure 2–14. Hundreds of studies have been carried out using this device. The most popular subjects have included the influence of space versus distributed practice and various studies in which motivational

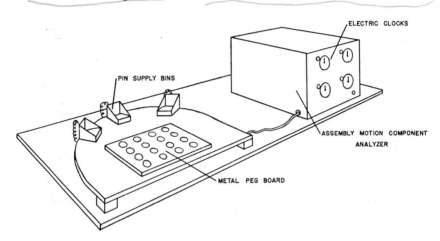

FIGURE 2–13.   Electronic assembly motion analyzer. This analyzer uses a double relay system of two pairs of recording amplifier relay units and clocks. One pair registers the time of the grasp and loaded transport movements, and the other the time of the assemble and empty transport movements. The task shown is to assemble pins in a plate. (Courtesy of Smader, R., and Smith, K. U.: Dimensional analyses of motion. VI. The component movements of assembly motion. J. Appl. Psychol., 37, 308-314, 1953. Copyright 1953 by the American Psychological Association, and reproduced by permission.)

FIGURE 2–14.   Rotary pursuit test. The subject tries to keep the stylus tip in contact with the target set near the edge of a revolving turntable. The score is the total time "on target" during the test period. (Courtesy of Fleishman, E. A.: *The Structure and Measurement of Physical Fitness.* Englewood Cliffs, N.J., Prentice-Hall, Inc., 1964.)

factors have been studied. Using a four-way stylus, permitting more than one subject at a time to participate, social-interaction studies have been conducted. When the speed is varied, research on transfer of training is possible. According to Fleishman, this device taps what is termed a "control precision" factor in the ability structure of humans, a quality also evaluated by the "Complex Coordination Test" in Figure 2–15. This device requires the subject to coordinate both stick and rudder pedals, reacting to lights on the board in front of him. The task reflects the interest in the 1940's and 1950's in the qualities contributing to effective flying skills.

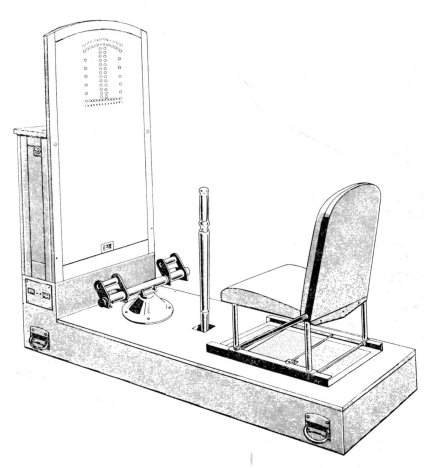

FIGURE 2–15. Complex coordination test. The subject coordinates stick and pedal controls to match the indicated positions of stimulus light patterns. The score is the number of matches in the time period. (Courtesy of Fleishman, E. A.: *The Structure and Measurement of Physical Fitness.* Englewood Cliffs, N.J., Prentice-Hall, Inc., 1964.)

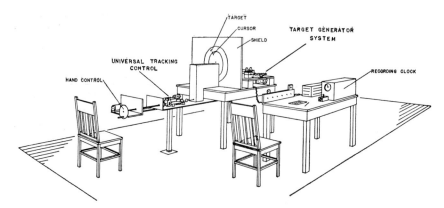

FIGURE 2–16. A controlled tracking device. The tracker uses a handwheel in order to make a cursor follow a moving target. Both actual movement of the cursor and the error in alignment are recorded graphically. Different motor controls can change the system to "velocity" and "aided" tracking. (Courtesy of Smith, K. U.: Learning and the associative pathways of the human cerebral cortex. Science, *114*, 117-120, 1951.)

Tracking studies of an infinite variety have appeared in the literature for the past 25 years. The tracker usually employs a handwheel as shown in Figure 2–16 or a combination of knobs to control the movement of a cursor (upward, downward, and to the sides). Targets moving in various ways are presented, to which the subject must match the mobile cursor. The tasks involve motor planning, visual-motor integrations, and, from a practical standpoint, resemble what must sometimes be done by radar operators and monitors of various types of military guidance systems. Sometimes the subject's movements operate the cursor in direct ways; at other times differential systems introduce various kinds of distortions and velocities into the system. One of the most interesting types of tracking studies has been that in which the operator's (subject's) characteristic errors and movements are programmed by computer and then the computer "takes over" the cursor, simulating the operator's characteristics. At times the duplication of the subject's characteristic errors and abilities has been so accurate that it is several minutes before the subject realizes that he is no longer in control!

Visual-Motor
Disruption and Reintegration

Mirror star tracing devices are used in studies exploring the effects of the disruption of visual and motor coordination. The object is to trace around the star's periphery, while watching the star only in the mirror. Scoring is based on accuracy (staying between the double lines of the

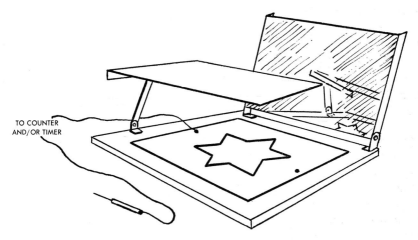

FIGURE 2–17. Mirror star tracing device to test effects of disruption of visual and motor coordination. (Redrawn from Carron, A. V.: *Laboratory Experiments in Motor Learning.* Englewood Cliffs, N.J., Prentice-Hall, Inc., 1971.)

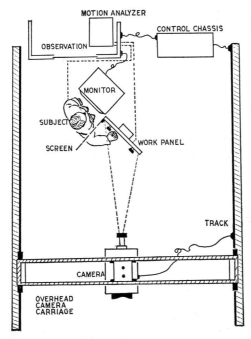

FIGURE 2–18. Instrumentation of a laboratory for systematic study of space-displaced and size-distorted visual feedback. (Courtesy of Smith, K. U., and Smith, W. M.: *Perception and Motion.* Philadelphia, W. B. Saunders, Co., 1962.)

star) and speed. This type of device is one of the precursors of the more elaborate electronically operated TV-monitor systems produced by K. U. Smith and others.

Beginning in the 1950's Karl U. Smith and his students devised numerous combinations of equipment that permitted them to study performance in motor tasks when visual "feedback" had been disrupted, by either inverting it or reversing it, or both. In the arrangement shown in Figure 2–18, the subject is dependent solely on what he sees in the monitor, which in turn depends on where and how the television "picks up" and sends the tasks that he is performing with his right hand. Using similar arrangements and a videotape arrangement that permits time-delays of visual feedback, Smith also altered time dimensions in a variety of visual-motor coordination tasks, that is, the subject saw himself performing the task at a slightly later time than he actually performed it. Although Smith's ingenuity and technical expertise have been lauded by many, he often failed to control for the more-than-a-single variable that could have influenced his results. For example, in the arrangement shown in Figure 2–18, it was impossible to determine whether the motor disruption the subject experienced was due to the fact that his arm was out to the side performing at an awkward and unfamiliar position, or whether the incoordination was due to the distortion of visual feedback produced by the TV-monitor system. A more thorough review of Smith's theories and work is found in Chapter 4.

Evaluation of Larger Muscles in Action

Stabilometers of a variety of constructions were used extensively in the 1950's and 1960's by Franklin Henry and his students and by others. The usual task was to attempt to stand on a tilting platform, to maintain balance, and to avoid touching contact points along the under edges of the platform. The one shown in Figure 2–19, by Singer, contains a recorder that measures extent of movement of the platform and the number of contacts. The device probably evaluates some combination of static and dynamic (moving) balance. Although often employed in studies that purportedly evaluate "gross motor ability," in practice the tasks also seem to tax fine adjustments of the feet and leg musculature.

Edwin Fleishman was the first researcher to administer really wide-range batteries of tests tapping gross motor abilities, and then to perform factor analyses on the scores obtained. Previous attempts to ascertain "basic motor abilities" on the part of the physical educators usually contained relatively limited batteries of tests, primarily tests assessing dynamic strength: push-ups, sit-ups, pull-ups, and "dips" on the parallel bars, together with a test or two of running agility and leg power. Fleish-

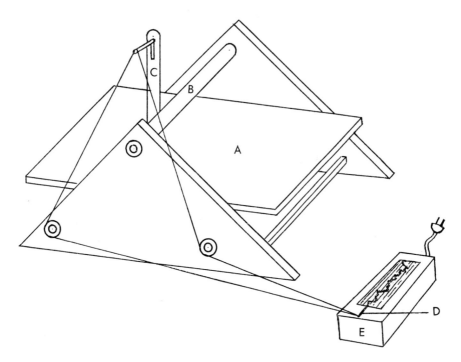

FIGURE 2–19. Stabilometer. Subject stands on platform (A) with his feet straddling axle (B). Lever arm (C) is attached to the platform. A cord extends from needle (D) to a point under the rear pulley to and around the far pulley to the lever arm where it is firmly attached. Another cord extends from the lever arm around the near pulley and is also attached to the needle. The needle records the extent of movement of the platform on graph paper inserted in the electric kymograph (E). (Redrawn from Singer, R. N.: Effect of spectators on athletes and nonathletes performing a gross motor task. Res. Quart. *36*, 473-482, 1965.)

man, on the other hand, included tests purporting to evaluate limb speed, as shown in Figure 2–20. In the first illustration (Fig. 2–20A), the score is the number of revolutions of the bucket a subject can make in a given time span. In Figure 2–20B, the score is number of times a subject can move his foot over the vertical partition in a given time period.

Tests of running agility and the quickness with which an individual can change the direction of his body were employed in Fleishman's batteries, together with a wider range of strength tests than had previously been employed. Figure 2–21 shows some of these tests, and the material in Chapter 11 reviews the results of these analyses. Since the turn of the century, various agility runs have been incorporated in batteries of tests devised by physical educators; the illustrations depict some of the variety of agility tests contained in Fleishman's work. The manner in which the

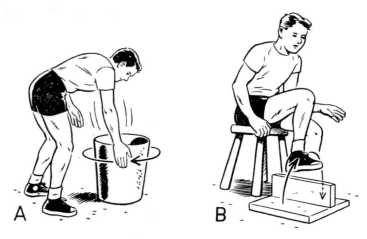

FIGURE 2-20. Tests to evaluate limb speed. (Courtesy of Fleishman, E. A.: *The Structure and Measurement of Physical Fitness.* Englewood Cliffs, N.J., Prentice-Hall, Inc., 1964.)

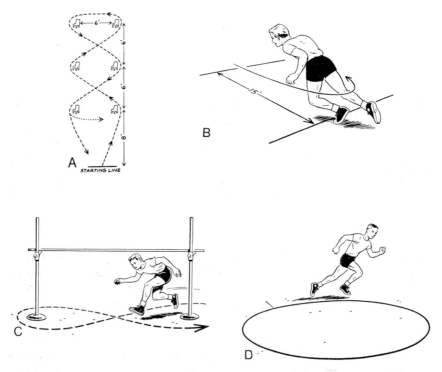

FIGURE 2-21. In the complex agility run (A), the score is the time taken to negotiate it. In the other illustrations (B-D), the score is based on the number of circuits (circular, figure eight, or back and forth) that can be negotiated in a given time period. (Courtesy of Fleishman, E. A.: *The Structure and Measurement of Physical Fitness.* Englewood Cliffs, N.J., Prentice-Hall, Inc., 1964.)

scores obtained from these and other tests are converted into physical ability "factors" is discussed in Chapter 10. In general, however, the more comprehensive the tests to which groups of subjects are exposed, the more "basic factors" are likely to emerge.

Analysis of "Effort and Shape" by Laban

In the early 1940's, Rudolph Laban developed a system of notation through which one may, in general terms, analyze several characteristics of human movement. His methods permit analysis of movement in and of itself, independent of any effects (e.g., a ball thrown) that may result. During the ensuing years, this system of "Labanotation" (or Kinetography Laban) has found an audience waiting to employ it not only in the field of dance, but also in both the esthetic and the remedial aspects of human motion.

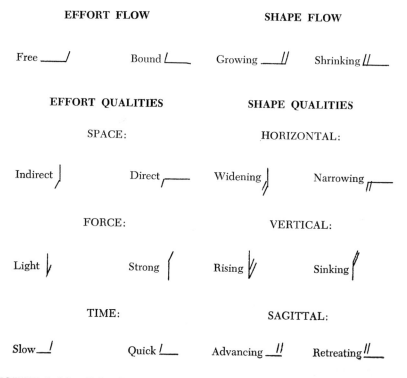

FIGURE 2–22. Laban's symbols for effort qualities of movement and their corresponding meanings. (Redrawn from Laban, R., and Lawrence, F. C.: *Effort*. London, MacDonald & Evans, Ltd., 1947.)

Laban[643] suggested that the "effort" qualities of movement can be described as *indirect* or *direct* in space, *light* or *strong* in force, and *slow* or *sudden* in time. Laban conceived of the "shape" qualities of movement as consisting of what he termed *widening* or *narrowing, rising* or *sinking, advancing* or *retreating*. He further suggested that the use of a system of 16 effort-shaped terms and their respective symbols facilitated the accurate description of what was termed "movement dynamics." These symbols and their corresponding meanings are shown in Figure 2–22. Laban's system of notation has encouraged many to explore movement possibilities to their fullest dimensions. The concepts and symbols arising from these have not, however, found great favor with the more scientifically minded.

The Motor Unit

In the 1960's a fascinating line of research dealing with the conscious acquisition of control over a single motor unit was conducted by Basmajian and his colleagues.[70] Fundamentally, the technique consists

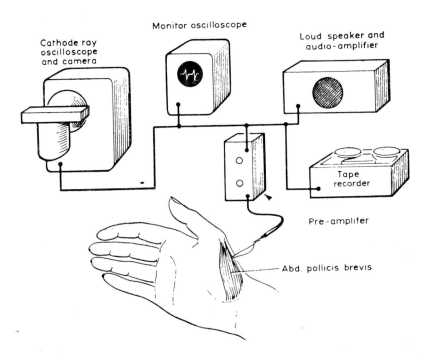

FIGURE 2–23. Technique used by Basmajian to provide subjects with feedback of activity of a motor neuron. (Courtesy of Basmajian, J. B.: Microscopic learning single nerve-cell training. In *Psychology of Motor Learning*. L. Smith (Ed.). Chicago, Athletic Institute, 1970.)

of providing human subjects with feedback activity of a motor neuron, through the monitoring of electromyographic signals (visual and/or auditory) (Fig. 2–23). A period of about 15 minutes is necessary for the subject to familiarize himself with the manner in which the apparatus responds to a range of movements and postures. A loudspeaker provides auditory feedback because the responses are usually so gentle that the subject is relatively unaware of a great deal of obvious muscle contraction. Although a variety of tasks may be presented using this general experimental set-up, the usual orientation involves first requiring the subject to isolate and maintain the regular firing of a single motor unit from among the 100 or more that a normal individual can recruit and display. When he is able to completely suppress neighboring motor units, the subject is asked to put the motor unit now under his control through one or more of several "tricks" including speeding up the rate of firing and the like.

Man in Space and the Measurement of Movement

Many efforts have been made during the past 25 to 30 years by human factors engineers to understand the integration of man and machines. Their efforts, particularly space exploration during the 1960's and early 1970's, have been characterized not only by how man moves under the pull of gravity, but also the complex actions of which he is capable in weightless space, during which rotation on all bodily axes is possible. Figure 2–24 shows systems of coordinates that, when translated into computer terms, have aided in the development of the dimensions and possible actions of which humans are capable while exploring outer space in some of the suits specially constructed for that purpose.

Summary

Many of the areas of study about human motor activity that are of concern to contemporary researchers have their precursors in the early days of experimental psychology. Studies of voluntary movement, of relationships between vision and movement, and of motor development antedate the turn of the century, whereas reports of the psychology of sport and similar topics are found in journal titles during the first two decades of the present century.

A recurring theme, which first appeared during the 1870's and 1880's, is the relationship between intelligence and motor activity and may be seen in many contemporary journals of education, physical education, and special education.

Much of the interest in human movement has been spawned by prac-

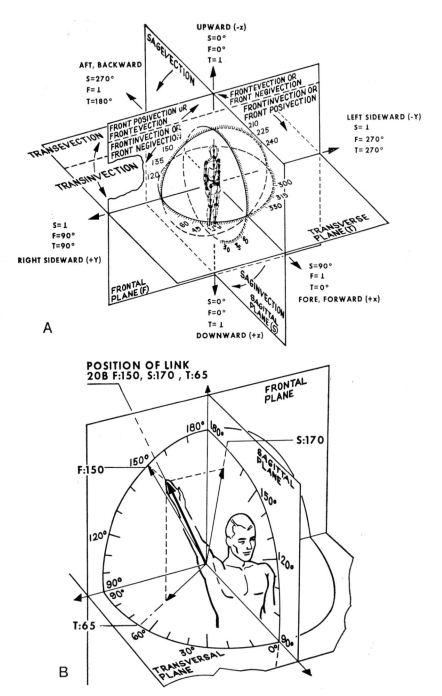

FIGURE 2–24. Examples of systems of coordinates that have aided in the development of the dimensions and possible actions of which men are capable in outer space. A, Global coordinate system (tentative), and B, shorthand notation. (Courtesy of Roebuck, J. A., Jr.: Kinesiology in Engineering. Paper presented to the Kinesiology Council, AAHPER Convention, Washington, D.C., 1968.)

tical problems in industry and education. Studies of handwriting behavior are found sprinkled throughout the decades, and research reports
about manual skills are still frequently found in the literature.

The development of electronic devices has not gone unnoticed by researchers dealing with motor performance and learning. In general, the
appearance of increasingly well-instrumented studies roughly parallels
increased knowledge about motor and perceptual-motor reactions. The
development of finite electronic monitoring devices has permitted studies,
similar to the ones described, that have been carried out by Basmajian
and his colleagues. With the possible exception of the work by Fleishman and by Franklin Henry and his students, relatively few sustained
research programs have focused in depth on movement abilities in
which the larger muscle groups are involved. Much of the work dealing
with gross motor skills and learning stems from one-shot efforts, the results of a single research and usually the reflection of an attempt to earn
an advanced degree.

Student Reading

Cratty, B. J.: *Physical Expressions of Intelligence.* Englewood Cliffs, N.J., Prentice-
Hall, Inc., 1972.
Brown, R. C., Jr., and Kenyon, G. S. (Eds.): *Classical Studies on Physical Activity.*
Englewood Cliffs, N.J., Prentice-Hall Inc., 1968.
Kroll, W. P.: *Perspectives in Physical Education.* New York, Academic Press, 1971.

II
PERCEPTION

3
PERCEPTION: AN INTRODUCTION

Vital to an understanding of man's movement behavior is knowledge about perception. It is the central portion of the situation-interpretation-action chain, leading to purposeful motor activity. Perception is a dynamic process, involving more than a response to sensory stimulation. It is a holistic term referring to meanings attached to an object, event, or situation occurring in spatial and temporal proximity to the individual. Perception is an ever-continuing, as well as an immediate, phenomenon, dependent not only on a situation's momentary core, but also on the context in which the event occurs and on past experience. The process involves organizing, feeling change, and selecting from among the complexity of events to which men are continually exposed, so that order may be attached to experience.

Recognition of the importance of the perceptual process arose from the observation that interpretation of an event by one individual did not always correspond to the meaning another might attach to the same facet of measurable reality. At the same time, however, within limits, prediction of perceptual interpretations seemed possible by controlling the nature of the sensations reaching sensory end-organs, the context in which these sensations were presented, and/or the individual's past exposure to similar objects and situations.

Research dealing with this "order within disorder," or the study of variables that modify and influence the meanings attached to the environment, has formed the basis of much of the experimental literature in psychology, psychiatry, personality theory, human engineering, and education. Therefore, careful consideration of these studies seems imperative for the student interested in the "why's" of human movement.

Sensation, Perception, and the Immediate Focus

Our perceptions are generally felt to depend on immediate sensations affecting our sensory end-organs, and, indeed, extensive literature concerned with psychophysics deals with quantitative aspects of this inter-

relationship. Perception also has been shown to be more than an awareness of immediate sensory stimulation. Events occurring in an individual's past and internal visceral changes also seem to play a part.

In essence, *perception* is more of an all inclusive term than is *sensation;*
it is usually viewed as a total pattern or "schemata" arising from many
sensations and results in a meaning that is more than the sum of its parts.
A perception (or percept) assumes a distinctive identity, independent of
the various kinds of sensations forming it.

Material elucidating perceptual phenomena is generally fragmented
into portions dealing with visual-spatial, olfactory, or auditory perception. Although these classifications probably are convenient, they are
somewhat artificial. Contemporary scholars emphasize the interdependence of the various senses in forming perceptual meanings.

Experimental and Theoretical
Approaches to the Study of Perception

Several avenues have been taken to the study of perception, including
the philosophical, the biological, and the behavioral. The latter classification might be further fragmented to include the psychophysical, the
sociocultural, or perhaps the phenomenal or holistic approach. Each of
these approaches seems dependent on the basic point of view and the
assumption as to which measurable or speculative aspects of perception
are most important to the total process.

Philosophical Approaches

The main argument among early Greek philosophers was whether judgment depends directly on the object and its direct influence on our senses
or whether imagination and the image formed from these sensations are
the main determiners of meaning.

The Stoics were the first to use the example of the *tabula rasa,* the
black wax tablet of the mind on which experience writes in the form of
direct sensory impressions of outer things. Later John Locke, in his *Essay
Concerning Human Understanding,*[700] suggested that, although the mind
may be conceived of as a blank piece of paper on which external sensations are inscribed, our *reflections* or internal senses also aid in forming
meanings from experience.

Bishop Berkeley[119] in the early 1700's argued at the other end of the
continuum by stating that the mind is the ultimate reality, that ideas are
primary. Despite this emphasis on thinking, Berkeley was the first to
classify sensation into the traditional five of sight, hearing, smell, taste,
and touch.

It remained for Thomas Reid[119] in the middle 1700's to differentiate between sensation and perception. A sensation was thought to be only an impression on an organ of sense, a perception, although dependent on sensation, was believed to be much more and included a conception of the object. The perception *was* the object, according to Reid.

These early philosophers eventually arrived at the concept of *associative fusion,* meaning that complex ideas are essentially built up of many sensations, perceived sights, sounds, or touch. A dog may be seen, heard, petted, and held and becomes a *dog* because of ideas inserted by several of the senses.

Two pathways were taken by those interested in perception at this point. On the one hand were those concerned with forming general behavioral categories in which to classify various perceptual phenomena. Research gained from introspective reports formed the basis of these classification systems. Descriptive categories included Wundt's[1229] characterization of sensations into two attributes, *quality* and *intensity.* Kulpe[119] added *duration* as a third category, and *extension* for sensations involving vision and hearing. Tichener[1104] added a fifth attribute, *clearness,* which pertained to the attention paid an object, whether it was central or marginal.

However, problems arose when an attempt was made to relate these attributes to concrete perceptual situations. It was initially difficult to demonstrate their general existence among all types of perceptual events. For example, when was a touch clear, or what constituted an intense color, and, more important, how could one equate a sound with a visual impression on a meaningful scale based on the attributes listed?

Psychophysical Approaches

A second more objective approach was taken as researchers attempted to measure more exactly the intensity of sensations affecting human beings. Psychophysical research was spurred by the scientific awakening of the nineteenth century and had as central concepts the ideas of *threshold* and *just noticeable differences.* General laws were derived by noting the point at which a majority of subjects in a controlled experimental environment reported a difference between two stimuli presented. Threshold studies included investigations of perceived changes in illumination, color, depth, and weight.

Fechner,[347] and later Weber,[119] published pioneer works in this area based on extensive studies. It was found that one sensation is reported just noticeably different from a second when it has been increased a constant percent of its total, rather than when increased a constant amount. The formula derived to explain this phenomenon became known as Weber's law. Although it was later found that the intensity of background stimulation modified threshold measurements between two presented stimuli, in general, Weber's law held true.

Research in psychophysics is based on three fundamental approaches: (1) The method of limits: a stimulus is gradually changed by discrete serial steps until a difference is reported by the subject. (2) The method of right and wrong cases: a stimulus is presented with a standard for comparison and a judgment is made as to whether the variable stimulus is equal to, less than, or greater than the original. (3) The method of average error: the subject is provided with a standard stimulus and with a method for changing the second stimulus. The average error is usually computed. This method of measurement is generally found in depth perception studies.

These three methods could be utilized to obtain information relative to five phenomena: (1) the absolute level of perception or the limits of audible frequency for sound or of visual color acuity, (2) the just noticeable difference or the amount of slight change to which the average subject reported being sensitive, (3) equivalents or thresholds of sensitivity in various parts of the body to similar types of stimulation involving the same kind of sensory receptor (Goldscheider,[442] for example, studied comparative sensitivity to movement in several of the joints when investigating kinesthesis), (4) sense-distance or comparison of just noticeable differences in various portions of scales of conscious judgments, and (5) sense ratios or the facility to multiply or to fragment judgments of stimulus intensity.

Studies in psychophysics marked the initial step toward quantification of perceptual judgments. In general, they were concerned with the efficiency of various sense organs, relying on subjects' introspections for evidence.

Biological Approaches

Perception may also be studied biologically. Two main avenues are utilized: (1) identification of anatomical structures that seem sensitive to various kinds of stimulation, and (2) analysis of various physiological processes that seem to influence perceptual judgment. Research in the former category has involved tracking nerve pathways or plotting functions performed by various portions of the brain. Investigations in the latter include studies of circulatory functioning, of blood chemistry, of enzyme action, and/or of hormonal secretion as affecting perceptual judgments.

Early researchers concluded that discrete portions of the nervous system, stimulated by sensory end-organ function, carried messages along specific pathways to identifiable portions of the brain. The messages were then thought to be received and to travel along labeled motor pathways producing movement. More contemporary investigations, however, seem to refute such simple explanations of behavior. It seems that, instead of single messages traveling over identifiable sensory and motor pathways, the receptors get hooked-up with one another, so that several receptors are usually communicating with the central nervous system at the same time. Further, it has been found that both broad-band and narrow-band receptors exist, the former reacting to the general nature of the stimulus, and the narrow-band receptors responding to selective aspects of the range of stimuli affecting the receptors.[811]

The picture was further complicated by finding that one receptor sometimes inhibits a second, just as one portion of the brain sometimes inhibits other portions. So instead of various sensory stimuli being simply added together to form a meaning in the brain, a vast number of summations and inhibitions take place concurrently to form the final sensory impressions.

Thus, the neat map of areas of brain functioning drawn by early researchers has become somewhat outmoded since it has been discovered that motor and sensory areas are firmly connected and sometimes seem to overlap. When one area of the brain is removed or destroyed through disease or injury, others will take over its function.

Recently, endocrine function has been explored as a possible effector of perception. Weber,[1162] analyzing and synthesizing research in perception, movement, personality, and endocrinology, concluded that endocrine malfunction not only affects movement variables, but also produces modifications in the process and organization of perceptual-motor activity.

Behavioral Approaches

The behavioral approach to the study of perception is most relevant to the central focus of the text. It is an avenue grounded in philosophy but using the experimental method to determine the effect of perception on behavior and the effect of various environmental variables on perception. Testing environments are usually created in which human subjects report their susceptibility to illusions, their impressions of events and objects, and the meanings they attach to what they see, hear, feel, smell, and/or taste.

In the general behavioral area, several subareas may be identified. Much research activity has revolved around the influence of perceptual facility on complex and simple motor activity. Literature of this nature is usually found in human factors and physical education journals and provides the bases for much of the material that follows.

A second subdivision of behavioral studies involves investigating the role of perception in the development of the total personality structure. It has been found that the manner in which we view and interpret the world and our relationships with reality are basic determinants of the total human character. Marked perceptual distortions of time, space, or body structure are sometimes indicative of personality disorders. Reports of studies concerned with the relationship of distorted perceptual judgments to the abnormal personality form a substantial portion of the literature on perception.

Another subdivision of research involves the experimental distortion of sensory input and the observation of the manner in which the subject functions to reorganize his relationship to the real world. Inversion of the visual field by various lens arrangements and reversal of the auditory functions of the two ears are examples of investigations in this area. Generally, it is presupposed that the manner in which the individual reorganizes the artificial experimental situation corresponds to the manner in which he originally began to interpret the world as he matured.

Research in these three broad areas generally involves the interpretation of three types of data: (1) *Informational* data include any simple means of informing the experimenter that a particular object, event, or situation is or is not present, through either a verbal statement, a movement, a nod of the head, or some simple manipulation. (2) *Response data,* including more active participation on the part of a subject, involve maze traversal, complex tracking movements, and the like. They require more than providing a simple negative or positive bit of information. (3) *Phenomenal data* are gleaned from perceptual studies and usually collected by the clinician.

In the present context, the primary concern is with data involving simple and complex movement responses to various perceptual events. The purpose of the present chapter is to form a structure and provide a general understanding of the perceptual process in order that perceptual determinants of movement behavior of normally adjusted human beings may be more clearly recognized.

Perceptual Theories

Throughout history, several theoretical positions have been advanced in the attempt to organize knowledge relating to the perception of the many facts in the complex environment. Generally these are rather broad statements representing a synthesis of philosophical thoughts and/or experimental findings. It is usually hoped that such statements will result in better predictions concerning the manner in which some phenomena of man, nature, or the physical world actually function. It is usually hoped that such formulations represent "truth" and, therefore, may eventually aid in the better control of some aspects of man's environment.

Several types of theories have been formulated in an attempt to explain the process of perception. Some are closely allied with identifiable philosophical trends. Others may be logically associated with various learning theories or to particular "schools" of psychology. Still others might be distinguished by the type of experimental evidence underlying their basic assumptions. Contemporary theories also may be grouped according to the relative emphasis placed on the individual, the immediate context, sociocultural factors, or past experience as molders of perception.

Within the present context, perceptual theories will be discussed in a historical framework, and the relative emphasis placed on various aspects of the perceptual environment will be brought out.

Sensation to Perception

Earliest thinkers held that we learn about our world through our senses, receiving discrete impulses from objects in the environment. This viewpoint was gradually expanded to include the concept that men also engage in imagery, in thinking about the received sensations, and that both the sensation and the integration were important. The emphasis, however, in these early theories was on a one-to-one relation between the object or event and the perceiving individual. The importance of the context in which the object was observed, the feeling of the individual about himself, his past experiences, and his sociocultural setting were usually ignored.

One of the first of the early theoreticians to recognize and emphasize the importance of perception over mere sensation was Wundt,[1229] who formulated the principle of *creative resultants* in 1912. He hypothesized that the product of our sensations is not merely a "sum of the separate elements . . . but represents a new creation." Reid[119] also postulated that perception was a fusion of conceptual and sensory processes. Expanding these concepts further, Helmholtz[119] suggested that unconscious inferences may also influence perceptions of the real world.

Core-Context Theory

Tichener's[1104] *core-context theory* was a forerunner of conceptual frameworks that attempted to explain perception as a dynamic phenomenon, rather than as a static mechanical process based on immediate sensation and situation. According to Tichener, perception consisted of a core of immediate sensations and of secondary sensations contributed by past experience. The learned context of the experience, therefore, was felt to vary considerably from individual to individual, whereas the immediate core remained relatively stable. Thus, variation in meanings could be attributable mainly to an individual's past experience with similar situations, objects, and events.

Boring[119] added support to the core-context theory by postulating that, although visual perceptions were initially dependent on the retinal size of the image (the core), exact estimation of size, distance, speed, and the like depended on the learned aspects of the context or the relationship to other objects. Woodworth[1225] also felt that cues and meanings are continually interacting, even when the organism is apparently at rest, and, further, that the perceptual process is a dynamic phenomenon.

Helson's[514] theory of adaptation level also is based heavily on the importance of past experience in the development of meaning. It was assumed that objects and events are isolated, identified, related, and ordered within frames of reference that are revealed in categorizing statements: for example, "This building is very tall," or "That is an angry man." The concept of "pooling" is central to Helson's theory. It refers to the idea that continual attempts to categorize depend on a rough average or "pool" of past experiences that influence quantitative and qualitative judgments of things. Three separate factors are felt to be important in the perceptual process, according to Helson: (1) the stimulus or object that gains attention, (2) other objects forming the object's immediate background, and (3) the effects of previous objects in the perceiver's past experiences that formed the "pool" or *residual stimuli*. Helson bases the *adaptation theory* on both psychological and physiological principles and was one of the first to emphasize the triad of object, background, and past experience as modifiers of perception.

Gestalt Theory

Much of the experimental literature relating to perception produced in the past 35 years has been related to one of the 134 "laws" developed by Gestalt psychologists. The Gestalt approach to the study of perception was the first to take the purely behavioral avenue. Experimental methods that were unrelated to previous experiments in psychophysics, physiology, or neurology were developed. Principles derived from this extensive program of experimentation underlie many of the perceptual tests presently found in the literature.

The word *Gestalt* means form or shape, and, more generally, a manner or essence. Basically, the system was instigated in protest against researchers who accepted only measurable behavior as experimental evidence and also against the psychophysicists who seemed preoccupied with physiological concepts.

The importance of whole meanings, independent of sensation, to the study of perception was first conceived by the German Wertheimer[1186] about 1910. His paper treating the apparent movement of quickly presented pictures, as occurs in the cinema, was published in 1912 and represents the first scientific exploration of gestaltic concepts.

This apparent movement in the cinema, or as Wertheimer termed it "phenomenonal movement" (or simply the phi-phenomenon), provides an example of the holistic gestaltic approach to the study of perceptual behavior. For what the Gestalt experimentalist would be interested in investigating is what is reported as *seen* as one views the movie, not the neurological-physiological processes that caused one to see the movement. For the gestaltist, the basic data are *phenomena,* or a *phenomenal experience*. One can see movement (phi) without being able to identify the successive pictures; one can describe an individual as "angry" without naming exact behavioral attributes constituting the emotion. A square may be formed of dots, of lines, either red or black, but it is usually seen as a square, not simply a sum of the parts. A whole form is usually perceived and reported, not the manner in which it is constituted.

While the gestaltist emphasized the total perceptual field, attention was also devoted to the central figure experience. The concept of *figure-ground* thus becomes important in the theoretical framework. The facility with which an individual perceives the figure (core or central object) of his experience, as opposed to the total field surrounding the object or event, was explored experimentally.

The concept of "good" form, or object consistency, is also central to gestaltic theory. It is based on the finding that an individual tends to preserve an object's basic shape, size, and/or color despite changes in background. For example, if an individual is quickly presented with a circle of dots (via a tachistoscope), it is reported as a circle. Likewise, if an incomplete circle is similarly presented, it is usually reported as being completed. This tendency for perceptual consistency and completeness (closure) is fundamental to gestaltic theory.

Gestaltic concepts, so frequently validated experimentally, have caused the particular "school" of psychology to become less identifiable in recent years. Gradually many of the concepts have been absorbed into general psychology. Most experimental studies have utilized tasks involving judgments of patterns in two-dimensional space, using vision.

The relation between various perceptual qualities, identified by Gestalt experimentalists, and accurate movement has just begun to be explored. An example is a study by Kreiger,[638] who found that the ability to distinguish simple geometric forms in more complex patterns was related to the facility with which tennis players adjusted their rackets to oncoming balls.

Transactional Theory

A more recent theory of perception is based primarily on external psychological and situational variables rather than on the internal anatomical-physiological fluctuations encountered in the sensory-tonic theory. "The transactional approach" suggests that a valid study of perception may be made only by considering all aspects of the dynamic event (or transaction) occurring between the observer and the object. It is held that the focus should be on the unique characteristics of identifiable situations, external to but including the observer, rather than on what environmental stimuli *do* to the individual.[571]

It is further suggested that each individual ascribes unique qualities to events in his "psychological environment," his temporary placement in time and space. These total events await perceptual interpretation for their very existence and do not achieve form as perceived, independent of real life situations. For example, it is felt that just to study a batter throwing a ball to an individual is not enough. Rather, to be valid such a study should involve consideration of the pitcher, of team members, and of other aspects of the situation as they affect the perceptions of the batter.

Although such a theory would seem to encourage research of such complex design that identification of influencing variables may prove difficult, such is not the case. Ames,[26] Ittelson, and others[571] have carried out carefully controlled studies in which many variables that may influence perception have received individual consideration. Generally, these investigations have involved either determining *discrepancies* between two events as perceived, or searching for *consistencies* among situations in slightly different contexts.

Although it is felt that "physiological excitation" is requisite to perception, more important factors are held to include objects and events of which the individual initially becomes *aware* and *significance* subsequently is attached to them. These assumptions and significances, it is suggested, correspond closely to weighted averages of previous experiences (Helson's "pooling"[514]) as they relate to the present situation. For example, when studying perception of events occurring in a seascape, supporters of the "transactional theory" would deem it important to find out whether the observer believed the beach to consist of large or small pebbles and whether birds flying among the rocks were thought to be large or small. It is only as these kinds of observer-assumptions are known, it is held, that one may correctly assess the accuracy perceptions of distance-speed-time-and-size formed by an individual who is viewing the scene.

It is further advanced that whether there is accurate or inaccurate correspondence between perceptual awareness and the actual environmental situation is central to the process of living. As a result, several important kinds of investigations involving the perception of movement in two-dimensional and three-dimensional space have been carried out in keeping with this theoretical framework. Some of these will be considered in Chapter 6, in which visual-space perception is discussed.

Sociocultural Theories

In addition to theoretical structures emphasizing sensory experience, the imagination, the perceptual field, and the tonus of the perceiver are those, usually advanced by the social psychologist, that place emphasis on the social and cultural context. These theories may employ a bio-logical-social approach or a gestaltic approach as found in Lewian field theory.

Initially, these theorists relied on observation and assertion concern-ing the role of instinctive factors in the molding of perceptual behavior. In 1918 McDougall[762] stated that perceptions are constructed from in-nate tendencies, leading to appropriate emotional responses related to survival and to physical activities involved with escaping danger.

Some social psychologists place emphasis on learned social perceptions. Experimental evidence by Munsterberg[825] at Harvard, for example, indi-cated that individuals in a classroom influence one another when report-ing on an objective situation, the number of dots placed on a screen. Allport,[24] following up Munsterberg's investigations, also demonstrated that group membership influenced individual perceptions, depressing qualitative judgments while adding to quantitative ones.

Sherif[996] in 1935 supplied the first experimental evidence concerning the influence of the social environment on perception. Using as stimu-lation the apparent movement of a single light in a dark room, the auto-kinetic effect, it was found that the individual learns to perceive as mem-bers of his group perceive and that the individual is progressively molded toward the group's perceptions of the illusion. Each group, it was found, established its own unique range and point of reference, and even if an individual was able to establish his own judgments first, convergence toward collective norms occurred as he was absorbed into a group. This convergence was even more marked if the individual was required to participate initially in a group. Sherif constructed curves to illustrate this convergence, or "the funnel-shaped relationship," characterizing in-doctrination of the individual in group perceptual norms.

Ten years later Schonbar[972] substantiated Sherif's findings using line-length estimation and height judgments as tasks. It was found that, when an individual was removed from the group, the collective perceptual norms persisted and that the longer an individual had been subjected to group influence the longer these norms persisted. Clark,[196] studying differences between men and women's interpretations of material bearing on a struggle between the sexes, and Bruner and Goodman,[145] studying the apparent size of coins judged by children from favored and sub-standard backgrounds, related the influence of the sociocultural environ-ment to individual perceptions of events, objects, and situations.

Anthropologists have also supplied objective evidence that individual

FIGURE 3–1.   The Miller-Lyre illusion.

perceptions are modified by the society in which one resides. For example, the staff of the Torres Straits expedition in 1898 found that certain native groups were much less subject to the Miller-Lyre illusion than were other groups (Fig. 3–1). It was hypothesized that the natives' frequent use of spears, the heads of which resembled part of the illusion, might have had some effect on their responses to the tests. McDougall and Rivers[984] in the same report noted that, although no differences were found in standard visual acuity test scores recorded by Murray Islanders and white Europeans, rather striking superiority of the native men was noted in their ability to spot objects on the distant horizon and to distinguish camouflaged coral fish against their natural backgrounds.

Borogas,[113] studying the Chuckhee, reported that these deer-hunting people, due to little opportunity to see colors in their native environment, seemed unable to sort accurately yarns of various hues. At the same time, however, these natives were able to distinguish more than two dozen patterns in the reindeer hide, differences that were not apparent to the investigating anthropologist.

Allport and Pettigrew[25] in 1941 found that the Zulus of Africa were not susceptible to an illusion resulting from a rotating trapezoidal-shaped window. This was attributed to the fact that rectangular-shaped windows, doors, square buildings, and the like were not normally found in their pastoral existence.

As the evidence mounted, psychologists began to use the phrase "in our culture" before generalizing about human perceptions, because it became apparent that cultural factors exert important influences on the development of meaning. As Frank stated: ". . . in every culture the individual is of necessity 'cribbed, cabinned, and confined' within the limitations of what his culture tells him to see, to believe, to do and to feel. . . ."[377]

The Perception of Physical Effort

Since 1958 an interesting program of research delving into what might be termed the "perception of effort" has been conducted in Sweden. This kind of judgment is an important quality to explore. It is based on the individual's perceptions of the effort he is expending and the feelings he encounters under varying amounts of exercise, such as changes in heart rate, modifications in respiration during exercise, and generalized mood states under different exercise loads.[117,118]

In general, it is found that rather exact psychophysical formulas may be applied to subjective feelings about changes in exercise load, and that, in general, these feelings closely parallel objective modifications in bodily processes during work, including increase in heart rate. Perceptions of exercise load have been placed in several categories: (1) feelings about a minimal effort, which are difficult to measure; (2) a "preference" level, which is an intensity preferred by a person for a given type of activity; (3) an "adaptation" level, which may closely correspond to "preference" level but at other times is closer to a stressful state; and (4) maximal intensity possible.

Among the psychological measurement tools employed by Gunnar Borg and others exploring this interesting phenomenon is the RPE Scale ("Rating Perceived Exertion") (Fig. 3–2), which permits an individual to attach one number of a 20-point scale to levels of exertion that are being experienced. The proponents of this scale claim that the numbers the subjects check relate closely to heart rate measured on the same individuals. For example, young men who report a RPE score of 17 are usually working at a task requiring a heart rate of 170, whereas correlations between these same ratings and officers' ratings of soldiers' endurance have been found to be moderate to high.

This type of psychological measure of perceived exertion has many practical applications, according to those researching it. The values obtained, for example, may be helpful when there is doubt about how much of a work load to place on an individual in a testing or a life situation.

6	
7	very, very light
8	
9	very light
10	
11	fairly light
12	
13	somewhat hard
14	
15	hard
16	
17	very hard
18	
19	very, very hard
20	

FIGURE 3–2. The RPE scale (the scale for rating of perceived exertion). (Courtesy of Borg, G.: The perception of physical performance. In *Frontiers of Fitness.* R. J. Shepard (Ed.). Springfield, Ill., Charles C Thomas, 1972.)

The close correspondence between the scores obtained and physiological measures of exertion makes the former a quicker and more easily obtained measure of work output in situations that do not call for precise levels of measurement; and most important, changes in adaptation level, which signal changes in physiological fitness, are easily measured using this type of assessment tool. And finally, instead of requiring individuals bent on self-improvement to carefully monitor heart rate or some other difficult-to-obtain measure, as they exert themselves, they may begin to rely on their subjective feelings of exercise stress, using the scale described.

This approach to the evaluation of the perception of effort has important implications for the measurement of motivational levels in athletes and in youth of average abilities; more important, the middle-aged woman and man may be guided more carefully in helpful conditioning programs when both the stress they perceive and the progress they make are psychologically *and* physiologically monitored.

Growth and Perceptual Change

The stages of growth through which humans pass seem to influence perception greatly, partly because of the changing and increasing complexity of the neuromuscular apparatus and sensory receptors and partly because of an evolving capacity to explore and to act. Developmental change and perceptual change are closely interrelated as the ability to attach meaning to and to act on various kinds of information bears a direct relationship to particular stages in development of the organism.

Siegel[1002] has hypothesized that three stages exist in perceptual-motor development: (1) the motor-somesthetic, (2) the motor-visual, and (3) the visual-motor. These are generally related to the manner in which man collects evidence about his environment. During the initial stage, the infant's sense of touch enables him to gain initial impressions of his world. The second stage involves confirmation of his motor exploration with visual impressions. Movement seems necessary to add substance to reality and to afford an accurate impression of size, shape, and depth. The final and most advanced stage involves, first, gathering distant impressions via visual cues and, later, confirming them with manipulative behavior.

The prolific Swiss writer Piaget[893] explained perceptual development through the use of central concepts, relatively independent of discrete sensory modalities. His key concepts are presented in nine volumes, published from 1923 to the present, on child growth and development, based on observations gathered in his research center at the University of Geneva. Although some critics have suggested that he has failed to keep abreast of contemporary statistical techniques, many provocative questions have been raised by Piaget's anecdotal records.

Piaget reported that the child passes initially through an egocentric stage during which a slow awareness of himself, distinct from a hazily perceived environment, is achieved. The emerging self, in turn, becomes the platform from which he observes and makes judgments about the world. Things and events then gain meaning in relation to his own feelings and experiences. The child's perceptual development, Piaget believes, involves the gradual emancipation from his egocentric mode of thought to what is termed the "participation stage."

Learning and Perception

Learning is intimately related to the perceptual process. Perception gives meaning to events, objects, or situations; whereas learning involves a series of ongoing perceptions or *perceptual change* brought about through repeated exposure to the same or similar objects and situations. Thus, learning may be thought of as perception with an added temporal dimension.

The effect of learned experience usually is strongest during the initial portion of the perceptual process, as the preparatory set or initial attitude toward the object or event is formed. Generally, as was pointed out during the discussion of Helson's[514] adaptation level theory, meaning is arrived at through an averaging process, a "pooling" of our past experience concerning similar situations or objects.

A second concept related to perceptual learning is *stability*. It is found that individuals generally attempt to create a stable environment, one similar to their previous experience, which they understand and in which they may function. Supporting this second concept are studies in which various kinds of sensations are reversed or distorted. The manner in which perceptual stability is relearned is noted. Examples are the experiments using inverted lenses resulting in an inverted view of the world. Generally it has been indicated that individuals can relearn the location of objects in an inverted visual field and can quickly make a readjustment when the lenses are removed.[1038]

Man seems to coordinate and stabilize his environment by the integration of several of his senses. For example, in the previous study, adjustment to the upside-down world is facilitated if the individual is afforded an opportunity to manipulate the strange environment. It seems certain that the more intimate the direct contact is with objects and events the more accurate are estimations of their characteristics. We have little real concept of the size and consistency of the moon, for example, whereas our perceptions of the buffalo nickel are reasonably accurate.

But, in addition to direct handling of objects, we also seem to learn about our environment through "mental manipulation." Kilpatrick[617] found that the real nature of rooms, which had been purposely distorted to encourage various misjudgments of size and shape of objects in them, could be accurately estimated when the subject was allowed to view the experimenter exploring room surfaces with a long wand or by throwing balls at the walls to demonstrate the actual tilt of the floors. Accurate estimation of the nature of the rooms and the objects in them was equally facilitated whether the subject manipulated the wand and threw the balls or merely *observed* the experimenter doing so.

Kilpatrick[617] thus proposed that two types of perceptual learning take place: (1) reorganization learning or the unconscious reweighing of visual cues after an illusion or misconception has been formed, and (2) formative learning or new perceptual ideas not dependent on cues offered by various exploratory types of behavior. It was concluded that the belief that "gross-overt action is necessary for perceptual modification is clearly wrong."[617]

Thus the perceptual process is intimately related to learning; they appear to be interacting behavioral phenomena. Learning is an attempt to organize and to give stability to the environment and may be carried out both by direct manipulation and by imaginal manipulation. As Hilgard pointed out: "The end result is, on one hand, a world in which we feel at home, because we know what to expect, and what we expect does not disagree too much with what we want."[533]

Perceptual Types

After exploring various perceptual qualities and attributes, investigators have sometimes attempted to categorize individuals according to the methods or approaches they characteristically use when structuring their space field. Although these "types" are generally related to general perceptual behavior, most of the tests on which classifications have been based evaluated abilities relating to space perception.

One of the most frequent ways of classifying individuals has been to place them in groups labeled *analytic, plastic* (or flexible), and *synthetic.* Research by George[418] indicated that at one extreme are individuals who actively analyze discrete portions of their space field and attempt to "see through" illusions and pull apart complex situations. At the other extreme are found individuals who tend to synthesize experience, to generalize rather than to analyze. In the intermediate portion of the continuum, of course, are people who seem to employ a flexible changing perceptual framework, depending on the nature of the event with which they are faced.

A more recently devised categorical system to describe individual differences in perception is the *visual* and *haptic* framework. In general, it has been found that some individuals characteristically perceive more easily through visual impressions, whereas others (the haptics) add the most meaning to their experience primarily through touch and kinesthesis.

Other researchers have found that some individuals are primarily dominated by vision when attempting to judge rod verticality within a tipped frame, whereas a second group of subjects seemed less susceptible to the visual context (the frame) and made independent judgments about the space field, based primarily on impressions of the central figure. It is thus hypothesized that some individuals are primarily *ground dependent* and others are *figure dependent* when making perceptual judgments.[1217]

In 1954, Holtzman and Klein[549] suggested the terms *levelers* and *sharpeners* with which to classify individual differences in perceptual functioning. This system was based on the observation that some individuals tend to accentuate differences between stimuli presented (the sharpeners), whereas others tend to minimize such differences (the levelers). The tasks utilized by these researchers consisted of judging the size of squares projected on a screen.

Research by Ryan[952] and others has pointed to the existence of another dichotomy with which to classify the manner in which people organize their environment. Utilizing measures of kinesthetic aftereffects and of pain thresholds, it has been concluded that there are both "reducers" and "augmenters" of stimuli. The former are individuals who reduce sensory input, who are motor-minded and relatively insensitive to their environment. On the other hand the augmenters are sensitive individuals who are relatively inactive themselves, and who are acutely aware of all components of their environment.[952] Placing these two types together in the classroom through the elementary school years and presenting the same learning experiences to them would seem to be fraught with peril, and yet this is exactly what usually happens.

Perhaps the physical educator can evolve learning experiences involving various movement tasks that will be more helpful in educating the active male "reducer" than are the present classroom activities that seem primarily to appeal to and aid the tranquil female "augmenter."

The Perceptual Process

As a summary of the theoretical discussion and the survey of various determinants and modifiers of perception, the following chart (Fig. 3–3) has been prepared. The process is presented as containing five parts, separate in time. The initial step deals with the preparatory set formation, or postural attitudinal modifiers within the perceiver, prior to the presence of the perceived object or event. This set, as has been stated, depends on "pooling" of the individual's past experience, the cultural and social expectations with which he is surrounded and his musculo-

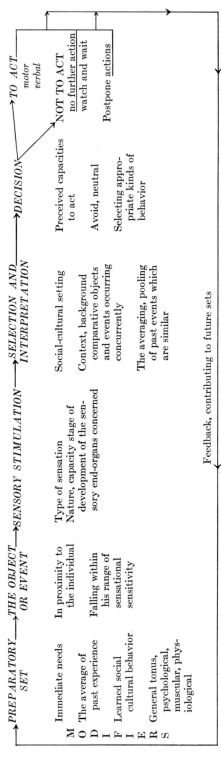

FIGURE 3–3. The perceptual process.

skeletal and visceral tonus. The preparatory set is also determined by unconscious past experiences and by visceral states of which the individual is relatively unaware.

The second part in the process occurs as the object or event begins to assume a distinct identity or form and is brought into spatial and temporal proximity to the organism. The event may be received by distance receptors, eyes and ears, or through surface receptors for pain, pressure, heat, and cold or possibly through kinesthetic receptors. In any case, the object or event must assume a distinct identity and become located in time and space so that it may affect one or more of the sensory end-organs.

The third step in perception comes as the event or object stimulates one of the sensory end-organs. In order to accomplish this, the object must emit stimuli that fall in the sensory range of human receptive organs. It must not be too small, have too limited a sound or range, or move too rapidly. Although formation of a perception involves more than a mere recording of sensory information, most perceptions begin in this manner. We usually do not perceive something that has not affected one or more of our sensory end-organs, although we may be stimulated without perceiving.

The fourth and vital step is the selection and interpretation stage. This is the heart of the process, when the incoming stimuli are differentiated, selected, and given meaning. The objects or events perceived are related to others in the immediate present and to events occurring in the past, through categorizing and classifying statements and thoughts. The average of the individual's past experiences with similar objects is compared to the present situation, and a quantitative or qualitative value judgment is made.

From this fourth stage a decision is made concerning the manner in which the perceiver will interact with the event. Important at this point is the individual's perception of his capacities to act or to deal with the situation. The individual may decide to move or to act, to assume a momentary attitude of inaction, to act at some future time, or to ignore the event. In general, however, an experimenter must require some kind of reaction either verbal or motor in order to confirm whether the perceiver attaches meaning to the facet of experience with which he has been confronted. Such concepts as intelligence and motor coordination rest on the appropriateness of the individual's choice of actions. The quality of the individual's response and the outcomes of his actions are related to his whole personality structure.

The final step in the process points to the dynamic nature of perception. It involves reinterpretation and evaluation of the decision that feed back to prepare the organism for future perception and activity. This feedback concerning the appropriateness of response, or lack of response, contributes markedly to the formation of future preparatory sets and to learning.

The perceptual process is thus a continuous and unending chain of events. We are continually coming into range of various objects. We select some for interpretation, ignore others, and act on our interpretations during all waking moments. The quality of the responses contributes to intelligent behavior, movement coordination, and the total personality.

The Components of Perception

Perception has been discussed theoretically as though it were a unitary concept. Experimental evidence, however, reveals that the process involves qualities measurable in a variety of tasks. Contrasting performance in various perceptual tests through factorial techniques has resulted in the identification of several groups of perceptual abilities.

Most of these qualities have been identified through tests of visual perception, but in any case they were selected for review because of their generality without regard to specific sense modalities. Some of these factors depend on the ability to locate quickly a central object in a complex background, to remain unconfused by various illusions, or to structure an object out of fragmented parts. As a result, intelligent discussion of various perceptual components, by necessity, involves a parallel analysis of the content of tests purporting to isolate such factors.

Perceptual Selection

One of the central factors influencing perception relates to the manner in which we select central objects from their backgrounds and our relative dependency on the central figure, or its surroundings, when making perceptual judgments. Research concerning the *figure-ground* phenomenon constitutes evaluation of the factor of *perceptual selection*.

Research in figure-ground concepts began in 1912 when the German Gestaltist Edgar Rubin[943] found that the field of visual perception is normally divided into two parts. The figure is the focus of attention, and the ground or surrounding context appears further removed, less clear, and lacking in detail. The central object is seen bounded by a contour and is perceived as a whole; the ground, on the other hand, has an indefinite shape and outline. The figure dominates the ground, is more impressive, and is better remembered.

The figure-ground phenomenon appears to be one of the basic organizing components of perception. It may be illustrated by experimental findings reported by Holzman and Klein[549] utilizing a task similar to that used by Wapner and Werner[1144] in exploring the sensory-tonic theory. A luminous rod was suspended in a dark room, surrounded by a luminous frame. Both the rod and the frame could be rotated independently. When the frame was rotated so that it was not aligned with the rod, some subjects were still able to make accurate adjustments of the rod, others could not. In other words, some subjects seemed to be influenced most by the context (the "ground" represented by the frame), whereas others were influenced most by the figure (the luminous rod) when making judgments of verticality. Some individuals were thus found to be "field dependent," and others "figure independent." These classifications seemed reliable over a period of time.

Kurt Goldstein,[445] the German psychiatrist, among others, holds that the flexibility and naturalness with which we select various objects from their background determine the consistency with which we perform motor and intellectual tasks. Perceptions of figure-ground relationships seem related to basic emotional factors and operate to determine sensory thresholds to various kinds of stimulation.

Perceptual Speed

Consistently emerging as a basic aspect of perception in most factorial studies is the speed with which perceptual judgments are made and acted on. Individuals scoring high on tests purporting to evaluate this quality generally evidence little "blocking" of responses; their reaction times are relatively short, and their perceptual judgments are acted on expeditiously.

Typical of tests evaluating perceptual speed is a matching task requiring the quick selection of one of five airplane silhouettes in one column that match those in the second row of five such figures.[935] A second task frequently used to evaluate perceptual speed involves the quick determination of words, parts of which have been erased. Rapid adaptation to the dark also seems to identify perceptual speed. The subject was presented with an illuminated screen on which a projected letter had been obliterated by bright light. A score was obtained by timing the interval between the removal of the light and the subject's correct identification of the now perceptible letter.[1101]

The speed factor emerges when responses required on a perceptual test are timed. Such a quality is probably related to innate reaction time, to a general alertness quality of personality, and to the quickness with which one is able to synthesize, organize, and draw inferences about various kinds of objects and events.

Perceptual Flexibility

Perceptual flexibility is the willingness to proceed from one fixed concept or form to a second. It involves the perception of an object in a variety of positions and situations. It infers that the individual, while accurately perceiving a given structure or object, is able to imagine it in a variety of positions. Perceptual flexibility may also be termed *perceptual imagination,* the ability to "shake-off" one attitude about an object and assume another. Tests that evaluate the ability to manipulate two simultaneously presented objects, or to engage in two movements at the same time, also evaluate perceptual flexibility.

Tests that require imagined changes in position of various objects, or prediction of movement of parts in statically presented mechanical systems, are related to perceptual flexibility. The ability to manipulate mentally two-dimensional patterns and solid figures, as represented in surface-development or unfolded solids tests, involves perceptual flexibility. In tasks of this nature, one must match a solid figure with the correct two-dimensional pattern of the figure as it might look if unfolded onto a flat surface. Tasks evaluating the resistance to one form in order to visualize a second and locating pictures of geometric design in more complex pictures also evaluate perceptual flexibility. A motor task involving two simultaneously made movements is another test of perceptual flexibility. The subject is required to touch styluses, held in either hand, as rapidly as possible to two separately numbered discs. A score is obtained by totaling the number of simultaneous touches on the same numbers.

Perceptual Structuring

A fourth general component of perception involves the ability effectively to structure a task, synthesize a form, or organize a situation despite the presence of illusions and distractions or the presence of other types of conflicting forms, activities, or objects. It also refers to the ability to draw whole meanings from fragmented evidence and to differentiate accurately between various kinds of objects and situations.

Structuring occurs after the individual selects the object from its context and, in a sense, involves the final stage of the perceptual process previously diagrammed. Tasks that evaluate the ability to construct forms and obtain whole meanings from fragmented materials seem to evaluate this quality also. Hilgard[533] has suggested that an important goal of perception includes this "achievement of definiteness and stability in the environment." Perceptual structuring refers to the success with which this is carried out.

The term *closure* is frequently utilized to identify a factor similar to perceptual structuring. Tests involving the identification of words and objects through reference to scattered incomplete or distorted visual cues evaluate the efficiency of perceptual closure. Examples of tasks in this category are the Hidden Digits test in which the subject is presented with 12 squares, each containing a multitude of small dots. The object is to distinguish letters or digits, or letters written in scripts, formed within the speckled patterns. Tests of perceptual efficiency also include some that evaluate perceptual speed and those that involve the distinguishing of simple geometric designs from within more complex ones.

The four basic factors of speed, flexibility, selection, and structuring are not felt to be mutually exclusive, nor do they constitute a complete list. Thurstone,[1101] in one of the first factorial studies of perception, identified 12 factors. Roeff,[935] in another analysis, isolated 18 elements, including a verbal factor, a memory factor, and a psychomotor factor. Identification of perceptual categories, of course, depends on the constituents of the test battery, the type of statistical treatment utilized, and the experimental focus.

The four general perceptual factors of speed, flexibility, structuring, and selection represent large *families* of elements. Their interrelationships are apparent from an inspection of the nature of tests purporting to evaluate each quality. Perceptual selection, for example, is partly dependent on the efficiency with which the individual is able to distinguish figure-ground relationships and the speed with which judgments are made. Perceptual efficiency is also related to perceptual speed.

Summary

Perception is the dynamic process of attaching meaning to objects, events, or situations occurring in the spatial and temporal proximity of the individual. It is a process involving organizing, feeling change, and selecting among the complexity of events with which men are continually confronted. It involves the attention-set, an object, sensory stimulation, and interpretations with the resultant decision. Some clinicians and researchers have formulated classification systems based on the manner in which it is purported that individuals habitually organize experience. It has been suggested that people differ in predictable ways in the amount of information they take in, as well as in the manner in which stimulus elements are organized.

Perceptual theories have evolved from those merely emphasizing sensations, and the manner in which they are organized, to those emphasizing the overall sociocultural context in which the event or object is perceived. Research reveals that general components of perception include perceptual selection, involving figure-ground concepts; perceptual flexibility, denoting the freedom to modify perception; perceptual structuring, involving the efficiency with which various objects are related and formed and the concepts of closure, leveling, and sharpening; and perceptual speed, indicating the rapidity with which judgments are made based on sensory information.

Student Reading

Borg, G.: The perception of physical performance. In *Frontiers of Fitness.* R. J. Shephard (Ed.). Springfield, Ill., Charles C Thomas, 1972.

Boring, E. C.: *Sensation and Perception in Experimental Psychology.* New York, D. Appleton-Century Co., 1942.

Dember, W. N.: *The Psychology of Perception.* New York, Henry Holt & Co., 1960.

Helson, H. (Ed.): *Theoretical Foundations of Psychology.* New York, D. Van Nostrand Co., 1951, Chapter VIII, "Perception."

Ittelson, W. H.: *Visual Space Perception.* New York, Springer Publishing Co., Inc., 1960.

Sherif, M.: A study of some social factors in perception. Arch. Psychol., *187,* 1-98, 1935.

Thurstone, L. L.: The perceptual factors. Psychometrica, *3,* 268-275, 1938.

Wapner, S., and Werner, H.: Sensory-tonic field theory of perception. J. Personality, *18,* 88-107, 1949.

Werner, H., and Wapner, S.: Toward a general theory of perception. Psychol. Rev., *59,* 324-338, 1952.

Wertheimer, M., and Beardsley, D. C.: *Readings in Perception.* Princeton, N.J., D. Van Nostrand Co., 1958.

4
PERCEPTUAL-
MOTOR RELATIONSHIPS

In recent years researchers in psychology, education, and related disciplines have begun to take a closer look at the relationships between perception and movement. The frequent appearance in the literature of the terms *perceptual-motor* and *sensory-motor* is indicative of the fact that the interactions of input to output are being scrutinized more and more by contemporary scholars. Some of the findings from studies in which the perceptual bases of motor activities have been explored offer obvious guidelines for the improvement of instruction in motor skills, while other information emanating from these investigations contributes to more basic understandings of how humans perceive, move, and develop during the earliest months of life.

Perception and Motion:
Developmental Perspectives

Some writers have speculated that perception and motion in the developing infant are inseparable, that adequate perceptual development is directly dependent on the acquisition of adequate motor competencies and that, if the infant lacks movement capacities and/or is denied movement experiences, he will probably evidence concomitant perceptual inadequacies. Piaget and others have argued for the imperative nature of the sensory-motor period that undergirds the ability to perceive, to interpret, and to think.

I believe that this type of "lamination theory" is inadequate to explain the complexities of human maturation and the acquisition of intellectual competencies of children and adults who either lack or have seriously impaired movement capacities. I have attempted to construct a more elaborate theoretical framework by which to explain the development and interactions of perceptual and motor attributes.[261] The theory proposes that the attributes of the infant or child develop along several parallel channels, reflecting verbal, motor, perceptual, and cognitive changes. These channels undergo a diffusion or branching as the child grows older, while numerous bonds are formed between these four channels. As the child ages some of these bonds may have to be obliterated in order for him to function more efficiently.

Reviewing some of the experimental evidence that supports this "lattice-work" theory may reveal the manner in which various perceptual attributes are related to indices of motor development in the maturing infant. Furthermore, the available evidence makes it clear that, at times, certain visual-perceptual abilities emerge, proliferate, and evolve relatively independent of any type of movement behavior or motor skills.

One example of the manner in which movement and visual perception first develop independently and later become welded together in various ways is illustrated in the emerging drawing behavior of infants and children.[261] During the first days following birth an infant can visually discriminate between various geometric figures placed over his crib. At about eight months of age, he begins to "exploit objects" as he hits blocks together, stacks them, and, in general, finds different things to do with them. These manipulative attributes proliferate, and when he reaches 18 months of age he usually begins to find that he can make interesting marks with crayons and pencils on tables, walls, and sometimes even on paper. Not until the age of three or four years, however, will enough strong "bonds" be formed between the infant's previously developed abilities to perceptually discriminate between the characteristics of geometric figures and his motor capacities to draw them accurately. Indeed, one of the first geometric figures *perceptually* recognized by the infant seems to be the triangle, whereas this same figure is one of the last that he can draw accurately. Not until about the age of six or seven years can a child draw accurate triangles, and he may be eight years or older before he can draw symmetrical diamonds. At varying rates, these same sequences of initial independent development of perceptual and motor attributes that are later welded together are also illustrated by data from studies in which an infant has been asked to discriminate between solid three-dimensional figures, including cylinders, cubes, and spheres. By the age of 20 *days* he is able to discriminate between the shapes of these figures, as well as between three-dimensional objects and two-dimensional ones (discs, squares, and the like).[261] And yet, not until about the age of 10 *years* can he be expected to draw these same figures accurately.

In perhaps the most provocative work carried out with infants during the 1960's, Siqueland,[1014] at Brown University, found that, by six weeks of age, an infant may be taught to suck at just the correct intensity, on a tube that controls the focus of a picture placed in front of him, to focus the picture correctly. Essentially, Siqueland demonstrated that an infant can employ his sucking apparatus as means to ends other than those for which it is normally employed. Moreover, an infant of this age, by learning to suck a given number of times a minute, can be taught to keep a picture in focus. Careful observations of an infant under these experimental conditions have revealed that after a short time the infant apparently learns how to integrate the sucking responses, vision, and head-turning reactions into a helpful and meaningful triad; so that for increased periods of time the infant may keep his gaze toward the picture, perceive whether it is clear, and, as a result, modify the strength and frequency of sucks. Siqueland suggests, after reviewing this research, that "one striking thing about human infancy is that the infant's sensory apparatus yields information far beyond the capacity of the motor apparatus to use it."[1014]

A dramatic example of the wedding of perception and motion in older children is the manner in which perceptual and motor attributes become bonded as children learn to intercept small balls projected toward them from a distance. Again the perceptual components of the task seem to emerge earlier than do the motor competencies. Also, the final bond between the appropriate perception and motion is formed in the child several years before the necessary motor and perceptual components appear separately.

At birth, the infant is attracted briefly by moving objects. By the age of six months he can usually track, using both eyes, the movements of objects placed over his crib in both vertical and horizontal directions through arcs of about 90 degrees. At about the age of one year, he learns how to walk, and by two years will start to run. During his second year, he may trap a large ball. But by the age of five or six years he still has little idea of where small balls projected from a distance will finally stop. Not until the age of nine or ten years, according to the research of Williams,[1208] can a child move accurately and quickly to small balls projected in his direction from some distance; objects that he may have been capable of visually tracking perfectly by the age of about two years. In Williams' investigation children from six to 12 years of age were tested in their ability to predict the landing site of a ball projected so that they could view only the initial part of the arc. One at a time, the children were placed under a large roof. They saw a ball-throwing machine at the end of the roof, and, after the ball was projected, they attempted to run to the spot under the roof where they felt the ball would land (if the overhead roof did not stop it). The subjects stood on switches connected to the ball-throwing machine and to a stop-clock, so that reaction time as well as accuracy of their responses could be determined.

As children mature numerous instances can be cited in which pre- viously formed bonds between perceptual and motor traits are "erased." For example, the one-year-old infant must carefully watch his moving feet as he makes his first tentative efforts to walk. By the age of two or three years this visual-motor bond has disappeared in the normal child; he no longer has to watch his feet while walking. Many other simple and complex tasks, when first mastered by the infant, require that strong bonds be formed between visual-perceptual processes and movement; whereas his later performance apparently is not dependent on an inordinate amount of guidance from his eyes.

In addition to the formation and dissolution of bonds between various perceptual-motor attributes, it also seems apparent that a marked dependence on one channel of attributes (vision) may tend to blunt the development of the other channel (movement). At the same time, if the maturing child engages in too much movement (is hyperactive), it may impair the development of attributes in the other channels.

The findings from the research by Burton White and Richard Held[1191] offer evidence of the possible interference of visual activity by the early awareness of movement capacities. Babies exposed to experimental conditions that include an inordinate amount of handling and visual displays of various types (e.g., watching stabiles placed over the crib) evidenced an average *delay* in the onset of "hand-regard" of more than three weeks when compared to infants who had not been exposed to this type of visual environment.

As can be seen from Table 4–1, however, when the groups in White and Held's study who had "massive enrichment" once began to exhibit voluntary interactions with their environment, the quality and quantity of physical contacts exceeded those exhibited by groups who had been given less (or no) visual enrichment. Thus, it was assumed that, although visual enrichment delays the onset of hand-regard, once the motor apparatus has been activated in the "enriched group" the inclination and/or ability to deal directly with things placed in their space field was accelerated.

In summary, the available data concerning the perceptual-motor relationships in the maturing infant suggest that visual-perceptual attributes mature before the motor abilities to which some of the perceptual attributes may be paired later. The successful early development of skills that depend on visual-motor coordinations is heightened by the formation of helpful bonds between perceptual and motor attributes, previously independent of one another. As the skill becomes ingrained into the child's memory, however, his performance may be marked by the apparent dissolution of a formerly helpful perceptual-motor bond.

It appears that, although the development of some perceptual attributes may depend on movement experiences, the efficient human animal also may structure his space field vicariously, without the need for direct contact. Although this latter "tactic" is more likely to be employed by the child whose motor capacities are blunted in some way, the normal child also quickly gains concepts of three-dimensional space without the need

TABLE 4-1.   Comparison of Prehensory Responses Among All Groups

RESPONSE	OBSERVED IN	TOTAL N	MEDIAN AND RANGE OF DATES OF FIRST OCCURRENCE (DAYS)
SWIPES AT OBJECT	13	13	
UNILATERAL HAND RAISING	15	15	
BOTH HANDS RAISED	16	18	
ALTERNATING GLANCES (HAND AND OBJECT)	18	19	
HANDS TO MIDLINE AND CLASP	15	15	
ONE HAND RAISED WITH ALTERNATING GLANCES, OTHER HAND TO MIDLINE CLUTCHING DRESS	11	19	
TORSO ORIENTED TOWARDS OBJECT	15	18	
HANDS TO MIDLINE AND CLASP AND ORIENTED TOWARDS OBJECT	14	19	
PIAGET-TYPE REACH	12	18	
TOP LEVEL REACH	14	14	

Courtesy of White, B. L., and Held, R.: Plasticity of sensorimotor development in the human infant. In *The Causes of Behavior: Readings in Child Development and Educational Psychology*, 2nd Ed. Rosenblith, J. F., and Allinsmith, W. (Eds.). Boston, Allyn and Bacon, Inc., 1966. Reprinted by permission.

for direct contact even before he acquires the capacities for concrete manipulative or locomotor experiences.

Physical educators, when attempting to engender sports skills in normal youngsters or to improve the movement attributes of atypical children, must aid in the formation of helpful bonds between perceptual and motor attributes, for example, when they teach youngsters to track and intercept a soaring ball. At other times they must help children to become more efficient by "erasing" the bonds between visual-perceptual events and movements that elicit less efficient functioning, e.g., watching the hand while writing or the feet while walking and running.

Educators who attempt to improve the perceptual-motor functioning of children should be well acquainted with the manner in which various movement attributes change and proliferate as children mature, and they should become familiar with the literature dealing with ocular maturation and the maturation of perceptual functions. Movement may aid in the development of certain perceptual attributes, but, to be scholarly, precisely what perceptual attributes can be modified by exactly what types of movement experiences should be delineated when devising active curricular experiences intended to promote perceptual development. (For a more detailed analysis of the visual-perceptual development of infants, see Cratty.[261])

The "Held Effect"

Held and his colleagues[509,510] at MIT have explored the influence of "self-induced movement" on the emergence of various perceptual attributes in both animal and human subjects. When animals (kittens) were used they were placed in a situation in which they could both walk and look or in one in which they could only look at their surroundings. Held's kittens were reared in the dark and then confronted with one of the two conditions mentioned. One group was permitted to pair active movement with their initial visual experiences (the kitten walking unobstructedly in Fig. 4–1); whereas the second group was permitted only passive movement, was carried, through the space field (the confined kitten in Fig. 4–1). The actively trained kittens developed normal sensory-motor coordinations, reacting to approaching objects with an eye blink response, and evidenced positive supporting reactions by reaching out with their paws when brought toward surfaces. The passively trained kittens failed to react in these ways until they had been free for several days.

To study visual-motor integration in human subjects, Held and his colleagues employed several kinds of apparatus. In the apparatus shown in Figure 4–2, the ability to locate the intersection of the lines viewed

FIGURE 4–1. Active and passive movements of kittens were compared in this apparatus. The active kitten walked about more or less freely; its gross movements were transmitted to the passive kitten by the chain and bar. The passive kitten, carried in a gondola, received essentially the same visual stimulation as the active kitten because of the unvarying pattern on the wall and center post. Active kittens developed normal sensory-motor coordination; passive kittens failed to do so until after being freed for several days. (Courtesy of Held, R.: Plasticity in sensory-motor systems. Sci. Amer., *213*, 85-95, 1965. Copyright © 1965 by Scientific American, Inc. All rights reserved.)

in a mirror was tested. One group of subjects was allowed to see their hands while they were trained; the other group was not.

In the task shown in Figure 4–3, Held tried to replicate with human subjects the general essence of the studies carried out with "dark-reared" kittens. While wearing distorting prisms, the subject is asked to make judgments concerning target placement, e.g., what is "straight ahead" and the like. One group of subjects is placed in the situation shown and

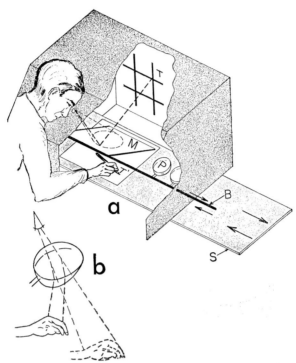

FIGURE 4–2.   Schematic representation of the apparatus designed by Held and Gottlieb to study visual-motor adaptation. Subject views his hand through the prism (P) during the training period. During the test period, the bar (B) is moved so the subject views only the target (T) in the mirror, apparently at T'. (Courtesy of Held, R., and Gottlieb, N.: Technique for studying adaptation to disarranged hand-eye coordination. Percept. Motor Skills, 8, 83-86, 1958. Reprinted with permission of authors and publisher.)

passively moved through a space field. Their responses to the task are compared to those of a group of subjects permitted to walk actively through the cylinder. In general, Held found that the best adjustment to the prismatically distorting conditions following these training experiences occurred in subjects who were permitted active movement rather than in those who were moved passively through the cylinder (as shown in Fig. 4–3).

Although Held and his colleagues at first suggested that basic visual-motor integrations occur in the lower levels of the midbrain, as the result of more recent experiments it has been suggested that these integrations occur at higher levels of the neurocortex. Judd[600] and others, in similar experiments, afforded their subjects information to think about concerning the amount of distortion that was occurring. They found that these kinds of distortions also could be resolved through thought.

Several other researchers during the 1960's and early 1970's, apparently intrigued with Held's work, have attempted to replicate his findings and have introduced experimental refinements in order to understand better the possible influence of various "input" variables on the data they obtained. Often these scholars have been unable to duplicate the findings of Held.

FIGURE 4–3. Passive transport of a subject wearing prism goggles while viewing a random scene is depicted. Purpose of the apparatus was to test the hypothesis that subjects moving actively through such a scene, which looks the same with or without prisms, would show a degree of adaptation to the prisms, whereas subjects moved passively (as shown) would not. Tests showed a link between visual and motor processes in the central nervous system by altering the correlation between motor outflow and visual feedback. (Courtesy of Held, R.: Plasticity in sensory-motor systems. Sci. Amer., *213*, 85-95, 1965. Copyright © 1965 by Scientific American, Inc. All rights reserved.)

4

In 1966, Singer and Day[1007] obtained negative results when they studied the relationships between active and passive responses after adaptation to "optically transformed vision." As a result, they suggested that the adequacy of postexposure measurement needed refinement in Held's work. Weinstein, Sersen, Fisher, and Weisinger[1167] also failed to replicate the "Held effect" in an experiment dealing with visual adaptation in 1964.

In 1966, Templeton and his colleagues[1091] suggested that Held's experimental conditions (passive versus active movement) constituted a "weak form" of training, and they proceeded to prove that, if subjects were given specific knowledge of results during training (e.g., exactly how much their hands had been distorted by viewing them through the prisms), post-training adaptation occurred whether the subjects had engaged in active or passive movement during the training interval.

Despite the controversy surrounding Held's work, his experiments with kittens are considered "classics" even by his critics. Fishkin[353] and Wilkinson[1206] have begun to explore in more detail the manner in which hand positioning, estimated visual displacement of targets, visual versus only kinesthetic feedback during training, and the time-delay between training and subsequent testing for the effects of adaptation influence the amount, kind, and direction of visual reorganization shown by human subjects. Thus, Held has been criticized for failing to control adequately the speed with which his relevant experimental variable subjects moved voluntarily under distorting conditions. At other times it has been pointed out that he did not encourage mediation in his experiments with men, treating them much like his animal subjects. Held's main contribution was the opening of an interesting and provocative area of research, potentially of use to the human factors scientist, the child development expert, and the scholar interested in the integration of perception and movement in skill acquisition.

Kilpatrick,[617] as a result of reviewing the findings from experiments using distorted rooms, suggested that perceptual organization occurs in two primary ways; (1) some percepts are the result of direct motor interactions with the environment, and (2) others are made vicariously from inspecting and thinking about the forces, movements, and other phenomena in space that are caused by the efforts of others.

French,[216] after polling subjects concerning how they made judgments about space, suggested two ways to achieve high scores on various perceptual tests: (1) to cognitively analyze the situation, and (2) to integrate sensory information without conscious effort. As they mature, children probably engage in both processes, depending on the type of perceptual judgment they are required to make and the unique experiences and capacities they possess.

After finding that perceptual judgments in infants are divisible into several distinct and independent factors (visual acuity, visual tracking, distance perception, depth perception, fractionalizing space, and the like), Olin Smith[1030] suggested that perceptions of depth (the relative distances of objects in relation to the perceiver) may be aided by loco-motor and manipulative activity, whereas judgments of distance (the relative distances between objects in space) are the result of separate perceptual processes.

The Neogeometric
Theory of Human Motion

Held allowed a period of time to elapse between the training and the testing of his subjects, in order to give evidence that the visual-motor distortions had been overcome. In contrast to this method, Karl U. Smith[1025] conducted numerous investigations of the manner in which people are able to resolve various kinds of visual-motor distortions in more dynamic ways. Generally, his subjects had to resolve various kinds of electronically created confusions and, at the same time, had to achieve accurate scores in various kinds of motor tasks. Moreover, Smith usually placed the subject's body and/or limbs in continuous motion while presenting problems in visual-motor integration and/or in the temporal dimensions of simple and complex coordinations.

In a typical experimental arrangement Smith used in his earlier work (Fig. 4–4), while observing a TV monitor the subject attempted to engage in a continuous tracking-like task, moving a pencil through a prescribed course. The TV camera can be moved to various points around the space field and the image can be inverted and/or reversed. Thus, the arrange-ment enables the experimenter to literally "pluck the eyes" from the head of his subject, and then to determine the manner in which the created distortions are resolved and the limits of tolerance for this kind of illusion. In another arrangement, Smith used a videotape of a task's visual dimensions as a feedback to his subjects. Transmission can be delayed from a few milliseconds to a second or more.

These experimental arrangements are rudimentary compared to some of the more contemporary ones employed by Smith and his colleagues at the University of Wisconsin. Rather exact monitoring devices have been applied to study the nature of eye movements and various neuro-physiological parameters, including brain wave patterns, heart rate, and respiration rate during the execution of numerous types of motor tasks. The results from hundreds of experiments have led Smith to formulate what he terms a "Neogeometric Theory of Human Motion," in which he attempts to explain, with reference to the concept of feedback, the basic nature not only of motor behavior, but also of physical exercise, muscle metabolism, social behavior, and the functions of the autonomic nervous

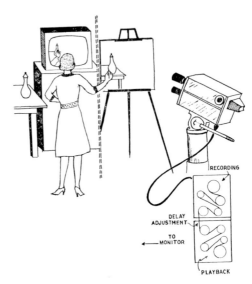

FIGURE 4–4. This test uses a dual videotape recording system to delay the visual feedback of motion. The magnitude of delay depends on the length of the interval between recording and playback. (Courtesy of Smith, K. U.: *Delayed Sensory Feedback and Behavior.* Philadelphia, W. B. Saunders Co., 1962.)

system. Although there is not space here to thoroughly pursue the theory, Smith[1026a] contends his experiments point to theoretical constructs that are better alternatives to standard psychological descriptions of behavior than are stimulus-response, Freudian, or Gestaltic terms.

Smith suggests that visually guided motor behavior can be studied with reference to several component levels of motion, including postural travel manipulative movements that in turn are mediated by what he terms "detector neurons" that detect differences in the spatial patterns of stimulation and regular movements based on this kind of search. Although Smith admits that evidence for the existence of these classifications of "detectors" has been demonstrated only indirectly (Smith and Smith,[1025] p. 128), he further contends that postural movements are regulated by older subcortical structures, transport movements (of the limbs) by bilateral structures of the new cerebellum and cortex, while manipulative behavior is integrated by cortical mechanisms.

Although, at times, Smith's theorizing is imprecise and not in accord with what is known about the complexities of neural functioning, his contributions to the understanding of feedback mechanisms in motor learning have been numerous and substantial. His experiments with distorted vision and temporal delays have established beyond doubt the rather exact pairing of vision and movement, together with a time dimension necessary for the production of accurate perceptual-motor behaviors.

Smith's recent work, outlining how gross bodily movements and the regulation of respiration and eye movements integrate, become "smoothed," and otherwise parallel the learning of complex motor skills, has elucidated the functioning and integration of mechanisms that, when explored further, may contribute to a better theoretical as well as practical understanding of the perceptual and physiological parameters of skilled learning.

However, Smith often overgeneralizes by incorporating rather crude experimental measures and procedures in elaborate electronic systems. His earlier experiments on displaced vision have been criticized by Howard and Templeton[553] and others for the failure to differentiate between the effects of two relevant variables on the production of accurate movement; the visual field has been moved from the front of the performer's body and has also been distorted in time and space. Often the motor tasks were not amenable to precise measurement of speed versus accuracy dimensions. Smith, like many others (Barsch, Kephart), is seemingly overpreoccupied, indeed, even hypnotized, with the importance of peripheral feedback mechanisms as keys to the understanding of all human behavior. He seems to perceive the human being as a kind of mindless wind-up toy, a kind of helpless servomechanism moving through an endless sequence of irrevocable social, motor, and perceptual experiences. Thus he does not really come to grips with the possibility of an individual making choices, of the self-determination of behavior. Such questions as *why* an individual sits down at a table to do a motor task in the first place and why a person chooses to "break into" or out of the social chains of events that are portrayed in his more recent writings are not adequately answered in the massive literature he and his students have produced. Some of Smith's axioms and postulates seem contrived and often are based on rather superficial data. For example, he states that "tactual tracking" is markedly superior to visual guidance, while portraying rather crude "experiments" in which subjects either watched the hands of another move and attempted to keep pace (visual tracking) or, while blindfolded, touched the fingertips of another person (tactual tracking). Citing this "evidence," Smith suggests that the vast amount of evidence showing quite clearly the superiority of vision over touch in the production of motor accuracy is invalid, and that "vision can never supersede the tactual modes of control."[1026a]

Thus, although every serious student of visual-motor or perceptual-motor behavior should thoroughly pursue Smith's experiments and writings, as they are indeed a treasure trove of practical and applied experiments that should lead to other experiments, the student should not conclude that prolific experimentation is a substitute for sound and meaningful theorizing, and that the quantity of reseach carried out is an inevitable precursor to penetrating generalizations. (For another review of Smith's research and theories, refer to Howard, I. P., and Templeton, W. B.: *Human Spatial Orientation.* New York, John Wiley and Sons, 1966, pp. 375, 381. This text also contains the most comprehensive review of all aspects of perception and motion presently available.)

The Sensory-Tonic Theory

Whereas the Gestaltist seemed primarily concerned with the complex visual field as a modifier of meaning, Werner and Wapner, in their sensory-tonic theory, suggest looking through the other end of the camera lens. They propose that perception depends equally on the general attitude (or tonus) of the perceiving individual and on the visual field. The term *tonus* is used broadly and means "the state of organismic tension as evidenced by the visceral as well as by somatic (muscular-skeletal) reactivity . . . to the dynamic (motion) and to the static posture status of the organism."[1183]

This theory holds that sensory experience and the status of the organism have equal importance in the total perceptual situation. It is based on the major assumption that the tonus factors of the organism exert a direct influence on the formation of meaning. Experimental literature from psychiatry, psychology, neurology, and physiology is drawn on to add substance to this theory.

Werner, Wapner, and Chandler[1185] carried out research that led directly to the formation of the theory. In a dark room the subject was placed erect with his head immobilized and was required to adjust visually a luminescent rod to the vertical. Using the perceived vertical as a control (subjective zero), it was found that when tonus in one neck muscle was increased by stimulation of its motor nerve, significant angular displacement of the rod to that side occurred. Similar results were obtained when strong auditory stimuli were sounded in one ear. The subject reported that the rod seemed to tip toward the side of the stimulated ear.

In another study by the same investigators, the subject was blindfolded and relied on his sense of touch to judge rod verticality. Induced muscular imbalance and unequal auditory stimulation affected kinesthetic judgment of the vertical in the same manner as described in the previous research. More recent research indicates that tactile sensation is also affected by postural tonus. Taken together, the results of these experiments are interpreted as indicating that perceptions can be altered significantly in several sense modalities when the tonus of the organism is modified.

A second important concept of the sensory-tonic theory is termed *vicariousness* or *equivalence.* This may be illustrated best by reference to the Krus, Werner, and Wagoner[641] experiment in which a subject stands in the center of a striped cylinder that rotates around him. Two perceptions are reported in this situation: (1) When the screen is moving, the subject reports watching it and he usually turns his whole body in the direction the screen is rotating. (2) When the screen is stopped suddenly, his movement also stops. However, he still perceives his body apparently moving in a direction opposite to the former rotation of the screen and a point in front of the screen apparently moving in the opposite direction.

The interpretation of these phenomena is that sensory-tonic energy may be released through body movement or may be expressed in perceptual illusions of motion. This fluctuation between the sensory experience as perceived and movement as perceived is termed *vicariousness* or *equivalence* and infers that sensory and tonic factors interact to exert equal influence on perception.

Werner and Wapner[1183] suggested that the sensory-tonic theory integrates well with those emphasizing the importance of the body-image, perception of the self or of the ego in the perceptual process. In addition, research dealing with the effect of various visceral states on perception also lends substance to the sensory-tonic theory. Thus, according to the supporters of this theory, the general tonus, the attention-set, and the state of tension assumed by or induced in the human organism seem intimately related to the perception of external objects and events.

Although the experiments inspired by the sensory-tonic theory are numerous, their findings are often contradictory and puzzling. A recent perusal of these investigations led one group of reviewers to label the theory a "wordy, oversimplified, poorly defined set of ideas." Although it is apparent that *something* occurs to visual perceptual judgments when bodily tonus is altered, exact delineation of the perceptual outcomes of various alterations of the motor sensorium is difficult to establish. For example, Sziklai[1086] found that loading the subject with a weighted vest caused his eye level to shift downward. Glick[439] found that the subject's eye level moved upward when the subject pressed down with his hands forcing his chin up against a spring and downward when his subject pressed up with his hands forcing his head down against a spring.

In both these experiments, it is obvious that changes in muscular tonus are occurring, but essentially they should be equalized by the opposing forces applied by the subjects, and thus no visual displacement should have occurred. Other experiments, studying the effects of auditory stimulation as a function of changes in muscular tonus and visual perception of apparent verticalness by Werner, Wapner, and Chandler[1185] in 1951 and Chandler[185] in 1961, produced data that contradict the primary tenets of the theory, which were established in earlier studies using body tilt instead of sound as the critical variable.

In conclusion, the findings from studies on the sensory-tonic theory of perception do not always appear to support the primary suppositions in the model espoused by its advocates; thus, although various kinds of interactions between perceptual measures and various changes in bodily tonus exist, at this point it seems that these data still need a unifying theory.

Comments

I hope that the foregoing discussion will convince all but the least sophisticated that the interactions between visual, perceptual, and motor processes are indeed complex. Although the studies of Held, Smith, and the scholars at Clark University are provocative, the data have produced more interesting questions than definitive answers, and these gentlemen have taken pains in their own writings to point out this fact.

Indeed, certain perceptual processes are important in the production and modification of skill performance. Perhaps, as Fleishman and others have pointed out (see Chapter 14), they are more important in the beginning than in the later stages of learning, but even this proposition needs further elaboration for a wide variety of skills.

Many of the theorists who attempt to link perception and motion in definitive ways seem preoccupied only with peripheral processes, to the almost total exclusion of central and higher processes, processes that seem unique to the human animal, both young and old. Organisms other than man can think, but only man can think about his thought processes. It appears that more concentration on the manner in which cognition, motion, and the simpler perceptual processes interact would be more fruitful than endless experimentation that repeatedly rediscovers the obvious fact that, if one cannot directly view one's own movements in unfamiliar tasks, rather marked incoordination occurs.

Despite the tenuous and exploratory nature of the available data relating perception and motion, many persons have devised rather elaborate motor education programs purporting to enhance a wide list of perceptual attributes of normal and of atypical children. Others, on studying the work of Wapner and Werner, have decided that school desks must be tilted at an exactly prescribed angle, or that children must have their heels raised so that both legs are even, thus minimizing the perceptually distorting tendencies of strained sitting and standing postures; this, despite the facts that, even while the body moves, the eyes can stabilize the visual field and that children assume an indeterminable number of postures in a given minute of school time. At this point, we should not assume that all motor experiences will either influence or be influenced by visual or auditory perceptual experiences just because much of the time, as Smith's work points out, voluntary motion depends on visual-perceptual factors. Just because most fire engines are red trucks does not mean that all red trucks are fire engines!

The emphasis on the perceptual qualities in voluntary motion inspired by the previously reviewed research has had helpful influences on those attempting to understand, to analyze, and to teach motor skills better, including athletic skills. Many coaches, for example, are beginning to teach for transfer from their drills to game situations by incorporating in their drills the perceptual components inherent in the game. Shooting drills in basketball often include guards waving their hands; kicking drills in football are likely to include on-rushing linemen; and a ball-throwing machine that simulates the movements of a pitcher has recently been developed for baseball players.

The material in this chapter was meant only as a brief introduction to the research that pairs perception and motion. A more thorough look at this work has been taken by Howard and Templeton,[553] and further reference to the perceptual components of motor performance and learning is found in several chapters of this text, including the two immediately following on kinesthesis and instructions, and in Chapters 11 and 17 on motor performance and motor learning.

Summary

Voluntary motor performance seems intimately tied to the visual-perceptual components of the task, including the manner in which the individual organizes his own movements, the ways in which he integrates information about the changes he perceives in the task, and the way in which he interprets information emanating from missiles and bodily extensions (bats, sticks, rackets) he may employ.

The purportedly sophisticated research on this topic, although pointing to the specificity of perceptual-motor integrations, presents more questions than answers. Karl Smith's work indicates that the individual can "tolerate" relatively little visual-perceptual stress in feedback components while performing a motor task, and even less when the temporal arrangements of the sight movement and its "feel" are modified so that they are no longer synchronized. Richard Held has inspired a number of questions by his classic work with "dark-reared" kittens, but others have had difficulty replicating his results with human beings, finding that higher processes involving the interpretation of knowledge of results may be more important than whether the individual engages in passive or active movement training in order to resolve visually distorted conditions.

The truly exciting work of Fantz,[344a] Bowers,[123a] and others, in which it was discovered that the human infant can engage in a remarkable number of reasonably sophisticated visual-perceptual judgments long before he can interact with his environment through his own efforts, should cause many to pause before setting out to "mold perception through movement." Indeed, it seems valid at this point, as Bowers suggests, that man's reasonably high place on the phylogenic scale endows him from birth with relatively sophisticated visual-perceptual processes in his nervous system.

The findings emanating from students and others interested in the sensory-tonic theory of perception are both provocative and puzzling. That bodily tonus in highly precise experimental situations alters certain definable perceptual judgments seems beyond doubt. However, a unifying theory, encompassing the multitude of often contradictory findings, seems vitally needed.

The most helpful outcomes of the previous research have been the thoughts it has inspired, thoughts of scholars and practitioners alike about the importance of sensory input and about understanding how people perceive while they act instead of being mindlessly concerned only about actions in and of themselves. I hope that, as the chapters that follow are read, a clearer understanding will be obtained about the manner in which perception and motion are related in various ways, as well as the manner in which they may operate separately at times.

Student Reading

Cratty, B. J.: Visual perceptual development. In *Perceptual and Motor Development in Infants and Children*. B. J. Cratty (Ed.). New York, The Macmillan Co., 1970.

Held, R., and Freedman, S. J.: Plasticity in human sensorimotor control. Science, *142*, 455-461, 1965.

Smith, K. U., and Smith, T. J.: Feedback mechanisms of athletic skills and learning. In *Psychology of Motor Learning*. L. E. Smith (Ed.). Chicago, The Athletic Institute, 1970.

Whiting, H. T. A.: *Acquiring Ball Skill*. London, G. Bell and Sons, Ltd., 1969.

5
KINESTHESIS: THE PERCEPTION
OF MOVEMENT POSITION AND TENSION

During the past 150 years various degrees of scientific attention have been paid to perception arising from movement and muscular tension. This interest has sometimes coalesced around attempting to discover the neurological underpinnings of kinesthesis, while at other times work has been done at the behavioral level. Most of these latter studies require subjects to report when their limbs are changed in position or to duplicate static positions of various kinds without the use of vision.

With the development of sensitive electronic apparatus in the 1940's and 1950's it has become possible to delineate rather exactly just what kinds of receptors seem to result in various kinds of kinesthetic adjustments to tasks. At the behavioral level, some of the best studies were carried out before the turn of the century. Sadly, the majority of the work since that time has often consisted of one-attempt efforts, without the benefit of solid theoretical bases. Indeed, it could be said that measurement of kinesthesis has probably provided almost as many physical educators with advanced degrees as have studies of strength and fitness.

A global survey of the available literature raises more questions than answers. While the neuroanatomical bases of various kinds of kinesthetic judgments are starting to become clear, it is more difficult to locate solid theoretical fabrics in the behavioral studies. It is particularly difficult to determine just how the findings from a majority of these studies contribute in applied ways to our understanding of voluntary motor activity. This difficulty of pairing data with practicalities seems to be caused by at least two incongruencies: (1) Most studies of kinesthesis involve rather static, discrete, and usually slowly executed positioning movements; whereas in life situations movements are rapid and flowing. (2) By definition kinesthetic judgments exclude the use of vision, whereas again in the "real world" people seldom consciously exclude vision from their motor experiences.

From a theoretical standpoint other difficulties are encountered when interpreting the available studies, in addition to the problem of their rapidly increasing number. Authorities are not always in agreement about how to define kinesthesis. Some definitions include a wide range of positionings, muscular tension changes, movements of the limbs and hands, as well as changes in the position of the total body, both passive and active. In these more global definitions it is often difficult to determine differences in sensations and perception that might be arising from muscle joints and tendon receptors, versus those that combine with these sensations and begin in receptors located in the vestibular system, pressure and touch receptors in the skin, as well as visual imagery, which might be occurring even though the subject is momentarily blindfolded. Indeed, the blind scoff at studies that purport to hold principles for the blind, in which blindfolded but sighted subjects have participated, suggesting that the sighted but blindfolded immediately "turn on" visual images while doing the task, imagery that is not always at the command of the blind, particularly the congenitally blind.

Methodological problems reside in most studies of kinesthesis, problems about which many researchers are not always cognizant. For example, since the turn of the century it has been demonstrated continually that positioning movements executed without vision are influenced in marked ways by the just-prior position of the limbs, and yet this variable is seldom (if ever!) accounted for in studies of kinesthesis.[265] Whether, after an initial positioning, a subject places his hands in his lap or keeps them on the table and the time they remain in these positions will influence to a rather significant degree the nature of subsequent judgments of their position that he may be called on to make.

Studies purportedly involving "passive positioning" of the subject's limbs by the experimenter contain similar problems. In the vast majority of investigations of this type, no effort has been made to determine just how much active involvement by the subject takes place while his arm is purportedly being positioned by the researcher; voluntary movement could easily be monitored, controlled for, and perhaps reduced through the use of the extremely accurate electronic monitoring equipment now available.

Thus, my primary thrust in presenting the following information is both to encourage the reader to be cautious when attempting to apply "knowledge" from studies of kinesthesis and to inspire researchers to "clean-up" experimental protocols and perhaps probe deeper experimentally in order to produce a model by which a unifying "picture" of kinesthesis can be obtained.

Definitions

Historically, the terms *proprioception* and *kinesthesis* have often been employed synonymously, although contemporary scholars often differentiate between the two. Bastian[71a] in 1883 was reportedly the first to apply the term "kinesthesis" to sensations of movement. In 1906 Sherrington[999,999a] used the more global term "proprioception" to connote not only the movement sense, but also perceptions formulated by sensations arising from the vestibular apparatus, pressure and tactual sensations from the skin, and other cues giving the individual an awareness of his total body position in space. Thus, from a historical standpoint, "kinesthesis" appears to be a more restricted term than does "proprioception."

Recently, more expanded definitions have been employed to delineate the meaning of the term *kinesthesis*. Scott[973] in 1955 defined kinesthesis as "the sense which enables the determination of the position of body segments, as well as their rate, extent and duration of movement, the position of the entire body, as well as the characteristics of total body movement." Scott's definition excludes little in the way of sensory information, and could include judgments made with and without vision. Magruder also formulated a similar, rather global, definition, so broad that it loses precision.

More helpful is the definition formulated by Sage[960a] in which he excludes feedback arising from visual, auditory, or verbal sources, stating that kinesthesis is the discrimination of the positions and movements of body parts, based on information *other than* (italics mine) visual, auditory, or verbal. Thus, Sage infers that kinesthesis is judgment that is nonvisual in nature, involving changes in the muscle tension, limb and body positioning, and the relative position of body parts.

Even more succinct is the statement formulated by Howard and Templeton.[553] They suggest that kinesthesis is most comprehendible as a "behavioral term," and includes the discrimination of body parts, of movement, and of amplitude of movement of body parts, made both passively (with assistance) and actively. They, like Sage, are careful to exclude visual and auditory information. They also seem to exclude the influence of information arising from the vestibular apparatus accompanying changes of the total body, since they suggest that kinesthesis can be defined as the "discrimination of the positions and movements of *body parts* (italics mine), based on information other than visual, auditory or verbal." It is this final definition that I find most acceptable and on which the remainder of the information in this chapter rests.

Since before the turn of the century experimenters have attempted to determine the interactions of vision and kinesthetic cues in the production of precise positioning. In 1882 Bowditch and Southard[123] studied visual and nonvisual positioning precision. For visual positioning the subject had an opportunity to see where he was pointing. For nonvisual positioning accuracy the blindfolded subject's arm was first positioned passively. He then had to put his arm down and return it to where he thought it had been positioned passively. They found, as did later

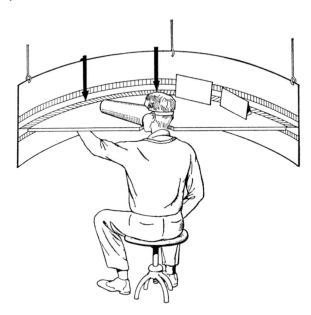

FIGURE 5–1.   Schematic representation of the apparatus used by Edgington (1953) to study the accuracy of pointing to a visual target when the subject cannot see the position of his arm. (Courtesy of Howard, I. P., and Templeton, W. B.: *Human Spatial Orientation.* New York, John Wiley & Sons, Publishers, 1966.)

experimenters, that vision was far more accurate than was blindfolded kinesthetic positioning.

Later experimenters devised ingenious apparatus, such as that used by Edgington[318a] in 1953 (Fig. 5–1), with which he studied the ability to point to a visible target without being able to see the pointing arm, i.e., pair vision with kinesthetic positioning. The subject's head is first positioned toward an arrow. He then moves his arm from the side of his body, holding it at shoulder level, and tries to point to the arrow. A board at chin level prevents him from seeing the position of his arm.

Even though detailed histologic structure of the anatomical reference points just discussed is being revealed quite clearly with the high-amplitude electronic monitoring equipment now available to neuro-anatomists, controversy exists concerning the exact ways in which the receptor and effector systems and organs mediate kinesthetic judgments.

Some disagreement exists concerning the role of the muscle spindles in the formation of kinesthetic judgments; for example, some researchers suggest that they are of little importance, believing instead that the joint receptors are more important in the judgment of movement and position of the limbs and body. Some suggest that kinesthetic awareness is largely a product of the central nervous system, citing evidence that includes the ability to continue simple movements after various kinds of "blockages" have been applied to joints and muscles involved. (It is unlikely that most of these techniques, which generally involve deadening a limb by cutting off the blood circulation with a cuff for a prolonged period of time, affect the deep-seated joint receptors.)

In any case, the reader should recognize that isolating the exact neural mechanisms that mediate a given measure of kinesthesis is an extremely complex undertaking and is highly specific to the measure involved. Most of the time kinesthetic judgments are a function of both peripheral receptor and effector systems and portions of the central nervous system.

Historical Look at Kinesthesis

According to Boring,[119] it was Vater in 1741 who first discovered the spindles in muscles, but they were described more fully by Paccini in 1835. Tendon receptors were described in 1876, and were more fully analyzed by Golgi in 1880. These fibers subsequently have been referred to as Golgi spindles.

The importance of kinesthesis to the perception of space was noted as early as 1820, when Brown pointed out that "our muscular frame" forms a "distinct organ of sense, which enables perception of spatial extensions to take place."[140] More recent factorial studies by Thurstone,[1101] Roeff,[935] and others have included a kinesthetic factor as being important when forming accurate and rapid judgments about spatial configurations.

The early psychophysicists used the reported perception of weight differences to establish several basic laws and to quantify measurement methods. Weber's law rests on such experimentation, holding that the just noticeable difference between a held weight and one held previously usually required a 1/40 increase.

Goldscheider[442] in 1898 completed classical research concerning the nature of the muscle sense by determining thresholds for passive movements in various parts of the body. He was the first to classify kinesthesis into the several components of sensitivity of muscular action, of tendon displacement, and of articulatory surfaces.

About the turn of the century, experimental studies of kinesthesis were numerous. Underscoring the popularity of research exploring the various aspects of the muscle sense was the reference to "The Great God Kinesthesis" at a meeting of the Society of Experimental Psychologists held during the early part of the twentieth century.

Much of the present-day knowledge about the neurological mechanisms underlying kinesthesis arose from the development of electronic amplifiers and their adaptation by Adrian for the recording of a single sensory nerve ending, and from the studies by Matthews in the 1930's examining the muscle spindles in frog and in mammals.

Learning and Kinesthesis

Early learning theorists, notably Gutherie,[474] suggested that conceptual frameworks are largely dependent on the chaining of movement responses. Men were believed to think primarily by remembering minute movements of the vocal apparatus in the formation of word symbols, to imagine through passively visualizing movements, and to perceive through establishing patterns in eye muscles. Among the studies lending support to these "learning through movement" theories was that by Carter[176] in 1936. He found that traversal of a maze resulted in quicker learning when unusual muscular tension was produced by springs embedded in the stylus than when these movement cues were absent.

The study of kinesthesis as behavioral phenomena became less intense in the intervening years as new experimental approaches were undertaken and as theoretical frameworks based on more central concepts were devised to explain learning and perception. For example, in 1930 Honzik[550] and others refuted the importance of kinesthesis in learning when their studies showed that mice could find their way through mazes after the nerves carrying movement sensations had been severed.

Contemporary Research

Recently, kinesthesis has been accorded more attention in the experimental literature. Contemporary research has included factorial analyses of a multiplicity of kinesthetic measures and further explorations of kinesthetic thresholds. Several variables have been found to influence the perception of kinesthetic thresholds. As early as 1909, Thorndike[1094] pointed out that exact laws concerning threshold phenomena might be questioned, due to the fact that practice was demonstrated to alter the sensitivity both to perception of held weights and to length of arm movements. He also pointed out that experimental conditions (e.g., how the weight was held) might negate previously devised "laws."

Contemporary research by Holway and Hurvich[548] lends support to Thorndike's beliefs. It was found that the weight-lifting task used by Weber to determine laws explaining just noticeable differences depended substantially on the manner in which the weight was held. Sensitivity to weight was found to be greatest when the shoulder was the fulcrum, intermediate when the elbow was, and least when the wrist was.

Although Slocum[1021] found that kinesthetic sensitivity was not significantly altered by fatigue, Leuba[678] found that duration, load, and rate of arm movement influenced judgment of their extent. Cleghorn and Darcus[200] discovered that sensibility to movement at the elbow joint was more pronounced when the joint was extended than when it was flexed; Comalli[208] found that muscular tension affected tactual kinesthetic judgments of size. Such research lends further support to Thorndike's earlier assertion that many measures of kinesthetic thresholds are relative and subjective.

Factorial studies,[973] carried out by physical educators at the University of Iowa, have resulted in the isolation of several general kinesthetic qualities, although rather low correlations are obtained between various tests of body positioning. Static and dynamic arm positioning, thigh-leg positioning, and various movements utilized in maintaining balance are among the best measures of kinesthesis identified after the scores of a large number of tests were analyzed.

Kinesthesis and Human Engineering. After World War II, human factors engineers became interested in the accuracy with which individuals can position and move their limbs without vision. Usually such basic knowledge is then applied to the placement of instrument controls and similar man-machine problems.

A recent contribution to the evaluation of thresholds was made by Ronco.[937] He developed a kine scale with which to evaluate sensitivity, defining kine as the subjective magnitude of movements, 1 inch in length, made by the arm. Ronco found that estimates of the magnitude of movement in the horizontal-medial plane were related exactly to the distance moved. He presented a precise mathematical formula of this relationship.

The Neuroanatomy of Kinesthesis

Because behavioral measures of kinesthesis are so varied, so are the processes that serve to undergird them. In general, however, the primary receptors involved in tests of kinesthesis are those in the body, mainly in the joints, tendons, and muscles. The judgments made, however, are usually dependent not only on the quality and interactions of these peripheral proprioceptors, but also on the involvement of higher neural structures, notably the cerebellum, parts of the reticular formation, and the somesthetic and motor areas of the cortex. In general three primary receptors are usually considered the main ones employed when forming kinesthetic judgments. They are the muscle spindles, the Golgi tendon organs, and the pacinian corpuscles. They generally are regarded as being influenced by changes in muscular tension and in joint angle that in turn send information to parts of the cortex and cerebellum for mediation and interpretation.

Muscle Receptors

Muscle spindles are interspersed among muscle fibers and are found in most muscles of the human body. They are a specialized form of muscle fiber containing contractile components as well as sensory endings. The sensory end-organs are confined to the outer sheath of the spindle, surrounded by a lymph-filled capsule in the central section of the spindle. This capsule seems to protect the end-organs from shocks.

The sensory ends in the spindle are of two types, primary and secondary. Primary endings are always present and are found in the equitorial region of the spindle, whereas the secondary endings are located in the proximal and distal ends of each equitorial region. These two types of endings have slightly different functions. The primary endings signal when the muscle is stretched, affording information about both the rate and the length of the stretch. The secondary endings, on the other hand, primarily transmit information concerning length. Thus, there seems to be a differentiation of the "signal" from the muscles, based on the different anatomical features of the two types of endings and their location in the spindle.

Periodically, particularly during isometric contractions, both types of spindles may evidence a "pause" during which they do not fire. Under tension the spindles fire. When quick contraction takes place, the tension on the spindles (being parallel with muscle fibers) is also released and the sensory end-organs cease firing until the "slack" in the spindle is taken up by the contraction of adjacent muscle fibers.

Changes in muscular tension are recorded more quickly and more sensitively by the spindles than by the tendons. It is generally believed that the impulses from the spindles enter the spinal cord through the sensory or dorsal roots, and once inside initiate monosynaptic reflexes, such as the stretch reflex. Other fibers from the spindles project into the cerebellum, but do not seem to reach the higher centers, e.g., the cortex.

Impulses coming from tendon receptors differ in several ways from information coming from the muscle spindles. The tendon's sensory end-organs are not as sensitive to low levels of tension, as are the muscle spindles. The tendon organs sometimes discharge during the time the sensations from the spindles "pause." Moreover, the tendon end-organs respond to active contraction as well as to passive stretch of the muscles.

More and more attention has been paid recently to a subsystem of receptors in the muscle spindles. This system is composed of what are termed "gamma" fibers, which are found in these contractile muscle fibers and innervate them. In general, this type of spindle ending has several functions, according to contemporary research: (1) one function is to maintain reasonable resting levels of tension in the muscle itself by a closed-loop feedback, peripheral circuit. (2) Another is to aid in the maintenance of appropriate tension levels in stabilizing or lengthening muscles when their opposites are in dynamic, voluntary contraction. This function is possible because of the relationships between the "gamma efferent system," portions of the cerebellum, and parts of the brain stem, notably the reticular formation. (3) The gamma efferent system also maintains the tension of the muscle spindle during the "pause" between muscular contractions. If this were not done the spindle would become flaccid during muscular contraction and would cease to function. (4) The gamma system also seems to prepare the muscle for vigorous voluntary contractions by subtly adjusting pre-performance tonus to optimum levels. (For a more detailed discussion of this system see Granit[460] and Howard and Templeton.[553])

Joint Receptors

There are two primary types of nerve endings in the joint that probably contribute to changes in joint angle and joint position: Golgi-type endings similar to those found in the tendons, and "spray-type" endings that resemble Ruffini endings found in the skin. Receptors in the joint capsule are seemingly not affected by muscular tension changes, and thus appear isolated from sensations of variations in tonus and external loading. It is probable that joint receptors interact more closely with receptors indicative of change in skin tensions, which accompany modifications of joint angle, than they do with receptors in the muscle spindle itself. Fibers from the joint receptor system project to the sensory cortex itself. The discharge of receptors in the joint and the activation of neurons in the cortex show a discrimination, some being activated when small joint angles are involved and others seemingly triggered only when a more macroscopic change in the joint angle occurs.

Thus at the peripheral levels, several sets of receptors are working, at times apparently independently, at other times interchangeably, and at still other times in close coordination. Much of the time the receptor systems are acting in conjunction with visual impressions and auditory cues; whereas in tests of kinesthesis, when external cues are purportedly reduced or removed, they interact much of the time with information from the vestibular apparatus and pressure receptors in the skin.

Furthermore, when a so-called coordination problem seems to occur, involving lack of awareness of finite changes in limb position, slight muscular tension changes, and the like, the condition may be caused by peripheral nerve damage, a defect in the ascending or descending pathways, and/or lesions in the reticular formation in the cerebellum or sensory-motor cortex, structures that interact in concert with the peripheral kinesthetic receptors just described.

The Measurement of Kinesthesis and the Results

Considered as behavior, the measurement of kinesthesis has a number of dimensions. The problems of studying kinesthesis are highlighted by the fact that when two or more measures obtained from the same group of subjects are compared, they correlate either not at all or only very slightly with each other. Thus, from a statistical standpoint, these measures are highly specific. Even when the same measures are compared, if the body segments from which they have been obtained differ, the correlations are likely to be low or nonexistent.

Kinesthetic measures may be of several types. They may reflect various kinds of thresholds, including the perception of slight movements of the limbs, when slowly displaced by the experimenter. The thresholds of the differences in hand-held weights formed the bases of many of the early psychophysics experiments in Welhelm Wundt's laboratory in Leipzig during the late 1870's. The thresholds to slight changes in the velocities of movements have also been studied. Kinesthetic measures may be made while the subjects are actively engaged in various positioning and repositioning efforts, or while the experimenter is moving their limbs for them, termed "passive movement." They may be made while the individual reacts slowly and precisely to various positioning tasks, while he is in action, or while he perceives actively moving parts of the measurement equipment. The device developed by Franklin Henry is an

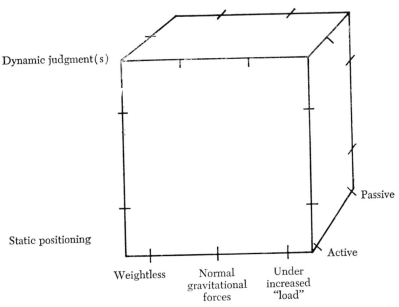

FIGURE 5–2. A three-dimensional chart depicting some of the more important dimensions of the measurement of kinesthesis. A given experiment may be located as a point, residing on the surface or within the cube, depending on whether active or passive movement is involved, whether or not the subject is placed under some "load," and the degree to which the measure obtained uses a dynamic movement task or a static one.

example of one designed to collect the latter type of impression. And finally, kinesthetic judgments may be assessed while the individual is under normal gravitational force or in situations in which this force has been reduced or increased.

A variety of measurement techniques will be outlined briefly in the following review together with some of the findings that resulted from their application. Rather thorough reviews of this subject may be found in Howard and Templeton[553] and in Sage.[960a]

Threshold Measures.   In experiments of threshold a subject is moved by the experimenter in various ways, and, without vision, is required to report when he first feels that a change of position has taken place. Variables that must be controlled include the speed with which the limbs are moved, the direction in which they are moved, how they are held, and the exact position of the body.

Passive Movement

In 1898 Goldscheider[442] investigated thresholds for passive movement in various parts of the body, determining that movements of 0.2 to 0.4 degree of displacement were sensed at the shoulder joint when the arm was moved at the rate of 0.3 degree per second. In the 1930's, Laidlaw and Hamilton[647] found similar thresholds in a passive displacement study. They also found, as did Goldscheider, that the hip and shoulder joints were the ones most sensitive to displacements when limbs were passively moved by the experimenter.

Direction and Extent of Passive Movement.   Cleghorn and Darcus[220] discovered that a subject could detect movement of a joint far easier than he could determine the *direction* of the movement. The limbs had to be moved at the rate of 1.8 degrees per second before their direction was perceived, whereas after being moved only 0.2 degree per second the subjects reported that movement was taking place, without being able to detect its direction. Usually flexion movements are more easily detected than are extension movements.

Few studies are available dealing with the ability to detect the distance that passively moved limbs traveled. However, in 1933, Van Skramlik[1172] passively moved a subject's arms a given distance at 60 centimeters per second. He then asked the subject to indicate the same distance his arm was moved between 1 and 5 centimeters per second. The distance of the faster movement was estimated as contrasted to his perceptions of the slower movement.

The studies that researchers carried out on so-called passive movement have uniformly failed to control for the degree of voluntary involvement by the subjects themselves. When scholars begin to monitor the active involvement of subjects in experiments, more confidence may be placed in the resultant data.

Active Movement

Active Positioning and Movement. In contrast to the previously outlined studies, numerous investigations have incorporated tasks in which the subject, while blindfolded or with vision excluded, first locates a point or moves in a specified way, and then attempts to replicate the position or movement. The experimenter, instead of guiding the subject's initial attempts, simply gives instructions, watches, and records. Thus, the subject first actively responds in various ways, and then attempts to reproduce as closely as possible his first response. A second protocol that is sometimes employed is to request a subject to match the positioning of both limbs in the same place, e.g., touch them to the opposite sides of a thin plate held in front of the body, or, one foot at a time, point to the same place.

A wide variety of positioning movements have been evaluated in research on kinesthesis. In the ones shown in Figure 5–3 the subject first actively, while blindfolded, positions his limbs, and then tries to replicate his initial position. In other experiments the subject is passively positioned (the experimenter guides his arm or hand), and then actively (without assistance) or passively (with assistance) he tries to reproduce the original position. In general, it is easier to replicate positions directly in front of the body than those to the sides or markedly above or below the middle of the body.

Active first positioning usually produces better repositioning than if the experimenter guides the hand to the initial position; whereas guidance (while the subject verbally confirms when a position has been reached) during the repositioning often results in better scores than if the subject is permitted to find the original point himself.

In another study by Cratty and Williams,[269] blindfolded subjects were asked to inscribe a line from a midpoint directly in front of their body. This experiment illustrates active positioning, rather than simple replication of a static position as shown in Figure 5–3.

The findings from these studies reveal that many had the proving of theoretical assumptions as their primary thrust, and others were pointed toward more applied problems. For example, in the target-pointing problem in Figure 5–3B, the data revealed where aircraft controls requiring precise nonvisual (or nonattentive) response should be placed in the cockpit; in the investigation by Cratty and Williams[269] the tendency of the blind, in the absence of external cues, to veer while walking was studied.

In a classic study, Fitts and Crannell[357] placed 24 different targets perpendicular to, and 28 inches from, a line extending from the blindfolded subject's shoulder. The task was to locate these various targets accurately. The hands were started from the front of the body. The most

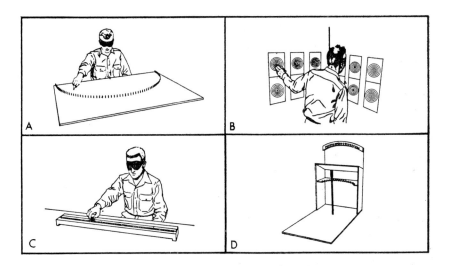

FIGURE 5–3. Tests of kinesthesis that require kinesthetic discrimination. In these tests the blindfolded subject must (A) reach a certain peg or (B) mark a certain target in response to verbal instructions. In tests (C) and (D), he reproduces certain movements with a knob or stick control. (Courtesy of Fleishman, E. A.: An analysis of positioning movements and static reactions. J. Exp. Psychol., 55, 13-24, 1958.)

accurate movements were made in front of the body and slightly below shoulder height. The most common error was reaching too low. Three variables usually contribute to accuracy in this kind of task, the original position of the pointing hand, the reaching distance, and the location of the terminal point relative to the subject's body.

The findings from other investigations in this category revealed the following: usually accuracy is greater in the space field directly in front of the subject, possibly because of the frequency with which such judgments are normally paired with vision. Kinesthetic judgments made close to the body are generally more accurate than those made further away. Preferred hands and legs are more accurately placed than are nonpreferred limbs, perhaps reflecting the influence of use in the development of kinesthetic sensitivity.

Cratty and Williams, studying the tendency of the arm to veer when the subject was requested to move it "in a straight line away from the body," found no significant hand differences; but in general the tendency was for the right arm to veer toward the left, and for the left arm to veer toward the right.

Woodworth[1220] made one of the more classic studies of the dynamics of kinesthesis in 1899. He studied over 100,000 voluntarily made pencil movements to determine the interactions of speed and accuracy. When doing division problems the faster the movement had to be executed, the more difficult it was for the subject to reproduce the exact length of the initial movement—up to 40 beats per minute accuracy remained constant, but at higher speed accuracy gradually decreased as the movements became more explosive. However *without* vision, accuracy seemed to improve with the increases in speed, particularly with the preferred hand. Woodworth concluded from the results of this and similar experiments, that accuracy of voluntary movements depends on the acuity of the sensory modality involved and the degree of deliberateness permitted by the experimenter.

During the present century, numerous studies of the accuracy of voluntary movement executed actively by the subject have been carried out. In 1957, Siddall and his colleagues[1001] studied the speed and accuracy of horizontal movements executed toward both sides, and at varying distances from the body. They found that errors of extent (how far) were greater than errors of direction (angle from the body). Other studies demonstrated that outward movements are made more accurately than inward movements, and intermediate-length movements are reproduced more accurately than extremely short (tend to be overestimated) or long (tend to be underestimated) ones. (For a more thorough review of these studies, see Howard and Templeton[553] pp. 84-90.)

Active Movement Under Load. There has long been a theoretical argument concerning whether movements under load, or tension, are made more accurately than free ones. During the 1920's and 1930's several studies of tension-kinesthetic judgment relationships were undertaken. As early as 1890 Loeb[702] found that when muscles were in slight contraction movements were often underestimated, whereas if greater contraction was produced they were overestimated. More recently, a number of scholars have investigated the effects of loading the moving limb while it traversed various distances. Bahrick and his colleagues[54] in 1955 found that "loaded" movements (via a spring resister) did not improve the spatial accuracy of rotary movements or of triangular movements, although with practice under load the rotary movements improved.

Some recent researchers, notably Christina,[189] Schmidt,[970] and Adams,[7] have stressed the importance of additional proprioceptive input in the anticipation of successive parts of a complex motor act. As a result, an "input hypothesis" has been formulated. It suggests that kinesthetic feedback from early parts of a movement is used as internalized cues for the timing of later portions, and thus through continued exposure to a skill the learner acquires specific stimulus characteristics that cue succeeding portions of the task. In support of this hypothesis these workers have found that adding proprioceptive input (usually raising tension) of certain movements aids in their acquisition in contrast to movements that are not subjected to this same overload. Vision was not excluded during performance.

Reproduction of Muscular Tension Levels. Some researchers have studied the ability of people to reproduce levels of muscular tension. At times the subject is taught to reach a certain poundage on the dynamometer. The experimenter then determines how closely the subject can reach this level without being able to see the results on the dynamometer. In another task the subject attempts to reproduce an absolute measure, e.g., to tighten his grip so that the dynamometer is 100 pounds. At other times the subject is required to fractionalize a given measure, that is, to reproduce a given percentage of his maximum, e.g., to tighten half as hard as before.

In 1945, Hick[528] required his subjects to push or to pull against a force, using a visual display for feedback, and then to increase or decrease the force they were applying a given amount. Errors generally involved overestimation, usually from 5 to 15 percent. Arthur Slater-Hammel,[1017] with this type of approach, found slight differences in the favor of athletes over nonathletes.

Maintenance of Position Under Dynamic Conditions

Research by Franklin Henry[516] underscores one of the many areas in which little is known concerning kinesthetic perception. Henry evaluated what he termed "kinesthetic adjustment" with an apparatus that required the blindfolded subject to stand with his right arm flexed and his hand against a movable hand-hold on the testing instrument. Thus, leg, arm and shoulder muscles, as well as joint receptors, were involved in the discrimination. As the cam shown in Figure 5–4 revolved, an uneven pressure was exerted by the machine against the subject's hand, which he was expected to hold in a constant position, exerting consistent pressure. Using a "difference analyzer" at the lower ends of the two vertical bars, the degree of the subject's ability to maintain constant pressure was recorded, as shown. This apparatus evaluates rather dynamic kinesthetic adjustments, instead of only the accuracy of retaining kinesthetic images of relatively simple positioning tasks.

Although a reasonably close correspondence occurred between average perception of pressure changes reported and ability to respond by maintaining a constant pressure, the slight adjustment made by the subjects under the latter conditions was so low that it was below the threshold for pressure adjustment, thus implying that a reflexive mechanism was operative.

Henry's findings suggest further investigations to explore what kinds of kinesthetic perceptions and adjustments occur reflexively at relatively unconscious levels and what types of movement positioning depend on

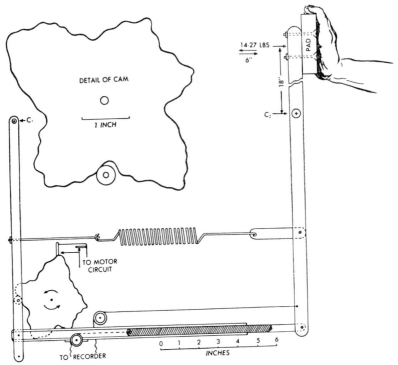

FIGURE 5–4. A, Diagram of the kinesthesis test apparatus. B, Kinesthesis test. The subject is of course blindfolded during the actual testing. (Redrawn from Henry, F. M.: Dynamic kinesthetic perception and adjustment. Res. Quart., *24*, 176, 1953.)

relatively conscious awareness by the individual. Is the fact that such measures are moving or rapid, or are confined to certain positions or parts of the body, the influencing factor? Further exploration of dynamic kinesthetic sensitivity to irregularly produced changes of pressure and position and to other types of stimulation seems needed.

The exact role that kinesthesis plays in the control of skilled movements is not always apparent. Chernikoff[188] points out that, although reaction time to passive dropping of the arm has been found to range from 120 to 130 milliseconds, it is not fast enough to permit voluntary control of movement solely through kinesthetic feedback circuits. It was suggested that the higher brain centers select a response pattern, and any correction of the movement, once under way, is difficult. This is seen most clearly as one attempts to correct an initiated ballistic movement (e.g., throwing or batting). Kinesthesis is probably of greater importance in the control of slow movements. In addition, awareness of a limb's position when beginning a ballistic action probably depends on kinesthetic feedback.

The "feel" of a movement after its completion (awkward, smooth, or jerky) also probably depends on kinesthetic sensitivity. Kinesthetic feedback from the eye and neck muscles aids in the formation of perceptions of depth and movement in the visual field. The formation of an accurate body image also is related intimately to sensations received from the various kinesthetic receptors. It is probable, however, that learning a complex movement is not entirely dependent on kinesthesis but is a product of total perceptual organization.

Another important area of investigation involves the question of whether general kinesthetic patterns are formed as a movement is rehearsed or whether kinesthetic sensations serve as discrete links in a chain while a complex serial action is practiced. Numerous maze studies, using both animals and men, suggest that both alternatives may be operative, depending on the type of evaluative instrument used, the nature and complexity of the subject's nervous system, and the kinds of cues available.

The manner in which kinesthetic sensations integrate with sensations from the viscera and from surface indices of pain, pressure, and temperature, as well as the relationship of kinesthetic measures to balance, seems worthy of further study. Kinesthetic cues are rarely the sole means through which the individual perceives his movements. In the following sections visual-kinesthetic and vestibular-kinesthetic relationships are explored briefly.

Kinesthetic Distortions

In 1933, Gibson[426] noted that subjects wearing prisms reported that straight edges not only looked curved but also felt curved to the touch. This observation prompted him to carry out further research by which he found that manipulation of a curved surface would also produce sensations of opposite curvature to a flat plane. Gibson's research and subsequent work by Kohler and Dinnerstein[635] in 1947 gave impetus to numerous investigations concerning the phenomenon termed *kinesthetic aftereffect.*

Wertheimer and Leventhal[1187] found that, with a high degree of satiation (movement in an initial task), the residual aftereffects persisted for as long as six months. Corah[218] found that the amount of attention given to the initial task seemed to influence the amount of aftereffect experienced; while Bakan and Weiler[57] found that the extent to which the subject was actively (moving a body member versus just holding an object) perceiving an object influenced the amount of aftereffect produced. In general, therefore, the literature suggests that the state of the organism (alertness) and the amount and the nature of the satiation affect the magnitude of aftereffects. Attempts to relate susceptibility to aftereffects to other performance and personality measures have generally failed.

Kohler[635] proposed that the aftereffect phenomenon is caused by some alteration of cerebral electrotonus, which carries over to create subsequent perceptual distortion. The after-discharge, previously mentioned as a property of a nerve impulse, is an important consideration in this context.

Kinesthetic Aftereffects from Gross Action Patterns. The majority of studies dealing with kinesthetic aftereffects have utilized tactual-manipulative activity rather than tasks involving movements of the entire body and/or of large muscle groups. However, it is common in the gymnasium or on the athletic field to experience aftereffects that arise from gross action patterns. For example, trampoline jumping is usually followed by a perceived inability to jump well on the floor. The batter who repeatedly "hefts" a weighted bat prior to using one of regulation weight seems intent on producing a favorable aftereffect. The common parlor game of standing in a doorway, pressing the arms against both sides of the frame, and then stepping away to let them rise, seemingly of their own volition, is another instance of a gross kinesthetic aftereffect (the Kohnstamm effect). Indeed, in all cases in which some overload is applied in an effort to improve athletic performance (to develop "strength"), the *immediate* effect of removing such an excess results in a kinesthetic illusion or aftereffect.

In a pilot study by Cratty and Hutton,[267] they demonstrated that locomotor activity of blindfolded subjects could produce aftereffects. Sixty subjects were divided into two groups of 30 each. One group guided themselves 10 consecutive times through pathways curved sharply toward the right, the other 30 moved 10 times to the left. When they were immediately placed in a straight test pathway, aftereffects were evidenced by their reports of curvature opposite to the direction in which they had been satiated. A typical delay curve was recorded. In recent years continued research on kinesthetic aftereffects using manual tasks, both limb and total body activity, led to the following conclusions:

1. The aftereffect is maximal immediately after satiation with the initial task, and then disappears slowly, leaving a residual aftereffect which may be temporary or permanent.

2. Magnitude of the aftereffect generally increases as a function of the duration of the time the satiation task is engaged in, until an optimum point is reached.

3. When attention is distracted from the inspection task, the aftereffect is reduced. Conversely when attention is heightened, as when movement is involved in the inspection task, the aftereffect is increased.

In subsequent work on this topic, sponsored by the National Science Foundation, my colleagues, Duffy[265] and Amatelli,[263] and I found that the occurrence of these aftereffects was highly task specific. When total action patterns were employed (e.g., walking blindfolded through curved and straight pathways), the aftereffects were relatively independent of tactual cues given by the railings forming the pathways.

The research by Richard Nelson and Michael Nofsinger[843] suggests that, although perceptual distortions may be *perceived* after a previously loaded limb is moved under "speed stress," there is a likelihood that there will be no significant changes in performance. The study by James Raack[907a] indicated that, if performance in a leg extension task is tested just after load is removed, slight but significant changes in leg speed may be elicited. In any case, more research is needed on this question. Although the findings of Nelson and Nofsinger are provocative, their subjects numbered only 24 and the time between removing the overload and testing for arm extension speed was not reported.

Research on kinesthetic aftereffects in arm-positioning movements indicates that if previous movements and/or positions are not well controlled they are almost certain to cause significant distortion in subsequent positionings. Thus, data from many previous studies of kinesthetic perception are highly questionable to say the least.

Kinesthesis and Athletic Skill

Kinesthetic test scores seem to differentiate broadly between proficient and average motor performers. Wiebe,[1200] using 20 tests of kinesthesis, found significant differences in the scores of varsity college athletes and nonathletes. Slater-Hammel,[1017] using the ability to repeat muscular tension levels recorded on an electromyograph as a kinesthetic measure, found that the constant errors were less for physical education majors than for liberal arts students.

In 1953, Roeff[935] reported administering eight tests of kinesthesis to 200 students in physical education classes. She obtained a significant positive relationship between these tests and the Scott motor ability test. In 1952, Norrie[856] also found differences in the kinesthetic measures she obtained from students judged "good" and "poor" by the physical education instructors. Most of the tests involved replicating limb positions, balance, and body positioning.

The quality of studies exploring relationships between measures of kinesthesis and sports skills and/or athletic ability varies markedly. Moreover, comparison of the results is difficult because of the difference in measures of kinesthesis employed, as well as the differences in definitions of "athletic ability" or "good motor ability" employed. Most of the time the relationships between static measures of kinesthesis and dynamic movement tasks are either absent or significant but not high enough for predictive purposes. The lack of marked correlations is probably due to the difference in the velocities involved in the two tasks. Most sports skills require rather rapid judgments or judgments made prior to or following a ballistic movement, too rapid for conscious control during its execution. On the other hand, measures of kinesthesis are usually obtained while the subject acts in a rather deliberate manner. Indeed, the speed with which the judgments are required, although critical, is seldom controlled.

One promising approach to resolving these dilemmas is the work of Mumby,[823] in 1953, who, employing a task similar to that designed by Henry,[916] found relationships between the ability to maintain a constant pressure against a surface moving in an irregular manner and wrestling ability. More research involving dynamic judgments, rapid judgments, and those under "loads" approximating those encountered in sport is likely to afford more information about kinesthetic perception as it relates to athletic skills, than is now available.

It is probable that certain subskills in various sports require more acute kinesthetic adjustment than do others, particularly those in which the athlete is expected to perform various movements or posturings without using vision, for example, a handstand in gymnastics. Kinesthetic qualities of various kinds may also serve to enhance skills at various levels of learning. While the factorial work of Fleishman, exploring successive influences of kinesthetic, motor, and perceptual factors during skill acquisition, has been criticized in recent years by Bechtol and others, his data reveal that there is a divergence of learning curves obtained in a two-handed coordination task when groups are separated on the basis of a "kinesthetic sensitivity" measure (determining slight differences in hand-held weights). This task illustrates the tendency of whatever is reflected in the measure of kinesthetic sensitivity to become more important in skill acquisition during the later stages of learning. Additional work of this nature, employing both static and dynamic measures of kinesthesis, together with a variety of perceptual-motor skills, could prove illuminating.

Heightening Kinesthetic Awareness

Clinicians and experimenters have attempted to heighten awareness of kinesthetic impressions with various techniques. These techniques fall into several categories: (1) teaching sports skills to blindfolded subjects, (2) reducing or adjusting muscular tension by relaxation training, and (3) therapeutically reducing the symptoms of major motor problems (cerebral palsy) with various kinesthetic therapies. (A more thorough review of this research may be found in Vanek and Cratty[1130] and Cratty.[247a])

Teaching sports skills to blindfolded subjects is generally not highly effective. The feedback apparently is not precise enough during the initial stages of learning to produce highly significant differences when contrasted with the usual methods. Perhaps studies that explore the worth of kinesthetic training at later learning trials would produce more promising results. However, the usual method is to introduce beginners to a skill while they are blindfolded, a practice that is not likely to elicit positive results, since spatial, mechanical, and cognitive factors are usually more important during the initial stages of skill acquisition.

Widdop,[1199] in a modification of this approach, found that he was able to elicit certain positive changes in kinesthetic awareness after training with ballet activities for which form-fitting leotards were worn. He hypothesized that the tactual impressions involved would contribute to the changes in the measures of kinesthesis he employed.

There has been a long history of interest in the manner in which heightening an individual's awareness of subtle changes in muscular tension contributes to his ability to display more appropriate emotional, intellectual, perceptual, and athletic abilities. Inspired by the work of Jacobson[576] in this country and by Schultz and others in Europe, these methodologies have been used with varied success by athletes, their trainers and coaches, as well as educators, psychologists, psychiatrists, and physical educators. The subjects for this work have included the psychotic, the athlete, the hyperactive child, and the retarded youth. Most of the time the results of the training elicited positive results. Many athletes in Eastern Europe, for example, apparently engage in some kind of behavioral adjustment in which gaining a heightened self-awareness plays at least a part.

The reduction of hyperactivity by relaxation training has been effective at times in changing the attention span of the hyperactive and/or retarded youngster. At other times, this training has been proved effective in modifying measures of anxiety in both children and adults.

However, because there are highly individual patterns of muscular tension emanating from unstable or stable persons when they are placed under stress, further work is needed to determine just what patterns of muscular tension can be modified by this kind of "kinesthetic training."

Recently in the eastern part of the United States, a "movement" purporting to aid the severely brain-damaged child (afflicted with cerebral palsy) to gain more control of his movements through "kinesthetic teaching" has arisen. The method involves blindfolding the child, so that when stroked and moved in various ways, he gains a heightened awareness of his actions, body parts, and body surfaces. Although the advertisement for the "product" does not parallel available research, the approach is potentially a helpful one. It should be noted that in the past therapists have employed this type of approach, for at least part of the time, when working with youngsters and adults afflicted with these kinds of problems. (Additional material about the relationships between the adjustment of muscular tension and motor performance is found in Chapter 15, Stress, Anxiety, and Tension.)

Vestibular Kinesthetic Functioning

Studies in the sensory-tonic theory of perception, research in balance and kinesthesis, and a knowledge of the neurological basis of movement, all point to the inseparability of kinesthetic sensations and sensations arising in the inner ear in giving information concerning the total body position in space.

Investigations of vestibular functioning were undertaken as early as 1820 by Purkinje. His main contribution was the discovery of an after-effect of rotation in an opposite direction if rotation in the original direction was slowed or stopped suddenly. Flourens,[374] another physiologist, at about the same time found that tampering with the semicircular canals of pigeons caused balance problems. In 1873 Mach demonstrated that rotation subjected each canal of the inner ear to specific pressures, depending on the plane in which the individual was rotated. Mach was one of the first to develop a device in which a human could be rotated about two axes. This was the forerunner of many more complex mechanisms of the same type.

The Vestibular Apparatus

The vestibular apparatus basically consists of three clear tubes filled with a fluid (endolymph) and encased in a bony labyrinth. The canals lie in three planes, and each contains hair cells supporting calcium carbonate particles (*otoliths*) that transmit linear accelerations of the body to neural impulses. Thus, as the head is oriented in different positions relative to gravity, the differential strain on the hair cells signals this displacement.

Two general kinds of sensitivity arise from the vestibular apparatus: (1) an awareness of tilt in various planes from the upright, and (2) an awareness of change in acceleration or turning of the body on one of its axes. In recent years, particularly with the advent of space travel, extensive research programs have been instituted to determine the exact manner in which these organs function and the precision of the information supplied.

Fleishman[363] tested the accuracy of the perception of verticality without visual cues. Blindfolded subjects were required to adjust a chair to the upright after it had been displaced. Greater accuracy was achieved when the head was held in a fixed position, and greater accuracy was achieved when the subjects were displaced to the left rather than to the

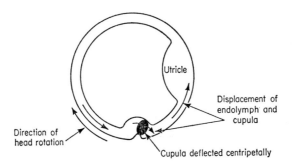

FIGURE 5–5. Schematic diagram of a vestibular canal showing the complete fluid circuit. The arrows depict the consequences of a clockwise rotation of the head in the plane of the canal. (Courtesy of Howard, I. P., and Templeton, W. B.: *Human Spatial Orientation.* New York, John Wiley & Sons, Publishers, 1966.)

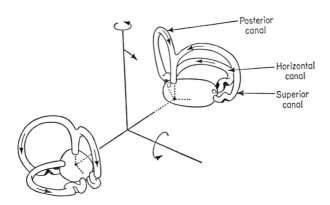

FIGURE 5–6. The arrangement of the vestibular canals on each side of the head. (Adapted from Groen, 1961) (Courtesy of Howard, I. P., and Templeton, W. B.: *Human Spatial Orientation.* New York, John Wiley & Sons, Publishers, 1966.)

right. Additionally, both the magnitude and the speed of the displacement influenced the precision of adjustment at various stages of practice. The subjects showed a high degree of consistency in their return to the upright; however, the accuracy of their adjustments was highly specific (many could adjust after being tilted to the right with accuracy, but not after being tilted to the left).

In general, it is difficult to isolate perception of tilt from other pressure and kinesthetic sensations. The straps holding an individual on any of the various tilt-tables overpower the vestibular sensations and become the dominant way in which information is received. In fact, studies of individuals who have had their otoliths removed or injured indicate that their sensitivity to the upright is nearly equal to that of those who have no such problem. Cues from the vestibular apparatus, as well as kinesthetic sensations from the neck muscles and other portions of the body, seem to override vestibular functioning with vision removed. With vision, a severe alteration in the visual field is necessary to produce distortions in the upright (e.g., removing all light except a tilted luminous rod).

In agreement with the original studies of Mach, Groen and Jongkees[467] found that minimum perception of angular acceleration for man is about 0.5 degree per second. Thresholds for tilt are less definitive and depend on the experimental conditions.

The studies of Witkin and his associates[1213–1217] point to the interaction of vision and postural cues when forming perceptual judgments about body verticality and about qualities of the visual field. Three primary tasks have been utilized in this research: (1) The tilting room-tilting chair test. The apparatus consists of a chair in a small room, both of which may be tilted laterally by either the experimenter or the subject seated in the chair. (2) The rod-and-frame test. This test measures the perception of position in the visual field. It consists of a luminous square frame and a luminous rod in a darkened room, each of which can be tilted independently. As a further variable, the subject's body may be tilted to either side when he attempts to judge the position of the rod and/or frame. (3) The apparatus in the third test is similar to that in the tilting room-tilting chair task, except that the entire room and chair can be rotated so that it is more difficult for the subject to utilize gravity cues acting on his body when attempting to adjust himself or the room to the upright.

Although this apparatus has been used in a variety of studies, they all create a conflict between visual and postural factors of perceived upright. Therefore, each represents a problem of integrating conflicting sensory experiences and arriving at a single perceptual judgment. The results of these investigations suggest that there are wide differences in the type of cues (visual or postural) individuals utilize when constructing their perceptions of positions in space and of their own bodies. Usually, however, the subjects "go along with the field" to a varying extent and base their judgments of verticality (of themselves or of the rod in the frame) on their surroundings (the tilted room or the luminous frame). The findings also indicate that individuals are remarkably consistent concerning the manner in which they arrive at their perceptual judgments in the tasks.

In general, it appears that man does not depend on the vestibular apparatus alone. Highly developed otolith organs are noted in the shark which lives in a comparatively weightless environment. The organs seem to assume less importance in man, however, because his visual apparatus and kinesthetic receptors seem to play more important roles than do vestibular sensations. The vestibular apparatus operates in close cooperation with other systems (kinesthetic receptors, visual apparatus, and other perceptual and motor systems) to contribute to the accuracy of total body movement. More research emphasis has been recently placed on the functioning of the vestibular apparatus in man in space.

Visual-Tactile-Kinesthetic
Structuring of Proximal Space

Research concerning kinesthetic visual relationships points to the conclusion that each sensation operating independently results in the formation of a different perception than that which results when several sensations are used together. When objects can only be seen, they often assume a different character than when they also can be explored manually. On the other hand, when objects can only be manipulated, different qualities are often assigned to them than if the eyes can see what the hands are doing.

Gibson[429] has pointed to the important difference in the perception formed by active touching of an object by the individual versus his being touched by the object.

Two types of research support the interdependence of tactual-motor-visual cues when making qualitative judgments of nearby objects. Studies by Bartley,[65] Zigler[1242] and others emphasize the importance of visual imagery in the formation of perceptions of manipulated objects when simultaneous visual inspection is prevented. Factorial studies by Thurstone,[1101] Guilford,[470] and others point to the importance of kinesthetic imagery in "mentally manipulating" seen objects.

Gibson[429] suggests that in some respects vision and touch register the same information and the same experience, when that experience is close to the body.

In 1953 Bartley[65] tested the hypothesis that visual imagery is operative in perception, even when tactual-kinesthetic cues are the only ones available. In visual judgment of size, near objects are generally perceived as larger than those further away. Bartley felt that, if visual imagery was important to tactual-kinesthetic perception, square blocks that were manipulated without vision might be judged larger when placed close to the individual than when located further away. His findings support the theory that factors influencing the judgment of distance and size with vision also function when only tactual-kinesthetic cues are available.

Zigler and Barrett,[1243] in a similar study, found that individuals depend on visual imagery to form accurate perceptions of forms pressed against portions of the arm and hand. Both researchers suggested that, since tactual-kinesthetic cues seem inadequate in themselves for the comprehensive judgment of qualities of objects in space, visual imagery becomes indispensable for the complete integration of tactual-kinesthetic cues.

If visual imagery is important to the tactual-kinesthetic perception of objects, the reverse also seems to be true. A kinesthetic factor consistently emerges in factorial studies relating many tests of visual perception. Generally, this attribute refers to the ability to "mentally rearrange" or structure objects perceived in two-dimensional space, while imaginarily moving them in a third dimension.

The "hands" test is heavily loaded with the kinesthetic factor. The problem is to determine quickly whether the hands pictured in a variety of positions are left or right hands. In the "flags" test the task is to determine which of several flags placed in various positions is identical to a standard flag. Such tasks, it is believed, involve kinesthetic imagination, since they require that objects in space be mentally manipulated to change their relationship to the perceiver or to similar objects. Although generally no overt movement response is required of those tested, the ability to achieve a high score in such measures is believed to depend on the facility to accurately imagine movement. Gibson[429] further emphasized the similarity between tactual and visual perception when he outlined the properties of objects that are manipulated with the hands. Their similarity to the traditional gestaltic principles gleaned from a consideration of visual perception is striking.

When handled, objects transmit an impression of *rigidity*. An observer can distinguish between two surfaces on an object: one is yielding, the other rigid, independent of visual cues. A second quality is termed *unity* by Gibson, and is suggested by that fact that when an object is felt with two or more fingers the sensations form a unitary perception of form, even when various combinations of fingers are used and that these combinations constantly change. *Stability* is another perceptual quality gleaned from manipulative activity; even as the hands and fingers move over the object, if it is fixed, it is perceived as stable in space. *Weight* is a fourth perceptual quality gained from manual-tactile activity. The whole neuromuscular feedback system (finger joints, wrist joints, and arm joints) contributes to the impression of relative and/or absolute weight of the handled object. Utilizing a task in which an individual had to match an unseen irregular object with one that was in view, it was determined that the final quality gained from manual activity was an extremely accurate concept of *shape*. Noting the similarity of these qualities with other perceptual qualities gained from "pure" visual sensations and auditory sensations, Gibson proposed a theory of perception. It holds that perception is relatively independent of sensation; the perceptual "permanence" underlying the ever-changing sensations that bombard the human organism is the crucial operation, not the separation of the sensory inputs and their later integration (through the learning process) into perceptual judgments.

Summary

Kinesthesis covers a category of nonvisual judgments evaluating the individual's awareness of limb and body movement, positioning, and changes in muscular tension. The interest in this subject has had a long history in experimental psychology and neurology and has, at times, formed the bases for learning theories and for models that attempt to explain perceptual processes.

Neurologically, kinesthetic impressions are the result of interactions at the peripheral and the central levels, including joint, tendon, and muscle receptors, mediated by portions of the sensory and motor cortex, the cerebellum, the reticular formation, and other parts of the brain stem. Some measures of kinesthesis require the integration of vestibular cues with tactual impressions. Some observers have even suggested that many blindfolded tasks call heavily on visual imagery for their execution.

When measured, kinesthesis is found to be a multi-faceted phenomenon. There are generally low intercorrelations between measures of kinesthesis and kinesthetic distortions or aftereffects. Measures of kinesthesis involve positioning the limb (without vision), either passively or actively, and then attempting to reproduce the position, still without vision. Other measures include steadiness tests, attempting to replicate measures of muscular tension, and attempting to move the limbs or body through circuitous pathways without vision.

Methodological defects in studies of kinesthesis are numerous. Often the experimenters have failed to control the nature and duration of movements or positions made just prior to the measures obtained, and much of the time so-called "passive positioning" or "passive movement" is accompanied by varying degree of active participation by the subject.

Kinesthetic methods to teach sports skills are limited in their effect. Weighted objects, when swung, make normal ones *seem* lighter, but probably do not significantly change performance. Blindfolded practice of sports skills also has limited effects. More helpful are various methods of relaxation training in which attempts are made to heighten an individual's perceptions of residual muscular tensions that, in various ways, may interfere with athletic performance, emotional stability, and classroom learning.

The relationships between motor learning and kinesthesis are complex and often unclear. Often static positioning tasks are not predictive of the quality of more rapidly executed sports skills; although recent studies incorporating more dynamic measures of kinesthesis hold promise for a more thorough illumination of causal interactions between ballistic skills, and the awareness of limb position, speed and amplitude of movement, and changes in muscular tension.

Student Reading

Howard, I. P., and Templeton, W. B.: Kinaesthesis. In *Human Spatial Orientation*. Howard and Templeton (Eds.). London, John Wiley & Sons, 1966, Chapter 4.
Smith, J. L.: Kinesthesis: a model for movement feedback. In *New Perspectives of Man in Action*. C. R. Brown, Jr., and B. J. Cratty (Eds.). Englewood Cliffs, N.J., Prentice-Hall, Inc., 1969.

6
VISION AND
VISUAL-SPACE PERCEPTION

Literally thousands of observations and scientific studies on visual behavior and visual space perception pertinent to an understanding of
the dynamics of movement and tracking behavior are important to performance and learning in various sports and physical activities. Although
during the 1930's and 1940's many of these investigations were theoretical and did not relate directly to ball skills and other visual-perceptual components of sports, more recently experiments that have clarified
problems important to those dealing with young children or with experienced athletes in game situations have increased.

Time and space do not permit a comprehensive review of all the pertinent studies of this highly complex area of investigation in this chapter.
I believe, however, that several of the principles discussed, particularly
those dealing with "dynamic visual abilities," are highly relevant and
potentially practical for students of human movement.

Early Development of
Spatial-Visual Abilities

Increasingly ingenious and scientifically sophisticated experiments,
some of which have been reviewed in Chapter 4, are beginning to
elucidate the manner in which an infant begins to deal with visual-space,
and, more importantly, how vision and movement are integrated in increasingly precise ways as an infant matures. The classic studies of
Walk and Gibson[1138] explored the awareness of depth perception in a
variety of animals and in human infants by the use of "visual cliffs" constructed from tables whose tops were half clear plate glass. The subjects
were placed on the "solid" side and encouraged to crawl toward the
"cliff." Those who retracted, the authors hypothesized, evidenced an
awareness of depth perception. These investigators concluded that all
animals, when locomotion is possible, give some evidence of perceiving
depth. Depth perception, they theorized, is largely innate, although it
is aided at times by learned cues.

117

Awareness of movement by infants seems to occur at an extremely early age. Haith[477] found that visual movement suppressed non-nutritive sucking movements in infants 24 to 48 hours old! Other investigators[331] report similar findings in young infants. The investigation by Dayton and his colleagues,[289] who used electro-oculography for the recording of both eye movement and eye position, presented findings supporting the conclusion that newborns innately possess more highly developed fixation and following reflexes than was formerly realized. According to Twitchell,[1115] infants' projection of their limbs in space occurs only following the emergence of their instinctive grasp reaction and its integration with visual mechanisms. Bruner reports that, as early as 10 weeks of age, infants evidence antigravitational activity in their shoulder and trunk musculature when objects come as close as 10 to 12 inches. Following this diffuse and undifferentiated, largely reflex activity, infants begin to engage in *preskilled and precoordinated* activity (to use Bruner's terms), denoting the onset of directed voluntary activity.

Bruner[144] studied the emergence of further hand-eye coordinations in infants one to eight months of age. He placed an infant in a specially designed chair, tilted back 30 degrees, and supported him with a band across his stomach and between his legs. Initially, the infant pursues moving objects with his head for a brief period and changes his activity level (if resting, he becomes more active, or if active he becomes more (passive) when an object moves into view. By 10 to 12 weeks of age, the infant begins to evidence a "pumping behavior" with arm, shoulder and head while keeping his gaze fixed and actively working his mouth. And at this age, he often launches swinging movements, with the fist moving in the general direction of the object. By 3½ to 4½ months of age, the infant makes less explosive action and begins to reach toward the object slowly, hand open and mouth and tongue working, reaching it with one or both hands at the midline of his body. The sequence then, according to Bruner, is activation-reach-capture-retrieval and, finally, mouthing of the object.

At times during these early reaching attempts, the infant, like the more experienced athlete, seems to depend not only on visual abilities, but also even closes his eyes at times, still reaching for the object. Bruner suggested that the infant may be trying to cut off some distracting stimuli and prevent on overburdening of his channeling capacity, depending only on proprioception during the early reaching attempts. In essence, the infant seems to be trying to avert his gaze when reaching in order to reduce the complexity of the task! With continued practice, the infant's reaching and intercepting movements become more precise and uniform. Both near and far objects are reached for at the same speed and both heavy and light objects are lifted in a similar way.

By the age of 5 years, according to the research by Olin Smith,[1030] children seem to have at least five discrete and separate visual-perceptual abilities: fractionalization of space (evaluation of what is half-way between me and you), depth perception, tracking of moving objects, distance perception (judgment of relative differences between positions, independent of the observer), and visual acuity.

With continued maturation, the child begins to employ various components of his visual, oculomotor, and movement subsystems in increasingly precise ways. Sometimes he pairs components, as when hand-eye coordinations are brought to bear on a problem confronting him. At other times he uses the systems independently, as when he simply gazes and thinks or runs without obviously looking at his feet. By late childhood, he is able to see a ball thrown toward him with moderate speed from some distance, to run and place his body in a position to intercept it, and, finally, to position his hands to catch or trap the ball.

Perception in Stable Two-Dimensional Space

Most of the gestaltic "laws" of perception offer cues through which two-dimensional space is ordered. Since more elaborate treatment of these basic principles are in texts specifically devoted to gestaltic doctrine, notably those by Koffka[630] and Kohler,[634] only passing references will be made to the most prominent ones at this time. Many of these cues and perceptual principles apply only to material in two-dimensional space. Many, however, are also basic to similar principles, under different labels, that order events in three-dimensional space and aid in the formation of perceptions about object movements.

In Chapter 3, the figure-ground concept was mentioned as an important general factor of perception and was placed under the broad classification of perceptual selection. However, this same concept is more specifically related to the perception of two-dimensional and three-dimensional space. Most figure-ground tests involve two-dimensional diagrams; therefore, these concepts properly belong in this section rather than in the one that follows. One of the basic tenets of the figure-ground concept is the fact that centrally perceived objects are more clear than is the surrounding and usually more distant field. Such an idea relates to the "clearness" cue, a characteristic of the space field by which three-dimensionality is perceived.

A second important principle is *proximity*. In general, objects that are next to each other are integrated into patterned wholes. The closer objects are, it is believed, the more likely it is that they will be combined into a common meaning or figure.

The principle of *similarity* is also important when discussing the perception of two-dimensional space. Objects that are similar in color, shape, or intensity are generally more prone to be combined into a common perception than those that are not.

Closure, an important gestaltic principle previously mentioned as underlying *perceptual organization,* is also important when structuring perceptions in two-dimensional space. In general, incomplete figures are perceived as commonly known wholes. Thus partly erased words or incomplete pictures of animals or incomplete circles quickly presented with a tachistoscope are generally reported as the completed object.

Thus the interrelated concepts of closure, figure-ground, proximity, and similarity, while by no means forming a complete list, seem the most important when considering the manner in which humans perceive structures in two-dimensional space. These concepts have been the subject of considerable research during the past 40 years. Detailed inspection of this work is left to the reader, however, as the present focus and limits of space preclude a more extensive review.

Perception in Stable
Three-Dimensional Space

Most spatial perceptions leading to movement behavior rely on a three-dimensional world. With the exception of handwriting, the painting and drawing of pictures, and various man-machine tasks, most large muscle activities utilize three dimensions. Brief consideration, therefore, will be given to the nature of cues that serve to organize perceptions in a space capsule containing depth, as well as height and breadth.

Many of these cues seem to have been discovered first by prehistoric artists to lend reality to their cave drawings, and in most cases validity seems obvious. A detailed examination of the extensive research underlying these signposts will be omitted, because the main focus of this text is on movement rather than on perception. The material presented in this section is meant only to provide a basic background from which to consider perceptual-movement relationships and is not intended to be a comprehensive coverage of space perception.

One of the most important cues used to structure stable three-dimensional space depends on the fact that a near object overlaps and partly blocks out portions of objects farther away. This *interposition effect,* related directly to figure-ground principles, contributes to the accurate relative placement of more than one object in the visual field. It is one of the primary cues through which perceptions of depth are obtained and is not dependent on the simultaneous use of two eyes (binocular), but may be considered by a single eye (monocular). Most of the cues that follow are also monocular rather than binocular.

Objects or surfaces with textures (a plowed field, a cobblestone street, and the like) also give cues concerning the relative position of objects placed on them. *Texture cues* relate to the invariance principle which holds that smaller objects will be perceived as located farther away, while larger ones will be perceived as closer. Thus the near portion of the plowed field will appear to contain larger chunks of dirt, while the irregularities grow less distinguishable on the more remote areas of the field. As a result, objects on such a background can be located more exactly by pairing them with the size of the textured pattern they seem to be nearest. Recent research on the invariance principle suggests that the size-distance relationship is not so exact as was once believed. Epstein[332] suggests that size as perceived and size as measured are often different; thus the invariance hypothesis does not deserve a central place in explanations of space perception. Adelson[14] also explains that size-distance relationships are not exact, and the "feelings" may influence one independent of the other.

Related to the invariance principle is the use of *known standards* to perceive objects in three-dimensional space. Research suggests that the exact name attached to an object by the perceiver is the main determiner of its distance and/or size. For example, if a plain white card is thought to be a postage stamp, it will be perceived as closer, in the absence of other cues, than the same object labeled a playing card. Having the same size retinal image, individuals seem to be continually comparing objects in extended space to objects and quantitative standards familiar to them. The known-size cues used to structure three-dimensional space are related to Helson's[514] principle of *perceptual pooling*, discussed previously. This is the tendency to form judgments about similar objects by continual reference to the average of past experiences.

Linear perspective is another type of cue enabling the more accurate perception of three-dimensional space. The tendency of parallel lines to converge as they extend away from the observer offers depth cues on which spatial judgments are based. The numerous studies by Ames[26] and others involving the use of distorted rooms, which seem to shrink or enlarge objects placed in them when moved to various parts, are based on this principle. The sides and windows in such enclosures are changed, and the nature of the change is concealed from the observer by a coat of paint that obliterates the usually seen converging lines of wall-floor-ceiling intersections. The naive observer thus habitually constructs a normal space field based on his past experience in looking at such rooms and becomes confused when size-distance relationships are not as expected.

One of the primary cues afforded us when perceiving three-dimensional space is related to the placement of our visual apparatus, enabling the two eyes to converge on a single object. These binocular depth cues are obtained partially from the "additional-roundness" as the two eyes see slightly different portions of the same object. The perceptual integration of these two images helps to produce the effect of depth.

The primary manner in which binocular vision provides depth cues, however, depends on the various angles at which the eyes must be fixed by their controlling muscles to intercept and focus on objects at varying distances. Thus, kinesthetic sensations arising from eye muscle tensions, monocular depth cues, and the actual size of the retinal image are combined to form accurate distance-shape judgments of objects in extended space. Most of the depth cues rely on sensations received from a single eye.

Perception of Movement in Two-Dimensional and Three-Dimensional Space

The space field is rarely a stable one. Movements of objects in two and three planes continually influence perceptual judgment. Men structure many of their gross movements in response to movements in space. The assembly line worker acts on his perceptions of conveyor belt movements and on actions of his hands when manipulating the object passing before him. The radar operator tracks objects moving across his scope by manually operating dials controlling cross hairs. The athlete continually bases his actions on perception of dynamic qualities in space: balls coming toward him to be caught or batted, or runners to be thrown to or dealt with otherwise.

The picture is further complicated when more than one object is in motion. Two men run out for a pass; cars move in the background behind a tennis court; and the machinist must attend to the rotation of the lathe as well as movements of his tools.

Thus, consideration of movement in structuring perceptions of space seems imperative. Such percepts are often referred to, owing to their complexity, as *"events,"* and several investigations have been devoted to the factors influencing *event perception.*

Temporal Perception

Perception of movement in two-dimensional and three-dimensional space involves the integration of a time dimension with some of the cues identified previously. In general, when viewing movements in space, conscious or unconscious judgments must be made concerning the time that has elapsed as an object or groups of objects traverse distances in visual or auditory fields. A brief review of the types of variables affecting perception of time thus seems worthwhile. The purpose is to present information about temporal perception that is related to movement of objects in space, not to cover such an extensive area of knowledge comprehensively. The student is referred to reviews of research on temporal perception by Dunlap,[309] Weber,[1159] Gilliland et al.,[434] and Wallace and Robin[1140] for more complete information.

Temporal perception has been described as an essential characteristic of movement and is defined as comparative or absolute judgments of the amount of separation between two units.[434] Many kinds of factors have been shown to influence the estimation of time and, thus, to affect the perception of movements in space.

Motivation is one of the primary modifiers of temporal perception and relates to the attention or interest in activities occurring in estimated time intervals. According to research by Harton,[502] Elkine,[326] and others, interesting jobs seem to make time pass quickly. More monotonous tasks, which call for few difficult judgments, cause the same time interval to be estimated as longer.

In general, various internal physiological states do not influence perception of time, except when modified by unusual drugs or the like. Neither blood pressure, pulse rate, heart work, breathing rate, nor alpha rhythms of brain waves were found to be related to the ability to estimate time, according to Schafer and Gilliland.[966]

The developmental level of the perceiver, however, has been shown by Smythe and Goldstone,[1035] Elkine,[326] and others to influence the accuracy of temporal judgment. The estimations of children are extremely inaccurate and variable until around the age of 14 to 16 years when they begin to approximate the estimations of adults.

Estimations of time intervals are also related to the type of sensation delineating the interval. For example, Goldstone et al.[1035] found that visual cues are judged consistently longer than auditory cues of the same duration are.

The culture in which the individual is raised influences perception of time. Whether estimations are influenced by unique group feelings about time in the culture or also are influenced by the climate in which the culture is located is open to question. However, as findings by Renzende[917] indicate, the prevailing temperature influences perceptual inferences of this nature.

In a study relating the intensity of large muscle activity to time estimation, Kawasima[607] had subjects estimate time while moving their arms in 10-degree circles. When action was easy overestimation occurred, and when it was difficult, underestimation.

Specifically related to time-space concepts are findings by Abbe,[2] who studied the effect of a constant time interval, established by blinking lights placed varying distances apart, on time judgment. He found that the time interval judgments were positively related to the distance between lights.

The close relationship between perceptions of time and of space is further emphasized by Weber,[1160] who suggested that, if actual velocity of an object equaled the space through which it moved, divided by the time involved, the velocity of objects as *perceived* could also be computed by dividing perceived space by *perceived time*. Thus the perception of movements is intimately related not only to their patterning, direction, and complexity but also to the accuracy of time judgments concerning their extent.

Many theories have been advanced to explain variability in time estimation. A most reasonable one was advanced by Rosenzweig,[941] who suggested that the general level of tension or "need strain" in an individual during the time interval to be perceived is the vital factor in the formation of such a perception. Generally, if tension produces the need to complete the task and other variables produce a high motivational state, time intervals are usually underestimated. Maze studies by Berman[95] support this "need tension" theory.

The body contains no identifiable organ through which time may be estimated nor do any rhythmic physiological factors seem to influence the process. The accurate estimation of time seems mainly attributable to general qualities of the situation, psychological factors inherent in the type of activity engaged in during the time interval judged, the type of sensations delineating an interval, and the developmental level of the individual.

Perception of Movement in Two-Dimensional Space

Many of the principles governing the perception of movement in two-dimensional space are derived directly from those factors influencing judgments about static objects in a similar field. In some of the literature, only broad, obvious generalizations concerning perception of movement, without substantiating experimental research, are found, for example, the concepts of closure used to explain the perception of rapidly presented sequences of scenes which result in the integrated "moving" picture—the "phi phenomenon." The figure-ground principle operates to produce the apparent movement of the "autokinetic effect." (When a single stable light is the only stimulus in an otherwise dark field, it seems to move.)

One of the primary factors influencing perception of movement is the inherent defensive mechanism built into the human organism. Perception of movement is more accurate in the peripheral portions of the eye than in the central visual field.[924] This is believed to be part of a mechanism to alert the organism to danger more quickly when objects approach from the side.

Much of the early research in this area was concerned with establishing characteristics of thresholds to movement perception. Brown found that lower thresholds to movement result when objects are dull. Research by Leibowitz and Lomont[671] substantiates these findings. They[672] found that thresholds for the perception of movement are significantly lowered when grids are added to the visual field, enabling the use of invariant cues. Thresholds to velocity are lowered by as much as 48 percent by the addition of these cues.

Brown[142] found that larger objects are perceived as moving more slowly than smaller ones. There is a marked relationship between size and speed perception. If an object is doubled in size, its velocity is perceived as being half as fast. And, conversely, to make the doubled-in-size object appear faster, the velocity has to be doubled. Speeds are perceived as faster in the vertical than in the horizontal direction.[141]

Aubert[46] and later students attempted to determine how slowly a movement could be reproduced and still be perceived. A range of variability was noted. The movement-speed thresholds ranged from one to two minutes of arc per second to 10 to 20 minutes of arc per second, depending on the availability of various auxiliary cues.

Several researchers, notably Heider,[508] Michotte,[793] and Johannson,[582] have investigated the perception of reasonably complex movements of more than one object interacting to form spatial patterns. Generally, these investigators concluded that total relationships are perceived. Also, when a change in speed or in other characteristics in one portion of the pattern takes place, completely different perceptions are reported.

Michotte[793] utilized a complex projection machine that produced two moving, intersecting dots along similar and parallel arcs that caused an apparent recoil as the pathway of one contacted the pathway of the second. His findings coincide with those of Piaget[893] insofar as perceptions of physical causality were consistently reported; one dot recoiled from the second. The subjects said that they saw one dot "pushing" or "launching" the second as contact appeared to be made. In a second study using squares moving in relation to each other, Michotte again found that the paired movements of the objects were interpreted in terms of the living behavior of organisms. One square was reported to be "mad" at the second or "afraid" of it.

In 1944 Heider[508] obtained findings that agree with Michotte's. When a black circle was moved in and out of a larger triangle, the movements were perceived in terms of human motives and purposes: the smaller dot was reported as aggressively trying to move into the "house" (the triangle), for example. Most of the researchers in this field have concluded that perceptions of moving schemata seem to be made quickly, holistically, and somewhat superficially, rather than analytically. And, in most cases, these perceptions appear to coincide with the immediate needs of the observer.

Johannson,[582] the Swedish psychologist, reported on one of the more comprehensive research programs of the perception of movements in space. He used a complex projection machine that flashed dots of light on a screen, and could form various patterns. The colors could be controlled. The device was capable of moving the spots independently to form regular geometric pathways or to produce various irregular combinations of movements. Johannson requested his subjects to describe qualitatively the various phenomena they observed in this moving kaleidoscope. Parallel studies in this program investigated the effect of fluctuating auditory and cutaneous stimuli which were varied in intensity and could make various movement patterns. These studies were described by Johannson as investigations of "event perception."

In general, Johannson's findings paralleled those of Michotte insofar as his subjects reported perceptions of patterned wholes rather than analytical descriptions of discrete parts. For example, when a pattern was presented in which the end lights were moved in opposite directions while the central light remained fixed, the subjects consistently reported that a stick seemed to be tipping back and forth. They seemed to "fill-in" the space between the lights with an imaginary rod, thus illustrating the "closure" effect noted as characteristic of stable elements in two-dimensional space.

Johannson suggested that, when the objects were presented simultaneously, their various relationships, rather than their actual speeds, exert the most influence on perception, although at times both factors seem operative. For example, when two spots of light moving at different speeds were presented at the same time, the slower one seemed to form the "ground" or field for the faster one. In conclusion, Johannson hypothesized that the perceptions of total motion rather than the intensity of the sounds, the speeds of the lights, or the force of the tactile stimulation (puffs of air) occupy a central position in the reported perceptions. Almost invariably, the subjects used temporal terms when discussing their judgments of these dynamic movements.

More recent studies have further delineated factors underlying the ability to organize movements in space effectively. Gottsdanker[458] studied the ability of human subjects to detect gradual acceleration in moving objects. Gemelli[416] presented findings in 1954 suggesting that movement left to right in the space field is perceived as faster than movement in the opposite direction. Goldstein and Weiner,[444] in a more definitive study, however, asserted that movement from left to right is perceived as accurately as movement in the opposite direction. They further concluded that when more than one object is moving at the same time: (1) when objects cross, they reach a "region of proximity" in which the objects' movements influence the observer's perceptions of both, and, as the objects move farther from one another, perceptual distortions caused by their proximity are reduced; (2) movements of discs placed high in the space field are perceived as faster than simultaneously moving ones placed lower; (3) the object starting to move first is perceived as faster than the one starting later. These researchers also found that their subjects, when viewing movement in two dimensions, frequently reported an illusion that they were viewing the objects in a third dimension.

It is believed that the findings of these studies in "event perception" have important implications for the student of human movement. They point to the fact that all aspects of the dynamic situation contribute to judgments of movements in space. For example, when a tennis ball is struck and moves toward the perceiver, judgments of its absolute speed may be influenced by the speed and direction of other background movements—the pathway taken by the opponent after hitting the ball or, perhaps, the direction and velocity of cars moving in back of the tennis court.

Perception of Movement in Three-Dimensional Space

Few studies examining phenomena related to the perception of movement in three-dimensional space were carried out prior to World War II. The complexity inherent in designing such studies seems at times insurmountable, since not only can several objects move in various configurations in space, but the observer also can change position.

The term *movement parallax* has been coined to refer to several kinds of cues utilized to judge movements in three-dimensional space. This term refers to phenomena relating to the apparent differences in speed at which various objects at varying distances from the observer seem to be moving relative to him and to each other. It also refers to the change in an object's shape that seems to take place as an observer moves around to inspect a complex figure from several positions. A commonly noted effect is that closely placed objects seem to move faster and in a direction opposite to that of the observer, whereas the farther away an object is, the slower it is judged to be moving. If two objects are moving in the same direction at the same rate of speed, the near object seems to move faster, or if two objects are judged to be the same size, the faster one seems to be closer, provided other cues are eliminated or held constant.

The movement parallax phenomenon is extremely complex, however, and is often influenced by various, almost illusionary situations. For example, when an individual is in a fast-moving train, the telephone poles near to him seem to move rapidly in a direction opposite to that of the train and at a speed directly related to that of the speeding vehicle. However, when these near objects seem to move rapidly, distant hills are often perceived to move in the *same* direction as does the train. Gibson et al.[430] have conjectured that the movement parallax phenomenon involves two types of spatial experience, "empty depth" and "filled depth." The former experience involves the perception of one surface in front of a second, whereas a receding surface acts to achieve a heightened depth effect in the latter.

Accurate perceptual judgments under such complex conditions, of course, underlie the performance of many movement skills. For example, ball-tracking facility depends on correct interpretations of various movement parallax cues in a visual field.

Tschermak[1113] presented an extensive list of situations giving rise to problems in movement parallax, when using one eye. Among these situations in differential angular velocity of moving objects are the following: (1) Circular movement: equations for determining velocities of various objects placed at varying distances and moving around a stable observer are computed or, if the angular velocities are known, distances are computed. (2) Movement parallel to the observer: the problem is to determine whether the individual is looking at various objects. Objects also tend to come into the peripheral field, thus further complicating the problem. (3) Moving head, stationary objects: approximately the same formulas are valid, depending on whether the head is moving parallel to or around the stationary object.

Graham et al.[459] published findings derived from using a device that evaluated various problems involving movement parallax cues. The task required the subject to look at two needles, one above the other, against a uniform background. Both needles moved at a constant speed in a plane perpendicular to the individual's line of sight. One needle was firmly fixed; the other could be adjusted to an equal distance from the observer by a micrometer setting. Only one eye was used by the subject to make the judgments, thus the findings pertain primarily to monocular movement parallax.

Both Zegers[1240] and Graham[459] found an increase in ability to match distance between the two moving needles when the rate of movement increased. However, if speed was increased beyond a certain point, judgments of relative distance became impossible. They concluded that sensitivity to movement parallax cues is primarily based on the individual's ability to perceive differences in the angular displacements of the two objects.

Ittelson,[570] one of the most prolific researchers in visual-space perception, conducted several studies from which he drew the following generalizations:

1. If the observer is aware of the real distance of a fixed object, when he moves the object appears to remain stationary.

2. If the observer is unaware of the exact location of an object because of some environmental or experimental distortion, when he moves the object also appears to change position.

3. If an object is moving and the observer knows its correct distance, he will accurately perceive its velocity.

4. If moving objects are incorrectly located by the observer, their judged velocities are distorted.

Such generalizations support and parallel Weber's[1160] "Perceptual Velocity Equals Perceptual Speed Divided by Perceptual Time" formula previously reported.

The exploration and delineation of these principles outlined by Ittelson have been made possible by the development of apparatus during the 1950's and 1960's with which to evaluate "dynamic visual abilities," spawning the studies reviewed in the following section.

Measurement and Meaning of Dynamic Visual Acuity

From the middle of the 1950's, considerable interest has been shown in the evaluation of what has been termed "dynamic visual acuity," defined as "the ability to discriminate an object when there is relative movement between the observer and the object." The interest is an outgrowth of the realization that these qualities probably play a more important part in such activities as driving, flying, and ball-playing than does visual acuity of static objects in less dynamic situations. Indeed, research indicates that there is a decreasing correlation between measures of static visual acuity and dynamic visual acuity when the speed of the stimulus in the latter tasks is increased. Moreover, the speed of a baseball thrown by a pitcher, and observed from first base, is estimated to travel at an angular velocity of approximately 100 degrees per second, while balls in games such as Ping-Pong, volleyball, and tennis may pass through the visual field at even higher rates of speed. Several experi-

FIGURE 6–1. Checkerboard target. (Courtesy of Burg, A.: Visual acuity as measured by dynamic and static tests: a comparative evaluation. J. Appl. Psychol., *50*, 460-466, 1966. Copyright 1966 by the American Psychological Association, and reproduced by permission.)

mental arrangements and stimuli have been employed in devices purporting to evaluate dynamic visual acuity. Ludvigh and Miller projected a C-shaped stimulus with a mirror arrangement so that the stimulus moved at various speeds across their subject's space field. The opening to the "C" was made to vary (left, right, up, and down) so that the subject's task was to report in which direction the opening appeared as it quickly traversed the subject's field of vision.

Burg and Hulbert[160,161] placed a projector above the subject's head which cast the image of a cross in front of him. A grid was positioned in either the top, bottom, left, or right section of the cross. The other three sections had a dotted pattern whose color, when moved, approximated that of the cross-patterned section. The subject had to report which section contained the checkerboard pattern (top, bottom, left, or right) (Fig. 6–1).

With the apparatus described, several conditions have been imposed: monocular vision with the head fixed or free to rotate in a horizontal plane, or binocular vision with the head fixed or free to rotate in a horizontal plane.

In general, significant changes in the ability to score high on tests of dynamic visual acuity are evident in increasing age and when the speed of the stimulus is increased. The lack of correlation between scores obtained at lower speeds and those at higher speeds has suggested that static visual acuity depends on simple ocular processes, the ability to resolve and focus on a stimulus; dynamic visual acuity depends both on the resolution processes in the ocular system and on oculomotor coordination, in which the head, neck, and gross eye movements interact.

After a series of tests of dynamic visual acuity given to Air Force cadets, Ludvigh and Miller suggested that individuals can be placed in two statistically different groups: "velocity susceptible" and "velocity resistant." In the former group are persons whose ability to make quick visual-perceptual judgments breaks down when the speed of the stimulus is increased; whereas persons in the latter group (velocity resistant) are not as easily disturbed when the speed is increased. Superior athletes in "velocity important" sports (all other things being equal) are more likely to be classified as "velocity resistant." It is unfortunate that little research has been conducted validating this hypothesis in situations requiring accurate anticipatory motor responses.[714–717]

Variables Affecting Dynamic Visual Acuity

In the ocular capabilities of the performer, a number of factors intrinsic and extrinsic to the task are likely to affect scores on tests of dynamic visual acuity. The influence of extrinsic factors was studied by Ludvigh who found that, with a target having an angular velocity of 90 degrees per second, visual acuity still improved at an illumination of 500 foot-candles. It is probable that illumination of many night games is less than optimal for the judgment of the velocities inherent in the contest. Ludvigh further explained that high illumination is necesary in dynamic conditions because the motion of the retinal image serves to reduce intensity contrast, which can be increased only by higher levels of illumination.

Although extensive work has not been done on the subject, Ludvigh and Miller suggested, as a result of their research on dynamic visual acuity, that visual tracking of rapidly moving objects is more difficult in a horizontal than in a vertical plane. The scarcity of data on this topic suggests that more detailed work, controlling for such variables as head-neck movement, target speed, and amplitude of arc should be performed before definitive conclusions are drawn.

The efficiency of at least two kinds of eye movements interact with scores obtained from tests of dynamic visual acuity. It is known that smooth eye movements can be exercised in response to relatively low angular velocities of the targets. After target speeds are increased more than 40 to 50 degrees per second, the pursuit task essentially depends on the quality of rapid jumping movements (saccadic movements) of the eye. Furthermore, efficient eye movements during ball games probably depend on the degree to which the individual can adjust his eye movements (probably at the unconscious level) to the variation in ball speed, since balls rarely travel at constant speeds in games. Further complicating the picture are recent indications that, as an individual anticipates the need to begin to track a rapidly moving object, he unconsciously suppresses saccadic movements of his eyes so that there is an initial and brief period of stability prior to the initiation of the rapid jumps needed to actually stay with the moving object once it appears.

It is well known that humans periodically blink. Investigators have found these blinks to last 40 to 300 milliseconds. Some researchers have explored the incidence and rate of eye blink as possible important influencers of performance in tasks requiring judgments of rapidly moving objects. Subsequent studies, however, have shown that this is a relatively insignificant factor. Individuals can exercise some voluntary control over this "blink reflex," suppressing it when appropriate. Experience, as well as attention and interest, can apparently prolong the period of time between eye blinks.

Practice is another factor that was investigated as possibly being important in the modification of scores on tests of dynamic visual perception. In general, effects of practice are more pronounced when target speed is rather rapid, 110 degrees per second, and slight or nonexistent at slower speeds. Moreover, when learning effects are measured, learning is found to take place rather quickly.

Exposure time also markedly affects the ability of persons to make rapid and accurate judgments about moving objects. The reaction time of the eyes prior to their initial interception of a moving target is a potentially important variable. Reaction time is 150 to 200 milliseconds. It may be an important factor in ball games when a player has only a brief time before he has to make a judgment about direction and velocity. Studies by Kay[608] and more recently by Whiting[1196] have shown that information during the later stages of a ball's flight may not be as important as information organized during the initial portions of it, which is more likely to be received accurately if reaction time to the initial presentation of the stimulus is small. Unfortunately, I am aware of no data outlining whether this response time can be reduced.

Closely related to the latency of the eye to intercept moving targets is the phenomenon termed "eye drift." This movement essentially is an anticipatory eye movement in the direction of the on-coming target (ball), which may occur *before* the object begins its movement. At higher velocities there is sometimes a slight, but rapid, "flick" of the eyes in the anticipated direction of flight. The quality, speed, and direction of these drifts or flicks, although not fully understood, may have an important bearing on ball-playing ability. Hopefully, further research will clarify the importance of this factor.

One of the more interesting relationships between visual perception and movement has been explored in studies dealing with the role that exercise plays in the modification of both visual acuity and dynamic visual perception. Studies by Whiting[1196] and by Krestovnikov (reported by Graybiel et al.[461]) suggested a positive relationship between exercise and visual functioning, which at times has elicited an improvement of as much as 45 percent in measures of acuity.

The Dynamics of Ball Anticipation

In the late 1960's and early 1970's Whiting and his colleagues[1193-1195] at Leeds employed various modifications of an apparatus designed to study dynamic visual acuity and the ability to intercept a ball swinging through a pendulum-like trajectory.* In the apparatus shown in Figures 6–2 and 6–3, a ball could be illuminated during its entire trajectory or only intermittently during its course. In a dark room it was possible to study the amount of visual information necessary for ball interception, as well as the effects of training. With experience gained while the ball

---

* In our pilot studies, however, we failed to obtain significant correlations between children's ability to intercept a ball swinging pendulum-like on a string and their ability to catch a ball bounced to them. Thus, the ability to track and to intercept a ball under these two conditions may not be as comparable as Whiting assumed. In Whiting's studies such variables as individual differences in manipulative abilities needed to catch the ball were also not controlled.

was lit continuously, some subjects began to need very little information concerning the ball's trajectory. They depended mainly on a visual cue (the lit ball), received near the beginning of the ball's swinging arc. Indeed, during the later trials, some subjects learned to intercept the ball in total darkness! Whiting concluded that this same training effect occurs in the acquisition of ball skills on the playground and athletic field, and that more experienced athletes, with excellent anticipatory skills, need very little visual inspection of on-coming balls in contrast to the less mature or less experienced individual.

Numerous variables influence the ability of players to interact and perform well in ball games, including factors that reflect the precision with which players judge rather quickly the rapidly moving objects in such contests. With the increased use of these and other measures of

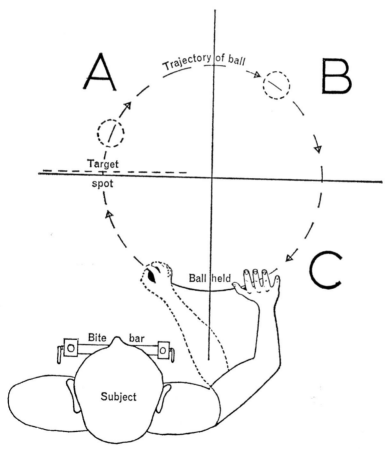

FIGURE 6–2. Plan of apparatus table showing quadrants (A, B, C) in which ball could be illuminated. (Courtesy of Whiting, H. T. A.: *Acquiring Ball Skills: Psychological Interpretation.* London, G. Bell & Sons, Ltd., 1969.)

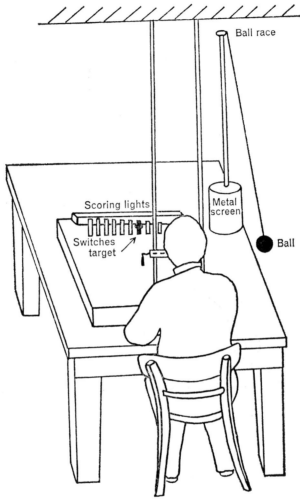

FIGURE 6–3. Modified table-skittles apparatus. (Courtesy of Whiting, H. T. A.: *Acquiring Ball Skills: Psychological Interpretation.* London, G. Bell & Sons, Ltd., 1969.)

dynamic visual acuity, it is expected that the role of visual perception will come to be delineated more exactly in many sports in which these visual abilities are potentially important.

The Role of Auditory Perception in Structuring Space

Sounds integrated with visual impressions make possible a more accurate estimation of the nature of events in three-dimensional space. The sound of the ball hitting the catcher's mitt permits the pitcher to make better judgments of speed when sound is paired with a visual impression of the ball's movement toward the plate. Sounds help localize objects in space and provide important cues in forming perceptions of reality.

The importance of sounds in space perception is given new meaning when sounds are eliminated or when some visual-auditory distortion is introduced into an experimental situation. For example, isolation in a non-echoing soundproof room has been found to have a quite disturbing effect, since the individual is removed from the familiar sounds that formerly aided him to localize himself and adjacent objects in space better.

Further illustrating the marked dependence on visual-auditory integration when forming perceptions about spatial events was Snyder and Pronko's[1038] distorted vision study. During the initial days of the experiment, the subject repeatedly mentioned the disconcerting effect of hearing cars and other objects approaching from one direction, while seeing them converging from the opposite one. Until these diverse sensations were resolved, stable perceptions about movements could not be formulated.

The nature of "auditory-space" has been the focus of experimental concern to various degrees during the past 130 years. Although initially psychologists doubted that sounds could provide knowledge about space, because sounds have no size, researchers began to perform experiments in sound localization that indicated the importance of auditory cues when structuring the space field. As early as 1887 Lord Rayleigh[913] performed simple experiments in sound localization. First, he found that, when his assistants were seated in a circle around him, he could locate and identify them when they spoke with more accuracy than he could describe the location of tuning forks placed in the same manner. Rayleigh also discovered that sounds could be located with more accuracy when they were produced in front of the body than when produced at the sides.

Several researchers around the turn of the century, including Matsumoto[746] and Scripture[976] at Yale in 1887 and Pierce[896] in 1901, constructed "sound-cages" with which to surround their subjects. They were designed to pinpoint various localizing phenomena and to test popular theories of auditory-space perception. Some researchers argued that intensity rather than location was the most important variable when identifying objects in space. Others suggested that the functioning of the balancing mechanism in the middle ear integrated with auditory impressions to form perceptions about auditory space.

Wallach[1141] showed that the kinesthetic sensation produced by head movements integrates with auditory sensations to provide perceptions of auditory space. If the head is permitted to move when sounds are produced, a more accurate judgment of their location is made than if the head is immobilized. Freedom of head movements also aided long-distance perception of the location of sounds.

The most widely accepted theory concerning localization of sound involves the concept of *dichoticity*, or the nearly simultaneous stimulation of the two ears by different kinds of sound qualities in the left-right space field. Thus, it is believed that a mechanism similar to binocular vision operates in localization of sound. A comprehensive explanation, however, would have to include the integration of auditory-kinesthetic sensations, and, when the eyes are used, various visual factors.

Vision and Visual Perception in Athletics

Even the most casual observer is aware of the importance of visual judgment in the faster moving sports. However, the measures of these abilities have not been applied to athletics in many programs of continuing research. Although most of the generalizations and principles dealing with dynamic visual acuity, discussed in the previous section, are appropriate in this context, few measures of this nature have been applied to athletes and to sports contests. Two types of studies are needed if deeper insights into the visual components of sports are to be gained. (1) The attributes of superior performers must be analyzed, and the visual abilities of inferior, average, and superior performers must be compared. (2) Factor analyses incorporating not only measures of athletic achievement (e.g., batting averages), but also measures of motor and visual abilities are necessary to understand the dynamic interactions between physical and visual attributes and their contributions to success.

As can be seen from inspecting the following material, findings relative to the role of visual and perceptual abilities in sport are conflicting. With continued work by researchers such as Whiting, more definitive answers to the questions posed by the presently available data should be forthcoming.

Generally, the earlier investigations compared perceptual-motor activities having highly dissimilar input qualities. For example, a test of static depth perception, involving the slow and deliberate alignment of rods in a tube, was often compared to fencing, basketball, or baseball skill—activities requiring rapid response to moving objects in space. The task of contemporary researchers, it seems, is to produce standardized measures of dynamic event perception that more closely approximate the real world of moving objects. Comparisons between scores achieved in such tasks and motor performance measures should produce higher perceptual-motor correlations than have thus far been obtained.

Some investigators who compared perceptual-motor functioning found that efficient visual-space perception differentiates between broad categories of motor performers. Olsen[863] found that athletes score higher in measures of reaction time, depth perception, and visual apprehension than do nonathletes. Visual apprehension was evaluated by measuring the capacity to deal with several objects, letters, or words in a single span of attention. The actual task included the quick presentation, with a tachistoscope, of several squares in sequence, each containing four to 13 small dots. The subject's score depended on his ability to make a quick accurate estimation of the number of dots presented. Winograd[1211] also reported findings implying that perceptual tests may aid in broadly classifying motor performers, but that perceptual-movement measures are not related in finer limits. Differences were found between varsity baseball players and nonathletes in several tests of visual efficiency, including binocular depth perception. However, he failed to obtain significant correlations between perceptual tests and specific performance measures (batting averages, runs batted in, and the like). Montebello,[809] as reported by Miller,[796] also found that baseball players have greater sensitivity to depth cues than nonplayers have, while finding no significant correlations between batting averages and perceptual functioning.

Graybiel,[461] reviewing research carried out during the 1952 Olympics, found that perceptual tests not only differentiate between performers and nonperformers but also permit finer discriminations to be made between athletes. Moderate correlations were found between performance in tennis, football, and other sports and depth perception.

Bannister and Blackburn[61] reported in 1931 that athletes (Rugby football players) have significantly larger distances between their eyes (interpupillary distances) than nonplayers. He felt that such an arrangement, facilitating the establishment of binocular depth cues, contributes to their superior playing ability. Although these findings remain unsubstantiated, studies clarifying the relationships between anthropometric measures, eye functioning, and physical performance are otherwise absent from the research.

Peripheral vision or the ability to perceive objects in a large angular span, usually on the horizontal plane, has been found to be an important factor relating to motor skill performance. The basic measure usually obtained is the span of vision encompassed when the head is held immobile in the medial plane. Graybiel[461] reported that, when peripheral vision is eliminated, more difficulty is experienced in motor task performance than when central vision is eliminated. In 1955, Gill[433] noted significant differences in peripheral perception of athletes and of nonathletes, and also that these differences persist after weeks of practice. Although McCain[754] found only slight differences in the peripheral vision of high-school athletes and of nonathletes, Stroup,[1074] studying basketball players, found that significant differences do exist in measures of visual sensitivity. In the latter study, peripheral vision was evaluated by a test that involved the perception of two rotating targets placed at two extreme edges of the visual field and moved through a range of 220 degrees. Thus, "the-field-of-motion" perception was evaluated, and probably a greater range was found than if only the sighting of static objects had been used.

Several researchers have taken motion pictures of the eyes and heads of sports performers in an effort to determine their overall visual behavior when tracking objects. Mott,[818] exploring the relationships between eye movements and performance during the beginning stages of four experimental motor skills, found that individuals whose eye movements are smooth perform better than do those whose movements are jerky and shift abruptly from object to object, involving many fixations.

Ocular balance also was investigated by Krestovnikov,[961] comparing 194 untrained subjects and 25 tennis champions. He found that the champions evidence significantly less deviation in the directions their eyes are fixed when in a position of rest (evaluated by noting the positions of the eyes' axes) than do the eyes of the nonathletes. Thus he indicated that the athletes have a more efficient oculomotor apparatus than do the untrained subjects. Krestovnikov also discovered that the athlete's oculomotor balance is less likely to be disrupted by visual fatigue than is the same measure in nonathletes. In 1954, Alfred Hubbard and Charles Seng[560] at the University of Illinois constructed an apparatus to study eye movements during baseball batting. Using the set-up depicted in Figure 6–4, they took movies at 24 to 48 frames per second. The research revealed that, although batters use pursuit movements of the eyes with the head fixed when tracing a pitched ball, most of the time their tracking movements stop when the ball is 8 to 15 feet from the plate.

The researchers also determined that head movements are kept to a minimum when tracking fast-moving objects coming toward the observer. Little head movement accompanies the visual tracking of incoming balls pitched 50 to 90 miles per hour. The evaluation of tracking ability through the use of an eye-movement camera holds great promise in the future. Such a device, by projecting a beam of light into the cornea and gathering the reflection in a camera that simultaneously photographs the subject's visual field, can produce a film of the visual field with a spot of light indicating where the individual was looking. The advantage to the use of such an instrument over the cinematographical analyses described above is obvious.

Two studies indicate that visual-motor integration breaks down when objects coming toward or departing from the observer exceed certain speeds. Hubbard and Seng[560] found that baseball batters were unable to track speeding baseballs thrown toward them when the balls were 8 to 15 feet from the plate. They suggested that further visual tracking is

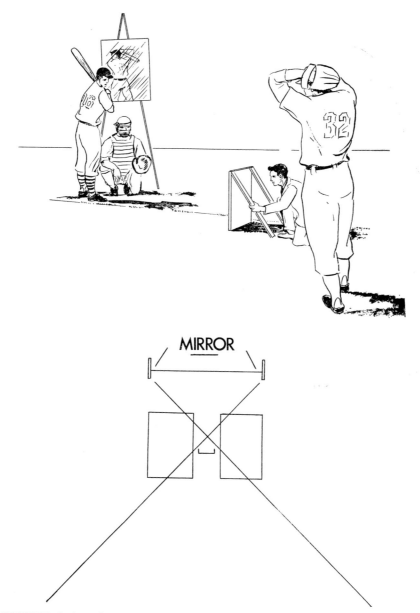

FIGURE 6–4. The mirror was actually behind the batting cage and the movie camera was 15 to 20 feet from home plate when the pictures were taken. (Redrawn from Hubbard, A. W., and Seng, C. N.: Visual movements of batters. Res. Quart., 25, 44-59, 1954.)

not only impossible, but impractical, because the movement (the bat swing) designed to intercept the object has already been initiated and cannot be stopped, even if perceptions of the ball's course *were* modified.

An unpublished study by Stull, reported by Miller,[796] suggested that the speed with which an object *departs* from the perceiver may be a factor influencing the efficiency of perception. He hypothesized that a basketball shot by an individual in the usual manner leaves him too rapidly to produce efficient binocular convergence. He suggested, therefore, that basketball shooting accuracy primarily must be due to the use of monocular, rather than to binocular, depth cues.

Two studies of a more general nature illustrate the manner in which several kinds of tests are utilized to determine the contribution of general perceptual factors to accurate movements in space. Kreiger[638] found that a moderate correlation exists between scores in a standard test of figure-ground perception and the ability to adjust a tennis racket to incoming balls thrown from various angles by a mechanical device. Thus figure-ground perception seems related in this case to perceptual anticipation, since it was found that about a 25 percent common variance exists between the two scores.

One of the most comprehensive perceptual-motor comparisons was completed in 1960 by Donna Mae Miller.[796] One hundred and sixty-two subjects, men and women recognized as champions, near-champions, or low-skilled performers in volleyball, basketball, fencing, swimming and diving, and gymnastics, were used. The battery of perceptual measures included those evaluating speed, orientation in space, spatial visualization, tests of closure, the McCloy Blocks test, and two tests of static balance. The main differences found by Miller between outstanding sports performers and low-skilled persons were balance, depth perception, closure, and the Block tests. Little difference was found between champions and near-champions on these same tests. Men scored significantly higher than did women on tests of spatial visualization, a factor that correlates with the findings of other researchers.

The significant correlation found between depth perception and balance confirmed the findings of previous investigators who held that vision is an important factor in maintaining balance. The importance of balance in performance was indicated, since the balance scores were found to provide the most valid indication for distinguishing between differing levels of sports ability. Miller concluded that champions in the various sports included evident measurable (although in most cases slight) differences in visual perception and are consistently superior to the intermediate performers. Marked differences were found when comparing high-level to low-level sports performers.

Relatively few investigations have attempted to delineate procedures with which visual-space perception might be improved. Several of these have been concerned with lowering recognition time of balls traveling in space. Haskins,[503] for example, found that the use of training films is beneficial in shortening the time necessary to perceive the direction of a tennis ball accurately.

Smith[1031] also found that, by using photographically portrayed targets, her subjects habitually underthrew distant targets and overthrew near ones. Furthermore she found that throwing at visually presented space fields that were affixed to the eyes of the subjects was helpful in studying some of the variables of the situation and that the motor responses of her subjects seemed to combine with visual perceptual cues to afford an accurate judgment of distance.

Despite the findings that certain measures of visual perception and acuity seem to be better in populations of athletes than in nonathletes, there is more than one investigation indicating that athletes' visual abilities may not be superior to the norms or to those of nonathletes. Banister and Blackburn[61] found that ability in ball games appears to be independent of visual acuity since many of the good players they measured were below normal in these measures. They concluded that visual-muscular coordination may be more important than is pure visual ability.

Measures of accommodation in athletes have also been investigated by Krestovnikov in Russia (reported by Graybiel et al.[461]). It would seem that the ability to quickly adjust the visual focus from near to far would be an important attribute in athletes. However, Krestovnikov found little difference between the athletes and the nonathletes he tested. To explain this, Sanderson suggested that the lack of differences in accommodation could be due to the fact that most visual judgments in athletics occur at intermediate ranges, whereas the most marked individual differences in the ability to accommodate are found either close or at a distance.

Winograd[1211] also found that many of the varsity baseball players he tested revealed visual defects and subnormal visual acuity. In 1940, following a thorough analysis of several of the visual abilities of athletes, Tussing found that many highly skilled performers are well below normal in visual acuity, oculomotor balance, and depth perception.[961]

These findings, coupled with the data reflecting positive relationships between measures of visual acuity, depth perception, and peripheral vision cited previously, suggest that ability in ball games depends on a multitude of complex variables and that many reasonably successful athletes in these types of sports are probably successful for reasons other than the abilities reflected in measures of vision and visual perception. Players scoring poorly in some of these measures may be able to compensate with superior motor abilities, better than average anticipatory responses from prolonged experience, and/or good visual-motor coordination, which until recent years often has not been measured except in tests evaluating dynamic visual ability.

Summary

Perceptions of the space field primarily depend on visual and auditory information integrated with temporal judgments. Perception of stable two-dimensional space may depend on gestaltic qualities of closure, figure-ground, proximity, and similarity, whereas the principles of known standards, linear perspective, texture, and interposition become important when forming perceptions of stable three-dimensional space.

The study of movement in two-dimensional and three-dimensional space has been referred to as *event perception,* and perceptions of this nature are linked with the judgment of time. The perception of movement in space is a function of the size of the objects and their luminescence, as well as their speed and other available cues. When two or more objects move in the same space field, they are generally interpreted as assuming some human function (one may be perceived as pushing another, or one may be reported as being a house with another trying to get in). In general, when complex movements of several objects are initiated in the space field, the total field is perceived as a dynamic whole, with relationships between the objects rather than their discrete functioning being most often reported. Judgments of velocities in three-dimensional space depend on the position and movement of the observer, the perceived distance of the object from the observer, and the perceived size of the object in motion.

The ability to make various judgments of moving objects varies with age, with the speed of the object, and with the arc through which the object is moved. Levels of illumination, various anticipatory responses of the eyes, and whether smooth tracking movements or saccadic movements are necessary also significantly alter the scores obtained from devices evaluating dynamic visual acuity. However, marked individual differences exist in the ability to make accurate judgments about rapidly moving stimuli, prompting one experimenter to label people either "velocity resistant" or "velocity susceptible."

The development of apparatus with which to evaluate dynamic visual acuity and of devices with which to evaluate the manner in which balls are tracked and intercepted holds promise for more definitive work relating athletic ability and success to visual and visual-perceptual attributes. At the present time, the findings from studies comparing visual and visual-perceptual abilities of athletes and nonathletes are mixed. The presently available data, however, do suggest that many athletes with inferior ocular qualities may compensate and play well, relying instead on experience and/or superior motor abilities.

Student Reading

Gibson, J. J.: *The Perception of the Visual World.* Boston, Houghton Mifflin Co., 1950.
Graybiel, A., Jokel, E., and Trapp, C.: Russian studies of vision in relation to physical activity and sports. Res. Quart., *26,* 480-485, 1955.

Ittelson, W. H.: *Visual Space Perception.* New York, Springer Publishing Co., Inc., 1960.

Sanderson, F. H.: Dynamic visual acuity and ball-game ability. Unpublished paper, Perceptual-Motor Skills Unit, Department of Physical Education, University of Leeds, 1969.

Vernon, M. D.: *A Further Study of Visual Perception.* New York, Cambridge University Press, 1954.

Whiting, H. T. A.: *Acquiring Ball Skill: A Psychological Interpretation.* London, G. Bell & Sons, Ltd., 1969.

7
INSTRUCTION

One of the more obvious types of sensory information available involves explicit directions. The manner in which the performer organizes this information, the placement of the information relative to performance of the task, the manner in which the directions are given, and the quantity of information available influence the learning and the performance of motor skills.

From the beginning of time men have guided the learning of other men. Skills needed for survival were transmitted from generation to generation before the dawn of recorded history. During the past 500 years, the writings of educators have reflected their keen interest in the influence of teaching methods on learning. More recently, scientists of human behavior have conducted carefully controlled experiments to determine more exactly the influence of instruction on learning efficiency.

Four types of instruction operate in any learning situation: (1) instruction tendered to the learner by another individual, (2) instruction that the learner acquires by himself, (3) instructions elicited from the task itself, and (4) information the learner gains from the monitoring of his own movements, either when they take place or after their execution. In this chapter, however, the main emphasis will be placed on instructions in the form of guidance extended to the learner from an external source in a somewhat deliberate manner.

The learning of a motor task does not necessarily depend on another's instructions. With regard to the process of acquisition, skills may be ranged on a continuum. At one end are those that can be learned most efficiently through continual guidance, correction, and instruction. At the other end are tasks mastered through a trial-and-error process. Most skills, however, lie somewhere in the central portion of the scale. Because man's complex sensory-motor apparatus facilitates interpersonal communication, most skills are more quickly acquired by attending to an external source of information than through internal adjustments to successes and failures.

The relationships between learning efficiency and instruction are extremely complex. In addition to the dichotomy based on the relative emphasis on instruction versus trial-and-error learning, the problem may be considered from three other viewpoints: (1) a time dimension, considers the instruction most appropriate for various stages in the learning process, (2) the extent to which instruction is designed to affect or to utilize various sensory end-organs, and (3) instruction from external sources, those elicited by the situation, and those acquired by the learner.

In a temporal consideration of instruction and motor learning, three stages emerge: (1) *Pre-performance instructions* include those that give the learner advanced knowledge concerning the extent or difficulty of the problem, or perhaps a description of the mechanical principles involved. During this initial stage an attempt is usually made to promote a "readiness to act" on the part of the learner, sometimes termed a "positive mental set." (2) Instructions during the second stage of learning, the actual *performance phase*, may include manual guidance, visual demonstration, verbal directions, and the like. (3) The *task-completion phase* generally contains instruction giving knowledge of the results. These three stages, it should be emphasized, are not usually independent but frequently overlap. For example, as an individual gains knowledge of his success on an initial phase, he is frequently in the process of completing a second movement. Performance in various serial-learning tasks exemplifies this overlapping phenomenon.

Instruction may also be classified according to the type of sensory experience involved: (1) *verbal instruction* of various kinds, (2) *visual guidance*, demonstrations, film viewing, and the like, (3) motor practice, *manual guidance* offering kinesthetic feedback of the movement to be acquired, and (4) various *combinations* of motor-visual, visual-verbal, motor-verbal, or motor-visual-verbal instruction. Numerous investigations have been concerned with the relative efficiency of one type of instruction when contrasted with another in learning motor skills.

Instruction may also be typed according to the degree to which it is designed to motivate the learner as opposed to merely extending him information. The type, nature and quantity of instruction are the important variables influencing the learning and performance of motor skills. The purpose is generally to achieve greater flexibility of behavior, while aiding the learner to analyze the task at hand. Instruction is the attempt to aid in the quick elimination of "bad" work methods or to prevent incorrect habits from forming, while facilitating neuromuscular adjustments to the movement desired.

Instruction has been shown to aid most the intellectually able and to reduce individual performance differences caused by structure.[422] In some situations, the absence of instruction, with the subsequent lack of knowledge concerning results, *prevents* learning from taking place. A comprehensive consideration of the influence of instruction on learning is imperative if greater understanding of the manner in which motor skill is acquired is to be gained.

Developmental Dimensions

The extending of formal instruction seems to have varied effects on children and youth of various ages. The types of instructions that seem to "work" best probably vary not only as a function of maturity, but also may be related to sex. Although present data are somewhat incomplete, specific instruction of children in the primary grades is likely to have a positive effect even on rather basic and purportedly "naturally acquired skills."

Wild[1204] and others have demonstrated that children as young as six or seven years, left to their own devices, may acquire mature throwing patterns, perhaps consciously or unconsciously copied from their peers. At the same time, evidence of the correct mechanical principles of throwing are often not seen even as late as high-school age in girls, and in some boys.

During the first and second grades, according to the data collected by Dusenbury,[311] children may be taught to throw efficiently and accurately. The studies of Sparks[1042] and Taylor[1088] indicate that instruction may also have a positive effect on jumping skills during these same years.

Malina,[729] studying the improvement of throwing behavior in high-school boys, found that accuracy is more difficult to improve than are throwing distance and velocity. Only after a two-week period does accuracy begin to improve (three practice sessions a week). Moreover, these more mature subjects seem to be able to incorporate information relative to improving the speed and velocity of their throwing behavior more easily than they could deal with information expected to improve accuracy.

Several thousand college and university physical education teachers tacitly assume that their efforts do indeed aid their students to gain skill. For the most part, their efforts are probably helpful to their students, but the result of a pilot study by Nelson[841] may cause some to pause and reflect. He divided male college students into two groups, one of which was given formal instruction while the second was permitted only to play in matched singles competition. The latter group of students were encouraged to "think and explore" when they encountered problems in skills acquisition. At the conclusion of the study, the noninstructed group recorded a higher level of skill than did the closely guided one. Nelson suggested that, when mature students are encouraged to develop their own unique styles and to concentrate on the individual problems they encounter, they progress more markedly than if their uniqueness is ignored in a mass-instructional situation.

Needless to say, the results of Nelson's study do not suggest that all students simply be left to their own devices when attempting to acquire skills. These data do point, however, to the importance of teaching for individual differences, at times, and for permitting exploratory practice by individuals independent of direct and often overstructured control by an instructor. Probably this kind of self-practice is most effective with mature learners and for those who do not desire or need to achieve extremely high levels of skill.

Numerous other developmental guidelines may be followed when teaching skills to children of various ages. For example, when working with smaller, younger children, care must be taken to place a visual demonstration in the restricted visual field of the youngster. A demonstration by a child of similar size is often desirable. Moreover, in younger children manual guidance in the youngster's own frame of reference (e.g., moving the child's hands, while facing in the same direction he is facing) is also important.

With the initiation and completion of further studies in this area, even more definitive guidelines for teaching motor skills to children of various ages and sexes should be forthcoming.

The Placement of
Instructions in Time

The initial type of instruction placed in a time dimension consists of directions that attempt to prepare an individual for learning and might be termed the *task-preparation phase*. Instruction at this stage generally has several purposes: (1) to provide a "warm-up" or readiness to learn the skill (sometimes referred to as creating the correct "mental set"), (2) to make the learner familiar with performance principles indigenous to the task, and (3) to give the individual information concerning the general severity duration, or difficulty of the task (sometimes termed the "amount-set").

Verbal instructions seem most important during the initial stage of learning. However, their complexity should not exceed the comprehension limits of the learners. Verbal pre-training is best kept to a minimum, especially in learning tasks containing rapid movements. Slowing of the movement to keep pace with a memorized verbal formula, especially during the later stages of learning, usually is not desirable. Verbal and/or written directions can, however, effectively point to similarities between the task to be learned and the individual's past experiences. They help to motivate the learner and also transmit knowledge of mechanical principles and spatial relationships involved in performance.

A visual demonstration is often a helpful method of task preparation. The demonstration may be copied, however, only to the extent to which the learner is able to identify with the demonstrator and to see himself in the role of the performer. Observation of a complex demonstration might have a detrimental effect.

Manual guidance during the pre-performance stage is also effective in transmitting knowledge of the spatial relationships, the speed of movements desired, or the force needed. Many times, however, movements that are too enthusiastically guided by an instructor may delay the learner in gaining the "feel" of the task. In some cases, because of inexpert guidance, muscles opposite to those that are to be used later in the task may be forcefully brought into play.

During this pre-performance stage, therefore, one may apply any of the various kinds of instruction: visual, manual, or verbal. Reference to Fleishman's research dealing with the importance of "nonmotor" factors, however, seems to indicate that such pre-task training should be mainly concerned with transmitting mechanical principles and knowledge of spatial relationships.[367-372] Research concerning the "amount-set" and its influence on performance and learning indicates that knowledge of the extent and complexity of the task is also important during this initial phase in the learning process.

The second time stage in the learning of a motor task, the actual performance, may be termed the *guidance phase*. It is during this period that corrections enabling the individual to mold his movements into increasingly exact patterns with perhaps a more precise application of force are made. Guidance of performance may come from manually moving the limbs or body of the learner or from interpolated verbal or visual directions. It should be remembered, however, that a learner may be "overcoached" during this period. For example, he may be working partially on a trial-and-error principle, and continual directions may impede self-correction. The learner may be attempting to concentrate on the whole task. Too complex a correction with minute attention to detail may serve to obliterate a feeling of the whole movement. Sharply spoken verbal criticism may obliterate the kinesthetic sensations being used to gain the "feel" of the movement.

During Performance

Instruction during performance not only may consist of visually presented demonstrations and materials, verbal directions, or the opportunity to engage in guided practice, but also may be characterized by the general emphasis placed on various aspects of performance. Instruction emphasizing speed versus accuracy, correcting the wrong movement as opposed to emphasizing the correct way to move, or placing relative emphasis on praise or reproof has varying effects on learning during this intermediate phase.

A primary consideration during the performance phase seems to be determining the appropriate quantity of correction and guidance to be offered as well as deciding the quality involved. The instructor should be sensitive of the transition from cognitive aspects of the task to the more basic movement or motor aspects.[872] Individuals should not be preoccupied or made overly concerned with analysis of the task during the performance phase; such an academic approach may actually impede acquisition. It is best to place emphasis on moving rapidly and accurately and on the vigorous and/or accurate use of force during the performance phase. Recent research by McGuigan[771] indicated that motor activity may interfere with verbal information if both impose on the individual during task performance. Thus, extensive analysis should be kept to the preliminary phases.

Following Performance

At the final stage of learning, "knowledge of results" is of vital importance to the later improvement of skill. Such knowledge may come from internal movement cues or from various types of external instruction. The instructor should be sensitive to information the learner has been able to obtain from internal cues, as well as the nature of the activity and the opportunity afforded to obtain knowledge of results. For example, when learning to swim, little visual information is obtained by the learner, since his face is usually submerged during a large portion of the practice period. Basketball free-throw shooting, on the other hand, is accompanied by continual verification of success or failure; the learner is able to see the accuracy achieved by each effort. Most learning has been found to be greatly facilitated by immediate knowledge of results. This is true also of gross motor activities.

Types of Sensory Input

As seen from the preceding analyses, instruction may be considered in a time dimension, the review of research will be organized in categories primarily based on the relative emphasis the instructor places on various types of sensory information. In the following section, the relative importance, most effective place in the learning process, the type of task most facilitated by visual, verbal, and motor guidance, or combinations of these three categories will be discussed. Research dealing with "knowledge of results" is accorded a separate section at the end of the chapter.

Verbal Instructions

As has been noted, the most effective placement of verbal instruction seems to be during the pre-performance phase and during the initial stages of performance. This assertion is based on the need for mechanical principles and for knowledge of spatial relations that are important during the initial stages of learning. Research also indicates that it is important to communicate a knowledge of the amount of the task to be accomplished during the initial stage of learning.

Most research indicates that verbal rehearsal of the task is most effective in paired-association skills, including the pairing of numbers with letters, colored lights with movement responses, and in nonsense syllables. However, Sackett[959] also found that the learning of a serial-type task (a maze) was facilitated by verbal rehearsal of the complexities of the pathway.

The instruction can have various degrees of relevancy to the task. As McAllister[751] and others have pointed out, increasing the specificity of instructions produces marked performance increments. Generally, such rehearsal of task elements is considered to offer a "warm-up" period and seems more effective as time devoted to it is increased.[733] Extensive pre-practice verbalization also seems to help an individual gain more initial proficiency when the task is one with which the learner has had little experience.

Mechanical Principles. A second reason for verbal pre-training is to transmit the mechanical principles of the task. If such instruction facilitates performance, it might be assumed that some general ability to analyze the task underlies performance. The early study of Judd[600] substantiated this contention. As boys were instructed in the principles of light refraction and then asked to hit an underwater target with a bow and arrow, their accuracy was little affected when the depth of the water was suddenly changed. A second group, receiving no such instructions, had difficulty adjusting to the changed conditions.

Hendrickson and Schroeder,[515] duplicating Judd's conditions, attempted to determine the role of "insightful" motor learning. However, these investigators believed that, in addition to transfer resulting from a knowledge of the principles involved, other factors are also important when the conditions are changed. Individual fluidity of behavior (willingness to change response patterns), ability to formulate the principles, the manner in which the principles are presented, and habits of verifying self-judgments are also important when using the knowledge of principles to learn a motor skill.

Subsequent studies seem to disagree on the extent to which knowledge of principles affects learning. Daugherty[282] found that the teaching of kinesiological principles positively affected the accuracy and force applied to sports skills. Coville,[223] on the other hand, found that a detailed knowledge of principles underlying ball bouncing, a combined tennis and badminton skill, and archery practice does not seem to facilitate performance.

Again, consideration of the research does not offer absolute answers. The nature of the task and the ability of the learner to understand and to apply basic performance principles seem to determine the extent of their effect on learning efficiency. The manner in which the principle is presented also seems to be an important variable.

Amount-Set. Advance knowledge of the amount and/or complexity of the task has also been shown to influence learning efficiency. Several results of investigations of the influence of the amount-set on learning have been published during the past 30 years. The initial studies, usually dealing with arithmetic tasks, indicate that, when the amount of work with which the learner is faced encourages initial slow performance, a "pacing" effect occurs.[100] Later investigators studied the effect of the amount-set on motor activities. Usually, when individuals are faced with a given number of strength efforts, the amount of force exerted in the initial trials decreases with the number of pulls, indicating the same "pacing" effect seen in the performance of "mental" tasks.[107,850]

The subtle influence of the exact knowledge of the extent of the task on performance was clearly illustrated in Katz's[601] study of 1949. When asked to "run to that post" (180 yards away), individuals ran the first 60 yards in an average time of 10.8 seconds. Informed of the exact distance of the post, a second group ran the initial 60 yards in a mean time of 10.2 seconds. Katz[601] concluded that the duration of the work and the output of the individual are conditioned by the nature of the task and the material into which it fits as a part.

An extensive program of research by Gunnar Borg[118] in Sweden has explored in some detail the pacing effects and modifications of work output influenced by an individual's perceptions of his own efforts. The more zealous student should consult this interesting work for a clearer look at this psychological phenomenon.

It is also possible that pre-performance perceptions of a task's complexity influence pacing effects, and that, as a result, the specific nature of pre-task preparation with instructions about the complexity of the task might conceivably influence subsequent efforts by the learner. However, to my knowledge, research dealing with this hypothesis is not presently available.

Speed versus Accuracy. Few researchers have been concerned about the relative influence of emphasizing speed versus accuracy when teaching motor skills. Studying gross motor skills, Solley[1040] found that speed probably should be emphasized from the initial stages of learning and that accuracy gained at slow speeds is generally lost when a movement becomes more rapid. When speed is a predominant factor in the performance of skill, early emphasis on speed is best. Solley believed that when both speed and accuracy are important, equal emphasis on both probably produces the best results.

In more recent work, Robb[929] also found that practice of a specific arm movement task at less than final speed is detrimental to performance; while Malina,[729] in his 1963 study of throwing improvement in high-school boys, suggested that even though emphasis on both speed and accuracy is made by an instructor, the learner may be able to incorporate *either*, but not both at the same time, in his performance. Malina found that information about speed and accuracy functioned differently at different points in the practice program. Instructions on accuracy proved more difficult for his subjects to deal with than was information to improve speed.

In one sense, such principles relate to the whole versus part question. When concentrating on speed, the individual must generally attend to the whole movement, rather than become concerned with components of the movement pattern. Thus, as recommended in Chapter 18, acquiring as much of the whole as can be perceived under conditions similar to those surrounding the final performance desired generally produces the best learning. Limits, however, certainly must exist. If practice of a movement at full speed so obliterates its components and/or presents too much of the whole for a learner to comprehend, slowing down the initial practice is desirable. Following a knowledge of spatial relationships, a rapid movement cannot be said to be learned until it can be performed at full speed. This is generally accomplished with more facility if the initial practice is carried out at full speed.

Negative versus Positive Directions. During actual performance of the task and during the learning process, correction of the learner's movements may be either positive or negative. Emphasis may be placed on what *to* do or what *not* to do. Basically, the traditional question of positive or negative reward is involved.

The findings of experimentations with rats have been verified in later studies with human beings. Wang[1143] and Silleck and Lapha[1004] found that positive instructions are better than merely extending the individual information concerning his inaccuracies when performing a maze task. Having subjects name the error after it is identified is beneficial, and verbal information during initial portions of the task is most helpful. Langfeld[654] also found that, when the subjects are moving a stylus down a groove, being told to "go down the center of the groove" has a more beneficial effect on performance than being requested to "avoid the sides of the pathway." These researchers, however, usually qualified their findings. They suggested, for example, that the *tester* may be more important than the type of information given or whether praise or blame is extended.[654] The relative spacing of negative or positive instruction may prove an important factor when assessing their effectiveness.[1143]

Some early investigators attempted to determine whether the practice of "wrong" responses is facilitating to the acquisition of a motor skill. The researchers point out that this kind of negative practice may help to bring to the attention of the learner the movement components to avoid as he practices the skill.

Manual Guidance

In addition to attending to verbal instruction, individuals may be guided manually when performing a task. The purpose is generally to mold movements into the desired forms through the manual correction of movements. Both Koch[629] and Lundgate[719] found that manual guidance is beneficial (as opposed to trial and error) when learning small maze tasks. Generally, manual guidance is more effective during the early stages of learning before incorrect habits are formed. If introduced too soon, the individual may not have the opportunity to explore the general nature of the task. If guidance is given too late in the learning process, habits may become fixed, and the learner may become confused. The effectiveness of guided practice depends largely on the task and the criterion of learning efficiency established. Guidance during the initial part of the learning process, however, generally results in quicker learning.

Combinations of Instruction

Verbal versus Manual. In 1934 Chase[187] compared the relative effectiveness of verbal instruction and manual guidance in the learning of a small stylus maze task. While manual guidance seems to facilitate early learning, no real advantage is seen in final achievement. Chase believed that the learning of a spatial pattern becomes a discerning process as practice is continued and that continued reliance on kinesthetic feedback might prove detrimental during the later stages of learning.

Audio-Visual Materials in Teaching Movement Activities

Traditionally, films have been used in physical education to introduce new activities and to enable students to improve their motor skills more quickly. Films of a desirable model for action have been used to depict skills, and to an increasing degree are being used to present to the learner a graphic description of his own learning efforts.

In the past several years, some investigations attempted to delineate the way in which films may be utilized most effectively in the teaching-learning situation. Contrary to what might be assumed, the findings do not always support the idea of the film as a good teaching tool. The investigations by Brown and Messersmith,[139] of tumbling instruction, and by Nelson, of golf, for example, revealed that loop films added to demonstrations do not result in any significant difference in ability between the control and experimental subjects.

On the other hand, Lockhart,[701] studying beginning bowlers, and Watkins,[1155] evaluating baseball skills, found that motion pictures exert a positive effect on the attributes measured. The study by Priebe and Burton[904] also gave findings suggesting that audio-visual aids are at least as effective as are conventional methods in the teaching of sports skills. Harby,[488] Murnin[826] and others, using loop films to teach such athletic skills as tumbling and basketball free-throw shooting, found that repeated motion picture demonstration is as effective as an instructor's live demonstration, but that a live demonstration is more helpful when individual coaching and correction are added.

Several principles must be kept in mind when attempting to achieve better physical performance with audio-visual aids. (1) An optimum speed of verbal information should accompany the film. If the words are spoken too fast or too slowly, less effective learning takes place. (2) The two-dimensional film may not be as effective as a three-dimensional live demonstration. (3) The film should be presented in close temporal proximity to the desired change in performance. If the performance and film are separated by too long a period, a great deal of positive transfer may not take place. (4) The spatial relationships between the performer and the task must be kept in mind. Roshal[942] found that portraying knot-tying from the viewpoint of the performer was more effective than filming a mirror image of the task. (5) Films may be more effective in the teaching of complex skills than of simple ones. (6) Films depicting movements are more effective than presenting static pictures of parts of the movement.

Videotape Feedback

The development of videotape feedback systems and their decreasing cost have encouraged many coaches and physical educators to employ them when teaching athletic skills to individuals or groups. Just as in the case of research about the effectiveness of films, however, the research on videotape feedback is not completely supportive of this dramatic way to present visual information relative to performance. In 1969, Penman[880] found no difference in the ability of beginning tumblers to perform, after they were exposed to videotape feedback of their performance efforts. Similar negative findings emanated from an investigation by Gasson[413] in the same year, involving beginners in badminton.

On the other hand, positive findings supporting the use of videotape were obtained in studies using the golf swing as the task, and in an investigation in which beginning swimmers were used as subjects; significantly better performance on a parallel bar skill through the use of the videotape playback technique was found in another study.

The admittedly sparse data suggest that positive results in the use of the videotape feedback system will be obtained in subjects who are moderately advanced in their skill progression and are thus able to evaluate their own performance well while observing the results. Moreover, performers who cannot easily see their performance while executing it (swimmers and gymnasts) are more likely to be helped by the immediacy provided by videotape playback systems, than are those whose successful performances are apparent to them while they are performing (badminton players, runners, broadjumpers, and the like).

Athletes whose visual fields undergo several distortions as they execute their tasks (pole vaulters, advanced tumblers, and trampolinists) are likely to be greatly aided by the videotape machine, particularly if their skills, at analysis, or the skills of an attending instructor or coach are compatible with the detailed and vivid information from such an arrangement. On the other hand, beginners whose skills at analysis are not sharply honed and/or who may be embarrassed by having to observe a concrete example of their ineptitude might be aided less by confrontation with the combination of a television monitor and videotape machine.

Comparisons of Visual, Verbal, and Manual Cues

Karlin and Mortimer[604] compared the relative effectiveness of visual versus verbal cues on the learning of a crank-turning task (crank had to be turned at exactly 99 rpm). Since the subject was permitted to consult a monitor, visual cues proved superior to verbal information on retention over a 24-hour period.

Numerous studies have compared the relative effectiveness of visual cues and motor cues obtained from manual guidance on the learning movement. The tasks utilized have usually been fine motor skills, finger mazes, pursuit-rotors, and the like. A dearth of studies using human subjects in gross motor tasks compared the relative effectiveness of visual cues to kinesthetic or movement cues on learning and performance.

One of the first studies illustrating the superiority of visual guidance over nonvisual guidance of movement was carried out in 1882 by Bowditch and Southard.[123] They found that blindfolded subjects in a finger-aiming task performed more accurately when they were given prior visual inspections of the target than when their fingers were manually directed to the target. Although Ammons[30] found no difference between pursuit-rotor performance following visual inspection of the task and moving through the task blindfolded, most experimenters found that vision provides important information in learning a motor task. As Miles[795] states: "No delays in action are occasioned by vision. It does not get in the way or occupy valuable space, it does all its coaching from the sidelines."

Many different degrees and variations of visual guidance in experimental situations have been attempted. Summarized by Miles,[795] they include: (1) full normal vision during all trials, (2) interrupted or fragmentary visual control, (3) blurred visual control, caused by aging, drugs, and similar conditions, and (4) distorted visual control, using mirrors or other refracting surfaces that cause disagreement between visual and tactile impressions.

In general, the accuracy of visual practice over manual or kinesthetic feedback has been supported in numerous studies with stylus or finger mazes[173,795] and with pursuit-rotors, and by Smith and Harrison,[1029] with a three-hole stylus punchboard. Robb,[929] in a 1968 study, also found that, when acquiring an arm movement pattern, concurrent visual feedback is superior to concurrent proprioceptive feedback coupled with graphs of accuracy that are studied following performance. Not only does the research show that visual inspection is more effective than manual guidance in determining spatial relationships during the initial stages of learning, but also that judgments of roughness, length, or curvature may actually be distorted if learned kinesthetically.[936] Thus, visual cues (films, demonstrations, or the like) are superior to movement cues when learning skills. Attempts to teach a skill by first blindfolding the learner are not as effective as permitting the individual simultaneously to perform and to attend to visual cues.

Manual guidance and verbal instructions prove most effective during the early stages of learning; the learner receives an awareness of the mechanical principles involved (verbal) and a knowledge of the spatial relationships and task complexities involved in the performance. Moreover, instruction of all kinds appears most effective during the initial stages of the task and may interfere with speed and force of movements during the later stages of learning.

Spaced correction by manual guidance, verbal instruction, and demonstrations should be most effective during the later stages of learning. Thus, the relative dependence on trial-and-error learning and closely instructed practice would seem to shift during the various stages of learning. More instruction is desirable during the initial stages to correct movements and to prevent the adoption of incorrect habits. More trial-and-error learning seems beneficial as the learner approaches his psychophysical limits during the later stages, although with correct instruction early in the learning process, fewer errors should be evidenced during these later stages.

Whenever possible, visual demonstration should be utilized and is superior, when gaining accuracy of movement, to manual guidance and to kinesthetic practice without vision.

Instructions to Retain a Skill

As individuals begin to learn and to perform a motor skill, they have various conceptions relative to the necessity to repeat the performance at a later time. They may assume that the immediate performance will be their only exposure to the skill. On the other hand, they may be aware that they will have to perform the skill some time in the future. Information about the necessity to retain a skill can be given before, during, or following a learning program.

Relatively few investigators have attempted to evaluate the influence of instructions about the necessity to retain a skill on its retention. It seems, however, that if this information is tendered at the start of the learning schedule, greater retention of the skill results. From two investigations, Lavery[664] found that instructions given prior to practice that a task would be evaluated at a later time aided in its retention, whereas no difference was noted when these instructions were given at the completion of the learning schedule. Sanderson[962] came to similar conclusions from an earlier investigation. Thus individuals seem to learn differently when they are aware of the need for retention from when they feel their exposure to the task is to be of rather short duration. A more thorough discussion of other factors influencing retention of skills is found in Chapter 19.

Knowledge of Results and Information Feedback

Knowledge of results may come in the nature of verbal information, visual confirmation of accuracy, speed, or some other success criterion, or through the feel of a completed movement. The effect of knowledge of results can be considered from several standpoints: (1) the relative spacing of this knowledge and the effects of spacing on learning efficiency, (2) the relation of knowledge of success on the performance of various kinds of tasks (strength efforts, athletic skills, or laboratory tasks), and (3) the effect of delaying the knowledge of results on learning efficiency. Seashore and Brevalas[980] point out that the extent to which knowledge of results is effective also may depend on the alertness of the learner in evaluating his success. Therefore, the factor influencing the knowledge of results involves the little-studied "self-estimation" factor. To what extent is the individual able to predict prior to attempting a task how well he will do and to determine at the completion of a task how well he did without the benefit of an external source of information?

An early study by Arps,[40] using a strength task (a finger ergograph), indicated a trend seen in subsequent research. The amount of work and the rate of work are positively influenced when the subject is constantly informed of how hard he pulled on the ergograph. Muscular efficiency increases, it was hypothesized, because knowledge of results operates to facilitate changes in the nervous system, as well as to help the learner maintain his attention on the task.[101] Howell[558] confirmed these findings in a later study. He used graphs indicating force and speed of limb movements that proved effective when learning the sprinting start. A masked group, unable to see the results of their efforts following each attempt, did not enjoy the same success.

Spencer and Judd,[1044] however, with a perceptual-motor skill (drawing dots that were the extension of lines), found that improvement seemed to take place when knowledge of results was lacking. Although at a loss to explain this phenomenon, they hypothesized that improvement was possibly due to the subject's general familiarity with the nature

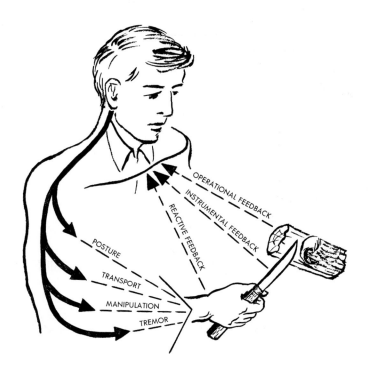

FIGURE 7–1. Parameters of feedback control of instrumental behavior. The complexity of the feedback components inherent in the task itself is illustrated. Feedback in motor tasks frequently comes from external sources (a teacher). Various kinds of tasks depend on the use of different types of feedback in the situation. (Redrawn from Smith, K. U., and Henry, J. P.: Cybernetic foundations for rehabilitation. Amer. J. Phys. Med., *46*, 379-467, 1967.)

of the task. They concluded that, with subsequent practice, a plateau would probably be reached.

Crafts and Gilbert[228] found that nonspecific knowledge of accuracy in a stylus maze did not produce greater learning. Subjects were informed when they were "below average" in performance, but no comment was made when they were average or above the mean. Crafts attributed this finding to the fact that the college students' exact knowledge of results proves to be of no help, since they generally are aware of how well they are doing in most tasks. In the absence of any extrinsic rewards or punishments, motivation was not greatly affected when some of the students found they were not doing well. Kneeland's[627a] research on self-estimation seems to corroborate Craft's findings.

Studies of this nature, as well as more recent work by Bell[85] and Smoll,[1034] indicate that information feedback (or knowledge of results), although it must be precise and specific, at the same time must be matched to the ability of the individual to comprehend it and to incorporate it in subsequent movements. Smoll, for example, found that specific information concerning the velocity at which a bowling ball had been rolled, if given within a tenth of a second, was as helpful as if given within a hundredth of a second. That is, there seemed to be an optimum level of specificity of information that was helpful to the subjects in his study, which, if exceeded, did not result in additional improvement.

Greenspoon and Foreman,[463] with a line-drawing task, found that, as students attempted to draw a line exactly 3 inches long, their learning efficiency was directly affected as knowledge of their accuracy was increasingly delayed for periods of 19, 20, and 30 seconds. The most effective learners were those who obtained *immediate* knowledge of results. If knowledge of results is offered too quickly following the completion of a skill or subskill, the individual may not be as favorably affected as if this information is delayed for several seconds. In general, a five-to-ten-second delay seems to produce the best improvement, permitting the feel of the skill to "set in," prior to asking the performer to interpret some kind of external information about the quality of his efforts.[665]

Frederick's 1968 study[379] reflects the same principle with respect to learning a gross motor skill. Employing a dart-throwing task, Frederick found that delays of knowledge of results occurring one, three, and 10 seconds after performance, proved detrimental to performance. The experimental arrangement permitted the target to be lighted after the throw was made, either immediately or after the time delays described.

Bilodeau and Bilodeau,[103] studying the effect of spacing knowledge of results, found that learning to move a large lever a given distance was facilitated by the number of times knowledge of accuracy was obtained and not by the various ways in which this knowledge was spaced throughout a series of trials. They also found, as did Greenspoon et al.,[463] Arps,[40] and others, that learning *did not* occur when knowledge of results was lacking.

At the same time the complexity of the task influences whether any positive benefit is derived from knowledge of the performance level achieved. Chapanis[186] found that knowledge of results produced no significant change in ability to perform tasks that were simple repetitive exercises (pressing a button in response to a light cue).

Thus the effectiveness of knowledge of results seems to depend on the form in which this knowledge is attained, the complexity of the learner and of the task, and the immediacy with which the knowledge is received. Retention is often best when knowledge of performance level is received a few seconds after the task is completed, and spaced knowledge of results from an external source is sometimes more effective than continual feedback from the performer's visual-motor feedback system. A degree of specificity of information feedback is helpful to the learner, and, if exceeded, is often reflected in further improvement in skill.

Contemporary Trends

Several contemporary trends dealing with the manner in which motor skills may be taught and incorporated in physical education and athletic programs are evident in the literature. Youths' strivings for increased independence and relative freedom from undue controls have influenced some physical educators to adopt less authoritarian methods than have sometimes been used in the past; whereas some deplore permissiveness in any form, whether in a high-school physical education class or a college classroom.

Those teachers and coaches who are extending decision-making to their students are often rewarded by the results. Muska Mosston[816a] and Jack Scott,[972a] among others, have been in the forefront in advocating more participation by students in the processes and decisions surrounding athletics and physical education. Mosston's suggestions, I believe, are particularly helpful, since they reflect a gradual assumption of the structure of teaching-learning situations by students, when it is obvious that students are ready to assume responsibility for their own actions and decisions. Mosston essentially suggests that decisions about the educational process be gradually transferred to students, allowing them first to choose modifications of the task presented to them, later to take over evaluative decisions from the teacher, and finally to make decisions about planning a lesson. The components and objectives of a lesson should be placed in the purview of students when it is apparent that their previous involvement has not led to chaos.

Recent texts I have written reflect a similar trend. They indicate how teachers of both secondary and elementary physical education classes and athletic teams, in operational ways, can encourage students to exercise their various intellectual abilities, including their problem-solving attributes and their academic skills. Research investigating the worth of these approaches to academic enrichment, as well as to the teaching of sports skills, has also provided positive support for these approaches. Contemporary investigations of the results of programmed teaching on the acquisition of motor skills by Farrell[346] and by Newman and Singer[1010] reflect further attempts to study the possible effects of the introduction of new methods.

Summary

Although instruction may be self-administered or arise from the nature of the task, the types of instruction discussed in this chapter were those deliberately tendered by another individual to the learner. In a temporal framework, three stages emerge: (1) *pre-performance* instructions contributing to the general learning set and including amount and intensity of the task, its general nature, and similar information, (2) instructions given during actual performance, and (3) the *task-completion* information offering the learner the knowledge of his success or failure. Instructions may also be classified according to the type of sensory experience they involved: verbal instructions; visual guidance, such as demonstrations, the viewing of films, and the like; and manual guidance. In addition, various combinations of these have been researched.

In many cases the available literature offers only tentative cues relating instruction to skilled performance. The following statements are believed to be valid ones.

1. Pre-task instructions should transmit the principles of the task and the spatial components of the task. Instructions may be in the form of a visual demonstration of written or verbal information and should be compatible with the learner's ability to comprehend.

2. Instructions during the performance of the task should not interfere with the learner's focus on the necessary movement patterns but rather should supplement performance. They should be visual demonstrations or a minimal amount of manual guidance.

3. Instructions following performance should give the learner knowledge of his success or failure or degrees thereof. The immediacy and clarity of this post-performance information seem to exert a direct and positive influence on his success in subsequent attempts.

4. Advanced information concerning the amount, duration, and intensity of the task, if exact, leads to more vigorous performance by the learner than does incomplete, incorrect, or no information concerning the "amount-set." The pacing effect is almost always evident when an individual performs a series of tasks, with the effect being more pro-

nounced if no knowledge concerning the exact limits of the task is obtained beforehand.

5. Early emphasis on speed seems important, if speed is a vital part of the task. However, emphasis on speed to the exclusion of spatial accuracy during the initial stages of learning may only prove an impediment during the later stages of learning.

6. Directions emphasizing what to do facilitate quicker learning of a motor skill than do directions on what not to do.

7. The most accurate type of sensory input when learning a motor task is visual inspection. However, manual guidance, visual demonstration, verbal description, and practice are best combined for effective learning.

8. If an individual is given information that he must retain the task prior to a learning program, retention is greater than if this information is extended to him at the completion of the learning process, or is omitted entirely.

9. Videotape and filmed instruction are effective when the visual displays are adequately analyzed and when the maturity and intelligence of the learner permit him to apply the information he received in subsequent attempts to perform the skill.

10. Specific information feedback produces better subsequent learning performance than does vague or general information about prior effort.

Student Reading

Bilodeau, E. A., and Bilodeau, I. McD.: Variable frequency of knowledge of results and the learning of a simple skill. J. Exp. Psychol., 55, 379-383, 1958.

Cratty, B. J.: *Physical Expressions of Intelligence.* Englewood Cliffs, N.J., Prentice-Hall, Inc., 1972.

Cratty, B. J.: *Teaching Motor Skills.* Englewood Cliffs, N.J., Prentice-Hall, Inc., 1973.

Daughtrey, G.: The effects of kinesiological teaching on the performance of junior high school boys. Res. Quart., 16, 26-33, 1945.

Greenspoon, J., and Foreman, S.: Effect of delay of knowledge of results on learning a motor task. J. Exp. Psychol., 51, 226-228, 1956.

Kantz, D.: Gestalt laws of mental work. Brit. J. Psychol., 39, 175-183, 1949.

Mosston, M.: *Teaching Physical Education.* Columbus, Ohio, Charles E. Merrill, Co., 1967.

Sackett, R. S.: The relationship between amount of symbolic rehearsal and retention of a maze habit. J. Gen. Psychol., 13, 113-128, 1935.

Solley, W. H.: The effect of verbal instruction of speed and accuracy upon the learning of a motor skill. Res. Quart., 23, 231-240, 1952.

III
MOTOR
PERFORMANCE,
ABILITY TRAITS, AND
MOVEMENT BEHAVIOR

8
NEUROLOGICAL
FOUNDATIONS
OF VOLUNTARY MOVEMENT

Despite emphasis on movement as *behavior,* an understanding of the nervous control of muscular action is necessary. Man is not a hollow tube, despite the view taken by some learning theorists, but a highly complex organism capable of receiving a vast number of messages through his sensory end-organs and of executing movements of remarkable complexity and variety. Some of the neurological mechanisms involved in the integration of movement output will be examined briefly, and an effort will be made to summarize recent findings concerning the neurological control of voluntary movement patterns.

Evolution of the Nervous System

Throughout the evolution of organic life on earth, examination of organismic control mechanisms reveals an accompanying developmental pattern. Living matter is modifiable. All organisms evidence mechanisms that facilitate irritability, contractility, and conductivity, characteristics that permit adaptation to changing conditions. Even the one-celled amoeba, capable of only avoidance or approach responses, evidences these basic qualities. Simple locomotion is facilitated by sequential contractions of cellular parts. To facilitate movement, a wave of excitability passes from one portion of the cell to another, just as a nerve impulse travels along branching nerve pathways in the human organism at a developmental level eons of years removed from the amoeba. In seeking or avoiding a stimulus, the amoeba thus evidences the three basic functions inherent to human neuromuscular control: (1) irritability (excited by stimuli), (2) contractility (controlled movement), and (3) conductivity (sequential undulations).

Among the higher mammals, more complex functioning is apparent due to the proliferating structures and mechanisms that have evolved in the nervous system. The increasing number of cells and structures permit more kinds of stimuli to be dealt with, while at the same time more complex action patterns become possible.

In general, the mechanism for nervous control appears to have evolved through three functional stages, from the ability to handle instinctual reflexes to simple learned movements to the highest level of behavior, evidenced primarily in the human being. At the lower level, innate stereotyped performance is integrated; at the intermediate stage, acquired adaptative behavior is monitored; and at the higher levels, abstract thinking, discrimination, symbolization, and communication are mediated.

During the course of evolution, the parts of the nervous system making their evolutionary appearance most recently did not displace more primitive structures. Less complex parts in the peripheral and spinal systems, on which the lower animals primarily depend for control, remain in the human nervous system. *Encephalization* is the term coined to denote the addition to and dominance of the more primitive structures by the higher components of nervous control. As will be discussed later, all portions of the human nervous system interact to provide a mutual series of checks and balances to facilitate the control of voluntary movement.

Basic Structures and Mechanisms of the Nervous System

The Neuron

The cell specialized for functioning in the nervous system is termed the *neuron*. It is different from other cells because of its characteristic fibrous processes (dendrites and axons) that permit a single cell to exert functional influence over a considerable distance. Although microscopic in diameter, a single neuron may extend from the feet to the base of the skull.

Neurons are found in the central nervous system (brain and spinal cord) as well as in nerve trunks and in peripheral nervous tissue in various nerve centers of the body. The neuron is usually covered by a myelin sheath, a white fatty tissue that reduces the effect of adjacent nerve fibers on each other and thus ensures the more exact transmission of an impulse. Complete development of the myelin sheath is believed related to performance of coordinated movement patterns and is completely developed sometime between the ages of four and seven years.

The neuron originates from the neural tube, the outermost layer of cells, in the embryo. At birth, man has his full quota of neurons. When a neuron is destroyed, it is not replaced.

The Nerve Impulse

The specialized function of the neuron is to conduct a nerve impulse, evidenced by a change in electrical potential, along the cell membrane.

The nature of the nerve impulse is studied by recording changes in electrical potential between active and inactive neurons with the use of delicate metering equipment. Through such techniques it seems that: (1) There is a *threshold of excitability,* which is a level of electrical stimulation that, unless exceeded, fails to elicit conduction through the nerve cell. (2) Positive and negative after-potentials are recorded. The duration of aftereffects depends on the extent of the previous activity and surrounding chemical conditions. (3) There is a maximum number of times that a given fiber can be stimulated in a given period, ranging from 100 to 1000 times per second, termed the *absolute refractory period* and is related to the length of time a neuron retains an impulse. (4) A single nerve impulse is governed by an all-or-none law, which suggests that a fiber responds to its limits or not at all, depending on whether its threshold of excitability has been exceeded. However, *summation,* the accumulative effects of two or more rapid and brief subthreshold stimulations that evoke a reaction by combining to exceed the threshold, can occur. (5) Nerve impulses vary greatly in speed from 120 meters per second to 17 meters per second, depending on the diameter of the neuron and its location and function in the nervous system. (6) Nerve cells evidence a kind of impairment through use (sometimes termed *fatigue*). After repeated stimulation, fiber recovery is impaired. Such a condition, however, does not correspond directly to general mental or muscular fatigue as the term is commonly used.

The Synapse

The term *synapse* has been given to the point of physiological space connecting a neuron to a neuron. It is the point between the axon of a neuron and either the cell body or dendrites of another. The synapse permits a complex of functional arrangements, because the axon leading from one neuron may branch and synapse with several other neurons.

Slightly more time is required for an impulse to pass through a synapse than to run along a single fiber. Because of the absence of a myelin covering at the synaptic junction, drugs have an easier access to the axon at this point. It has also been determined that a single synapse is capable of only one-way transmission of the impulse, thus establishing a regularity of functioning to the nervous system.

Two theories have been proposed to explain the manner in which an impulse traverses a synapse: (1) transmission is simply a summation of sufficient electrical potential to effect the crossing; and (2) a chemical substance, *acetylcholine,* secreted at some synapses enables one neuron to cause a second to discharge. These two concepts have been utilized as the basis for several learning theories. Summation of impulses seems necessary in order to traverse a synapse, since the available evidence renders it unlikely that a single impulse is capable of crossing this neural junction. In addition to synaptic transmission, the effects of one neuron on another may also be exercised as parallel fibers electrically activate each other. When neurons are placed in tight bundles, the excitability of adjacent fibers, caused by the effects of common electrical fields, may occur along their length.

The Motor Unit

The term *motor unit* was first used in 1925 by Liddell and Sherrington,[689] who defined it as a "motor neuron-axon and its adjunct muscle fibers." In general, a motor unit is a functional unit composed of a neuron lying in the peripheral portion of the nervous system, the ventral horn of the spinal cord, whose axon branches extend outward and terminate in groups of striated muscle fibers where they end in flattened oval-shaped end-plates.

Since there are many more striated muscle fibers in the body than there are myelinated nerve fibers that might innervate them, it is apparent that one nerve innervates many muscle fibers. Great differences are found in the innervation ratio for various muscles. In muscles that seem to demand immediate, quick, and precise actions, such as those of the eyes, the ratio is only 5:8, while in some of the larger muscles utilized primarily for locomotion and posturing, the ratio is greater, perhaps as much as 1:1775 in the large calf muscle (gastrocnemius) and 1:609 for the tibialis anterior muscle.[13]

Thus, the number of motor units in a given muscle and their innervation ratios affect the precision and range of contraction of which the muscle is capable. Muscles with many motor units are capable of fine coordinations. Muscles with few motor units, while at times able to exert more force, are less capable of precise, graduated action.

Previously outlined qualities of the neuron, of course, are applicable to the motor unit, of which the motor neuron is an integral part. It has been found that motor units have gradient thresholds; some begin firing to induce minimal contractions, whereas others do not fire until stronger contractions are required. Thus the intensity of muscular contraction is determined by the frequency and the number of motor units firing. Motor unit connections overlap in a particular muscle. As many as six motor units have been found to overlap, so that a bundle of three to 50 fibers may contain the axon endings from two or more motor units. Further complicating the picture is the fact that the rate of conduction of nerve impulses varies from fiber to fiber. Thus impulses that start at the same time in a receptor organ may arrive at the muscle fiber at different times.

Modifying the final muscular response are the nature of the muscle fiber that has been innervated and the action of muscles opposing the action of the one stimulated. For a muscle to move a body member, there must usually be a controlled movement of an opposing muscle.

The unique arrangement of the muscle fibers in bundles is also an effector of the final action produced. Some are placed across the line of pull (penniform), resulting in more force with a sacrifice of speed. Other fiber bundles are arranged parallel to the line of pull, thus making available all contractile power and resulting in a maximum range of motion. The fiber size is another factor and varies from 1 to 45 millimeters in length, while maximum diameters range from 0.01 to 0.10 millimeter.

Thus, at the periphery, controlled, forceful, and/or sustained movement depends on the innervation ratio, the number of motor units affecting the muscle, the duration and rate at which the stimulation occurs, the differential in nerve conduction rate, the arrangement of the muscle fibers, the nature of opposing muscular activity, and the size and formation of the fibers composing the muscle affected.

The Central Nervous System and the Control of Voluntary Movement

Structures

The Spinal Cord.   Basically, the spinal cord is a channel located along the back integrating reflexive and voluntary actions into a blend of total behavior. A cross-section view of the cord reveals columns of white matter on the outside and the characteristic "butterfly" of gray matter on the inside. The white matter consists of conducting tracts of myelinated nerve fibers, while the gray consists of cell bodies and unmyelinated fiber terminations.

Thirty-one pairs of spinal nerves connect the spinal cord with the peripheral parts of the body and are connected to the cord through a dorsal and a ventral root. The two general functions of the spinal cord involve conduction of impulses upward to higher centers and the conduction of impulses in the opposite direction. A third function is a reflex one—the integration of simple unlearned responses requiring no mediation by discriminative processes in the brain stem to discrete stimuli.

The Brain Stem.   Immediately at the upper extremity of the spinal cord lies the brain stem. Its primary structures are the medulla and further upward and dorsally the cerebellum. Although the medulla is primarily involved in reflexive coordination, the cerebellum is involved in the coordination of voluntary movements and acts primarily as a smoother or checkpoint through which movements initiated in the higher centers are mediated and controlled. The important *reticular formation,* a column of scattered portions of gray matter, is also located on the brain stem and contributes to the energy of cortically initiated movement, the production of muscle tone, and also may suppress or inhibit muscular activity. Moreover, evidence suggests that the reticular formation has connections to most major structures in the central nervous system. At the same time, certain cells in the spinal cord send axons directly to this structure. Branches from sensory pathways also find their way to this organ. Thus, the extensive network of innervation suggests that the reticular formation is partly responsible for monitoring both sensory and motor information and for coordinating the two. The reticular formation also serves to modify both general inhibitory and noninhibitory tendencies of the organism. This activation-regulation function comes through modifications in the sensitivity to input, as well as in changes of specific and general muscular tonus, in indirect ways.

The Cerebellum. The cerebellum is considered by most as the organ responsible for the precise timing of coordinated acts. Like the reticular formation, fibers from both sensory and motor pathways project into the cerebellum, as do fibers from the higher centers in the neurocortex.

Stimulation of the neurocerebellum results in general exhibition of muscular functions and tonus. Lesions in the cerebellum result in an atactic gait and/or tremors of the upper extremities.

The Cerebrum. The cerebrum, or cerebral hemispheres, consists of the corpora striata covered by the cerebral cortex. Two important landmarks of the cerebral hemispheres are folds that cause ridges called *gyri* and grooves or *sulci*. The two most important grooves are the central sulcus dividing the frontal and parietal lobes and the lateral fissure setting off the temporal lobe.

The cerebral cortex, or outer covering of the cerebrum, may be divided into two major subdivisions: (1) the neocortex, the newer in terms of evolutionary development, and (2) the allocortex, or "other" cortex. In general, the allocortex is concerned with visceral activity, smell, rage, and other emotional patterning. The neocortex, on the other hand, may be divided into lobes, as delineated by sulci and fissures, or according to the type of cell structure found in various areas.

The following generalized functions are attributed to the cortex: (1) in connection with the thalamus, it serves to arouse or alert the organism; (2) it organizes and interprets sensory impressions, including formation of a general body image; (3) it initiates and aids in the control of general motor functioning; and (4) the frontal association areas not specifically concerned with sensory or motor functioning are believed to involve perceptual memory, since stimulation of portions of this region may evoke images of familiar objects or scenes.

Two basic classifications of theories purport to explain cerebral functioning: nerve impulse theories and field theories. In general, the former theories suggest that the billions of cells in the cortex act as individual cells, much as the single tubes of an electronic computer may be activated. While not denying that patterns of neurons may fire together to create patterns of thoughts, perceptions, and the like, it is felt that a simple all-or-none principle of nerve excitation exists in the central nervous system much as is found in peripheral nervous functioning. The field theories, on the other hand, suggest that nerves in the central nervous system influence each other not only through the synapse but that generalized fields of electrical activity can be induced in the nervous system. Since nerve fibers may activate one another along their length, as well as at the synapse, credence is given to this argument. In pages which follow, a generalized field theory is further explored as a basis for explaining the coordination of voluntary movement.

Methods of Examining the Neurological Control of Motor Behavior

Ablation.   Ablation involves removing or destroying some portion of the central nervous system and then determining the alterations of functions that are produced. The method must be carefully examined in order to circumvent several difficulties: (1) careful appraisal of the extent of the tissue damage must be carried out; and (2) it is sometimes difficult to determine whether a change in function is due directly to removal of the structure or whether the structure acted as a check on the function of other portions of the nervous system.

Electrical and Chemical Stimulation.   A more frequent technique has been to stimulate portions of the nervous system electrically and then study the resultant responses. In general, it involves setting up a false nerve impulse. Men and animals have been studied in this manner in a variety of ways. A disadvantage lies in the inability, in most cases, to initiate a discrete impulse experimentally; the usual result is that several neurons discharge simultaneously, including those that might interfere with the response in which the experimenter is interested. It was through electrical stimulation of various portions of the cortex that the motor areas were initially mapped.

The electroencephalogram is an example of an electrical recording method used on the outside of the skull and is a routine procedure in clinical and experimental situations. Strychnine is the usual chemical applied to nervous structure to study its function. Occasionally, electrical and chemical stimulation are used concurrently, as when one is used to desensitize a given area, while the other is used to study more exactly the functions of another area.

Clinical Method—Functional Changes Induced by Structural Abnormalities.   Another frequent method of studying the relationship between neural structures and human behavior is through studying animals or men who have received some injury or are subject to some condition that apparently renders portions of their nervous system inoperative.

In general, however, attempting to predict alterations in behavior from knowing the various cerebral lesions in man becomes a perilous undertaking. Teuber[1092] and others have found that changes in behavior after various kinds of brain damage are not obvious; in fact, they often prove to be subtle and elusive and even go undetected. The adaptability of the human nervous system after damage to one of its parts, the taking-over of function from one structure by another, makes difficult the prediction of movement alterations by knowing the injury involved.

When studying human beings after injury or similar clinical problems, it is also difficult to determine what the patient was really like before his atypical condition occurred. Of paramount importance is not the performance after injury, but the change in performance or function produced by the injury to portions of the central nervous system.

Functions of the
Cerebrum and Associated
Structures and Voluntary Movement

With electrical stimulation, it has been possible to determine the areas of the cortex that give rise to each general kind of voluntary movement. In general, an area just in front of the central fissure, the precentral gyrus, might be termed the *motor area* and the effects of stimulation on one side of the cortex result in movements on the opposite side of the body. The upper part of the cortex gives rise to movements in the lower part of the body, whereas the lower portions of the cortex elicit movements in the upper part (facial region) of the body. In general, more finite movements (of face or hands) are controlled by relatively larger portions of the cortex than are gross, less accurate movements of the legs or trunk.

However, the exactitude of this "mapping" of the brain is open to question from several standpoints: (1) Repeated stimulation does not elicit the same precise effects. Such factors as the intensity and timing of the stimulations also seem to influence the observed functioning. (2) Other areas of the cerebrum, the somesthetic areas and various cortical suppressor areas (the corpus striatum and reticular formation) serve to reduce or increase activity. In addition, the cerebellum reduces and smooths movement.

In general, stimulation of a portion of the cortex fails to elicit an exact controlled or complex movement but rather produces a simple jerk or spasmodic action. It seems that all of the structures in the central nervous system must be continually activated and balanced in order to produce a complex movement response.

Pathways and Loops for the Transmission and Control
of Voluntary Movement

The human action system can be said to depend on both external and internal loops. Visual-motor integrations and other movement modifications, based on information from auditory sensations, verbal directions of others, and the like (external loops), form the basis for much of the material in the remainder of the book. We are concerned here with the internal neural loops that control movement.

It has been stated that all neural structures seem to cooperate to integrate and smooth voluntary movement, some facilitating, some initiating, whereas others inhibit and modify the form of the movement output. These modifications and controls may be represented by neural loops which represent mutually affecting pathways. These internal loops may be complex and dependent on internal control from remote reflexive and postural mechanisms located in the antigravity muscles of the trunk; proprioceptors located in muscles, tendons, and joints; or perhaps skin receptors receiving pressure cues. Some of these loops, however, are smaller and operate in the upper portions of the central nervous system, from cerebrum to cerebellum and corpus striatum and back again. These loops have two main functions: to restrain or inhibit movements, thus serving to smooth jerky and incoordinated movement patterns, and to strengthen the effect of patterns initiated at the cortical level.

In general, two major types of pathways have been shown to influence voluntary movement. At the lower level (termed the "Lower Motorneuron Keyboard" by Paillard[869]) is the functional organization represented by the medulla oblongata and spinal cord neurons which act directly on muscular systems. At the second (or cortical) level are the assembled neurons emanating directly from the cortex in what are termed the *pyramidal pathways.* Studies, reviewed by Tower,[1109] have indicated that these upper corticomotoneural tracks are essential in conveying impulses necessary for the manifestation of skilled movements.

The activation of motor units in the lower level initially depends on the creation of a central excitatory state contributed to by central elements. Thus the activation of peripheral muscle structure is carried out by "programs" established in the higher centers. The lower track, however, has the ability to control delicate movements through temporal patterning (pacing) of the impulses to the affected muscle.

Experimental findings[869] have confirmed that a direct corticomotoneural path exists from the central nervous system to the lower levels. These direct pathways from the cortex serve two main functions:[689] they contribute to the general excitatory state of the organism and, to facilitate general tension level, to the state of readiness for action; and they are "specific contributions to individual acts of performance."[689] Thus these centralized tracks have twofold roles, general and specific, contributing to the general state of arousal and to specific action patterns. Paillard,[869] in summarizing the research, concludes that ". . . The cortico-motorneuronal system . . . can be considered as the chief executor of skilled movements."

Electrical stimulation of the cortex in itself never gives rise to complex coordinated movement, although superior influences seem to initiate a skilled response. Therefore, final manifestation depends on activation from sensory structures in the cortex, smoothing by the lower portions of the brain stem, and peripheral and central feedback systems. The cortex, in the final analysis, seems to act as a funnel, or an integrator of movements, organizing a stream of patterned impulses from sensory structures in the periphery and in the central nervous system.

Bernstein's Model

The Russian physiologist-biomechanist, Nicholas Bernstein,[96] on the basis of his own extensive work, as well as on the research of others, has taken a position midway between those who suggest that the brain is modeled in very precise ways for the control of identifiable motor acts, and those who believe that the brain is, for the most part, made up of undifferentiated tissue that deals in general ways with input, integration, and output functions. In the late 1950's, Bernstein formulated a model by which he suggested one can better understand the neural regulation of motor acts. Although since the time the model was written more sophisticated research methodologies have become available through which to study the complexities of the nervous system, the concepts, questions, and ideas suggested by Bernstein's schema are valid today.

Essentially, Bernstein contends that voluntary and reasonably complex motor acts arise because of the presence of a motor problem confronting the individual. This problem (excluding day-to-day activities and demands) in turn evokes kinds of intellectual "modeling" by the individual, none of which is easily translated into neuroanatomical terms, including: (1) a model of what has related in the past to the present situation, (2) a model of the present situation, and (3) a "modelling of the future" or what might transpire in terms of the individual's own actions, as well as the result of his actions in the situation as he perceives it. Below these more global decision-making and perceiving functions, Bernstein writes, there are second-level and more subtle processes taking place. Among them are decisions about (1) "the degrees of freedom" possible in the contemplated motor act; that is, how accurate or inaccurate can the movement be in order to satisfy the situation and arrived-at criterion? These degrees of freedom reside not only in the spatial requirements of the movement, but also in the timing of the movement in answer to the question how fast or how slowly can I initiate the movement, and how rapidly can I, or must I, move once the movement has been started? (2) Once the movement is begun, or an initial movement is completed, the individual must then compare the results of his efforts with the actual "demand width" of the task. That is, he must decide whether the accuracy, force, and timing of the movement are within acceptable limits and, if not, whether they can be brought to within reasonable limits. This function, Bernstein suggests, is undertaken by "comparator devices" in the nervous system.

In Figure 8–1, Bernstein has labeled Sw (from the German *Sollwert*) the "required value" of the movement, Iw (Istwert) the actual value of the movement, and Δw the discrepancy between the required value and the actual value of the movement (Iw minus Sw), as detected by 4, the "comparing system." Thus, as Bernstein states, "every intelligent, purposeful movement is made as an answer to a motor problem, and is determined, directly or indirectly, by the situation as a whole." As learning takes place hypothetically, the size of Δw decreases, unless the movement is in the form of a gesture or other acts whose exact dimensions are not highly important. Repetition of the motor act is thus conceived of as a "problem-solving" situation with closer and closer approximations being made to what are "desirable" or "required" demands in situations calling for action. Bernstein and others who have studied the biomechanics of voluntary movement are quite aware of the inability of the human action system to replicate exactly an even moderately complex movement in successive trials. Thus, it is more appropriate to speak of *approximations* than of *duplications* of required movements.

Bernstein suggests in his model that the final motor output is a func-

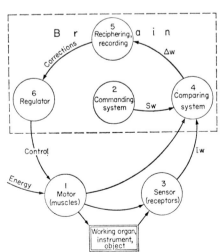

FIGURE 8–1. The simplest possible block diagram of an apparatus for the control of movements. (Courtesy of Bernstein, N.: *The Coordination and Regulation of Movements.* London, Pergamon Press Ltd., 1967.)

tion of the interaction of several types of neural mechanisms whose component parts contain numerous parts and interactions of their own. Both peripheral and central parts of the nervous system are important in the final output, and, as Bernstein emphasizes in several of his papers, once the movement has been initiated, gravitational forces, as well as environmental occurrences, may further serve to modify the action being taken.

Bernstein, like others, has been careful to categorize voluntary movements into those having several temporal dimensions. It is these dimensions, Bernstein believes, that are primarily reflected in the degree to which various kinds of modifications may be inserted prior to beginning the movement and/or once the movement has begun. It is obvious, he contends, that rapid ballistic movements require prior neural programming, whereas slower movements may be characterized by the degree to which some kind of "reprogramming" during their performance is both possible and desirable.

As can be seen, certain types of structures, including those regulating reciphering recording and those comparing and commanding, reside in the central nervous system (the brain in Fig. 8–1), whereas the motor and sensory systems are in the periphery. The importance of the correcting and comparing functions is reflected in the insertion of structures 4 and 6. Moreover, Bernstein, unlike several of his predecessors in Russia and some contemporary psychologists in the United States and abroad, *does not* view the regulation of voluntary movements as a kind of reflex-like, knee-jerk automated process, in fact, in some of his writings he is careful to point out that instinctive but complex animal reactions, such as the predatory behavior of fish, are a reflection of comparatively simple programmed behaviors that are stamped in the nervous system of animals. (Bernstein admits that we do not know exactly how.) In opposition to this, Bernstein is careful to point out that many human motor actions involve a number of higher level and less automated functions, including the formulation of conceptual models of what has been. what is now happening, and what might take place in the future.

Williams' Four Sequences

More recently Harriet Williams[1208] formulated a four-step sequence undergirding what she terms "perceptual-motor behavior" involving four overlapping stages governing the initiation and execution of a voluntary movement.

Step I: "Sensory Synthesis." Initially, the individual usually visually scans task components, instruments to be employed, and the total situation. Williams suggests that the level of activation for this initial stage is governed by the functioning of the reticular formation, together with the sensory stimulation received by the retina, and is passed to the higher cortical centers for evaluation concerning task characteristics including the size, shape, color, and spatial location of the object or task components.

Step II: "Sensory Interaction."   Occurring almost at the same time as Step I is a second cycle of events involving the comparing of sensory information with previously stored impressions. Thus, if a person is about to pick up a ball, this impression is compared with a vast (or lesser) amount of stored information concerning the location, size, and other characteristics of balls previously dealt with by the individual. Not only the cerebral cortex, but also structures in the brain stem and other subcortical structures may be important during this comparative phase.

Step III: "Initial Motor Activity."   The third step generally involves setting part of the motor apparatus into action as the result of a "central order" (pick up the ball) emanating from the cortex. The successful act then involves peripheral structures in the nervous system, motor neurons, and groups of neurons located in the spinal cord that have been readied by sensory activity occurring in the first three steps in the cycle.

Step IV: Further Sensory Information and Comparisons.   The next stage calls into play sensory information from the peripheral muscular structures and additional visual information from oculomotor activity. These two sources of information are conveyed at the same time to the central nervous system in order that subsequent judgments concerning the possible modification or continuation of the "central order" and/or modifications of the movement initiated can be executed by the individual. Williams concludes by stating that (1) perceptual-motor performance may be thought of as both a complicated and an overlapping group of sequential neural events; (2) motor activity may consist of at least two major subdivisions viewed neurologically, those involving "positional events" in which the total body is involved, and changes in positions and "manipulative events" in which smaller body parts are used to manipulate objects; and finally (3) the success of a motor act depends not only on the integrity of structures both central and peripheral that mediate the movement involved, but also on the structures that receive, inform, and otherwise integrate the results of *"sensory input"* into the complex feedback chain described.

The weakness of Williams' formulations lies perhaps in the fact that she does not attempt to explain the possible differences in neural function of rapid and ballistic versus slow and precise movements. These differences are discussed in other sections of the text (Chapter 5).

Summary

Through the course of evolution *encephalization*, the addition and dominance of primitive structures in the nervous system by higher components of nervous control, has occurred. In the human being, it appears that the higher centers, cortex, and associated structures function to integrate and funnel available sensory information and to initiate an appropriate movement output. The lower structures, cerebellum, reticular formation, and the spinal cord serve to monitor and smooth the action through a system of interdependent loops.

At the peripheral level, the motor units further modify the final response and exert the final control over muscular output. Primary variables influencing controlled muscle action at this level include the innervation ratio, the number of motor units affecting the muscle, the duration and rate at which stimulation occurs, differentials in nerve conduction rate, the nature of opposing muscle activity, and the size and formation of the fibers composing the muscle affected.

Student Reading

Hebb, D. O.: *The Organization of Behavior.* New York, John Wiley & Sons, Inc., 1949.

Harrison, V. F.: Review of the neuromuscular bases for motor learning. Res. Quart., *33*, 192-198, 1962.

Paillard, J.: The patterning of skilled movements. In *Handbook of Physiology.* Washington, D. C., Amer. J. Sociol., 1960.

Wenger, M. A., Jones, F. N., and Jones, M. H.: *Physiological Psychology.* New York, Holt, Rinehart and Winston, 1956.

Williams, H.: Neurological concepts and perceptual-motor behavior. In *New Perspectives of Man in Action.* R. C. Brown and B. J. Cratty (Eds.). Englewood Cliffs, N.J., Prentice-Hall, Inc., 1969.

9
"PERSONAL
EQUATIONS" IN MOVEMENT

The majority of studies involving motor performance and learning are concerned with optimum all-out effort. The subject in such experiments is usually informed that he should "do his best," exert "maximum effort," or move "as rapidly as possible." These experiments, while providing important information concerning performance attributes, tend to obliterate innumerable components of movement behavior that relate to how an individual *chooses* to move in the absence of some kind of exhortation for maximum effort. To an increasing degree these subtle components of motoric functioning are being accorded experimental attention. It is the purpose of this chapter to discuss these studies and to draw conclusions from them of importance to the physical educator.

In many tasks on the playground and in the gymnasium the manner in which the individual *prefers* to move will influence the total effort he exerts and the nature of the observable pattern elicited. The dance teacher is frequently confronted by evidence of these personal equations in movement as she attempts to encourage individuals in her charge to "break out" of well-established habit patterns involving rhythm; or perhaps to elicit movements within a larger amount of space than members of her class would prefer to use. Most performances in athletic skills represent a compromise between the maximum effort an individual can manifest versus what he *prefers* to do.

The available research indicates that there is a remarkable consistency in this kind of personal performance quality, both in action patterns[17,269,587] in which the total body is moving through space, in limb movements,[269,587] and in tasks involving smaller amounts of space.[926] This category of variables denoting a personal equation in movement might be termed *individual preferences in movement, personal equations of performance,* or perhaps *individual biases in movement behavior*. Essentially these components of movement seem to be the result of instructions the performer extends to himself prior to and during the performance of a motor task. These "personal equations" are also manifested in movement behaviors independent of structured performance situations—in walking, handwriting and similar daily activities.

In the pages which follow, material relative to *task persistence, personal rhythm, preferred speed,* and *spatial preference* will be discussed. *Task persistence* relates to individual differences in the inclination to continue performance while undergoing varying amounts of discomfort caused by continuing a task. "Personal rhythm" is obtained by experimental directions which ask the subject simply to "tap rhythmically," or instructions of a similar nature. "Preferred speed" is measured in tasks whose apparent emphasis is not upon speed, but upon accuracy, or by simply clocking movement patterns (walking) elicited from unsuspecting subjects. *Spatial preference* relates to the amount of space an individual habitually utilizes when moving. Studies involving naive subjects who are asked simply to "move their bodies to the music" have elicited data of this nature, as have studies evaluating the amount of space characteristically used by people when they have been asked to engage in a relatively unstructured manual skill.[926] These personal preferences, taken together, may be indicative of *personality* expressed in movement. During the 1930's several behavioral scientists become interested in these general movement attributes.

Early Investigations

Allport and Vernon carried out experiments in the 1950's that attempted to determine relationships between expressive movement and personality. The first battery of tests consisted of speed of walking, length of stride, handwriting measures, hand and finger tapping, estimation of distances, drawing of geometric figures, and similar tasks. Their first investigation resulted in the identification of three stable movement characteristics.[24]

Two of these characteristics seem related to the previously mentioned spatial preference. One was termed an *areal factor* by Allport, based on the amount of space characteristically used in tasks. Allport also identified a *centrifugal factor,* indicative of whether an individual typically made movements away from or toward his body during performances of various tasks. A third factor was named *emphasis* by Allport, and was identified by quantifying the amount of force and tension characteristically present in the performance of various finger tapping and handwriting tasks.

Further studies by Allport and Vernon purported to establish relationships between personality traits and various movement characteristics. Conversely they claimed that through observation of movement characteristics various personality traits could be predicted with moderate accuracy. However, Allport and his students warn the reader to proceed cautiously in the interpretation of the findings, stating that: "The unity of expression turns out entirely a question as to degree, just as the unity of personality is largely of degree. Expression is patterned in complex ways exactly as personality itself is patterned."[24]

In 1932 June Downey devoted a text to the elaboration and explanation of experimental findings that related "temperament" to movement. She used paper and pencil tests, together with handwriting analyses, to evaluate various movement traits which included speed of movement, freedom from tension, the tendency to vary a movement (flexibility), speed of decision, forcefulness, perseverance, and the like.[301]

From these groups of tests the following classifications were formulated:

1. The mobile type
2. The mobile-aggressive type, exploding with great force
3. The nonspecific type (difficult to classify)
4. The deliberate type, having great care for detail
5. The low-level type, easy-going, not forceful
6. The psychotic type, high degree of tension and little tendency to vary movements

Downey concluded that individuals might be characterized by their individual "profiles" based on the movement traits evidenced in these categories.

Although the reliability and validity of the test used by Downey were not established, this program represents one of the initial attempts to evaluate personal equations in movement. She is one of the first to show an awareness of the influence of tension on motor performance. Later researchers took a less global approach to the problem than did Downey, and usually investigated specific portions of this personal preference of movements.

Task Persistence

Various researchers in the past 30 years have attempted to determine whether a general quality termed *persistence* is evidenced when engaging in a variety of motor tasks. Although much of this work is not of a high caliber, the study by MacArthur in 1952 seems to point to the existence of a general factor involving the inclination of certain individuals to prolong their performances in a variety of tasks.[728]

MacArthur found, after intercorrelating 22 measures, that after intellectual differences were partialized out, a general persistence factor involving motor performance did exist. This investigator revealed that persistence was at least a dual factor, one part reflected in the relationships between various physical tasks, and the second in tasks of a more intellectual nature (how long an individual is willing to read from a book). This factor of motor persistence was revealed in correlations obtained from tasks that included the time an individual was willing to hold one foot straight out from the hip while seated, to hold his breath, to maintain hand-grip pressure, and to hold his arm extended at shoulder level. MacArthur's data also revealed that persistence under conditions involving some kind of social motivation (exhortation from others) seems to be a factor apart from the persistence evidenced by an individual in the absence of obvious social motivators.

Ryans,[957] Crutcher,[272] and others have also identified a general factor of persistence in a number of motor tasks. Thornton has isolated a general factor that he describes as "ability and/or willingness to withstand discomfort in order to achieve a goal," with high loading in "time holding breath, time standing still, maintained hand-grip, and similar measures."[1098] Rethlingschafer also named a factor "the willingness and/or ability to endure 'discomfort.'" Such studies involve the evaluation of a quality similar to pain.[183]

Although I am unaware of investigations relating such measures of persistence to vital capacity and other basic indices of optimum physical capacities, it is apparent that persistence could be an important variable influencing the results of experiments involving endurance, or in other studies in which repetitive movements lead to some degree of stress.

Typical of the methods used when evaluating persistence is first to obtain maximum capacity (grip strength) by asking the subject to maintain 50 to 75 percent of his maximum and then clock the length of time he is willing to do so. In common with the other *personal equations* discussed in this chapter, the experimenter must be certain that the subjects remain naive to the purposes of the investigation.

Although the physical educator and athletic coach frequently are heard to explain that encouraging a boy to persist in athletics will elicit similar fortitude when he is confronted with classroom lessons, the available data do not usually support this assumption, and the possibilities of research in this area are limitless. Determining whether persistence is a predictor of courage under stressful circumstances, studying the generality versus specificity of persistence, and relating persistence to the various measures of absolute capacity that undergird cardiovascular endurance would seem to be only some of the studies that could be profitably undertaken.

Personal Rhythm

Studies by Lewis,[687] Harding,[489] and others have presented somewhat inconclusive findings concerning the existence of a general factor of personal rhythm. Such a factor is studied by analyzing the speed an individual selects when directed to "tap rhythmically." In general there is a reasonable consistency in the measures obtained when the same limb is used in this kind of task on several trials.[877] At the same time, the contrasting of total body rhythm, foot tapping and finger tapping with various physiological measures, including heart rate, respiration rate, and the like, usually reveals low relationships.

Personal rhythm seems to be related to other kinds of sensory experiences. Dinner, Wapner, and McFarland[296] found that when an individual was asked to tap faster than he preferred, it led to an apparent shortening of an objective time period by the subject. On the other hand when he was asked to tap at a rate slower than he would usually choose, it led to an apparent lengthening of his perception of a time interval.[269]

Other characteristics of tapping behavior have also been explored as possible indices of personality. Eysenck[339] found that extroverts took more involuntary rests, after being instructed to tap rhythmically, than did introverts. Similarly subjects informed that their rate of tapping would be a criterion for admittance to a training course evidenced increased speed versus subjects who had already been admitted to a training program. Thus the personality of the subject as well as various motivating circumstances can alter personal tempo to a marked degree.

In general the identification of a personal tempo by asking an individual to engage in a few tapping tasks is a somewhat tenuous undertaking;[926] at the same time, given a specific tempo involving a single portion of the body, marked consistency is usually noted. Rimoldi found relatively consistent measures obtained on tests of personal rhythm between tasks administered several weeks apart.[926]

Preferred Speed

Relatively few investigations exploring preferred speed were carried out prior to the 1950's. In 1947 Kennedy and Travis[613] found a unitary speed factor when the scores obtained from a number of tasks were contrasted. These investigators coined the term "irritability" to indicate the general work rate evidenced by an individual. Frischeisen-Kohler[390] also suggested that a unitary speed factor exists, based on evaluation of preferred rates on tapping and on metronome tests.

Another study attempting to verify the existence of a general speed quality in movement was carried out by Harrison and Dorcus[500] somewhat earlier. Comparisons were made of the speed at which individuals characteristically moved, by measurement of their speed of arm and head movements in tasks in which speed was apparently not being evaluated. The speed with which the subjects walked to the experimental area was also measured without the subjects' knowledge. These investigators concluded that no unitary speed trait was present, although speed in specific tasks shows intertrial consistency.

In the most comprehensive study available, Rimoldi[926] found that both specific and general speed factors were evidenced when the work rate at which individuals preferred to perform various tasks were contrasted. Rimoldi used 59 measures in which 17 subjects participated; measures included those evaluating preferred speed in perceptual, cognitive, clerical, and motor tasks. The motor tasks included preferred arm-swinging speed of various kinds and in various planes, tapping tasks carried out by the feet, fingers and arms, and speed of walking. The perceptual tasks included various reaction and discrimination time problems. Writing activities were also included, as were reading speed, preferred metronome rate, cancellation speed, writing speed, and tests evaluating mental ability.[926]

Rimoldi found that habitual motor speed in various tasks evidenced moderate to high relationships, but that preferred speed in motor tasks was not indicative of the speed elicited when his subjects performed non-motor tasks. Two separate motor factors emerged, relative to preferred speed. One factor was composed of scores from tasks involving rhythmic and tapping movements; a second factor was composed of scores from tasks that required rather exact movement of the limbs (parallel movements of the legs while seated).

Rimoldi suggested that his data support the existence of different tempos, rather than acceptance of a universal one. For example, one could not predict preferred metronome speed by knowing the speed at which the same subject chose to bend his body. At the same time speed in bending the body is reasonably well predicted by knowing how fast the same person is willing to swing his arm. It is possible to predict speed of small movements by knowing the speed of large ones; prediction of movement speed by measuring preferred rate of drawing, for example, is not possible, based on the present data. Acceptance of the extreme "piecemeal viewpoint" relative to preferred speed is, Rimoldi concluded, not a sound approach. It seems, stated this investigator, possible to accept the existence of a motor speed factor of quite a general kind.

Rimoldi concluded that his study, as well as others, supported the existence of at least four areas in which the preferred speeds of performance are relatively independent of one another. These include speed of cognition, speed of perception, speed of reaction time, and speed of movement.

In common with the findings of Harrison and Dorcus[500] and of Frischeisen-Kohler,[390] Rimoldi found that the time between test periods has relatively little influence on the scores. Individuals are relatively consistent about the rate of movement when performing various kinds of motor tasks. Rimoldi concluded that "Each individual performs a particular act following a specific temporal pattern which he keeps constant." His chosen pattern seems to be, for him, the most economical way of performing. The speed of another person imposed on an individual's personal way of performing may prove detrimental.[926] The more recent study by Jones and Hanson also found marked consistency in measurements obtained 15 months apart, evaluating both time and space patterns evidenced when subjects arose from chairs.[587]

The available evidence thus supports the existence of a general factor indicative of preferred speed that is common to a number of motor tasks and relatively consistent over a time period. Although the correlations between preferred speed of movement, and maximum movement speed, and other physiological measures are low,[926] it seems that each individual has a characteristic and efficient movement speed that he prefers when performing a number of tasks. Further research as to how these temporal patterns are developed in children, the extent to which they are resistant to different kinds of external conditions, and their relationship to various other psychological and physiological measures seems indicated. Preference of personal tempos in movement is also probably related to an individual's perceptions of time; thus further research might also explore the relationship between various aspects of personal tempo in movement, and factors influencing the perception of time itself.

Of particular importance to coaches and to teachers of dance are the possible effects of the imposition of "unnatural" movement speeds on the performance of various tasks in which all-out speed is not requisite. The best procedure in such situations might first be to evaluate the effects of the individual's preference for speed when performing the task, and then proceed cautiously when attempting to inculcate any marked changes in the individual's chosen "movement speed."

Spatial Preference

Early observers of human behavior suggested the presence of a general spatial factor present in relatively unstructured movement tasks;[24] the experimental designs with which this quality was explored left much to be desired. More recent evidence from several sources indicates that there is a given amount of space through which individuals prefer to move their limbs and total bodies in relatively unstructured situations.

This general problem area has two primary questions that have been subjected to varying amounts of experimental exploration. (1) In a given type of task (line drawing, facing movements, dancing to music), just how much space do individuals prefer to utilize (how long a line do people prefer to draw?), and (2) are there individual consistencies in the space individuals utilize in several tasks and in the same task from trial to trial?

The first question has not been explored extensively. The available evidence, however, indicates that in various kinds of tasks there is a given distance people prefer to move despite directions from an outside source. When individuals are asked to draw a line 4 inches in length, they tend to draw a longer one; conversely people seem to resist drawing a line 15 inches long when requested to do so.

In another study it was found that when sighted and blind adults and children are asked to make facing movements of 90, 180, and 360 degrees while deprived of auditory cues (and sight in the case of the sighted), they were found to turn past 90 degrees by about 7 degrees, to underturn 180 degrees by about 10 degrees, and to underturn full turns by about 40 degrees. There thus seemed to be an amount of turning these subjects preferred despite experimental directions, probably somewhere between 90 and 180 degrees![269]

These findings are rather intriguing. It would seem that a simple factorial analysis might be helpful in the initial exploration of this phenomenon. The extent to which this kind of preference for space utilization in movements has long been speculated on in the clinical literature, however, relatively little objective work has been carried out.

Consistencies in individual differences in the amount of space utilized in various movement tasks have been also subjected to rather scant experimental treatment. The studies were initially concerned with writing movements both in structured handwriting tasks and in relatively unstructured activities.

Various modifications of the draw-a-person test have been explored as indicative of some kind of personality trait structure, usually without marked success. Similarly, graphologists have been diligently at work for years attempting to prove that character is reflected in handwriting with little to show for their efforts. The most recent review of the findings of the graphologists was by Vernon in 1953.[1135] By far the greatest number of studies have been concerned with attempts to match personality sketches or case studies with assessments from handwriting. The results of such studies are usually negative. Most of the European studies have failed to incorporate acceptable statistical procedures; and most of these seem to be based on the claims of intuition, rather than on scientific veracity.

Lewinson and Zubin[681] have presented a number of objective scorable scales and certain combined ratio scores that are claimed to be valid measures of handwriting characteristics. However, few investigations have been forthcoming utilizing these techniques. Perhaps Pophal, a research graphologist presently holding a chair in graphology at the University of Hamburg (Germany), will contribute research showing the relationships between personality and handwriting characteristics.

Generally the hypothesis that introversion and/or anxiety produces restriction in the amount of space utilized in various movements has little experimental verification. Exceptions are the studies by Craddock and Stern who found that introduction of stress produced a constriction in a design-copying task,[226] and the parallel findings of Brengelmann[130] relating confidence to the space utilized in a task involving the arrangement of figures around a radial pattern of lines.

A recent investigation by one of my students presents findings that seem an inroad to the understanding of spatial preferences in movement.[17] In this investigation, movement of the entire body was measured. Using 60 teenage girls with no previous dance experience as subjects, Ahrens requested that each one "move as she would like" to recorded music. One at a time the subjects were then left alone in a gym, and "watched" by a television camera of which they were unaware. The space they utilized was traced in an adjacent room with a monitor on which a grid was superimposed.

Three trials were given the subjects on three separate occasions. The scores were measures of the distance they moved, the number of squares in the grid they "visited," and the greatest distance they moved from the starting point.

Analysis of the data revealed remarkable consistencies in the amount of space the subjects used under the conditions described. Correlations exceeding .8 were obtained when the scores from the various trials were compared. In addition marked individual differences were evidenced in these spatial measures.

The investigation did prove the possibility of obtaining reliable measures from participation in a relatively unstructured movement task. It is believed that this investigation made an important contribution to our knowledge of human movement, and should be followed by others of similar intent, in which the influence of innumerable variables on spatial utilization might be explored. The additional factors might include various personality traits, stressors in the form of social harassment, verbal encouragement, and the presence of members of the opposite sex, of friends, and of disliked peers.

It is not difficult to locate various assumptions about the purported relationships between spatial qualities in movement and various other factors. Experimental verification of these associations are more difficult to locate, however.

Other "Personal Equations"

In addition to the four personal equations discussed on the previous pages, experimental evidence points to several other possible individual differences in movement characteristics that are consistent from task to task. For example, the work of Duffy indicates that there is a typical level of activation manifested in muscular tension and in other measures characteristic of an individual.[305] It is not unreasonable to suggest, therefore, that there is a personal equation, which might be termed *habitual force*, that may be evidenced in such tasks as handwriting, that in turn may correlate positively with various personality traits indicative of assertiveness.

Similarly individual differences in susceptibility or suggestibility to instructions probably exert an influence on the extent to which an individual asserts his personal movement characteristics versus accepting control and incorporating instructions from an outside source when moving. This *suggestibility factor* has been investigated by Sarazon and Rosenzweig[964] as revealed in relationships between body sway and susceptibility to hypnotism.

Further Investigations Needed

The available evidence is suggestive rather than conclusive. The amount of information presently available is not so extensive when compared to the bulk of data concerned with other problem areas contained in the text.

Further studies might explore the relationships between various motor tasks in which maximum performance is desired versus those in which various personal equations are exposed. The relationship between various structural and biological characteristics and individual preferences in movement also might be subjected to the scrutiny of the scientific method of problem-solving.

The relationship between selected measures of personality traits (introversion, extroversion, ascendency, aggression, hostility, succorance, and various manifestations of the personal equations described) would seem a fruitful field of investigation. Similarly the extent to which a movement as performed is influenced by some kind of personal preference versus maximum capacities is also an important avenue of scientific exploration. Contrasting various measures indicative of these personal equations with measures reflecting characteristic ways of perceiving should also prove interesting.

Overall these kinds of investigations should provide a deeper understanding of some of the subtle influences on perceptual-motor behaviors manifested by human beings. Correlation of these personal equations to various motor ability and motor learning scores might explain some of the findings presently attributable to "experimental artifacts." Consideration of these types of variables also might aid teachers to work more effectively with children in the classroom and on the athletic field and to accommodate better to individual differences in movement and perception evidenced by the students in their charge.

Summary

Performance data elicited from subjects under no specific instructions to perform maximally have revealed several classifications of attributes that may be defined as personal equations or personal preferences in movement. Persistence at a task is one of these. It is the inclination to continue performing under varying degrees of discomfort. Persistence at motor tasks seems independent of persistence at intellectual tasks. Other personal equations include personal rhythm, preferred speed, and the amount of space preferred in movements. In addition, the extent to which force is habitually expressed may be a sixth dimension in this category of movement attributes.

Student Reading

Eysenck, H. J.: *The Structure of Human Personality.* London, Methuen, 1953.
MacArthur, R. S.: The experimental investigation of persistence in secondary school boys. Canad. J. Psychol., 9, 42-54, 1955.
Rimoldi, H. J. A.: Personal tempo. J. Abnorm. Soc. Psychol., 46, 283-303, 1951.
Thornton, G. R.: A factor analysis of tests designed to measure persistence. Psychol. Monogr. 51, 1-42, 1939.

10
COMMUNICATION
THROUGH MOVEMENT

Closely related to investigation of personality-movement relationships is the study of the manner in which human actions may contribute to the communication process. Although early investigations were relatively subjective, having their genesis in phrenology, palmistry, and the like, in more recent years studies of movement communication are found in such respected fields as psychology, anthropology and sociology. As a result of the development of more objective evaluative instruments and sounder theoretical frameworks, studies in this area have become increasingly scientific.

Most investigations of movement communication are based on the assumption that interpersonal relations are facilitated as one becomes better able to assess and to utilize such factors as facial expression, posture, and gestures when judging meanings transmitted by another individual. Conversely, it is hypothesized that by failing to interpret correctly the thoughts expressed by another and by omitting consideration of accompanying movements, one may leave out an important dimension of interpersonal communication. Thus, much of the research seeks to gain general information that will enhance the productivity of various group endeavors.

Members of the performing arts have evidenced an interest in the manner in which movements communicate ideas, although little material that could be termed scientific has been forthcoming from this source. Acting "methods" recently coming into prominence have emphasized the subtle and overt use of bodily movements to communicate the intended emotions and ideas to the audience.

Expert dancers also have used an understanding of the manner in which gross limb and body movements suggest internal emotional states. Recent efforts by researchers in movement communication to evolve a shorthand system with which to describe various facial expressions bear a marked resemblance to systems of dance notation, which translate bodily movements to the printed page.

Literature in movement communication may be classified in several ways. Two main areas, for example, seem clearly delineated: (1) studies in *movement expression,* including the part overt bodily expression plays in communicating internal emotional states and various movement-verbal relationships; and (2) the study of *movement interpretation,* concerned with examining the variables that influence the manner in which individuals *judge* the movement behavior of others. In addition, recent investigations have considered actions manifested at three different levels, based on the area of the body involved in the movement; the study of *facial expressions, gestures* formed by the limbs and/or hands, and, at the gross end of the continuum, the manner in which posturing of the *total body* communicates meaning.

Two other important problem areas will be treated in the following pages. The first is concerned with whether gesture communication is innate or learned; the second, a close parallel, with what kinds of communicative movements occur of which the individual is unaware and what kinds are consciously sent and received.

Communicative
Movements: Learned or Innate?

As is the case with other facets of human behavior, motivation, personality, and the like, one of the major questions considered by various scholars is whether characteristics and individual differences in action cues are molded by sociocultural factors or whether they are determined by basic structural constituents of the organism.

Several lines of evidence support the viewpoint that movements and posturing are innate. Darwin, studying the relationship between animal emotions and their "facial" and bodily movements, concluded that many of these actions are functional in nature; for example, baring the teeth in anger enables the wolf to maintain a better grasp of his prey since it allows the teeth to become more effective as weapons. Since Darwinian theory naturally assumes that man has direct evolutionary linkages to the animals, it is therefore suggested that various human expressions have their basis in primitive action patterns.[281]

Cannon[167] offers another line of reasoning to support the innate nature of movement communication. Through numerous physiological studies investigating the characteristics of emotional states produced in dogs and cats, it was found that the methods by which they react to stress seem identifiable. Furthermore, these various rage and/or fear responses are mediated by subcortical portions of the nervous system. Since these do not depend on integration by the higher centers of the cortex, Cannon hypothesized that such innate movement responses to stress are "built-in" and not formed by learning.

Investigations in another area also support the contention that expressive movement communication may be inherited. Goodenough, studying the facial expressions of a ten-year-old child blind and deaf from birth, concluded that distinct movement patterns were evidenced, indicating rage, fear, disgust, and shame, that roughly corresponded to these same actions in sighted individuals. This was taken as evidence that such emotional states produce inherent kinds of gesture patterns unrelated to learning, as in this case the opportunity to observe others and to imitate them was, of course, not possible.[448]

Studies in growth and development provide further evidence. Watson,[1156] an early researcher in this area, concluded that three motion patterns are observable in the emotional patterns of infants. These he labeled x, y, and z and hypothesized that they represented evidence of fear, rage, and love, respectively. Since Watson noted that these three patterns were present in newborn infants, he suggested that such movement traits were innate.

Studies by Bridges,[131] however, suggested that Watson's findings might be questioned. He was unable to identify Watson's three patterns and proposed that the only significant movement pattern discernible in newborn babies is one of *general activity*. It is not until infants are about three weeks of age, Bridges argued, that other kinds of movement communication take place, including a *distress pattern*. At about two to three weeks of age, a *delight* pattern is noted to emerge, but not until the fourth month of age did movements that indicate *joy* become expressed in facial movements. Thus Bridges seems to infer that most patterns of movement communcation are learned rather than instinctive. It is interesting to speculate that the dissimilar backgrounds of Watson and of Bridges or the divergent frames of reference they employed may have resulted in their different interpretations of infantile action patterns.

Crying and Smiling in Infants

The crying response seems to be present at birth and initially is caused by internal discomfort. After the first month of age, the percentage of time given to crying decreases, reaching its lowest point at about four months. After four months, the time given to crying increases until about one year, and then decreases again to about eighteen months, according to Bayley.[76]

As the child grows, causes of crying become more related to external environmental conditions. The manner in which the child is handled and the like become increasingly important. After the child organizes his proximal world, strange objects or conditions seem increasingly to elicit a crying response.

Smiling is absent at birth and thus seems learned. Smiling does not appear until about the twentieth day with the total response developing during the third, fourth, fifth, and sixth months of age. By the age of six months, Buhler[149] found that the smile becomes a normal response to social stimulation and is utilized in communication.

In an ingenious study designed to determine various causes of smiling in infants, Spitz[1048] found that the human face, when presented to an infant between the age of three to six months, elicited a smiling response. This researcher then covered with a mask various portions of the face viewed by the infant to determine exactly what stimulated a smile. Was it movement, the eyes, the mouth, or what? On the basis of many observations, Spitz concluded that it is not another human face in itself that elicits a smiling response from infants, but a configuration of elements in a total stimulus pattern. This configuration was found to consist of two eyes combined with motion of various facial muscles, which could consist of nodding, sticking out the tongue, or some similar movement.

Movement and Emotion in Adults

Wenger,[1180] devoting considerable study to the electrophysiological activity of the autonomic nervous system, has produced findings that relate to movement communication. He found that there are about eight distinguishable patterns of electrical activity seemingly related to internal emotional states. Furthermore, he stated that: "There seem to be certain patterns, such as the flexion pattern in fear and pain, and the extension pattern in anger, as well as the unique relaxed 'bowed-back' flexion pattern in grief or depression."

Another question of prime importance, assuming that emotions and movements are moderately related, is whether one can objectively measure, and thus predict, one from the other. A pioneer study in this area by Meyers[789] suggested that in the case of anxiety this can be accomplished. He found that there was a significant positive correlation between rate of eye blink and anxiety.

The Culture
and Learned Movements

The view that emotional patterns expressed in movement are learned rather than innate is supported by anthropological studies. Anthropologists found long ago that peoples in various cultures use dissimilar gesture systems when expressing themselves. Cushing[277] suggested, from studying Zuni Indian sign language, that the more primitive the culture, the more the recourse to gesture communication. However, such a simple hypothesis is open to question when it is realized that, even in a given culture, a gesture may have different meanings for various situations and for different socioeconomic groups.

Misinterpretation or lack of knowledge about the characteristic gesture signs used by an ethnic group has caused the death of more than one anthropologist who mistakenly used gestures that threatened rather than signified friendship when first encountering an isolated tribe. The actions of actors in motion pictures produced in one country are often misunderstood, because of the habitual use of a different set of gestures in countries to which the films are exported.

Although a large number of gestures are culturally oriented and seemingly not dependent on innate characteristics, in most cases a one-to-one relationship between internal emotional state and movement cues is difficult to demonstrate. Indeed, in many primitive tribes, emphasis is placed on the concealment of internalized fear through the presentation of a relatively immobile countenance to the world.

Hewes[527] and other observers of various cultures found that there are a vast number of movement patterns characteristic of ethnic groups that apparently are learned, since they seem to be unique to specific groups. Such patterns have been used in studies of personality, status, and emotional state. For example, specific and nonspecific movement customs unique to citizens of the United States govern their actions while eating and playing. In some cases, the social group in which an individual belongs may be accurately identified through observing his mannerisms in various situations.

Although the instinctive versus learned question is difficult to resolve in relation to movement communication, it seems that rather intense emotional states result in innate movements of the face and body that indicate fright or fear. On the other hand, less intense kinds of communicative behavior, which transmit information or add a dimension to verbal behavior, seem largely a learned product of the cultural setting.

The learned patterns of movement expression seem to fall on a continuum, from actions of which the sender is totally unaware to those clearly practiced. Many of the more conscious patterns, such as shrugging the shoulders and turning the palms upward to indicate bewilderment, are used to augment, emphasize, and speed communication. Toward the subtle, reflexive end of the continuum lie minute facial expressions and overt flexings of the body of which an individual may be unaware.

The importance of such subtle clues is emphasized in an investigation by Eisenberg and Reichlane.[323] They found that observers could successfully differentiate between women labeled dominant and submissive, after the administration of a personality inventory, by observing films of the way they walked.

The contention that gesture patterns are both unique to the individual and culturally determined is supported by research by Hebb.[505] It was found that gestures were highly individualized in both animals and man. Observers of primates had to become familiar with each animal before they could correctly interpret the meanings of their gesture patterns. Similar findings were forthcoming when the gesture patterns of humans were analyzed.

Even primitive men evolved complex systems of movements that aided communication. Silent signals permitted the Bushmen to track game without using distracting verbal symbols. At times, these hand signals were given with accompanying actions denoting the motions of the animal indicated. Even more complex communicative movements are employed by the deaf and by teachers of hard-of-hearing persons, forming a complex system of communication involving letters, words, and phrases.

The Interpretation of Movement Cues

A number of articles have reported on the ability to interpret facial expression and larger bodily movements. The results often have been contradictory; however, the findings of one investigation seem worthy of review. Kline and Johannsen[625] found that correct interpretation of another's movements depends on the number of kinds of movements observed. And conversely, when viewing isolated portions of the body, less accurate estimates are possible. More accurate judgments are made when facial expressions, gestures, and posturing are observed in combination than when only one or two of these subdivisions were inspected. Kline et al. also presented evidence indicating that observations of moving pictures, rather than still pictures, resulted in more accurate judgments of emotions.[625]

Also important to correct interpretation of movement "language" is consideration of the context in which the action occurs. Research by Frijda[389] suggests that if the total situation is known, the judge may better project himself into it and thus become able to form more accurate judgment about the movements observed. For example, if expressions of joy are seen in a context that seems pleasant and happy, interpretation is not difficult. However, if these same gestures and movement patterns are viewed in a situation calling for grief, judgmental confusion is likely to result.

Although Ruesch and Kees,[948] among others, have supported the accuracy of Frijda's statements, relatively little research has been devoted to exploring the effect of the context on the interpretation of movement cues or the possible "overriding" of contextual cues by intense action patterns.

Innumerable cultural variations in communication gestures can be cited.[634] For example, the gesture meaning "come here" in America is used to denote "good-bye" in many parts of South America. Similarly stroking the chin in Italy means that the individual is "starting to grow a beard" because he is so bored with the speaker. The typical gestures of Jewish immigrants from Lithuania and Poland were studied by Efron, and it was found that they could be easily distinguished by reference to gesture patterns alone. The children of these immigrants, however, failed to utilize the amount or the kind of gestures that characterized their parents' efforts to communicate. Efron is one of the few individuals who has bothered to devise a reasonably objective system for coding gestures, although it is somewhat complex to use.[319]

These cultural variations, of course, indicate that the judgment of gesture patterns will be made more accurately by people of a similar background. Dusenbury and Knower found that ability to judge the meaning of gestures in one's own cultural context was good, but when people of one culture attempt to judge the communicative movements of another, little accuracy is possible.[310]

Although awareness of the cultural situation seems important to the interpretation of gestures, other variables do not. For example, Morrison[815] found that sex, intelligence, occupational rank, and religion do not seem to be related to the accuracy with which individuals are able to judge gesture-language.

During the 1950's, 1960's, and 1970's interest in parameters of communicative movement has increased greatly, reflected not only in the proliferation of scientific studies, but also in the appearance of popular books on the subjects (*Body Language*). Moreover, interested scholars have begun to explore further dimensions of the problem, presenting new ideas, and collecting highly provocative data. An example of one of the newer "offshoots" in this fascinating field is discussed in the following paragraphs.

Proxemics

In 1959 Hall[479] wrote about the presence of implied norms in various cultures, denoting the permissible ranges of distance between two individuals communicating verbally. Later, Hall, as well as Mehrabian,[776] began to explore some of the facets of posture, closeness, body-lean, eye-contact, interpersonal distance, and "openness" or "closedness" of the limbs that are apparent when two individuals communicate. Thus, Proxemics is the study of nonverbal clues that contribute to, detract from, or in some way influence interpersonal communication.

As early as 1932 James,[580] with 347 photographs in which positions of hands, trunk, feet, knees, and arms were systematically varied, found reasonable agreement among subjects shown these pictures on what he termed four "postural categories": (1) "approach": an attentive posture, usually a forward lean of the body; (2) "withdrawal": usually a drawing back or turning away posture; (3) "expansion": a proud, conceited, or arrogant posture, communicated by an erect or backward leaning trunk, overly erect head, and raised shoulders; and (4) "contraction": a depressed downcast or dejected posture, usually a bowed head, drooping shoulders, and sunken chest. In these four categories, the head and trunk positions were found to be the most important indicators.

In further research, Exline and his colleagues[335,336] found that when communicators prefer each other, there are not only posture cues, "forward leaning," but also a greater amount of eye contact. Machotka additionally found that arm postures indicative of "openness" further designated a positive attitude on the part of the communicator. Little noted that, when the communicators were closer, more positive interpersonal feelings were evident in one or both parties.

In a 1967 study, Argyle and Kendon[39] pointed out that a further important dimension to consider when evaluating nonverbal cues in the quality of interpersonal communication is a "relaxation-tension" scale. Further work indicated that this dimension is important when evaluating relative status of two or more communicators, the person of lower status, as would be expected, usually showing a greater amount of tension.

Studies of this dimension of interpersonal communication are proliferating at this writing. Findings emanating from these investigations should prove of assistance to many scholars interested in the behavioral sciences, to educators, to clinical psychologists, and to others interested in gaining a deeper understanding of the meanings of movement, as well as of human interactions.

The Measurement of Movement Interpretation

It is generally agreed that individuals continually interpret the gestures of others. In answer to the need for objective measuring tools with which to evaluate consistency of judgments, Morrison developed a Gesture Interpretation Test (GIT). The task evaluates whether individuals are consistent in the manner in which they interpret the emotions and meanings suggested by 37 outlines of individuals pictured in various postural and gestural attitudes.[815]

Morrison found that his subjects were able to attach meanings to commonplace postures, gestures, and apparent movements with some consistency. This is rather remarkable, because the pictures contained *no indication of facial expression.* The fact that even mentally abnormal individuals were able to judge the pictured postures accurately was interpreted by Morrison as indicating that ability in gesture interpretation is a skill formed early in childhood and is not easily forgotten.

Tactile Communication

Movement may communicate, of course, not only as the receiver observes the movements of another, but also as he is touched by another. In recent years, several researchers have indicated an interest in tactile communication, although little objective evidence has been forthcoming in this area.

Frank suggests that the growing infant reacts first to *signals,* then to larger and more complex kinds of tactile cues, or *signs,* and later to *symbols* that indicate still more complex meanings. Frank also discusses various cultural influences on tactile communication and suggests that personality development and increased tactile sensitivity are closely parallel.[378]

Summary

Movement communication is an important aspect of man's movement behavior. Mobile cues often accompany verbal expression, but at times stand by themselves to suggest meanings. Movements that communicate may be either learned or innate, depending on the intensity of the emotion directing them. The more intense emotional types of movement expressions are probably instinctive, whereas actions that only communicate information are largely learned and related to the culture.

An understanding of movement communication is important from several standpoints. Initially, it seems important for an individual to become sensitive to the exact meanings emanating from another; therefore, accurately interpreting movement cues heightens an individual's perceptions of the feelings, needs, meanings, and wishes of another. An understanding of the nature of movement communication is important also for the sender because more exact meanings can be transmitted, thus establishing clearer channels of interpersonal communication.

In also seems clear that when a total complex of movements is regarded, including facial, postural and bodily actions, accurate meanings may be interpreted or transmitted. And as Icheiser[569] has pointed out, failing to interpret movement cues properly may pose serious interpersonal misunderstandings.

A primary problem is the need for the development of objective measures of the ability to communicate through movement, as well as instruments to assess the ability to interpret movements. Morrison's GIT provides a vehicle through which investigators might better assess the manner in which individuals judge the posturing and gesturing of others.

It would appear that the primary area for further research concerns the nature of socially determined movements. Cooperative research among sociologists, anthropologists and psychologists might prove productive. More research also seems called for to explore the manner in which the sender becomes accustomed to utilizing the various gestures he is engaged in without thinking. In line with this problem, an investigation concerning the classification of various gestures into conscious and unconscious categories would be worthwhile.

The role of gestures in manipulating the behavior of others, either groups or individuals, the subject of a study by Stratton,[1068] also seems important for future consideration. No one who has ever attended a group meeting in education or business can deny the importance of the facial and bodily movements of ranking members to the channeling of discussion.

Student Reading

Birdwhistle, R. L.: Kinesics and communication. In *Explorations in Communication.* E. Carpenter and M. McLuhan (Eds.). Boston, Beacon Press, 1960, pp. 54-65.

Eisenberg, P.: Expressive movements related to feelings of dominance. Arch. Psychol., *211,* 1-130, 1937.

Ekman, P., Frirsen, W. V., and Ellsworth, J. B.: *Emotion in the Human Face.* Pergamon General Psychology Series. New York, Pergamon Press Inc., 1972.

Perl, W. R.: On the psychodiagnostic value of handwriting analysis. Amer. J. Psychiat., *3,* 595-602, 1955.

Ruesch, J., and Kees, W.: *Non-Verbal Communication.* San Francisco, University of California Press, 1956.

Talmadge, M.: Expressive graphic movements and their relationship to temperament factors. Psychol. Monogr., *469,* 1–30, 1958.

11
ABILITY TRAITS

Several definitions have been offered for the term *ability trait*. According to Fleishman,[362] an ability is a more general trait than that indicated by the term *skill*. He suggests that ability traits not only may underlie, to varying degrees, the performance of a group of skills, but also are rather "enduring traits," which are relatively difficult to modify in the adult. Thus, when approaching a given skill, the individual brings his "collection" of ability traits that are honed (or acquired through inheritance) to varying degrees of proficiency, collectively contributing to his initial and later successes at acquiring proficiency in the task confronting him.

English and English[329a] define ability trait in a quite different way, indicating that it is the "power" to perform *an act* (italics mine), physical or mental. Thus, this definition is highly task-specific, whereas the meaning applied by Fleishman and his colleagues indicates an underlying, more enduring, and more general characteristic. For the purposes of the discussion that follows, Fleishman's more general meaning will be attached to the term *ability trait*.

Numerous physiological and anatomical factors limit an individual's ability to utilize force (depends on the contractile strength of various muscles), to move with speed (governed by the mass of the limb or portion of the body moving), and to react quickly (depends on the type of stimuli reacted to), such as the speed of the nerve impulse, the complexity of the movement to be carried out, and the state of the organism (fatigue and the like). Within these capacity limitations, however, individual motor performance is extremely variable. Two men of similar physical makeup, having the same scores on strength tests and other measures of physiological capacity, might vary markedly when asked to perform a complex motor skill. Our concern, therefore, is not in defining absolute limitations of movement, speed, reaction time, or strength but of determining how performance potentials might be reached in these limitations. Basic to the achievement of performance is whether one can cultivate fundamental factors that seem to underlie a number of tasks or whether a skill is highly specific.

Are Ability Traits
General or Specific?

The answer to the question whether motor skill is task-specific or general in nature is complicated by several kinds of problems. (1) How are the two skills being compared with correlation techniques, by looking at "clusters" in factorial studies or by examining transfer (the effect of performing one task on the performance of a second)? (2) Is heredity versus environment or nature versus nurture being equated with generality and specificity? (3) What efforts have been made to control such variables as learning and the relative dependence on sensory information (visual control) when comparing the two tasks? (4) What is a motor skill, is it a simple arm-swing, involving reaction time and movement speed or is it a complex act involving spatial accuracy?

Trends in the Research

Research delving into specificity versus generality has shown the following trends during the past 60 years. Initially subjective investigations carried out during the early 1900's indicated that various general performance characteristics do *exist*. The research by Downey[301] and by Allport[24] and a study by Garfiel[411] are examples. During the 1930's, as intelligence testing was separated from evaluation of motor skills and as more objective measures were developed for performance, research indicated the specific nature of motor skill. Investigations by Perrin,[886] Seashore,[981] and others substantiated the independent nature of skilled performance.

In the late 1950's and the 1960's Franklin Henry and his colleagues[516-525] demonstrated that tasks involving movement, speed, reaction time, and strength seem largely based on factors unique to the movement. Although at times their concept of a coordinated movement seemed somewhat narrow and appeared to exclude tasks emphasizing spatial accuracy, these findings have generally served to shake the traditional concept of "general coordination" formerly espoused by physical educators. That some individuals seem to be "well coordinated" was explained in several ways: (1) They are able to perform well because they possess a number of specific performance qualities. (2) They frequently place themselves in a position, or the culture encourages them, to practice a number of activities. Thus their success is only the result of extensive practice. (3) Their general personality results in a need for success or approval in motor skills, so they are motivated to work hard to improve performance in a number of tasks.

First applied to the analysis of mental abilities, factor analytic techniques have become increasingly important in the analysis of motor skill. During and following World War II, studies employing this technique, a collective statistic permitting one to draw meaning from multiple correlations, have proliferated.

Correlational Techniques
to Determine
Generality or Specificity of Skill

One of the most direct methods of determining whether factors are common to two or more motor skills is to compare performances through correlation techniques. A correlation coefficient relates the order in which a group of individuals is ranked (from least to most proficient) in one task to their ranking in a second.

If an individual's score in shooting basketball free throws can be predicted by knowing the accuracy with which he is able to throw a baseball, it might be said that a general "throwing-for-accuracy" factor underlies performance of the two skills. If no such prediction is possible, since the subjects seem to reshuffle the order in which they rank on the two tests, the two skills may be considered specific measures of performance.

To interpret a correlation coefficient correctly, one must square it to determine the extent to which proficiency in one skill may contribute to the other. The final number achieved is in the form of a percentage of "common variance." Thus a correlation coefficient of $+.45$ between push-ups and sit-ups indicates that the ability to perform sit-ups probably contributes about 20 percent ($.45^2$) to the ability to do push-ups. The word *probably* was used in the previous sentence insofar as a relationship (evidence in a correlation coefficient) may not indicate *causality*. Thus a logical examination of the two tasks or groups of tasks, which are related statistically, must be made in order to reach a valid conclusion concerning the actual relationship.

The Specificity of Movement Time, Reaction Time, and Strength. In recent years studies demonstrating that movement time, reaction time, and strength are largely independent and are combined in specific parameters to produce a simple, direct movement have proliferated. Examination of the underlying peripheral structures controlling motor output, the *motor unit* (discussed in Chapter 16), demonstrates the anatomical possibility of such specificity.

Neuromotor specificity has been demonstrated in the time-honored measure of grip strength. Henry and Smith[524] presented findings that pointed out that individual differences in strength were 54 percent specific to the hand tested, but a general hand strength accounted for only 46 percent of grip pressure.

In a series of studies, Henry, Whitley, Smith, and Lotter[520,524,525] demonstrated the independence of strength and maximum arm speed. In addition, limb speed and limb reaction (time taken to initiate the movement after the stimulus is given) were demonstrated to be largely independent. Arm mass and speed of movement were also found to be independent phenomena. Nelson and Fahrney,[842] on the other hand, obtained moderate to high relationships between measures of strength and movement speed. In this study angular velocity was measured in an elbow flexion movement, whereas in the studies by Henry and his colleagues the movement speed measure was usually elicited by a movement that combined angular and linear velocities of the limbs. Helen Eckert[318] also found moderate correlations between speed of limb movement and strength when linear velocity was employed as the measure of speed.

While working in this program, Henry discovered that response time increased when more complicated movements were to be initiated, and he suggested that a "memory drum" theory might explain the basics of neuromotor reaction.[518] He proposed that an unconscious mechanism channels stored information to the appropriate neuromotor coordination center, thus causing the desired movement. The lengthened reaction time prior to a complex movement therefore may be explained by the increased time necessary for the more diverse pattern of impulses to manifest itself.

The contributions of these researchers have been important in the understanding of rather direct motor acts. Their terminology might be criticized, however, since they generalize findings obtained from simple movement speed experiments to explain "the high specificity of neuromotor *coordination skills*."[525] In one frame of reference, coordination seems to imply the monitoring of neural impulses involved in muscular contraction that control a rather direct simple movement (e.g., a horizontal arm swing). In another context, "coordination" might be construed as a series of movements of varying speeds and force combining into a motor act of a more complex nature. Basically, the question seems to be whether coordination implies internal integrations of the nervous system that produce finite variations in a simple act or whether it means complex outward manifestations of movement. The studies of Henry et al. seem to imply that the former definition is the more acceptable. However, acceptance of the latter meaning of coordination indicates a broader outlook rather than a rejection of processes underlying the former.

Factor Analysis

With increasing frequency, researchers have employed factor analytic techniques in efforts to analyze the basic components of motor skill and learning. Although a detailed analysis of this technique is beyond the scope of this text, an attempt will be made to explain some of the basic assumptions that underlie this helpful mathematical tool.

Essentially, a factor represents a "cluster" of test scores that intercorrelate highly with one another. For example, if we have 12 tests and five correlate highly with one another, a single factor has been identified; if four or more of the test scores correlate with one another but not with any of the initial five, a second factor has been identified.

In addition it can be determined how predictive of the total factor a single test score is by obtaining a "factor loading." This loading is a number, in the form of a correlation coefficient, that represents the relationship between the total factor and one of its parts; conversely, awareness of the degree to which a given test may load in one or more factors (or clusters) enables a more thorough analysis of the subabilities that underlie the performance of the test.

Some of the 12 test scores may not correlate with any other score, and thus they represent specific abilities, unrelated to other attributes common to the other tests in the battery. The practical outcomes of factor analysis include the identification of common factors that can be incorporated into a testing or training program. Similarly, if a number of tests that purportedly evaluate different attributes are given to a population, the application of factor analysis may reveal that fewer tests can be utilized, since there may be a marked overlapping between the qualities evaluated on the tests. Initial exploratory studies in relatively unresearched areas are best accomplished by simply obtaining numerous measures and then ascertaining those that seem to "cluster." This saving of time and effort in many testing and research programs is a helpful outcome of this statistical method.

It must be kept in mind, however, that the value of factor analysis is not intrinsic to the method but depends on the insight and interpretative abilities of the individual employing the technique. The experimenter, for example, by subjective judgment, originally selects items for inclusion in his battery; after the computer helpfully arranges his scores in clusters, he must, with his best insight, name the factors, utilizing his knowledge about what *seem* to be common basic attributes underlying the performance of the related tasks. In addition, the type of factorial analytic technique selected by the investigator influences the nature of the clusters obtained.

The reader is directed to tests by Fruchter[392] and by Harmon[493] to obtain a detailed account of various factorial techniques. Over the years, researchers have searched for general factors that seem to underlie the performance of more than one task. They seem interested in constructing a framework in which skilled performance can be considered rather than in merely dismissing motor skill as specific. Independent "clusters" of correlations in studies by McCloy[757a] and Jones[589] of gross motor skills and by Fleishman and his colleagues[358-373] of both fine and gross tasks indicate that it is possible to isolate basic, although independent, factors contributing to the performance of various types of motor tasks. McCloy,[757a] following a survey of studies concerned with this question, concluded that 10 factors contribute to the performance of gross motor skills: (1) strength, (2) dynamic strength or energy, (3) ability to change direction, (4) flexibility, (5) agility, (6) peripheral vision, (7) good vision, (8) concentration, (9) understanding the mechanics of movements, and (10) absence of disturbing emotional complications.

Guilford[470] evolved a matrix of factors in 1958, by reviewing the work of McCloy, Fleishman, and others, by which psychomotor ability can be classified. The independent "clusters" of abilities, previously noted, are apparent in Table 11–1. Broad areas seem to consist of the accurate utilization of space, the maximum and immediate use of force and balance, and the ability to move rapidly. The independence of these "clusters" is revealed when it is noted that many are present only in the functioning of specific parts of the body.

A large program of factorial studies was given impetus during the late 1940's and early 1950's by the United States Air Force, owing to its desire to learn more about pilot skills. These studies, in turn, bred further studies that concentrated on the analysis of gross motor skills and various fitness qualities. These studies constitute an important contribution to the literature for three major reasons: (1) A large number of subjects were used, in some cases 500 to 700 individuals participated in the testing programs. (2) A larger variety of skill and capacity tasks

TABLE 11–1.   Matrix of the Psychomotor Factors, with Columns for Kinds of Abilities, and Rows for Parts of the Body*

	Strength	Impulsion	Speed	Static Precision	Dynamic Precision	Coordination	Flexibility
Gross body	General strength	General reaction time		Static balance	Dynamic precision	Gross body coordination	Flexibility
Trunk	Trunk strength						Trunk flexibility
Limbs	Limb strength	Limb thrust	Arm speed	Steadiness	Aiming		Leg flexibility
Hand-finger		Finger tapping speed		Hand aiming	Finger and hand dexterity		

*Courtesy of Guilford, J. P.: A system of psychomotor abilities, Amer. J. Psychol., *71*, 164–174, 1958.

were included in these batteries of tests. (3) A more careful selection of these skills was made to include tasks evaluating a wide variety of performance traits. The recent investigations fall in two major areas: those investigating the components of manual dexterity and those concerned with the analysis of gross motor skill and capacity.

Components of Manual Skill

In one of a series of studies concerned with manual skill, Fleishman and Ellison[366] obtained findings that further point to the specificity of motor performance. Using 760 subjects and 22 tests of manual dexterity, including paper-and-pencil tests and apparatus tasks, five primary factors were isolated.

1. *Wrist-finger speed* was the initial factor identified and was evaluated with paper-and-pencil tests that involved tapping speed independent of accuracy.

2. *Finger dexterity* was the second factor and it has been repeatedly identified in factorial studies of manual skill. Tests that evaluate the rate and accuracy of the manipulation of small objects by the fingers delineate this performance quality.

3. *Speed-of-arm movement* was the third factor identified, and as we shall see later (p. 210) is perhaps only a component of a larger factor termed *speed-of-limb movement*. This factor was identified through the application of various arm-aiming tasks, with an accuracy component.

4. *Manual dexterity* was identified by tasks that involve rapid and precise hand-and-finger movements, as opposed only to finger movements.

5. *Aiming* was the fifth component of manual skill identified by Fleishman and Ellison and involved hand-eye coordination. It appeared most clearly when the aiming required great precision (attempting to place a pointer in a small circle).

Further studies by Fleishman and his colleagues resulted in the identification of additional abilities, shown graphically in Figure 11–1.

Thus it is apparent that manual skill of adults involves several kinds of qualities. The influence of findings of this type has been to expand the kinds of tasks included in batteries to screen the selection of industrial employees.

Components of Gross Action Patterns

Although the initial studies identified a general gross coordination factor involving the integration of arm and leg movements, more recent investigations with a broader range of tasks and a larger number of subjects have further dissected such apparently "pure" qualities as strength, flexibility, balance and the like. In one of the most recent and

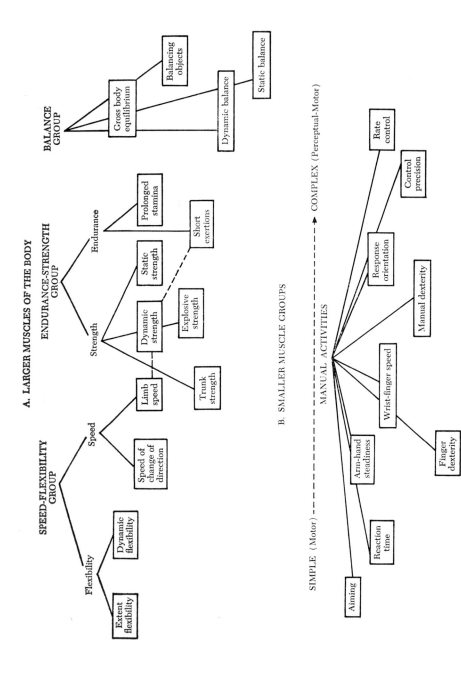

FIGURE 11–1. Motor ability traits.

comprehensive of these, Fleishman, Thomas, and Munroe[373] used 30 tests of gross motor ability. Six primary factors were identified.

1. *Speed-of-change-of-direction* was the initial factor isolated. It was evaluated by tests that include the quick propulsion of the total body in running tasks, and is related to the ability to mobilize energy quickly.

2. *Gross body equilibrium* is seen in the performance of various static and dynamic balance tests, and is evaluated by the length of time an individual can balance on an edge of a balance beam, as well as the proficiency with which an individual can walk a narrow beam (dynamic balance).

3. *Balance with visual cues* was isolated as a separate balance factor, and is apparent in tests of static balance performed with the eyes open.

4. *Dynamic flexibility* involves the ability to execute repeated trunk and/or limb movements quickly. The tasks involve speed in the movements through a wide range of motion.

5. *Extent flexibility* is evaluated by tasks requiring the demonstration of range of motion of the back and trunk in slower stretching movements than are necessary in dynamic flexibility tasks.

6. *Speed-of-limb movement* was identified as a performance quality, although it was originally hypothesized that arm speed and leg speed were separate components of performance. It is evaluated by tasks involving both leg speed (foot tapping) and arm speed (number of arm circles in a time period).

Components of Muscular Force: Strength

Another factorial study[311] further analyzed strength tests. Thirty carefully selected strength-endurance, flexibility tasks were given to 201 subjects. It has been suggested that strength lies in three broad areas: dynamic, explosive, and static. This investigation hypothesized that some more specific kinds of "strengths" might lie in these general areas. Specifically the role of endurance in strength tests was also investigated, as was the possibility that strength is specific to various muscle groups (e.g., flexor strength versus extensor strength). It was finally purposed to discover tests that would provide the best assessments of the various strength qualities. Seven factors were identified.

1. *Dynamic strength* is evaluated by chin-ups and push-ups to limits in specific time periods (15 seconds), dips on the parallel bars, and similar tests of arm strength. Since the best measures involved arm support tasks, as might be expected, height and weight are negatively correlated to performance in these kinds of measures.

2. *Static strength* is evaluated by tasks in which force is exerted against immobile objects. This factor seems rather general and involves

muscle groups in the hand, arm, back, shoulder and leg, and is common to both flexor and extensor muscle groups.

3. *Explosive strength* emphasizes the ability to expend a maximum of energy in one explosive act and is measured by tasks that extend to both the arm and shoulder regions (softball throw; vertical jump).

4. *Trunk strength* involves tasks that primarily evaluate abdominal strength.

5. *Weight balance* is the ability to handle and manipulate weights with both arms and feet. The number of pulls or pushes in a short time period (usually 20 seconds) evaluate this quality.

6 and 7. A questionnaire polling athletic experience was administered to the subjects and a scoring system was applied to the amount and type of experience the subjects reported. Relating this score to their performance scores resulted in the identification of two subfactors that, taken together, were termed *athletic experience: general.* This previous experience in athletics, however, seemed divisible into two components involving two patterns of participation: one pattern was a football-basketball-track combination, and the second was a basketball-baseball combination.

The bulk of Fleishman's factorial work has impressed many scholars. Some psychologists have recently taken the program to task for several methodological and theoretical reasons. Among the most energetic critics is Bechtoldt who, with others, has claimed that factor analysis is only an exploratory tool, and that to arrive at the degree to which various qualities may be common to two or more tasks, the evaluation of transfer effects is more productive. The critics further point out that Fleishman too frequently revises his hypotheses concerning the nature of the factors isolated, as well as what tests contribute most to a given factor.

Individuals unsophisticated in factor analytic processes, although perhaps not able to weigh these arguments in a productive way, should note that the results of *any* factor analysis depend on the nature of the scope and the constitution of the tasks analyzed, the factor analytic methods employed to treat the data, the age and nature of the subjects, as well as the subjective judgment of the researcher who finally names the factors. These same limitations are present in Fleishman's work, as they would be in that of any researcher employing this type of collective statistic. At the same time, within the limitations outlined, Fleishman's data are a reasonably valid picture of the motor abilities of young adult men confronted with the tests described.

Contemporary Studies.   Factor analytic techniques have continued to be employed by many researchers in further efforts to understand basic constituents of motor performance measures, as well as in attempts to fragment the "motor personality" of the human animal. Margaret and Chester Harris,[499] for example, carried out a detailed study of flexibility with this statistical technique(s) in 1963. Using measures indicative of single- as well as multiple-joint flexibility, they found the scores they obtained to be highly task-specific, with few clear-cut general factors emerging.

Practice and
Basic Skill Constituents

Two early studies searched for general factors that might emerge as the result of *practice*. In 1913 Hollingworth[546] found that, as motor skills were practiced, positive correlations increased: from 0 to +.28 at the fifth trial, to +.32 by the twenty-fifth, to +.39 by the eightieth and to +.49 by the two hundred and fifth. The tasks included those evaluating complex coordination, tapping, and various discrimination problems. Hollingworth concluded that a "true sampling of ability" emerged as learning progressed. It was hypothesized that other variables, such as momentary attitude, motivation, and initial methods used, became less important as practice is continued.

In 1943, Buxton and Humphries[164] also attempted to ascertain the effect of practice on generality of motor skill and arrived at findings disagreeing with those of Hollingworth. Nine cycles of tests, in which pursuit-rotor, fine motor skill, and other tasks covering a three-hour period were used, produced a drop in positive correlations, from +.25 to +.16. It should be noted that in this latter study only nine trials were allowed in each task, whereas Hollingworth's subjects participated in over 200 trials.

In recent years, research using various tracking tasks confirms the findings of Hollingworth. Correlations between scores on the same task increase as practice prior to the first score is continued, suggesting that the factorial structure of visual-motor tasks becomes simpler as learning progresses. Therefore, it has been hypothesized that, due to the multiplicity of factors present during the early stages of learning, relationship between the early trials of two tasks could be expected to be low, but when trials in two tasks are compared after considerable learning has transpired, more intertask generality can usually be demonstrated. Jones,[589] among others, suggests that with increasing practice, pre-experimental experience exerts a decreasing influence on performance. Adams,[10] in research for the Air Force, obtained higher intertask correlations between final than between initial trials and also found that final performance level can be predicted better by extratask measures than by intratask measures.

Fleishman[369] published a report of a study relating predictability of motor performance to the stage of learning. His findings imply that, although at times relative predictability may change as the task is learned, the same task factors are probably present throughout the learning process; they change only in percentage of involvement. Some abilities were shown to increase in importance, whereas others were demonstrated to decrease as learning progressed in various hand-eye-foot coordination tasks. Thus whether generality or specificity is demonstrated during the learning stages of various tasks probably depends on the ingenuity of the researcher in devising tests that will best correlate to the factors of paramount importance during the stage in the learning process under consideration.

More recently other researchers have explored further Fleishman's hypotheses dealing with the changes of ability structure as a function of learning. Like Fleishman, Hinrichs[542] found that task-specific factors fluctuated as a function of learning a rotor-pursuit task in a study completed in 1970.

Inherent Versus
Acquired Motor Characteristics

The traditional question concerning the importance of heredity versus environment also is important to the discussion of specific versus general factors in motor performance. One could assume that general factors depend on constitutional factors, whereas specific factors depend on the opportunities an individual has had to explore his environment. A study by Goodenough and Smart,[451] indicating that more general factors are present when children's motor performance scores are compared, and investigations revealing the same phenomenon when performance scores of the feebleminded are compared add substance to such a position. Studies of Co-Twin Control on maturation, summarized by Gesell,[418a] further suggest that basic motor activities involve inherent capacities.

In a classic study carried out in 1939, Myrtle McGraw[770] explored the nature-nurture question by "training" one of two identical twins in a variety of manipulative and gross motor tasks, including ascending incline slopes, jumping, and tricycling. She found that, at the conclusion of training, trained twin Johnny usually manifested greater motor coordination and daring in physical tasks in contrast to the untrained Jimmy, who remained somewhat awkward and timid. However, McGraw concluded that any alteration of performance by early training depends on the degree to which a given activity is already learned when exposed to enrichment, and by modifications of body mechanics and emotional and attitudinal factors surrounding the task's performance and learning: whereas later in life no significant differences in their emotional and intellectual makeup that might have been attributed to the early training were observed.[770]

In a study in 1959, I[230] obtained moderate to high correlations between father and son performance in the 100-yard dash (+.49) and the broad jump (+.80), from measures taken at the same time of life and on the same facilities. Although such relationships may result from opportunities to run and to jump that the father afforded his son, no significant correlations were found between the father's scores and the son's scores in more complex gross body skills (bar vaulting and ball throwing). Recent studies by Smith and his colleagues[1025] indicate that improvement of movement speed seems to resist practice, whereas manipulative ability (as part of the same complex task) shows marked improvement under the same conditions. Taken together, one might hypothesize that locomotor speed and efficiency are basic inherent factors, but accurate and complex movements of the upper limbs are more dependent on experience. However, further research is needed to explore this supposition.

A Classification System for Sports Skills

Sports skills can be studied from a number of theoretical or applied viewpoints. To cite only one way, skills can be classified according to whether they are "open" or "closed," depending on whether the responses to be made are relatively predictable and based on what the performer himself does, or whether the responses are highly variable and depend on quickly changing conditions in the environment of the skill and/or by one's opponent(s).

More precisely, however, it is possible to place sports skills (or any skill for that matter) on continua that relate to the degree to which invariance or variety is required. To add another dimension to the model, the response characteristics can be separated from the performance characteristics, and as a result, an attempt can be made to determine whether variability is required (or permitted) in the response or in the *results* of the action.

This three-way classification system is presented in Figure 11–2. To elaborate further, certain skill situations permit little variability in response characteristics, e.g., rifle shooting in a specified style, or the clean and jerk in competitive weight lifting (although at least two styles are acceptable under the rules, the "squat" and "split" clean). The gymnast practicing a prescribed "move" or "routine" is another example of this type of skill.

Moving further across the "degree of variability of response" dimension in our model, there are situations in which a variety of responses may be observed, but within limits, such as the several ways to shoot a free throw. At the extreme end of this continuum would be the modern dancer, composing her or his own routines, in which a wide variety of responses are often permitted and desirable.

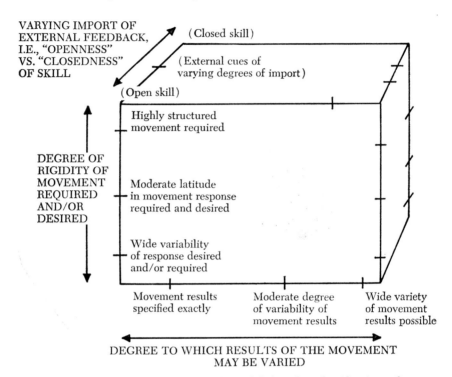

FIGURE 11–2. **A three-dimensional model for the classification of sports skills.**

With regard to the variability permitted or required in the *results* of the motor act, here again various skill situations can be placed at various points on the scale. The machinist must turn out a part with precise limits, despite a variability in response components that he may evidence as compared to other machinists and intertrial variability in his own performance curve. The basketball player is permitted a variety of shots (set shots, jump shots, lay-ups), but at the same time the *results* of these efforts are tightly prescribed—to put the ball, from top to bottom, through an 18-inch hoop placed horizontal to the floor. Passing a basketball, on the other hand, would be placed farther across the scale, suggesting that, in this instance, a wide variety of passes must be mastered, and in various situations a number of results, e.g., the ball arriving high, low, and the like, might be appropriate.

The final dimension of our model suggests that skills may vary according to the degree to which visual feedback is important for subsequent execution. A skill may not necessarily be classified as *either* open or closed, but may vary along a scale denoting the importance of feedback from sources external to the individual's response mechanism.

This variability in the importance of external cues, of course, is some-times reflected in the manner in which skill changes as it is practiced, with shifts toward the "closed" end of the scale expected as the result of practice. Whiting's work dealing with the interception of balls, which has led to theorizing by Adams and others, supports the validity of this important dimension in the classification of athletic skills.

There are other important dimensions of skill, some of which are alluded to in this chapter, so that the model described in this section should be considered as an attempt to provoke thought, rather than as an absolute. It is a model similar to this, however, that has inspired some contemporary sport psychologists, notably Berger, to suggest that certain kinds of sport situations tend to attract individuals who have a high need for structure and a parallel rejection of ambiguity; on the other hand, there are sports in which personality traits reflecting the ability to deal with complexity and ambiguity may enhance performance and learning.

A Four-Part Model of Perceptual-Motor Functioning

Fitts,[354] a pioneer researcher in the area of human factors, has identi-fied general capacities of movement found to be typical of individuals performing a variety of perceptual-motor tasks. Among the qualities considered were amount of information assimilated, facility in dispelling psychological interference ("noise"), channel capacity (ability to receive information and to organize it), and rate of movement. He concluded that:

> The performance capacity of the human motor system plus its associated visual and proprioceptive feedback mechanisms, when measured in information units, is relatively constant over a considerable range of task conditions, reflecting a fixed capacity for monitoring the results of on-going motor activity, while at the same time maintaining the necessary degree of organization with respect to magnitude and timing of successive movements.[354]

Consideration of the information contained in the previous chapters leads to the conclusion that a four-part theory of perceptual-motor be-havior is tenable. Underlying performance of movement tasks are several levels of general abilities, which, although somewhat independent, nevertheless explain the individual consistencies and differences exhibited in performance.

The argument concerning the specificity or generality of skill permeates the contents of this text, appearing not only in this chapter but also in the discussion of the transfer of training, motor educability, and in the sections dealing with anxiety and motivation. In general, the major conflict arises when skills are measured and compared, as contrasted to the observation that some individuals seem generally "coordinated" and are apparently able to perform and to learn a variety of perceptual-motor activities well.

Arguments concerning the generality or specificity of behavior have their genesis in literature dealing with the human intellect. Spearman,[1043] around the turn of the century, and later Thurstone,[1100a] Guilford,[470] and others suggested that cognitive behavior is highly specific and could be fractionalized into several parts. The previously described research by Fleishman[371] and Seashore[981] also gives impetus to the supposition that perceptual-motor functioning is highly specific.

The theoretical model shown in Figure 11–3 attempts to explain perceptual-motor performance in both general and specific terms. Spearman[1043] spoke of both a "g" (general) factor and an "s" (specific) factor in intelligence, whereas Kelley,[610] Burt,[163] Eysenck,[341] and Vernon[1134] share the opinion that human behavior is molded by a general or universal factor in addition to a hierarchy of second-level factors.

The theory assumes that four kinds of variables influence performance output. At the basic level are what have been termed *behavioral supports*[238] and include general aspiration level, state of arousal, ability to analyze a task, typical amount of muscular tension present, and the individual's need for and susceptibility to social stimulation. These basic *supports* are believed to influence a variety of human behaviors in addition to perceptual-motor performance, including verbal and cognitive abilities.

The second part consists of two types of attributes—personal equations of movement (described in detail in Chapter 9) and ability traits (described in this chapter). Generally these two types of attributes interact in the formation of performance. Personal equations in movement influence motor behavior more when the situation is unstructured, and maximum performance is not required. On the other hand, ability traits are more closely related to performance when optimum effort is expended. The ability traits change when performance is sustained, influencing perceptual-motor behavior in a direct way, and they do not exert the comprehensive effects on other categories of human behavior as do the *general supports* mentioned previously.

Unique performance factors are components of the performance situation that result in the marked skill specificity seen in the various experimental studies cited. Such variables as the social stimulation in the performance, the instructions (or lack of them) about task performance, the unique spatial and force requirements of the task, and the performer's past experience in the same and in similar tasks are placed here.

The importance of the various parts may change as a function of age and intelligence. For example, young children are probably influenced more by the basic behavioral supports than are older children and ado-

UNIQUE PERFORMANCE FACTORS

Specific Instructions
Force and Accuracy Components
of Task
Social Conditions Present
(etc.)

4

ABILITY TRAITS

Static Strength
Dynamic Balance
2 Agility
Hand-Finger Speed
(etc.)

PERSONAL EQUATIONS

Persistence
Preferred speed, tempo
Space Used   3

(etc.)

BEHAVIORAL SUPPORTS

Aspiration
Tension
Arousal Level

Social Needs
Analytical Ability
(etc.)

1

FIGURE 11–3. Four-part theory of perceptual-motor performance.

lescents. Retarded persons, perhaps unable to profit from specific past experiences to any degree, also may exhibit perceptual-motor functioning that depends more on the basic behavioral supports than on the unique performance characteristics of the task and situation.

Several types of investigations suggest themselves from inspection of this theoretical structure. For example, the generality or specificity of human skill may depend on the extent to which vision is incorporated into the task's performance. The generality or specificity of aspiration level, of situational anxiety, and of persistence in the performance of tasks needs further clarification. Particular emphasis in future studies should be placed on the importance of various perceptual factors that are important to the performance and the learning of motor skills.

Summary

The definition of ability traits used in this chapter alludes to a general trait that may underlie the performance of a number of motor tasks. For the most part, these traits have been identified as the result of factor analytic techniques applied to a battery of perceptual-motor tasks.

The number and kind of tasks analyzed, the type of subjects, and the biases of the experimenter influence the type, number, and name of the factors or traits emerging from these studies.

The question of specificity versus generality of skill was discussed in connection with correlative studies, and the influence of such variables as maturation, learning, and practice on the degree to which two or more skills are related was presented.

Several models for the classification and analysis of sports skills and of perceptual-motor skills in general were presented. Three dimensions of the model dealing with sports skills include (1) the degree to which the skill is open or closed, (2) the degree to which variability in response is desired or permitted, and (3) the degree to which the result of the performance is permitted to vary. Causality of motor performance was discussed through the use of a four-part model, including factors and conditions specific to a performance situation, basic motor and perceptual ability traits, personal equations, and, finally, basic behavioral supports.

Student Reading

Fleishman, E. A.: *The Structure and Measurement of Physical Fitness.* Englewood Cliffs, N.J., Prentice-Hall Inc., 1964.

Fleishman, E. A., and Hempel, W. E., Jr.: Factorial analysis of complex psychomotor performance and related skills. J. Appl. Psychol., *40*, 132-136, 1956.

Guilford, J. P.: A system of psychomotor abilities. Amer. J. Psychiat., *71*, 164-174, 1958.

Henry, F. M.: Increased response latency for complicated movements and a "memory drum" theory of neuromotor reaction. Res. Quart., *31*, 28-34, 1960.

IV
PERFORMANCE MODIFIERS

12
INDIVIDUAL DIFFERENCES

Early studies of the psychology of human intellectual and motor performance often employed one subject. A single professor (examiner) seated himself across the table from one student (subject). Alternately they proceeded to test each other and draw conclusions from their feelings and conversation, as well as from the scores they collected.

With the new statistical concepts of the 1920's and 1930's, this type of intuitive experiment was relegated to obscurity, as being unscientific and too narrow a sampling of human tendencies. Replacing the one-to-one introspection and observation were more elaborate experiments involving large groups of subjects.

This newer "group psychology" had certain advantages, but at the same time tended to obliterate individual differences in the scores obtained from single subjects, differences that, if carefully scrutinized, would have proved highly provocative, as well as forming the bases for further fruitful investigations. During the past decade, some experimental psychologists interested in general learning, as well as motor learning, again have begun to examine carefully the fluctuations of an individual as he performs in various ways, and the manifestations of performance and learning differences. These newest inroads have uncovered several types of individual differences in performance and learning of both motor and mental tasks, differences that may stem from a variety of causes. These types of individual differences can be categorized as follows.

I. Intra-individual differences: Fluctuations of performance and learning on the part of an individual that are noted in successive performance trials or while he is learning a given task.

II. Inter-group differences: Differences in the manner in which various categories of persons perform and learn. These differences are the result of factors other than individual idiosyncratic behaviors, and include dissimilarities that might be attributed to the person's status in the following subdivisions.

a. Maturation and age: Some differences may be attributable to variations in capacities and inclinations caused by age and/or maturation.

b. Sex: More and more psychologists have begun to pinpoint differences in the emotional, social, and physical makeup of the sexes.

c. Race: With increased study, there seem to be real and significant racial differences emerging that are reflected in measures of motor performance and learning, some noted in children as young as five years of age.

d. Personality traits: These differences are often reflected in the distinct ways that motor skills are performed and learned.

e. Physique or body-build: Persons with the same type of physique tend to participate in the same kinds of sports. The interactions of physique, personality, and motor performance are subtle, complex, and yet interesting.

f. Intelligence: Intellectual differences often cause variations in the manner in which individuals and groups acquire, analyze, perform, and learn motor skills.

g. Perceptual propensities and unique motor attributes: These qualities can at times markedly change the manner in which motor skills are performed, acquired, and retained.

The above listing is by no means complete. There are probably marked differences in the intellectual strategies employed by people of various subgroups, which could change motor performance increments. Further complicating the problem is the separation of the various factors listed, and then determining their influence on physical output. For example, differentiating between intelligence, opportunities, and maturation is a difficult, if not impossible, undertaking; and the racial differences obtained often are more a reflection of the differences in socioeconomic setting than of race.

The following discussion does not try to sort out and resolve all the theoretical, social, and philosophical implications of the study of individual differences. I have attempted both to inform the reader of how various factors can cause reasonably predictable changes in performance, and to make the scholar more sensitive to the manner in which people, who are different from himself, may respond in situations calling for varying degrees of physical effort.

Intra-individual Variations

When attempting to learn a new task or when performing a well-learned one, it is common to experience "ups" and "downs." Even among so-called champions performance often fluctuates. Golf experts do not do well in all tournaments, and basketball stars have good days and "off" days.

In the 1960's several scholars, including Franklin Henry[519] and his students, became interested in the fluctuations people evidence when performing and learning motor tasks. The research has attempted to answer several questions: (1) Do the fluctuations an individual evidences tend to be predictable at various stages of learning and from task to task? (2) Can people be classified according to whether they habitually vary a great deal or only minimally? (3) Are individual fluctuations from trial to trial more marked during the early or later stages of skill acquisition? (4) Is intra-individual variability more marked in simple tasks or in complex tasks? (5) What other characteristics tend to predict whether persons are relatively stable performers, or whether they will have performance curves with a jagged pattern, reflecting obvious inconsistencies?

At this point tentative answers can be formulated for some of these questions; the answers to other questions require further research. (The measure most often used is to obtain the variability or spread of scores around the subject's mean score on a given task.) Several difficulties plague researchers on these related problems: (1) the difficulty in separating the individual fluctuations in consistency due to the subject from those fluctuations caused by experimental artifacts, such as slight differences in the testing environment or subtle modifications in the experimenter's behavior; and (2) separating the fluctuations in the subject's basic capacity to respond from the inconsistencies caused by changes in the subject's attention, mood, and attitude.

Despite these problems in measurement, some tentative answers to the questions posed above emerge. For example, practice in relatively simple motor tasks does not usually result in increasingly marked individual variance, as contrasted to more complex tasks. And even in complex tasks, intra-individual variance often stays relatively constant as a function of practice; although in several studies inconsistency increased after the initial trials for three or four trials, and then became relatively constant, with the exception of decreased variability with practice found in one study in which the stabilometer was used (see Chapter 2, p. 32).

Furthermore, the degree to which an individual evidences inconsistencies in his performance is not highly correlated to the level of absolute performance he may be exhibiting, except during the early stages of learning. That is, good performers seemingly are as likely to evidence inconsistencies as are poorer performers.

The findings are mixed when the degree of consistency or inconsistency that people evidence in a particular task is evaluated. It appears that there is moderate consistency in individual variability (variability is not random), although some individual variability is caused by the specific task being performed. Correlations between measures of variability, as would be expected, are closer in highly similar tasks than in dissimilar tasks.

Intergroup Differences

In addition to random and regular individual fluctuations in task performance and learning, important differences in motor performance and motor learning measures are elicited from various groups of people. Some of these differences are obvious to all. Young children perform and learn in ways different from adolescents, adults, or the aged. Retardates engaging in physical tasks exhibit characteristics at variance with what we expect from normal youngsters or adults.

Other group differences are not always obvious. There appear to be racial differences, even in the young, reflecting qualities of physical performance that appear in adolescence or young adulthood. Certain perceptual preferences, ways of organizing and conceptualizing motor tasks, and various motor abilities undoubtedly modify the manner in which people perform in action situations.

But even in the more obvious categories, race, sex, age, intelligence, and the like, it is helpful not only to casually note that there *may* be certain differences in how the various groups perform, but even more important, to determine just why these differences occur. Discovery of the differences and the reasons for them is sometimes sought from a theoretical standpoint, but such a search also has several potentially practical outcomes. Curriculum planning may be expedited when the movement capacities and learning abilities of a given group can be described exactly (retardates, for example). Second, deeper insight into the processes that influence the movement capabilities of the so-called normal or average child or adolescent is sometimes obtained from learning in some detail about how various age or intellectual groups differ from one another.

Sex

Even in young children it is possible to discern differences in the manner in which they perform physical skills. Boys as young as three or four years seem to use more of their bodies when throwing than do girls of the same age; although girls usually outperform boys in motor tasks requiring precision and accuracy (hopping, drawing, and the like). Young boys, on the other hand, often outdo most of the girls in their class in activities requiring force and/or speed, including running for speed, throwing for distance, standing broad jumping and similar vigorous activities. (A detailed discussion of sex differences in motor abilities may be found in Cratty.[261])

Both Goodenough and Brian[449a] and Hicks[527a] reported that boys are superior to girls in ball-throwing tasks at three years of age. Jenkins[581] also found that, although sex differences were less marked at seven years than at younger ages, boys were superior in both standing and running broad jump, and in the baseball throw. Only in the jump reach test were greater age differences than sex differences noted. Hartman found that sex differences became more pronounced after five years of age, and item intercorrelations ranged from .4 to .66 when comparing the jump reach and dash scores with performance on the hurdle jump.[501a]

Despite these early differences, it is difficult to separate the influence of nature and nurture. Are young boys imitating the more vigorous and mechanically correct masculine "models" in their homes or neighborhoods, or is there something innate in their makeup that impels them to perform better in more vigorous activities? Are the girls aping the more restricted "feminine" movements of their mothers, or is there something biologically different that makes them approach the vigorous activities more conservatively?

Rather basic structural and muscular differences, which in turn may be expected to modify performance of the two sexes, appear rather early in life. In 1956, Rarick and Thompson[910] found that from an early age the male has more muscle tissue compared to body weight than does the female, and he is stronger per unit of body weight than is his feminine peer.

Later in life these differences become more pronounced due to the appearance of the male hormone, testosterone, which elicits greater muscular strength. Although girls reach adolescence almost two years earlier than do boys, by the time both have matured* the differences in strength are quite marked, whereas differences may be less distinct in other activities (Fig. 12–1).

Differences in motor ability appearing during the adolescent years are due to more than variations in muscle density, strength, and biochemical makeup. Cultural norms, expectations, and pressures also play an important part in what adolescents and young adults of either sex choose to participate in. Often, when performance curves of girls are plotted from the scores of activities they participate in during these years, the fluctuations are marked.

In 1940, Espenschade[334] used a variety of tests, such as throwing for distance, jumping, standing broad jump, jump and reach, the Brace test, and agility run, to study the motor performance of adolescents. Her findings emphasized the growing divergence of performance manifested by girls and by boys during this period of life. Espenschade found positive relationships between physical maturity and performance among the boys, whereas these relationships were not demonstrated when the same indices were compared for girls. She found further that strength and performance of boys were related, but the same measures were unrelated for girls. These findings seem to indicate that, as adolescence is reached, girls fail to perform to their potential, whereas boys utilize their fullest

---

* Appearance of curly pubic hair and presence of nocturnal emissions in boys and initial menstruation in girls are employed as maturational signposts.

capacities to do well in motor skills. Espenschade found that the mean performances of boys increased in all events during adolescence, but girls reached maximum performance levels at about 14 years of age, and then the levels gradually declined. This trend held true whether age was determined chronologically or through evaluation of skeletal maturity. Masculine interests in vigorous games correlate with masculine personality characteristics,[829] but the same clear-cut relationships between onset of maturational indices and various personality attributes do not usually appear in studies when girls are the subjects.

In *The Adolescent Society*, sociologist James Coleman[207] makes frequent reference to the influence of cultural demands on movement attributes. Findings concerning adolescent values, parental values that influence adolescents, and teacher-administrator expectations of adolescents are summarized. Numerous interviews were conducted and questionnaires collected from pupils in ten high schools in a variety of socioeconomic settings.

Coleman found that almost half the boys wished to be remembered after high school as athletes, rather than as leaders in other activities,

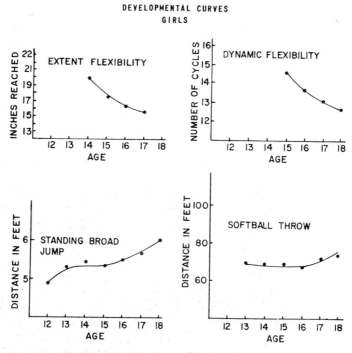

FIGURE 12–1. Physical proficiency in relation to age and sex. (Courtesy of Fleishman, E. A.: *The Structure and Measurement of Physical Fitness.* Englewood Cliffs, N.J., Prentice-Hall, Inc., 1964.)

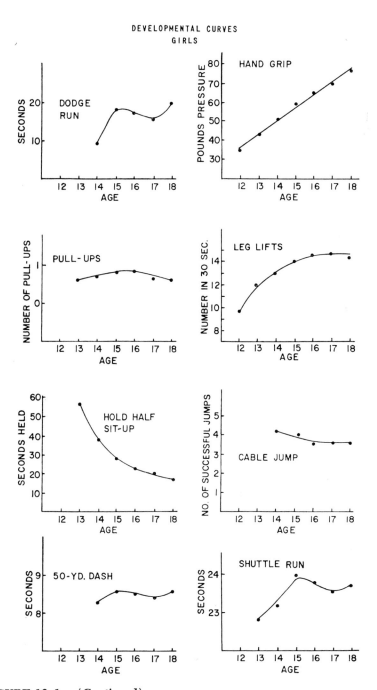

FIGURE 12–1. (*Continued*)

DEVELOPMENTAL CURVES
BOYS

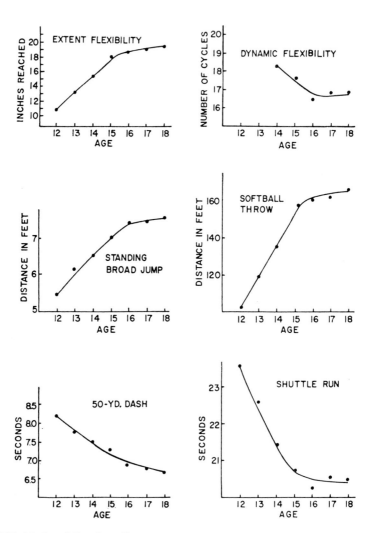

FIGURE 12–1.   (*Continued*)

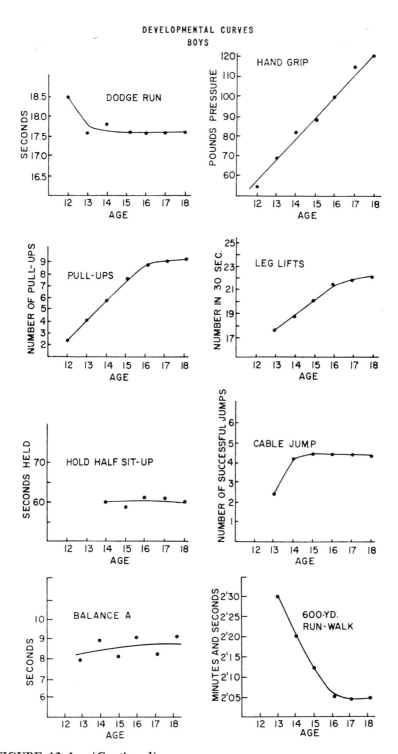

DEVELOPMENTAL CURVES
BOYS

FIGURE 12–1. (*Continued*)

231

brilliant scholars, or the most popular. Male membership in the leading school social groups was mainly attributed to participation in athletics. Other qualities, such as appearance, common sense, and sense of humor, took a back seat to movement skills. Only in schools located in an extremely high socioeconomic setting did the athlete-scholar outweigh the athlete in popularity, but in no case did the outstanding male scholar seriously threaten the athlete's popularity.

Adolescent girls, on the other hand, could succeed socially by being attractive, well dressed, and coming from a family with above-average cultural advantages (e.g., a college-educated father). But even the girls could enhance their prestige through association with some aspect of the boys' athletic program, such as cheerleading.

Coleman points out that both parents and colleges sustain the image of athletics as the road to success. Although parents do not wholeheartedly support their offsprings' values, they do contribute to their children's social goals by encouraging them to participate in athletics. In one school surveyed, Coleman found that, although six high school athletes were offered college scholarships, the outstanding male scholar was ignored by recruiters in higher education.

In addition to contributing to group approval, the adolescent's feelings of worth are decidedly affected by the extent to which he achieves success in athletics. Jones[588] discovered that, among boys scoring lowest in strength, most tended toward social introversion, felt a lack of status, and showed feelings of inferiority. On the other hand, boys scoring in the upper extremes in strength seemed to experience no such negative feelings about themselves and, on the whole, evidenced favorable personality traits, reflected in healthy aggressiveness and the attainment of leadership roles. A follow-up to this study was carried out 27 years later, using the same subjects. The remarkable consistency found in the personality trait scores of the subjects points to the importance of early maturation and physical ability in the formation of rather stable systems of behavioral characteristics.[995]

During adolescence boys are encouraged, threatened, and offered every cultural sanction to participate in and, above all, to excel in athletic skills, but girls are often discouraged from placing too much emphasis on athletic participation. Jones[590] found that approval was generally given to girls having a moderate interest in tennis, golf, and swimming in higher socioeconomic groups. Care had to be taken, however, that the girl did not participate at too high a competitive level. Thus, during adolescence both boys and girls are introduced more precisely to what the American culture considers to be appropriate adult feminine and masculine behavior, including the intensity and type of athletic skills in which they may participate.

It is a general observation that both pre- and postadolescent boys often take a less deliberate approach to the acquisition of sports skills than do their female counterparts. The girls, perhaps sensing that they cannot muscle through the tasks, on the whole seem more prone to analyze the tasks prior to executing them.

Numerous other variables influence sex differences when females and males are confronted with physical performance situations. For example, boys are more likely, even as young children, to express physical aggression than are girls, and are less likely to feel guilt anxiety about the aggression they do express, according to a summary of the work on this topic by Maccoby.[723a] Girls are found more likely to evidence "dependency behaviors" in a variety of situations, than are boys. Tests of gender identification, containing game choices, almost invariably denote games of aggression as "male," while there is usually an absence of these types of games among the choices considered appropriate for "females."

Other less apparent changes in *relationships* between motor performance measures are a function of age. Several recent studies point to the probability that, as people mature, they exhibit less "generality" when performance measures in various tasks are contrasted, that is, there is a decreasing correlation between task performance as individuals become older, which may be due to a number of factors. Most probably the differential and specific effects of experiences become increasingly unique with age. Corroborative data for this general trend are found in an investigation by Carron,[174] who found moderately high generality of performance in his younger subjects, seven and 11 years of age, when scores in two reaction-time tests were contrasted, but this generality (moderately high intercorrelations) diminished in 15- and 17-year-olds. Additional research, incorporating a broader spectrum of motor and perceptual-motor tasks and a larger range of subjects of both sexes, should further clarify the manner in which this principle manifests itself in the ability patterns of children and youth.

Relatively few comprehensive studies have been carried out in which sex differences in motor *learning* have been systematically investigated. The available data have been collected from tasks found only in the laboratory. In 1961, Bachman,[50] with a stabilometer and a "free-standing" ladder-climbing task, found no sex differences in the shape of the learning curves obtained, although males performed better on the two tasks than did females. Ammons[32] also noted significant superiority of males over females in the often-employed rotary pursuit task. In a review of his work, Ammons reported that marked sex differences only appeared in subjects older than eight years of age.

Thus, untangling the relative effect of the numerous variables as they influence sex differences in physical performance is a difficult undertaking. The task is made more taxing by the absence of systematic data, collected over a time span and employing a variety of tasks. In future investigations, I hope that such confounding variables as socioeconomic level and social expectations, as well as personality traits, such as achievement needs, are better controlled than they were in the previously published works on this topic.

Age

Obvious age differences exist in the acquisition of motor skill. In some of the most interesting and recent work, Jerome Bruner[144] suggests that the earliest hand-eye coordination skills, in relation to objects, occur in the following sequence: (1) The infant takes hold of objects handed to him at the middle of his body. (2) Then he uses one hand to facilitate the actions of the second. Bruner's task required the infant to raise a transparent lid from a box with one hand and to remove an object from the box with the other hand. (3) Next, the infant reaches for an object placed behind a barrier. Bruner calls this "detour reaching." (Piaget also believes that this type of activity is an important developmental milestone. He terms it the awareness of "object permanence"; the child is aware of the existence of objects he cannot perceive directly, is beginning to engage in visual imagery of unseen objects, and is evidencing the rudimentary beginnings of important cognitive processes.) (4) Finally, the infant is able to hold a large object so that he can handle a fine object attached to it. Bruner terms this the "differentiation of power and precision grips."

Bruner suggests that these and other steps in the early acquisition of skill denote that the infant is beginning to realize and potentiate various stored "programs" that he will continue to use throughout his life not only to master skilled motor tasks, but also for various problem-solving operations more closely linked to cognitive-intellectual work.

The early acquisition of skill, together with the growth of the inclination and propensity to move and to explore, is not only a function of the quality of the motor components of the infant's action system, but also reflects the experience and enrichment afforded to his sensorium, particularly his visual apparatus. In several investigations, one of which was reported in Chapter 4, Burton White and his colleagues[1191] first carefully collected developmental guidelines reflecting both visual and motor accompaniment, and then altered the amount and quality of visual-perceptual enrichment afforded to infants 20 to 200 days of age. Their data confirm the supposition that the quality of early visual enrichment is later reflected in the quality of the infant's visual-motor responses to events and objects in his environment.

In addition to studies based on observations and statistical analyses of group and individual performance data, the relative effect of environment and heredity on the acquisition of motor skill has been investigated.

The studies usually attempted to determine whether motor skills taught to one of two identical twins significantly affected the performance levels attained or whether the untaught twin acquired motor acts relatively independent of environmental support in the form of specific instruction. Although the variables present in such studies are difficult to control (for example, the twins must be kept apart or they will teach each other), the general approach is an interesting one. The advantage of using identical twins is that their hereditary characteristics are alike, and thus changes in performance can be primarily attributed to variables introduced experimentally.

In general, the findings emphasize the importance of inherent qualities in the formation of locomotor and manipulative activities during the early years of life. Hilgard[533] compared twins, one trained in ring tossing, walking board skill, and paper cutting, the other one was untrained. He found that performance differences on all tests were as similar to each other at the end of a training period as they were at the beginning. In another study, Gesell[420a] reported that the stair-climbing ability of twins remained remarkably alike despite instruction afforded one. Training in cube behavior and in language skills has also failed to produce marked differences in later testing.

Contrary evidence, however, has been presented by McGraw,[769] who found that the trained twin, Johnny, learned to swim at 10 months, to dive at 13 months, and to skate at 16 months of age. However, the preponderance of findings from co-twin investigations emphasizes the overriding importance of maturation and inherent qualities in the formation of motor skills during the early years of life.

The method of co-twin control has merit only if uniovular twins are used and the training period is preceded by a measurement period during which their initial differences are carefully noted. In addition, the training period should be carefully controlled, and the final measurements recorded exactly. With these precautions, studies of this type can provide additional insight concerning the roles of maturation and learning in the formation of movement behavior.

Movements of the infant have been subjected to several classification systems which have attempted to list, step-by-step, the kinds of movement occurring during the various periods of infancy. The California Infant Scale of Motor Development is typical and consists of 76 items listed in order of difficulty. An infant is checked to determine the ones he is capable of performing. Other systems and scales presented by Thompson[1093] and Shirley[996a] are similar in nature. In general, voluntary movements of infants fall into the following categories: (1) postural control, including movement of the entire trunk and random postural activity; (2) active efforts at locomotion, such as turning, stretching, and attempting to crawl; (3) start of walking movements; and (4) anticipatory and selective visual-motor regard using the hands and upper limbs, including prehension, approaching, grasping, and releasing objects. The appearance of movement behavior in these categories overlaps considerably and occasionally occurs simultaneously. Locomotion and prehension, for example, are frequently seen at the same time.

Muscular strength and control develop rapidly during the early months. By four months of age most babies can lift the head and neck from a prone position and about a month later can sit with some support. Control of the body proceeds from total bodily adjustments to finer movements, with development generally proceeding from the head to the feet (cephalocaudal) and from the midpoint to the extremities.

During the first 15 months motor and mental abilities are inseparable,[75] but after this time test scores seem to diverge. However, Piaget[893] suggests that children's concepts of time, space, and force continue to be based on their initial manipulatory experiences.

After the age of two years, more differentiation between tasks occurs, and the rapid growth patterns tend to slow. Motor abilities, which had been more closely related during infancy, tend to become more specific, a trend that continues into adulthood.[75]

Following the acquisition of the ability to walk, variations of gross body locomotion become possible. Hopping, skipping, and standing on one leg soon follow. Gutteridge[474a] reported that about 42 percent of the children she studied were jumping well at three years of age, at four and one-half, 72 percent were successful, and at five years, 81 percent showed proficiency. Children are closer to six years of age before they can hop skillfully. Galloping is not usually seen in three-year-olds, according to Breckenridge and Vincent.[128] The ability to skip is acquired after the child learns to gallop, at about the age of five and one-half to six years.

Jones[597] studied the development of the motor skills of two-, three-, and four-year-olds as they became proficient in the use of various wheeled toys. After numerous systematized observations of the use made of trucks, bicycles, tricycles, and the like, although basic performance seemed to depend on maturation, the development of skill was more attributable to practice. Higher skill and more self-reliant play when using this kind of equipment were attributed to prior experience with older playmates, previous availability of play materials, and previous participation in an outdoor play area.

It would seem that at a rather early age environmental supports markedly affect maturation in determining the quality of motor activity participated in.

Movement behavior in childhood (five to ten years) becomes stable as growth decelerates. More exact movement patterns become possible, and the child seems to enjoy the acquisition of skill for its own sake and to experience joy in movement much as does a young animal. The years of childhood mark a transition from early developmental patterns of postural adjustment and unfolding of manipulative behavior to the adolescent skill in specific sports. It is during this period that major emphasis should be placed on basic activities (throwing, running, jumping, and the like), so that a smooth progression is made into the movement behavior socially desirable in adolescence.

Carpenter,[172] Seils,[983a] Jenkins,[581] and others have formulated test batteries to evaluate performance characteristics of primary age children (five, six, and seven years). Hartman, using the hurdle jump, and Wild, using throwing, have attempted to evaluate performance with specific kinds of tasks.

Latchaw,[662a] Cumbee et al.,[273] and Glassow et al.[438] have studied the motor abilities of children (seven to ten years) with test batteries, while Cron and Pronko[270a] and Seashore[978a] have reported research evaluating the balancing ability of children from the ages of seven to 12 years.

Frequently, the tester imposes test batteries designed to evaluate the motor ability of children and attempts to assess the performance of rather basic movements—running, stand and running broad jumps, throwing for accuracy and distance, speed of running, and such activities. Jenkins,[581] Seils,[983a] and Carpenter[172] report that no significant correlation was obtained between height, weight, and performance in this kind of task. Most researchers, however, report that performance in most of the tasks improves from grade to grade. As Carpenter[172] states: ". . . some kind of maturation is an important factor in molding performance of these movements."

Using a more refined measure of maturity than did earlier investigators, Seils[983a] found that relationships did exist between skeletal maturity and gross motor performance items, including throwing and catching by both boys and girls and jumping by girls. Seils' findings pointed to two main trends that emerge during this period of life, the growing importance of body-build (a negative relationship between weight and jumping ability) and the growing specificity of motor skill performance.

Underscoring the importance of learning on motor ability scores even during childhood, was Jenkins' finding that girls were superior to boys in a task closely resembling hopscotch, a favorite pastime of the girls in his sample.

Numerous researchers, using batteries and single performance measures, have attempted to analyze and isolate basic factors of motor performance during the primary years. McCaskell and Wellman[755] used a multi-item battery, Vickers et al.[1135a] employed a modified Brace test, Hartman[501a] studied ability in the hurdle jump in relation to other gross measures of performance, and Carpenter[172] and Cumbee et al.[273] constructed batteries consisting of tasks assessing balancing ability, speed, strength, and the like. Their search for a single general performance measure proved unsuccessful. Hartman found that the hurdle jump score was no better than the scores of a number of other tests in predicting overall score in a battery that included throw for distance, 35-yard dash, and similar tests. Both Carpenter and Cumbee used factorial techniques in attempting to isolate basic motor performance qualities evidenced during primary years. Although they found marked specificity, both identified a factor related to the speed with which the subjects were able to move the total body. Carpenter isolated general factors of strength and ball handling (including scores on baseball and volleyball throws for distance and catching ability). Cumbee also identified factors relating to arm and hand velocity, as well as balance of the total body and facility in balancing objects.

As adolescence (ten to eighteen years) is reached, three interrelated forces combine to alter movement attributes. (1) A growth spurt, accompanied by hormonal fluctuations, serves to change body shape and size and to alter performance potential. (2) These body-build changes tend to affect the individual's feelings about himself, which, in turn, affect performance. (3) Changing cultural demands are felt concerning the kinds of acceptable movement tasks to engage in (both as to type and intensity). Critical to the personality development of adolescent boys is whether they are early or late maturers. Studies by Mussen[830] and Weatherly[1157] point to the fact that late maturation handicaps personality development, while earlier maturers exhibit more stable personalities.

In 1962, the results of an investigation, sponsored by the Office of Naval Research,[370] were published. With tests that evaluated flexibility, throwing ability, strength, agility, trunk strength, and the like, the physical fitness of 20,000 boys and girls between the ages of 12 and 18 years was tested. This investigation represents one of the most extensive testing programs of motor performance ever carried out with the nation's youth under reasonably controlled conditions.

The findings of this investigation indicated the following general trends when the data were plotted for each task by age. Most of the curves for boys showed negative acceleration; improvement was noted to a "critical" age, after which there was little improvement. Exceptions occurred on tests of grip, which presented a linear relationship to age; on a test of abdominal strength (hold one-half sit-up), showing no increase from the age of 14 to 18; and a test of dynamic flexibility showed a decrease up to the age of 16 years.

The curves plotted, based on the girls' scores, indicated the following trends: (1) Decrease in running speed up to age 15, some improvement through 17, then a decrease to age 18 years. (2) In the softball throw and broad jump there is relatively little improvement to age 16 or 17, after which some improvement is evidenced. The investigator believed that the number of tasks in which the girls evidenced little or no improvement during these years were a reflection both of the maturational phases of female development and of a waning of interest and participation in athletics.

It is during the adult period (past twenty years) when youthful maturation processes are completed and the degenerative effects of aging have not yet been felt, that experience exerts the most pronounced effects on motor performance. During this period, the most efficient performance of both manual and gross motor skill may be manifested, if the individual continues to participate in and to benefit from past experience. Welford[1173] has presented a chart that diagrams the relative influences of learning and of physiological capacities on skill performance during adulthood (Fig. 12–2). The chart indicates that, during adulthood, experiences and capacity exert equal and sometimes opposite effects on performance, with the performance measure obtained being a resultant of these two forces. "A" represents absolute organic capacities, "B," experience. These two curves, of course, are also dependent on the nature of the task as well as on individual differences in strength, endurance, and similar qualities.

Thus, performance and the capacity to learn physical skills become stabilized during adulthood and are not subjected to the intergroup variability evidenced during childhood and old age. The peaks of strength and endurance are reached during the early twenties, and skilled performance largely depends on practice and experience. Bachman[49] found

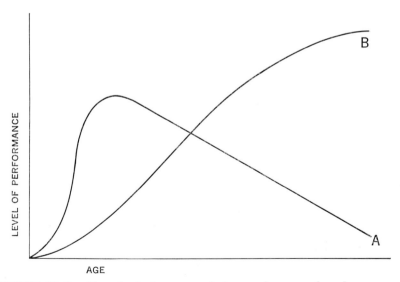

FIGURE 12–2. Hypothetical curves relating performance based on organic capacities (A) and on experience (B) with age. (Courtesy of Welford, A. T.: *Aging and Human Skill.* New York, Oxford University Press, 1958.)

9

no significant differences in various age groups 25 to 49 years when he measured the ability to learn two gross motor tasks: one a balancing task, the other a ladder-climbing task. Studies such as these lend further support to the premise that performance becomes relatively stable during adulthood.

During later adulthood, motivational factors impinge on the individual and affect his willingness and inclination to perform. The adult, past the age of 40, becomes less inclined to learn new skills and tends to use recreational skills learned during childhood and adolescence. Having passed through the years during which all-out achievement, both physical and mental, was stressed, the individual enters his later years attempting to obtain maximal satisfaction and gratifications out of what has been termed "the prime of life."[1173]

Few studies have been directed toward adult capacities in motor performance; those available have been primarily directed toward comparing adult performance to old-age performance. Most of the studies, of course, have used college-age youth, since students were most readily available to the investigator. Exceptions are studies by Pierson[898] and Mendryk,[782] both of whom utilized movement and reaction tasks as performance criteria, and Ammons, who used a complex visual-motor coordination task. Mendryk found that college-age subjects evidence significantly better reaction and movement times than did 12-year-old boys and 48-year-old men. Pierson found that correlations between movement time and reaction times increased in the older age ranges. Ammons reported significant improvement in the ability to perform the pursuit rotor task, measured from the ages of six through 16 and 17 years. Their data suggest that, after this period, performance remains relatively constant until about the age of 30 to 35, then it slowly declines to the age of 70. Their subjects have been college students, as well as prison inmates, and their studies have been conducted over a considerable period of time. Noble et al.[852] and Shepard et al.[994] also carried out studies that compared the performance of individuals from the ages of eight to 87 years on two complex coordination tasks. In common with findings on similar studies carried out by other investigators, it was found that improvement continued until about the age of 16 years by girls, and to the age of 20 by boys, after which a decline in performance was noted. The middle years of life are usually productive of the best performance on complex coordination tasks, with men usually being superior to women.[994]

In 1964, Clyde Noble and his colleagues[852] conducted one of the more elaborate studies of the effects of age and sex on motor learning. The task involved reaction time in response to an array of red and green signal lamps (discrimination reaction time apparatus previously used by the Air Force). Six hundred subjects ranging in age from 8 to 87 years were tested. Although the authors admit the difficulty of separating the effects on the scores due to maturation from those due to other factors, including transfer from similar experiences and from nonspecific experiences, they found that: (1) The two sexes were quite similar in performance and rate of growth until the age of about 16 years, after which the females began a linear decline into their 70's. (2) The males continued to improve until they were 20, after which they also evidenced a decline.

Success in skilled movements during adulthood is largely attributable to the opportunities the individual has had to practice, and it is during this period of life that the best scores in manual skills are recorded. Proficiency in gross movement tasks, however, tends to decline slightly, especially during the later years of adulthood, although the ability to acquire new skills remains rather stable until the fifties are reached.

No distinct signposts indicate when an individual should be termed "old." Entry into this period of life may be measured in a variety of ways, both by evaluating performance and by assessing biologic functioning. It is a common experience to observe individuals in their sixties performing intellectually and physically in a manner superior to persons 20 years their junior.

Difficulties arise, however, when attempting to obtain a fair sampling of older-age subjects for testing. Mortality, occupational influences, motivation, and similar variables often confound the findings. When evaluating work output in an industrial plant, for example, it is frequently found that older workers who were not performing well have been removed from the job, so that all who remain are well above average in ability. Despite these difficulties, however, it is possible to obtain relatively valid findings from such investigations. In the main, they have pointed out that, just as during infancy and childhood, performance of the aged becomes more variable, because the effects of experience and a lowering of physical capacities seem to influence individuals to varying degrees.

Differences in movement speed have been identified in the aged. A lowering of reaction time seems to be caused by a lessening of the ability to integrate input to output in the central nervous system, rather than to movement capacities at the peripheral level.[623] Older subjects evidence less endurance, particularly in the performance of large muscle tasks. Changes in task complexity more markedly lower performance of the aged than of younger performers. The learning of new tasks becomes more difficult, particularly in the oldest age ranges, and the capacity to retain information on a short-term basis also seems to suffer in old age.

Perceptual changes that are relatively independent of the lowering of visual acuity occur. Perceptually, the older subject appears less flexible. Increased visual-motor integration seems to be needed as the older individual performs tasks that are performed by the younger subject relatively independent of close visual guidance. The older individual thus appears to become less "plastic" in perceptual-motor performance and in measures of muscle elasticity. Szafran[1083] suggests that, in old age, a "blurring" of visual-motor perceptions occurs.

Older adults also tend to be more disturbed by various stressful conditions associated with performance. Studies indicate that elderly workers tend to withdraw from assembly line tasks that involve strict pacing, particularly if the rate is determined by the output of younger workers.[1173]

Research has been carried out to determine the reasons for the slowing of perceptual-motor performance during old age. Although Miles[794] first suggested in the 1930's that slowing was due to a decreasing capacity of the neuromuscular system at the peripheral level, findings from more recent research seem contradictory. Singleton[1012] and others believe that the slowing of performance, particularly those tasks "loaded" with perceptual judgments, is primarily attributable to a lowering of integrative capacity in the central nervous system. Older people seem able to "program" their movements only for a short sequence and in a relatively short time period and are forced to hesitate between movements in a complex series. Hicks and Birren[530] have suggested that decrements in motor performance in the aged may be caused by dysfunctions of the basal ganglia.

Age and Motor Learning. Three important characteristics are manifested with regard to learning motor skills as old age approaches: (1) Older people seem to require and to seek more information about a task, many times facts that are irrelevant to actual performance. (2) Long-term retention is less affected by old age than is short-term memory of immediately needed performance elements. (3) The learning of new tasks becomes more difficult, but performance in tasks that have been practiced over long periods of time does not seem to suffer.

The older learner seems to need stronger "input" cues. Younger individuals engaged in a chain-throwing task found little need for extraneous cues, but older subjects went about carefully acquiring all possible information.[1081,1173]

It is a common observation that older people recall incidents out of the *distant* past with some facility. However, experimental evidence by Brown,[1173] with a grid-plotting task, suggested that the inability of the older subjects to remember short-term directions probably lowered their performance and learning rate It was felt that the material had been presented too rapidly for full comprehension, because the older subjects seemed ignorant of important directions.

One of the pressing questions needing further research is determining how much of the slowness to learn is attributable to an increased "carefulness" on the part of the older subjects and how much to decreasing *capacities* to integrate and move.

Race

The findings from many studies of so-called racial differences often are questionable because of the failure to control the social-cultural factors that may contaminate the outcomes. Further problems, when investigating differences in motor ability and learning between various racial groups, are differences in body conformation and constitution, including bone and muscle density, and variations in the onset of maturity, often noted as significant when races have been contrasted.

For example, it is sometimes noted that Black children in the ghetto evidence superior gross motor abilities but inferior fine motor abilities, including drawing, when contrasted to white middle-class youngsters. However, obvious influences on such data include the probably greater freedom accorded the Black youngsters in rough play situations and the sometime shortage of writing, printing, and coloring materials available to them.

Differences in physique among superior athletes of the various races have been studied by Tanner.[1087] He found, after measuring, photographing, and somatotyping 137 track and field athletes at the 1960 Olympics, that the Black athletes had longer arms and legs, as well as slimmer hips and calves, than did the white athletes he evaluated. He further noted that these differences held true despite the event in which the athlete was participating, even weightlifting.

The data reflecting racial differences in motor ability are superficial and just beginning to emerge. For example, it has been found that Black youngsters can run faster than can white children; and in another study it was found that young Black children are able to follow complex rhythm patterns better than are comparable white subjects.

In a pilot study completed recently by one of my graduate students, he[115] found that the mean scores of 30 Black youngsters, at the age of five years, were superior to the mean scores of a similar number of white children, in tasks reflecting throwing distance, speed of running (30 yards), strength of hand-grip, and balance ability. Although in this investigation the race of those gathering the data was similar to the two groups of children being tested, and the socioeconomic levels of the two groups were similar, the subject population was small and experimenter effects could still have influenced the data. Because the experimenters were not rotated among the racial groups of subjects, the effects of race could not be separated from the effects of the testers.

There is little doubt, however, that the percentage of Black athletes participating in professional football and basketball is larger than the percentage of Black people in the United States. But again, separating the effects of cultural motivation and the few channels of financial success open to Black youngsters from the effects of the inherent differences in the athletic endeavor is difficult if not impossible.

Worthy and his colleagues[1227,1228] found that Black athletes seemed to excel in sports and at positions that required them to react to the responses of others, and were not found as often in self-spaced sports. For example, Blacks were found to be superior in shooting field goals (reactive), but white athletes were found to excel in shooting free throws (self-spaced). Although Worthy contends that eye color, as well as race, could influence the degree to which Black athletes react well to unexpected situations, the latter suppositions are open to question.*

Thus, the available information is more suggestive than definitive. Studies are needed that include longitudinal efforts that follow children of various races and record their performance fluctuations for a period of years, controlling for such variables as intelligence, economic circumstances, personality trait indices, and selected motivational variables (need achievement and the like). Such studies are more likely to result in helpful findings than are compartmentalized, sporadic efforts by graduate students or university faculty members. In any case, individuals dealing in physical performance situations with members of minority races should be aware of differences in attitudes about achievement, fluctuations in anxieties about failure, and the relative importance of physical success and toughness that are found in the various racial and ethnic subgroups in the United States today. This increased awareness will hopefully lead to greater sensitivity about the problems of minority races, which in turn could result in more productive associations of coach-teacher and athlete-student, than are sometimes seen.

Physique and Personality

The effect of physique influences even the motor performance of nursery-school-age children. Cunningham,[275] with several kinds of gross motor tasks, found that performance of preschool children depended more on body-build than on instruction or verbal ability. Walker[1138a] found that relationships existed between Sheldon's classifications of body-type and various kinds of behavior, at the ages of two, three, and four years. Positive correlations were obtained between mesomorphy and observational ratings of "energetic," "good gross motor coordination," "competitive," and the like. However, a negative correlation was obtained between mesomorphy and fine coordination in this age group. Walker also found that other physical types showed the expected results when their behavior was observed and recorded. The thin ectomorph tended

* A Black student of mine hypothesized, after inspecting these findings, that his ability to react well in sports was engendered in childhood, at which time he found himself constantly trying to get out of the way of slaps headed his way . . . and of the rival gang's excursions into his area.

to have "poor gross coordination" and, in general, evidenced other attributes in contrast to those of the mesomorph. The infant endomorph was found to be self-assertive, revengeful, easily angered, and competitive. No significant correlations were found relating motor behavior to endomorphy as has sometimes been found in the studies of older children.

Rather early in life, often on entering school, the child develops attitudes about physical performance in general and about more specific values that attract him toward or repel him from various sports and games. Many of these general feelings stem from basic and inherent activity needs he may have possessed since birth, and from the influences of parental attitudes about physical activity. In one recent study, a student of mine obtained correlations ranging from .6 to .7 between the physical performance of a group of children and parental attitudes about physical activity.

Also propelling the child entering late childhood and early adolescence toward rather specific sports is the degree of success he experiences, success that, at least to some degree, depends on the relationship between his physique and the requirements of the sport. Thus, rather early in life, the chain of events depicted in Figure 12–3 becomes operative.

By the time young adulthood is reached, superior athletes in given sports have, within limits, body builds that permit them to achieve success. In 1967, Hirata[542a] found that rather definitive body-build types had apparently gravitated toward various sports in Olympic competition. Gymnasts and divers who, when they are smaller, turn more efficiently were indeed smaller and shorter than the taller and leaner volleyball players playing the front line, and basketball players. Activities requiring short bursts of power attracted preponderantly stout and muscular athletes; whereas events requiring endurance, Hirata found, attracted men who were small and lean, thus making them more like endurance "machines."

In addition to an expanding awareness of what he can and cannot do, based at least in part on his physique, the maturing child or adolescent

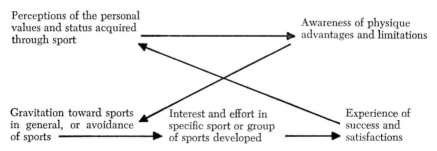

FIGURE 12–3. The diagram depicts the complex interactions between physique, emotional tone, and physical performance.

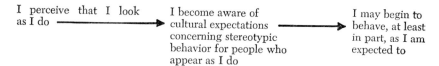

FIGURE 12-4.

also begins to perceive other types of relationships between his physique and the world and people around him. People may begin to comment about some apparent divergency in his body build. Society reacts differently to the extremely muscular type from what they do to a heavy obese youth. Different cultural expectations and pressures impinge on the thin youth, the tall muscular girl, and the small-boned petite girl. These expectations not only revolve around stereotypes about how people with various physiques are expected to perform physically, but also about how they may be expected to behave in a total way. Thus, another chain of events, of a more global nature, also begins to form in the life of the maturing youth (Fig. 12-4).

These types of perceptions have long interested philosophers and scientists alike. One reviewer cites nearly 300 authors who have been interested in body-build and the relationships between the body, mind, and personality, including Aristotle and Hippocrates.

Since the beginning of this century, moderate scientific attention has been paid to comparisons of physique and personality, stemming from the work of Kretschmer[639] in 1925. With 70 measures of physique, this German psychiatrist postulated that three types of physique exist (asthenic—lean; athletic—muscular; and pyknic—fat and round) which he believed were rough predictors of certain personality types and personality disorders.

The interesting study by Mizuno and his colleagues[806] in Japan points to the manner in which youth harbor ideals about body-build characteristics that are often at odds with their actual build. For example, the boys in his sampling (from several countries) expressed the wish to be taller and heavier than they actually were; but the girls from the nations surveyed expressed a wish to be taller and more slender. It was further found that the youth from nations in which the average height was short (Japan) tended to be molded, at least in part, by their national norms, and, in this case, did not wish to be as tall or as large as did the youth from countries peopled by larger Caucasians.

Some of the most definitive work in this field since 1940 has been conducted by Sheldon and his colleagues. Following publication of *The Varieties of Human Physique* in 1940, which presented classification techniques for categorizing the physical structures of men, Sheldon further explored the relationship between personality and physique. This study resulted in *The Varieties of Temperament* published two years later.[993] Although philosophers historically have often referred to the "appearance-behavior" relationship, it remained for Sheldon to demonstrate objectively that personality and structure may be related.

Calling on the "trait" concept as conceived by Allport, Sheldon isolated three "clusters" of personality qualities. These he termed *viscerotonia, somatotonia,* and *cerebrotonia.* The individual high in *somatotonia* was characterized as needing physical adventure and having a strong inclination for vigorous physical activity. Further research associated these characteristics with the *mesomorphic* (muscular) physique. The sociable, gluttonous, affectionate characterization of the fat person (the *endomorph*) was found to be a true one. The rotund individual usually scored high on the *viscerotonia* scale. The third personality-physique complex identified was the withdrawn and restrained *cerebrotonic* (the *ectomorph*), who possessed a linear build.

The relationships between physique and personality studies by Sheldon can be explained in several ways: (1) Individuals respond not only to their environment but also to how their environment previously reacted to their appearance (or to their apparent capacity for movement). (2) Physique and temperament are further linked by fostering commonly accepted stereotypes on individuals: the fat-jolly, muscular-active, and thin-withdrawn types are familiar dichotomies. (3) A third explanation is that environmental influences mold both temperament and physique. Thus, the overprotective mother or the athletic father is probably as influential in determining personality by manipulating the environment as parents are in shaping the bodies of their offspring through the transmission of their genes.

Several scholars have questioned the scientific basis of somatotyping. Most statistical analyses of body-build measures produce scores arranged on a linear continuum, rather than scores clustering into the three-part classification hypothesized by Sheldon. There is no scientific basis for the assumption that fat, thin, and muscular physiques arise from the three primary germinal layers.

Subsequent research has often failed to establish the close relationships between physique and personality which Sheldon proposed. For example, Hood, after surveying physique-personality trait relationships of 10,000 subjects (using the MMPI), concluded that "any relationships between physique and personality throughout the entire population are of a very small magnitude indeed."[551] Similarly Reiter found that body-build was not related to items on Edwards Personal Preference Scale.[915]

On the other hand, Davidson and McInnes[283] found a high relationship between personality traits and physical types in young children. Individuals generally behave as they view themselves capable of behaving.

For example, Cortes and Gatte[220] found high relationships between physique and the *subjects' own ratings* of their temperament.

In several studies, David Sleet[1018] has found that subjects viewing pictures of individuals possessing various physiques are likely to assign stereotypic social roles to them, despite the fact that they had had no opportunity to observe directly the individuals in a social context.

Structuring of the body image is not confined to childhood but continues throughout life. Moreover, these changing perceptions of "what I am . . . what I can do, and what I look like" invariably mold the performance attitudes and the performance capacities of adults. Sometimes these self-perceptions are modified by conditions that result in rapid changes, for example, amputation, viewing films of oneself, or experiencing difficulty when performing a previously mastered skill. More often, however, self-structuring during late childhood and adulthood involves more gradual change.

Some tests of changing self-perceptions depend on the manner in which the child or adult projects himself into various pictures,[282] ink blots,[983] or similar configurations. The draw-a-person test is also used as a measure of body image. Some of these tests derive scores from the accuracy with which an individual can touch his body parts, and the body parts of a man in a picture.[87a] A recently developed tool attempts to meet the criticism of the previous tests and avoid the necessity for verbal mediators by asking the child to imitate the gestures of the experimenter,[92] incorporating gestures made both with the arms and with the hands.

Harlow's[491] study of the character dynamics of body-builders and of the manner in which they attempt to alter radically their body structure and reshape its form to stabilize their personality structure points to the manner in which the body may become a springboard for a basic personality adjustment in later life. However, whether modifications imposed on the body by the gaining of muscle or by the sudden loss of fatty tissue effects changes in perceptions of space seems to require further research.

Clifton and Smith[201] completed studies of the change in self-concept by college men and women after they had viewed motion pictures of themselves. They found that variations in the direction of more positive self-assessments were evident after the subjects were permitted to see themselves executing a throwing movement. Shifts in self-concepts were not evidenced, however, after the students had viewed themselves in walking, jumping, and running activities. This study is believed to illustrate that perception of the performing self may undergo change well past childhood if individuals are presented with vivid evidence of their performance.

Several types of research instruments purporting to evaluate self-perceptions of body size, including direct questionnaire selection of silhouettes as to "me" and "ideal" body or body part size and shape, are available. Dillon[295] devised a test to evaluate the accuracy of an individual's perceptions of his body size. With ropes attached to a wooden frame, the subject is asked to adjust the components of the frame to duplicate his perceived height and width. Fisher[351] found that men who were committed to the idea of male superiority and had high aspirations of personal power consistently overestimated their height with this device. In summary, however, the individual differences in physical performance and learning occurring from variations in physique and personality are varied and often subtle. Some additional relationships between personality and performance are reviewed in Chapter 9, Personal Equations in Movement, Chapter 10, Communication Through Movement, and Chapter 15, Anxiety, Stress, and Tension.

Intelligence

The nature of human intelligence has interested many scholars during the eras of written history. As would be expected, the dawn of science, together with an interest in measuring things, spawned a parallel interest in measuring intelligence. Since the first measures of human perception and motor performance were occurring at the same time in the psychological laboratories of Europe and the United States, it was also to be expected that these two types of measures would be contrasted. Thus, during the latter part of the last century several investigations, some using the then new tool termed "correlation," contrasted the manner in which people ranked on tests of simple reaction time, movement speed, and kinesthesis with measures of vocabulary, problems, and the other crude assessments then available to evaluate intellectual function. (For a more thorough review of the early history of ability testing, both mental and physical, see Cratty.[257])

Although these early correlative studies generally pointed to the independence of scores obtained from simple movement tasks and intelligence measures, interest in the interaction of these two components of the human personality strongly manifests itself today. This contemporary concern for the roles of movement and intelligence is seen in literature of several types, only a portion of which is surveyed on the following pages.

Several pitfalls should be avoided or at least noted when studying the influence of intelligence as a factor influencing individual differences in motor skill performance and acquisition. (1) There is wide disagreement concerning valid definitions of intelligence. (2) The interaction of numerous other factors with intelligence often contaminates the conclusions drawn from causal or correlative studies. (3) The influence of intellectual factors on skill acquisition may vary depending on the level and the type of skill under consideration, as well as on whether comparisons are made during the initial, middle, or final stages of skill learning. (4) Human intelligence has been found to be multi- rather than unidimensional. Researchers have identified as many as 145 separate and independent intellectual abilities, which in turn may be analyzed in four or five dimensions. Thus, when working on movement-intellectual relationships one should specify in rather precise ways just what intellectual ability, or abilities, one is employing in the various kinds of comparisons.

Illustrating one of these dilemmas is the examination of motor skill performance in retarded persons at various intellectual levels. When sampling the motor responses of retarded children and youth, generally the lower they are on the intellectual scale the greater the amount of motor ineptitude and difficulties with skill acquisition they evidence. As would be expected, the less capable "trainables" (I.Q. usually 30 to 50) not only perform less well, but also have more difficulty acquiring skill than do the more capable "educables" (I.Q. 50 to 80). However, if one attempts to determine why these differences occur, it becomes difficult to separate the influence of several interacting variables. Many trainables are afflicted with rather generalized neurological impairments that cause problems in basic motor ineptitude, as compared to fewer neurological problems affecting motor functioning found in groups of educables. Trainables do not usually adopt helpful work methods when deciding how to perform motor tasks, as contrasted to the usually more ingenious educables. All groups of retarded children may lack motor competencies partly because of the difficulty of finding programs of physical education suitable to their needs, and partly because of the disinclination of "normal" youngsters to include them in their games. Thus, although the motor abilities of retarded children are often found to be "different" and sometimes inferior to those of so-called normal youngsters, the reasons for these differences are varied, interwoven, and difficult to isolate.

The research, however, does suggest that, if one aids retarded children to conceptualize about the elements of the skill they are about to attempt by giving them a greatly increased amount of verbal pretraining, they can often evidence learning curves similar to those of normal children. Moreover, to an increasing degree it has been demonstrated that, if enriched physical education programs are provided for these youngsters, their fitness levels may be significantly changed, and often brought to the levels seen in youngsters without mental handicaps.

The learning of motor skills by retardates may also suffer from the fact that many such youngsters attend poorly to whatever tasks confront them. Indeed, Zeaman and House[1238] have proposed that one of the primary factors separating retarded children from normal children is the inability of the former to focus their attention efficiently and for prolonged periods of time. Basing their "attention theory" primarily on the results obtained from two-choice visual discrimination problems, Zeaman and House have suggested that the shapes of the learning curves obtained from subjects at various points along the intellectual scale do not differ; what differs are the number of trials each group apparently must engage in prior to giving their attention to the task.

In summary, the correlative studies indicate that when tasks of increasing difficulty are compared to I.Q., moderate to high correlations will be found between the two types of measures; whereas scores from straightforward fitness tasks (measures of simple reaction time) are unlikely to be even slightly predictive of the I.Q. levels of the subjects. Furthermore, the same diffusion effect previously discussed as a function of age is seen when surveying factor analyses of the abilities of retardates at various levels on the intellectual scale. In general, higher intercorrelations are likely to be found between measures obtained from trainables than from the more capable educables, and even more specificity of motor and intellectual functioning is seen when the scores of normal children of similar ages are factor analyzed. Recently completed research by Rarick and previous work by Johs Clauson confirm the validity of this relationship between attribute specificity and mental age.

Thus, it is to be expected that fewer *intertask* differences will be obtained between scores from retarded children low on the intellectual scale, than are seen in the same comparisons of normals' scores. The inability of the retardate to arrive at sound and helpful work methods and to profit from past experiences obtained in motor skill situations is likely to make *intra-individual* variability higher than is seen in normal youngsters and adults.

Among superior athletes in Eastern Europe where the main studies have been carried out, it is often found that a minimal I.Q. is necessary to achieve superiority, usually set at about 115 to 120. At the same time, the numerous and independent intellectual subabilities identified by Guilford and others have not been extensively analyzed as they interact with specific game situations, individual skills, and various sports, either in this country or abroad, except for the pilot studies by Thorpe and West[1099] exploring game sense and intelligence.

It is probable that the greatest individual differences in skill learning due to intellectual variation among subject populations occur during the initial (analyses) stages of skill acquisition. The quality of preplanning of pre-performance sequencing and of similar stages prior to the exertion of all-out physical effort, which is usually seen later in learning, is probably where intellectual differences are most likely to manifest themselves and to influence the shape of the performance curves elicited.

Asymmetry

It has been found that all moving organisms evidence various kinds of asymmetrical functions. It is thus to be expected that one of the more complex animals, man, also manifests a variety of functional imbalances, asymmetries that are likely to influence his ability to learn and perform motor acts in rather distinct ways. The young child may or may not be consistent in hand use; the older person cocks one or the other "good" ear in the direction of conversation. The blind (and the sighted, while blindfolded), in the absence of sound and other externally orienting cues, evidence functional asymmetries of gait as they veer and spiral when trying to walk in a straight line. For years many child psychologists have been interested in and often greatly concerned about what is sometimes termed *cross-dominance* or *cross-preference,* the inclination to use the left eye while writing with the right hand (or the reverse combination). (The most detailed and penetrating discussion of these many ramifications from a behavioral, neurological, and educational standpoint is found in Hacaen.[475])

Although there is some disagreement among researchers, hand dominance appears very early, during the first three or four months of age. This is evidenced and reflected in movements of the total musculature, including head turning, leg use, body rotation, and the like.[431] Marked individual differences in the extent to which lateral dominance is manifested become apparent. Some individuals are totally left- or right-handed, whereas others evidence unilateral control. Jenkins,[581] for example, found that only 3.3 percent of the subjects tested at five years of age were both left-handed and left-footed, whereas about 7.7 percent were *left*-handed and *right*-footed. In general, the dominant hand influences early skill acquisition, and the nondominant hand is used frequently for supporting or stabilizing the body while the other is in use.

As more and more evidence accumulates about the influence of these types of variables on intelligence as well as motor performance and learning, the following statements are believed to be fair and valid assessments of the state of the current knowledge.

1. Normal children are as likely to evidence cross-preference (in eye-hand preference) as are retarded youngsters. This type of failure to match asymmetrical preferences is not related either causally or in a correlational manner to intelligence or speech, as many clinicians still believe. Extensive evidence, including the recent study by Tyler,[1116] indicates that hand-preference and cross-dominance are not predictive of the degree to which new skills are learned. It is also probable that central processes, independent of hand-use, influence unilateral motor performance to a marked degree. Eberhard's study,[317] indicating that as much bilateral transfer as learning takes place by observation, offers one

block of supporting data. More recently, Provins and his colleagues,[905] who found reasonably high intercorrelations between performance on typing and writing tasks when the efforts by the two hands were compared, also substantiate the importance of cortical processes underlying hand use in the formation of precise motor output.

2. The hand preference noted shortly after birth sometimes seems to "go away" as the child observes his feet while walking, but in general, is well established by six or seven years of age.

3. Hand preference often varies as the child undertakes different tasks. Some rating scales involve a seven-category system, placing children in either extremely right- or left-handed groups, or assigning them to groups reflecting mixed preferences, depending on the tasks employed.

4. It is generally more efficient for the child if he does not frequently change the hands he uses while performing and acquiring skills, from handwriting to ball throwing.

5. Both eye preference and foot preference are more difficult to assess than is hand preference. Foot preference is usually not as consistent and distinct as is hand preference. Often eye preference measures are a function of the test employed, rather than due to the asymmetries of eye functioning inherent in the child.

6. Most functional asymmetries are, at least in part, due to heredity. In one study, for example, it was found that about 42 percent of the children from marriages in which both parents are left-handed throw with their left hands. The percentage of left-handed children drops to 17 percent from marriages in which only one partner is a sinistral, and to 2 percent in children from marriages in which neither parent is left-handed.

7. Superior athletic performance apparently is not retarded by left-handedness, as evidenced by the study carried out by Uhrbrock.[1117] Based on the responses of 144 "nationally known" athletes, he found that the percentage of "right" responses (reflecting both right-handedness and right-footedness) was less than that found in a similar population of students whose interest in athletics was considered "nominal."

In summary, the preponderance of evidence suggests that, although left-handed children are different from right-handed children, and, at times, special accommodations must be made while they perform skills, such as changing the arm-desk arrangement for them, the fact that an individual is right-handed, left-handed and/or has various combinations of hand-eye preferences is not likely to affect the quality of the effort he is likely to evidence when performing and learning motor skills. Of course, there are times in athletic training when it is desirable to help an athlete use one or the other hand, such as when learning to bat as a switch hitter, or when learning to use both hands in four-way handball. These instances pose special skill-learning problems that have not been thoroughly explored in the available literature; although it would be assumed that an individual scoring toward the middle of a seven-point hand-preference scale is likely to have less difficulty acquiring skill in the nonpreferred hand than is a person who is markedly either right- or left-handed.

Summary

Numerous variables and conditions modify motor learning and performance in addition to factors closely associated with the incidence and type of practice engaged in. Maturation exerts significant variations in motor output, and personality and physique are often even more important modifiers of movement attributes and performance capacities. In general, the greatest variations in performance are seen in the very young and the very old, with motor performance remaining relatively consistent during the middle years of life.

Various unique functional asymmetries also exert effects on motor performance and learning. Hand preference, eye preference, foot preference, and ear preference are only some of the ways in which the human action system functions in "imbalanced" conditions that, individually or collectively, often affect performance accuracy as well as force. However, these asymmetries in motor functioning, when modified or as exhibited, do not exert significant influences on intellectual, perceptual, or academic functioning as some persons believe.

Some of the most interesting recent studies of motor performance and learning have begun to explore the manner in which human beings tend to exhibit variation in their performances. Data from these studies of intra-individual differences are contributing a great deal to our knowledge of the consistencies as well as the inconsistencies of human perceptual-motor functioning.

Student Reading

Cratty, B. J.: *Perceptual and Motor Development of Infants and Children.* New York, Macmillan, 1970.

Cratty, B. J.: *Physical Expressions of Intelligence.* Englewood Cliff, N.J., Prentice-Hall, Inc., 1972.

Fleishman, E. A.: Individual differences and motor learning. In *Learning and Individual Differences.* R. M. Gagne (Ed.). Columbus, Ohio, Charles E. Merrill Publishing Co., 1967.

Hacaen, J., and Ajuriaguerra, J. de: *Left-Handedness, Manual Superiority and Cerebral Dominance.* New York, Grune & Stratton, 1964.

Henry, F. M.: Individual differences in motor learning. In *Psychology of Motor Learning.* L. Smith (Ed.). Chicago, Athletic Institute, 1969.

Rees, L.: Constitutional factors and abnormal behavior. In *Handbook of Abnormal Psychology.* H. J. Eysenck (Ed.). New York, Basic Books, Inc., 1961.

13
MOTIVATION

The terms *motivation* and *motive* are used in many contexts. The criminologist constantly searches for the motives believed to be the roots of asocial behavior. Worker incentives are studied in the effort to increase production. To create a realistic drama, the playwright must attempt to construct a believable interplay of his characters' motivations.

Throughout history, the why's of man's behavior have provoked philosophical and scientific speculation. The early Greeks suggested that actions could be attributed simply to the seeking of pleasure or to the avoidance of pain. Contemporary research also reflects a similar, although at times more complex, interest in motivation. About one-third of the experimental work in the behavioral sciences deals with the elusive concept of motivation. Drive, need, motive, or some similar construct has been utilized to explain fluctuations in learning curves, to account for individual performance and/or perceptual differences, and to describe more clearly the total personality complex.

Motivation is a broad term, referring to a general level of arousal to action. It is derived from the Latin *movere*, meaning literally to *move*. The term *motive*, on the other hand, is usually considered a specific condition contributing to performance and to the general motivational level. The words *drive* and *need* also assume many varied and subtle meanings, depending on the type of evidence utilized for their objectification. In general, the term *need* refers to a rather internalized deficiency, something the organism *lacks*. The concept of *drive* involves the positive concept of *the impetus to action*. In some cases the two terms may be independent of one another. For example, an individual may require (need) some chemical addition to his system in the form of a dietary supplement but lacks the drive to acquire a vitamin preparation that might remedy the situation. Drives consist of variables that impel the organism to action. They are usually thought of as existing in varying degrees in the organism at all times, and only when various theoretical and/or experimental thresholds are exceeded do they become identifiable. Motives are theoretical constructs that attempt to explain the reason individuals select certain behavior and activities in which to engage, the reason people engage in tasks for extended lengths of time, and the reason an activity is performed with varying degrees of intensity.[424]

In many theoretical frameworks, however, differentiation among the terms *drive, need,* and *motive* is quite difficult. In any case, a drive can be conceived of as an initiator of action, whereas a motive refers more to the direction the action will take. A need is construed as an organismic deficiency, either psychological or physiological, that may or may not lead to action.

In a broader sense, however, the concepts of drive and motive are usually expanded to refer not only to factors that initiate some facet of behavior but also to conditions that sustain and direct actions once they have been started. Thus *motives and drives are factors that underlie and support the general motivational level of the individual by initiating, molding, and sustaining specific action patterns.*

Theories of Motivation

The effects of the general motivational level and of the specific motives seem to permeate the total performance situation. They influence the initial attitude of the individual, his preparatory "set," and his state of readiness for action. A motive may also be thought of as an intervening variable between perceptual-input and motor-output. In addition, motivation plays an important part in the evaluation of an action once it has been completed. Was the experience satisfying and worthy of repetition? Or was it unpleasant and to be avoided in the future? A thorough consideration of the role of motivation must include an examination of factors that affect events in the total behavioral chain, as well as conditions that simply trigger and mold performance.

The concept of motivation, therefore, is an important one to the scientist and philosopher attempting to gain a comprehensive understanding of human functioning. Speculation about the subject has led to many obtuse questions that have been treated in various theoretical frameworks. (Madsen,[726] Bindra,[108] and Young[1234] have discussed motivational theory as related to learning and perception; Berg and Bass[90] about the role of social motives; Rethlingshafer[918] has related motivation to personality theory; and Berlyne[94] has examined the role of curiosity, exploration, and manipulation as related to motivation.) Are motives innate or learned or both? Is it valid to consider unconscious motivations? Are motives physiological, psychological, or socially determined, or do their origins emanate from all three sources? Is there a general drive state, or are motives to action specific in nature? Is motivation merely the avoidance of pain and the seeking of pleasure, or are more complex factors operative? What is the relationship of motivation to learning, to perception, and to personality theory?

Despite the limited scope of the present discussion of motivation, certain of these questions will be dealt with briefly. The final portions of the chapter are concerned with general conditions that contribute to the motivated state, and with the kinds of actions that in themselves seem to constitute motivating experiences (play, exploration, and manipulation).

Instinct, Drive, and Learned Behavior Theories

Around the turn of the century, it was hypothesized that man's behavior was largely governed by unlearned action patterns, or *instincts*, that enabled him to survive by dealing more effectively with his environment. For example, fighting was believed to be the manifestation of the aggressive instinct. Such activities as working and playing were also believed to be instinctive.

In recent years, instinctual theories of motivation have lost favor since the reasoning seems circular. "People behave as they do because they have built-in mechanisms compelling them to act as they do" seems to constitute an unsatisfactory explanation for the many varied and seemingly self-directed activities in which human beings participate. A second main criticism of the instinctual theory is that it assumes that activity either is occurring or is not occurring. This was questioned when, following the development and use of the electroencephalograph, neural activity seems to be present even during trance-like states.

Need-Primacy Theories

A second view of human motivation was proposed by theorists who hypothesized that human behavior could be attributed to four or more primary drives. All human actions, the theorists suggested, could be traced finally to activities that satisfied physiological deficiencies, such as hunger, thirst, elimination, and sexual appetite. The primary exponents of drive theory, Hull and Freud, differed primarily in the emphasis they placed on conscious and measurable drives versus unconscious drive mechanisms, and the degree to which they believed that the sex motive was an instigator of human behavior.

Again, however, such a mechanistic approach to motivated behavior found many critics. The general human tendency to seek activity and to master a task for its own sake was noted. To play, to manipulate, and to explore seemed unrelated to any of the visceral needs that drive theorists suggested were basic. The drive theorists also seemed to view the human being as an inert machine, "turned-on" only when the internal need to survive was present.

Closely associated with the need-primacy or drive-reduction theories of Freud and Hull is the concept of homeostasis introduced by Cannon[167] in the 1920's. Homeostasis refers to the general and specific processes that enable an organism to maintain its physiological integrity by balancing internal adjustments with external and internal stresses. It is assumed that, as imbalances occur, built-in regulators act to return the organism to a state of equilibrium. Although such a doctrine would seem to support the drive-reduction concept, Cannon himself has suggested that organisms at times seem to seek imbalance by undertaking self-directed activities as stimulating kinds of undertakings.

Multifactor Theories

In order to explain many of the complexities of human behavior, various theories suggesting that motives may be effective at various levels and that there are classes of factors seeming to affect human performance were proposed. Tolman,[1105] for example, speaks of *primary needs* (hunger, thirst, and the like), *secondary needs* (socially related, such as affiliation and dominance), and *tertiary needs* (learned behavior involving various kinds of goal-directed activity).

Murray[828] and McDougall[762] both produced systems of basic needs that were dependent on the individual's social environment, rather than simply on his physiological constitution. Murray's list included such factors as: affiliation—liking for people; aggression—moving against people; dominance—drive to dominate people; and cognizance—exploring, asking questions, and the like. McDougall's list of socially important motives included the exploring tendency, the aggressive tendency, the gregarious tendency, and the dominating or self-assertive tendency. Thus theoretical systems that were relatively independent of basic tissue needs began to be developed.

Theories of this nature generally rested on "the functional autonomy of drive" concept first outlined by Allport. In general, it was proposed that, although activity initially might have a physiological basis, movement later becomes independent and self-sustaining as a motivator in its own right. The need to complete a task once it is started, the need to master a job for its own sake, and other such facets of human behavior seem to be explained better by such liberalized theoretical frameworks than by the simpler need-reduction or instinctual theories of Hull and Freud.

Trends in Construction of Motivational Theory

Several threads are discernible from a review of the literature dealing with theories of motivation. For example, one of the most popular approaches to motivation, as old as human thought, was the hedonistic theory. It suggested that the seeking of pleasure and the avoidance of pain are the mainsprings of human activity. Later experimentalists, unhappy with such a simple dichotomy for the explanation of human motivation, devised the complex classification systems previously reviewed.

Although it had long been noted that pain could be elicited by stimulating various portions of the brain electrically, more recently Miller[801,802] and others have found that, through the use of finite deep-penetrating electrodes, animals can be stimulated so that they apparently receive pleasurable sensations. If it can be assumed that such stimulation produces generalized feelings of pleasure, as the experimental findings seem to indicate, the hedonistic theory again becomes more tenable. Langworthy[655] and others have become concerned with the role of nonspecific neurons, making up controlling mechanisms in the brain that modify arousal level, alertness, and emotionality. The reticular activating system has come in for more than its share of study in this respect.[655] Others have become interested in the influence of external bodily manifestations of emotion and general regulating systems in the nervous system. Gellhorn, for example, has been concerned with the role of bodily and facial contortions that influence emotional states by sending impulses to the posterior hypothalamus, thus influencing hypothalamic balance. Gellhorn[415] suggests that muscular facial patterns arouse diffuse hypothalamic-cortical control systems, while the sensory-motor area in the cortex is excited by way of the specific afferent system from tactile and proprioceptive facial receptors.

In general, however, the overall trend seems to be in the production of more liberalized theoretical frameworks, expanding the list of human motives to include such activities as manipulation, exploration, and play. A longitudinal survey of the writings of single experimentalists also reflects this more accepting tendency. At the beginning of their careers, some scholars in the behavioral sciences reflect an exclusive dependence on measurements obtained from animal experimentation. Later in their careers, however, these same researchers seem to acknowledge the existence of motives in observable behaviors that are more resistant to strict experimental treatment. It is believed that the final theory reviewed in this section reflects this latter trend.

Capacity-Primacy Theory

A theory in keeping with the diversity and complexity of man's movement behavior has been termed the *capacity-primacy* or *behavioral-primacy theory* by its proponent, Woodworth.[1225] In general, it is hypothesized that the organism has a basic need to interact with its environment and that the manner in which this interaction takes place is determined by individual capacities for movement.

This theory is similar to a drive-system suggested by Goldstein,[445] which included the need to actualize one's capacities. However, the behavioral-primacy theory is more direct. Goldstein suggested that self-actualizing activities are based on unconscious motives, whereas the capacity-primacy theory implies that activities may be satisfying for their own sake.

Woodworth's theory[1225] is a protest against the failure of the need-primacy theories to predict the activities, interests, and motives of human adults and, in particular, to explain the play activities of animals and children. The theory suggests that, because men have hands to manipulate their environment, a need exists to handle objects, just as the winged bird must fly and the web-footed duck must swim. However, in the simplicity of the theory lies its weakness. For, indeed, the reasoning seems somewhat circular. That "man moves in complex and in unstructured ways because he possesses the musculature which encourages movement" does not constitute the most sophisticated explanation. In any case, it is believed that Woodworth's theory holds the most promise for explaining the diverse and sometimes unstructured forms of movement behavior engaged in by man.

Achievement Needs Theory

The most comprehensive look taken into motives-related mastery has been by Atkinson and his colleagues dealing with what they termed *achievement needs*. Obtaining scores from the Thematic Apperception Test, which purportedly reflects degrees of needs for mastery and/or achievement, they have conducted research exploring such variables as age, sex, and type of task. At times scholars working in this framework have also placed their subjects in categories reflecting either high or low achievement needs, and then studied their behaviors in various performance situations reflecting either mental and/or motor competence. Achievement needs also have been studied in relation to various measures of anxiety.

In general, Atkinson[44] hypothesizes that the effort expended by various individuals is a reflection not only of the need to achieve, but also, to varying degrees, of the need to avoid failure. It has also been hypothesized that persons who are highly anxious about their achievement, and the parallel need to avoid failure, will select moderately difficult tasks in which the chances for failure are minimal.

Other assumptions devised as a result of investigations into achievement needs are: (1) Those who have the highest needs to achieve may evidence less strong affiliative needs. (2) There may be marked sex differences in achievement needs, depending on the related nature of the task confronting the individual. (3) The specificity of achievement needs probably increases as a function of age; that is, the younger the child, the more valid it is to postulate the existence of a somewhat general need to achieve, but when considering older youth and adults, it is often more helpful to determine in just what types of tasks and situations they value achievement, or fear failure.

Suprisingly, there seem to have been few studies and fewer consistently applied programs of research in which achievement needs have been studied in contexts in which tasks involving motor performance and learning have played an important part. The few exceptions represented at the present time seem to be classified best as pilot studies, and for the most part are reflections of attempts to obtain advanced degrees. Although academic performance often has been evaluated with scores from the TAT reflecting achievement needs, it is probable that researchers in physical education lack the background and experience necessary to administer and interpret this projective test adequately.

The Measurements of Motives

The assessment of human motives has proved to be difficult. Three general approaches have been used: (1) direct self-reports about attitude, feelings of anxiety, and the like; (2) indirect means by use of the psychiatric interview or various projective tests; and (3) the behavioral approach, either by studying performance under various kinds of motivating conditions or by introducing various punishing variables, such as delaying the task.

Surwillow[1078] has listed nine specific motivational conditions that are characteristically utilized in the laboratory situation: (1) intrinsic interest of the task; (2) social incentives; (3) scores, which encourage improvement; (4) monetary rewards; (5) suggested importance of performance, i.e., in determining norms; (6) social-competitive, performing the task with others; (7) reward for improvement; (8) threat of punishment; and (9) administration of punishment. Note is generally taken of the effect of these variables on actual performance scores and on resultant fluctuations in learning curves. Although seldom utilized, another method may hold promise in the evaluation of motivational level. Since the estimation of time seems to be related to the motivational state of the individual during the time period to be judged, a time-estimation task, in conjunction with various other tasks, might prove to be a valid measure of motives and/or of general motivational level.

Atkinson[44] has presented several criteria by which motivational measures might be judged: (1) The measure should sensitively reflect the presence or the absence of a motive or its variation in strength. (2) The measure of a motive should reflect variations only in that motive. (3) The measure should be valid and related to similar methods purporting to evaluate the same motive. Atkinson and others have reported, with regard to this last criterion, that observations, self-reports, and other measures of motivation generally fail to correlate, further indicating the difficulty of obtaining a valid measure of motivation.

One of the first, and certainly the most ambitious, research programs designed to evaluate adult motives was carried out by Thorndike[1096] and published in *The Psychology of Wants, Interests and Attitudes* in 1935. Thorndike used various kinds of cognitive tasks, interpolated and accompanied by motivating conditions, to study what was termed the "law of effect." Innumerable situations in which various kinds of social approval or disapproval, various negative rewards such as electric shocks, and monetary rewards were used in order to investigate their effect on the performance of a number of mental tasks. In general, it was found that adult motives could be molded by various kinds of external conditions. Typical is the experiment in which subjects' opinions concerning the artistic merit of Christmas cards changed after a training period in which choices of the best cards were given approval when they corresponded to those previously selected by a group of art critics (Experiment 62). Much of the more recent work concerning the effect of various motivational states on motor skills and physical performance measures has utilized Thorndike's general approach to measurement.

Questionnaires

Questionnaires with which to collect and tabulate self-reports of the motivational state of the individual also have been utilized in the past. Some require a yes-no choice; others provide a five-point breakdown by which the individual can indicate the degree to which he believes something to be true about himself and the way he feels. Obtaining reliable responses to questionnaires is often difficult, however, because an individual's constellation of values may shift between the first and second administration of these evaluative tools.

Indirect Methods

The various indirect measures of motivation seem to impose even more impressive difficulties. These assessments often occur in psychiatric interviews, since hidden meanings in the subject's use of words, verbal mistakes, or the manner in which the individual moves and expresses himself in general are searched for. Most of these methods require extensive clinical experience before interpretations become valid and reliable. Examples are the Rorschach ink-blot test, the Thematic Apperception Test, and similar devices that require the individual to place his own interpretation on relatively vague and generalized forms and/or situations.

Perhaps the most accurate method of evaluating motivation is the interposition of various motivational conditions in the performance situation and then the measurement of performance fluctuations. Most often, these variables include differing kinds of instruction, the imposition of various stressors, such as interrupting the task, or the introduction of varying social conditions in the experimental situation. Performance fluctuations are generally studied as a function of the nature and degree of the motivational variable introduced.

Hypnotism and Motivation

Hypnotism has been used as a direct and an indirect technique to determine motivation-performance relationships. Hypnotic suggestions have been used in attempts to induce superior performance beyond the individual's "normal" capacities. In most cases, when such a variable has been introduced, marked variations in the individual's usual motor output have been induced. Two primary types of changes are involved: those specifically suggested by the hypnotist, including traditional alterations of reaction time and muscular tonus; and movement changes that seem to occur spontaneously.

Several investigations have been carried out concerning the effect of hypnosis on muscular strength. Wells,[1178] with a hand dynamometer, found that he could induce increased or decreased strength as desired. However, it was more efficient and reliable to suggest a decrease in strength than an increase. Hatfield[504] substantiated Wells' findings in regard to an increase in strength as the result of hypnotic suggestion. Johnson and Kramer[584] have obtained findings that a hypnotic suggestion of failure is consistently more reliable in producing decrements in the ability to repeatedly press a dumbbell than are suggestions to increase performance.

Since it appeared probable that continued pressure on some strength-testing devices, e.g., a hand or arm dynamometer, causes pain, researchers have attempted to induce greater strength by introducing the suggestion of "no-pain" during the hypnotic state. Marked increases in arm strength resulted from this kind of suggestion.

Work capacity has also been increased by hypnosis. In general, resistance to fatigue and work prolongation can be significantly effected by suggesting to the individual that he is less likely to feel the pain of tissue impairment during hard work. The usual task has been repetitive work with various kinds of dynamometers. Examples of studies in this area are those by Nicholson,[846] Williams[1207] and Manzer.[734] Johnson, Massey, and Kramer,[585] however, found that no significant increases in performance were evidenced on a bicycle-riding task under hypnotic suggestion.

In addition to investigations concerning the effect of hypnosis on involuntary smooth muscle actions, several investigators have studied the effects of suggestion on voluntary muscle control. Measures of steadiness have been studied the most frequently. Weitzenhoffer,[1170] presenting a review of studies in this area by Eysenck and others, found that induced suggestions of "relaxation" improved steadiness measures more than direct suggestions to "be accurate." There seems to be a lack of investigation involving the effect of hypnosis on the voluntary motor control in more complex tasks, perhaps due to measurement and safety problems.

Johnson et al.[585] utilized hypnosis in an ingenious way to assess the effectiveness of pre-performance warm-up. All subjects were placed under a hypnotic trance, and then half the subjects engaged in warm-up activities that were forgotten in the post-hypnotic state. Their findings indicated that warm-up may be a variable related to motivation, since no significant performance differences were noted between the two groups in a post-hypnotic performance test.

In general, the findings of such studies suggest that man is capable of much more in terms of physical performance than he actually exhibits. Inhibitory factors, which sometimes can be removed through hypnotic suggestion, seem to depress performance, particularly during the adult years. It is believed that further investigations, with more complex movement tasks, might prove worthwhile. A more comprehensive understanding of human motivation might be gained through hypnosis, by gradually "peeling-back" performance blocks that have perhaps been built up throughout the individual's lifetime.

Motives and Movement

The general and specific conditions that modify movement performance will be explored next. In the initial section, factors that contribute to the general motivational level will be discussed, including the arousal-level concept, the "what is it?" reflex, and the formation of the pre-performance "set." The second section will deal with more specific motivating conditions, including the effects of restriction, fatigue, competition, reward versus punishment, social facilitation, group interaction, and similar variables, as they affect motor performance.

Factors Contributing to the General Motivational Level

Arousal to Action.   Basic to an understanding of the manner in which motives affect the individual is the concept of arousal. The general readiness of the individual to act may be placed on a continuum, from a deep trance-like sleep to the hyperactivity characteristic of the mentally ill. Most individuals function in range somewhere near the midpoint, although individual fluctuations occur daily and hourly. Ryan and others[951] have found that an individual's basic level of arousal, measured by galvanic skin response, affects gross motor control.

The arousal curve is a more comprehensive construct than the previously discussed idea of tension level, although there is, of course, an overlapping of the two concepts. The tension level may be thought of as the upper portion of the arousal curve. When plotted in relationship to performance both curves assume the same U-shaped pattern, indicating that there is an optimal level of arousal (or tension) within which the most efficient motor performance may occur. This optimum generally depends on the nature of the task. The arousal level of an individual is a function of where he may be on several kinds of psychophysiological cycles that impinge on him at a given moment. These cycles are as short as a heart beat or as long as the menstrual cycle, and include the 24-hour sleep cycle. Other cycles consist of annual fluctuations of various physiological indices that indicate the willingness or readiness to act.[42]

The extent to which motives may affect performance depends directly on the point in the arousal curve at which the individual may be functioning momentarily. The higher his state of arousal, to a point, the more susceptible he is to various kinds of environmental conditions that may encourage him to move. However, a point is reached at which the individual may be thought of as overaroused (motivated), and to preserve his integrity, he may either blot out environmental stimuli or be unable to move efficiently because of excess tension.

The "What Is It?" Reflex. When the individual has been induced at least to notice some kind of motivating circumstances or stimuli, general skeletal musculature changes are noted. The head and total body orient to the direction of the object or event, the eyes become more adaptable to light, and previous movements are halted as general muscular tonus is raised. Pavlov[877] has termed this general pattern in animals *the "what is it?" reflex* to indicate bodily manifestations showing that the organism is ready to react to some portion of its environment. This state of attention is further characterized by changes in brain wave patterns, the slower waves present in lethargic states are replaced by the faster alpha waves. Visceral changes also prepare the organism for action.

Following these general and specific indices of readiness by the skeletal and muscular systems, the sensory organs, and the central nervous system, a decision is made to act or not to act. This state of attention indicates that a motive to move has not gone unnoticed, the potential to move has been improved, and the probability for action has been enhanced.

The Performance "Set." Following the impingement of some event on the attention of the organism, a specific readiness or "set" is produced. During this period, the human performer begins to adjust to the demands of the task, including self-instruction concerning his capabilities to perform the task, the amount or intensity of the impending task, and the specifics related to task performance (see Amount-Set, Chapter 4).

In general, this prefocusing may be related to a short-term or long-term view of the task. Information in this area suggests that a mixed-set may be produced (responding to one kind of stimuli and not responding to another). The research by Henry[518] and his co-workers suggests that the more complex the task the individual is "set" for, the longer will be his reaction time.

Motives Affecting Movement

Restriction from Movement as a Motive to Move. It is a common observation that, when children are required to sit still for long periods of time, as in the traditional classroom situation, they tend to evidence heightened activity needs when released from such restriction. Restraint thus has seemed to build up a backlog of action that needs an unusually large amount of expression.

Systematic studies by Shirley,[997] with animals, support the assumption that inactivity, induced by forcing the animals into small cages, results in an increase in activity on their release. Hill[541] obtained similar findings; however, his data suggest that there is an optimal time of restriction that will produce the most post activity and, if exceeded, less activity will be the outcome.

There also seems to be an optimal or typical amount of time during which restriction can be tolerated by human beings, and this seems to be related to maturational level. The time during which an infant will tolerate restriction of his movements is relatively short, whereas an older child can be restrained longer without apparent frustration or discomfort.

However, I am not aware of research with human subjects that treats the relationship between restriction and the subsequent activity levels. Although common observation indicates that the need for movement is increased by restrictions, there is little objective evidence as to the exact relationships involved. Hyperactivity certainly follows restriction and restraint has a physiological genesis, but other factors also seem operative.

Fatigue as a Negative Motivation. The phenomenon of fatigue is a little understood parameter of human performance. Few deny its existence, yet most researchers are unable to agree on a single definition. Bartley and Chute,[67] following an analysis of innumerable experimental viewpoints gleaned from psychological and physiological sources, suggest that fatigue may be regarded as a condition occurring to the whole person caused by a conflict situation in which the general attitude of the individual might be termed *aversion*.

In addition, Bartley and Chute suggest that the term *impairment* be used to refer to actual tissue conditions that indicate the accumulation of waste products of activity, and *fatigue* be construed as an attempt to retreat or escape from the situation that has become too difficult to contend with. They further suggest that impairment does not necessarily accompany fatigue, that inactivity can lead to fatiguing boredom, and that moderate and changing activity is less likely to prove fatiguing.

Man seems to abhor doing nothing. Thus the concept of fatigue as aversion is important when studying motivation. Although physiological impairment, if carried to individual limits, certainly curtails performance, boredom elicited by inactivity or sustained participation produces the same disinclination to move. There seems to be an optimal level of activity, more specifically of interesting complex activity, required to keep fatigue to a minimum. Anticipation of boring or repetitive work can be fatiguing or can produce a state of fatigue before the task is begun. Whereas anticipation of an interesting, though perhaps a somewhat taxing, task may produce an exhilaration that is antithetic to fatigue.

Thus fatigue may be evaluated by collecting subjective reports from the subjects pertaining to the monotony of the task, by noting performance decrements during sustained activity, and by various physiological indices signifying various kinds of tissue impairment due to prolonged periods of time at a task. The feelings people have about performance and their attitudes toward various components of physical endeavors influence their achievement both in direct and in subtle ways. For example, in a recent study by Smith and Bozymowski,[1022] they found that warm-up aided performance on an obstacle course only for those participants who expressed prior positive attitudes about the influence of warm-up on performance. Individuals who expressed the opinion that warm-up would not aid performance failed to perform better after warming up.

A recent and interesting "field" study of fatigue was conducted by Hagerman,[476] using the performances of pentathlon champions in a 1966 Australian competition. After comparing measures of fatigue to subsequent performance scores in the shooting, riding, and running events, he concluded that participants whose physical constitutions seemed best able to deal with fatigue scored best in the endurance events of the rigorous program.

Further laboratory studies of fatigue and physical performance are continuing in several parts of the world. Borg and his colleagues[117,118] at the University of Stockholm are examining perceptions of work and subsequent prior effort, and their findings are highly provocative.

Schmidt and others in this country are exploring in precise ways the influences of fatigue on both motor performance and learning. In general, Schmidt[968] found that carefully regulated, "artificially induced" fatigue prior to learning and performance (using the Bachman ladder climb) seemed to influence performance more than it did the ultimate levels of learning reached. It thus seems that localized muscular fatigue influences the muscular performance components of the task that modify immediate performance more than the conceptual factors that may contribute to a rather long-term and stable change in performance.

Rewards, Punishment, and Movement. One of the most investigated phenomenon in educational literature concerned with motivation is the relative effect of rewards and punishment on mental and motor performance. Much of this interest gained impetus from early studies by Thorndike dealing with motivation or his "law of effect." Usually the effects of reward were found to be far superior to those of punishment and that punishment with a reward following was more motivating than punishment alone. Innumerable findings have supported the influence of this "law of effect" on performance and learning. For example, Locke[698] found a .42 correlation between pursuit rotor performance and a "liking" score.

Simple monetary reward will elicit more physical work by human subjects than the absence of reward. In a recent series of studies, for example, Toppen[1107,1108] found that more work was elicited when increased payments were made to college students engaged in a repetitive strength-endurance task. Similarly, payment by the "piece" was more effective in raising work output than were wages at an hourly rate. Borg and his colleagues also have studied the effects of monetary rewards on physical performance. Their conclusions are in line with what would be expected, that is, individuals for whom money is important work harder under monetary reward; whereas those for whom money is not important do not work significantly harder for monetary reward.

In general, when attempting to relate the effects of rewards and punishments to motor activity, many variables make the relationship difficult to investigate. Initially, the movement itself, if the behavior-primacy theory is accorded validity, may prove to be motivating for its own sake. The optimal tension level principle is also operative. Conditions that are rewarding to one individual and serve to raise tension to an optimum may cause a second individual to perform badly when the desirable level is exceeded.

Punishment, on the other hand, frequently elicits fear and anxiety. Thus, the relative value of punishing or giving approval when performing a motor task varies from individual to individual. In addition, the form of the reward, the individual offering verbal encouragement, and similar variables all affect the reward-punishment-performance relationship.

Suggested Task Failure as a Motive to Achieve. One of the most frequently manipulated variables is suggesting to the subject that he is either failing or exceeding accepted norms. This is referred to as "failure-stress" if the latter condition is introduced. Utilizing this technique, interesting findings have been reported by Bayton and Conley.[77] With a manipulation task, they found that success or failure, before the introduction of suggested failure, determined the effect of such stress on performance. After initial success (manufactured by the experimenter), the introduction of suggested failure tended to spur performance to greater heights, since the individual seemed to attempt to sustain the feeling of status he had gained during prior trials. On the other hand, if failure was introduced during the early trials, later performance was impeded.

Leshman[676] also has presented findings suggesting that the aspiration level of the performer and his stated expectations determine performance decrement when some kind of failure-stress is introduced. Using a pattern-form problem, muscular tension became greater when experimentally suggested failure followed stated realistic expectations than stated unrealistic expectations. Tension levels also increased with failure and decreased with success.

Motivating Types of Movement Behavior

Some types of movement behavior in themselves seem to constitute motivating experiences. Of particular interest are the actions that have been labeled play, manipulation, and exploration and that seem to be manifestations of a basic need of the organism to deal with his environment. Play, manipulation, and exploration are interrelated kinds of behavior. For example, play seems to result in the individual exploring his environment more fully, as when various movement patterns that in another context might be imperative for survival are tried out. At the same time, exploration and manipulation appear so satisfying that they might be classified as play. In the following pages a discussion of these activities and the forces that seem to mold them, of the various forms they seem to take, and of theoretical frameworks that purport to explain their existence is presented.

Play

No one the least sensitive to the nature of children and animals can deny the existence of playful behavior. As Gavin Maxwell[750] states in a charming story outlining his friendships with several pets in the remote regions of England, ". . . Otters are extremely bad at doing nothing." The same statement might be applied to most animals and certainly to most children.

Play is a spontaneous activity motivating for its own sake. It is engaged in throughout the entire hierarchy of the animal kingdom in various forms. Playful behavior has been studied by the anthropologist, the naturalist, the psychologist, and experts in child development. It may be observed when fish jump from the water, when monkeys swing from trees, and when puppies and children play chase in the backyard. As Huizinga stated in *"Homo Ludens"* (*Man the Player*):

> Play is older than culture, for culture, however inadequately defined, always presupposes human society, and animals have not waited for man to teach them their playing.[561]

Characteristics of Play.   In general, the young of the species engage more in playful behavior than do older members. Welker,[1177] comparing exploratory and playful behavior of three young and three older chimpanzees, found that the younger ones played for more extended periods of time.

Playful activity contains elements of surprise and is usually marked by a distinct beginning and ending, as though tension has been alleviated. Play generally takes place in a social context, because a child usually plays with another child or with a member of another species.

Playful behavior seems to involve a wide degree of individual differences in both animals and man. Organisms differ both in the kinds of movements they manifest and in the specific forms they choose to express playful moods.

Theories of the Purpose for Play.   As many reasons have been postulated for the existence of play as have been advanced to explain motivation in general. In close alignment with instinctual theories of motivation was the explanation advanced by Groos,[468] who suggested that play is an instinctive act whose purpose is to dispose of surplus energies. Many persons attempt to justify exercise and physical education totally on the same premise today (that activity simply uses up energy that, in another form, might prove disruptive or destructive to society). Tolman[1105] reemphasized this viewpoint in 1932 when he stated that animals and man seem to be trying to achieve a harmonious fatigue.

Several criticisms of this theory were forthcoming. It was suggested that if play was meaningless as an educative device, why did the play activities of children so resemble the kinds of motor behavior necessary for the adult of the species? The young child pretends to drive a car, and the kitten's aimless pouncing on a ball suggests mice-catching skills needed later for survival. To further weaken the "surplus energy" theory of play, scientific inquiry failed to identify structures in the human organism that might conceivably store up this "energy" and then later release it in the form of play.

Another theory suggested that play is simply a joyful release. It was proposed that play was some kind of mystical expression by the individual. Such an explanation, while satisfying to some, failed to suggest any kind of experimental verification and, indeed, seemed circular.

A utilitarian explanation also has been advanced for the existence of play-like behavior. Beach,[78] following a review of theories of play, suggested that joyful movement serves a useful function. Since the young of the species engage most in playful pursuits, he assumed that the purpose of play was to build up a store of movements necessary to optimal functioning in later life.

It is my feeling that playful behavior might indeed fulfill a number of functions in addition to being the manifestation of a basic need for activity or of a general excitatory state of the organism. Play seems to provide for a release of tensions, and, at the same time, its imitative quality seems to prepare the young for the adoption of adult responsibilities. In addition, playful behavior seems satisfying in and of itself, apart from more useful consequences. In summary, play is the manifestation of motive to move, to explore, and to manipulate the environment.

Exploration and Manipulation in Animals and Man

Just as a basic need for self-expression in play seems to be present in the animal and human organism, there also seems to be a basic curiosity drive that is expressed in manipulative and explorative activities. Exploration involves movement of the total organism, whereas manipulation usually involves limb and finger movements. The two types of behavior are thus similar and differ primarily with regard to the amount of space occupied during their expression.

Several basic factors seem to channel and to mold the type and quantity of exploratory and manipulatory behavior. Two of the most important of these are the *novelty* and the *complexity* of the situation or objects. In addition, as is true of play, younger people usually engage more frequently and for more extended periods of time in exploratory and manipulatory behavior than do older individuals.

Novelty. The role of novelty in establishing and encouraging exploratory behavior has been examined in some detail by Berlyne.[94] In general, this author suggested that there are several kinds of novel situations that may direct attention to an object: (1) *relative novelty,* when something is new as compared to a similar but different past experience, and (2) *absolute novelty,* when an object or situation is unique to the individual's entire range of past experiences. In addition, Berlyne speaks

10

of short-term and long-term novelty, depending on whether the newly encountered situation is similar to experiences occurring in the recent or in the distant past.

Two hypotheses are presented by Berlyne to explain the motivating effect of novelty on manipulatory and exploratory behavior: (1) the *habituation hypothesis,* suggesting that novel objects are motivating simply because they have not yet had a chance to lose the intriguing qualities that all objects originally possess; and (2) a second theory proposing that novelty represents a *conflict* in the individual, an imbalance or tension that may be alleviated only by exploring and manipulating the new situation.

Complexity. A second contributory factor in the initiation of exploratory and/or manipulatory behavior has to do with the complexity of the object or situation. In general, objects or situations that are too simple do not seem to encourage exploratory behavior, while, on the other hand, an object or situation may be too complex to draw the organism's attention. In short, there seems to be an optimal level of complexity in the new situation that will encourage the organism to engage in a maximal amount of exploration and manipulation.

Illustrative of research focused on manipulation and exploration are studies by Welker[1177] using chimpanzees as subjects. Blocks of various shapes and colors were presented to the primates and the following measures were recorded: (1) total responsiveness based on the total number of five-second periods during which an animal touched any object, (2) number of contacts, (3) shifts, or the number of times touch shifted from one object to another, (4) withdrawals, or the number of times the subjects withdrew from the experimental situation, and (5) a listing of the objects touched, the number of different objects touched and the length of contact, and the average length of contact with each object of a given classification.

Welker found that novelty, or the introduction of new or different blocks of a more complex nature, resulted in an increase in the total responsiveness score. On the other hand, a decrease in responsiveness measures was noted when the object presented was less complex than previous ones, e.g., not as colorful or as intricate in shape or form. In addition it was found that, with repeated presentation of the same blocks, a decrease in the various responsive measures was recorded, indicating that the principle of saturation was operative. A significant decrease in responsiveness, for example, was noted when comparing scores recorded on the first day (during the ten-minute experimental period) and scores collected on the third day of the nine-day experiment.

Welker also found that, in addition to novelty and complexity, the *proximity* of the object to the animal seemed to be an effective variable. The blocks placed in the row nearest the chimpanzees were handled more frequently than were those placed in a row farther away. More recent research has elaborated on the findings presented by Welker. Menzel[785] also found that, although at times primates may be initially fearful of complex stimuli, they handle complex objects more than the simpler ones after their anxiety is dissipated. Menzel found that objects of a maximum size elicited the most manipulatory behavior by primates; objects that were too big or too small, on the other hand, elicited only a moderate amount of inspection by his subjects.

Sackett[958] found that early environment influences the tendency to manipulate objects. Jungle-reared monkeys manipulated and handled more complex objects than did their cage-reared cousins.

Children are being used more frequently in contemporary experiments dealing with the influence of novelty and complexity on manipulatory behavior.[292] Similar to the findings of studies in which primates are used, it has been found that complexity elicits more activity than does simplicity,[982] and novelty encourages more interest than does familiarity.[498]

The personality of the child, as well as his age and sex, influences his reaction to novel situations. Mendel[781] found that, although the preference value of a toy increased as a direct function of its novelty, younger children, as well as those who were scored high in anxiety by their teachers, preferred less novelty than did the older children and those with low anxiety scores. Similarly, the boys preferred more novelty than did the girls.[781]

The observations of Piaget,[894] Gesell,[418a] Halverson,[576] and others confirm the extent to which an infant seizes every opportunity to manipulate and to explore his environment. It is believed that no comprehensive theoretical explanation of human motivation can exclude this persistent and universal human activity.

Summary

Motivation refers to the reasons why people select various tasks, as well as why they seem to persist in them for various periods of time once selected. The terms *arousal* and *activation*, on the other hand, are coming to connote variables that undergird the intensity of physical effort.

Theories of motivation include those based on concepts of instincts and basic drives, and those advocating the importance of physiological needs, psychological needs, and social needs. The capacity-primacy theory of motivation suggests that the multiplicity of activities, interests, and movements engaged in by man need not depend on innate physiological drives, but may depend on innate capacities. The existence of play, manipulation, and exploratory behavior is best explained by such a theoretical framework.

A general condition contributing to the motivational state is the individual's state of arousal. On presentation of the task, the "what is it?" reflex is usually noted. General postural adjustments necessary to take in sensory information are indicated, in turn producing a general readiness or "set" prior to task performance.

Specific motives to move or not to move include restriction from movement, fatigue (task-aversion, boredom), and specific rewards or punishments. Conditions that raise general tension level may affect the performance of different individuals in different ways, depending on prior level of efficiency and general complex of personality traits.

Play, manipulation, and exploration are specific kinds of movement behavior that seem self-sustaining, motivating experiences in their own right. The intensity of these activities depends on the age of the participants and on the complexity and novelty of the situation.

Student Reading

Asch, S.: *Social Psychology.* Englewood Cliffs, N.J., Prentice-Hall, Inc., 1951.

Cratty, B. J.: Motivation. In *Psychology in Contemporary Sport.* Englewood Cliffs, N.J., Prentice-Hall, Inc., 1973, Chapter 8.

Fowler, H.: *Curiosity and Exploratory Behavior.* New York, The Macmillan Co., 1965.

Gates, G.: The effect of an audience upon performance. J. Abnorm. Soc. Psychol., *18,* 334–344, 1924.

Maslow, A. H.: *Motivation and Personality.* New York, Harper & Row, Publishers, 1970.

Rethlingshafer, D.: *Motivation as Related to Personality.* New York, McGraw-Hill Book Company, Inc., 1963.

Vernon, M. D.: *Human Motivation.* London, Cambridge University Press, 1969.

Welker, W. I.: Some determinants of play and exploration in chimpanzees. J. Comp. Physiol. Psychol., *49,* 84–90, 1956.

Woodworth, R. S.: *Dynamics of Behavior.* New York, Henry Holt & Co., 1958.

Young, P. T.: *Motivation and Emotion.* New York, John Wiley & Sons, Inc., 1961.

14
SOCIAL MOTIVES

Since before the turn of the century experimental psychologists have studied the effects of different social conditions on various measures of physical performance. The conclusions of these investigations, although often apparently contradictory, form one of the most important sources of information available concerning the psychosocial parameters of human motor activity. Such factors as the audience, competition versus competitive behavior between two or more persons, and the influences of social rewards have been explored. Still another important dimension of this problem involves the important but often subtle influence of cultural and/or ethnic expectations on the quality and quantity of vigorous and accurate motor performance and learning. After the first few days of life, the behavior of human infants begins to be influenced in direct ways by their parents and by others with whom they come in contact. Throughout childhood and adolescence and into adulthood, individuals performing a variety of tasks are influenced to varying degrees by the presence and by the encouragement or, at times, the disapproval of others.

Social motives may be defined as variables that mold human behavior and are an integral part of the social context in which the behavior is observed or measured. There are several dimensions to this type of impetus to action.

Initially, the effect of various "unseen audiences" on the performance of individuals or groups might be considered. These "absent" spectators include subcultures against which a person compares his performance, and perhaps parents and colleagues who might later judge the results of his efforts even though the activity be undertaken in solitude. The subtle influence of broad sociocultural variables is another example of a type of "absent audience" influencing performance.

Another classification includes social motives that may be identified in situations in which two or more persons are performing the same or related tasks at approximately the same time. Research dealing with competition, cooperative behavior, group interaction, interpersonal communication, leadership, and group cohesion is concerned with information of this nature.

The number of investigations dealing with various sociopsychological variables have proliferated in recent years. Many of these studies, in order to elicit exact performance measures, have employed a variety of motor tasks, particularly when children have been used as subjects. The following information is selective rather than comprehensive. However, a consideration of the points raised in these pages, I believe, will enable an educator to become more effective in his efforts to mold and to change the movement attributes of others.

The Effects of
Observers on Performance

A single observer or a group watching one or more individuals perform may evidence various kinds of behavior. The viewers may passively look on while a person performs, they may gesture or by their facial expressions express support or disapproval of his efforts and/or they may verbally reinforce or "razz" individual or group efforts.

An increasing amount of literature suggests that even passive, silent observation will elicit obvious or subtle performance changes by individuals or groups. McBride and his colleagues[753] found that the proximity of the experimenter to the subject elicits measurable changes in the galvanic skin responses of the latter, a reasonably reliable measure of activation influencing a variety of motor attributes. Furthermore these same experimenters found that whether the experimenter was standing to the front, back, or side of the subject also altered the electrophysiological measure.

As early as 1897, Triplett[1111] reported that the presence of an audience caused both negative and positive performance fluctuations in a reel-winding task and in competitive bicycle riding. In a more recent study, Gates[414] also found that an audience influenced different individuals in diverse ways when they were attempting a test of manual dexterity. Gates varied the size of the audience from a single experimenter to a small group of six onlookers to a large group of about 100. Overall, it is becoming increasingly clear that the audience effect is comparable to other factors that tend to heighten the arousal-activation levels of performers. Thus, like other "activators," an audience is generally a disrupter of complex acts and of poorly learned tasks; whereas the presence of spectators (whether friendly or hostile) is likely to facilitate the performance of simple direct and of well-learned actions, from sports skills to laboratory tasks. Kenyon and Loy[614] reported that a small group of spectators had no significant influence on the performance of a simple motor task.

The sex of the observer relative to the sex of the performer has been found to influence performance in many tasks. Generally, individuals perform best and for more sustained periods when in the presence of the opposite sex. A number of investigations have explored this cross-sex effect, demonstrating important lessons for experimenters when collecting data from human subjects and illustrating important principles for educators interested in changing the movement attributes of adults and children.

In a series of studies carried out from 1961 to 1965, Hill and Stevenson[537] found that the skilled performance of adolescent girls improved in the presence of male experimenters who verbally reinforced their efforts. It was found that testing by a member of the opposite sex increased competitiveness and anxiety about the task, as well as the desire to please the experimenter. Stevenson suggested that this effect is more pronounced in female subjects tested by males. However, the research by Bendig[86] concluded that the reverse is true, stating that males seem to have higher needs for social approval.

Noer and Whittaker[853] elicited the cross-sex effect in an indirect way. With a mirror-tracing skill, improvements were elicited in girls by suggesting that "girls do twice as well as boys in this task, but you did not," and by suggesting the reverse to the male subjects in their experiment. It might be hypothesized that the cross-sex effect operates in a number of tasks and serves generally to activate the performer; thus perhaps it can be counted on to influence simple tasks positively while proving detrimental to more complex ones. However, the number of studies dealing with this problem are few, and the tasks examined under these conditions are extremely limited.

The cross-sex effect is often noted by coaches and others concerned with optimum performance. The exact parameters of this phenomenon await further investigations. For example, there is no information relative to the effect of female onlookers on the performance of males in a wide variety of tasks. Similarly there is little information relative to the number of onlookers of the opposite sex necessary to elicit the most improvement in performance. Less skilled performers might be assumed to be hindered in their efforts by the presence of a member of the opposite sex, whereas the reverse might be true when more proficient individuals perform. I know of no experimental evidence, however, confirming or disproving these assumptions.

The effect of onlookers on motor performance also appears to be a function of age. Stevenson[1064] suggests that with increasing age children become more aware of various aspects of social reinforcers. Missiuro[805] fixes the age at which children's motor performance becomes positively affected by onlookers at six years. Improvement was noted in an endurance task by his subjects at this age. Prior to this age the children were noted to be generally activated by the presence of an audience, but they did not direct this heightened arousal into measurable improvement in performance.

The personality of the performer also influences his susceptibility to the audience effect. Bendig[86] found that individuals who had high achievement needs were most influenced by onlookers. Cox[225] also found that, when boys were asked to perform a marble-dropping task for sustained periods, those with low-anxiety scores performed best in the presence of a number of types of spectators, including their parents, peers, teachers, and strangers. Those who scored high in measures of anxiety performed best when only the experimenter was present.[225]

Some scholars have recently suggested that youths and adults who evidenced the most insecurity and/or fear in front of an audience are those who, as children, received inordinate amounts of parental punishment and disapproval for failing at various tasks confronting them.

Thus to predict the effects of a silent audience on performance of skills, the age and personality of the performer, the nature of the task, the size and composition of the audience, as well as the sex of the onlookers as compared to the sex of the performers must be taken into consideration. Innumerable studies suggest themselves after a survey of the relatively scant literature available on this and related subjects. For example, little is known about the effects of experience on physical performance while a person is performing with an audience present. A 1965 investigation by Singer,[1011] comparing the performance of athletes and nonathletes in an experimental task, suggests that experience in front of audiences might be specific to the task, and may not generalize to any great extent.

More recent studies have attempted to explore the relationships of other personality and situational variables to performance in the presence of an audience. Martens[740] reported an investigation in which the relationships between learning and performance in front of an audience were compared to measures of arousal (galvanic skin response), as well as to scores reflecting anxiety (the Taylor scale). Although anxiety scores did not seem predictive of performance in front of an audience, subjects scoring high and low in anxiety exhibited changes in arousal indices when observed. The lack of a relationship between anxiety, performance, and learning in the presence of an audience in this investigation could have stemmed from the rather inexact measure of trait anxiety employed. A more helpful measure in this context is the scale to evaluate "state" anxiety recently developed by Spielberger.[1046]

Investigations exploring the influence of an athlete's feelings about an audience on his performance efforts also seem to be needed. Although Ogilvie and Tutko[861] have postulated that most superior athletes have negative feelings about all individuals who watch them, they have not presented data elaborating on the possible relationships between the intensity of these feelings and the various facets of sports performance.

Effects of Spectators' Comments

Spectators may verbally denote approval or disapproval of the efforts they are observing. Relatively few studies have been carried out in which the effect of negative verbal reinforcement on motor performance was studied, although negative reinforcement frequently occurs in athletic stadiums and on playfields. More numerous are investigations in which the influence of praise on physical performance has been studied.

Earlier studies of these questions utilized relatively few subjects and were rather inexact. Laird[648] found that the performance of seven fraternity "pledges" was severely disrupted when seniors "razzed" them for their efforts. A study by Latane and Arrowood[662b] established that verbal harassment during the performance of physical skills tended to depress scores on complex activities (pushing buttons to light cues), although it did serve to facilitate performance in simpler tasks.

Several investigations have compared the effects of negative and positive verbal reinforcers on motor performance. They usually found that verbal "punishment" elicits a heightened state of arousal resulting in more rapid or more intense efforts.[662b] At the same time negative verbal exhortation tends to disrupt complex performance. The effect of praise is heightened if the subjects have high needs for social approval, or are between the ages of five and six years.[688] As the difficulty of the task and the age of the subject increase, verbal exhortation seems to have less effect, and the performer's interest in the task affects the quality of his efforts more.[21]

Innumerable studies attest to the positive influence of praise on the execution of a variety of motor tasks. Recent studies by Kelly and Stephens[609] and by Strickland and Jenkins[1071] support this basic assumption.

In addition to praising an individual or group for performing during or prior to the task, onlookers may encourage optimum effort by various kinds of exhortation. Fleishman published findings in 1958 in which he demonstrated that encouraging trainee airmen to "do your best," "the results of this test are important to you" and similar kinds of support significantly improved performance on a rudder-stick coordination task. Additional insight into the effects of exhortation on motor performance is provided by Locke,[699] who found that the setting of specific performance goals influenced scores on a complex coordination task more positively than when subjects were simply encouraged to "do your best." It thus seems that encouraging the performer to attain reasonable goals is more helpful than simply exciting him with nonspecific verbal exhortations.

In general, younger boys and girls remain longer and work harder under conditions involving verbal approval. Similarly, performance increments usually are elicited in complex tasks when approval is extended by a friend rather than by a non-preferred peer. In younger children, avoiding criticism seems to be a more powerful motive to performance than does eliciting approval for their efforts. The more mature children, adolescents, and adults tend to work relatively independent of criticism or praise extended, deriving more of their satisfactions from an interest in the task itself.[21] Substantiating this observation are the data from a recent investigation by Roberts and Martens.[932] They found no significant difference in the performance of a complex motor task by groups of mature male subjects, some of whom were rewarded socially in positive ways and some of whom either were not rewarded at all or were given negative social reinforcement.

The influence of verbal exhortation on performance is a function of the age of the performer, his past experience at the task, and the nature of the task. Similarly, the previous relationships between the individuals offering encouragement or disapproval and the performers also influence the effects of this kind of social motivation.

The Motivating Effects
of Another's Performance

In addition to individuals changing the performance output of another by passively observing him, or more actively engaging in some kind of verbal reinforcement, people stimulate each other as they perform at the same time on work teams, and as they compete against one another as teams or as individuals. These effects include some kind of group or individual interaction involving the motor performance of two or more individuals, in contrast to social facilitation elicited by the mere presence of onlookers.

Competition. The American society of the 1970's is a competitive one, in which apparent success purportedly depends on the extent to which an individual can compete with his fellows in activities on which the culture bestows status. One of these activities involves the performance of physical skills. Competitive behavior in play is not confined to the American culture. McClintock and Martin,[757] as well as others, have found that competitive behaviors are common in both older and younger children in many cultures throughout the world.

Individual and team sports have been justified in school curricula partly because they have been hypothesized to inculcate competitive behavior in the participants. Competitive urges seem a rather basic component of the human personality, and, indeed, they are observed in the behavior of animals at the lower levels of the evolutionary scale.

All other things being equal, competition improves performance in simple strength tasks, as well as in tasks whose successful execution depends on simple speed and/or reaction time.[190] On the other hand, if the performers are relatively anxious and/or the task requires precision, competition may impede performance.

Generally, individuals who perceive themselves as competitive and able in the performance of some task, and the presence of two or more individuals who perceive themselves nearly alike in ability can be counted on to elicit competition. The competitors in motor skills must be reasonably mature, because usually little structured competitive behavior is elicited before the age of three years. The similarities and/or differences in the socioeconomic levels of the antagonists can also influence their tendency to compete. Lower-class individuals compete for different reasons and for different goals than do those more favored economically and socially. Differences in the economic levels of two competitors may influence their interactions; lower-class individuals may be reluctant to challenge those of a superior economic classification.

Competition can be considered a form of "social activation" and be expected to elicit performance changes accordingly. Simple tasks are improved, complex tasks are hindered; the performance of individuals working at below optimum levels of activation is improved, but the scores of those working at desirable levels may be depressed. Thus the effect of competition on performance is a function of the current level of activation of the performers, the difficulty of the task, the individual's past experience in competitive circumstances, and his perceptions of himself as a competitor in the situation he faces.

People usually perceive competitive situations as satisfying, despite whether they have won or lost. Similarly mutual attractiveness of pairs or between members of larger groups has been demonstrated to be enhanced if they have competed with one another.

Although competition seems a rather ubiquitous part of our society and an important component of social motivation, many facets of competition have not been explored experimentally, particularly in relation to motor performance and learning. Additional research might explore, in more depth, the relationships between various personality traits and competitive behavior, perhaps in determining whether a "competitive nature" is a product of early training in childhood or is elicited by needs immediate to the situation. Further investigations might also explore whether individuals generally tend to compete in a variety of situations or only in selected tasks.

Cooperation. Individuals motivate each other when they perform in unison. Parallel play is first noted in children at about the age of two years, when two children may engage in similar activity but do not interact directly. By the age of six years, however, children stimulate each other directly by forming groups to accomplish various tasks. Affiliation is motivating, and grouping together to perform motor tasks usually affects the performance of the task. Frequently the problem of studying the effect of group interaction on motor performance is complicated by the fact that individuals sometimes perform both cooperatively and competitively at the same time. People form groups and engage in cooperative behavior in order to compete favorably with a similar group acting as their competitor.

Moreover, several important maturational dimensions are necessary to study cooperative behavior in physical tasks. Seldom are young children able to work as cooperatively as older children. The younger child cannot always perceive the manner in which the task appears to his teammates and thus cannot interact with them in the precise ways in which older youth are able to do. Fry[393] found that even children as old as 9 to 12 years of age had a difficult time placing themselves in the role of another while performing a cooperative game, whereas the college-age students in this same investigation could do so and, with practice, could improve the results of their cooperative performance.

Generally groups perform tasks better than do individuals, because of a greater amount of what has been termed "resource input" available to groups. However, as the group gets larger, individuals are not motivated to exert maximum effort, because they may feel that their part in the total effort is diminishing; thus there is a measurable performance decrement by each individual. In one study conducted with a tug-of-war task, a decrease of 10 percent in individual effort was noted with the addition of each member over four.

Groups can be motivated to varying degrees by needs for affiliation or by needs for superior group performance. Studies by Cratty and Sage[268] and others have described the tendency for affiliative needs to sometimes interfere with optimum group effort. An excess of "social noise," it was pointed out, may at times distract the group from focusing on the task at hand. Recent investigations point to the sometimes interfering effects of needs for affiliation on needs for mastery present in groups confronted with physical tasks. Martens[741] found that members of college intramural basketball teams who evidenced high needs for affiliation did not perform as well as those who were more highly "task motivated." Studies in Europe in the 1960's echo this some finding. Hans Lenk[673] pointed to the excellent performance of a German rowing team despite, or possibly because of, intragroup conflicts. Studies in the United States dating back to those of Fiedler[349] in the early 1950's further support the suggestion that some athletic teams may contain members whose affiliative needs overbalance their need for effective team effort.

In general, however, there seems to be an optimum amount of "we feeling" necessary to keep the group working together and to permit the leadership to focus on the task at hand. However, if the individuals have formed the group primarily with affiliative motives in mind, their performance as a group may suffer.

Innumerable questions remain unanswered in the available literature. The work methods of the group may be more important than whether they are competing or cooperating in some task. Jones[596] has found that how a group divides its labor, or whether they divide it at all, may influence performance more than whether they are competing or cooperating.

Similarly the performance quality researched by Wiest et al.[1203] and Comrey and his colleagues[209-211] is an important variable to consider. Some individuals perform particularly well when interacting with another person in a motor task; they coordinate their movements with those of their teammates, anticipating the actions of the other group members with facility. Thus the performances of individuals in groups probably depend not only on the mutual stimulation they afford one another, but also on the extent to which they can integrate their movements in a common task.

Gaining Status
Through Physical Performance

The gaining of status in childhood, adolescence, and adulthood depends on innumerable qualities and a variety of situations in which human beings may interact. Generally, status is bestowed on group members who perform well the activities valued by the group, and on those who enable the group to perform well by overcoming blocks to their efforts and by proposing helpful performance techniques. As the growing child reaches the age of five or six years, physical ability contributes to some degree to his social acceptability and status in the play group. Fighting ability and superior motor performance have been found to enhance the status of older children.

The status conferred by athletic prowess is reflected in various personality measures of growing boys. Research has documented the tendency for boys proficient in an ability to evidence traits that reflect the status this ability has bestowed on them by their social groups. In general, these good-performing young males are more ascendant and socially outgoing than are boys who are less proficient motorically. Early maturation, which enhances basic physical capacities of males, also correlates with personality traits denoting social adroitness.[830]

By the time adolescence is reached, athletic prowess has become an overriding means for boys to achieve status. Coleman,[207] in the discussion of his findings in *The Adolescent Society,* points out that almost half the boys interviewed wished to be remembered after high school as athletes rather than as leaders in activities, scholars, or the most popular. Male membership in leading social groups was mainly attributed to participation in athletics rather than to such qualities as appearance, common sense, and sense of humor. Although Coleman's findings might not be applicable to all communities or to adolescent societies of the 1970's, they hold important implications for understanding the influence of social motives on the performance and value systems of adolescent boys in our society.

The effects of early maturation and physical proficiency on the development of positive social skills carry over into adolescence and even into adulthood. In 1938, Jones[595] carried out an investigation that revealed a relationship between physical development and social adjustment of boys. In 1965, a follow-up to this investigation used the same subjects, now adults. These men tended to retain the same constellation of personality characteristics they had evidenced as boys. The late-maturing retiring youths grew up to be somewhat withdrawn men. Conversely the outgoing early-maturing boys retained their ascendant behaviors in adulthood. Thus the advantages of early maturation on boys contribute to a positive self-concept that continues into adulthood.

Girls in our culture, of course, do not derive the same status benefits from exhibiting proficiency in sports skills. Although there are some indications that girls are beginning to participate more in vigorous games, in general a girl must be selective as to the sports she attempts and be careful not to exhibit too intense an effort to excel.

Status cannot be derived from proficiency in a variety of motor tasks—only in those involving large muscle activity deemed important by the culture. A chicken-and-egg relationship exists between status and physical prowess. Boys who excel in motor skills achieve status and, having achieved it, continue to pursue its source. At the same time, individuals with high needs for status tend to work harder and to practice longer in various physical skills so that they may achieve social prominence. The "need for social approval" scored on various personality questionnaires is frequently correlated with proficiency in various gross motor activities.[266]

Summary

Individuals are motivated by numerous components of the social clime when performing and learning motor skills. The presence of an onlooker results in performance fluctuations, particularly if the spectator is a member of the opposite sex. More explicit modifications in performance result if the audience voices approval, disapproval, or simply attempts to elicit maximum effort. The effect of such facilitation is a function of the nature of the task and the maturity of the performer. Measurable indices of motor performance in children below the age of six or seven years do not seem to be affected to the same extent as are those of children a few years older. As the child matures into late childhood and early adolescence, however, verbal exhortation by an onlooker begins to have less effect, and performance begins to be influenced more by the nature of the task, its novelty, and its complexity.

Competition and cooperative behavior in individual and group performance situations are at times difficult to separate. Competition is motivating in itself, independent of whether it results in individual or group success. However, if individuals are successful in groups, the attractiveness of the group is heightened, as is the cohesion of the members involved. If affiliative needs of individuals in a group are paramount to their needs for success in the task at hand, performance may suffer. Although an optimum amount of group cohesion seems to be necessary in order to elicit maximum group efforts, facilitate communication, and make the most efficient use of the leadership available, groups whose members form primarily to satify social needs usually do not perform as well as groups whose primary reason for collecting together is to execute a task successfully.

Status seeking is an important social motive, particularly influencing the peer group relationships of growing boys in our culture. Early maturation together with the concomitant physical prowess—biologic maturity—forms a base of success that results in the appearance of personality traits involving ascendancy and social competence extending into adolescence and adulthood.

Student Reading

Coleman, J. S.: *The Adolescent Society*. New York, Free Press of Glencoe, 1961.
Cratty, B. J.: *Social Dimensions of Physical Activity*. Englewood Cliffs, N.J., Prentice-Hall, Inc., 1967.
Cratty, B. J.: *Psychology in Contemporary Sport*. Englewood Cliffs, N.J., Prentice-Hall, Inc., 1973.
Kenyon, G. S.: *Sociology of Sport*. Chicago, The Athletic Institute, 1968.
Loy, J. W., Jr., and Kenyon, G. S.: *Sport, Culture, and Society*. New York, Macmillan Co., 1969.
Martens, R.: Effect of performance of learning a complex motor task in the presence of spectators. Res. Quart., *40*, 2, 1960.
Rosen, B. C., and D'Andrade, R.: The psycho-social origins of achievement motivation. Sociometry, *22*, 185–218, 1959.
Sage, G. H.: *Sport and American Society*. Menlo Park, Calif., Addison-Wesley, Co., 1970.
Scott, J.: *The Athletic Revolution*. New York, Free Press, 1971.

15
ANXIETY, STRESS, AND TENSION

Many meanings have been assigned to the terms *stress, anxiety,* and *tension.* The definitions sometimes have depended on the viewpoint of the researcher, the situation in which observations were made, or the measures employed. For example, with regard to *tension,* it is often reported that experimental subjects were "too tense" to perform movement tasks well. In another context, it is sometimes observed that an individual evidences extreme "nervous tension" when attempting to meet the demands of life. In the first case, tension refers to a momentary task-related state, whereas the second describes a personality trait.

The meaning of the word *stress* has undergone change during the years. Earlier behavioral scientists considered the affecting situation as stress, while at other times definitions were based on changes in performance characteristics. More recent medical researchers have inferred that stress is an intervening variable located between the situational input and the movement output. It has been further suggested that stress is best determined through biochemical analyses of various types.

Pinpointing the meaning of *anxiety* poses similar problems. Early Freudian psychoanalysts and many contemporary clinicians consider anxiety as a general fear of impending events based on *unconscious* motives and on circumstances in the organism's forgotten past. On the other hand, experimental psychologists have recently coined the terms *manifest anxiety* and *free anxiety,* suggesting that this syndrome of fear is a reportable and *conscious* experience.

A historical look at the manner in which stress, tension, and anxiety have been interrelated also indicates that shifts of opinion have taken place. Early researchers often used stress and tension as interchangeable concepts, with stress assumed always to produce tension, while tension was considered indisputable evidence of the former. More recent investigations, however, suggest that stress is an internalized kind of preparation to meet an immediate or future threat, and tension is now considered to be a related, but separate and more peripheral, behavioral manifestation involving muscular contraction. It is further suggested that, although tension *may* be in response to emotional arousal, it can also be induced simply by increasing the task load.

Interrelating the terms *anxiety* and *stress* also has produced problems. In general, however, stress seems to be determined by the situation and is a rather short-range phenomenon. Anxiety, on the other hand, is usually considered to be a general and continuing state of the organism, a personality characteristic.

Stress and anxiety, however, are intimately related in several ways. The literature suggests that repeated exposure to stressful situations results in heightening general anxiety. In addition, a highly anxious individual evidences internal stress reactions to a wider range of events than does a non-anxious person and reacts more strongly to situations which to most would result in relatively mild reactions.

In summary, *anxiety appears to be a general fear or foreboding, a personality trait marked by a lower threshold to stressful events. Stress is an internal reaction, an intervening variable between situation and performance, evidenced by a marshaling of resources to meet a threat. Tension, on the other hand, is overt muscular contraction caused by an emotional state or by increased effort.*

Whatever definitions are attached to these terms, it is usually found that stress and anxiety are manifested in increased muscular tension. And, since the focus of this book is on overt movement behavior, also a product of the skeletomuscular system, the failure to consider these major factors in performance would be a serious omission. The establishment of more clear-cut boundaries between these terms and the demonstration of their interrelationships will be attempted in the pages which follow. First, various theoretical viewpoints, which have been proposed, together with a "how-are-they-measured?" approach, will be discussed. It is hoped that, as stress, tension, and anxiety are related to movement behavior in the final portion of each section, the definitions presented above will assume more exact dimensions.

The Nature of Anxiety

To maintain internal balance, the organism must function with a certain level of anxiety always present. For anxiety, in its broadest sense, refers to the general state of alertness. It is related to the body's alarm system and provides for vigilance against disruptive forces in the environment. One must be anxious when crossing a street and transmit this anxiety to his children in order to ensure their survival in the modern city. However, performance problems arise if anxiety-produced arousal is too great. If the organism is continually threatened, Malmo and Davis[731] suggest, heightened general anxiety, measured by increased muscular tension, is the result. Some psychiatrists utilize the term *anxiety* only in a pathological context, while suggesting that fear is a healthy respect for situations and objects that are actually threatening.

Anxiety is a central idea in Freudian psychodynamics. It is related to the ego concept, which is defined as the portion of the personality that interacts with actual situations in the real world, rather than with imagined events. It is suggested that, while the environment can reward and bring pleasure to the individual, it can also threaten and punish him. Freud[388] hypothesizes that anxiety floods the ego when it is overwhelmed with continual threats of pain and/or destruction with which the organism is unable to cope. It is further held that the dangers and insecurities of constant and pronounced threats will cause the individual to become generally anxious.

Initially, Freud emphasized that anxiety was primarily produced through frustration of sexual urges. Later experimental evidence, however, proved this assertion to be rather untenable. Freud divided anxiety into three categories, ranging from normal apprehension of real situations (*reality anxiety*) to the fear of punishment for future transgressions (*neurotic anxiety*). The third classification suggested was *moral anxiety*, or the fear of punishment for socially disapproved behavior.

Others differentiate between *general anxiety* and *situational anxiety*, the latter term denoting a specific fear. It has been suggested that with increased exposure to a task situational anxiety tends to dissipate.[64]

The Freudian concept of anxiety, however, depended directly on the existence of unconscious forces and was difficult to objectify experimentally. Contemporary psychological researchers, in a search for measures that would permit more exact investigation of anxiety and its relationship to objective performance measures and to other personality variables, have evolved simpler and more direct definitions. Terms that assume that anxiety may be verified best by the collection of reportable *conscious* behavior on the part of the individual have recently been coined.

In 1953, Janet Taylor[1089] developed a test to measure what she called *manifest anxiety*. It was based on the direct self-reports by the subjects. The device was validated by including responses that indicated marked differences between groups of "normal" individuals and those who had been clinically classified as needing psychiatric aid because of the general feeling of fear constantly attending them. This tool has been used, with some modifications, in numerous experimental studies during the past ten years.

Contemporary researchers have coined the terms *state anxiety* to denote a rather impermanent condition that may be caused by specific circumstances or feelings, and *trait anxiety* referring to a permanent or stable personality dimension. Moreover, some have begun to develop measures intended to evaluate these separate anxiety concepts. For years the Taylor Scale of Manifest Anxiety has been employed together with the anxiety scale from the Institute of Personality and Ability Testing to evaluate "trait" anxiety. (Most of the time these scales have been employed incorrectly to evaluate conditions that by their very nature are transitory, e.g., prematch anxiety and the like.) More recently, however, Spielberger[1046] has published a scale that he purports evaluates both *trait* and *state* anxiety.

Basowitz et al.[71] have suggested the term *free anxiety* to distinguish general fear. They also suggested that previous psychoanalytic descriptions did not lend themselves to precise measurement. Basowitz defines free anxiety as "the conscious and reportable experience of intense dread and foreboding." The concepts of *free anxiety* and *manifest anxiety* bear a marked similarity insofar as both are identified through similar measuring devices and are not dependent on the identification of unconscious motivations.

Anxiety and Performance

The effect of anxiety on performance depends directly on the type of task considered. In most cases a heightened arousal state has been found to facilitate simple performances such as finger tapping, eyelid conditioning, and verbal memory tasks. On the other hand, as anxiety reaches a certain level, a breakdown of psychological and physiological integrative mechanisms is often seen to occur, resulting in less efficient performance in more complex tasks.

In another frame of reference, anxiety has a temporal relationship to performance. The level of anxiety evidenced prior to performance may be different from arousal during performance. Following a stressful situation, abrupt changes in reportable anxiety are often recorded. In general, anxiety levels increase prior to a dangerous situation until they become relatively high just before it is encountered. During performance, anxiety is often lessened, since the individual must concentrate on his own actions rather than on his internalized fears. Post-task anxiety may then abruptly rise as the individual seems to lower his defenses and admit his fear more freely. This rise in post-task anxiety has been reported by Basowitz et al.,[71] investigating paratrooper training (and termed "the end phenomenon"), as well as by Menninger[783] and others, investigating anxiety under wartime conditions. It has been noted, for example, that more breakdowns took place after a soldier was removed from the front lines and placed in the rear rest areas than occurred during actual combat.

Two other kinds of anxiety have been identified in several kinds of experimental and real-life situations. Subjects often differentiate between what has been termed *harm anxiety* and *failure anxiety*. In addition to fear of the actual conditions that may cause injury (harm anxiety), individuals may evidence equal or stronger anxiety concerning the fear that they might not "measure up" or would fail under the stressful conditions to which they are subjected. Caudill[183] has pointed out the importance of social pressures and the manner in which they contribute to stress and anxiety in considering the fear of failure, in addition to the real dangers in the situation.

High anxiety sometimes results in more activity on the part of the individual, but often this activity is pointless, inflexible, and rigid. Since anxiety operates to increase tension levels within the organism, as might be expected inefficient performance is the result in complicated tasks. It has even been found in studies by Brieson[132] and others that continued high anxiety will lead to physiological breakdown, measurable by nerve cell deterioration.

Still under investigation is the manner in which tension and anxiety interact to affect performance. Although earlier researchers suggested that anxiety and tension summate to affect performance, an investigation by Lovass[710] indicates that anxiety and muscular tension interact separately to affect performance. Fenz[348] has also obtained findings that suggest that anxiety and muscular tension are separate factors. Anxiety, Fenz concludes, involves a "deeper level of inhibition," whereas muscular tension is associated with overt activity.

The relationship of anxiety to performances of both a simple and complex nature has been demonstrated in studies of verbal and motor tasks. Matarazzo and Matarazzo[744] found that subjects scoring in the middle portions of an anxiety scale performed best on a small maze task, while those scoring at both extremes evidenced inferior performance. At times, heightened anxiety results in increased speed in simple conditioning tasks. However, as Matarazzo and Matarazzo[744] found in a maze problem and Taylor and Spence[1090] discovered when studying a verbal choice-point problem, more complex performance is adversely affected by anxiety. Additional evidence that complex tasks requiring fine coordinations or fine discriminations are impeded by higher levels of anxiety is provided by findings of Wechsler and Hartogs.[1163] These investigators found that individuals with high anxiety took significantly more time to learn a mirror drawing task than those with low anxiety. Of particular interest to these experimenters was the continual evidence of "graphomotor blocks," tense small strokes made in a small area, which was taken to indicate that the neuromuscular integration had broken down.

Farber and Spence,[345] studying complex motor learning involving a stylus maze task, also found that subjects with high anxiety were significantly retarded, particularly in areas of the maze containing difficult choice points. On the other hand, these experimenters found that these same subjects evidenced greater proficiency when their eyelid reflex was conditioned. It was concluded that the anxious and non-anxious groups differed primarily with respect to drive level, rather than to general learning ability. It was further suggested that the effect of variations in drive level on performance is a function of specific task characteristics.

Easterbrook[315] has proposed a theory that is closely aligned with much of the experimental data to explain relationships between performance and anxiety. He suggests that emotional arousal acts to reduce the range of cues that an individual can use, and that the reduction in cue utilization may either organize or disorganize performance, depending on the type of task considered. Initially, Easterbrook points out, the use of cues irrelevant to the task are eliminated, thus resulting in improved performance as initial levels of anxiety arousal are encountered. Later, as emotional arousal continues to rise, task-relevant cues become difficult to use, thus reducing performance levels.

Highly anxious individuals seem unable to adapt to novel situations. Their behavior is rigid and their integrative mechanisms, which permit efficient perceptual-motor control, seem to break down. This assumption is confirmed by the findings of Ausubel, Schiff, and Goldman,[48] who found that, although anxious and non-anxious subjects performed the same during the initial trial of a blindfolded maze task, on subsequent performances the highly anxious subjects were outdistanced. These researchers suggested that this was a lowering of the anxious subjects' "improvising ability" as the task progressed.

Anxiety, Induced Stress, and Performance

Numerous studies have been carried out to determine the effect of stressful events on the motor and verbal performance of subjects with high and with low anxiety. Lucas,[712] producing stress by a fear of failure, found that highly anxious subjects performed more poorly than did non-anxious individuals when learning a verbal task. High anxiety, coupled with an increase in motivation due to instruction, also was found, by Sarason and Palola,[963] to impede performance in arithmetic and code-substitution tasks.

Baker[60] presented findings, in a doctoral study, that illustrate the effect of stress on high- and low-anxiety performers of a task involving gross motor activity. The subjects were required to place their feet in a pattern drawn on a rapidly moving treadmill, much as a small girl would play hopscotch but involving more complex movements. The stress was an electric shock applied to the leg. It was found that significantly more errors were recorded by high-anxiety subjects (as measured on Taylor's scale) than were recorded by low-anxiety subjects under the same conditions. The base performances of the two groups without shock, however, were not significantly different.

Experimental work by Kempe[612] has suggested that individuals can be differentiated according to the habitual manner in which they react to stress. On the one hand are people who tend to respond to stress with a general increase in muscular tension, who seem to remain aloof from social convention and can intellectualize quite easily. On the other hand are individuals who act by way of the autonomic nervous system. People in the second classification are emotionally sensitive, worry a great deal, and have fears of not being accepted by others.

Stress is more disturbing to the performance levels of individuals who are highly anxious; at times, however, performances of these persons cannot be distinguished from those of the more tranquil subject until a stressor has been introduced into the situation. The effect of anxiety level on performance, therefore, is a function of the amount of stress perceived by the performer, his habitual manner of reacting to stress, and the complexity of the task.

Anxiety in Sport

Both clinical and experimental psychologists, as well as psychiatrists around the world, have recently begun to study relationships between anxiety and athletic performance. According to the literature, some fears found among athletes are: (1) fear of success (success phobia), (2) fear of failure, (3) fear of crowds, (4) fear of expressing their aggressions, and (5) fear of physical harm to their bodies.

Clinicians, working directly with athletic teams, have employed a number of strategies in order to reduce anxiety levels among high level competitors, including desensitization training, relaxation training, removing the threat of competition, removing anxious performers and/or coaches from each other's presence, helping the athlete come to terms with the positive signs that often accompany activation prior to competition, and long-term psychotherapy or psychoanalysis.

Athletes are essentially men under stress so that highly anxious individuals in the community of sportsmen are likely to have trouble adjusting to the demands of international competition. More detailed discussions of anxiety in athletes and ways of dealing with this problem are found in a recent text by Cratty,[258b] as well as one by Vanek and Cratty.[1130]

The Nature of Stress

Stress may be defined as a temporarily induced physiological or psychological imbalance, caused by an event the organism considers threatening. More specifically, several different approaches that place the concept of stress in a framework of total human functioning have been employed. In 1964, Cofer and Appley[203] presented what they believed to be important concomitants of stress, which they envision as a "state of the organism." These included: (1) stress is more extreme than the usual motivated state; (2) a threat must be perceived by the individual; (3) stress involves an interaction between the individual and his environment; and (4) the individual cannot cope with the situation in a normal manner.

Selye,[987] physician and biochemist, has proposed a general stress theory, based on research carried out over a period of 30 years. He observed that several kinds of bodily conditions were consistently present when various types of diseases or infections were diagnosed. He thus "bound these loose logs together" (observed facts), related them to solid supports (classical medicine), and evolved a general theory of stress, reported in 1956 in *The Stress of Life*. The basis of this theory involves the identification of a General Adaptation Syndrome (GAS), related to the nonspecific adaptation of the body to general impingement or to disruptive events. GAS is evidenced spatially, it is suggested, in adrenal, pituitary, and thymus gland activity by the mobilization of white blood corpuscles, as well as in internal visceral activity. Temporally, adaptation is believed to be divisible into the alarm stage, the resistance stage, and the exhaustion stage.

According to Selye, stressors are any disease, infection or injury, but also might include fatigue, aging, thirst, pain, as well as frustration and threat. Thus the theory is a broad one from which philosophical implications are derived concerning the manner in which one may optimally conduct his life.

Although earlier research often describes stress as a particular kind of event or situation that is likely to produce fear or task inefficiency, later investigation considers stress as an intervening stage between the situation and the performance. This is occasioned by the observation that individuals differ markedly in their reactions to a given stressful situation. An occurrence producing stress in one individual often has no measurable effect on a second. It has also been observed that reactions to stressors take different forms. For example, a person may evidence marked physiological changes of various kinds, but have no marked performance fluctuations. Others may undergo perceptual distortion, while seeming to perform well and perhaps showing no measurable physiological changes.

Thus the measurement of stress and the definition of the term are intimately related to other intervening variables such as motivation, drive, and fear. For example, under sufficient motivation, an individual often performs well under stress, but if the motivation level is reduced marked performance breakdown occurs. Martens[740] and others have considered the term *stress* synonymous with state anxiety.

Stress will be considered in the present discussion, therefore, as a performance affector lying between the event and performance (as suggested by Lazarus, Deese, and Olser[667] in their 1952 synthesis of the research on stress and performance). To facilitate the study of the stress variable, consideration will be given to the type of stressor and the manner in which performance is affected under stressful conditions. The term *stressor* will be used to indicate the event, activity, or impingement on the organism that produces stress.

The Measurement of Stress

Stress has been measured through the evaluation of various physiological functions, including cardiovascular measures and respiration, as well as finite biochemical changes resulting from hormonal activity. In addition, it has been evaluated by noting disturbances in perceptual organization and motor performance. Another measure of stress has been obtained by polling the subject directly about his level of concern during the application of a stressor, his ability to continue to perform under stressful conditions, and/or his feelings about an imminent stressor.

Generally, the measures selected are determined by the definition applied to the term *stress*. For example, if stress is considered to be a general reaction to events that disrupt normal homeostasis, then a wide range of measures is employed. If stress is considered to depend on specific kinds of situations, then fewer measures have been used.

Physiological Measures of Stress. Physiologically, the measures may be divided into those indicating that the body is preparing for some kind of action and those implying that normal functioning is temporarily suspended so that the organism can concentrate on meeting the interpreted threat. Most investigations utilize several kinds of measures, combining performance and psychological and physiological measures in order to obtain a comprehensive picture of the stress reaction. Examples are the studies by Funkenstein et al.,[398] Basowitz et al.,[71] and Wolf et al.[1218]

Investigations concerned primarily with biologic determinants of stress are too numerous to survey thoroughly in this text. Thus, in the pages which follow, only a sampling of the types of measures used in recent years is presented.

Several researchers have suggested that secretions of the adrenal gland and changes in the presence of the various kinds of blood cells indicate that stress is present. Particular interest has been paid to the production of eosinophiles. Ulrich[1118] used this latter measure to evaluate stress levels before and after physical performance stressors were introduced.

Blood pressure and respiration changes are other measures frequently used. Wolf et al.,[1218] in an extensive study of the effect of stressful life events introduced into an interview situation, used blood pressure change as a stress measure. Hellweg,[513] studying stress before both examinations and physical contests, utilized respiration as one of her measures.

Mirskey and Stein[804] suggest that the presence of antidiuretic hormones secreted in the thalamus are reliable and valid indices of stress. This measure is an example of one indicating that the usual bodily processes are being halted momentarily so that energies can be focused on the implied threat.

Basowitz et al.[71] based a rather extensive study of paratroop training stresses on the hypothesis that hippuric acid secreted by the liver constituted a valid measure of stress. Although his hypothesis was not verified, several measures and the strict controls under which the investigation was carried out contributed much valuable information. Basowitz found that the most predictive factors in differentiating potential paratroopers from those who might fail the training were the self-ratings of harm anxiety, while ratings of *failure anxiety* were not found to be highly predictive of success in training.

Selye suggested that pituitary secretion, which activates the adrenocortical hormone, ACTH, to produce a compound labeled F that, in turn, feeds back to the pituitary and decreases its activity, is a valid index of stress. Selye also pointed out that stress is accompanied by a decrease in rhythmic stomach movement, causing indigestion.

Increased palmar perspiration is often taken as a valid and reliable sign of stress. This is usually measured by collecting perspiration in a hand sponge and noting the volume. The study by Hellweg[513] is an example of one using this device. The most common measure of increased palm perspiration is the galvanic skin response (GSR). The GSR, used as early as 1915, measures differences in electrical resistance of the skin as the result of increased perspiration during stressful conditions. Through the use of two small electrodes applied to the hands, it provides a sensitive, although at times unreliable, measure of stress. It has been suggested, however, that this increased sweating of the palms is caused by the need to increase the efficiency of the grip, much as could be accomplished by spitting on the hands before grasping an axe handle. This assumption, however, lacks experimental verification.

Many other physiological measures have been utilized to measure stress, including skin temperature, pupil dilation, and salivary secretion. A dermographic measure often used is obtained by stroking the skin with a rounded instrument and recording the time between the whitening of the skin and the return of the normal pink color to the area affected. Analyses of urine and of blood and measurement of metabolic rate, muscular tremor, eyelid blink rate, and muscular action potential have also been used as stress indicators.

Perceptual Disturbance.   Several kinds of perceptual tests have been used in the study of stress. In general it is assumed, as Postman and Bruner[902] stated, that perceptual behavior is disrupted and becomes less accurate under stress than under normal conditions. The two perceptual measures most often found to be helpful are tests of closure and tests involving the ability to reproduce quickly presented geometric designs. It is assumed that individuals under stress are not as sensitive to quickly presented incomplete circles and produce more inaccurate figures (or may prove unable to draw anything) when presented with complex designs contained in the Bender-Gestalt test.

Direct Poll. In some investigations, less complex psychological measures have been utilized to evaluate stress. Basowitz et al.[71] and Eriksen et al.[333] simply polled subjects concerning the level of stress they were experiencing, or the level of performance they expected of themselves under prolonged stress. Eriksen concluded that "asking them" was the best way to predict individual performance under stress following the administration of psychological measures of personality, general adjustment inventories, and a group Rorschach test.

Performance Measures. Various verbal and motor performance measures have been used as sole indicators of stress. The assumption usually advanced is that stress is indicated by a disruption of complex verbal, mental, or motor activity. Basowitz et al.[71] used an arithmetic task that involved subtracting rapidly by three's from a large base number. The problem with these measures, of course, is that it is difficult to separate learning effects from changes caused by stressors. Castaneda and Palmero[180] and Benton and Whythe[88] base their measures of stress entirely on motor performance scores. Benton used a manipulation task, and Castaneda found that manipulation of a switch to light cues was stressful when changes in the task were introduced. Parson et al.[873] employed a hand steadiness test as a stress measure.

Changes in Muscular Tension. Various changes in muscular tension also have been utilized as stress measures. Studies by Wenger,[1180] Davis,[284] and Nidever[847] are examples. In general, these measures are more exact than the biochemical and/or psychological tests cited above. A more detailed review of these measures and of their relationship to various kinds of performance is found in the section concerned with tension and performance (p. 306).

Intercorrelations Among Measures of Stress. Although low correlations are usually found among various stress measures, a general fear pattern caused by autonomic nervous system functioning often is identified. In studies by Basowitz,[71] when a stressor was applied several times, vast individual differences were seen not only in the indices of stress measured when a large variety of tests were made, but also in the manner in which individuals adapted to stress. Holzman and Bitterman,[547] for example, found few meaningful relationships between perceptual, performance, and biochemical measures (urine analysis) after repeated administration of the stressor to the situation. Thus, there seems to be a difference in the manner in which individuals react and adjust to stressors, and the search for the most reliable and valid indicator seems likely to continue.

Stressors of Life and of the Laboratory. A number of kinds of stressors have been studied with respect to their influence on performance. The two broadest categories include stressors present in real-life situations and those experimentally induced. In addition, obviously disturbed individuals have been selected for study in the attempt to determine the kinds of stressors that caused the anxieties.

Various life situations have been studied relative to the production of stress, and several texts have been concerned with stressors operative in the "average" civilian community. Among these are *The Split Level Trap*[456] and Menninger's *Psychiatry in a Troubled World.*[783] These are clinical descriptions of the manner in which many aspects of daily living, such as raising children, attempting to succeed in business, and growing up, prove to be individual and group stressors.

Other experimental studies have been concerned with life stressors, but in more narrow confines. Funkenstein et al.,[398] for example, studied 125 Harvard students for a number of years, introducing several kinds of laboratory stress situations.

Many of these studies are concerned with participation in various kinds of training and with conditions which involve the continued application of stressors in wartime. Among these studies are *Men Under Stress*[466] by two World War II psychiatrists, *Patterns of Performance* by Ginzberg et al.,[435] and *War Stress and Neurotic Illness* by Kardiner and Spiegle.[603] The authors of these books arrive at some of the same conclusions regarding the performance and behavior of men placed under continual stressors, i.e., imminent annihilation.

The effect of war stressors seems to culminate in nervousness, fatigue becomes a problem, and neuromuscular control lessens in the simplest of tasks. Additional problems result when closely knit combat units suffer casualties and buddies are seen to die. These authors also mention that not only were the men fearful of direct physical harm, but also were "afraid of being afraid," of not measuring up as men and thus of "losing face" with their peers. In a 1965 essay, Welford[1175] documented the manner in which humans in wartime conditions and under other circumstances tend to break down when placed under continual stress.

Findings such as those discussed emphasize the importance of studying stress in a total life situation, rather than only in the laboratory. Basowitz et al.[71] write of the importance of examining stressful events in a total field of experience, since "Stress is an experience which cannot be defined independently of the life situation and the response to it." Caudill[183] also advocates the study of stress as a total action picture, involving individual physiological measures and small group interactions in close proximity to the individual, as well as consideration of cultural pressures.

Laboratory Stressors.   Stressors range from general and continual stressful situations of varying magnitudes, involving the close grouping of a number of stressful events, to situations in which stressful events occur rather infrequently. These latter circumstances are more compatible for study in the research laboratory. Numerous investigations have been carried out in recent years to determine the effect of various discrete kinds of stressors in controlled environments.

Four kinds of stressors are imposed on the human subjects in the research laboratory. The one used most often involves the introduction of various kinds of distractions, such as loud noises and electric shocks, and then studying their effect on the performance of various perceptual-motor tasks. One of the most interesting of these was the sonic-confuser used by Funkenstein et al.[398] This test involves the delayed feedback of one's own voice while speaking, which results in thoroughly confusing the subject's reactions. Various perceptual-motor and/or biologic measures are taken before, during, and after such sensory distractions are introduced.

A second main type of laboratory stressor involves the implication of task failure. This is accomplished in several ways: informing the subject that he is not performing up to required norms, presenting him with a task impossible to solve under highly motivated circumstances, or interrupting him before he can possibly finish. An example of a research program in which the failure stress was used extensively was carried out during World War II during the training of agents for the Office of Strategic Services. Since it was hypothesized that these trainees would later be subjected to real-life stress when operating behind enemy lines, every effort was made to determine and to predict how their performance might hold up under stressful situations.

As reported in *The Assessment of Men*,[865] the program included bridge-building tasks and other individual and group endeavors which were at times insolvable. Numerous times the trainees were informed that they had failed the training program and were asked to reveal their real names (they were given "cover" identities during their training). Although the data collected from such situations were highly subjective, this program contributed materially to the understanding of men's performance under stressful conditions.

A third method of creating stressful situations in a laboratory is to introduce a real-life stress during an interview and then to determine various physiological reactions. This method was utilized by Wolf et al.[1218] when studying hypertension. Individuals suffering from marked hypertension were interviewed in detail to determine the nature and cause of their disturbance, i.e., what in their lives had probably caused them to become tense and susceptible to stressors. After this was determined, a second interview situation was set up and the subject was prepared so that various cardiovascular measures could be obtained. After a period of relatively innocuous give-and-take between the subject and the investigator, a question relating to the stressful life event was suddenly introduced (e.g., "How is your alcoholic husband?").

The marked cardiovascular changes produced when such a stressor was introduced suggested that hypertension can be caused by situational disturbances in the total life pattern. It was also noted by these experimenters that the blood pressure changes were most marked when the individual seemed to need to express hostile aggressive behavior, but the expression was suppressed by an equally strong need to remain calm. As will be noted in the following pages, activity has been suggested not only as producing stress but as alleviating stress in the individual. It is suggested here that a blocking of activity proves stressful, and other experiments suggest that mild activity relieves internal stress.

Environmental Stress. Another kind of stress frequently studied involves the production of rather long-term environmental changes and may involve a sustained exposure to heat, cold, weightlessness, disorienting movements, and the like. Most of these studies, of course, involve the ability of the body to perform well while under conditions that might be met in a military situation or in space flight. In other testing programs, however, an environment simulating industrial work conditions has been reproduced, and the effects of such sustained stressors as heat and noise have been related to performance measures.

Illustrative of hundreds of investigations of environmental stress is the study by Brozek and Taylor.[143] Various motor tests, including two of strength, three of speed, and one of "coordination," were administered under five kinds of environmental stressors: acute starvation, semi-starvation, deprivation of sleep, heat stress, and hard physical work. Brozek and Taylor found that motor performance was more susceptible to deterioration under stress than sensory and intellectual functioning. Of the motor tests administered, however, only the reaction time measure showed significant change under all five stressors. Strength showed the greatest decrement under semi-starvation, whereas speed of tapping and speed of hand and arm movements exhibited greatest deterioration in acute starvation combined with hard work. In conclusion, the authors suggested that, rather than using one type of task, a battery of motor tests plus physiological indices best measure deterioration under stress.[143]

Although these and similar studies have contributed to general knowledge in this area, an extensive review of environmental stress research will not be undertaken, since the focus of the book is on individuals moving in reasonably normal environments. The reader is directed to summaries by Macworth[725] and others for further information.

Several problems loom large when attempting to assess the effectiveness of induced stressors in the laboratory situation. Initially, the assumption must be made that the induced stressor is as upsetting to the subject as it would be to the experimenter, and such is not always the case. For example, the subject's motivations and his past experience with similar distractions and/or tasks influence his reactions. In addition, great individual differences in psychological and physiological reactions to stress have been recorded.

One of the primary problems, when studying stress-performance relationships, involves cultural variables. As Funkenstein et al. point out:

> The judgment as to what are mature or immature stress reactions depends to a large extent upon the values and expectations imposed by the cultural or sub-cultural system . . . for it must be remembered that man is a member of society and a bearer of culture and that stress reactions of man outside this context could not be completely understood.[398]

The Effect of Stress on Performance

Many stressor-performance relationships have been investigated. Essentially they have included the pairing of the kinds of stressors mentioned previously to various kinds of perceptual, motor, and verbal functioning.

Mental Performance

Although the focus of this book is on movement behavior, some of the initial principles of the stress-performance relationship can be illustrated by considering various kinds of verbal tasks. The introduction of failure stress into a verbal learning situation usually causes a deterioration of performance.

In a failure-stress experiment involving the learning of nonsense syllables, Sullivan[1077] found that, although success produced the most rapid learning, failure was more harmful for an intellectually superior group than for an intellectually inferior group. The reverse of this is suggested in findings of research relating muscular tension to motor performance. Increased tension was found to facilitate the poor performers but to inhibit the better performers, who were assumed to be operating at or near their optimal levels of tension.

In an unusual study by Beam[79] in 1955, involving simple conditioning and verbal learning tasks participated in just prior to three stressful situations, it was found again that stressors facilitate a simple conditioning task but impair more complex verbal ones. The stressful situations included doctoral examinations, taking part in a dramatic production before a large audience, and giving an oral report in partial fulfillment of a course requirement.

Perceptual-Motor Performance

The results of investigations of the effect of stressors on perceptual-motor performance are similar to those involving verbal-motor performance tasks. In general, impairment is caused by either failure stress or situationally induced stressors when performing complex tasks. With simple motor acts, reaction time, movement time, and the like, the reverse seems true. Howell,[557] for example, found that time to move (including a summation of reaction time and movement time) was markedly improved when an electric shock was introduced.

Parsons, Phillips, and Lane,[873] on the other hand, found that muscular steadiness was retarded when a stress was introduced. McClelland and Apicella,[756] using a card-sorting task, also found that failure stress produced less efficient performance in a complex task.

A further problem, only superficially investigated, is whether stress reactions prior to physical exertion are similar to those prior to mental application. Confirmation of a generally stressful state regardless of the activity prepared for is shown in the findings of Hellweg.[513] It was found, however, that stress measured before physical activity (a game) resulted in higher blood pressure measures than stress measured before an examination. This might be taken as an indication that the organism seems to prepare itself for the specific type of task in which it believes it will ultimately take part.

Stress and Motor Learning

The effect of stressors on motor learning is a more complex problem, and various influences have been demonstrated during different portions of the learning process. Castaneda[179] points out that when stress was introduced a decreasing tendency to increase errors in a visual-motor task was noted. This was taken to indicate that a stress-adaptation factor was operative during learning. An investigation by Michael,[792] using a physiological measure of stress, also suggested that exercise can facilitate stress adaptation.

In general, however, various stress measures, when studied longitudinally, indicate that adaptability to stress depends on the situation and the personality of the individual. Holtzman and Bitterman[547] concluded, following a factorial study, that few positive relationships existed between various stress measures, including perceptual tests, urine analyses, and galvanic skin response. Parson, Phillips, and Lane,[873] hypothesizing the existence of a general stress-adaptation factor, were disappointed to find no significant correlations between circulating blood constituents, which were believed to be indicative of stress, and performance. They suggested that other psychological factors were important.

Basowitz et al.[71] also found that no significant correlations existed between performance tests, perceptual tests, physiological indices, clinical ratings, and other personal information. Funkenstein et al.[398] suggested that the various physiological patterns obtained in the data indicated that stress patterns were related to specific shifts in subjects' emotions (e.g., anger at the task or at the experimenter), rather than to the task itself.

Group Learning, Performance, and Stress

One of the most promising new directions in the study of the effect of stress on learning behavior has been outlined by Caudill.[183] This anthropologist suggests that stress may be considered only in a total individual-group context through examining group feelings about bereavement, injury, and the like. Substantiating his argument, Caudill reviews research that indicates that individuals in close physical and psychological proximity often evidence similar kinds of internal physiological reactions to stress. Quoting from a study by Watson and Kanter, Caudill[183] presents findings indicating that changes in the heart rate of the analyst and the patient are similar when various kinds of stress occur during the interviews. Such emotions as anxiety, hostility, and depression, with the expected blood pressure changes of the patient, were reflected in similar, but less marked, blood pressure changes of the therapist.

More directly related to the focus of the text is the study by Hill et al.[539] concerning the stress relationship evidenced by members of athletic teams working in close physical proximity and performing a similar movement pattern. It was found that, when comparing the reactions to stress by two Harvard crews with the use of an eosinophile count, the team that was noted to "swing together" evidenced less variability in this stress measure than did the crew that was not as successful. In another study with Harvard crews, Renold[916] found that, although individual differences existed, there were characteristic patterns in the level of blood eosinophiles in the crew, the coxswain, and the coach during and when preparing for the traditional race with Yale. Caudill suggested that such research might be extended to determine whether physiological responses among team members in sports such as football and basketball, in which individual roles are more differentiated, are also related.

11

Thus, the evaluation of the effect of stress on motor activity requires an exact definition of the type of activity, simple or complex, the nature of the stress measure utilized, the stage of learning, and the motivational level of the subject.

Fuchs[394] has recently presented an explanation for the effects of stress on motor performance which seems worthy of consideration. Initially, it is contended, human learning under normal conditions becomes progressively dependent on more complex servo systems in the nervous system, as increasingly subtle cues are attended to. However, with the introduction of some stress, a retrogression occurs; tension, which accompanied initial attemps to learn, returns, and the more finite aspects of the situation again become lost to the learner.

Tension and Performance

The close relationship between levels of muscular tension and motor performance involving simple and complex movements is obvious. However, the exact manner in which tension affects motor performance and learning is not always as is expected. It is obvious that, for movement to occur, a minimal level of muscular tension must be present. Indeed, research findings suggest that, if subjects are trained to relax completely, no work is possible, and in addition they seem unable even to engage in imaginative pursuits.

Various theories concerning the relationship of muscular tension to general psychological processes have been advanced. Initially, a "peripheral" theory was suggested by Davis,[285] which held that any changes in tension patterns were intimately related to psychological processes.

Meyer and Noble[790] advance one of the most comprehensive explanations involving the role of muscular tension and the manner in which it affects mental and motor performance. They hold that impulses from tension converge on motor patterns and interact with the responses, and further suggest that the effect of tension on performance depends on the amount of tension, the proximity of the tension to the performing limb, and the stage of practice during which the tension is induced.

There is an increasing amount of evidence that points to the existence of what has been termed *general muscular tension*. Goldstein[443] suggests that individuals may be ranged on a continuum from those who are relaxed to those who habitually exhibit an amount of muscular tension in excess of that needed to perform life's activities. The extensive review of the research in this area by Duffy[305] also brought this authoress to the conclusion that although tension is many times manifested in specific ways, and has specific influences on various facets of behavior, "there appears to be both some degree of 'generality' and some degree of 'specificity' in activation . . . activation is an organismic phenomenon, and it is recognized as such when we speak of an individual being relaxed or being excited, rather than of a particular system's showing this condition."[305,383]

The Measurement of Tension

Muscular tension may be requested by the experimenter of his subject, e.g., "keep your limb and/or body tense as you perform." But more precisely, it may be induced into the situation by subjecting the subject to a stressor. McTeer[774] and numerous other experimenters found that an increase in muscular tension was the immediate result of the administration of an electric shock. In addition, muscular tension may be introduced by placing an increased work load on the subject as he attempts to perform a motor task. Studies carried out during the 1920's and 1930's induced tension with this method. Muscular tension also may be increased by having the subject squeeze hand dynamometers or handle a given number of pounds of pressure or by having the subject maintain pressure on a hand pulley or a foot pedal.

From a review of the literature, Davis[285] suggests several ways in which tension levels have been measured. These included the measurement of pressure changes in the grip of various performing instruments (e.g., the handles of stylus mazes as in Stroud's experiment[1073]) or from the work or force with which subjects strike the keys of a typewriter or other type of experimental response key. More recently, the magnitude of electric impulses produced by muscular action itself, as measured by the electromyograph, has been used to determine tension levels. Computed in microvolts, it is generally assumed that the level of electric output of the muscle is a direct measure of the tension present. In addition, Davis[285] points out that tension has been measured by determining the resistance to movements offered by a limb or muscle, by recording slight movements of body parts, by recording electric properties of the skin, and by determining the magnitude of the stretch reflex of the knee.

Wenger,[1180] in an attempt to determine what constituted muscular tension, compared individual subjective ratings of children in respect to the levels of tension they evidenced. It was found that these judgments were reliable. This experimenter then attempted to determine what kinds of physiological variables correlated with the observational ratings. Galvanic skin response, respiration, diastolic pressure, and dermographic latency combined to produce a score that seemed to be most predictive of muscular tension.

Nidever,[847] a student of Wenger, combined some of these same measures to determine whether a general factor of muscular tension existed. He found that in 19 of the 23 muscle groups tested such a general factor did emerge. Age, body build, and the time of day the measurements were taken were also found to be important variables. This researcher found that mental work implied concomitant physical work, insofar as increased tension was found to occur in the frontalis muscles during a serial verbal learning task. Eason[313] found that the neck muscles seemed the best indices of general muscular tension.

Freeman,[382] in research carried out in 1933, found that individual differences affected muscular tension. It was found, for example, that increased tension more adversely affected the performance of younger subjects than of older subjects.

It appears that the measurement of muscular tension may be accomplished by several means. Although a general muscular tension factor does seem to exist, most of the investigations reviewed involve direct measures of the load of a secondary task (induced tension), the reaction to shock stressor, and the like. The measurement of electric output of a muscle or group of muscles has been undertaken experimentally only since World War II.

The Effect of Tension on Performance

In general, the findings presented for stress and anxiety hold true for induced tension. Bills[99] carried out the pioneer work on this topic.

Mental Performance. Mental tasks, if not difficult, usually are facilitated with induced tension. Bills[99] found that tension produced in his subjects by having them squeeze hand dynamometers in both hands benefited the learning of tasks involving paired association learning and nonsense syllables, memorizing and adding columns of digits, and reciting scrambled letters. Zartmen and Cason,[1237] on the other hand, found that solving complete arithmetic problems was not facilitated by having subjects keep a foot on a resisting pedal.

Freeman[383] studied both mental and motor tasks and found that tension load, which is optimal for one type of activity, may be detrimental to another. He also suggested that the more complex the performance, the more likely it is that a tension increment will inhibit efficient performance. Freeman also suggested that theoretically it should be possible to determine the optimal tension loads for various kinds of tasks.

Bourne,[122] studying the effect of tension produced by squeezing a hand dynamometer, also found that, while tension affected performance in a paired word task, retention of these same words was not affected. Meyer and other researchers[790] have confirmed the fact that, although tension seems to affect momentary performance, the integrative processes leading to retention (i.e., learning) seem less, if at all, affected.

Visual Perception and Muscular Tension

Numerous studies have attested to the influence of changes in muscular tension on visual activity. Dowling[300] found that motor activity (pushing and pulling a desk drawer) facilitated visual recognition. Similarly, Smock[1033] found that moderate grip tension maintained at three-eighths to five-eighths of maximum, produced the best scores on a task involving the quick recognition of briefly viewed shapes. Proprioceptive return from the muscles perhaps heightens general activation level which translates into changes in a number of kinds of behavior. Weybrew[1188] found that moderate grip tension caused a reduction in perceived length of time. Thus muscular tension seems related in a number of ways to the total sensorium.

The Effects of Induced Tension on Tension

Hellenbrandt[512a] and her student, Joan Waterland,[1153] have engaged in an interesting series of studies in which they proposed to examine the effect of prolonged efforts of maximum strength on involuntary patterns of muscular tension manifested concomitantly. In order to examine this phenomenon, thousands of photographs were taken of subjects exerting all-out effort on a wrist ergograph. As tension was maintained, the following observations were made: (1) there seemed to be an orderly expansion of involuntary motor responses which varied from subject to subject, but evidenced intra-individual consistency; (2) various reflexive patternings were seen—for example, the tonic neck reflex was elicited as the subjects usually inclined their heads toward the side on which the arm-flexion movement was being made; (3) the involuntary stress pattern of muscular contractions spread in an orderly fashion as voluntary tension was maintained, and was "immune to remodeling."

These researchers concluded that these involuntary muscular contractions indicate the body's reaction to exercise stress when voluntary control dissipates ("cortical noise" is minimal or absent). These involuntary flexions, extensions and grimaces are the result of the recruitment of reserve motor units under stress, and this recruitment proceeds in an orderly and expansive pattern in each individual. The findings of these investigations portray vividly the manner in which excess tension can facilitate and at times interfere with voluntary movement patterns. The photographs depict the manner in which specifically introduced tensions may "overflow" and affect a number of voluntary and involuntary movement patterns in portions of the body far removed from the source of the original effort.

Tension and Motor Performance. Numerous investigations have been devoted to the study of the influence of induced tension on motor performance. In general, the findings parallel those of verbal-tension comparisons. Some tasks, usually the less complex, have been facilitated by tension, but others, the more complex, are usually inhibited.

Consideration of the effect of tension on performance involves two auxiliary considerations. Freeman found that the relationship of the limb in which tension is produced to the performing member is important. The nearer the produced tension is to the performing hand, for example, the more such tension affects performance.[253] Courts[222] suggested that there are two kinds of tension: one reflecting effort and a second reflecting emotional upset. Although it is suggested that the effort tension facilitates performance while emotional tension inhibits it, little experimental work separating the two phenomena suggested by Courts has been undertaken.

The earlier studies used rather inexact means for determining and/or inducing muscular tension. But, in general, they were predictive of the findings of more recent investigations in which more sophisticated measuring devices were utilized. Duffy,[307] for example, used subjective ratings of the tension observed in children and concluded that tense children evidenced awkwardness in their movements, were weaker in a hand dynamometer test, and indicated less ability in a perceptual test involving the tracing of figures. In addition, Duffy observed that the tense youngsters showed less tendency to engage in direct physical contact with the other children, although their social contacts did not seem to be inhibited.

In 1932, Russell[949] used as a variable the experimenter's request to subjects "to tense," "to remain as normal," or "to consciously relax the body" when throwing a tennis ball for accuracy. He found that the normals threw best, the individuals who had been requested to relax were next, and as might be expected, the most inaccurate throwers were those who had been requested to keep their bodies tense. The validity of Russell's findings might be questioned, however, even if his manner of inducing tension is ignored, for Freeman[382] suggests that individuals trained to tense or to relax their bodies show benefits from such training in subsequent trials. It has been noted that induced tension has aided simple maze learning, the amplitude of the knee-jerk is greater, and finger-tapping rate is also improved. On the other hand, more complex performances, including mirror-tracing and the like, are often inhibited by an increase in tension levels.

Although it has been proposed that motor performance follows a U-shaped curve with regard to degrees of muscular tension induced (maximum performance, reaction time, and movement speed are elicited at the intermediate levels of tension), in a recent review Marten suggests that the available evidence does not support such a straightforward hypothesis between tension-arousal and motor performance. The data from studies by Marteniuk[737] indicate that, although reaction time followed the hypothesized trend (smallest at intermediate levels of pretask tension), movement time followed a linear relationship to induce tension. That is, the faster movement times were recorded when preliminary muscular tension was increased from zero to 5 through 10, 15, and 20 pounds. In 1969, Berger and Mathus[91] also found that a prerelaxed condition permitted greater velocities to be imparted to a weight-lifting task than when the muscles were pretensed just prior to performing the task.

Tension and Motor Learning. Stroud,[1073] one of the initial investigators to measure tension changes during the learning of a motor task, used the downward pressure his subjects exerted on a stylus in a maze problem as the tension score. He found that more tension occurred as the subject learned the more difficult portions of the maze, containing numerous cul-de-sacs, than was recorded when he traversed the easier portions of the pathway. He also noted that tension decreased as learning progressed, with the exception of an "end spurt" during the last trials. The subjects were informed that they had to complete three perfect trials to finish the experiment successfully. Therefore, as might be expected, tension levels rose during the final three trials, particularly the last one. Stroud also found that, when additional tension was added by requiring the subject to hold a pulley weight with the nonperforming hand, more tension also was evidenced in stylus pressure. Stroud explained his findings by using the concept of facilitation and hypothesized that the nerve impulses having different sensory origins summated to aid in the production of a response.

Daniel,[278] using action potential as a tension measure, obtained findings paralleling those of Stroud; as learning progressed, tension decreased. He also reported that a slight increase in action potential was noted just prior to the completion of the maze problem. Daniel also found that decreased tension was associated with error elimination, while increased tension produced greater speed. In general, when measured by action potential, tension levels were greater, the closer they were recorded to the performing hand.

Ghisseli[424] also found that as the individual learned a visual-motor task, tension tended to decrease. The tension measure used in this investigation was the pressure exerted on keys that were struck in response to light cues. Ghisseli did not find that an end spurt occurred, indicating a rise in tension level, since his directions omitted mention of a requirement involving the learning of the task to a given criterion. It has also been found that at times skill may improve with tension remaining constant. Eason[314] found that improvement in performance was recorded on a tracking task while muscular tension, measured in the neck muscles, remained the same.

Pretask Tension. Several investigators have studied levels of tension occurring in the period prior to task performance. It has been shown by Davis[286] that tension during this "set" period is usually gradually increased if the period is relatively short. If the fore-period is extended, however, the tension level often falls, suggesting that there is an optimal length of time prior to motor task performance during which an individual can prepare himself to best advantage. To cite an example, in Japan the referee of a Sumo wrestling match must decide when both contestants are in psychological resonance (called *ki ga au*) before starting the match. It is suggested that he is attempting to determine when both performers are at their optimal levels of tension, or at least at equal levels when he starts the bout. At times, four or five starts are attempted before the bout is permitted to progress.

Seen frequently in gymnastics, weightlifting contests, and track and field meets are athletes who attempt to raise their tension levels to the optimum prior to performance by pacing back and forth or by similar activities. A high tension level at the end of the fore-period results in shorter reaction time, according to Davis. When the fore-period was varied so that the performer was not certain when the task was to begin, reaction time was affected adversely. Davis suggested that the effect of tension plus glandular activity combined to influence pre-set conditions.

Theories Relating Performance to Tension

Several hypotheses have been advanced to explain tension-performance-learning relationships. Some investigators suggest that the constancy of kinesthetic stimuli as the result of tension raises the level of excitement in all muscle groups through cortex action. This heightened excitation level, which brings about a general readiness to act, results in increased speed and accuracy of performance.

Freeman,[380] on the other hand, first proposed that muscular tension levels, when increased, lower the threshold of excitability in the higher nervous centers, and, as a result, accurate complex performance may be inhibited. More recent investigations by Pinneo[899] and Kempe[612] point more clearly to the relationships between muscular tension and more basic neurological and physiological measures. Pinneo found that induced tension of the muscles with a hand dynamometer resulted in widespread changes in various indices of activation including heart rate, respiration rate, palmar conductance, frontal and occipital EEG, and EMG readings from passive limbs. Pinneo concluded that "proprioceptive return from induced muscular tension produces generalized behavioral and physiological effects in the reticular activating system." It thus seems that the relation of tension to total behavior is a function of the amount of tension induced, the unique characteristics of the nervous system of the individual, and the locale in which such tension occurs.

Relaxation and Performance

If there is an optimal tension level for a specific task, as the literature indicates, the present discussion would be incomplete without a brief reference to the role of *relaxation* and its relationship to performance. Several writers have presented programs for producing relaxation and for alleviating tension through various mystical or pseudoscientific approaches to mind-body problems. For example, one writer presents suggestions about the alleviation of tension that involve "transplanting the mind" to tension-free thoughts.

A widely accepted method for promoting relaxation was advanced in 1938 by Jacobson[576] and described in his book *Progressive Relaxation*. It embodies a principle of nervous re-education (learning to relax the total body) based on acquiring a heightened kinesthetic awareness of tension in specific muscle groups. Jacobson's method is concerned with dispelling *residual tension,* which is defined as the excess tension exhibited as an individual reclines on a couch and based on external signs and manipulative tests. Residual tension, he hypothesized, consists of "fine tonic contraction along with slight movements or reflexes." The underlying principle of the Jacobson method, therefore, is to heighten the self-awareness of tension so that the individual can more fully and efficiently relax. Thus, subjects are instructed first to tense various body parts fully, then to "let go" and relax. They are then asked to tense the same muscle group about half as much as they had done previously and then to relax again. Thus, it is hypothesized that, as the individual learns to induce tension progressively and to relax, he becomes able to recognize and to control minute amounts of tension in his body and to reduce residual tension to a minimum.

An unpublished study by Benson[87] in 1958 indicated that the application of the Jacobson method contributed positively to efficient total body movement. It was assumed that the ability to relax plays an important role in learning to swim and that training in relaxation would speed the learning process of beginning and intermediate swimmers. The swimmers who were given relaxation training progressed more rapidly than those who were not, and, although little improvement in swimming speed was noted between the control and experimental groups, the group trained to relax evidenced a generally lower tension level and a significant improvement in an arm stroke test. In addition, all the nonswimmers in the experimental group could swim at least 20 yards at the end of the testing period, while half of those in the control group could not.

Benson's study points out the continuous nature of the tension-relaxation continuum. Other, more recent studies also have supported the effectiveness of aiding individuals to perceive better their residual muscular tensions (relaxation training) on motor performance and skill learning. In 1971, Paben and Rosentsweigh[866] found that performing and learning a novel paddle ball task were facilitated most in subjects who were "taught how to relax."

Although numerous experimenters have been interested in the problem of inducing tension, relatively few have investigated the role of relaxation on gross human movement. It would seem that to move efficiently, or to promote efficient movement in others, one must clearly grasp the "optimal tension" principle, to be as proficient in producing increased tension in himself (or in others) as he is in achieving relaxation.

Summary

Anxiety appears to be a general fear or foreboding, a personality trait marked by a low threshold to stress. Stress is an internal reaction to a specific threatening situation. On the other hand, tension is overt muscular contraction caused by an emotional state or merely by increased effort.

The effect of anxiety and stressful situations on performance is a function of the task, of the general anxiety of the individual, and of prior practice in the task. In general, induced tension results in performance improvement in simple conditioning tasks and when an individual is performing at an inferior level in some more complex task. Stressful situations interfere with task performance of superior performers and in complex tasks.

It has been found that individuals interacting in close proximity often evidence similar kinds of internal reactions to stress. Exploratory research indicates that well-functioning athletic teams often are in accord physiologically, just as are the psychotherapist and his patient in the medical interview.

In general, it has been found that stress affects highly anxious subjects and disrupts both mental and motor performance. Stress is alleviated by moderate physical activity. General adaptability to stress is often evidenced, but with repeated stress a general anxiety state can be produced which may eventually lead to physiological breakdown. In addition, as the task is learned, tension levels decrease as the performer adjusts to the demands of the situation.

Student Reading

Basowitz, H., Persky, H., Korchin, S. J., and Granker, R. R.: *Anxiety and Stress, An Interdisciplinary Study of a Life Situation.* New York, McGraw-Hill Book Co., 1955.

Berger, R. A., and Mathus, D. L.: Movement time with various resistance loads as a function of pre-tensed and pre-relaxed muscular contractions. Res. Quart., *40*, 456–459, 1969.

Cattell, R. B.: The nature and measurement of anxiety. Sci. Amer., *226*, 225, 1963.

Caudill, W.: Effects of social and cultural systems in reactions to stress. New York, Social Sciences Research Council, June, 1958.

Cofer, C. N., and Appley, M. H.: *Motivation: Theory and Research.* New York, John Wiley & Sons, 1964.

Courts, F. A.: Relations between muscular tension and performance. Psychol. Bull., *32*, 347–367, 1942.

Cratty, B. J.: Attention, activation, and self-control. In *Human Behavior: Exploring Educational Processes.* Wolfe City, Texas, University Press, 1971.

Cratty, B. J.: Intellectual activity, activation, and self-control. In *Physical Expressions of Intelligence.* Englewood Cliffs, N.J., Prentice-Hall, Inc., 1972.

Cratty, B. J.: Anxiety. In *Psychology in Contemporary Sport.* Englewood Cliffs, N.J., Prentice-Hall, Inc., 1973, Chapter 11.

Easterbrook, J. A.: The effect of emotion on cue utilization and the organization of behavior. Psychol. Rev., *66*, 183–201, 1959.

Eysenck, H. L.: *The Dynamics of Anxiety and Hysteria.* London, Routledge and Kegan Paul, 1957.

Freeman, G. L.: The optimal muscular tensions for various performance. Amer. J. Psychol., *51*, 146–150, 1938.

Hammer, W. H.: A comparison of differences in manifest anxiety in university athletes and non-athletes. J. Sports Med., *7*, 31–34, 1967.

Hill, S. R.: Studies on adrenocortical and psychological response to stress in man. Arch. Intern. Med., 97, 269–298, 1956.

Jacobson, E.: *Progressive Relaxation,* Chicago, The University of Chicago Press, 1938.

Marteniuk, R. G.: Motor performance and induced muscular tension. Res. Quart., *39*, 1025-1031, 1969.

Martens, R.: Anxiety and motor behavior: a review. J. Motor Behav., *3*, 151–179, 1971.

Morgan, W. F.: Pre-match anxiety in a group of college wrestlers. Int. J. Sport Psychol., *1*, 7–13, 1970.

Paben, M., and Rosentsweigh, J.: Control of muscular tension in learning a novel gross motor skill. Percept. Motor Skills, *32*, 556-558, 1971.

Ryan, E. D.: Relationship between motor performance and arousal. Res. Quart., *33*, 168-172, 1962.

Selye, H.: *The Stress of Life.* New York, McGraw-Hill Book Co., 1956.

Spielberger, C. D., Gorsuch, R. L., and Lushene, R. E.: *The State-Trait Anxiety Inventory.* Palo Alto, Calif., Consulting Psychologists Press, 1970.

Vanek, M., and Cratty, B. J.: *Psychology and the Superior Athlete.* Toronto, The Macmillan Co., 1970.

Welford, A. T.: Stress and achievement. Aust. J. Psychol., *17*, 1–11, 1965.

V
MOTOR LEARNING, TRANSFER, AND RETENTION

16
NEUROLOGICAL AND BIOCHEMICAL BASES OF LEARNING AND RETENTION

Since early man began to have time to think, many of his thoughts have been directed toward the attempt to understand thinking itself. Early Greek philosophers speculated that in the head lay wondrous mechanisms which aided man to imagine, to dream, and to ponder. With the gradually emerging dawn of the age of science these inexact speculations have been translated into both simple and complex experimental designs.

Luigi Galvani, who discovered the nature of the electric properties of neural transmission in the late 1700's, has been designated as the father of experimental neurology. Contemporary researchers—Magoun,[728] Bures,[156] Paillard,[869] Olds,[1221] Hebb,[898] Sperry,[1045] Penfield,[838] and others —have further advanced knowledge about the central and peripheral nervous systems and their effects and controls on human behavior. These researchers have attempted to elucidate the apparent capacities of the human brain to carry out four major functions related to learning: (1) How is experience recorded in the nervous system? (2) Where are memory traces stored? (3) What are the biochemical and anatomical mechanisms for this storage? (4) How are learned experiences "called up" and utilized when appropriate?

In recent years the search for the answers to these and related questions has more and more come to occupy the time of the biochemist, the neurologist, and the physiologist. At times the background of the experimenter has, of course, determined the avenue traveled. At other times a productive "wedding" between the various disciplines has occurred, and the result has been a deeper and more penetrating analysis of these problems.

The experimenters constructing these neurological and biochemical "models" to explain learning and/or memory have been beset with several momentous problems. The remarkable experiments of Wilder Penfield[881,882] (see Chapter 19) have suggested that humans seem to have a record in their nervous systems of literally everything to which they have attended during their lifetime. Thus by the age of twenty years an individual has somehow recorded (although not consciously remembered) literally billions of "bits" of information. When the surgical patients of Dr. Penfield had their speech areas stimulated electrically, they reported a kind of "double consciousness," and could vividly recall the details of experiences in their past. When the electrical stimulation was removed, the imagery would stop, and when it was reapplied, the "picture" of the past would continue to unfold without interruption.

However, Penfield's studies indicated that the patients only reported components of the scene to which they paid attention at the time. They did not recall particularly critical periods in their life span, but related everyday situations in which they had participated. Consideration of this evidence has led researchers to speculate concerning the apparent need for memory storage units by the human brain that range from about 50 billion units[1137] to "only" about 30 billion units.[1221]

Thus, any theory of learning and retention has to present a sufficient number of structures and modifications of structures to contain the remarkable volume of information which is apparently absorbed by the human mind during a lifetime.

Individuals constructing neurological and biochemical models of learning and retention have attempted to deal with other problems of a similar magnitude. For example, there seem to be storage components in the mind involving memory of various durations. Man seems to be able to remember vividly events of the previous day, as opposed to occurrences of a week ago, and at the same time to recall some important events occurring many years in the past. These subjective experiences lead to several knotty questions, including the neurological and biochemical mechanisms that seem to implant certain "important" events and people in our nervous system, and the processes that result in a "blurring" of less vital events and situations.

Important questions related to the focus of this text revolve around whether there are differences in the memory storage characteristics of motor skills or whether learning depends more on thought than on movement. If, as some would have us believe, motor skills are more lastingly retained than are verbal materials, does movement somehow better impregnate the neural memory mechanisms than does simply thinking about or discussing a problem? Can one truly hypothesize a difference between motor learning and the learning requiring other kinds of behavior? Or, as some have suggested, are there no differences in learning at the neurological level? Or do the differences between motor learning and problem-solving, the forming of associations, and the selection and classification functions of the mind occur only at the periphery when the individual is engaged in some overt act evidencing the acquisition of a concept or a motor skill?

The answers to these and other questions are not neatly spelled out in the experimental literature. The following discussion contains more questions than answers, but recent scientific research presents hopeful evidence of a more scholarly approach by theoreticians and experimenters to the problems outlined above. Essentially no differences have been found at the neurological level between motor learning and any other kind of learning, but these differences *may* exist. The learning of a motor skill is different from pure problem-solving insofar as the nature of the input to induce retention has been different, and a movement or series of movements have accompanied the resultant learning. At the same time, whatever is stored triggers series of movements that, if practiced often enough, seem to rely less and less on conscious thought when they are performed. Further analyses of the biochemical and anatomical mechanisms accompanying the learning and re-practice of a motor skill thus probably will uncover several stages of mechanisms operative at different periods in the learning process; whereas events, problems, and associations formed more independently of volitional movements probably will not evidence similar successive bioneurological changes when they are remembered and reproduced.

Some of the models elaborated on in the following pages are based on examinations of the electric processes in the nervous system. Others are the result of biochemical analyses at the molecular or synaptic levels. Still others concentrate on various anatomical structures and the manner in which the elusive "engram"* is stored in brain tissue. In any case, these models are primarily the result of theoretical speculations, rather than of direct evidence relating changes in measurable behavior of humans to biochemical and/or neurological changes in the nervous system. The best that can be said for them at present is that they seem to provide only tentative answers to the difficult questions raised by the learning theorists. Further progress will probably be forthcoming when students of behavior acquire extensive knowledge of biochemistry and neurology so that an amalgamation of the knowledge about external behavior and internal functioning occurs. Improved research methodology should also contribute to further knowledge, including more refined techniques for chemical analysis of the intact and healthy human brain as the individual is confronted with various tasks, and the development of methods to examine the deeper lying electrobiochemical processes in the brain accompanying various kinds of human behavior.

Four classifications of neurobiochemical models for learning and retention can be identified. Both a molar and molecular model of neural

---

* An engram is a memory storage unit. The term was introduced into the literature in the 1920's. It usually has not been related directly to an anatomical structure.

functioning have been presented by various authors. Molar models of neural functioning are concerned with more gross anatomical and electrophysiological phenomena connected with learning, whereas the more molecular models delve into the location, retrieval, and disruption of discrete memory traces in the human and animal cortex.

A molar biochemical model of learning and retention is concerned with chemical changes occurring at the synaptic levels. The more molecular biochemical theories of learning and retention have focused on finite changes in the components of nucleic acid and similar substances in the nervous system.

Furthermore, theories attempting to explain some of the internal processes accompanying learning and retention can be classified according to their dependence on biochemical-anatomical concepts, or whether they focus on electrophysiological processes in the central and peripheral nervous system. Theories of this nature are often based on reasonably objective evidence due to the more sophisticated electromonitoring equipment which has been recently made available to researchers. Several theoretical constructs revolving around the electric properties of the brain are discussed in the following pages.

Molar Theories
of Neural Functioning

Theories of learning and retention utilizing anatomical concepts suggest that accommodations in the brain to repeated stimuli and situations involve a functional integration of innumerable brain structures facilitated primarily by cortical activity. Paillard[869] presents evidence that learning of motor skills is facilitated according to the extent to which the organism can break down previously established patterns. Examples taken from experiments in which the innervation to reciprocally functioning muscle groups has been reversed are drawn on to substantiate this hypothesis. These clinical studies indicate that the higher the organism resides on the phylogenic scale, the more able it will be in adjusting to differences from the normal innervation-muscle relationships. For example, the rat is seldom able to function adequately when surgical incoordination has been induced; the monkey can make some slight adjustments; but the human being, by inspecting and thinking about his attempts at motor re-education, is able to establish new patterns of movement between previously unrelated muscles and nerves.

Furthermore, such theories suggest that, when learning occurs, dependence on a variety of neural structures decreases. For example, as a motor act is acquired, there is less dependence on and involvement of the visual centers of the brain since the individual does not continue to need vision to accompany movement. Similarly, the speech centers become less involved in the total act as symbolic verbal behavior becomes less important as learning occurs. Such evidence indicates that the capacity to learn motor skills relates closely to the extent to which connections between the higher and lower centers of the brain controlling motor functions are related. The direct influence of the corticospinal system and the indirect influence of the reticular activating system have both been postulated as vertical integrators of the nervous system that are important in the acquisition of motor skills.

Modifications in more peripheral structures of the nervous system have also been considered to influence learning. The contact surfaces at the synaptic junction were once considered facilitative of learning. It was hypothesized that the presentation of a more extensive surface permitted greater contact between neurons that in turn facilitated transmission of the impulse over the synapse during the acquisition of the learned act. In recent years, however, more microscopic changes at the synapse are being accorded greater scrutiny.

It has often been speculated that, when an act is learned, its mediation is progressively assumed by structures in the lower motor levels. Lashley's[660] earlier data on this question, although far from conclusive, suggest that an acquired habit never becomes independent of the cortex. The refinement of feedback circuits, while making a well-learned skill seem almost reflex-like, in essence only seems to improve the delicate adjustment of the act in the later stages of learning.

A molar theory of neural functioning does not consider the nervous system as a simple tablet of wax needing only to be impregnated. But rather the nervous system is described as a delicate balance of interactions of complex mechanisms and structures in which learning serves to bring the complexity into various functional relationships that support the final behavior desired. Thus improved functional interactions rather than finite molecular changes are emphasized in these theoretical frameworks.

Electrophysiology, Learning, and Retention

Seemingly random and specific electric activity is synonymous with neural functioning. Even during the deepest sleep the human brain seems to function as a miniature electric motor and transformer. It is therefore not surprising that these electrophysiological processes have been explored as possible indices of learning and retention.

Lachman[645] has recently evolved an "oscillation theory" of brain function to explain learning capacity. He suggests that the amplitude of the oscillations of various brain wave patterns is indicative of the flexibility with which an individual brain functions, and thus is related to the extent to which an individual can organize, interpret, and acquire new patterns of behavior. Learning is facilitated, according to Lachman, to the extent to which the oscillations of a given individual's brain correspond to the complexity of the stimuli. He hypothesizes that the extent of these oscillations is evidence of the readiness of the brain to receive information, and that complex patterns are recorded less readily than are simple ones. However, if a complex pattern is somehow congruent with what Lachman calls "optimal brain recording points," it will be received more easily. Furthermore, the greater the variability of the brain activity level, the more effective the learning.

Lachman states that the best indices of "brain readiness," or receptivity, is a figure obtained by subtracting the lowest percentage of the alpha rate from the highest percentage, i.e., the alpha wave variation. This figure, it was found, correlates well with rote memory scores.

Russell[950] also alludes to the presence of electric activity in the brain when attempting to explain reminiscence—the tendency to learn even without practice. According to Russell, patterns laid down faintly in the brain after brief practice result in pathways through which the random and ever-present electric activity naturally flows with little resistance. With increased rest, these trace pathways thus become strengthened and result in better performance when the individual re-performs the act.

Several experimenters have studied, with some success, the extent to which a "memory trace" becomes ingrained in the nervous system by attempting to disrupt this integration at various periods after practice has been discontinued. Most of these experiments have been carried out with animals, but others have ascertained the extent to which electro-shock therapy has obliterated learning in human beings.

The influence of cortically introduced electric stimuli on various stages of retention has been studied in men and in animals. Generally, this electric impingement on the nervous system obliterates most of a skilled act when administered directly after the act has been practiced. When a delay is permitted, less impediment to retention is evidenced. Thus if the memory trace is given time to become ingrained into the nervous system, it seems to be resistant to destruction by an externally applied electric stimulus.

Typical of the research on this subject is the recent investigation by Weissman,[1168] who found that a shock administered to rats resulted in amnesia only when given within 40 minutes or less after learning. This tendency to consolidation of the memory trace in animals was originally hypothesized by Heriot and Coleman.[526] Experiments on humans corroborate this "consolidation" theory.

Experiments in which both animals and human beings have taken part attest to the presence of a three-stage memory mechanism: a short-term, medium-term, and long-term memory storage capacity. Electroshock administered a few minutes after learning tends to obliterate more of the learned response than shock after a delay of 30 minutes. Similarly, if the electroshock is administered more than an hour after some learned response has been acquired, little disruption in retention is elicited.

Some researchers have criticized these kinds of experiments on the grounds that the electroshock simply results in general trauma and avoidance by the animals, rather than in the disruption of specific memory traces for a given act. However, carefully controlled experiments by King[621] and others have indicated that consolidation of memory and experimental disruption can occur independent of fear and competing responses elicited by electric shock itself.

Experiments of this kind have also confirmed the frequent observation that the middle years of life are those in which learning is more likely to take place, and new skills acquired with least effort. Doty and Doty[299] found that memory consolidation takes longer among animal subjects of extreme ages (rats under 30 days old, and over 600 days old). Massed practice, as well as various electroshock and chemical inhibitors, delayed memory consolidation in the young and old animals, whereas animals intermediate in age were significantly less affected by the various noxious stimuli applied directly to the brain.

In human retention Eysenck[340] and others have hypothesized that there are two stages in the consolidation of the memory trace termed *primary consolidation* and *secondary consolidation.* During the former stage, retention is susceptible to retrograde amnesia in humans from loss due to electroshock and from a traumatic brain injury. After the second stage is reached, *secondary consolidation,* the learned acts tend to be protected against these traumatic influences. It has been suggested that both stages probably go on simultaneously, with primary consolidation lasting a matter of minutes immediately after learning, and secondary consolidation taking place over a longer period of time.

Although it had long been assumed that motor learning occurred in subtle ways at the motor unit level, it was not until the 1960's that instrumentation techniques, together with inquisitive minds, resulted in the exploration of what is termed "single nerve cell training." Basmajian[70] and his students at Emory University, with the apparatus described on page 40, began to determine first if this type of microscopic learning task takes place and, if so, under what conditions. Although still in the exploratory stages, this type of basic research has implications not only for the learning of sports skills, but also for the rehabilitation of individuals with various kinds of neuromotor problems of moderate or severe nature.

With the electromyographic techniques previously explained, it has been found that a single motor unit (a group of muscle fibers supplied by a single motor nerve cell) may be activated by an individual, despite the lack of any obvious or overt movement response by the entire muscle in which the implantation was made.

The measurement technique essentially consists of implantation of fine wire electrodes in a muscle. The subject is then asked to attempt to contract the unit (part of the muscle) involved. Information concerning whether the unit has "fired" or not is provided either by visual feedback on an oscilloscope or by a loudspeaker arrangement which emits a noise when the firing has taken place. After a period of 15 to 20 minutes, the subjects find that indeed they are able to activate the unit containing the implant. Several tasks are placed before them at this point. For example, they may be asked to isolate and maintain the firing of a single motor unit from among 100 or so that a normal person can recruit and display. After this kind of isolation has taken place, the subject may be asked to put the unit under control through various "maneuvers," to turn it up or down or to fire it at a given rate.

Among the most pertinent findings from this program of research are the following: (1) There are marked individual differences in the ability to control a given motor unit. (2) Attention level influences performance as it does most motor tasks, although after learning has taken place, continued firing is possible under distracting conditions. (3) Cross-transfer effects are seen between limbs, and retention of the skill is measurable and at times marked. (4) Superior athletes are sometimes more proficient at this kind of task than are nonathletes, despite the lack of observable motor activity while "firing" the unit. (5) However, for the most part there are not high correlations with this skill and standardized laboratory skill tests. (6) This type of task has been learned by children as young as three and four years of age, as well as by retarded subjects. (7) Reducing sensory input to the limb, by cuffing it to prevent adequate blood circulation (ischemia), reduces the ability to isolate a single unit. (8) Gross posturings, conscious flexions, and the like are not apt to fire the single motor unit under the conditions described.

Although at this writing a close "wedding" between the phenomena under discussion and their implications for voluntary gross movements has not been consummated, the possible future help to applied areas of physical therapy and rehabilitation, as well as to understanding the theoretical and neurological underpinnings of motor skill acquisition, is potentially great.

The Location of
the Memory Trace

Experiments with electroshock, as well as Sperry's classic "split-brain" studies, have attempted to ascertain the location of the storage areas for various types of memory traces.[1045] From studies by Zamora and Kaelbling[1235] and by Gottlieb and Wilson,[457] it was found that only when electroshock was administered to the dominant cerebral hemisphere was verbal recall affected (the left hemisphere in right-handed subjects). More difficulty was noted in the obliteration of memory traces by electroshock to the left hemisphere, in the latter experiment, when individuals of mixed dominance were subjects. In general, such investigations indicate that the more electroshock administered, the greater the resultant memory loss, indicating that quantitative aspects of the trauma influence memory and retention in rather direct ways.

Sperry's findings indicate that the memory of visual discrimination tasks seems to be duplicated in both hemispheres almost immediately after the learning has taken place. He sectioned the cortex of both cats and primates so that the corpus callosum was divided. When performed immediately after learning, this procedure produced no effects on learning. However, when the animals' brains were split prior to learning, they functioned almost as different animals (what had been learned with one eye, in the split-brain animals, was not learned by the covered eye when it was later exposed to the task).

In further elaboration of this approach and by utilization of drugs to depress one of the hemispheres in animals, Bures[157] and his co-workers produced competing reactions in either hemisphere. With the activity in one hemisphere depressed, the animals could be taught to avoid a box, and when the depressant had worn off in the initial half of the brain, the second was anesthetized and a competing response could be learned (e.g., to approach the box). The implications of these experiments are too global for a thorough review here, but in general they provide ingenious means for investigating the primary integration of memory traces and the manner in which memory traces compete, add, subtract, or otherwise interfere with one another.

Although initially the whole neuron was considered a possible candidate for memory storage at the molecular level, in recent years other structures have been hypothesized as possibly aiding in this critical function of the nervous system. Indeed the vast amount of input feeding into the nervous system during a lifetime makes it apparent that there are probably not enough single neurons available for this extensive classification and storage job.

Classical neurological doctrine attributed only a housekeeping function to the glial cells which compose about 75 percent of the bulk of the brain. These cells, tightly packed between the neurons, and having about a 10:1 ratio to neurons, are believed to participate in memory storage.[568] The finding that the neuron to glial ratio is greater during the middle years of life further substantiates this contention.[567]

It has been hypothesized that the glial cells, which lie within a millionth of an inch from the bodies and dendrites of the neurons, store information by modifying the specifics of electric conductivity to local spots on the neurons, thus further modifying dendritic currents. This arrangement permits much greater storage capacity in the brain than one holding that a single neuron is responsible for the storage of a single "bit" of information.

The findings of these investigations raise more questions than answers. However, it is clear from the results that human retention depends on traces of the activity residing somewhere in the cortex, which become deeply ingrained and resistant to forgetfulness after a period of time has passed. Furthermore, verbal memory seems to reside primarily in the dominant hemisphere, whereas the memory for other kinds of activities may be duplicated in the two sides of the brain. These findings also point to the detrimental influences of cerebral stresses on human retention, including not only drugs and electroshock, but massed practice! The presence of memory storages of short, medium and long duration is also substantiated by these ingenious experiments.

Biochemical Mechanisms for Learning and Retention

In the past ten years increasing attention has been devoted to the molecular mechanisms influencing learning and retention in men and animals. These more refined intraorganismic theories and experiments have stemmed from the previously cited investigations of retrograde amnesia, controlled electroconvulsive shock experiments, and research concerned with more molar aspects of synaptic functioning.

Initially experimenters considered the fact that a calcium increase at the synapse seemed to influence learning. Later, when it was found that neuronal activity increased the amount of ribonucleic acid (RNA) at the synapse, attention was turned toward various components of nucleic acid as a possible explanation of learning and retention.

Both deoxyribonucleic acid (DNA) and RNA are found in great abundance in the nervous system, and at the same time, their structures are complex enough to explain the numerous vicissitudes of human learning. A single DNA molecule consists of thousands of units (about 40,000), and there are about 800,000 DNA molecules in each person. It has been estimated that there is enough DNA in a single cell body to encode about 1,000 books.[404] DNA is found in the cell nucleus and RNA in both the nucleus and the cytoplasm. In nerve cells about 90 percent of the RNA is in the soma of the cell and about 10 percent in the dendrites.

By reference to DNA and RNA, theoretical statements have been advanced to explain both learning and retention. For example, the Belgian chemist Hyden suggested that a nerve cell responds differently to each new RNA molecule formed. This RNA molecule in turn shapes a protein molecule that then reacts with a complementary molecule causing the triggering of an inhibitory or excitatory substance across a synapse. If the impulse is familiar, protein molecules that will dissociate rapidly will already be present, thus a more rapid response will be forthcoming. Each cell may perpetuate a large number of unique patterns of RNA and protein. A giant RNA molecule may accommodate along its length to many different sequences shaped by different impulse patterns that have coursed through its neuron.[651] Acceptance of such a theory does not require strict localization of brain function, since a single RNA molecule can be a link in many neuronal networks.

Learning, it has been further hypothesized, occurs when the RNA from the surrounding glial cells is transferred into conducting neurons and subsequently into the protein-synthesizing apparatus of the neuron. Similarly, retention has been explained as occurring when a neural membrane becomes tuned by alteration of its protein structure. Indeed both functions can occur at the same time.[651]

Developmental changes in animals and men support the importance of RNA and DNA to the learning process. As would be expected, there is an increase with age in the ratio of glial cells to neurons.[404] Similarly, RNA in the motor nerve cells increases from the third year of age to the fortieth year, remaining constant until about the age of sixty, after which it declines sharply.

Since the early 1960's intravenous and oral doses of RNA and DNA have been administered to humans in attempts to improve learning and retention. Cameron[165] reported an experiment in which the aged and the senile were injected with RNA, resulting in improved memory. These researchers, while suggesting that RNA is essential for operation of memory, also pointed out that the evidence they presented was far from conclusive.

There is little direct evidence that these findings are as clear-cut as they seem. For example, Gaito[403] has pointed out that DNA may be too stable a molecule to function as suggested, whereas RNA may be too unstable a molecule. In addition, there is little experimental evidence directly linking the production and presence of RNA and DNA to specific changes in human behavior caused by practice. It is uncertain whether RNA and DNA participate in learning and retention in direct ways, or simply serve as stimulants or nutrients for the nervous system, thus facilitating the general receptivity of the neural structures in an indirect way.

Ignoring the possible inadequacies of these molecular theories of learning and retention, several experimenters have attempted to elicit transfer of training by the injection of refined and unrefined biochemical extracts from a trained animal to an untrained one. Initially, these experiments, carried out by McConnel and his colleagues, involved the feeding of flatworms that had been trained to respond to simple light cues to flatworms that had not been trained in this manner. The positive transfer noted prompted more refined experiments involving rats, in which RNA was extracted from the cortex of trained animals and intraperitoneally injected into untrained rats. Rats trained with food rewards to respond to both clicks and lights were found to transfer their training somehow to their untrained compatriots by way of the injections described.[574]

Jacobson[573] and his colleagues at the University of California at Los Angeles have apparently succeeded in eliciting intraspecies transfer by injections from hamsters to rats. Additionally, more elaborate controls enabled the experimenters to determine in greater detail the specificity of the transfer effects elicited from these kinds of experimental conditions.

Although Jacobson's findings are provocative, other experimenters have had problems replicating them.[455] In addition, it is difficult to determine how RNA injected into the peritoneum could reach the brain of the animal with biochemical obstacles, the "blood-brain barrier," interposed. In general, the questions such experimental findings pose include elucidating the biochemical mechanisms involved, outlining the extent to which the transfer effects are specific or general, and describing what behavior arrangements and biochemical agents are important in obtaining the transfer effects.[403]

The veracity of these experiments can only be proved after further attempts are made at their replication, and when additional refinements in their experimental methodologies are carried out, including more rigorous controls. In any case, they indicate that learning may someday be improved with the injection of certain biochemical substances. Although it will be several years before such chemical agents are available for experiments involving human learning, the fascinating possibilities for the improvement of motor performance and learning are apparent.

Although it is apparent that physical educators cannot observe the biochemical concomitants of learning and retention, it is equally apparent that no component of human behavior is without its neurological and biochemical bases. Understanding the concepts presented above should result in a more thorough understanding of learning in behavioral terms.

A Contemporary Model

Processes and Interactions in Time

Although the details of many processes and subprocesses important in the learning of motor skills are still not entirely clear, there is some neuroanatomical evidence that, when contrasted with behavioral mea-

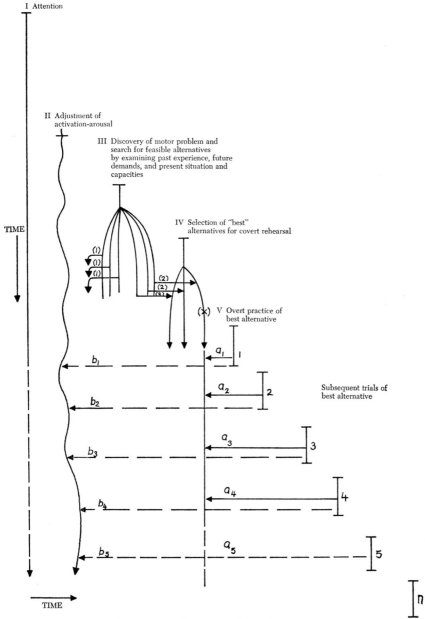

a = comparison of attempts with perceived "model"
b = feedback to arousal-activation dimension, to achieve best adjustment, productive of optimum performance.

FIGURE 16–1.   A model of motor learning processes.

sures of motor performance, the changes during practice suggest that the neurological model presented in Figure 16-1 may be viable. The schema admittedly is rather general, and assumes that the skill to be learned is a reasonably complex one, is not related closely to another one in the learner's past experience, and is a skill whose "good" performance depends on acquiring the ability to perform the movement not only with increasing accuracy but with increasing speed as well.

Learning a motor skill can be divided into several temporal phases, from the preparatory state to the initial confrontation of a situation that apparently calls for some kind of "motor decision" (to act or not to act), through the formulation of a "motor plan" to the initial and often erratic attempts at the task, and through the final stages that involve increasing automatization of the act. Further complicating the picture is the probability that more than one process occurs at the same time, while several purportedly discrete processes may overlap in time. For example, it is conceivably possible for an individual to be engaged in covert planning of subsequent parts of a motor act while actively engaged in performing the initial phases of the same skill. Moreover, it is also probable that memory processes occur at the same time as are acquisition processes, and alternative motor plans may be rehearsed mentally while the individual is in the process of completing and evaluating an apparently unsuccessful plan.

Contemporary writers, among them Koronski,[637] Bernstein,[96] Adams,[7] and Reynolds,[921] have dealt with several important theoretical questions relating to the topic under consideration. Among these conundrums are the following: (1) What kind of neurological feedback circuits operate during the performance of a motor skill? (2) What kind of feedback is *possible,* given what is known about the speed of nerve impulses and the speed of some ballistic skills? (3) What are the subtle interactions between the higher centers that initiate the *intent* of the movement with the lower centers, and with peripheral nerve structures that dictate the exact *form* the movement will take? (4) To what degree, if any, do the higher controlling mechanisms located in the cortex functionally "drop out" of the chain of neural events undergirding the learning of a skill during the later stages of acquisition?

To elaborate on the model presented in Figure 16-1, it is suggested in the upper left-hand corner that the individual must be attending to a potential "motor problem," and that his level of activation, as well as the degree of sensory acuity, which is partly influenced by activation and arousal level, must at least be capable of acquiring relative stimulus cues. Following this, his level of arousal is influenced by the imminent nature of a potential problem, which is discovered and examined at III. At this point the individual examines the present situation, his capacities, and his past experiences in similar situations, in order to search for feasible alternatives through which he can either solve the "problem confronting him," or avoid the problem altogether. If he decides to act, he will then (IV) begin to examine, through covert rehearsal processes, a fewer number (fewer than the multitude of feasible ones) of "best" alternatives. One of these (X) is then selected, a "mental model" is formulated (based not only on the temporal and spatial conformations of the movement, but also on the expected performance results), and a further decision is made (V) to "turn" the covertly rehearsed model into an actual movement. This process is similar to the "switching on" of subvocal speech to actual speech. The process is difficult in an immature nervous system (young children must often always accompany thought by word), a defective nervous system (the retardate usually evidences lip movements when reading), or an older nervous system (often the elderly voice their thoughts more than do those in the middle years of life). The performer then begins to engage in successive trials, #1 through n as shown.

During these "acted out" trials, several types of comparative processes are going on, as depicted by lines labeled $a_1 \ldots n$ and $b_1 \ldots n$. The lines (a) passing from each trial to line X, denoting covert rehearsal of "best" alternatives, suggest that as the movement is performed a constant comparison is being made between the movement (and its results) as *predicted and mentally rehearsed,* and the *actual* movement (and its results). As shown by dotted line a_5 at trial #5, this comparative process becomes less marked as the discrepancy between covertly rehearsed movement and the performance of the act becomes less distinct and finally unnecessary, as the result of learning.

A second important comparative process is also depicted on the model. Lines b_1 - - - n indicate that, as the performance trials occur, the individual experiments with various levels of activation (either consciously or unconsciously), as indicated by fluctuations in the line projecting from II, until a level that seems optimum for that task is achieved, thus reducing the necessity of continual comparisons as illustrated by the less distinct line b_5.

The model thus depicts several types of processes that are more important at certain points in the learning process than at others. The "solid" attention line I, for example, becomes less distinct as learning takes place, indicating less need for the individual to attend to the motor task itself (his growing ability to perform without undue attention directed to the movement). Thus he can spend more of his "attentional energies" on other relevant components of the performance situation, or on other thoughts not directly connected with the performance situation.

Also being "phased out" is the need for constant comparison of the motor act itself to some kind of a verbally and/or visually rehearsed model. At the behavioral level this suggests that, as practice continues, the skill may be said, as Adams suggests, to pass from a verbal-motor skill to a more nearly "pure" motor act.

Both the lack of necessity for comparison to mental models and the decreased necessity to attend to the more obvious motor and perceptual cues inherent in the situation suggest that, as learning takes place reflecting refinements in both speed and accuracy, the act becomes more automatized, and its execution more dependent on the instigation of a rather precise and total "program" of action emanating from the central nervous system, and sustained in a manner requiring less conscious control and more and more involvement of the lower centers of the brain.

Neurological-Anatomical Structures

If one accepts the foregoing model as viable, it then becomes possible to "tie in" neurological structures and functions to the various processes outlined. For example, it is usually found that aberrations, or lesions, in the brain stem (notably in the reticular formation and associated structures) result in inappropriate attention-arousal levels; conversely adequate functioning of the brain stem results in arousal levels that are appropriate to the situations facing the individual. To be more precise, when expectancies are more closely matched with actualities, there are less widespread signs of arousal in the brain stem. Greater inhibition of the reticular formation is often apparent. At this point, the intralaminar thalamic system becomes activated, which in turn affects more specific and exact regions in the neocortex than does the reticular system in the brain stem.

To an increased degree neurologists such as Sokolov,[1039] as well as educators and behavioral scientists, have come to the conclusion that appropriate attention and activation are the most important initial functions that are requisite for any kind of adequate learning, whether it be "motor" or "mental" in nature.

Closely aligned, structurally and functionally, with structures controlling activation, are some of those that seem to influence attention. However, it is becoming clear that adequate or inadequate attention is mediated not only by brain-stem structures, but by at least four or five other components of the nervous system, including the visual (occipital) centers to the rear of the brain, as well as portions of the forebrain.

The processes of recognition of a motor problem, of scanning memory mechanisms to discover related ones incurred in the past, and of scanning and selecting the possible motor act or acts that might result in the "best" solution to a "motor problem situation" are primarily the function of higher brain centers, according to most scholars. Bernstein, as well as Koronski, suggests that not only are such processes of vital importance prior to the execution of a motor act, but also that they take place in the neurocortex and closely aligned supporting structures. Koronski codifies memory traces for motor acts as "kinesthetic gnostic units."

The process of covert rehearsal of the best or selection of the best "motor solutions" has interested a number of neurologists, both recently and in the past. Often their attention has been drawn to the relationships between spoken and subvocally rehearsed speech. The division between a motor act as mentally rehearsed and the act as performed may at times be quite distinct. For example, individuals with the entire speech apparatus paralyzed still engage in subvocal internalized speech, just as the normal individual may quietly rehearse the verbal components of a motor task prior to or instead of performing it.

Thus, during the rehearsal period, several of the brain structures that mediate verbal behavior and those engaged in controlling certain aspects of vision are involved, either in conjunction with or exclusive of the motor centers of the cortex. Ideational components of speech are usually mediated in certain parts of the left cerebral hemisphere (regardless of whether the individual is left- or right-handed), while "spillover" into the motor centers of the cortex, while an individual is mentally rehearsing a motor task, may be caused by overactivation, e.g., a child or adult may begin to talk or even shout his formerly "silent" thoughts as he becomes more and more excited.

When overt practice is first begun, it is probable that the greatest number of neural structures are involved in its mediation, as compared to the first mental rehearsal phases and to the later learning stages. Not only do higher centers continue to function, together with the numerous structures mediating speech and vision, but now the person "calls in" the various structures that mediate voluntary movement. Indeed, it is difficult to determine which parts of the brain and nervous system are *not* likely to be involved during these initial action phases of skill acquisition. The cortex formulates a program, while the cerebellum aids in both timing and activation functions. Activation and arousal are also controlled at this phase by structures in the brain stem, and the visual centers in the occipital and frontal areas are usually necessary for close inspection of the task. Finally, even smells and sounds often contribute to "external feedback" needed for successful performance.

The peripheral structures in the nervous system are vitally involved. Basmajian's work (see Chapter 2) suggests that even at the level of the "motor unit" learning is taking place, since the neurons and muscle cells learn to "fire" in rather precise sequences, and in correct temporal relationships to each other.

Gradually, however, as skill is acquired, during which the differences between what the individual expects and how he acts are reduced, there is a subtle "phasing out" of certain behaviors, a reduction in the involvement of various components of the "thought-action" system which in turn must seemingly be accompanied by a parallel reduction in the quantity of neural activity necessary.

Recent investigations, with both animal and human subjects, are beginning to provide evidence that supports the decreasing necessity for people to compare and bring to cognitive awareness the various parts of a movement. It is at this point that the performer no longer feels the necessity of consciously comparing actual performance with what Reynolds has termed an "expectancy engram." Moreover, performance becomes "smoother" and less variable.

The suggestion that with skill acquisition there is a reduction in the number of brain regions involved is not an original idea, but has been previously expounded by several contemporary psychologists, including Welford and Broadbent. At the same time, recent studies with cats and other animals, both in this country and in Russia, seem to confirm the suggestion that during the initial stages of skill (and/or habit) acquisition temporary brain connections are formed, which are subsequently terminated as the result of practice (see Livanov, et al.,[696] Morrell et al.,[814] and Reynolds[921] bibliography).

Comments

Thus, from a neurological standpoint, it is becoming possible to explore the neurological underpinnings for behaviors and changes in behaviors that are observable as an individual is confronted with, begins to attempt, and finally acquires a motor skill. Identifiable neural mechanisms undergird the vocalizations, heard and unheard, that often accompany rudimentary attempts to learn a skill. Interactions in the brain mediate and thus explain the inordinate amount of mental activity that often precedes, and then sometimes continues to accompany practice in a complex motor act. Furthermore, there are ways of explaining, using anatomical-neurological terms, just how an individual changes as he acquires skill, how increased efficiency is reflected not only in a decreasing amount of muscular tension and visual attention devoted to the motor act, but also how apparently fewer of the internalized components of the nervous system take part in the performance of a skill practiced until it is automatic. In the following four chapters, the behavioral aspects of motor skill learning and retention will be examined more thoroughly.

Summary

Biochemical and neurological theories of learning and retention may be concerned with either gross or finite changes in the nervous system. These theoretical models attempt to explain how information is obtained, stored, remembered, and brought to recall when appropriate.

The various neuroanatomical theories of learning and retention have recently focused on the glial cells as possible repositories of information. The more molar neural theories, on the other hand, have been intent on explaining learning and retention by reference to the interaction of larger neural structures. Other theories have attempted to explain learning and retention by reference to structural changes at the synaptic level, or by reference to various electrophysiological changes that seem to parallel the acquisition and recall of information and skills.

To an increasing degree, contemporary neurophysiologists are beginning to discover the internalized functions and interactions between organs that support and explain various behavioral characteristics noted when an individual thinks about, attempts, and finally acquires proficiency in motor skill. These models, one of which is discussed in this chapter, aid in the understanding of why and how individuals learn skills. The following four chapters contain information in more detail concerning skill acquisition, employing measures of behavior rather than of neurological function. I believe, however, that a thorough understanding of the intricacies of motor skill learning demand at least a superficial understanding of the neural underpinnings of behavioral change, as well as of the precise nature of the measurable changes themselves.

Student Readings

Eiduson, S., Eiduson, B. T., Geller, E., and Yuwiler, A.: *Biochemistry and Behavior.* Princeton, N.J., Van Nostrand Publishers, 1964.

Jacobson, A. L., Fried, C., and Horowitz, S. D.: Planarians and memory: I. Transfer of learning by injection of ribonucleic acid. Nature, *209,* 599-601, 1966.

Luttges, M., Johnson, T., Buck, C., Holland, J., and McGaugh, J.: An examination of 'transfer of learning' by nucleic acid. Science, *151,* 834-837, 1966.

Magoun, H. W.: *The Waking Brain.* Springfield, Ill., Charles C Thomas, 1958.

Woolridge, D. E.: *The Machinery of the Brain.* New York, McGraw-Hill Book Co., 1963.

17
MOTOR LEARNING

Learning is defined as *the rather permanent change in behavior brought about through practice.* Based on this definition, *motor learning* may be termed a *stable change in the level of skill as the result of repeated trials.*

Learning is also explained as the *potential* to perform, and reference is made to motivation as one variable that sometimes invalidates the assessment of learning solely as depicted by performance changes. The findings of studies concerned with the effect of "mental practice" on skill acquisition also point to the validity of the "learning potential" concept. In addition to practice, learning a complex motor act may be facilitated by "thinking through" the movements and/or by viewing others perform. Skill improvement may thus be assumed to take place as the result of silent, inactive contemplation. These findings indicate that learning is occurring even though performance improvement measures are not recorded. The amount of "latent" learning achieved is later found by comparing the progress of the "thinkers" to the progress of groups who had no such opportunity.

These "mental practice" studies, as well as others that dealt with the types of cues influencing motor learning, also point to a basic difference between animal and human learning. The performance of humans is superior to that of animals because of many factors, such as greater facility in integrating movements and anatomical specialization. The paramount difference between animal and human learning, however, is that human beings attach symbols to a motor task, which usually result in an increased ability to remember and to organize information. Humans may rehearse a skill by prior manipulation of symbols whereas animals are unable to do so. Although reference will be made to animal experimentation when discussing theoretical considerations, because of this basic difference, emphasis will be placed on research investigating human capacities to learn motor skills.

Initially, it is also important to differentiate between the terms *performance* and *learning*, often accomplished by reference to a time dimension. *Learning* is a long-range change, demonstrable in retention measures collected over a period of time. *Performance,* on the other hand, is a one-attempt phenomenon influenced by such short-term variables as motivation, fatigue, and nutritive state.

Usually the so-called "learning curve" is actually a plotting of the individual's changes in "performance." Learning curves most often reflect performance as *expressed* rather than the degree of learning *acquired*.

The movement characteristics of human beings cannot be neatly designated as either learned or innate, however. There are increasing indications in the literature that perhaps a second kind of acquired behavior influences human actions. For the past 50 years zoologists have studied, with various degrees of objectivity, the phenomenon known as imprinting, which involves apparently automatic sets of behavioral sequences that seem to be "triggered" by specific events occurring early in the life of the organism. For example, the "following" response of chicks and ducklings is believed to be imprinted when the animals are exposed to a moving stimulus pattern during a critical period of their early life.

The studies by Goldfarb,[441] examining the influence of maternal deprivation on later development, the research by Brodbeck and Irwin,[138] concerning the emergence of speech behavior, the findings of Spitz,[1048] who studied factors that elicit smiling, the wolf-child histories summarized by Gesell,[420] and the investigations of Green and Money[462] of effeminate behavior in boys raise the possibility that at certain times in the lives of infants and children critical events trigger certain components of their motor behavior. Although the present evidence is suggestive rather than conclusive, it might be hypothesized that several facets of movement behavior may be the result of imprinting—including throwing, running, unique characteristics of gait and a variety of gesture patterns.

Introduction to Learning Theory

A learning theory is a set of theoretical assumptions that attempts to explain such phenomena as forgetting, retention, the role of practice, performance variations, learning limits, the influence of rewards, and the types of cues that cause learning to take place. Learning theories dwell mainly on two basic concepts and may be classified by the relative emphasis placed on each.

The initial dimension is the relative importance accorded *reinforcement* as a condition necessary for learning. Reinforcement, although a somewhat nebulous concept, may be defined as some *reward* in the learning situation, as obvious as satisfaction gained from hitting a target or approval from a coach, or as subtle as the lessening of tension or a feeling of task mastery. Opposing the theory that reinforcement is indispensable is the "contiguity theory," the concept that learning occurs when a stimulus (or event) and a response take place at the same time.

A second dimension with which learning theories are concerned is the nature of the sensory stimulation that causes the organism to respond. In essence the argument deals with whether an organism reacts to discrete stimuli (chained together, or in groups) or whether action is elicited by some meaning or significance attached to the situation or object. The former theories are termed "stimulus-response" (S-R) theories, and the latter "associative" or "field theories."

Learning theories may also be classified by more explicit criteria. Some are classified by the extent to which they emphasize central thought processes, as contrasted to simple muscular movement (central versus peripheral theories). Some researchers utilize objective mathematical formulas, while others use more subjective philosophical assumptions to explain learning. Other theories may be identified by whether more than one type of learning is presented to explain simple and complex performance, or intellectual versus motor behavior, and whether importance is attached to intermediate factors (emotion, reward, motivation, and the like).

In the following pages an attempt has been made to outline briefly theories that represent a sampling of the various conceptual frameworks for learning. An extensive review of learning theories is beyond the scope of the book and has been ably presented by Hilgard[534] and others.

Thorndike—S-R Theory

Thorndike[1095] developed one of the most accepted S-R learning theories and has had an important influence on educational practice from the 1890's to the present. Experimentation with animal and human subjects resulted in the hypothesis that learning consisted primarily of the strengthening of the connections (bonds) between stimulus and response. Important implications for both animal and human learning are contained in Thorndike's theory. *Motivation* is emphasized as an important intervening factor influencing learning. Consequently, Thorndike's "connectivism" may be considered an S-R theory emphasizing the importance of reinforcing or rewarding conditions.

Three laws of learning were proposed in this conceptual framework: (1) *The Law of Readiness* stated that learning is dependent on a readiness to act or prior "mental set," which facilitates the response. Generally, this preparation was believed to consist of physiological accommodations within the conduction units of the nervous system. (2) *The Law of Exercise* assumed that S-R connections were strengthened through *frequent* pairing. Later, it was expostulated that mere repetition did not strengthen the S-R bonds but that motivating conditions (including knowledge of results) were necessary for learning to take place. (3) *The Law of Effect* emphasized the importance of the annoying or satisfying results of the act in influencing the chance of its recurrence. In later experiments, Thorndike found that the effects of satisfaction and displeasure were not equal and that the satisfying results facilitated performance more than did punishment. Discussions of "Teaching Method," emphasizing the importance of reward as opposed to punishment on learning, indicate an acceptance of these later findings.

Thorndike suggested that learning was specific to the task at hand. Extension of the concept to motor performances has been referred to previously. His "transfer of identical elements" theory, holding that the practice of one task would contribute to proficiency in a second only when elements of the two are identical, is currently being tested by motor skill researchers.

Although Thorndike's assumptions did not deal specifically with learning athletic skills or gross motor performance, considerable attention was accorded to fine motor skills. Handwriting, typing, and other such classroom tasks were investigated and accorded as respectable a place in his research as were more "intellectual tasks." His "specificity theory" provided the impetus that prompted educators to include typing and other vocational courses in school curricula.

Thorndike is considered a behaviorist because he based theories on evidence obtained from direct and observable performance rather than from subjective reports of subjects. His contribution to the study of motor learning lies in the formulation of (1) the specificity theory, (2) the importance accorded motivation, and (3) the objective approach he took to the study of learning problems.

Gutherie—Contiguity Theory

Gutherie[474] was an S-R theorist who, while de-emphasizing reinforcement, placed importance on the occurrence of stimulus and response together in time. His theory was derived to a large extent from research based on study of kinesthesis. Gutherie hypothesized that all learning, complex and simple or verbal and nonverbal, consists of the contiguous pairing of movement stimuli and responses. He postulated that all thinking and remembering depend on the repetition of subliminal movements of the vocal apparatus. His experiments involved small animals— mice in mazes and cats in "escape" boxes. From the results, generalizations were extended to human learning. It was assumed that the gradual improvement in performance shown by sloping learning curves was the result of the joining of various pairs of stimuli and responses in complex tasks until a whole "family" of connections was formed.

The explanations reported by Gutherie have been rejected by many as too simple to explain complex human functioning. And later experimenters demonstrated that mice were able to learn maze pathways even when nerves carrying kinesthetic impulses were cut. However, the basic assumptions formulated by Gutherie deserve serious study because they have led to additional research concerned with movement learning.

Hull—Mathematical Model for Learning

Moving from more traditional S-R theories, Hull developed a highly objective theory based on animal experimentation. The central concept in this theory was habit formation. To explain learning phenomena occurring in the stimulus phase, variables intrinsic to the organism and various motor "output" variables, postulates involving exact mathematical formulas were devised. They were modified if subsequent experimentation proved them questionable. Hull's theory could be likened to Woodworth's S-O-R theory,[1225] with emphasis placed on the organism's integrating role, or "O," in the learning process.

Hull relied heavily on mathematical symbols to explain behavioral changes, quantifying the effect of the number of trials, the amount of reward, the intensity of the stimulus, and other variables in order to predict behavior more exactly in various experimental environments. From his experiments, Hull developed the concept of *habit strength* ($_sH_r$), which, he concluded, was the direct outcome of reinforced, spaced trials at a given task. The concept of *reaction potential* ($_sE_r$) is also central to the theory and represents the organism's *tendency* to respond. With these two terms, Hull explained learning in absolute performance units (habit strength) and in units of learning potential (reaction potential).

He considered seven "input" variables, including the intensity of the stimulus, the amount of reward, prior practice, drive, and the work required in responding. Several factors intrinsic to the responding organism included habit strength, strength from related habits, the extent to which a given stimulus affects the learner, and the variability of performance from trial to trial. The final "output" variables considered important included strength of reaction (reaction amplitude) and the persistency and endurance of unrewarded responses.

Hull proposed that at the basic level several primitive types of learning occur, including those based on inborn tendencies, adaptation to primitive situations, the ability to generalize and to discriminate, and trial-and-error learning. To explain complex behavior and learning at the final level, Hull presented concepts based on the integration of behavioral sequences through *anticipatory responses,* believed to be the steering mechanisms formed by conditions affecting the learner. It was from this latter concept that the formation of "families" of habits was explained.

Hull's theory is extremely complex, and further elaboration is beyond the scope of this discussion (see Adams[11]). His main contribution, however, was the objective manner in which learning was explained. Objectivity does not imply rigidity, however, since Hull's postulates were subject to change when experimental evidence seemed to warrant it.

Tolman—Sign Theory

Tolman[1105] was one of the first to emphasize the integrative function of the nervous system in contrast to concepts dealing with the formation of peripheral stimulus-response connections. It is assumed that human learning depends on the meaning (sign or significance) an individual attaches to situations or objects in his environment. The theory may thus be considered *molar,* or based mainly on the observation of total behavior, rather than *molecular,* or based on the anatomical-physiological phenomena underlying S-R theories.

Tolman was one of the first "field" theorists. He used the term "behavior space" (similar to Lewinian "life space") to represent the individual's immediate environment. Contradicting the findings of S-R behaviorists who felt that learning implied the acquisition of simple responses, Tolman postulated that organisms become familiar with places, that mice, for example, form "cognitive maps" of the maze pattern. The meanings attached to a situation were not assumed to be only spatial, since time factors and "logical" considerations were also proposed to aid in performing the task at hand.

Tolman considered behavior to be goal-directed and concerned with avoiding or approaching something in the environment. The concept of *confirmation* replaces *reinforcement* in Tolmanian theory. An individual is assumed to repeat an act when its consequences become known and predictable. The term *carthexes* (negative or positive) was coined to explain the relative attraction or repulsion individuals attach to objects or situations.

Tolman considered himself a strict behaviorist, concerned mainly with observable evidence. However, it was hypothesized that numerous "intervening variables" existed between the situation and the resultant behavior. Although the list of variables was often modified, it generally included demand, appetite, differentiation, motor skill, and bias.

Tolman was criticized for generalizing human learning from animal experiments. However, the findings of his "latent learning" studies carried out with animals, which indicated that maze learning unverified by performance might take place as maze exploration remained unrewarded, seem to be confirmed by "mental practice" research carried out with human subjects. It was explained that complex motor skills are learned because of the formation of "motor patterns" rather than because of the acquisition of movement stimulus-response chains. Motor learning was believed to depend on the perceptual process that resulted in meanings attached to the situation that in turn produced a readiness to act or to remain inactive.

Although some feel that Tolman's assumptions did not cover all problems of learning, many believe that the value of his theory lies in this incompleteness. It seems to have provided an impetus for further study which many more "complete" systems failed to do. The "cognitive-map," or "sign-significant" theory, forms a bridge between the strict behaviorists who deal only in S-R terms and the later Gestaltists who accorded an increasing importance to perceptual and central processes in formulating more "holistic" concepts of learning.

Gestalt Theory

In the 1930's, the simplicity of approach advocated by the S-R theorists was challenged by German psychologists who advocated the importance of insight in learning. These Gestaltists evolved a "field theory" based initially on the problem-solving behavior of apes. Learning laws were formulated, the validity of which depended on an accurate assessment of perceptual processes. Particularly emphasized was the sudden recognition of factors involved in a problem, with the subsequent correct action. This was in direct opposition to the trial-and-error concepts advanced by Thorndike in the United States at about the same time.

As was the case with Tolman's theory, Gestaltism may be termed "holistic." However, the latter conceptual framework depends more on introspective evidence and *anthropomorphic* observations, or putting oneself in the place of the animal, than did Tolman's theory. Awareness of relationships and meanings among various parts of a problem, among problems, and between the part and the whole is emphasized. Transfer of learning, or "transposition," is assumed to take place when patterns of dynamic relationships are found to be similar in two situations.

A most important contribution of Gestaltic learning theory was the emphasis on conceptualization, on cognition, and on thought. Even in primates the experimental evidence indicated that there seemed to be a point in the learning at which "sudden insight" was acquired by the animal, insight leading to the solution of various problems confronting the animal.

Woodworth, Skinner, and Miller

Several traditional theories combine concepts of the Gestaltists and the S-R bond psychologists as well as several views of reinforcement. Woodworth[1225] explained complex learning in terms of S-R sequences, and at the same time emphasized the importance of the perceptual process, dependent on both biological and behavioral cues (i.e., the need on the part of the organism to use its capacities). A framework of ideas is constructively based on a variety of evidence (behavior, introspection, and experimental observations). Although termed "eclectic" by some, Woodworth's functionalism seems to be a most comprehensive theory of learning and has been outlined in his publications appearing over a period of 60 years.

Skinner[1015] also reconciled certain aspects of the S-R and field theories by proposing two types of learning: (1) respondent behavior, smooth muscle activity elicited by an identifiable stimulus, and (2) operant behavior, movement of the skeletal muscle not necessarily caused by an identifiable stimulus, but which may result from the demands of the whole situation.

Neil Miller's liberalized S-R theory is another example of the more comprehensive theory formulation in recent years. He presented a broad definition of a *stimulus* as "anything to which a response can be learned," and *response* as "anything that can be learned to a stimulus." Thus, although specific biologic needs often determine initial behavior, the behavior may later prove rewarding in itself. This idea is similar to Allport's "functional autonomy of drive" concept and to Woodworth's emphasis on exploratory and play drives as basic human needs.

Information Theory

Although earlier learning theorists, particularly Hull, have utilized mathematical constructs when explaining modifications of human behavior, the more contemporary learning theories draw further comparisons between components of an electronic computer and the functioning of the human nervous system. Although it is doubtful that electronic engineers studied the brain and spinal cord before developing these complex devices, the reverse has been noted. Several contemporary learning theories use computer terms to explain human functioning.

The "feedback model," one of the central concepts in the science of cybernetics espoused by Norbert Weiner[1202] in 1948, and the "information theory," utilized by the human factors engineer in studying man-machine relationships, are two recent theories of this type. These conceptual frameworks were initially grounded in studies of communication theory. These two theories might be combined as shown in Figure 17–1. The boxes can represent either the components of an electronic sending-receiving system or the components of human-to-human or man-environment communication system. Motor learning can be graphically explained by referring to such a model. For example, when an individual learns a complex skill, such as shooting a free throw in basketball, kinesthetic

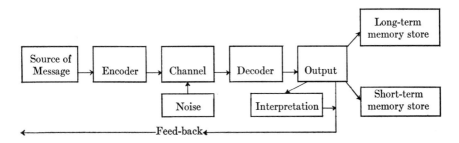

FIGURE 17-1. Information theory employs computer terms to explain information processing (encoder) and interpretation (decoder) by men. Critical in such a model is the concept of feedback, indicating that the human processor of information engages in a continual process of self-correction.

impulses are sent from the muscles, tendons, and joints performing a component of the movement and from the visual apparatus as the eyes observe the ball's pathway (or during the initial stages of the whole movement) and transmitted to the brain. These impulses are transmitted by the nervous system (encoded) through various channels, the individual then interprets them (decodes), a meaning is attached to them—hit or missed? (output interpretation), and relative success and reasons for it are stored in the components indicated. Feedback that might govern subsequent muscular adjustments involved in the second free throw occurs when impulses are sent to the muscles.

Learning adjustments and modifications may thus be represented graphically. In addition to the concepts pictured, such ideas as long-term and short-term memory stores have been utilized to evaluate the manner in which skills or concepts are retained over varying periods of time.

Numerous researchers have studied the implications of these various concepts. For example, the "channel" capacity of individuals has received considerable attention in an attempt to determine the volume of material that can be comprehended at one time, its nature, how many kinds of stimuli (vocal, movement, and the like) can be attended to, and what types of stimuli take precedence over others in an individual's "receiving channels."[137]

The psychological "noise" pictured refers to any type of block or impediment to communication. What kinds of blocks interfere most (emotional, physical, auditory, other)? Do the relative amounts of interference differ from individual to individual and from situation to situation? How can the sender discover the type of "noise" interfering with communication, and how can it be alleviated? These are some of the questions that have received experimental attention.

Although some persons might object to the mechanistic and somewhat inhuman sound of these terms, they are useful as a concise means of explaining problems of communication, perception, and motor performance.

K. U. Smith,[1026] in his experiments outlined in Chapter 7, has at times based his concepts and research on components of information theory, particularly on the concept of feedback as a critical ingredient in learning. Nicholas Bernstein,[96] whose theories were reviewed in the previous chapter, was an early initiator of some of the concepts later clarified by Norbert Weiner and other pioneers in information theory, cybernetics, and feedback mechanisms. As has been pointed out (Chapter 10), Bernstein suggests that learning of motor acts consists of rather constant "feedback" or comparative processes, because what is being performed is continually being compared to an ideal model conceived by the central nervous system.

Perceptual-Motor Learning

Descriptions

Difficulty is encountered when attempting to differentiate between motor learning, perceptual-motor learning, and any other kind of learning. Similarly, sharp distinctions between verbal learning and motor learning become impossible to make. Advocates of the theoretical models that follow often have voiced the opinion that differentiation between theories of skill learning and theories explaining learning in other terms is difficult.

Many explanations of learning are subjective, but their consideration should add depth to the study of learning of motor skills. Hilgard[534] has separated definitions of learning into two main types: (1) theoretical, concerning the essential conditions or processes believed necessary to enable learning to occur, and (2) factual, relating to observations of behavior in the physical world. The statements that follow may be classified as factual rather than theoretical.

Descriptions of motor learning are sometimes descriptions of how individuals appear to have behaved when learning a motor act. Anderson[36] has described learning as "a progressive organization of behavior" based on the opportunity to repeat experience for a sufficient amount of time. He holds, along with Thorndike and others, that locomotion is the basic skill, learned from the infant's crawling and climbing behavior to the gross body movements of the adult. Elements in the skilled act are identified by Anderson as including speed (a time element), strength (an energy element), and coordination (a quality element).

Sells[986] refers to a "plasticity" quality necessary for the learning of a motor skill. This concept, similar to Tolman's concept of "creative instability," implies that individuals who learn best are those who easily can change persisting movement characteristics.

Kingsley[622] has described skilled performance as "purposive action" and identified four acquisition stages: (1) instruction, or receiving external and internal cues; (2) formulation of the task, or gaining task understanding; (3) progress toward goal, or practice; and (4) completion. It is held that movements are revised during learning and that abbreviated and unnecessary components ("fractionations") are dropped out of the action. When learned, the skilled act is less likely to become disturbed by emotions and is accompanied by fewer accessory responses (e.g., words).

The Continuous Versus the Discontinuous Nature
of Skill Acquisition

There has been a considerable amount of investigation and speculation as to whether the acquisition of skill may be considered to be a continuous process, or whether it might be considered as fragmented into various identifiable components. The question determines not only the theoretical construct most amenable to use, but also the practical methods to elicit the most improvement in skill.

It is becoming increasingly clear from inspection of the experimental literature that the learning process can be fragmented into several components, indicating several phases in skill acquisition. Initially the learner seeks to discover the task components that are similar to or different from those he has known in the past. During this initial stage various perceptual components of the act are important, as well as the performer's ability to acquire directions relative to the task (his short-term memory) and similar cognitive attributes. Following the initial preparatory phase of learning, such factors as the ability to handle the various input information become important. For example, if the movement is rapid and continuous, the performer's ability to monitor kinesthetic input feed-in during the initial portion of the movement(s) influences the quality of subsequent performance. During this stage of learning the individual begins to organize discrete portions of the task into progressively larger components, as his perceptual-motor systems become increasingly capable of not only perceiving larger amounts of information, but become able to respond more qualitatively, evidencing a smoothing of motoric behaviors, and a higher and higher level of integration.

The final stages of skill learning have received relatively little attention on the part of researchers. However, the evidence is beginning to indicate that improvement in perceptual-motor functioning apparently continues to higher levels than was believed possible in past years. Not only are marks achieved by superior athletes indicative of increasing excellence, but recent information from researchers has advanced that subtle changes in ocular movements, in respiratory adjustments, and in similar concomitants of performance take place in the later stages of skill acquisition, which permit extremely high levels of achievement to be attained.[1023]

It thus seems that if skill acquisition is observed it would be judged continuous; but shifts in strategies, in response modifications, and in the manner in which task components are integrated enable us to identify discrete phases in the learning process. Further research is needed to identify the characteristics of these phases, in particular the unique components of the final levels of achievement.

Limits of Motor Learning

Dudycha[304] and Gagne and Fleishman[402] point to the importance of the acquisition of unconscious habits, although Gagne indicates that these are probably more important during the later stages of learning. Both consider capacity limits, divided by Dudycha into two types: (1) practical limits, or that with which the individual is satisfied, and (2) physiological limits, or the individual's highest possible achievement. The second type of limit is approached gradually. The factors determining physiological limitations include the nature of the nervous system, bodily proportions, the physical equipment measuring workout (speed of the typewriter), working conditions (temperature, noise), methods of learning (similar to Seashore's work methods concept[982]) and aspirational level (motivation). Gagne and Fleishman[402] explain that "we cannot expect human motor skills to have characteristics which exceed the capacity of the response mechanism itself."

Work by Karl U. Smith[1206a] and his students has further expanded on the processes possibly operative when higher levels of performance and/or learning are reached. Their data suggest that several kinds of automatic physiological-anatomical mechanisms are operative during the later stages of learning: (1) The eyes become paired more precisely with hand movements. (2) Subtle and unconscious changes occur in energy utilization, muscular contraction, and hormonal regulation. (3) Adjustments occur in brain wave patterns. (4) Subtle refinements of breathing rate and depth accompany well-learned skilled performance.

The Memory Drum Theory of Neuromotor Reaction

General theories of personality purporting to explain general human functioning are first-level theories. At the second level are the learning theories reviewed on the previous pages. In addition, there are third-level theories that attempt to explain specific types of human functioning. Such a theory is the "memory drum theory" espoused by Franklin Henry.[518]

Using "computer terms," Henry made assumptions based on the greater response delay that precedes the performance of more complex tasks. This phenomenon is interpreted to indicate that unconscious neural patterns acquired from past experience are stored in what may be thought of as a *memory storage drum*. The store is used when a movement skill is learned. The initial attempts to perform the new skill are awkward and carried out under conscious control if there has been no similar "program" previously recorded on the drum. He explained that, although some response delay is attributable to speed of nerve conduction, the minor "program" change necessary for a simple movement, once the "will to act" has been initiated, results in a shorter reaction time. A long complicated program of movements is more difficult to change and results in a delay of response to the complex task. Such a theory, it is believed, aids in explaining specificity of motor skill, as well as other phenomena related to motor learning.

A "Closed-Loop" Theory of Motor Learning

In 1971, Jack Adams,[9] whose previous interest in motor activity was reflected in writings detailing relationships between Hullian learning theory and motor learning, proposed what he termed a *"closed-loop" theory* of motor learning. After first thoroughly reviewing research pointing out the importance of various kinds of knowledge of results (KR) in the formation of initial models or "images" of the motor act, Adams then pointed out that "after a relatively large amount of training, learning can continue when KR is withdrawn." Adams suggests that, while peripheral proprioceptive feedback and visual and auditory information concerning the relative success of a motor act are important during the initial "verbal-motor" stages of skill acquisition, during the later stages of learning when the "perceptual trace" for the correct response has become strong enough to elicit relatively stable and "correct" performance, additional performance and learning are sustained not because of the operation of feedback chains in which external or even muscular cues are operative, but because of the functioning of "closed loops" in the nervous system, triggered by a preprogrammed "image" emanating from the cortex.

Thus, Adams suggests that motor learning proceeds at two levels: initially, skill acquisition depends on error correction, due to peripheral muscular feedback "circuits" and visual and auditory information, whereas later in the learning process, more central processes are operative. Adams, as well as others, has accumulated experimental evidence to indicate that, as movements gain speed, it becomes impossible to explain performance by referring to the relatively large amount of time that the nervous system needs to monitor kinesthetic information emanating from discrete parts of the movement itself. The work of Higgins[532] and others at Columbia University seems to confirm this latter assumption. Jones'[592] statements in 1970 that skill acquisition should be studied in two contexts, those processes influencing rate of improvement and those reflected in terminal level of proficiency, also reflect some of Adams' ideas and concerns. The interesting experiment, using computerized methods to vary the degree of feedback in a drawing task, by Smith and Sussman[1026] in 1969 also points to the validity of the dichotomy outlined by Adams. These authors suggest that motor learning is based not only on the processing of immediately available sensory information, but also on a dynamic "time spanning" process in which a record of the perception of past movements plays a vital part.

Among the directions for future research, which Adams suggests for his admittedly incomplete theory, are the following: (1) exploration of the nature of the two "images" or "traces" proposed by the theory, the "image" built up by initial peripheral feedback, and the more stabilized "trace" of the response residing in the central nervous system; and (2) elucidation of the mechanisms that permit "error detection" particularly when the movement becomes more rapid because of increased proficiency.

The Quantification of Learning

The gradual acquisition of a complex skill has been represented by numerical indices as well as graphic curves. Using performance measures recorded over a period of time, a "learning" score has been obtained by (1) subtracting the first score from the last, (2) dividing the number of trials into the total improvement record (a measure of learning rate), (3) averaging some portion of the trials (usually after a few "warm-ups"), (4) determining the extent to which some hypothetical or actual performance *limit* is reached, or (5) various combinations of these methods.

To obtain a valid measure of learning is not simple. Problems arise because of several complexities in the learning situation: (1) Usually the unique properties of the task determine the most appropriate learning score computed; methods proposed for one type of task mistakenly may be applied to another. (2) The measure of learning must be accomplished indirectly through performance measures, susceptible to many variables in addition to practice. (3) Most learning is a function not simply of the number of trials but also of their spacing. (4) Most measures of successive performance scores represent only a portion of the actual learning process. It is usually hypothesized that the first trial is really an initial performance level not affected by past experiences, an assumption which is seldom true. Previous experience in a similar or dissimilar task may facilitate or impede performance. Most measures represent only a portion of the learning taking place. Despite such problems, however, considerable thought and time have been spent in developing acceptable means for determining just *how much* skill an individual has acquired under various experimental conditions.

Although numerous investigations have dealt with objectifying verbal or cognitive learning tasks, several studies have been directed specifically toward quantifying the learning of motor skill. In 1955, McGraw[761] studied the validity of several possible measures of learning, including: (1) averaging all the scores, the first through the last, (2) finding the difference between the initial raw score and the final raw score, (3) summing up the highest or best trials and subtracting the sum of the initial trials, and (4) dividing the actual gain from the initial to the final trial by the possible gain from the initial to the highest possible score. Agreeing with other scholars, McGraw found that, by using the same raw data, a wide variety of "learning" scores could be obtained, depending on the method employed. He concluded that the most valid learning score could be obtained by any of the following formulas:

1. adding all the scores

2. $$\frac{\text{sum of highest successive trials} - \text{sum of first trials}}{\text{highest possible score} - \text{sum of lowest scores}}$$

3. $$\frac{\text{sum of highest trials} - \text{sum of first trials}}{\text{highest possible score} - \text{sum of first trials}}$$

4. $$\frac{\text{sum of trials} - \text{sum of first trials}}{\text{highest possible score} - \text{sum of first trials}}$$

The latter three formulas are termed "Per cent of Possible Gain Methods."

Learning and Performance Curves

In addition to using a single numerical index, the ubiquitous learning curve is frequently employed as a measure of learning. It should be remembered that, for the most part, so-called learning curves reflect only the individual's inclinations *to perform* at a given place and time and in a given task. Performance fluctuations on these curves do not always reflect the individual's basic learning capabilities but his temporary emotional highs and lows, as well as possible modifications in environmental conditions and/or instructions.

The graphic representation of the acquisition of skill in performing a task may involve several measures: (1) the decreasing amount of time necessary to perform the task; (2) some measure of accuracy, such as ability to hit a target; (3) a decrease in the number of errors com-

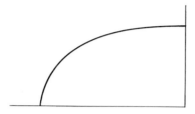

FIGURE 17–2.   A motor learning curve showing rapid initial improvement with a gradual decrease later in the learning process.

mitted when learning the task; (4) the percentage of success per trial, as compared to a real or hypothetical performance limit; or (5) a combination of two or more of the above measures. Ehrlich,[321] studying the accuracy of a fencing thrust as a motor skill involving total body skill and accuracy, recommends that curves should be constructed by analyzing performance from three points of view: (1) initial states, (2) rate of learning, and (3) maximal end points.

Learning curves represent the successive scores of an individual while he learns a task or of group means. Such graphs are helpful to illustrate "reminiscence," the effect of spacing on improvement, "transfer," the influence of other tasks on the task studied, a comparison of "whole versus part" practice, or other practice variables.

At times reference has been made in the literature to a "typically" shaped motor learning curve, generally assumed to be one indicating a gradual decrease in the amount of learning after initial quick improvement (Fig. 17–2). In reality, however, motor learning curves assume a variety of shapes, depending on the nature of the task, the practice conditions imposed, and the characteristics of the experimental situation or of the learner. Thus, although at times curves assume the shape shown in Figure 17–2, other curves are characterized by initially slow improvement, with a gradual increase in the amount of learning from trial to trial. This curve is characteristic when the task is difficult or when the attempts of a feebleminded subject are graphed (Fig. 17–3).

The general shape of the curve may depend on the measure used, motivation, or facilitating or distracting conditions. In addition, the amount of task analysis required, as determined by task complexity, has an influence on the shape of the learning curve. Many complex tasks might involve an error curve which would decline, whereas a curve based on the number of successful trials might move in the opposite direction. Superimposed, these two curves might appear as shown in Figure 17–4.

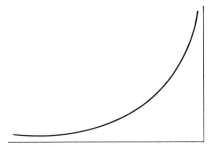

FIGURE 17–3. A characteristic motor learning curve when the task is difficult or the learner is slow.

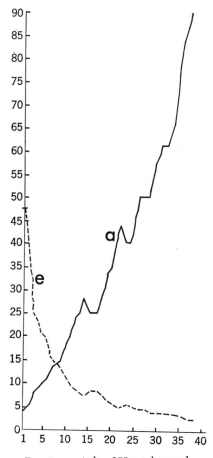

Practice periods: 200 catches each.

FIGURE 17–4. An error curve (e) superimposed on an achievement curve (a).

Although the general shape of a curve often differs, several general characteristics of such graphs have been studied by various researchers. In general, motor learning curves are characterized by an initial stage of relatively rapid improvement. Melton[779] has termed this "the discovery stage" of learning. During this initial phase the individual acquires a general knowledge of task components and of the goal to be achieved. Following the initial portion, a second part termed the actual "performance" phase occurs during which improvement is generally not so rapid, but more stable and more likely to be retained.

Noticeable in most curves indicating skill acquisition are performance fluctuations. Investigators generally attribute these to motivational conditions, fatigue, or other such temporary factors. In addition, a plateau may appear at several stages in the learning process. A plateau has been defined as a period during which relatively little improvement takes place. Plateaus in motor learning curves have been studied by several investigators. Some researchers have assumed that, if given enough trials, every motor learning curve will eventually evidence plateauing. Peterson,[887] however, found that a juggling task produced a learning curve without any plateauing. This is generally found to be true when a task is learned as a whole (Fig. 17–5).

A plateau is usually believed to indicate a period during which parts of a task are combined into "wholes." Although actual improvement in performance may not be demonstrated, it is assumed that the individual is gradually assimilating task components and will suddenly evidence this by "breaking out" of the plateau effect. Such a simple explanation is not always valid, however. Kao,[602] undertaking an extensive study of plateaus in motor learning curves, concluded that, when learning *simple skills,* plateaus may be due to fatigue, a change of methods adopted by a subject, or a subtle change in the experimental environment (e.g., shifting of the apparatus). When acquiring *complex skills,* Kao continued, plateaus result when individuals attempt to build complex patterns out of formerly independent ones. If success in an initial component leads

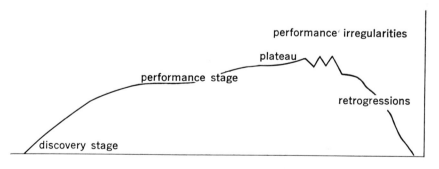

FIGURE 17–5.   A graph depicting stages in skill acquisition.

to immediate task facilitation, however, probably no plateau will be evident, and when individuals continuously attend to the "whole" of the task no plateaus will be evident.

Factorial Studies of the Learning Curve

Learning curves, as well as being linear, also have *thickness!* As has been seen, *a single performance measure* may be analyzed to determine the relative importance of various basic factors. Thus learning may be progressively analyzed (factored) to determine the relative importance of various basic qualities at several stages in the process of acquisition. Such studies are rare in the literature, and more are needed to provide a depth analysis of the learning process. An example of such an investigation was carried out by Fleishman and Hempel[367] in 1954. Scores were obtained at eight different stages of practice in a complex coordination test (making complex adjustments of an airplane stick and rudder in response to visual signal patterns). Their findings are summarized in Figure 17–6. As can be seen, the number of factors contributing to performance were more numerous during the initial stages and became fewer as learning continued. During the last four stages only three factors were present, whereas during the initial stages seven factors were apparent. There was also a shift in the "nature" of the factors. During the initial stages, "non-motor" or cognitive factors were more apparent (visualization of spatial relations, mechanical analysis, and the like). From the fifth through the last stage, however, the factors of psychomotor coordination, rate of movement, and a factor specific to the task predominated. Expressed as percentages during the early stages, "motor factors" contributed only about 29.5 percent and non-motor factors about 46.1 percent of the task. Later in the learning process the motor factors contributed about 74.5 percent and non-motor factors only about 10.5 percent.

Individual differences in learning may be affected by different factors during various stages of learning. Once the spatial relationships of a task are acquired, no further improvement may be possible or necessary, and other factors then assume increasing importance. The rise in the motor learning curve was considered by Fleishman and Hempel[367] to be the result of systematic transformations in particular combinations of abilities at various stages of practice. The task analyzed in this research was a basic skill needed to fly an airplane. It is believed, however, that generalities applicable to a wide variety of motor skills may be drawn from this research. The importance of correct verbalizing and of task analysis during the initial and later stages of learning appears to be statistically confirmed by these findings.

Investigations subsequent to the initial one by Fleishman and his colleagues have substantiated and elaborated on these findings. An investigation[368] in 1955 suggested that practice may exert an unequal effect on the numerous factors involved in the performance of a reaction time test in response to a visual stimulus. The performance score at one point in the learning process therefore appears to be a resultant of the changes in the unique combinations of abilities possessed by the performer at that point.

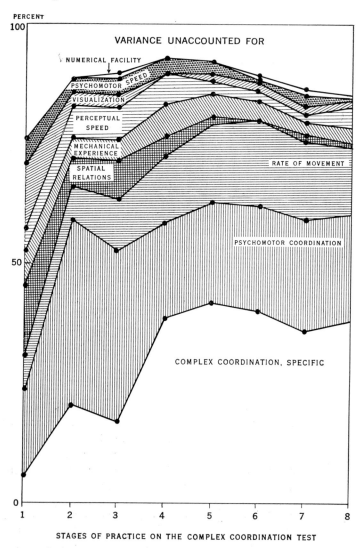

FIGURE 17–6. Percentage of variance (shaded area) represented by each factor at different stages of practice on the Complex Coordination Test. (Fleishman and Hempel, courtesy of Psychometrika.)

In a subsequent investigation[365] it was hypothesized that ideal training conditions, suited to the factorial changes in the task during learning, might facilitate final performance. Thus an investigation carried out in 1961 was based on the premise that, when it is known that a given ability may be important at a particular point in the practice schedule, verbal emphasis on that ability at the correct time will enhance learning. The findings indicated that such an approach is a sound one. The experimental group subjected to this type of carefully placed verbal emphasis performed significantly better at the final stages of learning than did two control groups receiving no such training. Such a program, of course, presupposed that the skill under consideration had been previously subjected to a longitudinal factorial analysis.

In a 1963 study, Fleishman and Rich[372] found that subjects scoring high in a test of "kinesthetic sensitivity" evidenced greater improvement in performance during the later stages of learning, whereas those scoring higher in a "spatial measure" were better initial learners but tended to plateau during the later stages of learning.

Subsequent studies at times have confirmed the hypotheses outlined by Fleishman and his colleagues. In 1968, Stallings[1049] found that visual spatial orientation was related to the initial stages of performance in a "two-handed speed pass" task. At the same time, critics of the basic assumptions underlying Fleishman's work have been active during the 1960's and 1970's. Bechtoldt[82] and Jones[593] published results in 1962 suggesting that it is conceptually invalid to compare transitional stages of ability on a single task with factors derived from factorial studies of batteries of motor performance tasks. Both Anderson[37] and Bechtoldt have recommended that comparisons of this nature are best carried out with analysis of variance and regression analysis. The mathematically inclined and statistically sophisticated student may wish to refer to Bechtoldt's 1969 summary[83] of the arguments surrounding Fleishman's work. In any case, it should be noted that the premises on which Fleishman's data are based are not without a number of scholarly critics at this writing.

Formulizing Motor Learning Curves

Motor learning curves are frequently "smoothed" or reduced to some hypothetical mathematical formula in order to offer greater clarity to the learning phenomena studied or to facilitate prediction of performance scores in trials not recorded, or conversely, to predict at which trial certain performance levels may be reached. When carrying out such a mathematical operation, however, several assumptions usually must be made: (1) that there is an initial trial before which no learning occurs, (2) that there is a fixed rate of learning evidenced, and (3) that, when contrasting two curves, the same parts of the learning process are comparable. The smoothing of learning curves, in addition, obliterates irregularities which in themselves might be worthy of study. Plateaus, retrogressions, and other irregularities are passed over when a learning curve is smoothed. Recent comparisons of the shapes of learning curves derived from the practice of a number of perceptual-motor skills indicate that their shapes are remarkably similar.[606] The shape of a motor learning curve of a sorting task, for example, is similar in conformation to that obtained when a pursuit-rotor task is practiced for a period of time.

The result of this similarity has been to encourage several investigators to attempt to determine the extent to which performance at the initial stages of learning correlates with performance during the later stages of learning of the same skill. The results of these experiments are inconclusive, but in general the closer the compared trials are in the learning schedule, the higher their intercorrelation. Welch[1171] found that the farther trials were from each other (in a ladder-climbing task), the less likely one was to obtain even moderate correlations. More recently, Jones[591] found that even the insertion of rest intervals had little effect on intertrial correlations.

Forgetting

In addition to "learning curves," "forgetting" curves have been investigated extensively. Although numerous studies have focused on verbal or cognitive tasks, little attention has been paid to the forgetting of motor tasks. In general, a "forgetting" curve is usually considered to be shaped as shown in Figure 17–7. It is characterized by rapid initial forgetting, which lessens as time passes.

Investigations concerned with the retention of motor skills generally obtain only a single performance measure after a period of prolonged inactivity, rather than studying successive performance drop-offs. Researchers in this area probably have been discouraged by the comparatively long period over which motor habits seem to endure.

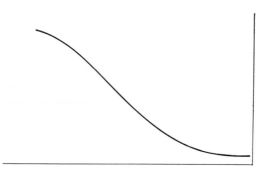

FIGURE 17–7. A forgetting curve.

Motor Educability

Motor educability has been defined previously as the general ability to learn a number of tasks quickly and accurately. It refers to the ability of an individual to accommodate to the requirements of several kinds of motor tasks. If such a factor exists, one should be able to identify persons who might be predicted to learn a wide variety of motor skills with a minimum of time and effort. Motor educability might, therefore, be termed *general motor intelligence*.

When we find individuals who seem to *perform* a number of skills well, it would logically follow that these same individuals also should be able to *learn* a variety of movements quickly. The close relationship between performance and learning has been previously discussed (p. 337). Such does not seem to be the case, however, since much of the experimental evidence argues against the existence of a general motor learning factor.

For years, Brace[125a] carried out studies with a stunt-type test as a measure of general motor ability. He incurred little success when attempting to discover a relationship between such general indices and the ability to learn motor skills. Gire and Espenschade[436] also failed to identify a general motor educability factor. In an elaborate study using several batteries of performance tests, no significant relationships were established between the scores obtained on the tests and the ability to learn different sports skills.

Generally, from such studies researchers conclude that even combinations of strength test scores provide only a fair index of ability to learn *simple* gross motor skills. A comprehensive factor involved in the learning of *complex* tasks seems more difficult to isolate.

In an attempt to show a relationship between the ability to learn two similar spatial patterns of different sizes, I[232] failed to find a significant correlation between learning proficiencies. However, a comparison of skills depending on the same kinds of sensory information or involving similar movement patterns might eventually lead to the identification of general learning factors.

In 1969, Marteniuk[739] also found that learning in two speed tasks, requiring similar but slightly different movements with the same arm, produced highly specific learning scores (only 9 percent common variance), while intertask correlations at the initial and final scores in the two tasks also indicated the lack of a general speed factor common to the two tasks since the r's were only .51 and .54 respectively.

The disturbing observation continues to be made, however, that some individuals seem to be able to learn quickly any skill to which they are exposed. At present, the subject is a controversial one. There is an indication, however, that these quick learners are highly motivated, possess above average strength, are able to analyze quickly and accurately the mechanics of a task, and are relatively free from excess tension which might impede performance. The isolation and identification of a single general motor educability factor, however, seem to be a tenuous experimental undertaking.

It is believed that when measures reflecting the quality of movement that occurs during learning (including assessments of smooth accelerations and decelerations, appropriate build-up of velocities that anticipate sudden application of force, and similar data which may be collected by the biomechanist) are collected and compared, one may begin to confirm what is generally observed about those who tend to be rather quick learners and those who seem to be "motor morons."

The motor educability question is related to the specificity versus generality argument concerning motor performance and to the validity of various learning and transfer theories. Further reference to this question is found throughout this book, specifically in the sections concerned with performance and transfer.

Student Reading

Bilodeau, E. A.: *Acquisition of Skill.* New York, Academic Press, 1966.
Bilodeau, E. A., and Bilodeau, I. McD.: Motor skills learning. *Annual Review of Psychology.* Palo Alto, Calif., 1961, pp. 243–280.
Connolly, K. J. (Ed.): *Mechanisms of Motor Skill Development.* New York, Academic Press, 1970.
Cratty, B. J.: *Teaching Motor Skill.* Englewood Cliffs, N.J., Prentice-Hall, Inc., 1973.
Knapp, B.: *Skill in Sport.* London, Routledge and Kegan Paul, 1963.
Melton, A. W.: *Categories of Human Learning.* New York, Academic Press, 1964.
Oxendine, J. B.: *Psychology of Motor Learning.* New York, Appleton-Century-Crofts, 1968.
Sage, G. H.: *Introduction to Motor Behavior: A Neuropsychological Approach.* Reading, Mass., Addison-Wesley Publishing, 1971.
Singer, R. N. (Ed.): *Readings in Motor Learning.* Philadelphia, Lea & Febiger, 1972.

18
PRACTICE FACTORS

As defined in the previous chapter, *learning* is a rather permanent change brought about through practice. In this chapter some of the ways in which practice conditions influence learning will be reviewed. Problems arise when comparing and evaluating research findings. Many different types of skills have been investigated from various theoretical points of view. In addition, many of the practice variables have not been subjected to rigid control. For example, when studying massing versus distributing practice, the majority of the investigators failed to control the subjects' activities during the rest periods adequately.

Further problems are caused by the various definitions of "learning proficiency." Confusion also results from the performance measures utilized. Some experimenters are concerned with accurate performance, others with speed, and still others with the elimination of errors. In any case, a review of the following studies has led to the conclusion that numerous questions remain unanswered. I hope that the ensuing discussion will not only aid the reader to summarize current knowledge but also stimulate students to give consideration to undertaking research on these topics.

The Nature of Whole
Practice Versus Part Practice

One of the questions with which experimenters have been concerned has been the relative influence on learning efficiency of practicing the *whole* of a task as opposed to first practicing its *parts*. Several combinations of whole-part practice have been investigated. In addition to practicing the entire task, as opposed to practicing all of its parts separately, the *progressive-part method* has also been studied. The latter technique consists of first practicing the initial two parts of a task, combining these into a whole, learning a third part, and then chaining this to the first two, adding a fourth section, and so on. This process is then continued until the entire task seems to be mastered. Card-sorting, typewriting, and stylus mazes seem the favored manual tasks studied, and basketball skills and various gymnastic activities the most favored gross motor skills.

Accurate interpretation of the results of research in this area requires the formulation of common definitions for the terms "whole" and "economy of learning." For, according to Seagoe,[978] often what is really measured is the extent to which an individual is able to concentrate on a task or the length of a subject's memory span, rather than the main problem in question.

The relative influence of various methods on what kinds of "economy of learning" is a second crucial question. Does economy mean elimination of errors, increase in speed or rate of learning, improvement of accuracy, or just what? Results of studies by Koch[629] and Barton[69] indicate that the assessment of the best methods depends on the definition of economy. The *part method* sometimes aids in quickly reducing errors, whereas the *whole method* usually results in more rapid learning to a given criterion.

It also seems that the relative efficiency of one method or a second depends on the nature of the task and on the characteristics of the learner.[914,978] One investigator points out that high intelligence, advanced age, and/or a task of closely related sequences favor the *whole method*. When practice is massed and the material is difficult, the *part* or *progressive-part* method is usually best. Other investigators indicate that retardates usually learn best by the part method,[543] and another researcher found that younger subjects learned best if the task was divided into component parts. Barton summarized this viewpoint by stating that to make "the units too large is to overwhelm the learner."

In general, a part method has been found to be wasteful of time, when the whole method suffices.[848] The time required to connect the various parts of a task and/or to break up previously formed associations between parts is wasted. This waste can be seen in the plateaus noted in learning curves. For example, when learning to type, progress is retarded when the learner changes from single letters to entire words, and later to phrases (Fig. 18–1). Similar plateaus are seen in the progressive performance measures of gross motor skills as time is required to chain parts together. No such loss of time is experienced if the task is learned as a whole.

Further illustration of the relationship between the "best" method to use and the task complexity is found in Cross' study of basketball skills.[271] He reported that to learn simple unitary movements (e.g., passing and catching) the whole method proved best. For movements of greater complexity (e.g., stop-pivot-and-shoot), however, quicker progress was obtained with a progressive-part approach. Briggs and Naylor,[134] utilizing a tracking task, also suggested that the relative efficiency of whole versus part training is a function of task complexity and task organization. *Complexity* is defined as the ability to process infor-

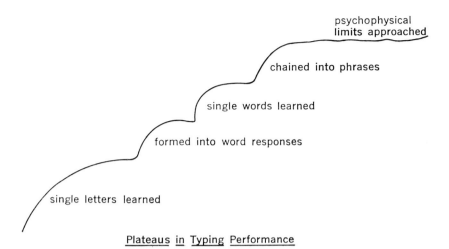

Plateaus in Typing Performance

FIGURE 18–1. The plateaus formed when component parts of learning to type are joined together.

mation; *organization* relates to establishing relationships between various task components.

The basic problem, therefore, seems to be to recognize the characteristics of motor "wholes." Seagoe[978] has helpfully synthesized "wholeness" into three statements: (1) It should be isolated and autonomous, an integrated unity. (2) It must have "form" quality. (3) It must be more than the sum of the parts; it must be a rational structure in itself. These criteria might be considered subjective, but when it is considered that a kip on the hi-bar has been found to be best learned by the whole method,[992] whereas a four-part stylus maze task is best learned by the progressive-part method,[878] Seagoe's criteria become clearer.

The findings of a study completed in 1958 by Niemeyer[848] point to a second hypothesis that may clarify when the whole or the part method of teaching will be most effective. When acquiring skills that involve complex interactions with an opponent (e.g., badminton and volleyball), the part method provides a sounder foundation. When learning movements that require no interaction, the whole method seems superior. Although the whole method seemed to result in a better understanding of team interactions during the final stages of learning, more accurate performance was recorded when the skills were broken down into components during the early stages of acquisition.

Results of Niemeyer's research[848] clearly demonstrated that learning to swim was carried out with far more efficiency when the whole method was used, perhaps owing to the fact that when learning a whole movement less time is needed later to integrate the parts. Subjects taught the stroke as a unit were able to swim sooner, farther, faster, and with better form than those taught by the part method. Group differences were particularly striking when the mean distances were compared at the completion of the study. Those taught the whole stroke averaged 845 yards, whereas the group learning the stroke by component parts averaged only 442 yards.

The task, therefore, seems to be to determine initially the characteristics and capacities of the learner and then to analyze the nature of the task. Quickest learning is generally obtained by practicing the "whole." If subsequent evaluation of performance suggests that the portions of the task selected or the task as an entirety proved too large and/or complex for acquisition, the progressive-part method would then seem to hold the most promise for efficient learning.

Massing Practice
Versus Distributing Practice

A frequently investigated problem has been the relative efficiency of massing versus distributing practice when learning various verbal or motor tasks. "Efficiency" usually refers to the final level of performance attained or to the amount of retention evidenced at the completion of the learning program after a period of interpolated rest. Performance improvement due to the introduction of rest intervals has been termed "reminiscence."

The influence of many combinations of massing and/or spacing practice on learning has been studied, including: (1) massing of practice with no rest intervals, (2) spacing of practice with rest intervals of a fixed duration, (3) initial massing of practice and gradually increasing the length of the rest intervals, (4) initial spacing and progressive massing or decreasing the length of rest intervals, (5) initial massing with irregularly introduced rests or the reverse, and (6) initial spacing with irregularly introduced periods of massed practice. The complexity of the problem becomes apparent when it is realized that the distributing or massing of trials *in a single practice session* may also be varied according to these numerous schedules.

Initially the concern of the investigators was with verbal or rote learning tasks. A number of tasks have been investigated in connection with the "reminiscence" effect, such as the classic studies of Ebbinghaus[316] and Lyon,[722] based on the retention of nonsense syllables. Although tasks of this nature continued to be investigated,[330,536] fine motor skills seemed to become a more popular evaluative tool, possibly because of the ease with which such performance can be scored. Typical of these later studies are the investigations of Ammons,[27] Reynolds and Bilodeau,[920] and Snoddy,[1036] with pursuit rotors; Cook[212] and Pechstein,[879] with stylus mazes; and Lorge,[705] with mirror-star tracing. Investigations of gross motor skills have appeared less frequently in the literature, although Harmon et al.,[494] using billiard playing, Lashley[669] and Young,[1233] using archery ability, Knapp and Dixon,[626] studying juggling skill and Neimeyer,[848] using volleyball and badminton, are representative of this latter category. More recently, E. Dean Ryan,[955] Stelmach,[1059] and others have used a stabilometer and a ladder-climbing task in laboratory studies of gross motor control.

The findings from study of reminiscence are, at times, somewhat conflicting. Initially, the early investigators flatly concluded that spacing was more desirable than massing of practice, especially when verbal skills were involved.[316,722] According to more recent studies, distributed practice also has been found to be effective in a variety of tasks. Improvement of performance in a pursuit-rotor task,[27] juggling,[626] inverted alphabet printing,[600,1006] and archery skill[1233] was found to benefit from distribution of practice. In 1964, Koonce and others[636] found that reminiscence in a pursuit-rotor task occurred after rest intervals of ten minutes, one, seven, 35, 70, 175, 365, and 730 days.

Less frequent are findings that advocate the efficiency of massed practice. Both Pechstein[879] and Cook[212] found massing to be the most effective method of learning small stylus mazes and advanced skills in volleyball. Young[1233] found that badminton was best learned when practice was massed, although Niemeyer[848] found the opposite to be true of badminton skill.

More recently Whitley,[1198] with a fine motor task ("foot tracking"), found that while performance was improved under distributed practice, learning was not. Whitley suggests that the conflicting findings in previous studies have resulted because only vague distinctions were made between performance and learning. Stelmach,[1060] in 1969, investigating reminiscence effects in gross motor skill and taking care to differentiate between learning and performance, came to conclusions similar to those of Whitley. He found that while performance improvements were elicited by distributed practice effects (on a stabilometer and ladder-climbing task), no significant learning differences were recorded when the two practice methods were compared.

Thus, recent data suggest that marked conflicts in findings are to be expected unless the distinctions between learning and performance are carefully accounted for. Marked differences in effects of practice distribution may depend on whether the skill studied is a fine or a gross motor task. In most instances, the contention is that massing of practice results in greater learning owing to the fact that each performance strikes a higher level of the forgetting curve of the previous performance.

Changes of Learning Schedule

Numerous studies have investigated the effectiveness of various combinations of massing and spacing during the learning process. Tsai,[1112] investigating mirror drawing, Harmon et al.,[494] studying billiard playing, Norris,[857] using a pursuit rotor, and Niemeyer,[848] studying three sports skills, found that initial massing with subsequent spacing of practice produced the highest performance levels. These findings are usually attributed to a "warm-up" effect, or to the provision of a "foundation of understanding." Harmon has termed this initial massing with the introduction of gradually prolonged rests the "additive" method.

Lashley,[659] among others, found that early spacing with the later massing of trials proved to be most effective. This is generally attributed to the fact that once initial success in the task is achieved, such factors as fatigue or boredom, which might interfere in a massed practice situation, are somewhat negated. More willingness to work as the result of task mastery is the hypothesis extended.

Zeaman and Kaufman[1239] obtained findings that indicate that fluctuating from a massed to a distributed learning schedule may affect individual differences. Subjects performing an inverted alphabet writing task retained their starting differences when spaced practice conditions were maintained, but lost their relative rankings when massed practice was introduced. It is interesting to note, however, that, when spaced practice was resumed, the original skill differences became apparent.

A series of interesting studies were conducted at Columbia University several years ago. They involved irregularly introduced massing or spacing of practice in the learning situation. Using mirror-star tracing as a task, Gentry[417] found that when rests were suddenly introduced into a massed learning environment, more learning resulted. Conversely, Lorge[705] found that when trials were massed late in a spaced learning situation, performance dropped to a level achieved by a second group who had engaged only in massed practice. Extending the findings of his colleagues, Epstein[330] concluded that retention seemed more related to performance achieved than to the type of practice.

Generally less reminiscence is evidenced during the later stages of the learning process, despite the arrangement of practice periods prior to reaching the limits of learning.[577]

Optimum Rest

Kimble[618] investigated the optimal amount of rest desirable between trials of pursuit-rotor tasks. Travis,[1110] with a gross-tracking skill, found that 20 minutes were better than five minutes and superior to time intervals as long as 120 hours. Kimble came to a similar conclusion, finding that the optimal rest interval was ten minutes. Ammons[27] also found that an intermediate amount of rest was best when learning a pursuit-rotor task. Several experimenters have found that best improvement is achieved when a day's rest is received.

It is interesting to note that Travis found that the performance of a gross motor skill (standing and attempting to keep a pointer on target) was aided by twice the rest time that apparently was desirable when performing and learning a fine motor task. Investigations of the relationship between fine and gross motor performance as a function of spacing or massing of practice seem to be lacking at the present time.

Results of several investigations indicate the advantage of 24-hour rests, as opposed to practice executed in a single day. Riopelle[927] and others have pointed to the advantage of interday rest as opposed to intraday rest in the improvement of performance. Although studies of this nature are common, there is some uncertainty as to whether improvement is due to the 24-hour rest, the sleep obtained, or a combination of conditions.

Most studies of the reminiscence effect do not specify the number of trials in a particular practice session or at least have not attempted to deal with this important variable. The research by Hilgard,[533] dealing with pursuit-rotor performance, is an exception, however. Although he found that the massing of practice in a single session proved initially most desirable, the spacing of trials in a single session became more effective later in the learning process. Plutchik and Petti[900] found that improvement in a pursuit-rotor task was more a function of the *relationship* between the time taken to perform the task and the rest between trials, rather than being dependent simply on the length of the rest period. No significant differences were found in the mean rate of learning between work-rest ratios of 40 to 20 seconds, 30 to 60 seconds, one to two minutes, two to four minutes, and five to two and one-half minutes. The findings suggest that there may also be an optimum work-rest ratio necessary for best performance and learning for a variety of tasks. However, at this point, data of this nature are based only on performance and learning of a pursuit-rotor task.

Reminiscence and Whole versus Part Learning

In 1921, Pechstein, following up on his investigation of the effect of massing in learning small stylus mazes, studied reminiscence as it related to whole versus part learning of a complex maze task. Several interesting conclusions were forthcoming: (1) If the problem is short, massing is best. (2) Connecting the units of a complex task is most economical when practice is massed. Thus, to learn a complex skill, break it into parts and learn the parts by massing practice. (3) Practice of the whole of a complex problem may strain the subject's capacity to analyze and to

13

eliminate unnecessary task components. Pechstein[879] termed this phenomenon the principle of "elimination."

Pechstein also found that the habitual acquisition (the principle of "mechanization") of a complex task was facilitated by using the part method and massing practice. Such practice, it was believed, facilitated the connection of the various parts of the task at the time when the subject was ready to make such connections.

Theories of Reminiscence

The interpretation and synthesis of reminiscence studies are often difficult because of the number of uncontrolled variables. For example, no control is usually exerted over what subjects do during rest intervals. Are they mentally rehearsing or reviewing the task? How are they being taught? How complex is the material being presented? What kinds of material are being learned—verbal, motor, or a combination?

Usually more improvement in "pure" skill results when rest intervals are introduced. Several theories have been formulated to explain this phenomenon, among them the belief that intervals in the practice session result in more forgetting of the incorrect than of the correct responses.[135,312] Other experimenters have concluded that spacing of practice seems to reduce fatigue which may be building up in the learning situation.

Snoddy,[1036] following 20 years of experimentation with the pursuit rotor, formulated a theory of primary and secondary processes in mental growth. The initial improvement evidenced in learning curves was believed to be caused by the spacing of practice and was termed "primary growth." Coming later, "secondary growth" was the result of massed practice.

Hilgard and Marquis,[535] rejecting Snoddy's theory, proposed a more conventional explanation to describe the reminiscence effect. They concluded that, with an overnight rest, forgetting is incomplete and that there is a residual gain from the previous day. "Learning," they believed, accounted for the relatively permanent growth base in the learning curve, "forgetting" for temporary losses.

Hull[562] viewed learning as the acquisition of "reaction potential" while "inhibiting" elements are building up, and believed that with distributed practice, inhibitory processes would largely disappear. Thus, he concluded, more improvement should result when practice periods are spaced. Adams[11] reported a detailed summary of the relationship of Hullian theory to the effects of massing and/or distributing the practice of motor skills.

Several authors have rejected the hypothesis that improvement takes place because of *rest intervals*. Webb,[1158] finding that no difference was obtained from massing or distributing practice on a pursuit rotor, concluded that the *method used* to perform the task was of paramount importance in achieving improvement. Others believe that reminiscence is more closely related to the performance levels attained prior to rest. Kimble[620] attributed improvement after intervals of rest to motivational factors ("reminiscence after twenty-four hours is largely ego-centered").

Eysenck[342] has suggested that reminiscence is a function of drive. His subjects with high levels of drive (produced by suggesting that their scores were critical for their acceptance to engineering school) evidenced higher reminiscence scores during the initial stages of learning but response inhibition ($_sI_r$) slowed their improvement because of rest during the later stages of learning a pursuit-rotor task. On the other hand, subjects who were already assured of acceptance to engineering training evidenced less response inhibition during the later performance trials.

Ammons,[34] among others, derived mathematical formulas to describe the optimal length of rest intervals to learn a pursuit-rotor task best. Goodenough and Brian,[449a] on the other hand, seemed to view the interpolation of rest intervals as an art rather than a science and advocated appropriate interruptions when undesirable habits appear to be retarding progress. Thus they conclude that the efficiency of massing or distributing practice is not based on absolutes.

In 1969, Eysenck[342] wrote that post-rest "upswings" in motor learning tasks may be caused by physiological factors, including a warm-up effect in the muscles when the task is performed again. Citing data indicating that optimum physical performance is elicited by achieving a desirable temperature level in the muscles, Eysenck points out that the effects of distributed and massed practice are greater in the more vigorous gross motor tasks, as well as in less vigorous tasks, when a moderately high body temperature is maintained between trials. Specifically, Eysenck claims that the available data point to several physiological causes for post-rest reminiscence effects in motor task learning and performance, including:

1. Subjects who are making the greatest effort, and thus generating the highest body heat, show improved performance during the pre-rest, as well as during the post-rest, stage.

2. Subjects who work hardest and are the most successful evidence the greatest pre- and post-rest upswings, since they tend to maintain higher temperatures in the body parts used to perform the task.

3. Although not specific to the task, exercise during the "rest" periods of the body parts to be used in the task is more likely to produce reminiscence effects than is exercise of the uninvolved body parts.

Although other contemporary researchers have presented evidence tending to make one skeptical of at least some of Eysenck's speculations, he has made an important contribution to our understanding of the theoretical and practical underpinnings of the "improvement because of spacing practice phenomena" often dealt with in the experimental literature.

In order to truly understand reminiscence, particularly in regard to the more complex, vigorous, and often fatiguing gross motor skills found in athletics, such variables as physiological measures of work output, psychological assessments of boredom, the duration of the work, as well as the duration and distributions of the rest periods, should be included in theoretical speculations.

There is a tendency for many reviewers of the literature on this subject, which is so heavily permeated with studies whose data have come from the pursuit rotor, to overgeneralize and to attempt to explain reminiscence of physical education skills in the same theoretical context. It is increasingly apparent that the pursuit rotor, a reasonably complex but ultimately boring task performed without accompanying physiological fatigue, is highly amenable to improvement because of distributed practice. Physical education and athletic skills, which are many times more straightforward and permeated with heavy demands on large muscle groups, do not always "follow the rules" governing reminiscence which have been derived from highly dissimilar laboratory tasks.

Additional Research Needed

A survey of the literature reveals that the question of whether massed or distributed practice produces more learning remains largely unanswered. Fleishman and Parker[371] found that initially re-learning was facilitated by distributing practice, but that in a short period of time there proved to be no difference in the amount of re-learning possible under massed or distributed conditions. Snoddy[1036] found that spacing practice increased accuracy while massing practice increased speed. These findings are largely confined to fine motor skills, however, and should be extended to determine whether this is also true of gross motor skill. More research also seems to be needed concerning the spacing of trials and massing of trials in a single practice session. Research in this area has been briefly reviewed, but much additional investigation appears necessary.

More extensive investigation of the nature of the task as it is affected by various practice conditions might be fruitful. Are there differences between fine and gross motor learning with respect to reminiscence? Does the nature of the sensory cues that are depended on when learning the task influence the effect of spacing practice? What are the roles of fatigue, motivation, and other such variables on reminiscence? What influences do a variety of work-rest ratios have on reminiscence in different perceptual-motor tasks? These are only some of the problems needing clarification.

The existent research, however, justifies several generalizations: (1) The amount of spacing of practice seems related to the type of task and to the stage of learning reached. (2) Initial massing of practice seems the most desirable means of acquiring a basis from which to proceed. Considering Fleishman's research concerning the multitude of non-motor factors present during initial stages of learning motor tasks, it is plain that such massing must be intelligently applied and be accompanied by knowledge of the tasks. It is also noted that largely motor tasks (e.g., nonvisual maze tracing) seem to be learned best by massing practice, whereas those requiring visual-motor coordination (e.g., juggling and pursuit rotors) seem to be affected most favorably by spacing practice. Such generalizations certainly might be questioned, however, when applied to gross motor skills because of possible fatigue during performance.

Research indicates that the optimal rest time is specific to the nature of the task. Thus, in the absence of exact formulas for the multitude of tasks possible in physical education and allied fields, one might well follow the course of action advocated by Goodenough and Brian[449a] —to employ mass practice initially after first analyzing the task to determine its requirements. If, following evaluation of performance, improvement seems to diminish or plateaus result, rest intervals can be introduced and their effect on progress studied.

The amount of reminiscence evidenced at a given point in the learning of a given skill depends simply on the interest of the performer in the skill rather than on more subtle factors. If the task is interesting, massing practice will produce the best results. If the performer is not challenged by the task, it is too difficult, or he is otherwise repelled by it, distributing practice will lessen the effects of these unpleasant feelings and produce the best learning.

Mental Practice

During the past 30 years, numerous studies have explored the effects of mental rehearsal, conceptualization, symbolic rehearsal, and similarly labeled exercises on the acquisition of skill. In general, the findings from these studies lead to the conclusion that some degree of mental practice combined with physical practice is beneficial to the learning of motor skills.

When reviewing data from mental practice studies, it is important to note that one can study only the influence of some kinds of *instructions* to perform, modification of performance strategy, mental rehearsal, and the like on actual performance measures. Obtaining *direct* assessments by physiological (usually electroencephalographic) measures of the mental processes involved when learning various intellectual and/or physical skills have not been highly successful. In general this research has:

1. Considered the best time to institute instructions to facilitate skill learning.

2. Instructed individuals to imagine themselves performing the skill, to verbalize the sequences in the skill (say it over in their minds), or to imagine themselves observing another individual performing the skill in order to improve skill performance.

3. Explored the influence of various personality and intellectual traits of the learners on skill acquisition.

4. Studied the influence of various degrees of complexity of skills on learners' abilities to rehearse the skills mentally.

5. Studied the effects of physical practice and the effects of simply permitting subjects to observe the performance of a motor task on skill learning.

6. Considered whether the frequency of opportunities and/or instructions to practice a skill mentally has produced task improvement and to what degree.

7. Explored the possible influences of varying combinations of physical practice with mental practice on the ultimate skill levels attained.

8. Studied the influence of instructions to rehearse a skill mentally on the retention of the skill after a period without practice has elapsed.

9. Explored the relationships between mental processes (thinking) and slight muscular responses in the larger muscle groups in skill learning.

Theories of Mental Practice

A number of attempts have been made to explain the reasons for the usually positive findings of studies exploring the effects of mental practice on motor skill. Some explanations revolve around the possible presence of finite muscular responses that purportedly accompany conceptualization of an action. Other researchers have proposed theories with references to mediating verbal responses that may insert themselves between perceptual conditions and motor responses.

Neuromuscular Theories

Results of research by Jacobson[575] and Shaw[991] have revealed that imagining a movement will produce recordable electric action potentials emanating from the same muscle groups that are called on when the movement is to be performed. This phenomenon has also been reported by Ulich[1119] and by Oxendine[867] in more recent studies. The effect also has been confirmed in the subjective reports of those engaged in mental practice studies who have stated, for example, that "during the second trial I felt fatigued in my hand."

Several other investigators have reported that movements of the eye muscles sometimes accompany mental rehearsal of motor skills and that in most cases these movements are similar to those that would be expected if the individual were actually performing the task. This tendency to elicit muscular responses during mental work has been termed "the carpenter effect," and has been defined as the tendency of one's imagination of a motion to produce muscular impulses that correspond to the overtly produced motion itself.

However, it is debatable whether the muscular responses occurring in mental practice studies are as precise as the responses when the movements are actually performed. For example, Oxendine[867] reported that, "during mental practices the total body was tense." He also wrote that some of his subjects rolled their heads and engaged in similar activities when asked to imagine themselves practicing on a pursuit rotor. In this investigation the soccer kick and basketball jump shot were employed, both of which are rather precise actions calling for well-regulated and sequenced acts.

In a recent pilot study, Ulich[1119] recorded the amount of electric potential emanating from the hands of 18 retarded subjects while they mentally practiced a finger dexterity test. He then separated the group into thirds, according to the amount of muscular tension they evidenced (high, medium, low) on an electromyograph. The greatest improvement in the task was recorded by the group evidencing a moderate amount of tension (95 percent improvement as compared to 50 percent and 56 percent for the high- and low-tension groups respectively). Ulich concluded that too much tension reflected disorganized and inefficient muscular impulses accompanying thought, whereas the low-tension group was probably not activated enough. On the other hand, the moderately activated group was most productive, since the muscular responses accompanying their thoughts more closely matched the actual demands of the task. It is believed that, before such a simple neuromuscular way of explaining the positive effects of mental practice becomes a tenable model, further research is needed in which not only the general presence of rather diffuse muscular tension is measured, but also the subtle changes of tension in various muscle groups are recorded in temporal sequences during the mental practice sessions.

Mental activity is often accompanied by a general heightening of muscular tension, a rise that may simply be a reflection of rather global activation-arousal, rather than due to the mental practice of a specific motor skill.

Ideational Elements Theory

One of the most significant differences between animals and men is the ability of the latter to attach symbols to motor tasks, which may result in better retention. Motor skill practice during the early phases of learning is often accompanied by what is termed "verbal mediation," self-directed subvocal verbal rehearsal of the skill attempted. Glanzer and Clark[436a] have suggested that most perceptual information is translated into word series that are retained until time for some kind of reproduction or interpretation. Acceptance of this principle leads to the speculation that thought influences the effects of mental practice on motor skill acquisition. Lambert and Ewert,[649] as well as Warden,[1147] found that verbalization of stylus maze tasks resulted in more proficient performance than when subjects were asked to rely on remembering muscular responses (the kinesthetic method). Warden concluded that there is a substitution of preformed unit responses (composed of muscular-word units?) that provide a helpful base (composed of a verbal pattern) for motor skill learning.

However, it is difficult to accept totally either an ideational-mediation model or a neuromotor model to explain the effects of mental practice or of observational practice on the acquisition of complex motor responses. For example, in several studies with complex tasks, the subjects tended more to rely on verbal self-descriptions and less to exhibit muscular tensions. Moreover, in the same task subjects evidenced highly individual differences and modified the various behaviors they manifested during mental rehearsal as the practice sessions progressed. Just as perceptual-conceptual elements seem to begin to "drop out" (in relation to their importance) as one practices a complex motor skill, so do general and specific muscular tensions as one mentally rehearses reasonably complex movement. Only when the imagined movement is a simple, direct, and forceful weightlifting task will strong muscle responses continue to be manifested during the entire period the subjects are requested to engage in mental rehearsal. Thus, the suggestion is offered that both verbal-cognitive and muscular elements involved during mental rehearsal periods change as a function of task familiarity and complexity.

When to Conceptualize

Several helpful studies have produced data relating to when mental rehearsal and the offering of instructions to mentally rehearse are most likely to aid the learning and performance of a motor skill.

From one of the most sustained programs of study of perceptual-motor skills, Fleishman[369] obtained findings that point to several practical guidelines in this general area. For example, factor analytic studies of the degrees to which various factors apparently contribute to the acquisition of several complex skills indicate that, during initial trials, various conceptual and perceptual factors are most important and contribute most to skill improvement. But during the later stages of learning, such motor competencies as reaction time and measures of kinesthesis correlated highest with the performance of complex criterion tasks used.

Follow-up research based on these findings studied the effects of insertion of instructions appropriate to the stage of learning in which the performer found himself. Thus, during the initial stages of learning, performers were carefully guided through the mechanical principles of the task and permitted to learn about the various spatial relationships of the movements they were to engage in.

During the later stages of learning, instructions concerning various movement qualities were inserted just before, as previous research had indicated, these kinds of abilities become important in skill improvement. The findings of this research program constitute some of the most helpful information emerging from the entire study of human movement capacities. For, with appropriate instructions and, hypothetically, with the appropriate concomitant mental activity elicited by these instructions, marked improvement was achieved and skill levels were reached that were significantly higher than were those attained by control groups. Stebbins,[1056] for example, has found that mental practice during the initial phases of learning a motor skill is as productive as physical practice during the initial trials. This finding would not be expected to hold true, however, if the same physical-mental practice comparisons are made during the later stages of skill acquisition.

Skills Most Improved by Mental Practice

The literature suggests that more complex skills, particularly those involving some kind of throwing-aiming hand-eye coordination, are most improved through mental practice. Relatively simple skills, involving few stages to be integrated, on the whole show little or no improvement with mental practice. The principle obviously arising from this finding suggests that mental practice will aid the learning of a specific skill to the degree to which mental factors are important in the skill's performance.

Individual Differences in Mental Practice Effects

For the past 300 years scholars have been aware of individual differences in human abilities. Although the first differences explored were such simplistic attributes as reaction time and the like; more recently, relatively subtle differences in imagery have been explored. Some of the strategies employed to study mental practice effects have included looking at how individual differences in the way people perceive and organize information influence how they covertly acquire skill.

The preponderance of evidence indicates that scores derived from standardized I.Q. tests are in no way predictive of practice effects, and data from other studies indicate that no sex differences seem to exist in the improvement of motor ability scores as a function of mental practice on five different tasks.

Start[1051] has found, however, that individuals higher in general measures of motor ability and in "game ability" generally derive more benefit from mental practice than do less physically able individuals. However, it is difficult to determine whether those high in motor ability are also those more highly motivated to improve in the experimental situations, or whether real differences in the various groups did indeed exist. It seems that familiarity with the task had an important influence on the percentage of physical versus mental practice that may result in optimum improvement. Among novice basketball players, for example, Clark[197] found that physical practice was almost twice as beneficial as mental practice, whereas with more skilled groups mental practice proved almost equal to physical practice.

Moderate correlations have been obtained (+.63) between percentage of improvement due to mental practice and various measures of visual memory. Whitley[1192] found that those subjects who could remember where on a quadrant various subjects had been placed were generally those who benefited more from mental practice of a physical skill.

However, no significant correlations were obtained between improvement in a mentally rehearsed motor skill and measures obtained from the Gottschaldt test of figure-ground perception. Measures of spatial relations obtained by Wilson[1210a] also failed to correlate with mental practice gains, and similar nonsignificant correlations were noted by Start,[1052] who compared measures of kinesthesis with improvement scores obtained when exposing subjects to a gymnastic skill.

In general, the data suggest that standard measures of kinesthesis, visual memory, figure-ground perception, and the like are not likely to be highly predictive of improvement in motor skill due to mental practice. However, the research is sparse and more sophisticated studies might reveal individual differences in perceptual abilities predictive of the manner in which at least a portion of the population could benefit from engaging in mental practice of motor skills.

Comparisons of Observation, Mental Practice, and Physical Practice

Various strategies can be taken when instructing people to engage mentally in the learning of motor skills. For example, an experimenter may present a highly structured list of directions, such as: "I want you to imagine yourself in the gymnasium, standing behind the throwing line and facing your target. When you feel you have done this as well as you are able, try to rehearse mentally the routine of throwing the ball at the target. Besides trying to see yourself, try to feel yourself going through the routine. Try to see and feel yourself picking up the ball, putting the ball behind you as you transfer your weight backward onto your rear foot in preparation for the throw. Try then to imagine the second part of the action, in which, having selected your point of aim on the target, you complete the throw with a forward twisting movement of the body and a forward movement of the arm and hand. Watch the ball during its flight. Remember the target has been dusted with chalk and the place where the ball strikes will remain clearly marked after the ball has rebounded from the target. Give this mark careful attention and in your next throw try to make any adjustments in your action and in the selection of your point of aim that you feel will result in a more accurate throw. I shall stop you in 15 minutes. Now quietly concentrate."

On the other hand, the experimenter may permit the subjects a period of time for both physical and mental practice of the skill, as Oxendine and Egstrom have done. Still other experimenters permitted subjects to observe the performance of a skill they were later to reproduce, but tendered no formal and structured instructions as to how the subjects might imaginably practice the skill.

In general, when the improvement of these groups is compared, the data are relatively consistent. Ulich[1119] found that the observation group improved 47.4 percent, the "mental training" group 63.2 percent, and the physical practice group 96.6 percent. The greatest improvement in a task of finger dexterity was achieved by a group given alternate physical and mental practice, and Ulich reports that the controls given no practice in the task improved only 20.3 percent on the second testing (Fig. 18–2).

Optimum Time

There seems to be an optimum time devoted to rehearsing a skill that is likely to produce the most improvement in motor skill. Twining[1114] found that about five minutes were as long as he could expect his subjects to concentrate on the task he asked them to rehearse mentally. Difficult to control in these studies, of course, is what enters the subject's thoughts when he is not instructed to rehearse mentally, and thus estimates about how long an individual really engaged in conceptualization about the skill are probably inaccurate. Shick[1000] also found that mental practice for three minutes was superior to mental practice for one minute in the acquisition of a volleyball skill.

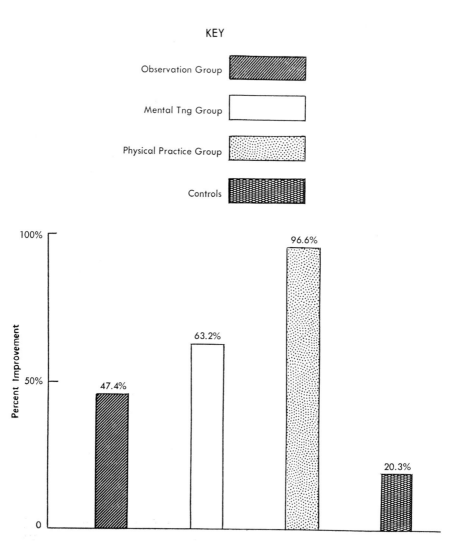

FIGURE 18–2. Comparison of improvement by observation, mental training, and physical practice on the same motor task. (Redrawn from data by
Ulich, E.: Some experiments on the function of mental training on the acquisition of motor skill. Ergonomics, *4,* 411-419, 1957.)

Some researchers asked their subjects to think about things other than the skill involved, and Cratty and Densmore[264] asked their control groups either to engage in a knot-tying task or to count backwards from 100 in a 1962 study of mental practice effects.

Alternating Physical Practice with Mental Practice

A number of researchers have compared the improvement of groups who have mentally practiced a task with the improvement of those who have engaged in varying amounts of physical plus mental practice. In general, their findings indicate that some combination is better than engaging only in mental practice. Egstrom's findings[320] indicate that the groups alternating physical and mental practice performed about equally as well as those engaging entirely in physical practice in a task that involved hitting a ball toward a target with their non-preferred hand.

Retention after Mental Practice

Relatively few studies have been carried out to determine the lasting influence of mental practice on motor skill acquisition. Oxendine[867] found that the retention of the various groups in his study did not differ significantly, and Sackett,[960] with a finger maze, obtained the same results. Rubin-Rabson,[944] studying piano playing ability, found that a group who employed physical practice initially and then a mental practice followed by physical practice, retained better, after a week had passed, than other groups who had either all physical practice or first practiced mentally and then physically.

Ulich[1119] also reports an interesting finding in a study that employed a finger dexterity test, and in which a six-month rest period was inserted between initial practice and later testing for retention. The two groups, one given all mental practice and a second in which mental practice was alternated with physical practice, not only retained best but even evidenced slight improvement. The other two groups, having had physical practice only, and "training" solely through the opportunity to observe the dexterity task, showed significant decrements! Owing to the scarcity of data, little can be done at this point relative to a valid interpretation of these findings, however.

Summary

Although often with conflicting results, studies of massing versus distributing the practice of physical skills generally indicate that, if the skill does not require a great deal of physical effort, distributing practice is best. On the other hand, if the task is taxing, one must carefully consider the ratio between the time devoted to practice and the time inter-polated between practice trials. Since much of the evidence relating reminiscence to motor skill learning has been based on tasks found only in the psychological laboratory, only superficial guidelines are available when dealing with tasks involving large muscle groups and vigorous effort.

Whole practice results in quicker learning if the learner is capable of grasping the "whole" tendered to him by his instructor or by the situation. When the learner is immature, the task is extremely complex, and/or the performer is retarded, progressive-part practice is often best. This method involves gradually building on one or more subresponses until the task is practiced in its entirety.

Although findings of several studies indicate that mental practice had little or no effect on the improvement of physical skill and strength, the majority of the research efforts have had positive outcomes. The re-searchers have found two to ten times as much improvement in groups asked to rehearse mentally (based on percentage of gain) as compared to groups without practice. However, the data emerging from the major-ity of the studies indicate that physical practice is from slightly better than mental practice to several times more effective in the case of studies where sheer physical output (endurance or force) is the main require-ment in the task.

Student Reading

Cratty, B. J.: *Teaching Motor Skills.* Englewood Cliffs, N.J., Prentice-Hall, Inc., 1973.

Cratty, B. J.: Mental components of motor skill learning. In *Physical Expressions of Intelligence.* Englewood Cliffs, N.J., Prentice-Hall, Inc., 1972, Chapter 8.

Oxendine, J.: Conditions for learning. In *Psychology of Motor Learning.* New York, Appleton-Century-Crofts, 1968, Part IV.

Richardson, A.: Mental practice: A review and discussion. Res. Quart., 38, 95-107, 1967.

Sage, G.: Conditions affecting motor skill acquisition and performance: Practice. In *Introduction to Motor-Behavior, a Neurophysiological Approach.* Menlo Park, Calif., Addison Wesley, 1971.

19
TRANSFER

Two factors basic to human learning are the ability to discriminate and the ability to generalize. The transfer concept is closely related to the latter quality and involves the tendency to draw from past experience when learning a new task. To define *transfer* merely as generalization, however, is similar to stating that green is greenness and white, whiteness. For clarity, *transfer* is best explained as *the effect that the practice of one task has on the learning or performance of a second.*

The basketball mentor strives to construct practice tasks that will be transferable to the game situation. The physical therapist is concerned with the re-education of an impaired limb when an adjacent member is exercised. The physical educator and industrial psychologist are interested in facilitating the learning of complex skills and in devising test batteries predicting proficiency in a variety of tasks. An understanding of transfer, therefore, is important to the athletic coach, the physical educator, the industrial psychologist, and the therapist.

In addition to the obvious "how-to-do-it-better" approach to the learning of skills, a review of the research dealing with transfer sometimes aids in the identification of basic task factors. If transfer is caused by the presence of identical elements in two tasks, identification of these elements usually results in a deeper understanding of movement constituents. Investigation of transfer also helps to clarify the generality and specificity question discussed in Chapter 10.

The extent to which transfer occurs among various mental and motor tasks has been at the core of educational theory for the past 100 years. Those educators advocating a formal doctrine of education believed that general habits, including the ability to think and reason, transferred from such school subjects as Latin and algebra to many tasks. At the turn of the century, however, many educational psychologists, on finding only slight transfer from one school subject to another, suggested that human functioning was highly specific. The controversy continues, and the extent to which practice of one task facilitates the learning of a second frequently rests on the kind of evidence the experimenter is willing to consider, as well as the kinds of tasks under consideration.

The transfer concept may be studied in several contexts. Transfer may be negative, positive, or have no influence. Practice of an initial task may facilitate, impede, or have no significant influence on the learning of a second.

Some investigators insisted that all adult learning and performance result from transfer from childhood experiences. McGeogh and Irion[767] suggested that, after "small amounts of learning early in the life of the individual, every instance of learning is a result of transfer." Hebb[507] pointed out that, when little or no "transfer" is noted when comparing adult skills, it is probably due to the fact that transfer from the individual's past experiences "must have been complete before the experiments began." In contrast are those researchers who contend that, because of the limited extent to which skilled movements are seen to transfer in studies using mature subjects, motor performance and learning are highly dependent on specific conditions connected with the immediate task.

On further consideration of motor skills research, several other classification systems become apparent. On the one hand are investigations dealing with cross education, or the bilateral transfer of skill and/or strength in the individual. These studies investigate the extent to which skill and strength are transferred from limb-to-limb (hand-to-hand, hand-to-foot, foot-to-hand). A second category deals with the influence of the performance and practice of one complex skill on proficiency in a second. In the second group are studies exploring the influence of verbal pretraining on a motor task, the transfer of task components to the completed act, the transfer of task principles, and the transfer of skills containing similar or different spatial dimensions, force requirements, and/or time intervals.

Following a brief historical overview of the problem, research on cross education will be discussed together with investigations of transfer between tasks. The influence of practice schedule and task complexity on transfer is also discussed in this section. The chapter concludes with a summary, including questions remaining to be answered concerning the transfer phenomena.

A Historical Look at Transfer

As pointed out by Wieg,[1201] interest in the problem of transfer between limbs dates back to the middle of the nineteenth century. Weber, in the United States, and Fechner, in Germany, both found that training of distance discrimination transferred from the trained hand to the idle one. In 1899, Woodworth[1224] discovered that the ability to draw straight lines was transferable between limbs. In 1892, Bryant[147] reported the same phenomenon when measuring the tapping ability of children at various ages. He also found that cross fatigue was independent of general body fatigue. Scripture,[976] working at the Yale Psychological Laboratory at the turn of the century, also noted, from the study of a tapping exercise, and from an investigation of the ability to thrust a needle into a small hole, that transfer of skill occurred between limbs of the body. Transfer studies concerned with the cross-education effect continued during the years and utilized stylus mazes,[214] adding machine tasks, mirror target practice,[127] and the like.

The first studies concerned with transfer between tasks mainly seemed based on mental problems. Although prior to 1900 educators assumed that such general qualities as attention to a task and the ability to reason transferred between various school subjects, Thorndike and Woodworth[1097] declared the opposite to be true. After studying a number of tasks they concluded that human functioning (both mental and motor) was specific. They believed that it was incorrect to be concerned with general qualities, such as sense discrimination, attention, memory, observation, accuracy, and quickness, which were purported to underlie a number of tasks, rather that an individual's mind works in great detail, adapting itself to the "special data of the situation."

Although subsequent studies have purported to examine transfer between various "motor" tasks, in reality most of the transfer studies utilize tasks relying heavily on verbal-cognitive functions. Various tracking studies by Lincoln and Smith,[691] rotary-pursuit tasks by Namikas and Archer[832] and others, as well as various paired association tasks, encourage the subject verbally to rehearse elements that might result in transfer. Studies concerned with "pure" motor acts are less frequent although those by Woodward,[1223] Cratty,[239] Henry,[520] Lindeburg,[692] and Nelson[839] point in this direction.

Theories of Transfer

Numerous theories have been devised to explain transfer of skill. While the identical elements theory and the general factors theory are the most popular, several others become apparent on a review of the literature. A third category might include statements that accept both a general and a specific explanation of transfer. A general Gestaltic concept of "transposition" has also been proposed. In addition, various neurological explanations attempting to explain transfer in anatomical terms have been reported. The concept of "nerve impulse diffusion" is representative of this latter classification.

General Elements Theory

An initial proponent of the general elements, or factors, theory was Judd.[600] He concluded that general instructions were transferable, since he found that individuals were aided in hitting a submerged target with an arrow when the principle of refraction of light was explained to them. Judd believed that motor accuracy was due to unconscious transfer from previous tasks to present movement needs and came about as a result of use of neurological pathways established for tasks performed earlier.

Results of several studies reported in the intervening years seem to substantiate the general elements theory first proposed by Judd. In 1921, Norcross,[854] from studying adding machine skill, concluded that transfer was due to emotional factors, mental readiness for the task, ability to concentrate on the task, freedom from distractions, and other general conditions. Woodward,[1223] from studying the transfer of training in two industrial skills, thought that, although the transfer might have been due to the presence of identical spatial requirements in the two tasks, it was more likely due to a similarity in the general work situations.

Harlow,[490] from his classic investigation of "learning sets," concluded that both children and primates evidenced the ability to begin at successively higher levels when problems of a single classification were presented to them. Both species seemed to be learning how to learn, and the author suggested that his data indicated that his subjects "can gradually learn insight."[490]

Seymour,[988] presenting a synthesis of transfer literature in 1955, suggested that transfer is merely evidence that individuals learn to select the most appropriate muscle groups to be used, resulting in less "fumbling" when performing industrial tasks. He thought that improvement was generally due to improving general methods rather than to transfer of specifics. Seymour concluded his synthesis with the suggestion that experiments investigating general principles of transfer rather than task minutia be conducted. In addition, Seymour believed that the study of individual differences in the ability to transfer experience should hold promise for the future.

Denny and Reisman,[293] after studying the role of anxiety in transfer, presented findings suggesting that general tension might impede transfer of skill. When attempting to transfer skill, individuals who scored high on Taylor's Manifest Anxiety Scale had more marked initial feelings of failure when the task changed and did poorly in subsequent attempts at the changed task. Individuals who were not anxious, on the other hand, were found to adapt more readily to a change of task and to benefit more from the previous task practice.

In 1952, Lewis and Smith[686] presented a summary of the prevalent arguments for a general factors theory of motor transfer. After finding that transfer was not impeded when specific stimuli and responses of a task were modified, they proposed a theory that attempted to explain the acquisition of proficiency in complex motor tasks and the simultaneous negative and positive transfer effects sometimes seen. Lewis and

Smith thought that five constructs were important in summarizing their argument: (1) *dexterity*, understanding the general task requirements; (2) *facilitation*, the tendency to respond to general unchanging features of a task; (3) *skill*, the ability to modify one's responses and to predict changes in the task situation while performing; (4) *interference*, the tendency, owing to past experience, to make inappropriate responses to any part of the task situation; and (5) *inhibition*, the tendency to suppress irrelevant or inappropriate responses. *Performance potential*, they concluded, was a function of all the tendencies to make appropriate responses or to inhibit inappropriate ones, minus some function of all tendencies to make inappropriate ones.

Identical Elements Theory

More numerous are the studies pointing out that transfer is possible only when elements of one task correspond exactly to those of the second. Generally, these elements are considered to consist of similar stimuli or responses that are identical. So, while the generalist speaks of common conditions resulting in transfer, the researcher advocating the identical elements theory is concerned with small bits of the tasks, in the form of discrete stimuli or responses, that are similar, rather than with patterns or meanings.

Baker and Wylie[58] and Namikas and Archer[832] reported findings that upheld the identical elements theory. Both, from rotary-pursuit tasks, found that greatest transfer occurred when the revolutions of their devices were similar. Individuals seemed to program their "memory drums" specifically for the task practiced, such as following a target at 60 r.p.m. rather than at 70 or 50 r.p.m.

Lincoln,[690] from studying tracking ability, and Smith and Von Trebra,[1027] after investigating the ability to manipulate knobs and to travel manually from one knob to another, and Gagne et al.,[399] from a study of the ability to press buttons when presented with light stimuli, all point to the specificity of skill and hold that transfer is due to similarity in responses or stimuli between two variations of the same task.

In general, such researchers theorize that a "gradient of generalization" related to stimulus or to response exists and that transfer will occur to the extent that similarities between either exist. In some instances, subjects generalize from stimulus to stimulus or recognize similarities in the elements that cue or trigger the movements of the task. In this context, the S-R specificist holds that *stimulus generalization* has caused the transfer. In other cases, it is felt that a similarity in responses facilitated transfer, that the subject, usually consciously, recognized the similarity in the movement responses required of him when performing the two tasks, and that *response generalization* has taken place.

Gestaltic Theory

In opposition to those advocating specificity of transfer, and slightly modified from the position taken by most generalists who attempt to explain transfer in neurological terms, stand the classic Gestaltic learning theorists who hold that transfer occurs when a pattern of dynamic relationships is discovered in two learning situations. "Transposition" is said to take place if the practice of one task facilitates the learning of a second.

"Transposition" may occur due to the presence of common patterns, configurations, or relationships. One learns, these theorists believed, from previous task experience through understandings, not through the discovery of piecemeal stimuli or discrete responses common to two situations. It is believed that through this type of understanding one is able to transfer his experience to a wider range of situations, rather than to the limited ones possible in stimulus-response terms.

In 1961, I[246] published results of a study that utilized Gestaltic terms to explain transfer. Studying the effect of small-pattern practice on large-pattern learning (with maze tasks of varying sizes), I found that practicing a small pattern while blindfolded facilitated large-pattern learning of a similar pattern, and that practice in a reverse small-pattern impeded large-pattern learning. Negative and positive transfer occurred, depending on pattern relationships. The subjects seemed to learn the tasks as patterned wholes and seemed to be unaware of the relationships involved, owing to the irregular shape of the maze pathways and the emphasis on speed in performance. I concluded that negative and positive transfer was explained best in Gestaltic terms.

Two-Factor Theories

In addition to general neurological factors theories, identical elements theory, and Gestaltic theory, several investigators suggest that transfer may occur from a combination of factors, both general and specific. This theory suggests that individuals not only transfer such generalities as "learning-how-to-learn" and "general work methods," but also learn new tasks through the acquisition of stimulus and/or response patterns.

This theory was advanced by Munn[824] when he studied the bilateral transfer of mirror tracing. He concluded that the formulation of method as well as discrete movements of the opposite hand probably caused transfer. Duncan[308] echoed this view when, after studying transfer in a lever-positioning skill, he concluded that "learning-how-to-learn," as well as "response generalization," had facilitated transfer. Wieg,[1201] after studying bilateral transfer in adults and children when learning cul-de-sac mazes, also believed that attention to the task, as well as attention to discrete cues, facilitated transfer from one maze task to another.

In 1921, Norcross,[854] after studying the ability to use an adding machine, held that various emotional factors, such as readiness for the task, as well as task specifics, influenced transfer. Swift,[1082] after studying the ability to keep two balls in the air with one hand, concluded that alterations in the central nervous system, as well as the ability to comprehend and to meet a situation, caused bilateral transfer. Meredith,[786] reporting results of research in 1941, also took an eclectic approach when explaining transfer. He thought that transfer depends on an individual's awareness of the usable common elements, verbalization of the task, and factors unique to the task.

From a theoretical standpoint, then, transfer may depend on (1) general factors underlying several tasks, (2) pathways in the nervous system, (3) the existence of identical elements (usually stimulus-response elements) common to two tasks, (4) the "transposition" of meanings, understanding, or configurations from one task to a second, and (5) a combination of factors, both general and specific. It would seem that the last explanation holds the most promise at the present time. Results of studies of tasks that can be analyzed in discrete elements (e.g., paired serial learning tasks and light to lever position tasks) generally support the identical elements theory, but results of more complex and integrated tasks support a generalized or Gestaltic approach. The careful student, however, most frequently seems to attribute the influence of one complex task on the performance and learning of a second to several kinds of factors, those accompanying the general experimental environment and conditions unique to the tasks compared.

Within the stimulus-response theory, Osgood[864] and others have attempted to delineate rather precisely just when one can expect positive transfer, negative transfer, or no transfer between two tasks. Correct application of these principles to the teaching of motor skills, including those found on the athletic field, is believed imperative. It is usual to find that the more nearly identical the stimulus elements (what the performer sees) and the response elements are, the greater the positive transfer elicited. Indeed, if both stimulus elements and response elements are identical, the individual will be engaging in successive practice of the same skill, and it is clear that most of the time practice produces improvement.

Most likely to elicit negative transfer are situations in the second skill in which the individual is required to react to the same stimulus, but in a different manner. He may have been schooled in a tip-in drill in basketball in which he is required to tip the ball off the backboard to a waiting teammate who in turn tips it back to him. In this situation, negative transfer to the same situation might occur; the stimuli are roughly similar in drill and game—a ball rebounding from a backboard. However, the motor responses required in each task are different. In the first instance the object is to tip the ball over the basket to a team-mate, whereas in the second situation (game), the intent is to tip the ball *into* the basket.

Usually, slight positive transfer occurs when the individual is exposed to different stimuli and required to make relatively similar movement responses. Learning to throw to first base is facilitated by drills in which the ball is thrown toward the shortstop from several directions. Indeed, in many drill situations it is desirable to expose the individual to a variety of stimuli (perceptual situations), similar to those that occur in the game or competition, so that he will be able to respond quickly to a variety of conditions.

Additionally, negative transfer may be elicited in situations that are apparently the same, but are actually different in terms of velocities, spatial dimensions of the task, and basic principles. Several years ago a student of mine was surprised to find that practicing an underhand throw in softball did not transfer positively to the underhand serve of volleyball. Her experiment contained a critical variable, however, she *told* her subjects that indeed the principles involved in the two tasks were the same. Although the tasks resemble each other superficially, in fact the weight and size of the two objects and the fact that in one task (volleyball serve) the action involves a striking motion whereas in the second it is a sweeping ballistic movement make the *real* principles in the two tasks different. If subjects assume that the general elements are the same, and practice follows this assumption, the subjects are likely to be confused and have less ability to perform and learn the second task.

Thus, two tasks may be similar enough to be confusing, causing negative transfer, and until the tasks are made almost identical no positive transfer is likely to occur. Illustrating this principle, Britt[136] found that, when two activities differed to the maximum in content, meaning, form, method of execution, and environment, negative transfer occurred. As the relative degree of similarity of one or all these factors was increased, more negative transfer occurred. A point was eventually reached, however, at which increasing the degree of similarity resulted in the performer's identification of the various factors. From this point on, the amount of negative transfer tended to decrease until, at the upper limit, all factors were identified and no inhibition occurred, with the exception of the effect of task repetition.

Additional fallacies concerning the effects of drill-to-game transfer of skill in athletics revolve around the slow strength-eliciting movements that some throwers employ in training and the rapid ballistic actions that are actually required to propel the javelin, baseball, or shotput in competition. Although the exact dimensions required to elicit positive transfer in regard to speed components of two throwing tasks are not precisely known, it *is* known that if the speed and load differences are as great as assumed by some manufacturers of commercial exercise equipment used to "improve" football, track, and baseball skills, there is a strong likelihood that either no transfer or even negative transfer will occur.

From a practical standpoint, it appears generally that, between a practice task and the focal or "reference" task, there may be no similarities in either general or specific elements, in which case, usually neither positive nor negative transfer effects can be measured. However, in many instances, it is probable that some elements (either specific or general) common in the two tasks will elicit positive transfer effects, and at the same time there may be other common elements that will cause negative transfer effects. Thus, the degree to which negative or positive transfer is measured depends on whether the *summation* of the negative transfer elements equals, exceeds, or fails to exceed the total of the common elements likely to produce positive transfer.

Thus, practice drills may produce positive transfer to game situations and for this reason are lauded, disseminated, and exploited by athletic coaches. However, in truth such drills may simply contain more positive transfer chainings than they do negative ones. When preparing practice drills, general and specific elements in both practice and focal tasks that elicit positive transfer should be maximized rather than simply designing drills that "seem to work well," which those unsophisticated in the analysis of skills and/or unfamiliar with principles governing transfer of training often do.

The Measurement of Transfer

Transfer may be evaluated in a number of ways: determination of whether practice and learning affect subsequent performance on a second task (or on the same task performed with another limb); whether initial practice affects later learning; and whether prior learning on one task affects subsequent learning on a second task. These possibilities may be measured as shown in Figure 19–1. Despite clear-cut guidelines, there is more than one conundrum that may plague a researcher experimenting with motor transfer effects. For example, the separation of the influence of mental elements from motor elements in the two tasks is often difficult if not impossible. Controlling the amount of mental practice the subjects engaged in between administrations of the task, as in most learning studies, is a second difficult matter, as is the problem of precise analysis of the stimulus and/or response elements in the tasks. Furthermore, variation in the quantity of learning permitted the subjects in either the "practice" or the "reference" task in transfer studies is likely to elicit a parallel variation in transfer effects. Finally, separation of the effects of

PERFORMANCE-TO-PERFORMANCE EFFECTS

Key

Experimental Subjects ─────────

Control Subjects ------------

LEARNING-TO-PERFORMANCE EFFECTS

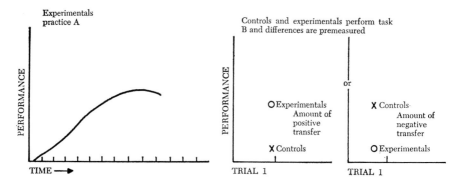

LEARNING-TO-LEARNING EFFECTS

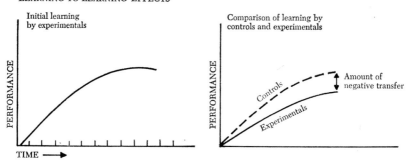

PERFORMANCE-TO-LEARNING EFFECTS

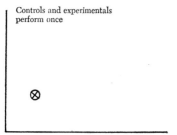

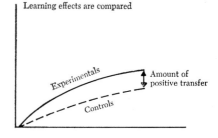

FIGURE 19–1.

massing practice versus distributing practice from the actual transfer effects elicited is also a formidable undertaking.

Further complicating the problem of the measurement of transfer is the determination of what transfer effects may have occurred in the final reference task from the previous experiences of the subjects. For example, it is likely that few positive transfer effects will be elicited in studies in which mature and intellectually capable subjects are employed because they are able to draw on extensive past experience and apply it to the final reference task, experience that overcomes the often short-term exposure to some practice tasks from which transfer is expected.

Additionally when studying transfer to a second task with a performance or learning curve, sometimes positive or negative effects will not become apparent until later in the learning process, when perhaps interfering or facilitating elements in the performance of the task, which related to those in the reference task, come into prominence; that is, there may either be a delay in the emergence of negative or positive transfer effects, or transfer effects noted initially in a performance curve may be obliterated after a series of practice trials. The early emergence and later obliteration of transfer effects were noted by Leonard et al.[674] when they studied transfer of rotary-pursuit learning. More studies similar to those by Vincent,[1136] in which transfer of perceptual components versus motor components of tasks was studied, should provide additional and valuable information on this aspect of motor skill transfer.

Illustrating the influence of past experience on positive transfer are the findings of Ann Clarke[198,199] and her colleagues in England, who consistently noted that retarded subjects transferred positive effects from one simple sorting task to another. The same positive effects probably cannot be measured in mature, intellectually capable individuals in whom transfer to the second sorting task occurred prior to entering the experimental situation, owing to their rich and remembered past experiences with sorting.

The Relationships of Tasks in Time

Theoretically, two conditions in the temporal placement of tasks are important in the study of negative and positive transfer effects. A task may be affected negatively or positively by tasks that have been practiced prior to the initial task (proactive transfer), or will be affected positively or negatively by a task or tasks inserted *after* an initial exposure to the reference task (retroactive transfer). These two conditions can be studied experimentally as shown in Figure 19–2. In both "experiments" one must be certain to equate the groups initially, and to vary the amount of task B to which the groups are exposed in order to determine the quantitative effects as well as the qualitative effects of transfer forward (proactive) or backward (retroactive) in time,

PROACTIVE TRANSFER

Experimental group	Practice task B	Perform (or learn) task A
Control groups	No practice	Perform (or learn) task A

RETROACTIVE TRANSFER

Experimental group	Practice task A	Practice task B	Re-perform task A
Control groups	Practice task A	No practice	Re-perform task A

FIGURE 19–2. **Experimental plans for the study of proactive and retroactive transfer. The proactive effects of task B on task A can be determined from the plan under proactive transfer, and the retroactive effects of task B on task A can be ascertained from the setup under retroactive transfer.**

Consideration of Figure 19–2 leads to many speculations concerning the effects of practice periods on weekend athletic contests. Is positive improvement from game to game due more to the result of previously played games or to interpolated practice? Is practice in certain drills prior to and following previous games more beneficial than is practice in others? Do the negative practice effects overcome the positive, or vice versa? Can the possibly negative transfer effects that occur proactively be overcome by inserting desirable drills into the practice periods during weekdays? Finally, what positive and negative transfer effects, which may occur both forward and backward in time, operate between drills, and between drills and contest?

Bilateral Transfer of Skill

Initial studies concerning the transfer phenomena came about when it was observed that the performance of a skill with one hand seemed to "teach" the same skill to the other hand. Such transfer from hand-to-hand is termed "bilateral" transfer. Although bilateral transfer has been studied from several standpoints and many kinds of motor and perceptual-motor tasks have been employed, much remains to be learned. Reviews of research concerning cross transfer were prepared by Wieg,[1201] Bray,[127] and Ammons.[30]

Many of the skills that were studied in order to determine the nature and conditions of cross education of skill have involved fine motor tasks or perceptual-motor skills. Wieg's[1201] cul-de-sac maze tasks learned blindfolded and Cook's[215] small irregularly patterned mazes are examples. One of the few studies in the literature dealing with a gross motor skill is that of Swift,[1082] in which he studied the transfer of juggling skill (keeping two balls in the air with one hand) from one hand to the other (hand-to-hand). The task, however, seems to depend heavily on cognitive and verbal elements.

In general, the research indicates that transfer from hand-to-hand of a skilled act always occurs to some degree. It is usually understood to indicate that skilled performance is a function of *central* rather than of *peripheral* processes in the nervous system. In early studies in this area by Woodworth[1224] and by Bray,[127] a motor task observed by the performer in a mirror was utilized. Woodworth[1224] used mirror star tracing; Bray[127] utilized target spotting with a pencil while viewing the act from a mirror. Both found that transfer not only occurred from hand-to-hand, but also from hand-to-foot and from foot-to-foot and from feet-to-hands. Cook[215] also noted that transfer between all four limbs of the body occurred when learning a maze task. Eberhard[317] published results of an investigation that make a valuable contribution to our knowledge of transfer, specifically the importance of visual and intellectual processes in the learning of visual-motor skills. He found that as much bilateral transfer occurred in a one-handed manipulative task as was derived when the subjects simply *watched* another individual perform the task first!

Researchers concerned with cross education of skilled performance have given many reasons for the phenomenon. Ammons,[30] summarizing studies in this area, suggests that the following are the usual rationale given for bilateral transfer: cues from verbal self-instruction, visual cues, relaxing effects of practicing a skill, general muscular tension accompanying the skill, body position and posture, movements of the entire body, eye movements, head movement, complex perceptual adjustments, formulation of principles of efficiency, familiarity with the general nature of the task, neural structure, past learning of highly similar skills, effects of fatigue, consistency and stability of approach, subliminal practice of the skill by the ostensibly idle limbs, solutions to problems in the handling of equipment, emotional adjustments, and feelings of confidence or boredom.

The questions seem to be, what kinds of practice conditions and tasks best facilitate transfer? And more important, will learning of a skill with one hand be facilitated by ambidextrous practice during the learning process? Few attempts seem to have been made to answer these questions, although Bray[127] suggests, from a mirror target hitting task, that cross education was present only during the initial trials, with later ones showing no such transfer. In addition, Allen[20] suggests that alternate practice from hand-to-hand of a mirror drawing task produced higher efficiency than massed practice with the same hand prior to attempting the skill with the second limb.

Studies have also shown that the effects of motivation further becloud the amount of bilateral transfer observed. Ammons[30] thought that the lowering of proficiency in a rotary-pursuit task, by high school girls in the upper grades, was probably due to motivation. He further suggested that, with a high level of motivation, a poorly transferable task would be frustrating and would probably produce extreme variability in performance. Likewise, a poorly motivated group might not exhibit the transfer expected due to a lack of attention to the details of the task or some such factor.

There is some conjecture, however, as to whether more transfer occurs from the dominant to the non-dominant hand, or whether the reverse is true, and whether such transfer is due to the dominance factor or to the general level of limb proficiency. In general, it seems that both factors are operative. Swift[1082] suggests that, in juggling a ball, the transfer from right to left hand was less when the proficiency of the left hand was lower. The same was found to be true by Briggs and Brodgen[133] from study of a pursuit task. This suggests that the amount of transfer is mainly a function of the proficiency of the limb *from* which or *to* which the transfer occurs. Wieg[1201] found that transfer of a maze skill was greater for adults than for children. Cook[215] also suggested that transfer is determined by the proficiency of the first limb trained.

The use of research findings concerning the transfer phenomena may be twofold: (1) Some experimental evidence may be used to study the effects of brain damage and of other injury to the central nervous system. Freeman[383] utilized bilateral transfer to pinpoint neurological functioning. (2) Transfer research can be utilized to identify the common components of two tasks or to identify discrete elements in a new task.

Ammons[30] suggested that a "reference" skill, the components of which have been identified, might be used in studying factors in a second task. However, greater objectivity needs to be achieved in pinpointing common factors that appear to be related to positive transfer between skills before the use of such "reference" skills can be applied with confidence to ordinary skill development.

Cross Transfer and Physical Education

What implications do the findings on transfer from hand-to-hand have for the physical educator? Most so-called gross motor tasks, such as ball throwing, involve fine adjustments. The finite adjustments of fingers, for example, are necessary when releasing a ball in a throwing act. It would seem that practice with both hands, the dominant and the non-dominant, might facilitate the learning of many such tasks by the preferred hand. If findings concerning the effects of fatigue on accuracy are valid, it would seem that one could practice longer with more positive results by utilizing the non-dominant hand and resting the dominant one. If skill is partially a function of the central nervous system, practice at the cortical level could continue, whereas localized muscular fatigue in a particular limb might impede continued practice with that member. Investigations of these concepts are absent from the literature.

Further research is needed to identify (1) the kinds of tasks that seem to transfer most effectively, (2) the reasons for bilateral transfer, and (3) at what point practice with the non-preferred limb should be introduced for best results. In addition, the important variable of motivation in relation to amount of transfer needs further investigation, as does the transfer of skills from hand-to-foot and from foot-to-foot. Soccer skills involve extensive use of the lower extremities, and from a practical standpoint, coaches of this sport might be interested in the extent to which the feet acquire movements first learned by the upper limbs and the extent to which practice of kicking with the left foot facilitates proficiency in the right leg.

Verbal-Motor Transfer

Transfer from hand-to-hand (or cross transfer) is sometimes facilitated by verbal self-instruction, solution of special task problems, or the formulation of principles relating to two tasks. Consequently, it seems important to examine the extent to which verbal pretraining transfers to the performance of a skilled motor act.

Many of the tasks used in studies in this area have consisted of paired-serial skills. Gagne et al.[400] used a panel of switches cued by visual signals. The correct pairings between a visual signal and a switch were practiced verbally. The extent to which verbal pretraining transferred to the motor act was studied and taken as the amount of speed achieved in the final visual-motor act. A level-positioning skill used by Battig[73] and the pairing of lights to switches studied by Baker et al.[58] are typical examples of the types of skill that seem best adaptable to verbal pretraining.

In most cases, a complex motor task involving discrete stimulus-response elements, either alone or in series, is facilitated by verbal rehearsal of the pairings desired. The practice of a verbal formula (e.g., "red light means number one switch" or "initial positioning of a lever," "blue light means switch number three") seems to transfer to the motor act. Subjects who received this type of training performed at a higher level than did those who received no such training.

However, there seems to be an optimal amount of preverbal practice. Baker[58] noted that small amounts of preverbal practice had no effect, and it was only when larger amounts were introduced that the light-to-switch skill was facilitated. Underwood,[1120] on the other hand, found that after a certain amount of verbal pretraining no improvement was noted later.

Verbal pretraining seems to facilitate a motor act that is easily translated to a word description. In addition to the kinds of paired serial tasks already described, McAllister[751] found that verbal pretraining facilitated a task in which the subjects were required to move a rod to various star points when they were confronted with colored light stimuli. Pretraining (with word formulas) seemed most helpful in reducing errors, rather than in improving speed in tasks of this nature.

The literature deals mainly with the effects of verbal pretraining in paired association acts. Motor acts involving fast or irregular movement patterns either have not been studied or are so difficult to reduce to a word formula that the results have been negative or simply have not lent themselves to verbal pretraining.

It would seem that the baseball coach, requiring accurate placement of the ball in discrete game situations, might rely on verbal pretraining. (Instruction, such as "With two outs and a man on first, a ball hit to the shortstop should be relayed to second base," might facilitate the motor act.) On the other hand, it appears doubtful that an excessive amount of verbal pretraining in an irregular and continuous movement pattern, such as is required in a tennis serve, would facilitate learning. In some cases, an excessive amount of verbal pretraining might result in impaired performance, as when the performer attempts to slow down a ballistic pattern to correspond to the time needed to translate the movement into a word formula.

Although further research is needed in this area, it appears accurate to assume that paired association tasks will probably be facilitated by a moderate amount of verbal pretraining, but movements of an irregular or rapid nature probably will not be greatly aided by pretask verbalizing.

Task-to-Task Transfer

Results of studies of transfer from one motor or spatial-motor task to another, using mature subjects, usually point to the specificity of motor skill. Lindeberg[692] studied the transfer of "coordination" exercises to sports activities and found none. Nelson,[839] from another study of gross motor activities, indicated that the deliberate teaching of principles for three pairs of sports skills produced negative effects. This may have resulted from incorrect statements or misunderstanding of the principles. For example, when transfer between tennis and badminton is compared, although the stimuli are similar (i.e., hitting an object with a racket), the responses required are quite different. Badminton requires wrist action; tennis requires movement of the entire arm. Slight transfer was found, however, between the initial learning of a tennis skill and a badminton skill.

Langdon and Yates[652] found little transfer among various manual skills closely approximating industrial tasks. Namikas et al.[832] and

Lordahl and Archer,[657] from studying the transfer effect between various conditions of pursuit motor performance, found that transfer to the same speed was highest, while Lordahl noted that, when the radius of the pursuit rotors was the same, the transfer was greatest. As Namikas et al.[832] pointed out, individuals seemed to learn a specific set of motor components.

Transfer from the Simple to the Complex

Should one expect more transfer from a complex task to a simple one, or is the reverse to be expected? Does the learning of a simple task facilitate the learning of a more complex one? The experimental evidence seems contradictory.

Lawrence,[666] from a discrimination task with animal subjects, found that transfer was greatest if learning occurred from the simple to the complex. Gagne, Baker, and Foster,[399] using human subjects on a similar task (hitting switches in response to light cues), found the reverse to be true, since the most difficult kinds of discrimination seem to transfer best to the simpler components of the task. Lewis, Smitt, and McAllister,[751] from a two-handed coordination task, found that transfer from a difficult to an easy task may be greater because the initial task requires more facilitation of the correct responses and inhibition of the incorrect ones. On the other hand, a simple skill might be performed without extensive learning, thus reducing or eliminating the amount of transfer found.

Seymour[988] noted that his subjects seemed to fumble less when learning the whole of an industrial task because more perception of the correct and appropriate muscle groups was required. He also found positive transfer from a part of an extremely complex task to the whole in his experimental findings. Lordahl and Archer discovered more positive transfer from simple to the complex than occurred in the reverse direction. With a pursuit-rotor task, greater transfer was found when the r.p.m.'s were increased from 40 to 60 than when the initial learning occurred at 80 r.p.m., and the secondary task was at 60 r.p.m. Scannell[965] made the size of a target either larger or smaller than the criterion size in order to study easy-to-difficult versus difficult-to-easy transfer effects. Perhaps the sizes of the targets did not differ significantly in this study since no positive effects of either condition were recorded.

Holding[545] concluded that transfer is not simply a function of the easy-difficult dichotomy, but is influenced by other factors. Mukherjee[821] also states that transfer is a direct function of initial ability attained rather than being dependent on the difficult-to-easy argument.

Thus, it would seem that whether more transfer can be expected from the simple to the complex, or in the reverse direction, is a function of the task and the experimental conditions. The question is further confounded when an attempt is made to objectify and equate "simple" and "complex" with "easy" and "difficult." Seymour[988] found that the whole of the task (the apparently complex aspect of performance) was actually performed easily because of its integrated nature. One might therefore conclude that, for practical purposes, most transfer can be expected to occur from the complex to the simple. The ability to master a difficult skill will certainly facilitate a less complex component. The problem is to select a complex skill for which the simple one is really a component and will not prove too difficult in initial mastery. If transfer is desired in the opposite direction (from simple to complex), again the initial, simple skill must be selected intelligently. Too simple a beginning probably results in little transfer, unless considerable overlearning has taken place.

Transfer of Motor Habits over Time Intervals

In the absence of studies with human subjects, we must turn to a series of articles by M. E. Bunch[151] and by others, who investigated the influence of time intervals between learning bouts on negative and positive transfer in animals' habits in mazes. In general, the longer the time interval, the less positive transfer between tasks.

Bunch's findings concerning negative transfer, however, are more complex. In general, if the interval between practice and re-test is not too great initially, negative transfer appears similar to that noted for positive transfer (i.e., a gradually decreasing function of the time interval). However, past a certain point in time, negative transfer disappears and positive transfer becomes evident, which in turn finally declines gradually toward a zero effect as the time interval is prolonged. As a result of this finding, Bunch concluded that whether one habit is antagonistic to another is a function of the interval between initial acquisition of the two habits, rather than a function of the relationship between task components.

Although it is often difficult to generalize from animal studies, it is believed that these findings suggest research that might prove helpful in understanding the transfer effect over a time interval in humans.

Fatigue and Transfer

Recently several experimenters, including Caplan[169] at Berkeley, have experimentally introduced activities intended to induce muscular fatigue to various degrees, followed by performance of a motor task. At times, the fatiguing activities involved the limb or body part to be used later in performing the task. At other times, they tried to fatigue the individual "generally," without specifically involving the arm or limb to be used later in performing the task.

In general, if extreme fatigue is achieved in the performing limb, negative transfer is noted in the performance of the motor task. Similarly, negative transfer also is elicited if extreme steps are taken to produce fatigue in the total body independent of the limb performing later.

On the other hand, if localized fatigue, which is nearly similar to but different from the muscular requirements later imposed on the limb or limbs used in the motor task, is produced in a specific muscle group, less negative transfer will result from this fatigue than will usually be forthcoming.

Henry[517] and, later, Fairclough[344] reported findings indicating that positive and negative transfer might be caused by motivating or inhibiting circumstances in the experimental environment rather than by the nature of the tasks studied. When experimental subjects were stimulated by sound or shock on their slower trials, reaction time showed a larger and more significant transfer than did movement time. When the shock and sound were omitted from the experimental conditions, transfer of training failed to occur. Thus, the transfer found under the experimental conditions was attributed to motivation by both the experimenters. It is interesting that no significant differences were noted between the transfer effects of a sound (a non-punitive type of reminder) and the shock (more punitive).

Transfer and Massed Practice

Negative transfer will occur between two tasks regardless of their relationships if too much massed practice is introduced in the experimental conditions. Nystrom et al.,[859] from a keyboard task, Reynolds et al.[920] and Kimble,[618] from a rotary-pursuit task, found that extensive massing of initial practice produced negative transfer.

A clear-cut example of the inhibiting effect of massed practice is described by Hall[478] from a mirror tracing task. He found that negative transfer occurred when the mirror was placed in various positions relative to the subject. He hypothesized that negative transfer might be attributed to fatigue resulting from the massing of tasks with little rest between each positioning of the mirror. A follow-up investigation allowed more time between trials (between 30 seconds and five minutes in sets of ten trials) and positive transfer occurred.

Transfer and Amount of Initial Learning

Transfer may also be influenced by the amount of learning accomplished on the initial task. Generally, if slight learning has occurred, little transfer will occur, whereas if extensive, dissimilar learning has

14

taken place on the initial task, negative transfer will usually take place. Duncan[308] underscored this when he concluded, following the study of a lever-moving task, that positive transfer was a function of both first task learning and task similarities.

Principles of Transfer

Some of the major principles of transfer derived from an inspection of the data include the following:

1. Transfer is greatest when the training conditions of two tasks are highly similar.
2. When the task requires the same response to a new but similar stimulus, positive transfer increases as the stimuli become more alike.
3. When the task requires the learner to make new or different responses to the same stimuli, transfer tends to be negative and increases as the responses become less similar.
4. If the responses in the transfer task are different from those in the original task, then the more similar the stimuli the less positive transfer will occur.
5. Continued practice in learning a number of related tasks leads to increased facility in learning how to learn.
6. Transfer is greatest if greater effort is extended during the early part of a series of related tasks.
7. Insight occurs with more frequency as extensive practice is gained in a series of related tasks.
8. Transfer can occur as the result of "cognitive links" formed between two tasks.
9. The greater the amount of practice on the original task, the greater the transfer.
10. Time elapsing between the original and transfer tasks is not critical unless specific details must be remembered.
11. Transfer is likely to be greater if the performer understands the general principles that are truly common to two or more tasks.

Questions for Further Experimental Work

Although general laws may be formulated from the experimental evidence available, a survey of the literature on transfer produces more questions than answers. Among these questions the following are most important:
1. To what exact factors can transfer be attributed—learning, experi-

mental conditions, work methods, motivational (positive and negative) conditions, or what?

2. Is bilateral transfer of strength actually a neurological phenomenon, or, as recent students seem to believe, does it result from the tensing and stabilizing of one side of the body as the other side applies force in some strength task?

3. To what extent is transfer affected by general experimental environments, the subjects' feelings about the experimenter, the task, or the rewards for successful performance?

4. What is the relationship of mental rehearsal, or pretask verbal training, to motor transfer? What kinds of motor tasks are facilitated or impeded by what kinds of verbal activity either preceding or interspaced with skill learning?

Summary

A better understanding of the available information on transfer of motor skill is important from a theoretical viewpoint in order that elements common to several motor tasks can be identified and applied to the teaching-learning situation. Interest in and research about this question extend back to the middle 1800's, and, while the initial concern was with verbal-mental problems, it now extends to a variety of motor and perceptual-motor tasks.

Theories explaining transfer include the general elements theory, the specific factors theory (or identical elements theory), and theories that incorporate both general and specific factors, as well as Gestaltic theories involving "transposition" concepts, referring to the presence of common patterns and the relationships between two tasks.

Extensive transfer of skill and strength can be demonstrated hand-to-hand (cross education) and hand-to-foot, whereas little transfer is generally found task-to-task. The cross-education effects are usually interpreted as indicating that skilled performance is a function of the central rather than peripheral processes in the nervous system. The lack of extensive task-to-task transfer, in general, supports the identical elements theory of transfer.

Generally, transfer seems to be facilitated in paired association tasks by (1) verbal pretraining, (2) first learning a complex task and then learning a simpler one, (3) spaced, rather than massed, practice, and (4) a high level of motivation, regardless of task interrelationships. Transfer is impeded (negative transfer occurs) when (1) the tasks are dissimilar, (2) a high level of learning is desired in the secondary task, and (3) fatigue is present. Skill transfer thus seems to be a function of intertask similarity and a result of general motivating or inhibiting conditions in the total learning environment.

Student Reading

Ammons, R. B.: "Le Mouvement," Current Psychological Issues edited by G. H. Seward and J. P. Seward. New York, Henry Holt & Co., Inc., 1958.

Bruce, R. W.: Conditions of transfer of training. J. Exp. Psychol., *16,* 343-361, 1933.

Cratty, B. J.: The influence of small-pattern practice upon large pattern learning. Res. Quart., *33,* 4, 1960.

Ellis, H.: *The Transfer of Learning.* New York, The Macmillan Company, 1965.

Lindeberg, F. A.: A study of the degree of transfer between quickening exercises and other coordinated movements. Res. Quart., *20,* 180-195, 1949.

Seymour, W. D.: Transfer of training in engineering skills. Percept. Motor Skills, *7,* 235-237, 1957.

20
THE RETENTION OF MOTOR SKILL

The practice of motor skills usually is based on the tacit assumption that remembering the task at some future time is desirable. An athlete practices daily for a weekend contest, the assembly line worker hones his skills in order to meet job specifications, and the astronaut rehearses docking procedures that will be used days and even months later in outer space.

The nature of human memory and of forgetting has long interested philosophers, psychologists, physiologists, and neurologists. Some of the early concepts of man's relationship to the universe were based on how the intellect is built on experience, and by the end of the last century experimental psychologists were becoming intrigued by the remembering and the forgetting of verbal material. The usual task used to test memory involved the rehearsal and the later replication of lists of nonsense syllables.

During the ensuing years the large bulk of the experimental literature dealing with human memory has concentrated on verbal rather than motor responses. During the past decade this interest in the retention of words and phrases has expanded greatly, while the research dealing with how people learn, recall, and sometimes fail to recall motor skills of various kinds has continued to be sporadic, and is usually not tied into any kind of viable model.

In contrast to much of the work in verbal learning and retention, the work on motor skill has usually come from applied psychologists, whose focus is on specific problems, without dependence on or development of helpful theories. Thus, although individual problems have been solved, helpful generalizations are, to a large degree, lacking.

Many important facts and principles about the retention of motor skills are largely unknown, owing to the scarcity of research. For example, little is known about the psychological mechanisms involved in short-term memory, and how this component of memory is involved when first learning a motor skill. Little also is known about how various motivational conditions contribute to or detract from retention, and about the relationships between verbal memory, motor memory, and the retention of motor skills heavily permeated with verbal components, or verbal tasks with physical parts.

Numerous methodological problems contaminate many available studies. As Adams[8] has pointed out, most of the studies of the retention of gross motor skills have not permitted the subjects enough distributed practice initially to permit the separation of reminiscence effects from true retention.

Similarly, the various theories of retention to be reviewed shortly have not been thoroughly explored with reference to movement tasks, and from a practical standpoint, not many studies are helpful in the formulation of pragmatic teaching principles.

Despite these limitations, however, knowing about what *is* available on this topic is important. Coaches, teachers, special educators, therapists, as well as industrial educators, usually do not want the efforts they and their patients and students are expending to terminate at the completion of a lesson, but hope the content will extend itself in time. I hope that the following material will result in a better understanding of this often fascinating component of human endeavor and will optimize the teaching of all varieties of motor skills.

In the following paragraphs several facets of this interesting problem area will be explored. Initially, some contemporary dimensions to understanding human memory will be discussed; next various theoretical models that explain human memory will be clarified; and finally various practical comparisons and applications will be presented. The final part of the chapter will attempt to offer practical guidelines for eliciting retention of motor skills.

Contemporary Dimensions

During the past 10 to 15 years interest in the problems surrounding human retention (memory storage) at both the neurological and the behavioral levels has increased. Some of the principles derived have little relevance to the retention of motor skill. Some problem areas that have been clarified with respect to verbal retention have not been studied as they pertain to the memorization of motor activities. Other facets of human memory have rather direct application and theoretical relevance to the retention of movements.

Duration

Quite a bit of attention has been paid recently to the categorization of memory, based on the apparent duration of the ability to replicate, recognize, or otherwise deal with a given task or event. It has become apparent that one may speak with validity of either *short-term* or *long-*

term memory, and some researchers contend that a third category, *medium-term memory*, exists.

Although much of the research has been conducted with written materials, a few studies dealing with long-term and short-term memory for motor skills are beginning to appear. Results of investigations indicate that it is efficient not to remember everything to which one is exposed, and that selection of appropriateness is a sign of intelligence.* Thus, much of what a person is confronted with is relegated to "storage" in short-term memory for at least a time, and then, if the event, object, concept, or movement is frequently rehearsed (or used), it is likely to become mentally and/or physically "embedded" into rather permanent long-term memory.

Short-term memory of motor tasks is probably important as an individual learns a complex skill, and tries to add each of the parts together in a progressive manner until the whole movement assumes a form of its own, separate and distinct from its parts.

Long-term memorization of many kinds of motor skills seems to happen at times as if by chance, particularly if the skill is important to the learner and has internal consistency and some degree of rhythm in its execution. In two studies by Swift,[1079,1080] ability in a ball-juggling task remained high over a six-year period; and the classic investigation by Hill[538] revealed that retention remained high in typing skills sampled at 25-year intervals. Several studies which will be reviewed shortly have attempted to determine what kinds of rehearsal and how much practice are likely to "drop" a skill from the short-term to the long-term "storage" area.

In Figure 20–1, the interactions of short-term (primary) and long-term (secondary) memory are diagrammed with other variables, including rehearsal and "noise" (psychological interference or stressful events). It is probable that the degree to which an event, object, or movement is likely to have enough meaning ascribed to it, permitting it to be retained in short-term memory, depends on whether it is related to some already well-engrained components of long-term memory.

Attention and Retention

It is becoming increasingly apparent that more important than the duration of time or the number of times a task is practiced is the *quality of attention* afforded the task by the learner. Lavery[664] and Sanderson[962] found that giving their subjects specific instructions that they would be expected to retain and to re-perform their tasks at a later time elicited

---

* It is not unusual to find retardates who engage in random, meaningless, although surprising, feats of memory, such as memorizing all the flight numbers during a visit to the airport, but remaining oblivious to what the numbers mean.

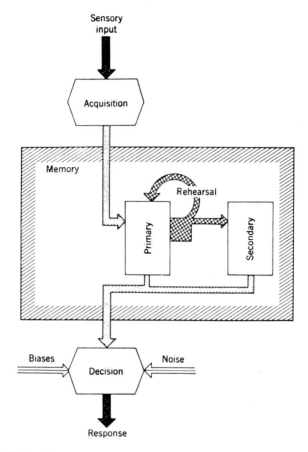

Sensory
input

FIGURE 20–1.   Interactions among the three different processes affecting the
subject's actions in a memory experiment. In the acquisition process, the
sensory input is encoded for the memory process. Items in primary memory
are rapidly forgotten, whereas items in secondary memory can be retained
for long periods of time. In the decision process, the output of the memory is
combined with the subject's biases to determine his response. Noise can be
considered to enter the process at this point. The loop labeled "rehearsal"
indicates the effects of this operation: to renew the strengths of material in
primary memory and to help enter it in secondary memory. (Courtesy of
Norman, D. A.: *Memory and Attention: An Introduction to Human Information Processing.* New York, John Wiley & Sons, Inc., 1969.)

more retention than was apparent in groups who had not been given
these instructions. It is probable that, when individuals are aware that
they will later be responsible for repeating a learning task, they practice
with better attention than if they are unaware or do not believe that
they must retain what they have learned.

Often hyperactive children are given medication in order to improve their attention span. Usually stimulants calm such children, since the stimulants activate the inhibiting centers in the central nervous system. We were surprised a few years ago to find that one such child evidenced marked improvement both in a balance task and in a writing task over a five-month period, during which he was administered this kind of medication. It is unlikely that the drug aided his motor processes directly. It is more probable that the child began to attend to his own movements while performing them, resulting in the dramatic improvement shown in Figure 20–2.

Approximation

It is increasingly apparent that seldom, if ever, is a motor skill performed precisely in the same way twice. Electronic equipment with which to analyze the characteristics of human movement is becoming more accurate than is the human sensorium, which informs the performer just how accurately and with what force he is executing a given movement. Thus, skill retention implies that an individual is able to reproduce a movement in a tolerable range, not that he can produce a skilled movement exactly as he performed it in the past. Furthermore, the performer's perceptions of how well he performed probably differ from individual to individual, and from observer to observer.

This "approximation" principle may sometimes deceive us into thinking that motor skills are remarkably amenable to retention over prolonged periods of time. That is, when an older individual attempts, after a period of years, to perform a task he learned as a youth, the degree of retention he is given credit for greatly depends on the observers' and his tolerance for range of variability. Thus, over a period of time, a seemingly well-retained task may actually vary markedly from the original skill, and yet rest well within the "toleration of difference range" of both the observer and of the performer.

Recognition of Performance

One of the methods, usually not employed for evaluating retention of motor skill, involves whether the individual recognizes an event, word, configuration, or some other kind of stimuli. This kind of assessment of retention is usually used when measuring the retention of material at the perceptual or conceptual level, rather than of a skill that must be recognized and reproduced by direct action. However, there may be times when retention of motor skill, at least to some degree, depends on memory processes of recognition, rather than solely on reproduction processes. For example, it may be important for an individual to rec-

PRE-TEST CONDUCTED, October 23, 1969
EMC
Part I

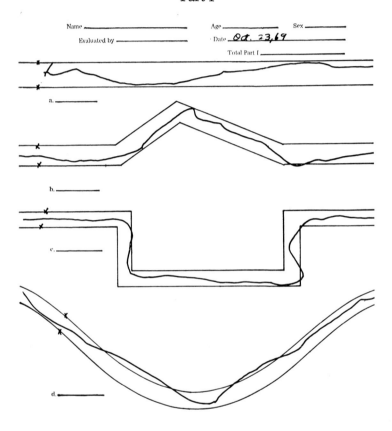

Name _____   Age _____ Sex _____
Evaluated by _____   Date _Oct. 23,69_ _____
Total Part I _____

a. _____

b. _____

c. _____

d. _____

A

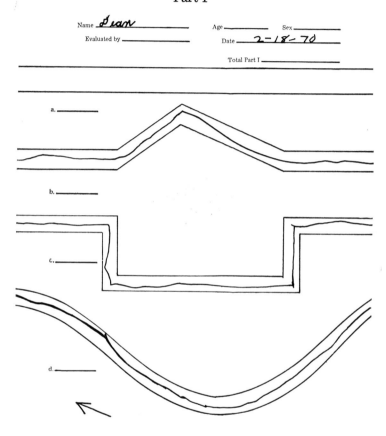

B

FIGURE 20–2. After approximately five months of medication intended to improve attention span, the boy whose work is shown above improved rather dramatically in hand-eye coordination, measured by requiring him to draw through the various "channels" without touching the edges. (A) Test conducted prior to medication and (B) test conducted following medication illustrate the importance of attention in motor control tasks. (Courtesy of Cratty, B. J.: *Human Behavior: Exploring Educational Processes.* Wolfe City, Texas, The University Press, 1971.)

ognize the "feel" of a previously learned skill when he attempts to re-perform it at a later date. To cite another example, it may be important for an individual to recognize at a later time a situation or set of stimuli that can be appropriately dealt with by a previously acquired motor skill. Indeed, if this type of stimulus cannot be recognized the appropriate skill cannot be "called-up" and used, and thus no evidence of its retention will be forthcoming.

Storage, Scanning, and Selection

A number of theoretical models attempt to explain, at the neuro-anatomical level, just how skill is learned and retained, and several of these were outlined in Chapter 13. At the same time, theoretical attention is being paid to the manner in which the memory mechanism is used when the individual "scans" what is available from previous experience, and how he selects an apparently appropriate response from those "on hand."

From the literature it is increasingly apparent that this scanning and selection process occurs rather quickly, and that a separate quality of intelligence, relatively independent of memory itself, interjects itself into the process, when an appropriate response is chosen. That is, the quality of an individual's retention of motor skill may not be entirely due to the number of skills he has learned, or how well he has learned each of several, but how intelligently he selects what is appropriate for a situation at some future time.

Memory Aids

Since the earliest civilizations men employed various memory aids, tricks, and at times exotic strategies that purportedly help an individual to remember. The ancient Greeks memorized speeches by imagining parts of the oration posted on the temple walls, and thus while speaking they mentally traveled from room to room reading from the manuscript they imagined there. This same interest in memory aids has persisted into contemporary times, evident from the various schools, publications, and lecture series that purportedly can "stretch," enhance, and otherwise bend the human memory.

Only slight scientific attention has been paid to these types of approaches with regard to verbal skills, and virtually no research is available supporting or rejecting the efficiency of various memory devices in the enhancement of motor skill learning and retention. Although instructors at times have children "sing" the components to the tennis serve or "say to themselves" how to perform a given skill or mentally rehearse in various ways during and after a practice session, little viable research that either condemns or supports such methods, particularly as they influence quality and quantity of attention, is available.

The Measurement of Retention

In one sense, whether one is dealing with a study of retention or of the influences of spaced practice on learning, improvement depends on the label placed on the effort by the experimenter. Many studies whose titles contain the phrase "short-term memory" incorporate intervals without practice lasting only a few seconds, whereas in other investigations of effects of massed versus distributed practice, some of the intervals between trials may last several times as long.

Traditionally, however, one of two methods of measuring retention has been employed. In the "percentage of gain" method, the attempt is made, after a period of no (without) practice which may last from a few hours to months, or even years, to determine how great a percentage of the performance level exhibited at the termination of the initial learning "bout" can be measured during the re-performance phase. Often this type of measure gives a clue as to whether the terminal level of performance reached during the initial practice "bout" is more a measure of relatively long-lasting "learning" or whether the initial level reached was a rather transitory "performance"! This method can be depicted as shown in Figure 20–3, where the "percentage of gain" is 80 percent, since that is the percentage of the initial level of performance reached on the first "bout" exhibited during the retention testing.

The second traditional way to measure retention is more qualitative and is based on the number of trials or amount of time apparently saved during the retention testing by previous practice. This "savings method" is based on the premise that retention is partly reflected in the fact that

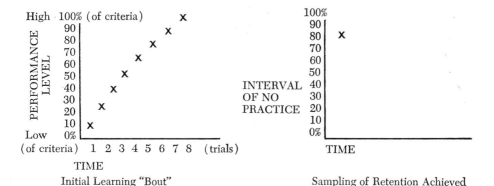

FIGURE 20–3. Diagram of the "percentage of gain method" of evaluating retention.

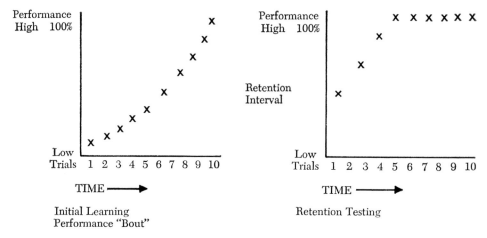

FIGURE 20–4. Diagram of the "savings method" of evaluating retention, i.e., time taken to reach prior performance criteria.

previously learned skills may be re-performed more quickly, and learned to some criteria level faster than skills to which there has been no previous exposure. In Figure 20–4, the "savings" are on the order of 50 percent, since the criteria score was achieved 50 percent faster during the final retention testing than during the initial exposure to the task. This method requires more elaborate experimental work, involving a second learning "bout," than the "percentage of gain" method.

In recent years, more sophisticated ways of assessing retention, some of which have been applied to motor skill, have been developed. Rivenes and Mawhinney[928] have employed methods outlined by Bilodeau, Sulzer, and Levy. In this type of analysis the changing interdependencies of the learned response, the recalled knowledge of results, and post-rest performance are studied. For anyone other than the college or university researcher, however, the two methods outlined above are potentially helpful and appropriate.

Theories of Retention

Theories of human retention are properly termed middle-level, or third- or fourth-level, theories, ranking well below learning or personality theories in scope, and essentially they constitute a portion of most learning theories. The theories of retention outlined below are largely based on findings from studies in which written material was employed. At the same time these theories have recently inspired several researchers to explore the nature of both short-term and long-term memory in their dimensions.

Decay

A discussion of the decay theory as related to human memory and forgetting is important for inclusion primarily as a historical footnote. Today few researchers believe that remembering and forgetting are simply a matter of the influence of time on the "memory trace," although that viewpoint was held by many during the early decades of this century.

In essence, this subtheory suggests that forgetting and remembering depend primarily on the time that elapses between initial learning and re-performance. It is usually further hypothesized that the greatest amount of forgetting occurs initially, with a decreasing amount of forgetting as time wears on. The latter assumption is primarily based on the quick forgetting noted when nonsense syllables are practiced, and then re-tested after a time interval.

The decay theory has fallen into scientific disrepute. It requires several difficult to accept hypotheses, including the hypothesis that the retention interval is "unfilled" (consists of empty time) with possibly interfering events. As early as 1932 McGeogh[764] wrote a compelling argument that an "interference" theory of forgetting and retention is a more valid hypothetical construct from which to proceed. Most reputable theoreticians now feel that the decay theory contributed at least one important variable, "time," to our understanding of human retention.

Trace Transformation

Gestaltic learning theorists explain retention and forgetting by reference to changes in the *configuration* of the memory trace. Essentially, they argue that the neural trace imprinted in the nervous system due to practice does not disappear because of a time interval of no use, but instead may gradually modify itself, change in various ways, so that re-performance reflects observable and measurable changes. They suggest that these "traces" initially laid down by exposure and practice may change owing either to neural events in the brain that often modify the initial trace to conform with what the individual has previously learned or to some "ideal" perceptual or motor configuration, or to external factors from similar experiences leaving similar traces which may then interact with the previously acquired skill.

From an experiential standpoint, most individuals who attempt to re-perform a motor skill have experienced this kind of subtle transformation after a period of no practice. The movement may do the job, but "feel" differently, or it may look the same but subtly differ in the velocity and/or in the power applied at various points. Again, however, strict experimentalists, notably Hebb,[507] attacked the theory outlined by the Gestaltists, relegating it to a historical niche similar to that occupied by the decay theory.

Interference

The most scientifically respectable theory in contemporary writings about retention of skill contains the concept of interference. Essentially, it is held that the amount or quality retained depends primarily on the nature of interfering events. While time is certainly needed to contain these events, the "decay because of time" concept has no place in this type of model.

More than one observer has suggested that the remarkable retention of motor skills which is often recorded is due to the fact that relatively few interfering motor "events" are experienced in everyday life during the retention interval extending from initial practice to re-performance; unlike the usually large amounts of verbal information that are likely to be encountered in the same retention interval.

Two subhypotheses are found in writings outlining interference theory. One suggests that the memory trace is intrinsically *eroded* by events following, or prior to, the practice of a given task. The other is that events build an inhibitory barrier to the re-performance of a memory trace, leaving the trace itself relatively intact. The latter assumption concerning the permanency of memory is further examined in the following section.

Interfering events, particularly with respect to the memory for written material, have been subjected to numerous analyses in a *temporal* framework. That is, interference effects due to events learned or practiced before the practice of the primary task have been studied (proactive inhibition); and the interfering qualities of events placed in the retention interval, thus taking place *after* the primary task has been practiced initially, have been studied (retroactive inhibition) (Fig. 20–5).

At least two, sometimes interacting, qualities in "interfering" tasks can hypothetically alter retention of some motor skill. The degree of similarity between the "reference" task and the purportedly interfering task is an important relationship, as is possibly the intensity of the interfering experience.

Relatively few studies have explored either proactive or retroactive interference effects, and the findings of those that have been conducted are based on a narrow range of tasks, and suggest that these interference

PROACTIVE INHIBITION

| Interfering event(s) | Reference task | Re-performance of reference task |

RETROACTIVE INHIBITION

| Reference task | Interfering event(s) | Re-performance of reference task |

FIGURE 20–5.   Proactive and retroactive inhibition.

effects may not be similar in motor skill retention and in verbal skill retention. In 1947, Lewis[682] did some of the initial work on this subject. In 1951, Lewis[684] and his colleagues carried out two studies using an apparatus similar to the complex coordination task pictured in Chapter 2, page 33. After first learning a set of responses in accord with the light cues presented on the "instrument panel," the apparatus was changed so that antagonistic movements were required to complete a match for the same set of lights.

As is usually the finding from studies dealing with retroactive interference using verbal skills, when the amount of interpolated learning of the interfering task increased, so did the amount of retroactive inhibition. Unlike the studies dealing with verbal skills, in which large amounts of learning on the reference task tended to decrease interfering effects of interpolated tasks, the opposite phenomenon seemed to take place in these experiments. Decrements due to the practice of the interfering task tended to *increase* as the amount of original learning on the reference task increased.

Thus, as Adams[8] has pointed out, the laws of interference that have evolved from research dealing with verbal tasks are not applicable to motor task interference and retention. At the same time, the usually interacting effects of intensity and similarity (or differences in stimuli and responses) between reference and interfering tasks have not been well researched to date. As is obvious, motor tasks often contain components that create not only psychological fatigue but real tissue impairment because of their intensity, a tendency that should make one even more cautious when drawing conclusions from the scarce data available.

There have been even fewer studies of motor skill retention using a research design to investigate proactive inhibition. In 1953, Duncan and Underwood,[308a] from a self-spaced motor task with discrete response components (positioning a lever in response to light cues), obtained negative results when the reference task was re-performed 24 hours later. These negative findings were obtained despite the fact that the initial task was practiced as many as 180 times. In recent years two other studies of proaction effects on short-term memory of motor responses have been conducted. In general, both of these, one by Stelmach[1061] and the second by Ascoli and Schmidt,[43] indicate that in short-term memory the similarity of the initial interfering task to the reference task and the retention interval influence the amount of retention. After reviewing their findings, Ascoli and Schmidt[43] suggest that the laws governing short-term memory of verbal and motor skills may be similar. Montague and Hillix,[808] however, found fewer interference effects in the short-term memory of motor responses, as contrasted to short-term memory of verbal responses. Thus, on the basis of the few findings available, it appears that perhaps short-term retention of motor skills acts in ways similar to that of retention of verbal skills in relation to interfering events. Perhaps this is true because of the importance of mental (verbal?) rehearsal in short-term memory tasks. On the other hand, in studies in which the retention interval has lasted 24 hours, it was found that the laws of interference derived from studies in which verbal skills are operative are not appropriately applied to the retention of motor skills. If these assumptions are deemed valid, it is highly possible that entirely different laws, relative to proactive and retroactive inhibition, also must be derived when comparing short-term and long-term memory of motor tasks themselves, laws that at this time are not easy to formulate because of the scarcity of viable data.

Memory Permanence and Overlay

Even before the turn of the century psychologists postulated that human memory is indeed permanently stored information. Freud also seemed to imply in his writings that memory is relatively permanent, although recall is governed by "motivated forgetting," and by psychic needs which result in distortions. Many modern definitions of learning contain the phrase "relatively permanent change."

Wilder Penfield's work[881,882] as a clinical surgeon supplies some of the most dramatic evidence that memory may be permanent. He performed craniotomies* in over 1,000 patients and discovered that the awake, conscious patient is able to report varied experiences when different portions of his brain are electrically stimulated during the operation. Although only rather vague reports are obtained from the patients when the sensory areas are stimulated, stimulation of the auditory cortex results in the report of sounds; when the motor areas are touched by an electrode, movements are elicited (or feelings of numbness); and when the visual areas are stimulated, patients report seeing lights and colors.

However, when certain parts of the cortex are stimulated, Penfield reports that his patients say they are experiencing a former time and place in great detail. The memory proceeds forward in time during the time the electrode is held in place, and then terminates when it is removed. Most exciting to Penfield was the fact that the experience may not have been a particularly important event in the life of the person, and that the details reported are often those not normally retained. Penfield concluded that memory, held together on a "thread" of time, is based on all experiences to which an individual consciously attends, and is relatively independent of the individual's ability to consciously recall experiences and events at a later time.

* A portion of the temporal lobe is exposed in order to relieve focal epilepsy, when medication fails.

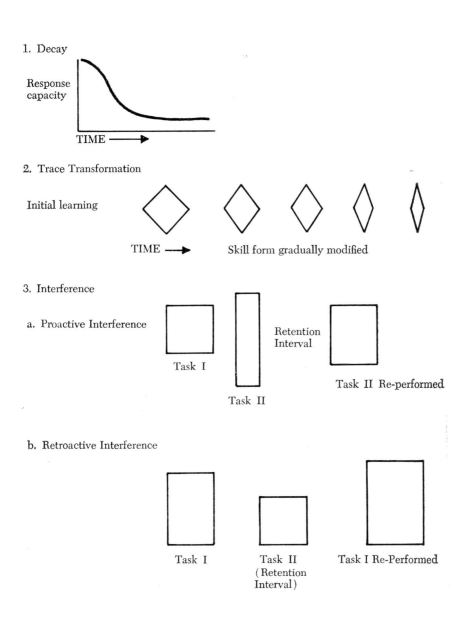

1. Decay

Response
capacity

TIME ⟶

2. Trace Transformation

Initial learning

TIME ⟶   Skill form gradually modified

3. Interference

a. Proactive Interference

Task I

Task II

Retention
Interval

Task II Re-performed

b. Retroactive Interference

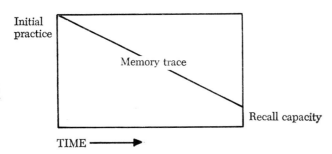

Task I

Task II
(Retention
Interval)

Task I Re-Performed

4. Permanence and Subordination

Initial
practice

Memory trace

Recall capacity

TIME ⟶

FIGURE 20–6.   Theories of human memory for motor tasks in diagram form.

417

Thus, in such a context, memory for physical acts, if attended to as they usually must be when they are performed and learned, is never forgotten, and any decrease in the efficiency experienced after a time has elapsed is due to some kind of subordination of the response, rather than to obliteration because of time or interfering events.

Schematically, the various theories of human memory for motor tasks appear as shown in Figure 20–6 from those suggesting that only time is important to the more complex ones incorporating the nature and timing of interfering events.

Most contemporary behavioral scientists espouse some variation of interference theory to explain human retention; although as has been pointed out, relatively little work has focused on the details of interference theories relative to remembering motor skills. Additional insight concerning the exact manner in which interpolated skills may either aid or inhibit retention and learning of motor tasks is found in Chapter 19, Transfer.

Facilitation of Retention

Of most interest to many readers of this text is a clear understanding of what variables and factors contribute to and detract from the retention of skill. Generally, of course, teachers attempt to cultivate conditions that facilitate retention and subordinate, negate, or reduce the effects of conditions inhibiting retention.

The types of factors, variables, and conditions that, in various ways, influence retention can be placed in several categories. Some are found in the way verbal instructions are given to the learner (see Chapter 7, page 158, Instructions to Retain a Skill). Other conditions are inherent in the task. For example, it is usually found that relatively rhythmic, continuous, and fluid motor tasks are retained more easily than those that are disconnected responses. Still other conditions that may elicit varying degrees of retention are found in the nature of the initial practice. Some researchers, for example, have explored the influence of massing versus distributing practice in time on retention measures; others have studied the effects of overlearning on retention.

Just as is true about the research dealing with retroactive and proactive inhibition of motor skill retention so is the research about ways to enhance retention and reduce forgetting of motor skills. It is fragmentary and does not fall in clear-cut theoretical categories. Despite these limitations, at least superficial hand-holds are available that, in at least cursory ways, may lead to effective teaching for retention.

However, the reader should be cautioned that some of the variables to be discussed, notably overlearning, definitely influence greater retention;

whereas other variables, including the practice conditions, are not as clearly outlined in relation to their effects on retention of motor skill.

Overlearning

It is a common observation that well-learned tasks are difficult to forget and easily retained. Prudy and Lockhart[907] suggest that the amount of original learning of gross motor skills (they studied balancing, throwing, and coordination movements) is a "valuable index" to retention. It is helpful to know how much overlearning can produce and predict reasonably good retention effects. It is surprising, therefore, that studies of the exact amount of overlearning that may be optimum, particularly for gross motor skills, are so scarce.

One of the first researchers to explore the degree of overlearning as related to retention was Krueger,[640] who in 1930 employed finger mazes, together with three amounts of overlearning, 100 percent (perfect performance), 150 percent and 200 percent (past criteria). Although he found that there was better retention after 200 percent of overlearning, as contrasted to 150 percent overlearning, the extra time needed to accomplish the 200 percent did not seem warranted. He thus concluded that 150 percent was the most efficient amount of overlearning to produce maximum retention effects.

Results of further studies by Bell[84] and Rubin-Rabson[944] also suggest that, while the degree of overlearning facilitates retention, a point may be reached at which increased time spent to overlearn a task will not be reflected proportionally in the amount of retention exhibited.

Merrill Melnick,[778] from a study of the ability to retain performance on a stabilometer, also found that 150 percent overlearning facilitated retention in most cases as much as did 200 and 300 percent overlearning, after a retention interval of one week and one month. However, subjects who received practice that resulted in 200 percent overlearning retained significantly more after one month than did subjects who had had no opportunity to overlearn the task.

Task Organization

Poems and songs learned in childhood are easily recalled and difficult to forget. It is also a common experience for an adult to mount a bike and ride it reasonably well even though he has not ridden one since childhood. Researchers have also been struck with the tendency of persons to retain rhythmic motor skills for long time periods without conscious effort or interpolated practice.

Some have suggested that the reason motor skills are seemingly retained better than verbal information is because the former are often fluid, containing closely integrated parts, whereas the latter are often nonsensical and discontinuous, composed of often unrelated parts. Leavitt and Schlosberg[670] suggest that what they term "task-organization" is the critical factor in determining how well one will retain a verbal or a motor skill; and Naylor and Briggs[835] suggest that an "arbitrary sequence" is more difficult to retain than a closely integrated one containing patterns of meaningful responses.

Indeed, results of a study in 1958 by Ammons[33] demonstrate quite clearly that a continuous two-hand tracking task (see Chapter 2, page 34) is more resistant to forgetting than are ones requiring discrete responses.

In 1962, Fleishman and Parker[371] found, from a compensatory tracking task, that after intensive initial training (17 daily sessions) retention effects were quite marked after time intervals of 9, 14, and 24 months. Indeed, retention even after 24 months was nearly perfect, and the subjects needed only a few minutes to recapture their original levels of learning.

In contrast, Neumann and Ammons[844] reported that discrete motor responses after retention intervals of one minute, 20 minutes, two days, seven weeks, and one year were difficult to retain. Indeed, after even 20 minutes marked forgetting occurred, and by one year it was complete. The task consisted of turning switches in order, determined by a buzzer reinforcement for "correctness." It should be noted, however, that in this type of experiment the quality of the motor response (turning a switch) is incidental to the marked degree of mental subvocal rehearsal which probably accompanies efforts to determine "correct" order of execution. Indeed, in this investigation 44 percent of the subjects, when interviewed, reported employing verbal mediation when executing the task.

Examining my own background I find that I can easily play melodies on a viola or a violin, which I last practiced at the age of 17; but translating the two types of music notation (the viola employs a special notation) to the fingers proves impossible 25 years later. The latter translation is relatively abstract and possesses no inherent meaning, whereas the melodies have internal form, consistency, rhythm, and fluidity.

Usually coaches and physical educators are interested in skills that are fluid in nature—swimming, running, jumping, skating, bicycle riding and the like. Thus, these skills apparently prove highly resistant to forgetting. At the same time if one closely analyzes various sports, it is obvious that they contain coherent rhythmic subskills, but other components of the sport are discrete and not as fluid in nature. An example is baseball, in which the throwing, catching, and fielding movements are graceful and possess internal coherence and form, but the *decisions* as to where to throw and under what conditions (score, number out, men on base, and the like) are discrete and require a great deal of practice and, indeed, may be based on opinion that varies from coach to coach! Basketball is similar in some ways. I can still execute most of the subskills (dribbling, shooting, foul shooting, and the like) reasonably well from my experiences in freshman basketball at UCLA 25 years ago, but the complex floor patterns and weaves we were taught by our coach at that same time completely escape me today.

Thus, in the absence of definitive research it would seem that certain parts of a sports practice may be retained easily, but those components that are not as fluid, depending more on discrete responses to specific situations, may not be. It is also unclear whether apparent retention of even so-called fluid movements, after a period of no practice, only *seem* to be retained well (one is given points for even attempting certain physical skills at older ages), whereas, in fact, even the continuous skills are actually considerably modified after periods without practice.

Moreover, it is probable that the difference between the retention of verbal skills and the retention of motor skills is not as diverse as we are often led to believe (Table 20–1). Indeed, when Van Tilborg[1131] attempted to control for difficulty in verbal and motor tasks, he found little difference in the retention of a raised finger maze, performed blindfolded, as contrasted to the learning of a verbal maze (in which one is presented with a pair of words, one of which is "correct" and which, when discovered, permits progress to a second pair of words, and so forth).

The research suggests that this apparently remarkable retention of continuous motor skills may be due to one or more of the following reasons: (1) Continuous skills are often overlearned, pleasurable, and engaged in for prolonged periods of time during initial exposure, resulting in high levels of performance that enhance retention. (2) Continuous

TABLE 20–1.   Retention of Verbal and Motor Skills

	VERBAL	MOTOR
Easiest to retain	Poetry	Rhythmic skills
Retained but with difficulty	Prose	Coherent but nonrhythmic acts
Difficult to retain	Words presented out of order	Skills with no internal relationship
Most difficult to retain	Nonsense syllables	"Nonsense" movements—those that one has not been previously exposed to and that are unrelated to sports or life

skills are perhaps less likely to be disrupted by interfering efforts taking place during the retention interval. (3) Methods of measuring retention may be inexact, with slight deviations from the original skilled performance having relatively little effect on the total outcome of the effort expended. (4) Re-practice of a continuous motor skill may "put together" both stimulus and response (represented by kinesthetic feedback), as well as feedback from watching the movement itself, more quickly than occurs when one attempts to recall written information. (5) The works of Laszlo[661,662] and others, who have manipulated the number of feedback channels, suggest that the retention of continuous motor skills may be enhanced because of the several channels of information available to the learner, such as subvocal rehearsal, the sight of his movements, and the sensations of the movement themselves.

Serial Order

Generally, when asked to learn and retain lists of nonsense syllables, subjects evidence best retention of the initial and final parts of the series. This recency-primacy effect is purportedly due to the delineating effects of the list's termination, and to the effects of initial exposure to the first part of the series. It is unclear from the available studies whether the order of presentation has an effect on the retention of movement tasks. This kind of effect was noted in the study by me[260] in 1963, but Singer[1010] failed to find the effect in a study using four volleyball skills in 1968. In the latter study, however, it is doubtful whether the effects would emerge due to the few skills in the series and the sophistication of the college-age subjects. Most theories concerning the rationale behind such effects suggest that the middle of the series is the most difficult to retain because the learner becomes overloaded by the initial portions, until his ability to retain "breaks down," a condition hardly likely with four skills.

Practice Schedule

Several investigators have explored the influences of the type of practice schedule on retention of skills, and the findings have been mixed. For example, Rubin-Rabson[944] found that whole versus part practice of piano skill (practicing with one versus two hands) had little effect on retention. Briggs and Waters[135] found that initial whole practice facilitated the retention of a tracking skill.

Investigating the effects of massing versus distributing practice on retention, Reynolds and Bilodeau[920] found no differences in retention scores recorded on pursuit-rotor and rudder-control tasks: Adams and Reynolds obtained similar findings two years later. Lewis and Low, from a two-dimensional tracking skill, found that a massed practice group retained best; but Jahnke and Duncan[579] obtained opposite results.

Thus, no clear-cut guidelines may be obtained from the available data. Comparison of the results of the various studies is difficult because of the dissimilarity in tasks, and the differences in initial levels of learning recorded. Thus, at this point one must conclude that a more important modifier of retention than practice conditions are the levels of initial learning and performance achieved.

An Overview

Other variables, including the "size" of the movement employed[1062] and whether the retention interval is "filled" or not,[227] have been explored as possibly influencing retention. It has been found that the "larger" the movement, the better it may be retained on a short-term basis, and the longer the retention interval the less the correlation between final learning and later retention scores. That is, whatever qualities are needed to learn well are not necessarily those required to retain well.

The available research is more noteworthy for its omissions than its content. There has been little attempt to control what the subject does during the retention interval, however difficult this may be. Furthermore, much work is required to separate the effects of physical fatigue from psychological boredom since they interact and probably influence both learning and retention. Unique to motor skill learning are the possible effects of localized and generalized muscular fatigue, independent of the psychological inhibitions to performing the task which may emerge.

The well-known Ziegarnik effect,* which has been demonstrated to influence the retention of written material, has not to my knowledge been researched using motor skills as tasks. Studies of this problem might well prove interesting and helpful.

Although the increased interest in short-term memory for simple motor acts has been well documented in the previous pages, there are not only contradictory findings emerging from this research, but there is little attempt by these scholars to construct models for understanding the nature of short-term "motor memory" in order to separate the possible effects of the degree of difficulty and/or of speed of the act, or to look at the interrelationships between short-term and long-term memory for simple and complex motor acts. It is believed that short-term memory may indeed influence the degree to which a reasonably complex skill is initially assimilated and the separate components added to form the completed act; but at this point these problems have not been investigated. Factor analyses of the retention noted in a number of types of

---

* The effect of discontinuation of a task, just prior to its completion, on learning and retention of completed parts.

motor skills might also reveal more about individual differences in retention and learning effects than is presently known.

The importance of "quality" of rest during both short and long retention intervals needs to be explored with regard to motor skill retention. Loratt and Warr, from a study in 1968, found that recall for verbal items is better after sleep than before. Similar studies dealing with the recall of movements are scarce.

Summary

Historically, the literature contains several rather striking studies indicating that motor skills are remarkably resistant to forgetting. Retention intervals of as long as 25 years have been interpolated between the initial and terminal practice of typing and similar skills with little decrease in ability or the quick resumption of initial levels of proficiency.

More recent studies have begun to refine our knowledge of what practice conditions and skill characteristics influence the recall and forgetting of motor activities, over both short and long periods of time. It is increasingly obvious that continuous, integrated tasks are more resistant to forgetting than are less cyclic acts, composed of discrete responses. Furthermore, overlearning is the quality in initial practice most likely to produce best retention and recall of a skill.

From some studies short-term memory has been found to be interfered with by the interpolation of similar motor tasks, in ways similar to the interference noted in verbal tasks; but from other investigations, it seems that short-term memory for motor acts is in some ways different from memory for written or verbal material.

The apparently good long-term memory for performance of motor tasks, as contrasted to retention of verbal or written material, seems primarily to depend on the rhythmic nature of most motor tasks, rather than because of any inherent differences in motor and cognitive components. Practice conditions are seemingly not as important predictors of the amount of retention of skill as are the amount of initial learning and the retention interval.

The problems needing further research are numerous. A more sophisticated theoretical comparison of verbal and motor retention is necessary. Studies of the interrelationships between short-term and long-term memory for skills are required. And finally investigations that control more closely the interactions between psychological boredom and physical fatigue, which may occur in the retention interval, would be helpful.

Student Reading

Adams, J. A.: Recall of motor responses. In *Human Memory*. New York, McGraw-Hill Book Co., 1967, Chapter 8.

Bilodeau, E. A.: Retention. In *Acquisition of Skill*. New York, Academic Press, Inc., 1966, Chapter 7.
Cratty, B. J.: Retention of motor skill. In *Teaching Motor Skills*. Englewood Cliffs, N.J., Prentice-Hall, Inc., 1972, Chapter 9.
Norman, D.: *Memory and Attention: An Introduction to Human Information Processing*. New York, John Wiley & Sons, 1969.
Norman, D. A. (Ed.): *Models of Human Memory*. New York, Academic Press, Inc., 1970.
Roy, J. E.: *Mechanisms of Memory*. New York, Academic Press, Inc., 1967.

21
AN OVERVIEW

In this final chapter, a summary of the material in the body of the text is presented in four primary divisions: (1) movement considered *functionally* through a discussion of behavioral "loops," (2) movement considered *qualitatively,* in terms of several performance continua, (3) areas of needed research, and (4) implications.

Behavioral Loops:
Movement Considered Functionally

From a review of the research on which the material in this text is based, a number of interacting chains of events both in and external to the organism are clearly apparent. These mutually effective happenings initiate, sustain, and modify motor activity.

The concept of behavioral loops is not original. Advocates of the information theory, as well as neurophysiologists, refer continually to the human "servo system," meaning that the human being acts as a self-correcting mechanism, constantly adjusting to changes in his external and internal environment. Smith's[1029] neurogeometric theory of motion also depends on the concept that perception and motion are inseparable units of behavior. As used in this book, however, "a behavioral loop" is a broader construct that includes a consideration of sociocultural factors and perceptual and physiological events, interacting within and external to the organism.

The concept of a behavioral loop emphasizes that a measurable "bit" of motor performance does not somehow function independently but depends on immediate and long-range functional loops composed of events external and internal to the organism. The following postulates are presented for consideration as basic concepts underlying the functioning of these dynamic chains.

1. Several loops operate simultaneously at various levels to sustain a single identifiable type of motor activity occurring in a specific time period. For example, when throwing a baseball, the individual depends on internal loops, or the mutual interactions among the cerebrum, cere-

bellum, and reticular formation, for the smoothing and monitoring of the movement at the neurological level. A larger loop, involving sensory feedback, relays the resultant "feel" of the throw to the central nervous system so that further modifications may be made. These might be termed internal loops. Externally, and operating simultaneously with the aforementioned internal loops, are visual-motor integrations that further serve to direct the throwing movement and to modify the intensity and placement of subsequent throws.

2. Some skilled activities rely more on internal loops than on external loops, and the relative dependence may change as the movement is learned or as the organism matures. For example, when writing his signature, an adult primarily depends on internal loops involving kinesthetic feedback. The adult can replicate his own signature without the use of vision. The young child learning to write his name for the first time relies on an external visual-motor loop and becomes less dependent on it only when he matures and acquires the necessary skill. Poulton[903] has termed activities primarily depending on internal loops "closed skills," and those requiring external feedback "open skills."

3. External and internal loops can function to modify performance immediately or over a long period of time. Skilled learning has been explained by Hebb[507] as consisting of the establishment and storage of functional, neurological loops (cell linkages or phase cycles) which are used when some act must be repeated. External loops may operate over long time periods. As the individual receives continual feedback from his environment in the form of social approval or disapproval, he gradually forms a "self" construct that modifies his subsequent movement behavior and determines whether he will even attempt new skills. Long-term loops offer feedback of performance and the social implications of success or failure.

4. The relative dependence on external loops may be reduced when learning occurs. For example, the automatization of a motor act generally requires less reliance on visual feedback in the later stages of skill acquisition.

5. Learning a new act, or eliciting a performance modification, consists of "breaking in" on an established loop with an effective event, cue, or stimulus. The result is the establishment of another loop, either in addition to or taking the place of the previous one. Usually the teacher or coach purposely introduces some type of interfering stimulus or perceptual event causing change. However, there is an optimal amount of interference (word cues) that can be introduced. Too strong an interfering event may break down some of the underlying external loops important to the performance of the desired movement.

6. Performance or learning difficulties occur when a loop is broken by

some interfering stress, without replacing it with a new functional loop. If instruction proves stressful, it may not contribute to the establishment of a new loop but rather break down an existing one. As a result, learning difficulties occur. Some type of stressful event may interfere with the normal internal monitoring loops in the nervous system, as well as the various functioning external loops. In contrast, the removal of a stressful event may aid in recalling some suppressed loop to a functional relationship, thus facilitating performance.

7. Retention of a skilled act involves the "calling-up" of a relatively stable loop and the re-performance of the skill. Repetition and over-learning seem to contribute to the stabilization and strengthening of such a behavioral loop.

8. External loops may be termed *complete* or *adjusted*. Complete loops are interacting chains of events primarily dependent on an individual's own actions and perceptions (e.g., hitting a tennis ball against a wall). The adjusted loop, however, depends on relatively unpredictable interpersonal events for its functional completion. Playing tennis with another person involves an adjusted loop; for, however the ball is hit by the performer, constant adjustments need to be made to the unpredictable actions of the opponent when returning the ball.

9. One might also refer to loops involving two or more people and those in which a single person interacts with a portion of his environment that does not react to him with verbal behavior and gestures. One is constantly forming and breaking various social loops when encountering and otherwise interacting with people in his immediate environment. The quality and nature of these human interactions form a potent source of stress and reward, as was pointed out in Chapter 14, Social Motives. People perform for and react to the approval and disapproval of others in more intense ways than if they are merely hitting a ball against a wall in the absence of competitors, onlookers, and/or teammates.

Continua: Movement
Behavior Considered Qualitatively

Because of the complexity of the human organism, an identifiable "bit" of movement behavior might be considered on several continua, scales that describe various *qualitative* differences between motor acts. Among these are the verbal-motor, the perceptual-motor, fine-gross, and simple-complex continua. As learning takes place, a motor act may shift from one portion to another on the same continuum. At the same time, a single motor act can be described as falling on different portions of several scales.

Verbal-Motor Continuum

Types of movement behavior may be classified in accordance with the extent to which word cues, either internal or external, contribute to or support performance. Usually irregular, rapid movements require fewer words. Activities that are relatively slow and composed of discrete movements, on the other hand, are better accompanied by word descriptions. The extent to which an activity is compatible with verbalization also depends on prior learning and the maturational level of the performer. Younger children depend less on verbal cues and more on imitation and kinesthetic "feel" of the movement. During initial stages of learning verbalization plays a more important role than during the later stages.

Perceptual-Motor Continuum

Activities may also be classified according to the extent to which they are perceptually "loaded," as opposed to consisting of responses to relatively simple stimuli. Here again, the perceptual loading, or the extent to which judgments or meanings need to be formulated prior to the motor output, varies as the task is learned. Usually less complex judgments are needed during the later stages of task acquisition.

Tasks in which a simple key-pressing or switch-turning reaction is required in response to light or word cues, while sometimes termed *motor,* actually seem heavily laden with perceptual factors. One of the problems, when reviewing studies of motor skills, is selecting those that seem to use "true motor activities" as evaluative tasks. Many of the so-called motor skill investigations have used tasks that are largely cognitive or perceptual in nature, with the motor component of the task being a relatively simple, unchanging, and minor portion of the behavior measured.

Force-Accuracy Continuum

Quantitatively, motor performance also may be considered as including or requiring varying amounts of force as contrasted to accuracy. Some researchers feel that motor activity is primarily a force-speed phenomenon; others emphasize spatial accuracy as basic. It is believed that force, spatial accuracy, and temporal factors (speed and/or rhythm) are all vital components of motor activity. The problem becomes one of analyzing the specifics of the task under consideration in order to determine which kinds of factors are important.

Visual-Motor Continuum

The classification of a task according to the extent to which visual cues are utilized in its performance also is important. Again, this can be a function of the stage of learning, with the initial portion of the learning process usually more dependent on visual cues than the later. It is often found that visual cues override the kinesthetic or movement cues. More accuracy can usually be achieved, however, when available visual information is used.

Fine-Gross Continuum

Seashore[979] compared the performance of fine motor skills versus gross motor skills. In general, such a classification depends on the size of the muscle groups involved, the magnitude of space used for the movements, and the amount of force necessary to complete the movement. A three-way breakdown has been suggested by Karl Smith[1025]: movements involving hand-finger manipulations, traveling movements of the limbs, and locomotor activities. Rather than discrete categories, however, a continuum might be constructed on which activities are arranged according to the amount of space needed for their execution. At the present time, however, no exact classification system has been evolved, and most writers continue to use a two-way system.

At the finite level are finger movements, tapping activities, and steadiness tests—movements that at times seem related to the physiological tremor rate of the individual. Gross motor skills have included arm movements, dynamic balance activities, and the like. I[232] have referred to a large locomotor maze as a "gross motor skill." However, when comparing such a task to that involving the rotary-pursuit apparatus, the need for a three-way classification becomes apparent.

The fine-gross continuum is closely related to the simple-complex continuum, because fine motor skills seem to be simpler than are gross motor activities which require stabilizing actions, the organization of a larger space field, and usually the total involvement of the performer.

Personal Equation versus Optimum Effort

A "bit" of motoric behavior can be classified as to whether it depends on some combination of an individual's personal equations (see Chapter 9) or whether it depends on ability traits measured under conditions that encouraged maximum effort. In general, task scores obtained when optimum effort is applied correlate highly with various ability trait measures, whereas samplings of movement behavior in which no such stress is imposed are primarily a manifestation of an individual's basic movement preferences.

Simple-Complex Continuum

The point on the simple-complex continuum at which a skill might be placed is based on a variety of conditions. It may depend on the

15

complexity of sensory information necessary or on the complexity of the movement pattern required. In still another context, classification of the skill might rest on the serial nature of the task or the stage of learning involved. When learning to type the initial portion of the process involves learning the location of letters and becomes more complex as word and phrase responses are required. Thus, the particular skill level at which the performer is functioning at the moment governs the point on a simple-complex continuum at which his motor activity would be located. The maturational level of the performer must also be taken into account in utilizing such a continuum. For example, skills that are simple for adults might be complex when infants or children attempt to perform them.

The extent to which perceptual judgments are necessary to execute a skill is an important criterion by which to judge the simplicity or complexity of that skill. Direct motor acts cued by a single stimulus could be termed simple, but complicated movements requiring frequent modifications because of unexpected or uncontrollable cues would be labeled complex.

Needed Research

Some topics related to movement behavior and motor learning appear frequently in the literature, whereas others have received relatively little attention. I believe the following general problem areas need further investigation.

The Neurological and Biochemical Bases of Learning and Retention

Innumerable research programs suggest themselves from a review of the material in Chapter 16. The influence of RNA and DNA on learning and the exact mechanisms involved need further investigation. Additionally, the relationships between various neuroelectrical measures and learning and retention are critically in need of further elucidation. Developmental studies of learning and retention as functions of the biochemical makeup, and the anatomical appearance of the human brain would be helpful. A continued effort should be made to elaborate on various interspecies differences in brain structure and function at various points on the phylogenic scale.

Anthropology and the Human Action System

Examination of the parallel evolvement of man's abilities to utilize his hands and of other indices of his social and intellectual development might reveal interesting insights into the manner in which movement characteristics contributed to the development of the other capacities. Evolutionary changes produced by operations on primates would be helpful in clarifying relationships between movement capacities and intellect.

The Development of Motor Attributes in Infants and Children

In child development, the unexplored problems seem endless. For example, few studies deal with the development of body awareness or kinesthetic maturation, or with the manner in which a child might gain a more stable concept of his physical self. The development of visual perception has received only cursory attention, and changes in the ability to move accurately with advancing age have been neglected in longitudinal investigations.

Verbal-Motor Relationships

Man not only moves but speaks. The relationships between these two types of behavior, however, have received little attention, except for comparative retention studies.

The Nature of Play, Manipulation, and Exploration

More objective studies seem needed in examining the parameters of play, manipulation, and exploration in children and adults. Although it is frequently suggested that children engage more in unstructured play than do adolescents, few objective studies have examined the intensity, emphasis, and duration of play and manipulative activities as a function of age. Restriction from movement as a motive to move also belongs in this general classification. Although animal studies have been carried out, I am unaware of investigations with human subjects.

Construction of a Tension-Performance Scale

Another fruitful area of investigation is the relation between tension level and optimum performance. Research in this area would require valid measures of tension, motivational or arousal level, and classifications of tasks that might be performed best in various portions of such a scale.

Movement Panaceas?

In recent years several clinicians have suggested that a variety of perceptual, cognitive, and emotional problems evidenced by children and adults can be ameliorated through practicing various kinds of perceptual-motor tasks. It has been suggested that by recapitulating various loco-motor sequences, visual and auditory perception, together with speech, may be improved.[290] Many of these theories have resulted in practices that are proving helpful to atypical children, but a considerable amount of experimental data is needed to further refine their use, and to suggest the scope as well as the limitations of the programs proposed.[930]

Longitudinal Studies of Learning and Retention

Studies of long-term retention of motor skills are needed. As Naylor and Briggs[833] pointed out, such research begins to assume important practical implications when man attempts to conquer space and must retain various kinds of instrument behavior in the confines of a space-ship over extended periods of time.

Kinesthetic Studies

Much information is needed concerning the nature and function of kinesthetic sensations. Among the problems are whether there are specific or general factors involved (although Scott[973] has published results of research in this area) and the manner in which kinesthetic sensations integrate with vestibular, visual, and pressure cues to form a total per-ception of movement. Investigations of the nature of kinesthetic after-effects at the finite and gross levels might also provide added knowledge. Experimental induction of a kinesthetic illusion, an aftereffect, in essence involves creating a short-term perception. It is believed that research in which an attempt is made to control some of the variables contributing to this kind of temporary distortion might shed light on the nature of kinesthetic perception.

Implications

It is believed that the following implications are important as a basis for understanding the general and specific factors that contribute to movement "output." These "threads" are found in several research areas concerned with motor performance and learning. They are important for the teacher who attempts to modify the movement behavior of others and for the performer who wishes to gain a more complete knowledge about his personal action patterns.

The Importance of Sociocultural Factors

Motor performance levels are usually affected by the social implica-tions of the immediate situation, as well as by the over-all cultural context in which the action takes place. As the individual learns a skill, he is concerned with not only task specifics but how the culture expects one of his age, sex, and background to perform. Thus, the performer is continually sensitive to the extent to which his performance level either coincides or falls short of cultural expectations. As an example, the concept of "failure-anxiety" (Chapter 15) suggests that a large portion of the apprehension experienced when one attempts to perform relatively hazardous movements may relate to the social consequences of failure.

Literature on growth and development outlines several social-performance relationships. The cultural expectations related to the performance of boys, as opposed to the performance of girls, are exacting. These demands of the society tend to channel the type as well as the intensity of motor activities engaged in by the two sexes, particularly when they reach adolescence. Society also exerts an influence over the movement patterns of the very young. The vigorous total body effort seen in the throwing behavior of two- and three-year-old boys, as opposed to the comparatively more restricted throwing ability of girls at this age level, has been attributed to differing cultural expectations.

Within limits, the teacher may manipulate the social clime immediately connected with performance. For example, judiciously selected team captains may enhance group performance. However, if just the obvious and proximal social dimensions are dealt with, only a portion of the complex cultural picture is being accounted for. The individual attempting to change the performance of another should be aware not only of the manner in which the task fits into the immediate learning situation but also of the way in which the hoped for action pattern coincides with the performer's perceptions of himself in a total socio-cultural context of family demands, community expectations, and national goals.

Both General and Specific Factors Contribute to Performance

Another important principle apparent from a review of the literature on skilled learning is that, in addition to task specifics, motor performance is molded by a number of general conditions. A four-part theory was presented in Chapter 11 elaborating on this concept. Although a single motor task may be analyzed in terms of specific components, such general conditions as motivational level, ability to interpret instructions, maturational level, the ability to vary force and tension, and similar qualities may contribute in a general way to performance of several kinds of motor skills.

Although identification of general coordination of adults generally meets with little success, at times general performance qualities of young children have been isolated. In addition, there seems to be a typical arousal level that an individual sustains through the day, which is probably influential in molding performance and learning.

A personality trait that might be labeled "need for achievement," "aspiration level," or "need for social approval" also appears to underlie the performance of a number of skills. Individuals who generally strive to succeed, whatever the nature of the task facing them, seem to score higher on motor skills tests.

An awareness of such general conditions underlying performance, however, does not negate the remarkable specificity of adult motor skill. The numerous studies cited in Chapter 18 point to the necessity for practicing the task at hand, rather than relying too heavily on general conditions, inherent physical qualities, or transfer from past experience.

Arousal, Tension, Motivational Level, and Performance

The concept of an optimal level of "trying" on the part of the performer is needed to perform a motor task most efficiently. An individual may evidence too much residual muscular tension for optimal performance or might be said to be too highly aroused or motivated to perform a desired movement successfully. On the other hand, the evidence also seems to indicate that motor performance may be impeded by a motivational state (or tension level) that is not high enough. The performance of simple direct movements, requiring moderate to large amounts of force, will usually suffer unless enough tension is summoned by the performer.

The athletic coach, and others hoping to elicit outstanding performance from individuals, should be particularly sensitive to this concept. The instructor who attempts to make all the members of a team "mad" at their opposition is perhaps ignoring this principle. On the other hand, the athletic leader, on noting the amount of tension already present in the individuals and evaluating the requirements of the task, would be following a sounder course of action if he encouraged some and relaxed others.

The Instructor and Motor Performance

Throughout the book an attempt has been made to describe conditions that contribute to individual variations in movement behavior, motor performance, and motor learning. A simple presentation of principles, formulas, methods, or guidelines for action in the teaching-learning situation would have been naive. Rather, the intent was to provide an appreciation of the complexity of the action patterns of man.

However, from a review of the preceding chapters, several broad implications related to formal instruction seem important to re-emphasize. Initially, the primary lesson to be gained is that an instructor should introduce an optimal amount of formal guidance at opportune times in the learning process. Too much formal guidance or too little may prove equally undesirable. For example, if an instructor attempts to give immature learners an exact awareness of the multitude of principles underlying their performance, more confusion than enlightenment may result. The educator should take into account the maturity of his students, their attention span, and the nature of the task, and then introduce formal guidance when he believes it is appropriate.

In general, the literature indicates that the maximal amount of guidance should be offered during the initial part of the learning process, taking care not to present an overabundance of verbiage when rapidly executed movements are to be assimilated. During the final stages of learning the student might be allotted time to engage in unguided practice, with the instruction imposed only to correct errors.

A second major implication when studying the instructor-performance relationship is that the teacher, if he is to be effective, should be able to utilize well several kinds of sensory input. This assumption is based on findings that individuals, at various portions of their lives, tend to change the type of sensory cues they habitually depend on when learning motor skills. In addition, for a given maturational level, learners often differ widely in the type or combination of learning cues that have the most meaning for them. The prediction of the type of cues a learner usually relies on in a variety of performance situations is an extremely tenuous undertaking. In a given task, some individuals may use word cues best and thus require a rather detailed verbal description of the movement. Others may learn best with a visual demonstration, and others may prefer to practice and to "feel" the movement kinesthetically. However, on changing the nature of the task, these same individuals will report dependence on different sensory cues, or combinations of cues.

The relative dependence on various kinds of sensory input often changes when various portions of the learning process are reached. The kinds of cues found to be best during the initial stages may hinder the student during the final stages of learning. Thus, to have the most desirable impact on the learning situation in the absence of the means to evaluate the manner in which his students learn best, the instructor should cultivate the ability to communicate in several sensory modalities: verbal instructions, visual demonstration, and manual guidance.

My primary purpose was to contribute to the development of two attitudes on the part of the student: (1) *sensitivity* and (2) *flexibility* in the teaching-learning situation. If one wishes to modify his motor attributes or those of another, he first of all must be *sensitive* to the numerous conditions that mold and channel performance. Secondly, cognizance of this multitude of factors should promote an attitude of *flexibility*. An instructor should be prepared and able to change the manner in which he approaches the instruction of a group or an individual, rather than to adhere to preconceived guidelines. Consequently, I hope that the future teacher, on considering the material in the preceding chapters, will be able to analyze the situation, the learner, the task, and his own attributes with greater facility and thus be able to modify the movement behavior of those in his charge more effectively.

Underlying much of the material in the preceding chapters has been the inference that, at certain levels, performance and learning are not divisible into motor and mental components. However, I hope that the reader has not assumed that movement has been considered the key from which all aspects of behavior—mental, emotional, and social—must stem. An attempt has been made, however, to point out that observable action is an imperative facet of human behavior, and through failure to understand movement behavior, one may glimpse only a portion of the totality of man.

Student Reading

Bloom, B. S.: *Stability and Change in Human Characteristics*. New York, John Wiley & Sons, Inc., 1964.

Cratty, B. J.: *Human Behavior: Exploring Educational Processes*. Wolfe City, Texas, University Press, 1971.

Gagne, R. M. (Ed.): *Learning and Individual Differences*. Columbus, Ohio, Charles E. Merrill Inc., 1967.

Melton, A. W.: *Categories of Human Learning*. New York, Academic Press Inc., 1964.

Norman, D. A.: *Models of Human Memory*. New York, Academic Press Inc., 1970.

Oxendine, J. B.: *Psychology of Motor Learning*. New York, Appleton-Century-Crofts, Inc., 1968.

Singer, R. N.: *Readings in Motor Learning*. Philadelphia, Lea & Febiger, 1972.

Smith, K. U., and Smith, M. F.: *Cybernetic Principles of Learning and Educational Design*. New York, Holt, Rinehart and Winston, Inc., 1966.

Smith, L. (Ed.): *Psychology of Motor Learning*. Chicago, The Athletic Institute, 1969.

REFERENCES

1. Abbe, M.: The spatial effect upon the perception of time. Jap. J. Exp. Psychol., *3*, 1-52, 1936.
2. Abbe, M.: Temporal effect upon the perception of time. Jap. J. Exp. Psychol., *4*, 83-93, 1937.
3. Abbey, D. S.: Age, proficiency and reminiscence in a complex perceptual-motor task. Percept. Motor Skills, *14*, 51-57, 1962.
4. Abel, L. B.: The effects of shift in motivation upon the learning of a sensory-motor task. Arch. Psychol., *29*, 1-57, 1936.
5. Abercrombie, M. L. J., and Tyson, M. C.: Body image and draw-a-man test in cerebral palsy. Develop. Med. Child Neurol., *8*, 9-15, 1966.
6. Adams, G. L.: Effect of eye dominance on baseball batting. Res. Quart., *36*, 3-9, 1965.
7. Adams, J. A.: A closed-loop theory of motor learning. J. Motor Behav., *3*, 111-150, 1971.
8. Adams, J. A.: *Human Memory.* New York, McGraw-Hill Book Co., 1967.
9. Adams, J. A.: Human tracking behavior. Psychol. Bull., *58*, 1, 55-79, 1961.
10. Adams, J. A.: The relationship between certain measures of ability and the acquisition of a psycho-motor criterion response. J. Gen. Psychol., *56*, 121-134, 1957.
11. Adams, J. A.: Some implications of Hull's theory for human motor performance. J. Gen. Psychol., *55*, 189-198, 1956.
12. Adams, J. A., and Dijkstra, S.: Short-term memory for motor responses. J. Exp. Psychol., *71*, 314-318, 1966.
13. Adams, J. A., and Reynolds, B.: Effect of shift in distribution of practice conditions following interpolated rest. J. Exp. Psychol., *47*, 32-36, 1954.
14. Adelson, D.: The relational influence of size on judgments of distance. J. Gen. Psychol., *69*, 319-333, 1963.
15. Adey, W. R.: Recent thoughts on the neuron model based on brain wave analysis. Paper given at Biomedical Engineering Symposium, San Diego, California, April 1961.
16. Adler, A.: *The Practice and Theory of Individual Psychology.* New York, Harcourt & Brace, 1927.
17. Ahrens, S. J.: Spatial Dimensions of Movement. Master's thesis, University of California, Los Angeles, 1966.
18. Alderman, R. B.: Age and sex differences in learning and performance of an arm speed motor task. Res. Quart., *39*, 428-431, 1968.
19. Alderman, R. B.: Reminiscence effects of inter- and intra-individual differences in pursuit rotor performance. Res. Quart., *39*, 423-427, 1968.
20. Allen, R. M.: Factors in mirror drawing. J. Educ. Psychol., *39*, 216-226, 1948.
21. Allen, S.: The effects of verbal reinforcement on children's performance as a function of type of task. J. Exp. Child Psychol., *13*, 57-73, 1965.
22. Allport, G. W.: *Personality, a Psychological Interpretation.* New York, Henry Holt & Co., 1937, pp. 566, 588.
23. Allport, G. W.: *Social Psychology.* Boston, Houghton Mifflin Co., 1924.
24. Allport, G. W.: *Studies in Expressive Movement.* New York, The Macmillan Co., 1933.

25. Allport, G. W., and Pettigrew, T. F.: Cultural influence on the perception of movement: The trapezoid influence among Zulus. J. Abnorm. Soc. Psychol., 65, 104-113, 324, 1957.

26. Ames, A., Jr.: Reconsideration of the origin and nature of perception. In *Vision and Action,* S. Ratner (Ed.). New Brunswick, N.J., Rutgers University Press, 1953.

27. Ammons, R. B.: Acquisition of motor skill: III. Effects of initially distributed practice on rotary pursuit performance. J. Exp. Psychol., 40, 777, 1950.

28. Ammons, R. B.: Effects of knowledge of performance: a survey and tentative thumbnail formulation. J. Gen. Psychol., 54, 279-299, 1956.

29. Ammons, R. B.: Effects of pre-practice activities on rotary pursuit performance. J. Exp. Psychol., 41, 187-191, 1951.

30. Ammons, R. B.: *"Le Mouvement"* Current Psychological Issues, G. H. Seward and J. P. Seward (Eds.). New York, Henry Holt & Co., 1958.

31. Ammons, R. B., Alprin, S. I., and Ammons, C. H.: Rotary pursuit performance as related to age and sex of pre-adult subjects. J. Exp. Psychol., 49, 127-133, 1955.

32. Ammons, R. B., and Ammons, C. H.: Decremental and related processes in skilled performance. In *Psychology of Motor Learning,* L. B. Smith (Ed.). Chicago, Athletic Institute, 1969, pp. 205-238.

33. Ammons, R. B., Farr, R. G., Block, E., Neuman, E., Marion, D. M., and Ammons, C. H.: Long-term retention of perceptual motor skills. J. Exp. Psychol., 55, 318-328, 1958.

34. Ammons, R. B., and Willig, L.: Acquisition of motor skills: IV. Effects of repeated periods of massed practice. J. Exp. Psychol., 51, 2, 1956.

35. Anastasiow, N. J.: Success in school and boys' sex role patterns. Child Develop., 33, 1053-1066, 1965.

36. Anderson, J. E.: *The Psychology of Development and Personal Adjustment.* New York, Harper & Bros., 1949, p. 152.

37. Anderson, T. W.: The use of factor analysis in the statistical analysis of multiple time series. Psychometrika, 28, 1-25, 1963.

38. Argyle, M., and Dean, J.: Eye-contact, distance and affiliations. Sociometry, 28, 289-304, 1965.

39. Argyle, M., and Kendon, A.: The experimental analysis of social performance. In *Advances in Experimental Social Psychology,* L. Berkowitz (Ed.). New York, Academic Press, Inc., 1967, Vol. 3, pp. 55-98.

40. Arps, G. F.: Work with knowledge of results vs. work without knowledge of results. Psychol. Monogr., 28, 125, 1920.

41. Asch, S.: *Social Psychology.* Englewood Cliffs, N.J., Prentice-Hall, Inc., 1951.

42. Aschoff, J.: Circadian rhythms in man. Science, 148, 1427-1432, 1965.

43. Ascoli, K. M., and Schmidt, R. A.: Proactive interference in short-term motor retention. J. Mot. Behav., 1, 12-16, 1969.

44. Atkinson, J. W.: *Motives in Fantasy, Action and Society.* Princeton, N.J., D. Van Nostrand Co., Inc., 1958.

45. Attneave, F., and Arnoult, M. D.: The quantitative study of shape and pattern perception. Psychol. Bull., 53, 452, 1956.

46. Aubert, H.: "Die Bewegungsempfindung." Arch. Ges. Psychol., 39, 347-370, 1886.

47. Ausubel, D. P.: *Theory and Problems of Adolescent Development.* New York, Grune & Stratton, 1954.

48. Ausubel, D. P., Schiff, H. M., and Goldman, M.: Qualitative characteristics in the learning process associated with anxiety. J. Abnorm. Soc. Psychol., 48, 537, 1953.

49. Bachman, J. C.: Influence of age and sex on the amount and rate of learning two motor tasks. Res. Quart., 37, 176-186, 1966.

50. Bachman, J. C.: Motor learning and performance as related to age and sex in two measures of balance coordination. Res Quart., 32, 123-137, 1961.

51. Bachman, J. C.: Specificity vs. generality in learning and performing two large muscle motor tasks. Res. Quart., *32,* 3-11, 1961.
52. Bahrick, H. P.: Retention curves—facts or artifacts? Psychol. Bull., *61,* 188-194, 1964.
53. Bahrick, H. P., Fitts, P. M., and Briggs, G. E.: Learning curves—facts or artifacts? Psychol. Bull., *54,* 256-268, 1957.
54. Bahrick, H. P., Fitts, P. M., and Schneider, R.: Reproduction of simple movements as a function of factors influencing proprioceptive feedback. J. Exp. Psychol., *49,* 445-454, 1955.
55. Bakan, P., Meyers, L. B., and Schoonard, J.: Kinesthetic after-effects and length of inspection period. Amer. J. Psychol., *75,* 457-461, 1962.
56. Bakan, P., and Thompson, R.: The effect of pre-inspection control measures on the size of kinesthetic after-effects. Amer. J. Psychol., *75,* 302-303, 1962.
57. Bakan, P., and Weiler, E.: Kinesthetic after effect and mode of exposure to the inspection stimulus. J. Exp. Psychol., *65,* 319-320, 1963.
58. Baker, K. E., and Wylie, R. C.: Transfer of verbal training to a motor task. J. Exp. Psychol., *40,* 623, 1950.
59. Baker, L. M.: *General Experimental Psychology.* New York, Oxford University Press, 1960.
60. Baker, R. F.: The Effects of Anxiety and Stress on Gross Motor Performance. Doctoral dissertation, University of California, Los Angeles, Calif., 1961.
61. Bannister, H., and Blackburn, J. H.: An eye factor affecting proficiency at ball games. Brit. J. Psychol., *21,* 382-384, 1931.
62. Barber, T. X.: Physiological effects of "hypnosis." Psychol. Bull., *58,* 390-419, 1961.
63. Barch, A. M.: Bi-lateral transfer of warm-up in rotary pursuit. Percept. Motor Skills, *17,* 723-726, 1963.
64. Bardach, J. L.: Effects of situational anxiety at different stages of practice. J. Exp. Psychol., *59,* 420-424, 1960.
65. Bartley, S. H.: The perception of size or distance based on tactile and kinesthetic data. J. Psychol., *36,* 401-408, 1953.
66. Bartley, S. H.: *Principles of Perception.* New York, Harper & Row, 1958.
67. Bartley, S. H., and Chute, E.: *Fatigue and Impairment in Man.* New York, McGraw-Hill Book Co., 1947.
68. Barton, J. W.: Comprehensive units in learning typewriting. Psychol. Monogr., *35,* 164, 1926.
69. Barton, J. W.: Smaller versus larger units in learning the maze. J. Exp. Psychol., *4,* 418-429, 1921.
70. Basmajian, J. B.: Microscopic learning single nerve-cell training. In *Psychology of Motor Learning,* L. Smith (Ed.). Chicago, Athletic Institute, 1970.
71. Basowitz, H., Persky, H., Korchin, S. J., and Grinker, R. R.: *Anxiety and Stress, an Interdisciplinary Study of a Life Situation.* New York, McGraw-Hill Book Co., 1955.
71a. Bastian, H. C.: *The Brain as an Organ of the Mind.* New York, Appleton, 1883.
72. Batson, W. H.: Acquisition of skill. Psychol. Monogr., *21,* 91, 1916.
73. Battig, W. F.: Transfer from verbal pretraining to motor performance a function of motor task complexity. J. Exp. Psychol., *51,* 371-378, 1956.
74. Battig, W. F., Nagel, E. H., Voss, J. F., and Brogden, W. J.: Transfer and retention of bidimensional compensatory tracking after extended practice. Amer. J. Psychol., *70,* 75-80, 1957.
75. Bayley, N.: The Development of Motor Abilities, during the First Three Years. Monographs for the Society for Research in Child Development. Washington, D.C., 1935.
76. Bayley, N.: A study of the crying of infants during mental and physical tests. J. Genet. Psychol., *40,* 306-329, 1932.
77. Bayton, J. A., and Conley, H. W.: Duration of success background and the effect of failure upon performance. J. Gen. Psychol, *56,* 179-185, 1957.

78. Beach, F. A.: Current concepts of play in animals. Amer. Natur., *79*, 523-541, 1945.

79. Beam, J. C.: Serial learning and conditioning under real life stress. J. Abnorm. Soc. Psychol., *51*, 543-551, 1955.

80. Beardslee, D. C., and Wertheimer, M.: *Readings in Perception.* Princeton, N.J., D. Van Nostrand Co., Inc., 1958.

81. Beasley, J. W., and Mendelson, J. H.: Effects of visual deprivation on nucleic acid levels in rat brain cortex. Recent Advances Biol. Psychiat., *7*, 101, 1966.

82. Bechtoldt, H. P.: Factor analysis and the investigation of hypotheses. Percept. Motor Skills, *14*, 319-342, 1962.

83. Bechtoldt, H. P.: Motor abilities in studies of motor learning. In *Psychology of Motor Learning*, L. Smith (Ed.). Chicago, Athletic Institute, 1970.

84. Bell, H. M.: Retention of pursuit rotor skill after one year. J. Exp. Psychol., *40*, 648-649, 1950.

85. Bell, V. L.: Augmented knowledge of results and its effect upon acquisition and retention of a gross motor skill. Res. Quart., *39*, 25-30, 1968.

86. Bendig, A. W.: Factor analytic scales of need achievement. J. Gen. Psychol., *90*, 59-67, 1964.

87. Benson, D.: Effects of Concomitant Learing in Relaxation and Swimming on Swimming Improvement. Unpublished study, University of California, Los Angeles, Calif., 1958.

87a. Benton, A. L.: *Right-Left Discrimination and Finger Localization.* New York, Paul B. Hoeber, Inc., 1959, p. 14.

88. Benton, J. A., and Whyte, E. C.: Personality dynamics during successful failure sequence. J. Abnorm. Soc. Psychol., *45*, 583-591, 1950.

89. Bentson, T. B., and Summerskill, J.: Relation of personal success in intercollegiate athletics to certain aspects of personal adjustment. Res. Quart., *26*, 8-14, 1955.

90. Berg, I. A., and Bass, B. M.: *Conformity and Deviation.* New York, Harper & Bros., 1961.

91. Berger, R. A., and Mathus, D. L.: Movement time with various resistance loads as a function of pre-tensed and pre-relaxed muscular contractions. Res. Quart., *40*, 456-459, 1969.

92. Bergès, J., and Lezine, I.: *The Imitation of Gestures.* Suffolk, England, The Lavenham Press Ltd., 1963.

93. Berkeley, G.: An essay toward a new theory of vision. In *Classical Psychologists*, B. Rand (Ed.). Boston, Houghton Mifflin Co., 1912.

94. Berlyne, D. E.: *Conflict, Arousal and Curiosity.* New York, McGraw-Hill Book Co., 1960.

95. Berman, A.: The relation of time estimation to satiation. J. Exp. Psychol., *25*, 281-293, 1939.

96. Bernstein, N.: *The Co-ordination and Regulation of Movements.* London, Pergamon Press, 1967.

97. Berridge, H. L.: An experiment in the psychology of competition. Res. Quart., *35*, 37-42, 1935.

98. Bielianskas, V.: Recent advances in the psychology of masculinity and femininity. J. Psychol., *60*, 255-263, 1965.

99. Bills, A. G.: The influence of muscular tension on the efficiency of mental work. Amer. J. Psychol., *38*, 226-251, 1927.

100. Bills, A. G., and Brown, G.: The quantitative set. J. Exp. Psychol., *12*, 301-323, 1929.

101. Bilodeau, E. A.: Motor performance as affected by magnitude and direction of error contained in knowledge of results. J. Psychol., *50*, 103-113, 1955.

102. Bilodeau, E. A., and Bilodeau, I. McD.: Motor skills learning. Ann. Rev. Psychol., *42*, 243-280, 1961.

103. Bilodeau, E. A., and Bilodeau, I. McD.: Variable frequency of knowledge of results and the learning of a simple skill. J. Exp. Psychol., *55*, 379-383, 1958.

104. Bilodeau, E. A., Bilodeau, I. McD., and Schumsky, D. A.: Some effects of introducing and withdrawing knowledge of results early and late in practice. J. Exp. Psychol., *58*, 142-144, 1959.
105. Bilodeau, E. A., Jones, M. B., and Long, M. C.: Long-term memory as a function of retention time and repeated recalling. J. Exp. Psychol., *67*, 303-309, 1964.
106. Bilodeau, E. A., and Levy, C. M.: Long-term memory as a function of retention time and other conditions of learning. Psychol Rev., *71*, 27-41, 1964.
107. Bilodeau, I. McD.: Performance of an effortful task with variation in duration of prior practice and anticipated duration of present practice. J. Exp. Psychol., *46*, 146, 1953.
108. Bindra, D.: *Motivation, a Systematic Reinterpretation.* New York, The Ronald Press Company, 1951.
109. Binet, A., and Simon, T.: *The Development of Intelligence in Children.* Baltimore, Williams & Wilkins Co., 1916.
110. Bladen, S. R.: An extensive experiment in motor learning and re-learning. J. Educ. Psychol., *15*, 313-315, 1924.
111. Blane, H. T.: Space perception among unilaterally paralyzed children and adolescents. J. Exp. Psychol., *63*, 244-247, 1958.
112. Blick, K. S., and Bilodeau, E. A.: Interpolated activity and the learning of a simple skill. J. Exp. Psychol., *65*, 515-519, 1963.
113. Bogoras, W.: *The Chukchee.* New York, G. E. Stechert & Co., 1909.
114. Bolton, T. L.: The relation of motor power to intelligence. Amer. J. Psychol., *14*, 351-367, 1903.
115. Bonds, R. V.: A Comparison of Movement Attributes Exhibited by Chicano, White and Black Children. Unpublished study, Perceptual-Motor Learning Laboratory, UCLA, Los Angeles, Calif., 1971.
116. Boreas, Th.: Experimental studies on memory: II. The rate of forgetting. *Praktika de l'Academie d' Athenes, 5,* 382, 1930.
117. Borg, G.: The perception of physical performance. In *Frontiers of Fitness,* R. J. Shephard (Ed.). Springfield, Ill., Charles C Thomas, 1972.
118. Borg, G., Cavallin, N., Edstrom, C-G., and Marklund, G.: Motivation and Physical Performance, No. 19. Reports from the Institute of Applied Psychology, The University of Stockholm, Sweden, 1971.
119. Boring, E. C.: *A History of Experimental Psychology,* 2nd ed. New York, Appleton-Century-Crofts, 1950.
120. Boring, E. C.: *Sensation and Perception in Experimental Psychology.* New York, Appleton-Century-Crofts, 1942.
121. Bourne, L. B., Jr., Kepros, P. G., and Beier, E. G.: Effect of post inspection delay upon kinesthetic figural after-effects. J. Gen. Psychol., *68*, 37-42, 1963.
122. Bourne, L. E.: An evaluation of the effect of induced tension on performance. J. Exp. Psychol., *49*, 418-422, 1955.
123. Bowditch, H. P., and Southard, W. F.: A comparison of sight and touch. J. Physiol., *3*, 232-254, 1882.
123a. Bower, T. G.: The visual world of infants. Sci. Amer., *215*, 80-97, 1966.
124. Bowers, L.: Effects of autosuggested muscle contraction on muscular strength and size. Res. Quart., *37*, 302-312, 1966.
125. Brace, C. L., and Montagu, M. F.: *Man's Evolution.* New York, The Macmillan Co., 1965.
125a. Brace, D. K.: *Measuring Motor Ability, A Scale of Motor Ability Tests.* New York, A. S. Barnes Co., 1926.
126. Brace, D. K.: Studies in the rate of learning gross bodily motor skills. Res. Quart., *12*, 181-185, 1941.
127. Bray, C. W.: Transfer of learning. J. Exp. Psychol., *11*, 443-467, 1928.
128. Breckenridge, M. E., and Vincent, E. L.: *Child Development, Physical and Psychologic Growth Through the School Years.* Philadelphia, W. B. Saunders Co., 1955.

129. Brengelmann, J. C.: Abnormal and personality correlates of certainty. J. Ment. Sci., *105*, 142-162, 1959.

130. Brengelmann, J. C.: Expressive movements and abnormal behaviour. In *Handbook of Abnormal Psychology*, H. J. Eysenck (Ed.). New York, Basic Books, Inc., 1961, Chapter III.

131. Bridges, K. M. B.: Emotional development in early infancy. Child Develop., *3*, 324-341, 1932.

132. Brieson, H. V.: A discussion of stress and exhaustion as a primary as well as a contributing etiologic factor in organic neurological disease. The Military Surgeon, *5*, 101, 1947.

133. Briggs, G. E., and Brogden, W. J.: The effect of component practice on performance of a level-positionary skill. J. Exp. Psychol., *48*, 375-380, 1954.

134. Briggs, G. E., and Naylor, J. C.: The relative efficiency of several training methods as a function of transfer of task complexity. J. Exp. Psychol., *64*, 505, 512, 1962.

135. Briggs, G. E., and Waters, L. K.: Training and transfer as a function of component interaction. J. Exp. Psychol., *56*, 492-500, 1958.

136. Britt, S. H.: Retroactive inhibition—a review of the literature. Psychol. Bull., *32*, 381, 1935.

137. Broadbent, D. E.: *Perception and Communication.* London. Pergamon Press, 1958, p. 338.

138. Brodbeck, A. J., and Irwin, O. C.: The speech behavior of infants without families. Child Develop., *17*, 145-156, 1946.

139. Brown, H. S., and Messersmith, L.: An experiment in teaching tumbling with and without motion pictures. Res. Quart., *19*, 304-307, 1948.

140. Brown, J. S., Knauft, E. B., and Rosenbaum, G.: The accuracy of positioning reactions as a function of direction and extent. Office of Naval Research N5 ori-57, 1947.

141. Brown, R. H.: Visual sensitivity to differences in velocity. Psychol. Bull., *58*, 89, 1961.

142. Brown, V.: Thresholds for visual movement. Psychol. Forsch., *14*, 249-268, 1931.

143. Brozek, J., and Taylor, H. L.: Tests of motor functions in investigations on fitness. Amer. J. Psychol., *67*, 590-611, 1954.

144. Bruner, J. S.: Processes of Cognitive Growth in Infancy. Heinz Werner Lectures, Clark University, Worcester, Mass., 1968.

145. Bruner, J. S., and Goodman, C. C.: Value and need as organizing factors in perception. J. Abnorm. Soc. Psychol., *42*, 33-44, 1947.

146. Bryant, W. L.: On the development of voluntary motor ability. Amer. J. Psychol., *5*, 123-205, 1892.

147. Bryant, W. L.: On the development of voluntary motor ability. Amer. J. Psychol., *4*, 123-204, 1892.

148. Buchner, E. F.: A quarter century of psychology in America: 1878-1903. Amer. J. Psychol., *14*, 402-416, 1903.

149. Buhler, C., as quoted in Young: Re Smiling. *Motivation and Emotion.* New York, John Wiley & Sons, 1961.

150. Bunch, M. E.: Retroactive inhibition or facilitation from interpolated learning as a function of time. J. Comp. Physiol. Psychol., *39*, 287-291, 1946.

151. Bunch, M. E.: Transfer of training in the mastery of an antagonistic habit after varying intervals of time. J. Comp. Physiol. Psychol., *28*, 189-200, 1939.

152. Bunch, M. E., and Lang, E. S.: The amount of transfer of training from partial learning after varying intervals of time. J. Comp Physiol. Psychol., *27*, 449-459, 1939.

153. Bunch, M. E., and McTeer, F. D.: The influence of punishment during learning upon retroactive inhibition. J. Exp. Psychol., *15*, 473-495, 1932.

154. Bunch, M. E., and Rogers, M.: The relationship between transfer and the length of the interval separating the mastery of the two problems. J. Comp. Physiol. Psychol., *21*, 37-52, 1936.

155. Burdeshaw, D., Spragens, J. E., and Weis, P. A.: Evaluation of general vs. specific instruction of badminton skills to women of low motor ability. Res. Quart., *41*, 472-477, 1970.

156. Bures, J., and Buresora, O.: Cortical spreading depression as a memory disturbing factor. J. Comp. Physiol. Psychol., *56*, 268-272, 1963.

157. Bures, J., and Buresora, O.: The use of Leao's spreading depression in the study of interhemispheric transfer of memory traces. J. Comp. Physiol. Psychol., *53*, 558-563, 1960.

158. Bures, J., Buresora, O., and Fifkora, E.: Interhemispheric transfer of passive avoidance reaction. J. Comp. Physiol. Psychol., *57*, 326-330, 1964.

159. Buresora, O., and Bures, J.: Interhemispheric synthesis of memory traces. J. Comp. Physiol. Psychol., *59*, 211-214, 1965.

160. Burg, A.: Apparatus for measurement of dynamic visual acuity. Percept. Motor Skills, *20*, 231-235, 1965.

161. Burg, A.: Visual acuity as measured by dynamic and static tests. J. Appl. Psychol., *50*, 360-466, 1966.

162. Burg, A., and Hulbert, S.: Dynamic visual acuity as related to age, sex and static acuity. J. Appl. Psychol., *45*, 111-116, 1961.

163. Burt, C.: *The Factors of the Mind.* London, University of London Press, 1956.

164. Buxton, E. E., and Humphries, L. G.: The effect of practice upon intercorrelations of motor skills. Science, *81*, 441-442, 1935.

165. Cameron, D. E., Solyom, L., Smed, S., and Wainrib, B.: Effects of intravenous administration of ribonucleic acid upon failure of memory for recent events in pre-senile and aged individuals. Recent Advances Biol. Psychiat., *5*, 365-373, 1965.

166. Cameron, P., and Wertheimer, M.: Kinesthetic after-effects are in the hands, not in phenomenal space. Percept. Motor Skills, *20*, 1131-1132, 1965.

167. Cannon, W. B.: *The Wisdom of the Body.* New York, W. W. Norton & Co., Inc., 1932.

168. Cantrell, R. P.: Body balance activity and perception. Percept. Motor Skills, *17*, 431-437, 1963.

169. Caplan, C. S.: Transfer of Fatigue in Motor Performance. Unpublished study, University of California, Berkeley, Calif., 1969.

170. Carlson, J. B.: Effect of amount and distribution of inspection time and length of delay interval on kinesthetic after-effect. J. Exp. Psychol., *66*, 377-382, 1963.

171. Carpenter, A.: The measurement of general motor capacity and general motor ability in the first three grades. Res. Quart., *13*, 444-465, 1942.

172. Carpenter, A.: Tests of motor educability for the first three grades. Child Develop., *11*, 293-299, 1940.

173. Carr, H. A.: The influence of visual guidance in maze learning. J. Exp. Psychol., *4*, 399-417, 1921.

174. Carron, A. V.: Motor performance and response consistency as a function of age. J. Motor Behav., *3*, 105-109, 1971.

175. Carron, A. V.: Physical fatigue and motor learning. Res. Quart., *40*, 682-686, 1969.

176. Carter, L. F.: Maze learning with a differential proprioceptive cue. J. Exp. Psychol., *19*, 758-762, 1936.

177. Carter, L. F., Haythorn, W., and Howell, M.: A further investigation of the criteria of leadership. J. Abnorm. Soc. Psychol., *46*, 589-595, 1951.

178. Carter, L. F., and Nixon, M.: An investigation of the relationship between four criteria of leadership ability for three different tasks. J. Psychol., *27*, 245-261, 1949.

179. Castaneda, A.: Effects of stress on complex learning and performance. J. Exp. Psychol., *52*, 9-12, 1956.

180. Castaneda, A., and Palmero, D. S.: Psychomotor performance as a function of amount of training and stress. J. Exp. Psychol., *50*, 175-179, 1955.

181. Cattell, J.: Mental tests and measurements. Mind, *15*, 363-380, 1890.
182. Cattell, R. B.: The nature and measurement of anxiety. Sci. Amer., *206*, 96-104, 1963.
183. Caudill, W.: Effects of social and cultural systems in reactions to stress. New York, Social Science Research Council, 1958.
184. Chan, D.: An apparatus for the measurement of tactile activity. Amer. J. Psychol., 77, 489, 1964.
185. Chandler, K. A.: The effect of monaural and binaural tones of different intensities on the visual perception of verticality. Amer. J. Psychol., *74*, 260-265, 1961.
186. Chapanis, A.: Knowledge of performance as an incentive in repetitive monotonous tasks. J. Appl. Psychol., *48*, 263-267, 1964.
187. Chase, W. P.: The role of kinesthesis in ideation maze learning. J. Exp. Psychol., *17*, 424-438, 1934.
188. Chernikoff, R., and Taylor, F. V.: *Reaction Time to Kinesthetic Stimulation Resulting from Sudden Arm Displacement.* Washington, D.C.: Naval Research Laboratory. NRL Report 3887, November 19, 1951.
189. Christina, R. W.: Movement-produced feedback as a mechanism for the temporal anticipation of motor responses. J. Motor Behav., *3*, 97-104, 1971.
190. Church, R. M.: The effects of competition on reaction time and palmar skin conductance. J. Abnorm. Soc. Psychol., *65*, 32-40, 1962.
191. Church, R. M., and Camp, D. S.: Change in reaction time as a function of knowledge of results. Amer. J. Psychol., 77, 102-106, 1965.
192. Churchill, A. V.: Visual-kinesthetic localization. Amer. J. Psychol., *78*, 496-498, 1965.
193. Clapper, D. J.: Measurement of Selected Kinesthetic Responses at the Junior and Senior High School Levels. Unpublished doctoral dissertation, State University of Iowa, Ames, Iowa, 1957.
194. Clarke, D. H., and Gentry, R. B.: Individual differences in hand-grip and elbow flexion fatigue. J. Motor Behav., *3*, 225-234, 1971.
195. Clarke, H. H.: *Physical and Motor Tests in the Medford Boy's Growth Study.* Englewood Cliffs, N. J., Prentice-Hall, Inc., 1971.
196. Clark, K. B.: Some factors influencing the remembering of prose materials. Arch. Psychol., *32*, 253, 1940.
197. Clark, L. V.: Effect of mental practice on the development of a certain motor skill. Res. Quart., *31*, 560-568, 1960.
198. Clarke, A. D. B., and Blakemore, C. B.: Age and perceptual-motor transfer in imbeciles. Brit. J. Psychiat., *52*, 125-131, 1961.
199. Clarke, A. D. B., and Cookson, M.: Perceptual-motor transfer in imbeciles: A second series of experiments. Brit. J. Psychiat., *53*, 321-330, 1962.
200. Cleghorn, T. E., and Darcus, H. D.: The sensibility to passive movement of the human elbow joint. Quart. J. Exp. Psychol., *4*, 66-77, 1952.
201. Clifton, M. A., and Smith, H. M.: Viewing oneself performing selected motor skills in motion pictures and its effect upon the expressed consciousness of self in performance. Res. Quart., *33*, 369-375, 1962.
202. Coan, R. W.: Factors in movement perception. J. Consult. Psychol., *28*, 394-402, 1964.
203. Cofer, C. N., and Appley, M. H.: *Motivation: Theory and Research.* New York, John Wiley & Sons, 1964.
204. Cogswell, J. F.: Effects of a stereoscopic sound motion picture on the learning of a perceptual-motor task. *Human Engineering Report SDC 269-7-32.* Special Devices Center, 1952.
205. Cohen, P.: Relationship of Performance in Two Maze Tasks. Unpublished Master's thesis, University of California, Los Angeles, Calif., 1963.
206. Coleman, G. R.: A laboratory for research in athletics. Res. Quart., *1*, 34-40, 1930.
207. Coleman, J. S.: *The Adolescent Society.* New York, The Free Press of Glencoe, 1961.

208. Comalli, P. E., Jr., Wagner, S., and Weener, H.: Effects of muscular involvement on size perception. Percept. Motor Skills, 9, 116, 1959.
209. Comrey, A.: Group performance in a manual dexterity task. J. Appl. Psychol., 37, 207, 1953.
210. Comrey, A., and Deskin, G.: Group manual dexterity in women. J. Appl. Psychol., 38, 178, 1954.
211. Comrey, A., and Deskin, G.: Further results on group manual dexterity in men. J. Appl. Psychol., 38, 116, 1954.
212. Cook, T. W.: Factors in massed and distributed practice. J. Exp. Psychol., 34, 325-334, 1934.
213. Cook, T. W.: Mirror position and negative transfer. J. Exp. Psychol., 29, 155-160, 1941.
214. Cook, T. W.: Studies in cross-education. Mirror tracing the star-shaped maze. J. Exp. Psychol., 16, 146-147, 1933.
215. Cook, T. W.: Studies in cross-education. Further experiments in mirror tracing the star-shaped maze. J. Exp. Psychol., 16, 679-700, 1933.
216. Cook, T. W.: Studies in cross education. Kinesthetic learning of an irregular pattern. J. Exp. Psychol., 17, 745-751, 1934.
217. Cooper, J., and Glassow, R.: *Kinesiology*. St. Louis, C. V. Mosby Co., 1963.
218. Corah, N. L.: Attention and kinesthetic figural after-effect. Amer. J. Psychol., 74, 629-630, 1961.
219. Corder, O.: Effects of physical education on the intellectual, physical, and social development of educable mentally retarded boys. Exceptional Child., 43, 357-364, 1966.
220. Cortes, J. B., and Gatte, F. M.: Physique and self-description of temperament. J. Consult. Psychol., 29, 429-432, 1965.
221. Costello, C. G., Herrera, B., and Holland, H. C.: The role of the interpolated stimulus in producing kinesthetic figural after-effects. Amer. J. Psychol., 76, 670-674, 1963.
222. Courts, F. A.: Relations between muscular tension and performance. Psychol. Bull., 39, 347-367, 1942.
223. Coville, F. H.: The learning of motor skills as influenced by knowledge of mechanical principles. J. Educ. Psychol., 48, 321-327, 1957.
224. Cowan, E. A., and Pratt, B. M.: The hurdle jump as a developmental diagnostic test of motor coordination for children from three to twelve years of age. Child Develop., 5, 107-121, 1934.
225. Cox, F. N.: Some effects of test anxiety and presence or absence of other persons on boys' performance on a repetitive motor task. J. Exp. Child Psychol., 3, 100-112, 1965.
226. Craddock, R. A., and Stern, M. R.: Effect of pre- and post-stress upon height of drawings in a perceptual-motor task. Percept. Motor Skills, 17, 283-285, 1963.
227. Craft, L. J., and Hinricks, J. V.: Short-term retention of simple motor responses. Similarity of prior and succeeding responses. J. Exp. Psychol., 87, 297-302, 1971.
228. Crafts, L. W., and Gilbert, R. W.: The effect of knowledge of results on maze learning and retention. J. Educ. Psychol., 26, 177-187, 1935.
229. Cratty, B. J.: Attention, activation and self-control. In *Human Behavior: Exploring Educational Processes*. Wolfe City, Texas, University Press, 1971.
230. Cratty, B. J.: A comparison of fathers and sons in physical ability. Res. Quart., 31, 12-15, 1960.
231. Cratty, B. J.: A comparison of selected pre-teaching competencies of transfer and non-transfer students. The Junior College Journal, 31, 78-81, 1960.
232. Cratty, B. J.: A comparison of the learning of a fine motor skill to learning a similar gross motor task, based upon kinesthetic cues. Res. Quart., 33, 212 and 221, 1962.
233. Cratty, B. J.: An investigation of motor educability. Percept. Motor Skills, 13, 179-181, 1961.

234. Cratty, B. J.: Assessing the Accuracy of Gross Human Movement. Proceedings of 65th Annual College Physical Education Association, 1961-62.
235. Cratty, B. J.: Assessing movement accuracy with a fluid-patterned locomotor maze. Percept. Motor Skills, *13*, 162, 1961.
236. Cratty, B. J.: The assessment of teacher sensitivity. Calif. J. Educ. Res., *13*, 2, 1962.
237. Cratty, B. J.: Athletic and physical experiences of fathers and sons who participated in physical fitness testing at Pomona College, 1925-1959. Calif. J. Educ. Res., *10*, 510, 1959.
238. Cratty, B. J.: A three level theory of perceptual-motor behavior. Quest, VI, 3-10, 1966.
239. Cratty, B. J.: Characteristics of human learning in an irregularly patterned locomotor maze. Calif. J. Educ. Res., *14*, 36-42, 1963.
240. Cratty, B. J.: Comparison of verbal-motor performance and learning in serial memory tasks. Res. Quart., *34*, 431-439, 1964.
241. Cratty, B. J.: *Developmental Sequences of Perceptual-Motor Tasks.* L. I., New York, Educational Activities Inc., 1967.
242. Cratty, B. J.: Effects of intra-maze delay upon learning. Percept. Motor Skills, *15*, 14, 1962.
243. Cratty, B. J.: The evolution of the human action system. Quest, VI, 10-21, 1965.
244. Cratty, B. J.: Figural after-effects resulting from gross action patterns: Part II. Perceptual alterations of veer by interpolated movement experience. Res. Quart., *36*, 22-28, 1965.
245. Cratty, B. J.: Figural after-effects resulting from gross action patterns: Part III. The amount of exposure to the inspection task and the duration of the after-effects. Res. Quart., *36*, 4, 1965.
246. Cratty B. J.: The influence of small-pattern practice upon large pattern learning. Res. Quart., *33*, 523-535, 1962.
247. Cratty, B. J.: Intellectual activity, activation, and self-control. In *Physical Expressions of Intelligence.* Englewood Cliffs, N.J., Prentice-Hall, Inc., 1972.
247a. Cratty, B. J.: *Motor Activity and the Education of Retardates.* Philadelphia, Lea & Febiger, 1969.
248. Cratty, B. J.: Motor learning. In *The Science and Medicine of Exercise and Sport,* Warren Johnson (Ed.). New York, The Macmillan Co., 1965.
249. Cratty, B. J.: On the Threshold. Merck Sharpe and Dohme Lecture at the Texas Institute of Child Psychiatry, Houston, Texas, 1965.
250. Cratty, B. J.: The perception of gradient and the veering tendency while walking without vision. Res. Bull., The American Foundation for the Blind, October 1965.
251. Cratty, B. J.: Perception of inclined plane while walking without vision. Percept. Motor Skills, *22*, 547-556, 1966.
252. Cratty, B. J.: Perceptual alternations of veer by interpolated movement experiences. Res. Quart., *36*, 361-366, 1965.
253. Cratty, B. J.: The Perceptual-Motor Attributes of Mentally Retarded Children and Youth. Monograph, Mental Retardation Services Board of Los Angeles County, August 1966.
254. Cratty, B. J.: Transfer of small-pattern practice to large-pattern learning. Res. Quart., *33*, 523-535, 1962.
255. Cratty, B. J.: Perceptual Thresholds of Non-visual Locomotion. Monograph, Part I, Department of Physical Education, University of California, Los Angeles, Calif., August 1965.
256. Cratty, B. J.: Personality and Individual Variations in Gross Movement Behavior. Paper presented to the So. Sec. of the Calif. Assn. for Physical Education, 1961.
257. Cratty, B. J.: *Physical Expressions of Intelligence.* Englewood Cliffs, N.J., Prentice-Hall, Inc., 1972.

258. Cratty, B. J.: The psychological bases of physical activity. J. Health, Phys. Educ., Recreation, 7, 71-72, 1965.
258a. Cratty, B. J.: *Psychology and Contemporary Sport.* Englewood Cliffs, N.J., Prentice-Hall, Inc., 1973.
259. Cratty, B. J.: *Psychology and Physical Activity.* Englewood Cliffs, N.J., Prentice-Hall, Inc., 1968.
260. Cratty, B. J.: Recency vs. primacy in a complex gross motor task. Res. Quart., 34, 3-8, 1963.
261. Cratty, B. J.: *Perceptual and Motor Development of Infants and Children.* New York, The Macmillan Co., 1970.
262. Cratty, B. J.: The veering tendency and the perception of gradient. *The New Outlook for the Blind,* August 1965.
263. Cratty, B. J., and Amatelli, F. E.: Figural aftereffects elicited by gross action patterns: The role of kinesthetic aftereffects in the arm-shoulder musculature. Res. Quart., 40, 38-45, 1969.
264. Cratty, B. J., and Densmore, A. E.: Activity during rest and learning a gross movement task. Percept. Motor Skills, 17, 250, 1963.
265. Cratty, B. J., and Duffy, K. E.: Studies of movement aftereffects. Percept. Motor Skills, 29, 843-860, 1969.
266. Cratty, B. J., and Eachus, T.: Correlates of Personality and Motor Performance in Two Maze Tasks. Paper presented at Nat. College Physical Assn., 1961.
267. Cratty, B. J., and Hutton, R. S.: Figural after-effects, resulting from gross action patterns. Res. Quart., 35, 147-160, 1964
268. Cratty, B. J., and Sage, J. N.: The Effects of Primary and Secondary Group Interaction upon Improvement in a Complex Movement Task. Unpublished study, University of California, Los Angeles, Calif., 1963.
269. Cratty, B. J., and Williams, H. G.: Accuracy of facing movements executed without vision. Percept. Motor Skills, 23, 1231-1238, 1966.
270. Cratty, B. J., and Williams, H. G.: Perceptual Thresholds of Non-visual Locomotion. Monograph, Part II, Department of Physical Education, University of California, Los Angeles, Calif., 1966.
270a. Cron, G. W., and Pronko, N. H.: Development of the sense of balance in school children. J. Educ. Res., 51, 33-37, 1957.
271. Cross, T. J.: A comparison of the whole method, the minor game method, and the whole-part method of teaching basketball to ninth-grade boys. Res. Quart., 8, 49-54, 1937.
272. Crutcher, R.: An experimental study of persistence. J. Appl. Psychol., 18, 409-417, 1934.
273. Cumbee, F.: A factorial analysis of motor coordination. Res. Quart., 25, 412-420, 1954.
274. Cumbee, F. Z., Meyer, M., and Peterson, G.: Factorial analysis of motor coordination variables for third and fourth grade girls. Res. Quart., 28, 100-108, 1957.
275. Cummins, R. A.: A study of the effect of basketball practice on motor reaction, attention and suggestibility. Psychol. Rev., 21, 356-369, 1914.
276. Cunningham, B. V.: An experiment in measuring gross motor development of infants and young children. J. Educ. Psychol., 18, 43-54, 1927.
277. Cushing, F. H.: Manual concepts. Amer. Anthropologist, 5, 289-317, 1892.
278. Daniel, R. S.: The distribution of muscular action potentials during maze learning. J. Exp. Psychol., 24, 621-629, 1939.
279. Dart, R. A.: *Adventures With the Missing Link.* New York, Viking Press, 1959.
280. Darwin, C. R.: *The Descent of Man, and Selection in Relation to Sex.* London, John Murray, 1875.
281. Darwin, C. R.: *The Expression of Emotions in Man and Animals.* New York, Appleton, 1872.

282. Daugherty, G.: The effects of kinesiological teaching on the performance of junior high school boys. Res. Quart., *16*, 26-33, 1945.
283. Davidson, M., and McInnes, P. R.: The distribution of personality traits in 7-year-old children. Brit. J. Educ. Psychol., *27*, 48-61, 1957.
284. Davis, R. C.: Methods of measuring muscular tension. Psychol. Bull., *39*, 329-346, 1942.
285. Davis, R. C.: The Relation of Certain Muscle Action Potentials to 'Mental Work.' Bloomington, Ind., Indiana University Publication, Science Series, 5, 1937.
286. Davis, R. C.: Set and Muscular Tension. Bloomington, Ind., Indiana University Publication, Science Series, 10, 1940.
287. Davis, R. C., and Payne, B.: The role of muscular tension in the comparison of lifted weights. J. Exp. Psychol., *27*, 227-242, 1940.
288. Dawson, W. W., and Edwards, R. W.: Motor development of retarded children. Percept. Motor Skills, *21*, 223-226, 1965.
289. Dayton, G. O., Jr., Jones, M. H., Steele, B., and Rose, M.: Developmental study of coordinated eye movements in the human infant. Arch. Ophthal., *71*, 871-875, 1970.
290. Delacato, C. H.: *The Diagnosis and Treatment of Speech and Reading Problems.* Springfield, Ill., Charles C. Thomas, 1963.
291. Dember, W. N.: *The Psychology of Perception.* New York, Henry Holt & Co., 1960.
292. Dember, W. N., and Earl, R. W.: Analysis of exploratory, manipulatory and curiosity behaviors. Psychol. Rev., *64*, 91-96, 1957.
293. Denny, M. R., and Reisman, J. M.: Negative transfer as a function of manifest anxiety. Percept. Motor Skills, *6*, 73-75, 1956.
294. Dickinson, J.: The role of two factors in a gross motor aiming task. Brit. J. Psychol., *60*, 465-470, 1970.
295. Dillon, D. J.: Measurement of perceived body size. Percept. Motor Skills, *14*, 191-196, 1962.
296. Dinner, B., Wapner, S., McFarland, J., and Werner, H.: Rhythmic activity and the perception of time. Amer. J. Psychol., *76*, 287, 292, 1963.
297. Domey, R. G., Duckworth, J. E., and Morandi, A. J.: Taxonomies and correlates of physique. Psychol. Bull., *62*, 411-426, 1964.
298. Dore, L. L., and Hilgard, E. R.: Spaced practice and the maturation hypothesis. J. Psychol., *4*, 245-259, 1937.
299. Doty, B., and Doty, L. A.: Effect of age and chlorpromazine on memory consolidation. J. Comp. Physiol. Psychol., *57*, 331-334, 1964.
300. Dowling, R. M.: Visual recognition threshold and concurrent motor activity. Percept. Motor Skills, *20*, 1141-1146, 1965.
301. Downey, J. E.: *The Will-Temperament and Its Testing.* Yonkers-on-Hudson, N.Y., World Book Co., 1923, p. 339.
302. Draper, W. R.: Sensory stimulation and Rhesus monkey activity. Percept. Motor Skills, *21*, 319-322, 1965.
303. Drazin, D. H.: Effects of foreperiod, foreperiod variability, and probability of stimulus occurrence on simple reaction time. J. Exp. Psychol., *62*, 43-45, 1961.
304. Dudycha, G. J.: *Learn More with Less Effort.* New York, Harper & Bros., 1957, p. 240.
305. Duffy, E.: *Activation and Behavior.* New York, John Wiley & Sons, Inc., 1962.
306. Duffy, E.: Muscular tension as related to physique and behavior. Child Develop., *3*, 200-206, 1932.
307. Duffy, E.: The psychological significance of the concept of "arousal" or activation. Psychol. Rev., *64*, 265-275, 1957.
308. Duncan, C. P.: Transfer in motor learning as a function of 1st task learning and inter-task similarity. J. Exp. Psychol., *45*, 1-11, 1953.

308a. Duncan, C. P., and Underwood, B. J.: Retention of transfer in motor learning after twenty-four hours and after fourteen months. J. Exp. Psychol., *46*, 445-452, 1953.

309. Dunlap, K.: Rhythm and time. Psychol. Bull., *8*, 230-242, 1911; *9*, 197-199, 1914; *11*, 169-171, 1916; *13*, 206-208, 1918.

310. Dusenbury, D., and Knower, F. H.: Experimental studies of the symbolism of action and voice. Quart. J. Speech, *24*, 424-435, 1938.

311. Dusenbury, L.: A study of the effects of training in ball throwing by children ages three to seven. Res. Quart., *23*, 9-14, 1952.

312. Easley, H.: The curve of forgetting and the distribution of practice. J. Educ. Psychol., *28*, 474-478, 1937.

313. Eason, R. G.: Effect of level of activation on the quality and efficiency of performance of verbal and motor tasks. Percept. Motor Skills, *16*, 525-543, 1963.

314. Eason, R. G.: Relation between effort, tension level, skill and performance efficiency in a perceptual-motor task. Percept. Motor Skills, *16*, 297-317, 1963.

315. Easterbrook, J. A.: The effect of emotion on cue utilization and the organization of behavior. Psychol. Rev., *66*, 183-201, 1959.

316. Ebbinghaus, H.: Memory: A Contribution to Experimental Psychology. Bureau of Publications, Teachers College, Columbia University, New York, N.Y., 1913.

317. Eberhard, U.: Transfer of training related to finger dexterity. Percept. Motor Skills, *17*, 274, 1963.

318. Eckert, H. M.: Linear relationships of isometric strength to propulsive force, angular velocity, and angular acceleration in the standing broad jump. Res. Quart., *35*, 298-306, 1964.

318a. Edgington, E. S.: Kinesthetically guided movements of head and arm. J. Psychol., *36*, 51-57, 1953.

319. Efron, D.: *Gesture and Environment*. London, King's Crown Press, 1941, p. 155.

320. Egstrom, G.: The Effects of an Emphasis on Conceptualizing Techniques upon the Early Learning of a Gross Motor Skill. Doctoral dissertation, University of Southern California, Los Angeles, Calif., 1961.

321. Ehrlich, G.: A method of constructing learning curves for a motor skill involving total body skill and accuracy. J. Appl. Psychol., *27*, 494-503, 1943.

322. Eiduson, S., Eiduson, B. T., Geller, E., and Yuwiler, A.: *Biochemistry and Behavior*. Princeton, N.J., D. Van Nostrand Publishers, 1964.

323. Eisenberg, P., and Reichlane, P. B.: Judging expressive movements. II. Judgment of dominance feeling from motion pictures of gait. J. Soc. Psychol., *10*, 345-357, 1939.

324. Ekman, P.: Body position, facial expression and verbal behavior during interviews. J. Abnorm. Soc. Psychol., *68*, 295-301, 1964.

325. Elkin, E. N.: Target velocity, exposure time and anticipatory tracking time as determinants of dynamic visual acuity (DVA). J. Gen. Psychol., *1*, 26-33, 1962.

326. Elkine, D.: De l'orientation de l'enfant d'age schdaire daus les relations temporales. J. Psychol. Norm. Path., *25*, 425-429, 1928.

327. Elliott, R.: A Comparison of Videotape Replay with a Traditional Approach in the Teaching of Selected Gymnastic Skills. Unpublished study, Colorado State University, Fort Collins, Colorado, 1970.

328. Ellis, H.: *The Transfer of Learning*. New York, The Macmillan Company, 1965.

329. Ellis, M. J., and Craig, T. T.: A note on the inferiority of retardates' motor performance. J. Motor Behav., *1*, 339, 1969.

329a. English, H. B., and English, A. C.: *A Comprehensive Dictionary of Psychological and Psychoanalytic Terms*. New York, David McKay, 1958.

330. Epstein, B.: *Immediate and Retention Effects of Interpolated Rest Periods on Learning Performance*. Teachers' College Contributions to Education, 949, 1949.
331. Epstein, W.: Experimental investigations of the genesis of visual space-perception. Psychol. Bull., *61*, 115-118, 1964.
332. Epstein, W., Pash, J., and Coney, A.: The current status of the size-distance hypothesis. Psychol. Bull., *58*, 491-514, 1961.
333. Eriksen, C. W., Lazarus, R. S., and Strange, J. R.: Psychological stress and its personality correlates. J. Personality, *20*, 277-286, 1952.
334. Espenschade, A.: Motor Performance in Adolescence. Society for Research in Child Development, 5, Serial No. 24, No. 1. National Research Council, Washington, D. C., 1940.
335. Exline, R. V.: Explorations in process of person perception: visual interaction in relationship to competition, sex, and need for affiliation. J. Personality, *31*, 1-20, 1963.
336. Exline, R. V., Gray, D., and Schuette, D.: Visual behavior in a dyad as affected by interview content and sex of respondent. J. Personality Soc. Psychol., *1*, 201-209, 1965.
337. Eysenck, H. J.: *The Dynamics of Anxiety and Hysteria*. London, Routledge and Kegan Paul, 1957.
338. Eysenck, H. J.: *Handbook of Abnormal Psychology*. New York, Basic Books, Inc., 1961.
339. Eysenck, H. J.: Involuntary rest pauses in tapping as a function of drive and personality. Percept. Motor Skills, *18*, 173-174, 1964.
340. Eysenck, H. J.: On the dual function of consolidation. Percept. Motor Skills, *22*, 273-274, 1966.
341. Eysenck, H. J.: *The Structure of Human Personality*. London, Methune, 1953.
342. Eysenck, H. J.: A new theory of post-rest upswing or "warm-up" in motor learning. Percept. Motor Skills, *28*, 992-994, 1969.
343. Eysenck, H. J., and Maxwell, A. E.: Reminiscence as a function of drive. Brit. J. Psychol., *58*, 43-52, 1961.
344. Fairclough, R. H., Jr.: Transfer of motivated improvement in speed of reaction and movement. Res. Quart., *23*, 1, 1952.
344a. Fantz, R. L.: Pattern vision in newborn infants. Science, *140*, 296-297, 1963.
345. Farber, I. E., and Spence, K. W.: Conditioning and extinction as a function of anxiety. J. Exp. Psychol., *45*, 116-119, 1953.
346. Farrell, J. E.: Programed vs. teacher-directed instruction in beginning tennis for women. Res. Quart., *41*, 51-58, 1970.
347. Fechner, G. T.: *Élemente der Psychophysik, II*, 311-313, 1860, Leipzig.
348. Fenz, W. D., and Epstein, S.: Manifest anxiety: Unifactoral or multifactoral composition. Percept. Motor Skills, *20*, 773-780, 1965.
349. Fiedler, F. E.: Assumed similarity measures as predictors of team effectiveness. J. Abnorm. Soc. Psychol., *49*, 381-388, 1954.
350. Fisher, S.: Body sensation and perception of projective stimuli. J. Consult. Psychol., *29*, 135-138, 1965.
351. Fisher, S.: Power orientation and concept of self-height in men. Preliminary note. Percept. Motor Skills, *18*, 732, 1964.
352. Fisher, S., and Cleveland, S. E.: *Body Image and Personality*. New York, D. Van Nostrand Publishers, Inc., 1941, p. 389.
353. Fishkin, S. M.: Passive vs. active exposure and other variables related to the occurrence of hand adaptation to lateral displacement. Percept. Motor Skills, *29*, 291-297, 1969.
354. Fitts, P. M.: The information capacity of the human motor system in controlling amplitude of movement. J. Exp. Psychol., *47*, 381-391, 1954.
355. Fitts, P. M.: Perceptual-motor skill learning. In *Categories of Human Learning*, Arthur W. Melton (Ed.). New York, Academic Press, Inc., 1964.
356. Fitts, P. M., Bahrick, H. P., and Noble, M. E.: *Skilled Performance*. New York, John Wiley & Sons, Inc., 1961.

357. Fitts, P. M., and Crannell, C.: Location Discrimination. II. Accuracy of Reaching Movements to 24 Different Areas, USAF Air Material Command Technical Report 5833, 1950.
358. Fleishman, E. A.: An analysis of positioning movements and static reactions. J. Exp. Psychol., *55*, 13-24, 1958.
359. Fleishman, E. A.: A comparative study of aptitude patterns in unskilled and skilled psychomotor performances. J. Appl. Psychol., *41*, 54-63, 1957.
360. Fleishman, E. A.: Component and total task relations at different stages of learning a complex tracking task. Percept. Motor Skills, *20*, 1305-1311, 1965.
361. Fleishman, E. A.: The Dimensions of Physical Fitness—The Nationwide Normative and Developmental Study of Basic Tests. Technical Report No. 4, The Office of Naval Research, Department of Industrial Administration and Department of Psychology, Yale University, New Haven, Conn., 1962.
362. Fleishman, E. A.: Individual differences and motor learning. In *Learning and Individual Differences*. Columbus, Ohio, Charles E. Merrill Books, Inc., 1967, Chapter 8.
363. Fleishman, E. A.: Perception of body position in the absence of visual cues. J. Exp. Psychol., *46*, 261-270, 1953.
364. Fleishman, E. A.: Performance assessment on an empirically derived task taxonomy. Hum. Factors, *9*, 349-366, 1967.
365. Fleishman, E. A.: A relationship between incentive motivation and ability level in psychomotor performance. J. Exp. Psychol., *56*, 78-81, 1958.
366. Fleishman, E. A., and Ellison, G. D.: A factor analysis of fine manipulative tests. J. Appl. Psychol., *46*, 96-105, 1962.
367. Fleishman, E. A., and Hempel, W. E., Jr.: Changes in factor structure of a complex psychomotor test as a function of practice. Psychometrika, *19*, 239-252, 1954.
368. Fleishman, E. A., and Hempel, W. E., Jr.: The relation between abilities and improvement with practice in a visual discrimination reaction task. J. Exp. Psychol., *49*, 301-312, 1955.
369. Fleishman, E. A., and Hempel, W. E., Jr.: Factorial analysis of complex psychomotor performance and related skills. J. Appl. Psychol., *40*, 2, 1956.
370. Fleishman, E. A., Kremer, E. J., and Shoup, G. W.: The Dimensions of Physical Fitness—A Factor Analysis of Strength Tests. Technical Report No. 2, The Office of Naval Research, Department of Industrial Administration and Department of Psychology, Yale University, New Haven, Conn., 1961.
371. Fleishman, E. A., and Parker, J. F., Jr.: Factors in the retention and relearning of perceptual-motor skills. J. Exp. Psychol., *64*, 215-226, 1962.
372. Fleishman, E. A., and Rich, S.: Role of kinesthetic and spatial-visual abilities in perceptual-motor learning. J. Exp. Psychol., *66*, 6-11, 1963.
373. Fleishman, E. A., Thomas, P., and Munroe, P.: The Dimensions of Physical Fitness—A Factor Analysis of Speed Flexibility, Balance and Coordination Tests. Technical Report No. 3, The Office of Naval Research, Department of Industrial Administration and Department of Psychology, Yale University, New Haven, Conn., 1961.
374. Flourens, M. J. P.: *Experiences Sur le Systeme Nerveaux*, Paris, 1825.
375. Fowler, H.: *Curiosity and Exploratory Behavior*. New York, The Macmillan Company, 1965.
376. Francis, R. J., and Rarick, G. L.: Motor Characteristics of the Mentally Retarded. U.S. Office of Education Cooperative Research Project, No. 152, (6432), University of Wisconsin, Madison, Wisconsin, 1957.
377. Frank, L. K.: *Society as the Patient*. New Brunswick, N.J., Rutgers University Press, 1949.
378. Frank, L. K.: Tactile communication. In *Explorations in Communication*, E. Carpenter and M. McLuhan (Eds.). Boston, Beacon Press, 1964, pp. 4-11.
379. Frederick, R. L.: A Study of the Effects that Delayed Knowledge of Results Has on the Acquisition of a Dart Throwing Task. Unpublished master's thesis, Bradley University, Peoria, Illinois, 1968.

380. Freeman, G. L.: Facilitative and inhibitory effects of muscular tension upon performance. Amer. J. Psychol., *45*, 17-52, 1933.
381. Freeman, G. L.: The optimal locus of 'anticipatory tensions' in muscular work. J. Exp. Psychol., *21*, 554-564, 1937.
382. Freeman, G. L.: The optimal muscular tensions for various performances. Amer. J. Psychol., *51*, 146-150, 1938.
383. Freeman, G. L.: Studies in the psycho-physiology of transfer: I. The problem of identical elements. J. Exp. Psychol., *2*, 521, 1937.
384. Freeman, F. N., and Abernathy, E. M.: Comparative retention of typewriting and of substitution with analogous material. J. Educ. Psychol., *21*, 639-647, 1930.
385. Freeman, F. N., and Abernathy, E. M.: New evidence of the superior retention of typewriting to that of substitution. J. Educ. Psychol., *23*, 331-334, 1932.
386. Freeman, R. B., Jr.: Figural after-effects: Displacement or contrast? Amer. J. Psychol., *77*, 607-613, 1964.
387. French, J. D.: The reticular formation. J. Neurosurg., XV, 97-115, 1958.
388. Freud, S.: In *Theories of Personality*, C. S. Hall and G. Lindsley (Eds.). New York, John Wiley & Sons, Inc., 1957.
389. Frijda, N. H.: Facial expression and situational cues: a control. Acta Psychol. (Amst.), *18*, 239-244, 1961.
390. Frischeisen-Kohler, L.: The personal tempo and its inheritance. Character Personality, *1*, 301-313, 1933.
391. Fromm, E.: *Man for Himself*. New York, Rinehart & Co., 1947, p. 112.
392. Fruchter, B.: *Introduction to Factor Analysis*. Princeton, N.J., D. Van Nostrand Publishers, Inc., 1954.
393. Fry, C. L.: A developmental examination of performance in a tacit coordination game situation. J. Personality Soc. Psychol., *5*, 277-281, 1967.
394. Fuchs, A. H.: Perceptual-motor skill learning. J. Exp. Psychol., *42*, 177-182, 1962.
395. Fuchs, A. H.: The progression-regression hypothesis in perceptual-motor skill learning. J. Exp. Psychol., *63*, 177-182, 1962.
396. Fulton, R. E.: Speed and accuracy in learning movements. Arch. Psychol., *5*, 1-53, 1945.
397. Fulton, R. E.: Speed and accuracy in learning a ballistic movement. Res. Quart., *13*, 30-36, 1942.
398. Funkenstein, D. H., King, S. J., and Drolette, M. E.: *Mastery of Stress*. Cambridge, Harvard University Press, 1957.
399. Gagne, R. M., Baker, K. E., and Foster, H.: On the relation between similarity and transfer of training in the learning of discriminative motor tasks. Psychol., Rev., *57*, 2, 1950.
400. Gagne, R. M., Baker, K. E., and Foster, H.: Transfer of discrimination training to a motor task. J. Exp. Psychol., *40*, 314, 1950.
401. Gagne, R. M.: *Learning and Individual Differences*. Columbus, Ohio, Charles E. Merrill Books, Inc., 1967.
402. Gagne, R. M., and Fleishman, E. A.: *Psychology and Human Performance*. New York, Henry Holt & Co., 1959, p. 493.
403. Gaito, J.: DNA and RNA as memory molecules. Psychol. Rev., *70*, 471-480, 1963.
404. Gaito, J., and Zavala, A.: Neurochemistry and learning. Psychol. Bull., *61*, 45-62, 1964.
405. Galambos, R.: Changing concepts of the learning mechanism. In *Brain Mechanisms and Learning*, Fessard, Gerard, Konorski, and Delafresnaye (Eds.). Springfield, Ill., Charles C Thomas, 1961, pp. 231-242.
406. Galambos, R.: Glia, neurons, and information storage. In *Macro-Molecular Specificity and Biological Memory*. F. Schmitt (Ed.). Cambridge, Mass., The MIT Press, 1962, pp. 52-54.

407. Gallahue, D. L.: The relationship between perceptual and motor abilities. Res. Quart., *39*, 948-952, 1968.
408. Ganz, L., and Day, R. H.: An analysis of the satiation fatigue mechanism of figural after-effects. Amer. J. Psychol., *78*, 345-361, 1965.
409. Gardner, E.: *Fundamentals of Neurology.* Philadelphia, W. B. Saunders Co., 1963.
410. Gardner, R. A.: Immediate and residual figural after-effects in kinesthesis. Amer. J. Psychol., *74*, 457-461, 1961.
411. Garfiel, E.: The measurement of motor ability. Arch. Psychol., *9*, 1-47, 1923.
412. Garvey, W. D., and Mitnick, L. L.: An analysis of tracking behavior in terms of lead-lag errors. J. Exp. Psychol., *53*, 373-378, 1957.
413. Gasson, I.: Relative effectiveness of teaching beginning badminton with and without an instant replay videotape recorder. Percept. Motor Skills, *13*, 399-402, 1969.
414. Gates, G.: The effects of an audience upon performance. J. Abnorm. Soc. Psychol., *18*, 334-344, 1924.
415. Gellhorn, E.: Motion and emotion: The role of proprioception in the physiology and pathology of the emotions. Psychol. Rev., *71*, 457-472, 1964.
416. Gemelli, A.: The visual perception of objective motion and subjective movement. Psychol. Rev., *61*, 304-314, 1954.
417. Gentry, J. R.: Immediate Effects of Interpolated Rest Periods on Learning Performance. Teachers College Contributions to Education, 799, 1940.
418. George, F. H.: Errors of visual recognition. J. Exp. Psychol., *43*, 202-206, 1952.
418a. Gesell, A.: *Studies in Child Development.* New York, Harper & Bros., 1948.
419. Gesell, A.: *Vision.* New York, Paul B. Hoeber, Inc., 1949.
420. Gesell, A.: *Wolf Child and Human Child.* New York, Harper & Bros., 1941, p. 107.
420a. Gesell, A., and Amatruda, C. S.: *Developmental Diagnosis.* New York, Paul B. Hoeber, Inc., 1960.
421. Geschwind, N.: Brain mechanisms suggested by studies of hemispheric connections. In *Brain Mechanisms Underlying Speech and Language*, F. L. Darley (Ed.). New York, Grune & Stratton, 1967, pp. 103-107.
422. Gesell, A., and Ilg, F. L.: *The Child from Five to Ten.* New York, Harper & Bros., 1946, pp. 227-237.
423. Ghent, L.: Developmental changes in tactile thresholds on dominant and non-dominant sides. J. Comp. Physiol. Psychol., *54*, 670-673, 1961.
424. Ghisseli, E.: Changes in neuromuscular tension accompanying the performance of a learning problem involving constant choice of time. J. Exp. Psychol., *19*, 91-98, 1936.
425. Gibson, H. B.: The spiral maze: A psychomotor test with implications for the study of delinquency. Brit. J. Psychol., *55*, 219-225, 1964.
426. Gibson, J. J.: Adaptation, after-effect and contrast in the perception of curved lines. J. Exp. Psychol., *16*, 1-33, 1933.
427. Gibson, J. J.: *The Perception of the Visual World.* Boston, Houghton-Mifflin Co., 1950.
428. Gibson, J. J.: Observations on active touch. Psychol. Rev., *69*, 477-491, 1962.
429. Gibson, J. J.: The useful dimensions of sensitivity. Amer. Psychol., *18*, 178-195, 1963.
430. Gibson, J. J., Gibson, E. J., Smith, O. W., and Flock, H.: Motion parallax in perceived depth. J. Exp. Psychol., *58*, 40-51, 1959.
431. Giesecke, M.: The Genesis of Hand Preference. Study No. 2. Committee on Child Development, University of Chicago, Monographs for the Society for Research in Child Development No. 5, National Research Council, Washington, D.C., 1935.
432. Gilbreth, E. F., and Gilbreth, L. M.: *Applied Motion Study.* New York, Grune & Stratton, 1917.

433. Gill, D. J.: Effect of Practice on Peripheral Vision on Reaction Time. Master's thesis, University of Illinois, Urbana, Illinois, 1955.
434. Gilliland, A. R., Hofeld, J., and Eckstrand, C.: Studies in time perception. Psychol. Bull., *43*, 162-176, 1946.
435. Ginzberg, E., Anderson, J. K., Ginsberg, S. W., and Merma, J. L.: *Patterns of Performance*. New York, Columbia University Press, 1959.
436. Gire, E., and Espenschade, A.: Relation between measures of motor educability and learning of specific motor skills. Res. Quart., *13*, 41-56, 1942.
436a. Glanzer M., and Clark, W.: Accuracy of perceptual recall: an analysis of organization. J. Verbal Learning Verbal Behav., *1*, 289-299, 1967.
437. Glaser, R. (Ed.): *Training Research and Education*. Pittsburgh, University of Pittsburgh Press, 1962, pp. 137-175.
438. Glassow, R. B., and Kruse, P.: Motor performance of girls age six to 14 years. Res. Quart., *31*, 426-433, 1960.
439. Glick, J.: The Effects of Static, Extraneous Stimuli upon the Localization of the Apparent Horizon. Master's thesis, Clark University, Worcester, Mass., 1959.
440. Glickman, S. E.: Perseverative neural processes and consolidation of the memory trace. Psychol. Bull., *58*, 218-233, 1961.
441. Goldfarb, W.: The effects of early institutional care on adolescent personality. J. Exp. Educ., *12*, 106-129, 1943.
442. Goldscheider, A.: Physiologie des Muskelsinnes: Gesammelte. *Abhandlungen II*, 1898.
443. Goldstein, I. B.: Role of muscle tension in personality theory. Psychol. Bull., *61*, 413-425, 1964.
444. Goldstein, J., and Weiner, C.: On some relations between the perception of depth and of movement. J. Psychol., *55*, 3-23, 1963.
445. Goldstein, K.: The organism, a holistic approach to biology. In *Pathological Data in Man*. New York, American Book Co., 1939.
446. Goldstone, S., Bond, W. K., and Lohamon, W. T.: Intersensory comparisons of temporal judgments. J. Exp. Psychol., *57*, 243-248, 1959.
447. Gomulicki, B. R.: The development and present status of the trace theory of memory. Brit. J. Psychol. (Monogr.), *29*, 1953.
448. Goodenough, F. L.: The expression of emotions in infancy. Child Develop., *2*, 96-101, 1931.
449. Goodenough, F. L.: Interrelationships in the behavior of young children. Child Develop., *1*, 29-48, 1930.
449a. Goodenough, F. L., and Brian, C. R.: Certain factors underlying the acquisition of motor skills by pre-school youngsters. J. Exp. Psychol., *12*, 127-155, 1929.
450. Goodenough, F. L.: *Measurement of Intelligence by Drawings*. Cleveland, Ohio, The World Publishing Co., 1926.
451. Goodenough, F. L., and Smart, R. C.: Interrelationships of motor abilities in young children. Child Develop., *6*, 141-153, 1935.
452. Gopalaswami, M.: Economy in motor learning. Brit. J. Psychol., *15*, 226-236, 1925.
453. Gopalaswami, M.: Intelligence in motor learning. Brit. J. Psychol., *14*, 274-290, 1924.
454. Gordon, K.: Group judgments in the field of lifted weights. J. Exp. Psychol., *7*, 398-400, 1924.
455. Gordon, M. W., Deanin, G. G., Leonhardt, H., and Gwynn, R.: RNA and memory: A negative experiment. Amer. J. Psychiat., *43*, 1174-1177, 1966.
456. Gordon, R. E., Gorton, K. K., and Gunther, M.: *The Split Level Trap*. New York, B. Geis Assn., Random House Distributors, 1969.
457. Gottlieb, G., and Wilson, I.: Cerebral dominance: Temporary description of verbal memory by unilateral electroconvulsive shock treatment. J. Comp. Physiol. Psychol., *60*, 368-375, 1965.

458. Gottsdanker, R., Frich, J. W., and Lockhard, R. B.: Identifying the acceleration of visual targets. Brit. J. Psychol., *52*, 31-42, 1961.

459. Graham, C. H., Baker, K. E., Hecht, M., and Lloyd, V. V.: Factors: Thresholds for monocular movement parallax. J. Exp. Psychol., *38*, 205-223, 1948.

460. Granit, R.: *Receptors and Sensory Perception*. New Haven, Yale University Press, 1955.

461. Graybiel, A., Jokl, E., and Trapp, C.: Russian studies of vision in relation to physical activity and sports. Res. Quart., *26*, 480-485, 1955.

462. Green, R., and Money, J.: Effeminacy in pre-pubertal boys. Summary of eleven cases and recommendations for case management. Pediatrics, *27*, 2, 1961.

463. Greenspoon, J., and Foreman, S.: Effect of delay of knowledge of results on learning a motor task. J. Exp. Psychol., *51*, 226-228, 1956.

464. Greenwald, A. G.: Skill and motivation as separate components of performance. Percept. Motor Skills, *20*, 239-246, 1965.

465. Griffith, C. R.: A laboratory for research in athletics. Res. Quart., *1*, 34-40, 1930.

466. Grinker, R. R., and Spiegel, J. P.: *Men Under Stress*. Philadelphia, The Blakiston Co., 1945.

467. Groen, J. J., and Jongkees, L. B. W.: The threshold of angular acceleration perception. J. Physiol., *107* 1-7, 1948.

468. Groos, K.: *The Play of Animals*. New York, D. Appleton & Co., 1898, p. 338.

469. Grossack, M. M.: Some effects of cooperation and competition upon small group behavior. J. Abnorm. Soc. Psychol., *49*, 341-348, 1954.

470. Guilford, J. P.: A system of psychomotor abilities. Amer. J. Psychol., *71*, 164-174, 1958.

471. Guilford, J. P. (Ed.): *Printed Classification Tests*. A.A.F. Aviation Psych. Program Research Reports No. 5, Washington, D.C., Government Printing Office, 1947.

472. Guilford, J. P.: The structure of intellect. Psychol. Bull., *53*, 267-293, 1956.

473. Gurnee, H.: Maze learning in the collective situation. J. Psychol., *3*, 437-443, 1937.

474. Guthrie, E. R.: *The Psychology of Learning*. New York, Harper & Bros., 1952, pp. 91 and 305.

474a. Gutteridge, M. V.: A study of motor achievements of young children. Arch. Psychol., *6*, 244, 1939.

475. Hacaen, H., and de Ajuriaguerra, J.: *Left-Handedness, Manual Superiority and Cerebral Dominance*. New York, Grune & Stratton, 1964.

476. Hagerman, F. C.: An investigation of accumulative acute fatigue in participants at the 1966 World Modern Pentathlon Championships, Melbourne (Victoria, Australia). J. Sport Med., *8*, 158-170, 1968.

477. Haith, M. M.: The response of the human newborn to visual movement. J. Exp. Child Psychol., *3*, 235-243, 1966.

478. Hall, B. E.: Transfer of training in mirror tracing. J. Exp. Psychol., *25*, 316-318, 1939.

479. Hall, E. T.: *The Silent Language*. New York, Doubleday, 1959.

480. Hall, E. T.: Silent assumptions in social communication. Disorders Comm., *42*, 41-55, 1964.

481. Hall, E. T.: A system for the notation of proxemic behavior. Amer. Anthropologist, *65*, 1003-1026, 1963.

482. Halverson, H. M.: The acquisition of skill in infancy. J. Gen. Psychol., *43*, 3-48, 1933.

483. Halverson, H. M.: A further study of grasping. J. Gen. Psychol., *7*, 34-64, 1932.

484. Halverson, H. M.: An experimental study of prehension in infants by means of systematic cinema record. Genet. Psychol. Monogr., *10*, 2, 1931.

485. Hammer, W. H.: A comparison of differences in manifest anxiety in university athletes and non-athletes. J. Sport Med., *7*, 31-34, 1967.

458   *References*

486. Hansen, F. C.: Serial action as a basic measure of motor capacity. Psychol. Monogr., *31*, 320-382, 1922.
487. Hanson, S. K.: A Comparison of the Overhand Throw Performance of Instructed and Non-instructed Kindergarten Boys and Girls. Master's thesis, University of Wisconsin, Madison, Wisconsin, 1961.
488. Harby, S. F.: Comparison of Mental Practice and Physical Practice in the Learning of Physical Skills. *Human Engineering Report SDC 269-7-27.* Special Devices Center, 1952.
489. Harding, D. W.: Rhythmization and speed of work. Brit. J. Psychol., *23*, 262-278, 1932.
490. Harlow, H. F.: The formation of learning sets. Psychol. Rev., *56*, 51-65, 1949.
491. Harlow, R. G.: Masculine inadequacy and compensatory development of physique. J. Personality, *19*, 312-323, 1951.
492. Harmon, D. B.: *Winter Haven Study of Perceptual Learning.* Winter Haven Lions Research Foundation, Inc., Winter Haven Lions Club, Winter Haven, Florida, 1962.
493. Harmon, H.: *Modern Factor Analysis.* Chicago, University of Chicago Press, 1960.
494. Harmon, J. M., and Miller, A. G.: Time patterns in motor learning. Res. Quart., *21*, 182-187, 1950.
495. Haromian, F., and Sugerman, A.: A comparison of Sheldon's and Parnell's methods for quantifying morphological differences. Amer. J. Phys. Anthrop., *23*, 135-142, 1965.
496. Harris, C. W., and Liba, M. R.: *Component, Image, and Factor Analysis of Tests of Intellect and of Motor Performance.* Cooperative Research Project No. S-192-64, University of Wisconsin, Madison, Wisconsin, 1965.
497. Harris, D. V.: Comparison of physical performance and psychological traits of college women with high and low fitness indices. Percept. Motor Skills, *17*, 293-294, 1963.
498. Harris, L.: The effects of relative novelty on children's choice behavior. J. Exp. Child Psychol., *2*, 297-305, 1970.
499. Harris, M. L.: A Factor Analytic Study of Flexibility. Paper presented to AAHPER Convention, St. Louis, Missouri, 1968.
500. Harrison, R., and Dorcus, R.: Is rate of voluntary bodily movements unitary? J. Gen. Psychol., *18*, 31-39, 1938.
501. Harrison, V. F.: Review of the neuromuscular bases for motor learning. Res. Quart., *33*, 59-69, 1938.
501a. Hartman, D. M.: The hurdle jump as a measure of the motor proficiency of young children. Child Develop., *14*, 201-211, 1943.
502. Harton, J. J.: The influence of the difficulty of activity on the estimation of time. J. Exp. Psychol., *23*, 270-287, 1938.
503. Haskins, M. J.: Development of a response recognition training film in tennis. Percept. Motor Skills, *21*, 207-211, 1965.
504. Hatfield, J. A.: *The Psychology of Power.* New York, The Macmillan Co., 1923.
505. Hebb, D. O.: Emotion in man and animal: An analysis of the intuitive processes of recognition. Psychol. Rev., *32*, 88-106, 1946.
506. Hebb, D. O.: Man's frontal lobes. Arch. Neurol., *54*, 10-24, 1945.
507. Hebb, D. O.: *The Organization of Behavior.* New York, John Wiley & Sons, Inc., 1949.
508. Heider, F.: On perception, event structure, and psychological environment. Psychol. Issues, 1, 3, Monograph 3. New York, International Universities Press, Inc., 1959.
509. Held, R., and Bossom, J.: Neonatal deprivation and adult rearrangement: complementary techniques for analyzing plastic sensory-motor coordination. J. Comp. Physiol. Psychol., *54*, 223-237, 1961.
510. Held, R., and Freedman, S. J.: Plasticity in human sensori-motor control. Science, *142*, 455-462, 1963.

511. Hellebrandt, F. A., Schade, M., and Carns, M. L.: Methods of evoking the tonic neck reflexes in normal human subjects. Amer. J. Phys. Med., *41,* 90-137, 1962.

512. Hellebrandt, F. A., and Waterland, J. C.: Indirect learning. Amer. J. Phys. Med., *41,* 90-137, 1962.

512a. Hellebrandt, F. A., and Waterland, J. C.: Expansion of motor patterning under exercise stress. Amer. J. Phys. Med., *41, 56-66,* 1962.

513. Hellweg, D. A.: Effect of Different Stress Situations on Emotional Response. Master's dissertation, University of California, Los Angeles, Calif., 1960.

514. Helson, H. (Ed.): *Theoretical Foundations of Psychology.* New York, D. Van Nostrand Publishers, Inc., 1951, Chapter 8, pp. 349-385.

515. Hendrickson, G., and Schroeder, W. H.: Transfer of training in learning to hit a submerged target. J. Educ. Psychol., *32,* 205-213, 1941.

516. Henry, F. M.: Dynamic kinesthetic perception and adjustment. Res. Quart., *24, 176,* 1953.

517. Henry, F. M.: Increase in speed of movement by motivation and by transfer of motivated improvement. Res. Quart., *22,* 219-288, 1951.

518. Henry, F. M.: Increased response latency for complicated movements and a "memory drum" theory of neuromotor reaction. Res. Quart., *31,* 448-457, 1960.

519. Henry, F. M.: Individual differences in motor learning and performance. In *Psychology of Motor Learning,* L. Smith (Ed.). Chicago, Athletic Institute, 1970, pp. 243-255.

520. Henry, F. M.: Interdependence of reaction and movement times and equivalence of sensory motivators of fast response. Res. Quart., *23,* 43-53, 1952.

521. Henry, F. M.: Personality differences in athletes and physical education and aviation students. Psychol. Bull., *38,* 745-755, 1941.

522. Henry, F. M.: Within Individual Variability. Paper presented at Research Section, Annual Conference S.W. District, Amer. Assn. Health, Physical Education and Recreation, Sacramento, Calif., 1969.

523. Henry, F. M., and Nelson, G. A.: Age differences and interrelationships between skill and learning in gross motor performance of 10 and 15 year old boys. Res. Quart., *27,* 162-175, 1956.

524. Henry, F. M., and Smith, L. E.: Simultaneous vs. separate bilateral muscular contractions in relation to neural overflow theory and neuromotor specificity. Res. Quart., *32,* 42-46, 1961.

525. Henry, F. M., and Whitley, J. D.: Relationships between individual differences in strength, speed, and mass in an arm movement. Res. Quart., *31,* 24-33, 1960.

526. Heriot, J. T., and Coleman, P. D.: The effect of electroconvulsive shock on retention of a modified 'one-trial' conditioned avoidance. J. Comp. Physiol. Psychol., *55,* 1082-1084, 1962.

527. Hewes, G. W.: The anthropology of posture. Sci. Amer., *196,* 123-132, 1957.

527a. Hicks, J. A.: The acquisition of motor skill in young children. *University of Iowa Studies in Child Welfare,* 4, No. f, University of Iowa Press, Ames, Iowa, 1929.

528. Hick, W. E.: The Precision of Incremental Muscular Forces with Special Reference to Manual Control Design. Report No. 642. Flying Personnel Res. Comm., Great Britain, 1945.

529. Hicks, J. A., and Ralph, D. W.: The effect of practice in tracing the porteus diamond maze. Child Develop., *11,* 156-158, 1931.

530. Hicks, L. H., and Birren, J. E.: Aging, brain damage and psychomotor slowing. Psychol. Bull., *74,* 377-396, 1970.

531. Hicks, V. C., and Carr, H. A.: Human reactions in a maze. J. Anim. Behav., *2,* 98-125, 1912.

532. Higgins, J. R.: Monitoring Motor Outflow During Performance of a Step-function Tracking Task. Paper presented at the 2nd Canadian Motor Learning Symposium, Wilberg (Ed.). Ontario, Canada, 1970.

533. Hilgard, E. R.: The role of learning in perception. In *Perception, an Approach to Personality*, R. R. Blake and G. V. Ramsey (Eds.). New York, The Ronald Press, 1951, pp. 95-120.
534. Hilgard, E. R.: *Theories of Learning*. New York, Appleton-Century-Crofts, Inc., 1948, p. 407.
535. Hilgard, E. R., and Marquis, D. G.: *Conditioning and Learning*, 2nd ed. New York, Appleton-Century-Crofts, Inc., 1961.
536. Hill, D. S.: Minor studies in learning and relearning. J. Educ. Psychol., 5, 375-386, 1914.
537. Hill, K. T., and Stevenson, H. W.: The effects of social reinforcement vs. nonreinforcement and sex of E on the performance of adolescent girls. J. Personality, 33, 30-45, 1965.
538. Hill, L. B.: A second quarter century of delayed recall or relearning at eighty. J. Educ. Psychol., 48, 65-68, 1957.
539. Hill, S. R.: Studies on adrenocortical and psychological response to stress in man. Arch. Intern. Med., 97, 269-298, 1956.
540. Hill, W. C. O.: *Man As An Animal*. London, Hutchinson and Company, 1957.
541. Hill, W. F.: The effect of long confinement on voluntary wheel-running by rats. J. Comp. Physiol. Psychol., 51, 770-773, 1958.
542. Hinricks, J. R.: Ability correlates in learning a psychomotor task. J. Appl. Psychol., 54, 56-64, 1970.
542a. Hirata, H., and Mizuno, H.: A study on ideal body-builds and personal traits. Res. J. Phys. Educ., 11, 132, 1967.
543. Hirsch, W.: Motor Skill Transfer by Trainable Mentally Retarded and Normal Children. Doctoral dissertation. University of California, Los Angeles, Calif., 1965.
544. Hoban, C. F., Jr.: *Movies That Teach*. New York, Dryden Press, 1946.
545. Holding, D. H.: Transfer between difficult and easy tasks. Brit. J. Psychol., 53, 397-407, 1962.
546. Hollingworth, H. L.: Correlation of abilities as affected by practice. J. Educ. Psychol., 4, 405-413, 1913.
547. Holzman, W. H., and Bitterman, M. E.: A factorial study of adjustment to stress. J. Abnorm. Soc. Psychol., 52, 179, 1956.
548. Holway, A. H., and Hurvich, L. M.: On the discrimination of mineral differences in weight. I. A theory of differential sensitivity. J. Psychol., 4, 309-332, 1937.
549. Holzman, P. S., and Klein, G. S.: Cognitive system principles of leveling and sharpening; individual differences in assimilation effects in visual time error. J. Psychol., 37, 105-122, 1954.
550. Honzik, C. H.: The role of kinesthesis in maze learning. Science, 84, 373, 1936.
551. Hood, A. B.: A study of the relationship between physique and personality variables measured by MMPI. J. Personality, 31, 97-107, 1963.
552. Horney, K.: In *Theories of Personality*, C. S. Hall, and G. Lindsley (Eds.), New York, John Wiley & Sons, Inc., 1957.
553. Howard, I. P., and Templeton, W. B.: Kinesthesis. In *Human Spatial Orientation*, I. P. Howard and W. B. Templeton (Eds.). New York, John Wiley & Sons, 1966, Chapter 4.
554. Howard, I. P., and Templeton, B.: *Human Spatial Orientation*. New York, John Wiley & Sons, Inc., 1966.
555. Howe, C. A.: Comparison of motor skills of mentally retarded and normal children. Exceptional Child., 25, 352-354, 1959.
556. Howell, F. C., and Bourliere, F. (Eds.): *African Ecology and Human Evolution*. New York, Viking Fund Publications in Anthropology, No. 36, 1963.
557. Howell, M. L.: Influence of emotional tension to speed of reaction and movement. Res. Quart., 24, 22-32, 1953.
558. Howell, M. L.: Use of force-time graphs for performance analysis in facilitating motor learning. Res. Quart., 27, 12-22, 1956.

559. Howland, C. I.: Experimental studies in rote-learning theory: VI. Comparison of retention following learning to same criterion by massed and distributed practice. J. Exp. Psychol., *26*, 568-587, 1940.

560. Hubbard, F., and Seng, C. N.: Visual movements of batters. Res. Quart., *25*, 42-57, 1954.

561. Huizinga, J.: *Homo Ludens* (Man the Player). Boston, Beacon Press, 1950.

562. Hull, C. L.: *Principles of Behavior*. New York, Appleton-Century-Crofts, Inc., 1943.

563. Humphrey, J. H.: Comparison of the use of active games and language workbook exercises as learning media in the development of language understandings with third-grade children. Percept. Motor Skills, *21*, 23-26, 1965.

564. Hunt, V.: Cerebral Palsied Youngsters, and Body-Image Problems. Unpublished report to the Faculty, University of California, Los Angeles, Calif., 1962.

565. Hutinger, P. W.: Differences in speed between American Negro and white children in performance of the 35 yard dash. Res. Quart., *30*, 366-368, 1959.

566. Hutton, R. S.: Kinesthetic after-effect produced by walking on a gradient. Res. Quart., *37*, 368-374, 1966.

567. Hyden, H.: Biochemical changes in glial cells and nerve cells at varying activity. In Proceedings of the Fourth International Congress of Biochemistry: *Biochemistry of the Central Nervous System*, v. 3, London, Pergamon Press, 1959.

568. Hyden, H.: Satellite cells in the nervous system. Sci. Amer., *205*, 62-70, 1961.

569. Icheiser, G.: Misunderstandings in human relations: A study in false social perception. Amer. J. Sociol., *55*, 2, 1949.

570. Ittelson, W. H.: *Visual Space Perception*. New York, Springer Publishing Co., Inc., 1960.

571. Ittelson, W. H., and Cantril, H.: *Perception, A Transactional Approach*. New York, Doubleday & Co., 1954.

572. Jackson, C. V.: The influence of previous movement and posture on subsequent posture. Quart. J. Exp. Psychol., *85*, 72-78, 1954.

573. Jacobson, A. L.: Learning in flatworms and annelids. Psychol. Bull., *60*, 74-94, 1963.

574. Jacobson, A. L., Fried, C., and Horowitz, S. D.: Planarians and memory: I. Transfer of learning by injection of ribonucleic acid. Nature, *209*, 599-601, 1966.

575. Jacobson, E.: Electrophysiology of mental activities. Amer. J. Psychol., *44*, 677-694, 1932.

576. Jacobson, E.: *Progressive Relaxation*. Chicago, The University of Chicago Press, 1938.

577. Jahnke, J. C.: Post-rest motor learning performance as a function of degree of learning. J. Exp. Psychol., *62*, 605-611, 1961.

578. Jahnke, J. C.: Retention in motor learning as a function of amount of practice and rest. J. Exp. Psychol., *55*, 270-273, 1958.

579. Jahnke, J. C., and Duncan, C. P.: Reminiscence and forgetting in motor learning after extended rest intervals. J. Exp. Psychol., *52*, 273-282, 1956.

580. James, W. T.: A study of the expression of bodily posture. J. Gen. Psychol., *7*, 405-437, 1932.

581. Jenkins, L. M.: Comparative Study of Motor Achievements of Children Five, Six and Seven Years of Age. New York, Teachers College, Columbia University Contributions to Education, 414, 1930.

582. Johansson, G.: *Configurations in Event Perception*. Uppsala, 1950.

583. John, E. R., and Killam, F. K.: Electrophysiological correlates of avoidance conditioning in the cat. J. Pharmacol. Exp. Ther., *125*, 252-274, 1959.

584. Johnson, W. R., and Kramer, G. F.: Effects of different types of hypnotic suggestions upon physical performance. Res. Quart., *31*, 469-473, 1960.

585. Johnson, W. R., Massey, B. H., and Kramer, G. F.: Effect of posthypnotic suggestions on all-out effort of short duration. Res. Quart., *31*, 142-146, 1960.

586. Jones, F. P., and Hanson, J. A.: Note on the persistence of pattern in a gross body movement. Percept. Motor Skills, *14*, 230, 1962.
587. Jones, F. P., and Hanson, J. A.: Time-space pattern in a gross body movement. Percept. Motor Skills, *12*, 35-41, 1961.
588. Jones, H. E.: The California adolescent growth study. J. Educ. Res., *31*, 561-567, 1938.
589. Jones, H. E.: *Motor Performance and Growth.* A developmental study of static dynamometric strength. Berkeley, Calif., University of California Press, 1949, p. 182.
590. Jones, H. E.: Physical ability as a factor in social adjustment in adolescence. J. Educ. Res., *40*, 287-301, 1946.
591. Jones, M. B.: Intertrial correlations and intertrial periods of rest. J. Motor Behav., *1*, 53-60, 1969.
592. Jones, M. B.: Rate and terminal processes in skill acquisition. Amer. J. Psychol., *83*, 222-236, 1970.
593. Jones, M. B.: Individual differences. In *Acquisition of Skill*, E. A. Bilodeau (Ed.). New York, Academic Press, Inc., 1966, pp. 109-146.
594. Jones, M. B.: Simplex Theory. U.S. Naval School of Aviation Medicine Monograph Series 3, Pensacola, Florida, 1959.
595. Jones, M. C.: Psychological correlates of somatic development. Child Develop., *33*, 899-911, 1965.
596. Jones, S., and Vroom, V. H.: Division of labor and performance under cooperative and competitive conditions. J. Abnorm. Soc. Psychol., *68*, 313-320, 1964.
597. Jones, T. D.: The Development of Certain Motor Skills and Play Activities in Young Children. New York, Bureau of Publications, Teachers College, Columbia University, 1939.
598. Jones, W. R., and Ellis, N. R.: Inhibitory potential in rotary pursuit, acquisition by normal and defective subjects. J. Exp. Psychol., *63*, 534-537, 1972.
599. Judd, C. H.: Movement and consciousness. Psychol. Rev., *7*, 199-226, 1905.
600. Judd, C. H.: The relationship of special training to general intelligence. Educ. Rev., *26*, 28-42, 1908.
601. Katz, D.: Gestalt laws of mental work. Brit. J. Psychol., *39*, 175-183, 1949.
602. Kao, D-L.: Plateaus and the curve of learning in motor skills. Psychol. Monogr., *49*, 1-81, 1937.
603. Kardiner, A., and Spiegle, H.: *War Stress and Neurotic Illness.* New York, Paul B. Hoeber, Inc., 1947.
604. Karlin, L., and Mortimer, R. G.: Effect of verbal, visual and auditory augmenting cues on learning a complex motor skill. J. Exp. Psychol., *65*, 75-79, 1963.
605. Karlin, L., and Mortimer, R. G.: Effects of visual and verbal cues on learning a motor skill. J. Exp. Psychol., *64*, 608-614, 1962.
606. Kaufman, H., Smith, J., and Zeaman, D.: Tests of generality of two empirical equations for motor learning. Percept. Motor Skills, *15*, 91-100, 1962.
607. Kawasima, S.: The influence of time intervals upon the perception of arm motion. Jap. J. Psychol., *12*, 270-289, 1937.
608. Kay, H.: Information theory in the understanding of skills. Occup. Psychol., *31*, 218-224, 1957.
609. Kelly, R., and Stephens, M. W.: Comparison of different patterns of social reinforcement in children's operant learning. J. Comp. Physiol. Psychol., *57*, 294-296, 1964.
610. Kelley, T. L.: *Crossroads in the Mind of Man.* Stanford, California, 1928.
611. Kelsey, I. B.: Effects of mental practice and physical practice upon muscular endurance. Res. Quart., *32*, 47-54, 1961.
612. Kempe, J. E.: An Experimental Investigation of the Relationship Between Certain Personality Characteristics and Physiological Responses to Stress in a Normal Population. Doctoral dissertation, Michigan State University, East Lansing, Michigan, 1956.

613. Kennedy, J. L., and Travis, R. C.: Prediction of speed of performance by muscle action potentials. Science, *15*, 410-411, 1947.
614. Kenyon, G. S., and Loy, J. W., Jr.: Soziale beeinflussung der leistung bei vier psychomotorischen aufgaben. In *Kleingruppenforschung und Gruppe im Sport*, G. Luschen (Ed.). Koln, Germany, Westdeutscher Verlag, 1966.
615. Kershner, J. R.: An Investigation of the Doman-Delacato Theory of Neuropsychology as it Applies to Trainable Mentally Retarded Children in Public Schools. Bureau of Research Administration and Coordination Area of Research Administration and Coordination Area of Research and Development, Department of Public Instruction, Commonwealth of Pennsylvania, October 1966.
616. Kientzle, M. J.: Learning curves, etc. J. Exp. Psychol., *36*, 187-211, 1946.
617. Kilpatrick, F. P.: Two processes in perceptual learning. J. Exp. Psychol., *36*, 187-211, 1946.
618. Kimble, G. A.: Evidence for the role of motivation in determining the amount of reminiscence in pursuit-rotor learning. J. Exp. Psychol., *40*, 248, 1950.
619. Kimble, G. A.: Performance and reminiscence in motor learning as a function of the degree of distribution of practice. J. Exp. Psychol., *39*, 500-510, 1949.
620. Kimble, G. A.: Reminiscence in motor learning as a function of interpolated rest. Amer. J. Psychol., *2*, 312, 1947.
621. King, R. A.: Consolidation of the neural trace in memory: Investigation with one-trial avoidance conditioning and ECS. J. Comp. Physiol. Psychol., *59*, 283-284, 1965.
622. Kingsley, H. L.: The development of motor skills. In *The Nature and Conditions of Learning*. New York, Prentice-Hall, Inc., 1946, p. 2.
623. Kirchner, W. K.: Age differences in short-term retention of rapidly changing information. J. Exp. Psychol., *55*, 352-358, 1958.
624. Klein, G., and Krech, D.: Cortical conductivity in the brain injured. J. Neurol., *21*, 118-148, 1952.
625. Kline, L. W., and Johannsen, D. E.: Comparative role of the face and face-body-hands as aids in identifying emotions. J. Abnorm. Soc. Psychol., *29*, 415-426, 1935.
626. Knapp, C., and Dixon, R.: Learning to juggle: I. A study to determine the effects of two different distribution of practice on learning efficiency. Res. Quart., *21*, 331-336, 1950.
627. Knapp, C., and Dixon, R.: Learning to juggle: II. A study of whole and part methods. Res. Quart., *23*, 389-401, 1952.
627a. Kneeland, N.: Self-estimates of improvement in repeated tasks. Arch. Psychol., *163*, 163-174, 1934.
628. Knitz, B. L., and Zaffy, D. J.: Short-term and long-term retention and task difficulty. J. Psychol., *59*, 229-232, 1965.
629. Koch, H. L.: The influence of mechanical guidance upon maze learning. Psychol. Monogr., *12*, 147, 1923.
630. Koffka, K.: *The Growth of the Mind*. New York, Harcourt Brace, 1929.
631. Koffka, K.: *Principles of Gestalt Psychology*. New York, Harcourt, Brace and Co., Inc., 1935.
632. Kogan, B. R. (Ed.): *Darwin and His Critics*. San Francisco, Wadsworth Publishing Company, Inc., 1960.
633. Kohler, W.: *Dynamics in Psychology*. New York, Liveright, 1940.
634. Kohler, W.: *Gestalt Psychology*. New York, Liveright, 1929.
635. Kohler, W., and Dinnerstein, D.: Figural after-effects in kinesthesis. In *Miscellanea psychologia*. Albert Michotte. Paris, Libraire Philosophique, 1947, pp. 196-220.
636. Koonce, J. M., Chambliss, D. J., and Irion, A.: Long-term reminiscence in the pursuit rotor habit. J. Exp. Psychol., *67*, 498-500, 1964.
637. Koronski, J.: *Integrative Activity of the Brain: An Interdisciplinary Approach*. Chicago, University of Chicago Press, 1967.

638. Kreiger, J. C.: The Influence of Figural-Ground Perception on Spatial Adjustment in Tennis. Master's thesis, University of California, Los Angeles, Calif., 1962.

639. Kretschmer, E.: *Physique and Character*. Translated by W. J. H. Sprott. New York, Harcourt, Brace and Co., Inc., 1925.

640. Krueger, W. C. F.: Further studies in overlearning. J. Exp. Psychol., *13*, 152-163, 1930.

641. Krus, D. M., and Wagoner, S.: Studies in vicariousness: Motor activity and perceived movement. Amer. J. Psychol., *66*, 603-609, 1953.

642. Kurz, R. B.: Relationship between time imagery and Rorschach human movement responses. J. Consult. Psychol., *27*, 273-276, 1963.

643. Laban, R.: *Effort*. London, MacDonald Press, 1947.

644. La Barre, W.: The cultural basis of emotions and gestures. J. Personality, *16*, 49-68, 1947.

645. Lachman, S. J.: A theory relating learning to electrophysiology of the brain. J. Psychol., *59*, 275-281, 1965.

646. Laidlaw, R. W., and Hamilton, M. A.: A study of thresholds in apperception of passive movement among normal subjects. Bull. Neurol. Inst., (New York), *6*, 268-273, 1937.

647. Laidlaw, R. W., and Hamilton, M. A.: The quantitative measurement of apperception of passive movement. Bull. Neurol. Inst., (New York), *6*, 145-153, 1937.

648. Laird, D. A.: Changes in motor control and individual variations under the influence of "razzing." J. Exp. Psychol., *6*, 233-246, 1923.

649. Lambert, J., and Ewert, P.: The effect of verbal instructions upon stylus maze learning. J. Gen. Psychol., *6*, 377-399, 1932.

650. Lambert, P.: Practice effect of non-dominant vs. dominant musculature in acquiring two-handed skill. Res. Quart., *22*, 50-57, 1951.

651. Landauer, T. K.: Two hypotheses concerning the biochemical basis of memory. Psychol. Rev., *71*, 167-179, 1964.

652. Langdon, J. N., and Yates, E. M.: Experimental investigation into transfer of training in skilled performances. Brit. J. Psychol., *18*, 422-437, 1928.

653. Langer, J., Heinz, W., and Wapner, S.: Apparent speed of walking under conditions of danger. J. Gen. Psychol., *73*, 291-298, 1965.

654. Langfeld, H. S.: Voluntary movement under positive and negative instruction. Psychol. Rev., *20*, 459-478, 1913.

655. Langworthy, O.: The neurophysiology of motivation. Amer. J. Psychiat., *122*, 1033-1039, 1966.

656. Lordahl, D. S.: Effect of the weight-contrast illusion on rotary pursuit performance. Percept. Motor Skills, *17*, 87-90, 1963.

657. Lordahl, D. S., and Archer, E. J.: Transfer effects on a rotary pursuit task as a function of first task difficulty. J. Exp. Psychol., *56*, 421-426, 1958.

658. Lasher, G. W. (Ed.): *The Processes of Ongoing Human Evolution*. Detroit, Wayne State University Press, 1960.

659. Lashley, K. S.: The Acquisition of Skill in Archery. Papers from the Department of Marine Biology, Carnegie Institute, Washington, 7, 105-128, 1915.

660. Lashley, K. S.: *Brain Mechanisms and Intelligence*. New York, Dover Publications, Inc., 1963.

661. Laszlo, J. I.: The role of visual and kinesthetic cues in learning a novel skill. Aust. J. Psychol., *20*, 191-196, 1968.

662. Laszlo, J. I.: Training of fast rapping with reduction of kinesthetic, tactile, visual and auditory sensations. Quart. J. Exp. Psychol., *19*(b), 344-349, 1967.

662a. Latane, B., and Arrowood, J.: Emotional arousal and task performance. J. Appl. Psychol., *47*, 324-327, 1963.

662b. Latchaw, M.: Measuring selected motor skills in fourth, fifth, and sixth grades. Res. Quart., *25*, 439-449, 1954.

663. Lavery, J. J.: The effect of one-trial delay in knowledge of results on the acquisition and retention of a tossing skill. Amer. J. Psychol., *77*, 437-443, 1964.

664. Lavery, J. J.: Retention of a skill following training with and without instructions to retain. Percept. Motor Skills, *18*, 275-281, 1964.

665. Lavery, J. J., and Suddon, F. H.: Retention of simple motor skills as a function of the number of trials by which KR is delayed. Percept. Motor Skills, *15*, 231-237, 1962.

666. Lawrence, D. H.: The transfer of a discrimination along a continuum. J. Comp. Physiol. Psychol., *45*, 511-516, 1952.

667. Lazarus, R. S., Deese, J., and Olser, S. J.: The effects of psychological stress upon performance. Psychol. Bull., *49*, 293-317, 1952.

668. Leakey, L. S. B.: *Adam's Ancestors.* London, Methune & Company Ltd., 1934.

669. Leavitt, J. L.: Reliability and specificity of individual differences in reminiscence. J. Motor Behav., *1*, 275-284, 1969.

670. Leavitt, H. J., and Schlosberg, H.: The retention of verbal and of motor skills. J. Exp. Psychol., *34*, 404-417, 1944.

671. Leibowitz, H. W., and Lomont, J. F.: *The Effect of Grid Lines in the Field of View Upon Perception of Motion.* Technical Report No. 54-201, March, 1954, Wright-Patterson Air Force Base.

672. Leibowitz, H. W., and Lomont, J. F.: *The Effect of Luminance and Exposure Time Upon Perception of Motion.* Technical Report No. 54-78, March, 1954, Wright-Patterson Air Force Base.

673. Lenk, H.: Maximale Leistung trotz innerer Konflikte. In *Kleingruppenforschung und Gruppe im Sport,* G. Luschen (Ed.). Koln, Germany, Westdeutscher Verlag, 1966.

674. Leonard, D. S.: Effects of task difficulty on transfer performance on rotary pursuit. Percept. Motor Skills, *30*, 731-736, 1970.

675. Lersten, K. C.: Transfer of movement components in a motor learning task. Res. Quart., *39*, 575-581, 1968.

676. Leshman, S. S.: Effects of aspiration and achievement on muscular tension. J. Exp. Psychol., *61*, 133-137, 1961.

677. Leton, D. A.: Visual-motor capacities and ocular efficiency in reading. Percept. Motor Skills, *15*, 407-432, 1962.

678. Leuba, J. H.: The influence of the duration and of the rate of arm movements upon the judgment of their length. Amer. J. Psychol., *20*, 374-385, 1909.

679. Levy, C. M., and Lam, D.: The psychology of memory—1968: a bibliography. Percept. Motor Skills, Monogr. Suppl. 1-V32, 1971.

680. Levy, S. L.: This way to self improvement. Personnel J., *38*, 373-376, 1960.

681. Lewinson, T. S., and Zubin, J.: *Handwriting Analysis.* New York, King's Crown Press, 1942.

682. Lewis, D.: Positive and negative transfer in motor learning. Amer. Psychol., *2*, 423, 1947 (Abstract).

683. Lewis, D., and Lowe, W.: Retention of skill on the SAM Complex Coordinator. Proc. Iowa Acad. Sci., *63*, 591-599, 1959.

684. Lewis, D., McAllister, D. E., and Adams, J. A.: Facilitation and interference in performance on the Modified Mashburn Apparatus: I. The effects of varying the amount of original learning. J. Exp. Psychol., *41*, 247-260, 1951.

685. Lewis, D., and Shepard, A. H.: Devices for studying associative interference in psychomotor performance: I. The Modified Mashburn Apparatus. J. Psychol., *29*, 35-46, 1950.

686. Lewis, D., Smith, P. N., and McAllister, D. E.: Retroactive facilitation and interference in performance on the two-hand coordinator. J. Exp. Psychol., *44*, 44-50, 1952.

687. Lewis, F. H.: Affective characteristics of rhythm. Psychol. Bull., *30*, 679-680, 1933.

16a

688. Lewis, M., Wall, A. M., and Aronfreed, J.: Developmental change in the relative values of social and non-social reinforcement. J. Exp. Psychol., *66*, 133-137, 1963.
689. Liddell, E. G. T., and Sherrington, Sir C. S.: Recruitment and some other features of reflex inhibition. Proceedings of the Royal Society Series: Series B, *Biological Sciences, 97*, 488-518, 1925.
690. Lincoln, R. S.: Learning a rate of movement. J. Exp. Psychol., *47*, 465-470, 1954.
691. Lincoln, R. S., and Smith, K. U.: Transfer of training in tracking performance at different target speeds. J. Appl. Psychol., *35*, 358, 1951.
692. Lindeburg, F. A.: A study of the degree of transfer between quickening exercises and other coordinated movements. Res. Quart., *20*, 180-195, 1949.
693. Lipman, R. S., and Spitz, H.: The relationship between kinesthetic satiation and inhibition in rotary pursuit performance. J. Exp. Psychol., *62*, 468-475, 1961.
694. Lipsitt, L. P.: A self concept scale for children and its relationship to the children's form of the manifest anxiety scale. Child Develop., *29*, 463-472, 1959.
695. Little, K. B.: Personal space. J. Exp. Soc. Psychol., *1*, 237-247, 1965.
696. Livanov, M. H.: The application of electronic-computer techniques to the analysis of bioelectric processes in the brain. In *Handbook of Contemporary Soviet Psychology*. M. Coe and I. Moltzman (Eds.). New York, Basic Books, Inc., 1969.
697. Lloyd, A. J., and Caldwell, L. S.: Accuracy of active and passive positioning of the leg on the basis of kinesthetic cues. J. Comp. Physiol. Psychol., *60*, 102-106, 1965.
698. Locke, E. A.: Interaction of ability and motivation in performance. Percept. Motor Skills, *21*, 719-725, 1965.
699. Locke, E. A.: The relationship of task success to task liking and satisfaction. J. Appl. Psychol., *5*, 379-385, 1965.
700. Locke, J.: *Essay Concerning Human Understanding*, London, 1690.
701. Lockhart, A. A.: The value of the motion picture as an instructional device in learning a motor skill. Res. Quart., *15*, 181-187, 1944.
702. Loeb, J.: Untersuchungen uber die Orientirung im Fuhlraum der Hand und im Blickraum. Pflueger. Arch. Gen. Psysiol., *46*, 1-46, 1890.
703. London, P., and Fuhrer, M.: Hypnosis, motivation, and performance. J. Personality, *29*, 321-333, 1961.
704. Loratt, D. J., and Warr, P. B.: Recall after sleep. Amer. J. Psychol., *81*, 432-435, 1968.
705. Lorge, I.: Influence of regularly interpolated time intervals upon subsequent learning. Teachers' College Contributions to Education, Columbia University, 1930, p. 438.
706. Lorge, I., Fox, D., Davitz, J., and Bremer, M.: A survey of studies contrasting the quality of group performance and individual performance, 1920-1957. Psychol. Bull., *55*, 28-49, 1958.
707. Lotter, W. S.: Interrelationships among reaction times and speed of movement in different limbs. Res. Quart., *31*, 147-154, 1960.
708. Lotter, W. S.: Specificity or generality of speed of systematically related movements. Res. Quart., *32*, 55-61, 1961.
709. Lovass, O. I.: The relationship of induced muscular tension, tension level, and manifest anxiety in learning. J. Exp. Psychol., *59*, 146-152, 1960.
710. Lovass, O. I.: Supplementary report: The relationship of induced muscular tension to manifest anxiety in learning. J. Exp. Psychol., *59*, 205, 1960.
711. Lowe, C. M.: The self-concept, fact or artifact? Psychol. Bull., *58*, 325-336, 1961.
712. Lucas, J. D.: The interactive effects of anxiety, failure, and intra-serial duplication. Amer. J. Psychol., *65*, 59-66, 1952.

713. Ludvigh, E. J., and Miller, J. W.: A Study of Dynamic Visual Acuity. Joint Project Report No. NM 001 075.01.01. U.S. Naval Sch. Aviat. Med., Pensacola, Florida, 1953a.

714. Ludvigh, E. J., and Miller, J. W.: An Analysis of Dynamic Visual Acuity in a Population of 200 Naval Aviation Cadets. Joint Project Report No. NM 001 075.01.07. U.S. Naval Sch. Aviat. Med., Pensacola, Florida, 1954b.

715. Ludvigh, E. J., and Miller, J. W.: The Effects on Dynamic Visual Acuity of Practice at One Angular Velocity on the Subsequent Performance at a Second Angular Velocity. Joint Project Report No. NM 001 501.09. U.S. Naval Sch. Aviat. Med., Pensacola, Florida, 1955.

716. Ludvigh, E. J., and Miller, J. W.: Some Effects of Training on Dynamic Visual Acuity. Joint Project Report No. NM 001 075.0.06. U.S. Naval Sch. Aviat. Med., Pensacola, Florida, 1954a.

717. Ludvigh, E. J., and Miller, J. W.: Study of visual acuity during the ocular pursuit of moving test objects. I. Introduction. J. Opt. Soc. Amer., 48, 799-802, 1958.

718. Luh, C. W.: The conditions of retention. Psychol. Monogr., 31, 3, 1922.

719. Lundgate, L.: The effect of manual guidance upon maze learning. Psychol. Rev. Monogr., 33, 33, 1923.

720. Luriza, A. R., and Klimovskiy, J.: On the organization of short-term memory by modality. Soviet Psychol., 8, 257-263, 1970.

721. Luttges, M., Johnson, T., Buck, C., Holland, J., and McGaugh, J.: An examination of "Transfer of Learning" by nucleic acid. Science, 151, 834-837, 1966.

722. Lyon, D. O.: Memory and the Learing Process. Baltimore, Warwick and York, Inc., 1917.

723. MacArthur, R. S.: The experimental investigation of persistence in secondary school boys. Canad. J. Psychol., 9, 42-54, 1955.

723a. Maccoby, E. E.: The Development of Sex Differences. Stanford, Calif., Stanford University Press, 1966.

724. Maccoby, E. E., Dowley, E. M., and Hagen, J. W.: Activity level and intellectual functioning in normal pre-school children. Child Develop., 36, 761-769, 1965.

725. Macworth, N. H.: Researches on the Measurement of Human Performance. Medical Res. Council Special Report Series, No. 268. London, His Majesty's Stationery Office, 1950.

726. Madsen, K. B.: Theories of Motivation, 2nd ed. Cleveland, Ohio, Howard Allen, 1961.

727. Magoun, H. W.: Darwin and concepts of brain function. In Brain Mechanism and Learning. A symposium by the Council for Internal Organizations of Medical Sciences, under UNESCO and WHO, J. F. Delafresnaye (Ed.). Springfield, Ill., Charles C Thomas, 1961.

728. Magoun, H. W.: The Waking Brain. Springfield, Ill., Charles C Thomas, 1958.

729. Malina, R. M.: Performance Changes in a Speed-Accuracy Task as a Function of Practice under Different Conditions of Information Feedback. Doctoral dissertation, University of Wisconsin, Madison, Wisconsin, 1963.

730. Malmo, R. B.: Activation: A neuropsychological dimension. Psychol. Rev., 68, 367-368, 1959.

731. Malmo, R. B., and Davis, J. F.: Anxiety and behavioral arousal. Psychol. Rev., 64, 276-287, 1957.

732. Malpass, L. F.: Motor skills in mental deficiency. In The Handbook of Mental Deficiency, N. R. Ellis (Ed.). New York, McGraw-Hill Book Co., 1964, pp. 602-631.

733. Mandler, G.: The warm-up effect: some further evidence on temporal and task factors. J. Gen. Psychol., 55, 3-8, 1956.

734. Manzer, C. W.: The effect of verbal suggestion on output and variability of muscular work. Psychol. Clin., 22. 248-256, 1934.

735. Marriott, R.: Incentive Payments System, A Review of Research and Opinion. London, Staples Press, 1961.

736. Marston, W., King, C. D., and Marston, E.: *Integrative Psychology,* Kegan, Paul (Ed.). New York, Harcourt Brace & Co., 1931.
737. Marteniuk, R. G.: Motor performance and induced muscular tension. Res. Quart., *39,* 1025-1031, 1969.
738. Marteniuk, R. G.: Individual differences in intra-individual variability. J. Motor Behav., *1,* 307-316, 1969.
739. Marteniuk, R. G.: Generality and specificity of learning and performance in two similar speed tasks. Res. Quart., *40,* 518-522, 1969.
740. Martens, R.: Anxiety and motor behavior: a review. J. Motor Behav., *3,* 151-179, 1971.
741. Martens, R.: Influence of participation motivation on success and satisfaction in team performance. Res. Quart., *41,* 510-518, 1970.
742. Martens, R.: Social reinforcement effects on preschool children's motor performance. Percept. Motor Skills., *31,* 787-792, 1970.
743. Martin, B.: Reward and punishment associated with the same goal response: A factor in the learning of motives. Psychol. Bull., *60,* 441-451, 1963.
744. Matarazzo, R., and Matarazzo, J. D.: Anxiety level and pursuit-rotor performance. J. Consult. Psychol., *20,* 70, 1956.
745. Matarazzo, J. D., Ulett, G. A., and Saslow, G.: Human maze performance as a function of increasing levels of anxiety. J. Gen. Psychol., *53,* 79-95, 1955.
746. Matsumoto, M.: Researches on acoustic space. Studies in Yale Psychology Laboratory, *5,* 1-75, 1887.
747. Matthews, P. B. C.: Muscle spindles and their motor control. Physiol., Rev., *44,* 219-288, 1964.
748. Matthews, B. H. C.: The response of a muscle spindle during active contraction of a muscle. J. Physiol., *72,* 153-174, 1931.
749. Matthews, B. H. C.: The response of a single end organ. J. Physiol., *71,* 64-110, 1931.
750. Maxwell, G.: *Ring of Bright Water.* London, Longmans, Green & Co., 1960.
751. McAllister, D. E.: The effects of various kinds of relevant verbal pretraining on subsequent motor performance. J. Exp. Psychol., *46,* 329-336, 1953.
752. McAllister, D. E., and Lewis, D.: Facilitation and interference in performance on the Modified Mashburn Apparatus: II. The effects of varying the amount of interpolated learning. J. Exp. Psychol., *41,* 356-363, 1951.
753. McBride, G., King, M. G., and James, J. W.: Social proximity effects on galvanic skin responses in adult humans. J. Psychol., *61,* 153-157, 1965.
754. McCain, S. R.: A Comparison of the Motion Perception Fields of Athletes and Non-athletes. Master's thesis presented to the University of Albama, University, Alabama, 1950.
755. McCaskill, C. L., and Wellman, B. L.: A study of common motor achievements at the pre-school ages. Child Develop., *9,* 141-150, 1938.
756. McClelland, D. C., and Apicella, F. S.: Reminiscence following experimentally induced failure. J. Exp. Psychol., *37,* 159-169, 1947.
757. McClintock, C. G., and Martin, J. M., Jr.: Development of competitive game behavior of children across 2 cultures. J. Exp. Soc. Psychol., *5,* 203-218, 1965.
757a. McCloy, C. H.: An analytical study of the stunt type test as a measure of motor educability. Res. Quart., *8,* 46-55, 1937.
758. McCloy, C. H.: Blocks test of multiple response. Psychometrika, *7,* 165-169, 1942.
759. McCord, J., McCord, W., and Thurber, E.: Some effects of paternal absence on male children. J. Abnorm. Soc. Psychol., *64,* 361-369, 1962.
760. McCormack, P. D., Binding, F. R. S., and McElheran, M.: Effects on reaction time of partial knowledge of results of performance. Percept. Motor Skills, *17,* 279-281, 1963.
761. McCraw, L. W.: Comparative analysis of methods of scoring tests of motor learning. Res. Quart., *26,* 440-453, 1955,

762. McDougall, W.: *An Introduction to Social Psychology*, 13th ed. Boston, John W. Luce Co., 1918.

763. McDougall, W.: *An Introduction to Psychology*. Boston, Bruce Humphries, 1926.

764. McGeogh, J. A.: The comparative retention values of a maze habit, of nonsense syllables, and of rational learning. J. Exp. Psychol., *15*, 662-680, 1932.

765. McGeogh, J. A.: The influence of four different interpolated activities upon retention. J. Exp. Psychol., *14*, 400-413, 1931.

766. McGeogh, J. A.: Forgetting and the law of disuse. Psychol. Rev., *39*, 352-370, 1932.

767. McGeogh, J. A., and Irion, A. L.: *The Psychology of Human Learning*, 2nd ed. London, Longmans, Green & Co., 1952.

768. McGeogh, J. A., and Melton, A. W.: The comparative retention values of maze habits and nonsense syllables. J. Exp. Psychol., *12*, 392-414, 1929.

769. McGraw, M. B.: *Growth: A Study of Johnny and Jimmy*. New York, Appleton-Century-Crofts, 1935.

770. McGraw, M. B.: Later development of children, especially trained during infancy: Johnny and Jimmy at school age. Child Develop., *10*, 1-19, 1939.

771. McGuigan, F. J.: The effect of precision, delay and schedule of knowledge of results on performance. J. Exp. Psychol., *58*, 79-84, 1959.

772. McGuigan, F. J., Hutchens, C., Eason, N., and Reynolds, T.: The retrograde interference of motor activity with knowledge of results. J. Gen. Psychol., *70*, 279-281, 1964.

773. McIntyre, J., and Humphries, M.: Reminiscence in pursuit rotor reaction time. Percept. Motor Skills, *18*, 39-42, 1964.

774. McTeer, A.: Changes in group tension following electric shock in minor tracing. J. Exp. Psychol., *36*, 735-742, 1933.

775. Medinnus, G. R.: Adolescents' self-acceptance and perceptions of their parents. J. Consult. Psychol., *29*, 150-154, 1965.

776. Mehrabian, A.: Orientation behaviors and nonverbal attitude communication. J. Commun., *2*, 33-66, 1967.

777. Melcher, R. T.: Children's motor learning, with and without vision. Child Develop., *4*, 315-350, 1934.

778. Melnick, M. J.: Effects of overlearning on the retention of a gross motor skill. Res. Quart., *42*, 60-69, 1968.

779. Melton, A. W.: Learning. In *Encyclopedia of Educational Research*, W. S. Munroe (Ed.). New York, The Macmillan Company, 1950, pp. 668-690.

780. Melton, A. W.: Implications of short-term memory for a general theory of memory. J. Verbal Learning Verbal Behav., *2*, 1-21, 1963.

781. Mendel, G.: Children's preferences for differing degrees of novelty. Child Develop., *36*, 452-464, 1966.

782. Mendryk, S.: Reaction time, movement time, and task specificity relationships at ages 12, 33, and 48 years. Res. Quart., *31*, 156-162, 1960.

783. Menninger, W. C.: Yesterday's war and today's challenge. In *Psychiatry in a Troubled World*. New York, The Macmillan Co., 1948.

784. Menzel, E.: Individual differences in the responsiveness of young chimpanzees to stimulus size and novelty. Percept. Motor Skills, *15*, 127-134, 1962.

785. Menzel, E., Davenport, R., and Rogers, C. M.: Some aspects of behavior toward novelty in young chimpanzees. J. Comp Physiol. Psychol., *54*, 16-19, 1961.

786. Meredith, G. P.: The transfer of training. Occup. Psychol., *15*, 61-76, 1941.

787. Merriman, B. J.: The relationship of personality traits to motor ability. Res. Quart., *31*, 163-173, 1960.

788. Metheny, E.: Some differences in bodily proportions between American Negro and white, male college students, as related to athletic performance. Res. Quart., *10*, 148-151, 1939.

789. Meyer, D. R.: On the interaction of simultaneous responses. Psychol. Bull., *50*, 204-220, 1953.

790. Meyer, D. R., and Noble, M. E.: Summation of manifest anxiety and muscular tension. J. Exp. Psychol., *55*, 599-602, 1958.

791. Meyers, J. L.: Motor learning and retention: influence of practice and remoteness on individual differences. Res. Quart., *39*, 278-284, 1968.

792. Michael, E. D., Jr.: Stress adaptation through exercise. Res. Quart., *28*, 50-54, 1957.

793. Michotte, Van den Berch, A.: Perception and cognition. Acta Psychol., *11*, 70-91, 1955.

794. Miles, W. R.: Age and human ability. Psychol. Rev., *40*, 99-123, 1933.

795. Miles, W. R.: The two-story duplicate maze. J. Exp. Psychol., *10*, 365-377, 1927.

796. Miller, D. M.: The relation between some visual perceptual factors and the degree of success realized by sports performers. Doctoral dissertation, University of Southern California, Los Angeles, Calif., 1960.

797. Miller, G. A., Galanter, E., and Dribham, K. H.: *Plans and the Structure of Behavior*. New York, Henry Holt & Co., Inc., 1960.

798. Miller, J. L.: Effect of instruction on development of throwing for accuracy of first grade children. Res. Quart., *28*, 132-137, 1957.

799. Miller, L. K.: Eye-movement latency as a function of age, stimulus uncertainty and position in visual field. Percept. Motor Skills, *28*, 631-636, 1969.

800. Miller, N. E.: Central stimulation and other new approaches to motivation and reward. Amer. Psychol., *13*, 100-108, 1958.

801. Miller, N. E.: Experiments on motivation. Science, *126*, 1271, 1957.

802. Miller, N. E.: Learnable drives and rewards. In *Handbook of Experimental Psychology*, S. S. Stevens (Ed.). New York, John Wiley & Sons, Inc., 1961.

803. Mingione, A. D.: Need for achievement in Negro and white children. J. Consult. Psychol., *29*, 108-111, 1965.

804. Mirskey, I. A., and Stein, M.: The secretion of an antidiuretic substance into the circulation in response to noxious stimuli. Science, *118*, 602, 1953.

805. Missiuro, W.: The development of reflex activity in children. In *International Research in Sport and Physical Education*, E. Jokl and E. Simon (Eds.). Springfield, Ill., Charles C Thomas, 1964, pp. 372-383.

806. Mizuno, T., Hirata, H., Aoyama, S., Chan Shi, J., and Ishikawa, N.: An international comparative study of body concepts of youths. Res. J. Phys. Educ. (Japan), *12*, 120-125, 1968.

807. Moeller, G., and Chattin, C. P.: The palmar perspiration index and pursuit tracking. Percept Motor Skills, *15*, 463-473, 1962.

808. Montague, W. E., and Hillix, W. A.: Intertrial interval and practice interference in short-term motor memory. Canad. J. Psychol., *23*, 73-78, 1968.

809. Montebello, R. A.: The role of stereoscopic vision in some aspects of basketball playing ability. Master's thesis, Ohio State University, Columbus, Ohio, 1953.

810. Montessori, M.: *Dr. Montessori's Own Handbook*. New York, Frederick A. Stokes, 1914.

811. Morgan, C. T.: Some structural factors in perception. In *Readings in Perception*, D. C. Beardslee and M. Wertheimer (Eds.). New York, D. Van Nostrand Co., Inc., 1969, pp. 3-36.

812. Morgan, W. F.: Pre-match anxiety in a group of college wrestlers. Int. J. Sport Psychol., *1*, 7-13, 1970.

813. Morin, R. F., Grant, D. A., and Nystrom, C. O.: *Temporal Predictions of Motion from Intermittently Viewed Light Stimulation*. Technical Report No. 54-69, January 1954. Wright-Patterson Air Force Base.

814. Morrell, F., and Jasper, H. H.: Electrographic studies of the formation of temporary connections of the brain. Electroenceph. Clin. Neurophysiol., *8*, 201-215, 1956.

815. Morrison, A. V.: Individual differences in the ability to interpret gestures. Doctoral dissertation, University of California, Los Angeles, Calif., 1961.
816. Moss, C. S.: *Hypnosis in Perspective.* New York, The Macmillan Company, 1965.
816a. Mosston, M.: *Teaching Physical Education.* Columbus, Ohio, Charles E. Merrill Books Co., 1967.
817. Mosso, A.: Ueber die Gesetze der Ermudung Untersuchungen. Arch. Anat. Path. (Paris), 5, 89-243, 1890.
818. Mott, J. A.: Eye movements during initial learning of motor skills. Doctoral dissertation, University of Southern California, Los Angeles, Calif., 1954.
819. Mountcastle, V. B., Poggio, G. F., and Werner, G.: The relation of thalamic cell response to peripheral stimuli varied over an intensive continuum. J. Neurophysiol., 26, 804-834, 1963.
820. Moylan, J. J.: Kinesthetic figural after-effects: Satiation or contrast. J. Exp. Psychol., 67, 83-90, 1964.
821. Mukherjee, B. N.: Transfer of two-hand coordination skill as a function of initial ability level. J. Gen. Psychol., 67, 215-223, 1962.
822. Muller, G. E., and Pilzecker, A.: Experimentelle Beitrage zur Lehre Vom Gedachtniss. Z. Psychol., 1, 1-300, 1900.
823. Mumby, H. H.: Kinesthetic acuity and balance related to wrestling ability. Res. Quart., 24, 327, 1953.
824. Munn, N. L.: Bilateral transfer of learning. J. Exp. Psychol., 15, 343-353, 1932.
825. Munsterberg, H.: *Psychology, General and Applied.* New York, D. Appleton & Co., 1914.
826. Murnin, J. A., et al.: Daylight Projection of Film Loops as the Teaching Medium in Perceptual-Motor Skill Training. *Human Engineering Report SDC 269-7-26.* Special Devices Center, 1952.
827. Murray, H. A.: *Explorations in Personality.* New York, Oxford University Press, 1938.
828. Murray, H. A.: A functional theory of personality. In *Theories of Personality.* C. S. Hall and G. Lindsley (Eds.). New York, John Wiley & Sons, Inc., 1957.
829. Mussen, P. H.: Some antecedents and consequences of masculine sex-typing in adolescent boys. Psychol. Monogr., 75, 2, 1961.
830. Mussen, P. H., and Jones, M. C.: Self-conceptions, motivations and interpersonal attitudes of late and early maturing boys. Child Develop., 28, 243-256, 1957.
831. Nachmias, J.: Figural after-effects in kinesthetic space. Amer. J. Psychol., 66, 609-612, 1953.
832. Namikas, G., and Archer, E. J.: Motor skill transfer as a function of intertask interval and pre-transfer task difficulty. J. Exp. Psychol., 59, 109-112, 1960.
833. Naylor, J. C., and Briggs, G. E.: Effect of rehearsal of temporal and spatial aspects on the long-term retention of a procedural skill. J. Appl. Psychol., 4, 120-126, 1963.
834. Naylor, J. C., and Briggs, G. E.: *Long-Term Retention of Learned Skills, a Review of the Literature.* Laboratory of Aviation Psychology, Ohio State University and Ohio State University Research Foundation, August 1961.
835. Naylor, J. C., Briggs, G. E., and Reed, W. G.: The Effects of Task Organization, Training Time, and Retention Interval on the Retention of Skill. USAF 6570th AMRL Tech. Docum. Report AMRL-TDR-62-107. Wright-Patterson Air Force Base, Dayton, Ohio, 1962.
836. Naylor, J. C., Briggs, G. E., and Reed, W. G.: Task Coherence, Training Time, and Retention Interval Effect on Skill Retention. J. Appl. Psychol., 52, 386-393, 1968.
837. Nelson, D. O.: Effect of slow-motion loop films on learning of golf. Res. Quart., 29, 37-45, 1958.
838. Nelson, D. O.: Leadership in sports. Res. Quart., 37, 268-275, 1966.

839. Nelson, D. O.: Studies of transfer of learning in gross motor skills. Res. Quart., 28, 364-374, 1957.
840. Nelson, G. A., and Henry, F. M.: Age differences and interrelationships between skill and learning in gross motor performance of ten and fifteen-year-old boys. Res. Quart., 27, 162-175, 1956.
841. Nelson, N.: A comparison of two methods of teaching badminton skills. Unpublished study, Department of Health and Physical Education, Austin Peay State University, Clarksville, Tenn., 1968.
842. Nelson, R., and Fahrney, R. A.: Relationships between strength and speed of elbow flexion. Res. Quart., 36, 455-463, 1965.
843. Nelson, R. D., and Nofsinger, M. R.: The effect of overload on speed of elbow flexion and associated aftereffects. Res. Quart., 36, 156-165, 1965.
844. Neumann, E., and Ammons, R. B.: Acquisition and long-term retention of a simple serial perceptual-motor task. J. Exp. Psychol., 53, 159-161, 1957.
845. Nichols, R. C.: A factor analysis of parental attitudes of fathers. Child Develop., 33, 791-802, 1962.
846. Nicholson, N. C.: Notes on muscular work during hypnosis. Bull. Johns Hopkins Hosp., 31, 89-91, 1920.
847. Nidever, J. E.: A Factor Analytic Study of General Muscular Tension. Doctoral dissertation, University of California, Los Angeles, Calif., 1960.
848. Niemeyer, R. K.: Part versus whole methods and massed versus distributed practice in the learning of selected large muscle activities. Proceed. College Phys. Educ. Assn., 5, 122-125, 1958.
849. Nishi, T.: A new tentative theory of visual space perception. Part II. Tohoku Psychol. Folio, 17, 1-20, 1958.
850. Noble, C. E.: Amount-set and length difficulty function for a self-paced perceptual motor skill. J. Exp. Psychol., 46, 435, 1953.
851. Noble, S. G.: The acquisition of skill in the throwing of basketball goals. School and Society, 16, 640-644, 1922.
852. Noble, C. E., Baker, B. L., and Jones, T. A.: Age and sex parameters in psychomotor learning. Percept. Motor Skills, 19 935-945, 1964.
853. Noer, D., and Whittaker, J.: Effects of masculine-feminine ego involvement on the acquisition of a mirror-tracing skill. J. Psychol., 56, 15-17, 1963.
854. Norcross, W. H.: Experiments on the transfer of training. J. Comp. Psychol., 1, 317-363, 1921.
855. Norman, D. A. (Ed.): Models of Human Memory. New York, Academic Press, 1970.
856. Norrie, M. L.: The relationship between measures of kinesthesia and motor performance. Master's thesis, University of California, Berkeley, Calif., 1952.
857. Norris, E. B.: Performance of a motor task as a function of rest at different points in acquisition. J. Exp. Psychol., 45, 260-264, 1953.
858. Noton, P., and Stark, L.: Eye movements and visual perception. Sci. Amer., 223, 34-43, 1971.
859. Nystrom, C. O., Morin, R. E., and Grant, D. A.: Transfer effects between automatically-paced training schedules in a perceptual motor task. J. Gen. Psychol., 55, 9-18, 1956.
860. Nueman, M. C.: A comparison of traditional versus programed methods of learning tennis. Res. Quart., 39, 1044-1048, 1968.
861. Ogilvie, B. C., and Tutko, T. A.: The psychological profile of Olympic champions. Proceedings of 1st International Congress of Psychology of Sport, Rome, 1965.
862. Oliver, J.: The effects of physical conditioning exercises and activities on the mental characteristics of educationally sub-normal boys. Brit. J. Psychol., 34, 155-165, 1958.
863. Olsen, E. A.: Relationship between psychological capacities and success in college athletics. Res. Quart., 27, 79-89, 1956.
864. Osgood, C. E.: The similarity paradox in human learning: a resolution. Psychol. Rev., 56, 132-143, 1949.

865. O. S. S.: *The Assessment of Men*. New York, Rinehart, 1948.
866. Paben, M., and Rosentsweigh, J.: Control of muscular tension in learning a novel gross motor skill. Percept. Motor Skill, *32*, 556-558, 1971.
867. Oxendine, J. B.: Effect of mental and physical practice on the learning of three motor skills. Res. Quart., *40*, 763-775, 1969.
868. Oxendine, J. B.: Visual and kinesthetic perception. In *Psychology of Motor Learning*, J. B. Oxendine (Ed.). New York, Appleton-Century-Crofts, 1968.
869. Paillard, J.: The patterning of skilled movements. In *The Handbook of Physiology*, section I, Neurophysiology, 3, J. Field (Ed.). Washington, D.C., American Physiological Society, 1960, Chapter 67, pp. 1679-1708.
870. Palmer, R. D.: Development of a differentiated handedness. Psychol. Bull., *62*, 257-272, 1964.
871. Palmer, R. D.: Hand differentiation and psychological functioning. J. Personality, *31*, 446-461, 1963.
872. Parker, J. F., Jr., and Fleishman, E. A.: Use of analytical information concerning task requirements to increase the effectiveness of skill training. J. Appl. Psychol., *45*, 295-302, 1961.
873. Parsons, O. A., Phillips, L., and Lane, J. E.: Performance on the same psychomotor task under different stressful conditions. J. Psychol., *38*, 457-466, 1954.
874. Patrick, G. T. W.: The psychology of American football. Amer. J. Psychol., *14*, 104-117, 1903.
875. Patten, E. F.: The influence of distribution of repetitions on certain rote learning phenomena. J. Psychol., *5*, 359-374, 1938.
876. Patterson, G. R., and Anderson, D.: Peers as social reinforcers. Child Develop., *35*, 951-960, 1964.
877. Pavlov, I. P.: *Conditioned Reflexes*. Translated by G. V. Anrep. London, Oxford University Press, 1927.
878. Pechstein, L. A.: Alleged elements of waste in learning a motor problem by the 'part method.' J. Educ. Psychol., *8*, 303-310, 1917.
879. Pechstein, L. A.: Massed vs. distributed effort in learning. J. Educ. Psychol., *12*, 92-97, 1921.
880. Penman, K.: Relative effectiveness of teaching beginning tumbling with and without an instant replay videotape recorder. Percept. Motor Skills, *28*, 45-46, 1969.
881. Penfield, W.: The interpretive cortex. Science, *129*, 1719-1725, 1959.
882. Penfield, W.: Memory mechanisms. Trans. Amer. Neurol. Ass., *76*, 15-31, 1951.
883. Penfield, W., and Roberts, L.: *Speech and Brain Mechanisms*. Princeton, N.J., Princeton University Press, 1959.
884. Pepper, R. L., and Herman, L. M.: Decay and interference effects in short-term retention of a discrete motor act. J. Exp. Psychol., *83*, 165-172, 1970.
885. Perl, R. E.: The effect of practice upon individual differences. Arch. Psychol., *21*, 159, 1933.
886. Perrin, F. A. C.: An experimental study of motor ability. J. Exp. Psychol., *4*, 25-57, 1921.
887. Peterson, J.: Experiments in ball-tossing: The significance of learning curves. J. Exp. Psychol., *2*, 178-224, 1919.
888. Peterson, J.: Review of Tolman "purposive behavior in animals and man." Amer. J. Psychol., *45*, 177-178, 1933.
889. Pew, R. W., and Rupp, G. L.: Two quantitative measures of skill development. J. Exp. Psychol., *90*, 1-7, 1971.
890. Phares, E. J.: Effects of reinforcement value on expectancy statements in skill and chance situations. Percept. Motor Skills, *20*, 845-852, 1965.
891. Phillips, M., and Summers, D.: Relation of kinesthetic perception of motor learning. Res. Quart., *25*, 456-469, 1954.
892. Phipps, S. J., and Morehouse, C. A.: Effects of mental practice on the acquisition of motor skills of varied difficulty. Res. Quart., *40*, 773-778, 1969.

893. Piaget, J.: *The Construction of Reality in the Child*. New York, Basic Books, Inc., 1954.
894. Piaget, J.: *Play, Dreams, and Imitation in Childhood*. Translated by C. Gattegno and F. M. Hodgson. New York, Norton, 1951.
895. Pick, H. L., Jr., and Hay, J. C.: A passive test of the Held reference hypothesis. Percept. Motor Skills, *20*, 1070-1072, 1965.
896. Pierce, A. H.: *Researches on Acoustic Space*. Studies in Yale Psychology Laboratory, *5*, 1-209, 1901.
897. Pierson, W. R.: Comparison of fencers and nonfencers by psychomotor, space perception and anthropometric measures. Res. Quart., *27*, 1, 1956.
898. Pierson, W. R.: The relationship of movement time and reaction time from childhood to senility. Res. Quart., *30*, 227-230, 1959.
899. Pinneo, L. R.: The effects of induced muscular tension during tracking on level of activation and on performance. J. Exp. Psychol., *62*, 523-531, 1961.
900. Plutchik, R., and Petti, R. D.: Rate of learning on a pursuit rotor task at a constant work-rest ratio with varying work and rest ratios. Percept. Motor Skills, *19*, 227-231, 1964.
901. Porteus, S. D.: *The Maze Test and Clinical Psychology*. Palo Alto, Calif., Pacific Books, 1959.
902. Postman, L., and Bruner, J. S.: Perception under stress. Psychol. Rev., *55*, 314-323, 1948.
903. Poulton, E. C.: On prediction in skilled movements. Psychol. Bull., *54*, 467-478, 1957.
904. Priebe, R. E., and Burton, W. H.: The slow motion picture as a coaching device. School Review, *47*, 192-198, 1939.
905. Provins, K. A., and Glencross, D. J.: Handwriting, typing and handedness. Quart. J. Exp. Psychol., *20*, 282-286, 1968.
906. Pryor, H. B., and Stolz, H.: Determining appropriate weight for body build. J. Pediatrics, *3*, 608-624, 1933.
907. Purdy, B. J., and Lockhart, A.: Retention and relearning of gross motor skills after long periods of no practice. Res. Quart., *33*, 2, 1962.
907a. Raack, J. D.: Kinesthetic After-Effect and Movement Speed. Master's thesis, University of California, Los Angeles, Calif., 1965.
908. Ragsdale, C. E.: How children learn the motor types of activities. 49th Yearbook. Chicago, University of Chicago Press, 1952.
909. Ragsdale, C. E.: *The Psychology of Motor Learning*. Ann Arbor, Mich., Edward Bros. Press, Inc., 1930.
910. Rarick, L., and Thompson, J. J.: Roentgenographic measures of leg muscle size and ankle extensor strength of seven-year-old children. Res. Quart., *27*, 321-332, 1956.
911. Rasch, P. J., and Mozee, G.: Neuroticism and extroversion in weight trainers. J. Phys. Mental Rehab., *17*, 53-56, 1963.
912. Rathbone, J. L.: Relaxation. Bureau of Publications, Teachers' College, Columbia University, New York, 1943.
913. Lord Rayleigh (J. W. Stauttis): Acoustical observations. Phil. Mag., *5*, 456-464, 1887.
914. Reed, H. B.: An experiment on the law of effect in learning the maze by humans. J. Educ. Psychol., *26*, 695, 1935.
915. Reiter, H. H.: Relation of body build to personal preference among college males. Percept. Motor Skills, *21*, 34, 1965.
916. Renold, A., et al.: Reaction of the adrenal cortex to physical and emotional stress in college oarsmen. New Eng. J. Med., *45*, 754-757, 1951.
917. de Renzende, M. N.: An experiment on the perception of time. Arch. de Brasil, *2*, 40-55, 1950.
918. Rethlingshafer, D.: *Motivation as Related to Personality*. New York, McGraw-Hill Book Co., 1963.
919. Rethlingshafer, D.: Relationship of tests of persistence to other measures of continuance of activities. J. Abnorm. Soc. Psychol., *37*, 71-82, 1942.

920. Reynolds, B., and Bilodeau, I. McD.: Acquisition and retention of three psychomotor tests as a function of distribution of practice during acquisition. J. Exp. Psychol., *44*, 19-26, 1952.
921. Reynolds, D. V.: Towards a Theory of Complex Motor Skills—A Neural Model. Proceedings of 2nd Canadian Psycho-Motor Learning and Sports Psychology Symposium. R. E. Wilberg (Ed.). University of Windsor, Canada, 1970.
922. Rhodes, A.: A comparative study of motor abilities of Negroes and whites. Child Develop., *8*, 369-371, 1937.
923. Richardson, A.: Mental practice: a review and discussion. Part I. Res. Quart., *38*, 95-107, 1967.
924. Riddoch, G.: Dissociation of visual perception due to occipital injuries with especial reference to appreciation of movement. Brain, *40*, 15-17, 1917.
925. Riley, E., and Start, K. B.: The effect of the spacing of mental and physical practices on the acquisition of a physical skill. Aust. J. Phys. Educ., *20*, 13-16, 1960.
926. Rimoldi, H. J. A.: Personal tempo. J. Abnorm. Soc. Psychol., *46*, 283-303, 1951.
927. Riopelle, A. J.: Psychomotor performance and distribution of practice. J. Exp. Psychol., *40*, 390, 1950.
928. Rivenes, R. S., and Mawhinney, M. M.: Retention of perceptual motor skill: an analysis of new methods. Res. Quart., *39*, 684-689, 1968.
929. Robb, M.: Feedback and skill learning. Res. Quart., *39*, 175-184, 1969.
930. Robbins, M. P.: The Delacato interpretation of neurological organization. Reading Res. Quart., *37*, 59-77, 1966.
931. Roberts, G. C.: Effect of Achievement Motivation on Risk Taking Choices of Men and Women. Paper presented to the AAHPER Conference, Houston, Texas, 1972.
932. Roberts, G. C., and Martens, R.: Social reinforcement and complex motor performance. Res. Quart., *41*, 175-181, 1970.
933. Roe, A., and Simpson, G. G. (Eds.): *Behavior and Evolution.* New Haven, Yale University Press, 1958.
934. Roehrig, W. C.: Psychomotor task with perfect recall after 50 weeks of no practice. Percept. Motor Skills, *19*, 547-550, 1964.
935. Roeff, M.: A factorial study of tests in the perceptual area. Psychomet. Monogr., *41*, 8, 1953.
936. Roffell, G.: Visual and kinesthetic judgments of length. Amer. J. Psychol., *48*, 331-334, 1946.
937. Ronco, P. G.: An experimental quantification of kinesthetic sensation: Extent of arm movement. J. Psychol., *55*, 227-238, 1963.
938. Rose, J. E., and Mountcastle, V. B.: Touch and kinesthesis. In *Handbook of Physiology,* vol. 1. J. Field (Ed.). Washington, D.C., American Physiological Society, 1959, pp. 307-429.
939. Roseborough, M. E.: Experimental studies of small groups. Psychol. Bull., *50*, 275-303, 1953.
940. Rosen, B. C.: and D'Andrade, R.: The psycho-social origins of achievement motivation. Sociometry, *22*, 185-218, 1959.
941. Rosenzweig, S.: A dynamic interpretation of psychotherapy oriented towards research. In *Contemporary Psychopathology,* S. S. Tomkins (Ed.). Cambridge, Harvard University Press, 1943, pp. 235-243.
942. Roshal, S. M.: Effects of Learner Representation in Film-Mediated Perceptual-Motor Learning. *Technical Report SDC 269-7-5.* Special Devices Center, 1949.
943. Rubin, E.: An abridged translation by Michael Wertheimer of *Visuell Wahrgenommene Figuren.* Copenhagen, Glydendalske, 1912.
944. Rubin-Rabson, G.: Mental and keyboard overlearning in memorizing piano music. J. Musicol., *3*, 33-40, 1941.

945. Rubin-Rabson, G.: Studies in the psychology of memorizing piano music: II. A comparison of massed and distributed practice. J. Educ. Psychol., *31*, 270-284, 1940.

946. Rubin-Rabson, G.: Studies on the psychology of memorizing piano music: III. A comparison of the whole and the part approach. J. Educ. Psychol., *31*, 460-476, 1940.

947. Rubin-Rabson, G.: Studies in the psychology of memorizing piano music: VII. A comparison of three degrees of overlearning. J. Educ. Psychol., *32*, 688-696, 1941.

948. Ruesch, J., and Kees, W.: *Non-Verbal Communication*. Berkeley, Calif., University of California Press, 1956.

949. Russell, J. T.: Relative efficiency of relaxation and tension in performing an act of skill. J. Gen. Psychol., *6*, 330-343, 1932.

950. Russell, W. R.: *Brain, Memory, Learning*. Fair Lawn, N.J., Oxford University Press, 1959.

951. Ryan, E. D.: Competitive Performance in Relation to Achievement Motivation and Anxiety. Paper presented to the National Convention, Minneapolis, Minnesota, 1963.

952. Ryan, E. D.: Kinesthetic Figural After-effects and Athletic Performance. Speech presented to National Convention of American Association of Health, Recreation and Physical Education, Chicago, Illinois, 1966.

953. Ryan, E. D.: Relationship between motor performance and arousal. Res. Quart., *33*, 428-432, 1962.

954. Ryan, E. D.: Reminiscence in Stabilometer Performance as a Function of Prerest Distribution of Practice. Paper presented to the Research Section, S.W. District CAHPER Convention, Long Beach, Calif., 1963.

955. Ryan, E. D.: Retention of stabilometer and pursuit rotor skills. Res. Quart., *33*, 593-598, 1962.

956. Ryan, E. D.: Retention of stabilometer performance over extended periods of time. Res. Quart., *36*, 46-51, 1965.

957. Ryans, D. G.: An experimental attempt to analyse persistence behavior: I. Measuring traits presumed to involve persistence. J. Gen. Psychol., *19*, 333-353, 1938.

958. Sackett, G. P.: Manipulatory behavior in monkeys reared under different conditions of early stimulus variation. Percept. Motor Skills, *20*, 985-988, 1965.

959. Sackett, R. S.: The influence of symbolic rehearsal upon the retention of a maze habit. J. Gen. Psychol., *10*, 376-398, 1934.

960. Sackett, R. S.: The relationship between amount of symbolic rehearsal and retention of a maze habit. J. Gen. Psychol., *13*, 113-128, 1935.

960a. Sage, G.: *Introduction to Motor Behavior: A Neurophysiological Approach.* Menlo Park, Calif., Addison-Wesley, 1971.

961. Sanderson, F. H.: Dynamic Visual Acuity and Ball-Game Ability. Unpublished paper, Perceptual-Motor Skills Unit, Department of Physical Education, University of Leeds, Leeds, England, 1969.

962. Sanderson, J.: Intention in motor learning. J. Exp. Psychol., *12*, 463-489, 1929.

963. Sarason, I. G., and Palola, E. G.: The relationship of test and general anxiety, difficulty of task, and experimental instructions to performance. J. Exp. Psychol., *59*, 185-191, 1960.

964. Sarason, S., and Rosenzweig, S.: An experimental study of the triadic hypothesis: Reaction to frustration, ego-defense hypnotizability: II. Thematic apperception approach. Character Personality, *11*, 150-165, 1942.

965. Scannell, R. J.: Transfer of accuracy training when difficulty is controlled by varying target size. Res. Quart., *39*, 341-350, 1968.

966. Schafer, V. G., and Gilliland, A. R.: The relationship of time estimations to certain physiological changes. J. Exp. Psychol., *23*, 545-552, 1938.

967. Schendel, J.: Psychological differences between athletes and non-participants in athletics at three educational levels. Res. Quart., *36*, 52-67, 1965.

968. Schmidt, R. A.: Performance and learning a gross motor skill under conditions of artificially induced fatigue. Res. Quart., *40*, 185-190, 1969.
969. Schmidt, R.: Proprioception and the Timing of Motor Responses. Proceedings of 2nd Annual Canadian Motor Learning and Sports Psychology Symposium, R. B. Wilberg (Ed.). University of Windsor, Canada, 1970.
970. Schmidt, R. A., and Ascoli, K. M.: Intertrial intervals and motor short-term memory. Res. Quart., *41*, 423-438, 1970.
971. Schneider, C. W., and Bartley, S. H.: A study of the effects of mechanically induced tension of the neck muscles on the perception of verticality. J. Psychol., *54*, 245-248, 1962.
972. Schonbar, R. A.: The interaction of observer pairs in judging visual extent and movement. Arch. Psychol., *28*, 299, 1945.
972a. Scott, J.: *The Athletic Revolution.* New York, The Free Press, 1971.
973. Scott, M. G.: Measurement of kinesthesis. Res. Quart., *26*, 324-341, 1955.
974. Scott, R. H.: The psychology of the body image. Brit. J. Med. Psychol., *24*, 266, 1954.
975. Scripture, E. W.: Cross education. Pop. Sci. Monthly, *56*, 589-596, 1899.
976. Scripture, E. W.: Recent investigations at the Yale Laboratory. Psychol. Rev., *6*, 165, 1899.
977. Scripture, E. W., Smith, T. L., and Brown, E. M.: On the education of muscular control and power. Studies from the Yale Psychological Laboratory, *2*, 114-119, 1894.
978. Seagoe, M. V.: Qualitative wholes: A re-evaluation of the whole-part problem. J. Educ. Psychol., *27*, 537-545, 1936.
978a. Seashore, H. G.: The development of a beam walking test and its use in measuring development of balance in children. Res. Quart., *18*, 246-259, 1947.
979. Seashore, H. G.: Some relationships of fine and gross motor abilities. Res. Quart., *13*, 259-274, 1942.
980. Seashore, H. G., and Brevalas, A.: The function of knowledge of results in Thorndike's line drawing experiment. Psychol. Rev., *48*, 155-164, 1941.
981. Seashore, R. G.: Individual differences in motor skills. J. Gen. Psychol., *3*, 38-66, 1930.
982. Seashore, R. H.: Work methods: An often neglected factor underlying individual differences. Psychol. Rev., *46*, 123-141, 1939.
983. Secord, P. F.: Personality in faces. Genet. Psychol. Monogr., *49*, 231-279, 1954.
983a. Seils, L.: The relationships between measures of physical growth and gross motor performance of primary grade school children. Res. Quart., *22*, 244-260, 1951.
984. Seligman, C. G.: The vision of the natives of British Guinea. *Report of the Anthropological Expedition to Torres Straits*, 1901, A. C. Haddon (Ed.). New York, Cambridge University Press, 1961.
985. Selling, L. S.: An experimental investigation of the phenomenon of postural persistence. Arch. Psychol., *3*, 118, 1940.
986. Sells, S. B., and Berry, C. A.: *Human Factors in Jet and Space Travel.* New York, The Ronald Press, 1961.
987. Selye, H.: *The Stress of Life.* New York, McGraw-Hill Book Co., 1956, p. 324.
988. Seymour, W. D.: Transfer of training in engineering skills. Percept. Motor Skills, *7*, 235-237, 1957.
989. Shard, M., and Blum, J. M.: Group performance as a function of task difficulty and the group's awareness of member satisfaction. J. Appl. Psychol., *49*, 151-154, 1964.
990. Shaw, M. E.: Some motivational factors in cooperation and competition. J. Personality, *26*, 155-169, 1958.
991. Shaw, W. A.: The relation of muscular action potentials to imaginal weight lifting. Arch. Psychol., *35*, 1-50, 1940.
992. Shay, C. T.: The progressive-part vs. the whole method of learning motor skills. Res. Quart., *5*, 62-67, 1934.

992a. Sheldon, W. H., Dupertuis, C. W., and McDermott, E.: *Atlas of Men: A Guide for Somatotyping the Adult Male at All Ages.* New York, Harper & Bros., 1954.

993. Sheldon, W. H., and Stevens, S. S.: *The Varieties of Temperament.* New York, Harper & Bros., 1942.

994. Shepard, A., Abbey, D. S., and Humphries, M.: Age and sex in relation to perceptual-motor performance on several control-display relations on the TCC. Percept. Motor Skills, *14*, 103-118, 1962.

995. Shepard, A., and Cook, T. W.: Body orientation and perceptual motor performance. Percept. Motor Skills, 8, 327-330, 1958.

996. Sherif, M.: A study of some social factors in perception. Arch. Psychol., 8, 187, 1935.

996a. Shirley, M. M.: *The First Two Years,* Vol. 1. Minneapolis, University of Minnesota Press, 1931.

997. Shirley, M. M.: Studies in activity: II. Activity rhythms; age and activity; activity after rest. J. Comp. Psychol., 8, 159-186, 1928.

998. Sherrington, C. S.: On the anatomical constitution of nerves of skeletal muscles: some remarks on recurrent fibres in the ventral spinal nerve roots. J. Physiol., *17*, 211-258, 1894.

999. Sherrington, C. S.: On the proprioceptive system, especially in its reflex aspect. Brain, *29*, 467-482, 1906.

999a. Sherrington, C. S.: *The Integrative Action of the Nervous System.* New York, Scribner, 1906.

1000. Shick, J.: Effects of mental practice on selected volleyball skills for college women. Res. Quart., *41*, 88-94, 1970.

1001. Siddall, G. J., Holding, D. H., and Draper, J.: Errors of aim and extent in manual point to point movement. Occup. Psychol., *31*, 185-195, 1957.

1002. Siegal, A. I.: A motor hypothesis of perceptual development. Amer. J. Psychol., *66*, 301-304, 1953.

1003. Siipola, E. M., and Hayden, S. D.: Exploring eidetic imagery among retarded. Percept. Motor Skills, *21*, 275-286, 1965.

1004. Silleck, S. B., Jr., and Lapha, C. W.: The relative effectiveness of emphasis upon right and wrong responses in human maze learning. J. Exp. Psychol., *20*, 195-201, 1937.

1005. Silver, A. W.: The self concept: Its relationship to parental and peer acceptance. Dissertation Abstracts, *19*, 166, 1958.

1006. Silver, R. J.: Effect of amount and distribution of warming-up activity on retention in motor learning. J. Exp. Psychol., *44*, 88-95, 1952.

1007. Singer, G., and Day, R. H.: Spatial adaptation and aftereffect with optically transformed vision: effects of active and passive responding and the relationships between test and exposure responses. J. Exp. Psychol., *71*, 725-731, 1966.

1008. Singer, J. L., and Herman, J.: Motor and fantasy correlates of Rorschach human movement responses. J. Consult. Psychol., *18*, 325-331, 1954.

1009. Singer, R. N.: Massed and distributed practice effects on the acquisition and retention of a novel basketball skill. Res. Quart., *36*, 68-77, 1965.

1010. Singer, R. N.: Sequential skill learning and retention effects. Res. Quart., *39*, 28-35, 1968.

1011. Singer, R. N.: Effect of spectators on athletes and non-athletes performing a gross motor task. Res. Quart., *36*, 473-483, 1965.

1012. Singleton, W. T.: Age and performance timing on simple skills. In *Old Age and the Modern World.* Edinburgh, C. & S. Livingstone, 1955, pp. 221-231.

1013. Singleton, W. T.: The change of movement timing with age. Brit. J. Psychol., *65*, 166-172, 1954.

1014. Siqueland, E. R.: Conditioned Sucking and Visual Reinforcers with Human Infants. Unpublished paper, Brown University, Providence, R.I., 1967.

1015. Skinner, B. F.: *The Behavior of Organisms.* New York, Appleton-Century-Crofts, 1938, p. 437.

1016. Slater-Hammel, A. T.: Effect of blinking upon reaction time measures. Res. Quart., *25*, 338-345, 1954.
1017. Slater-Hammel, A. T.: Measurement of kinesthetic perception of muscular force with muscle potential charges. Res. Quart., *28*, 153-159, 1957.
1018. Sleet, D. A.: Physique and social image. Percept. Motor Skills, *28*, 295-299, 1969.
1019. Sloan, W.: Motor proficiency and intelligence. Amer. J. Ment. Defic., *55*, 394-406, 1951.
1020. Smith, G. J.: The Concept of Group Cohesion and Its Significance in Physical Education and Athletics. Paper presented to the Sociology of Sport Section, CAHPER Convention, Victoria, British Columbia, Canada, 1969.
1021. Slocum, H. M.: The effect of fatigue induced by physical activity on certain tests in kinesthesis. Dissertation Abstracts, *13*, 1084-1085, 1953.
1022. Smith, J. L., and Bozymowski, M. E.: Effects of attitude toward warmups on motor performance. Res. Quart., *36*, 78-85, 1965.
1023. Smith, K. U.: *Cybernetic Principles of Learning and Educational Design.* New York, Holt, Rinehart, & Winston, 1965.
1024. Smith, K. U.: Feedback Theory and Motor Learning. Paper presented at the North American Society of Sports Psychology, Chicago, Illinois, 1966.
1025. Smith, K. U., and Smith, W. M.: *Perception and Motion.* Philadelphia, W. B. Saunders Co., 1962.
1026. Smith, K. U., and Sussman, H.: Feedback analysis of stuttering function in motorsensory learning and performance. J. Appl. Psychol., *63*, 521-526, 1969.
1026a. Smith, K. U.: Feedback mechanisms of athletic skills and learning. In *Psychology of Motor Learning*, L. E. Smith (Ed.). Chicago, Athletic Institute, 1970.
1027. Smith, K. U., and Trebra, P. V.: The dimensional analysis of motion: IV. Transfer effects and direction of movement. J. Appl. Psychol., *36*, 348-353, 1952.
1028. Smith, L. E.: Individual differences in maximal speed of muscular contraction and reaction time. Percept. Motor Skills, *21*, 19-22, 1965.
1029. Smith, L. E., and Harrison, J. S.: Comparison of the effects of visual, motor, mental, and guided practice upon speed and accuracy of performing a simple eye-hand coordination task. Res. Quart., *83*, 299-307, 1962.
1030. Smith, O. W.: Developmental studies of spatial judgments by children and adults. Percept. Motor Skills, *22*, 3-73, 1966, Monograph Supplement I-V22.
1031. Smith, P. C., and Smith, A. W.: Ball throwing responses to photographically portrayed targets. J. Exp. Psychol., *62*, 223-233, 1961.
1032. Smock, C. D., and Holt, B. G.: Children's reactions to novelty: An experimental study of 'curiosity motivation.' Child Develop., *33*, 631-642, 1962.
1033. Smock, C. D., and Small, V. H.: Efficiency of utilization of visual information as a function of induced muscular tension. Percept. Motor Skills, *14*, 39-44, 1962.
1034. Smoll, F. L.: Effects of Specificity of Information Feedback on Learning a Motor Skill. Paper presented at the National AAHPER Conference, Houston, Texas, 1972.
1035. Smythe, E., and Goldstone, S.: The time sense: a normative genetic study of the development of time perception. Percept. Motor Skills, *7*, 49-59, 1957.
1036. Snoddy, G. S.: Evidence for two opposed processes in mental growth. Lancaster, Pa., Science Press, 1935, p. 103.
1037. Snoddy, G. W.: An experimental analysis of a case of trial and error learning in the human subject. Psychol. Monogr., *124*, 28, 78, 1920.
1038. Snyder, F. W., and Pronko, N. H.: *Vision with Spatial Inversion.* Wichita, Kansas, University of Wichita Press, 1952.
1039. Sokolov, E. N.: Neuronal models and the orienting reflex. In *CNS and Behavior*, M. A. B. Brazier (Ed.). New York, Josiah Macy, Jr., Foundation, 1960, pp. 187-276.

1040. Solley, W. H.: The effects of verbal instruction of speed and accuracy upon the learning of a motor skill. Res. Quart., *23*, 231-240, 1952.

1041. Solomons, G., and Solomons, H. C.: Factors affecting motor performance of four-month-old infants. Child Develop., *35*, 1283-1296, 1964.

1042. Sparks, N. E.: A Study of the Effectiveness of Practice in the Development of Certain Motor Skills in First Grade Children. *Illinois State Normal University, Studies in Education*. No. 158, 1950.

1043. Spearman, C.: General intelligence objectivity measured and determined. Amer. J. Psychol., *15*, 201-293, 1904.

1044. Spencer, L. T., and Judd, C. H.: Practice without knowledge of results. Psychol. Rev., *29*, 185-198, 1905.

1045. Sperry, R. W.: Cerebral organization and behavior. Science, *133*, 1749-1757, 1961.

1046. Spielberger, C. D., Gorsuch, R. L., and Lushene, R. E.: *The State-Trait Anxiety Inventory*. Palo Alto, Calif., Consulting Psychologists Press, 1970.

1047. Spitz, R. A.: The smiling response: a contribution to the ontogenesis of social relations. Genet. Psychol. Monogr., *34*, 57-125, 1946.

1048. Spitz, R. A., and Wolf, K. M.: The smiling response: a contribution to the ontogenesis of social relations. Genet. Psychol. Monogr., *34*, 57-156, 1946.

1049. Stallings, L. M.: The role of visual-spatial abilities in the performance of certain motor skills. Res. Quart., *39*, 708-713, 1968.

1050. Starbuck, W. H.: Level of aspiration. Psychol. Rev., *70*, 51-60, 1963.

1051. Start, K. B.: The influence of subjectively assessed 'games ability' on gain in motor performance after mental practice. J. Gen. Psychol., *67*, 159-173, 1962.

1052. Start, K. B.: Intelligence and improvement in a gross motor skill after mental practice. Brit. J. Educ. Psychol., *34*, 85-90, 1964.

1053. Start, K. B.: Relationship between intelligence and the effect of mental practice on the performance of a motor skill. Res. Quart., *81*, 644-649, 1960.

1054. Start, K. B., and Richardson, A.: Imagery and mental practice. Brit. J. Educ. Psychol., *34*, 280-284, 1964.

1055. Stauffacher, J. C.: The effect of induced muscular tension upon various phases of the learning process. J. Exp. Psychol., *21*, 26-46, 1937.

1056. Stebbins, R. J.: A comparison of the effects of physical and mental practice on the learning of a motor skill. Res. Quart., *39*, 714-720, 1968.

1057. Steel, W. I.: The effect of mental practice on the acquisition of a motor skill. J. Phys. Educ., *44*, 101-108, 1952.

1058. Stein, J. U.: Motor function and physical fitness of the mentally retarded: a critical review. Rehab. Lit., *24*, 230-242, 1963.

1059. Stelmach, G. E.: Efficiency of motor learning as a function of inter-trial rest. Res. Quart., *40*, 198-202, 1969.

1060. Stelmach, G. E.: Short-term motor retention as a function of response similarity. J. Motor Behav., *1*, 37-42, 1969.

1061. Stelmach, G. E., and Barber, J. L.: Interpolated activity in short-term memory. Percept. Motor Skills, *30*, 231-234, 1970.

1062. Stelmach, G. E., and Wilson, A.: Kinesthetic retention, movement extent and information processing. J. Exp. Psychol., *85*, 425-430, 1970.

1063. Stennett, R. G.: The relationships of performance level to level of arousal. J. Exp. Psychol., *54*, 54-61, 1957.

1064. Stevenson, H. W.: Social reinforcement with children as a function of CA, sex of E and sex of S. J. Abnorm. Soc. Psychol., *63*, 147-154, 1961.

1065. Stevenson, H. W., and Allen, S.: Adult performance as a function of sex of experimenter and sex of subject. J. Abnorm. Soc. Psychol., *68*, 214-216, 1964.

1066. Stolnick, R. S., Liebert, R. M., and Hilgard, E. R.: The enhancement of muscular performance in hypnosis through exhortation and involving instructions. J. Personality, *33*, 37-44, 1965.

1067. Stoltz, H. R., and Stoltz, L. M.: Adolescent problems related to somatic variations. In *Adolescence*, 43rd Yearbook N.S.S.E. Part I. Chicago, University of Chicago Press, 1944.

1068. Stratton, G. M.: The control of another person by obscure signs. Psychol. Rev., *28*, 801-814, 1921.

1069. Stratton, G. M.: Vision without inversion of the retinal image. Psychol. Rev., *4*, 341-360; 463-481, 1897.

1070. Strickland, B. R.: Need approval and motor steadiness under positive and negative approval conditions. Percept. Motor Skills, *20*, 667-668, 1965.

1071. Strickland, B. R., and Jenkins, O.: Simple motor performance under positive and negative approval motivation. Percept. Motor Skills, *19*, 599-605, 1964.

1072. Strong, C. H.: Motivation related to performance of physical fitness tests. Res. Quart., *34*, 497-507, 1963.

1073. Stroud, J. B.: The role of muscular tension in stylus maze learning. J. Exp. Psychol., *14*, 606-631, 1931.

1074. Stroup, F.: Relationship between measurement of the field of motion perception and basketball ability in college men. Res. Quart., *28*, 113-118, 1957.

1075. Stuart, I. R., Breslow, A., Brechner, S., Ilyus, R. B., and Wolpoff, M.: The question of constitutional influence on perceptual style. Percept. Motor Skills, *20*, 419-420, 1965.

1076. Suddon, F. H.: Paced and self-paced performance on simple motor task. Percept. Motor Skills, *16*, 247-254, 1963.

1077. Sullivan, E. B.: Attitude in relation to learning. Psychol. Monogr., *36*, 169, 1927.

1078. Surwillow, W. W.: A new method of motivating human behavior in laboratory investigations. Amer. J. Psychol., *71*, 432-436, 1958.

1079. Swift, E. J.: Memory of a complex skillful act. Amer. J. Psychol., *16*, 131-133, 1905.

1080. Swift, E. J.: Memory of skillful movements. Psychol. Bull., *3*, 185-187, 1906.

1081. Swift, E. J.: Relearning a skillful act: An experimental study in neuro-muscular memory. Psychol. Bull., *7*, 17-19, 1910.

1082. Swift, E. J.: Studies in the psychology and physiology of learning. Amer. J. Psychol., *14*, 201-251, 1903.

1083. Szafran, J.: Changes in age and with exclusion of vision in performance at an aiming task. J. Exp. Psychol., *44*, 111-118, 1951.

1084. Szafran, J.: Experiments on the greater use of vision by older adults. In *Old Age in the Modern World*. Edinburgh, E. & S. Livingstone, Ltd., 1965, pp. 231-235.

1085. Szafran, J., and Welford, A. T.: On the relation between transfer and difficulty of initial task. Quart. J. Exp. Psychol., *2*, 88-94, 1950.

1086. Sziklai, C.: Effect of Body Position and Muscular Strain on Space Localization, as Measured by the Apparent Eye-line. Master's thesis, Clark University, Worcester, Mass., 1961.

1087. Tanner, J. M.: The physique of the Olympic athletes, Rome, 1960. In *International Research in Sports and Physical Education*, E. Jokl and E. Simon (Eds.). Springfield, Ill., Charles C Thomas, 1964.

1088. Taylor, G. E.: A Study to Determine the Influence of Training on Performance of Selected Second and Fifth Grade Children in the Throw for Distance and the Standing Broad Jump. Unpublished master's problem, University of Wisconsin, Madison, Wisconsin, 1953.

1089. Taylor, J. A.: A personality test for manifest anxiety. J. Abnorm. Soc. Psychol., *48*, 285-290, 1953.

1090. Taylor, J. A., and Spence, K. W.: The relationship of anxiety level to performance in serial learning. J. Exp. Psychol., *44*, 61-66, 1952.

1091. Templeton, W. B., Howard, I. P., and Lowman, A. E.: A passively generated adaptation to prismatic distortion. Percept. Motor Skills, *22*, 140-141, 1966.

1092. Teuber, H. L.: : Some alterations in behavior after cerebral lesions in man. In *Evolution of Nervous Control from Primitive Organisms to Man*, Allan D. Bass (Ed.). American Association for the Advancement of Science, Washington, D.C., *52*, 157-194, 1959.

1093. Thompson, M. E.: A study of reliabilities of selected gross muscular coordination test items. Hum. Resour. Res. Cent. Res. Bull., *52*, 128-140, 1952.

1094. Thorndike, E. L.: A note on the accuracy of discrimination of weights and lengths. Psychol. Rev., *16*, 340-346, 1909.

1095. Thorndike, E. L.: *Fundamentals of Learning*. New York, New York Teachers College, 1935.

1096. Thorndike, E. L.: *The Psychology of Wants, Interests and Attitudes*. New York, D. Appleton-Century Co., 1935.

1097. Thorndike, E. L., and Woodworth, R. S.: The influence of improvement in one mental function upon the efficiency of other functions. Psychol. Rev., *8*, 247-261, 1901.

1098. Thornton, G. R.: A factor analysis of tests designed to measure persistence. Psychol. Monogr., *51*, 1-42, 1939.

1099. Thorpe, J. A., and West, C.: Game sense and intelligence. Percept. Motor Skills, *29*, 326, 1969.

1100. Thune, J. B.: Personality of weightlifters. Res. Quart., *20*, 296-306, 1949.

1100a. Thurstone, L. L.: The perceptual factor. *Psychometrika*, 3, 1-17, 1938.

1101. Thurstone, L. L.: Some primary abilities in visual thinking. Chicago, University of Chicago, Psychometric Laboratory Report, 59, 1950.

1102. Thurstone, L. L.: The vectors of the mind. Psychol. Rev., *41*, 1-32, 1934.

1103. Tibbits, C., and Donahue, W.: *Aging in Today's Society*. Englewood Cliffs, N.J., Prentice-Hall, Inc., 1960.

1104. Tichener, E. B.: *A Beginner's Psychology*. New York, The Macmillan Co., 1916.

1105. Tolman, E. C.: *Purposeful Behavior in Animals and Men*. New York, The Century Co., 1932, p. 463.

1106. Tolman, E. C.: There is more than one kind of learning. Psychol. Rev., *56*, 144-155, 1949.

1107. Toppen, J. T.: Effect of size and frequency of money reinforcement on human operant (work) behavior. Percept. Motor Skills, *20*, 259-269, 1965.

1108. Toppen, J. T.: Money reinforcement and human operant (work) behavior in piecework-payment and time-payment comparisons. Percept. Motor Skills, *21*, 907-913, 1965.

1109. Tower, S. S.: In *The Precentral Motor Cortex*. 2nd ed., P. C. Bucy (Ed.). Urbana, Ill., University of Illinois Press, 1949, p. 149.

1110. Travis, L. E.: The effect of a small audience upon hand-eye coordination. J. Abnorm. Soc. Psychol., *20*, 142-146, 1925.

1111. Triplett, N.: The dynamogenic factors in pacemaking and competition. Amer. J. Psychol., *9*, 507-533, 1897-98.

1112. Tsai, J. C.: Shifting of distribution of practice in maze learning. J. Exp. Psychol., *40*, 639, 1950.

1113. Tschermak, S. S.: Uber Parallaktoskopie. Pflueger. Arch. Ges. Physiol., *241*, 454-469, 1939.

1114. Twining, W. E.: Mental practice and physical practice in learning a motor skill. Res. Quart., *20*, 432-435, 1949.

1115. Twitchell, T. E.: The automatic grasping responses of infants. Neuropsychologia, *3*, 247-259, 1965.

1116. Tyler, R. W.: Lateral dominance as a factor in learning selected motor skills. J. Motor Behav., *3*, 253-258, 1971.

1117. Uhrbrock, R. S.: Laterality of champion athletes. J. Motor Behav., *2*, 285-290, 1970.

1118. Ulrich, C.: Measurement of stress evidenced by college women in situations involving competition. Res. Quart., *28*, 160-172, 1957.

1119. Ulich, E.: Some experiments on the function of mental training in the acquisition of motor skills. Ergonomics, *10*, 411-419, 1957.
1120. Underwood, B. J.: *Experimental Psychology.* New York, Appleton-Century-Crofts, 1949.
1121. Underwood, B. J.: Interference and forgetting. Psychol. Rev., *64*, 49-60, 1957.
1122. Updegraff, R.: The Visual Perception of Distance in Young Children and Adults, a Comparative Study. University of Iowa Studies, Studies in Child Welfare, 4, 4, 1948.
1123. U.S. Department of the Army: A factor analysis of spatial relations items. Personal Res. Br. Rep., *31*, 978, 1952.
1124. Van Alstyne, D., and Osborne, E.: Rhythmic responses of Negro and white children, 2 to 6. Monogr. Soc. Res. Child Develop., *2*, 1948.
1125. Vandell, R. A., Davis, R. A., and Clugston, H. A.: The function of mental practice in the acquisition of motor skills. J. Gen. Psychol., *29*, 243-250, 1943.
1126. Vandenberg, S. G.: Factor analytic studies of the Lincoln-Oseretsky test of motor proficiency. Percept. Motor Skills, *19*, 23-41, 1964.
1127. VanderMeer, A. W:. The economy of time in industrial training: an experimental study of the use of sound films in the training of engine lathe operators. J. Educ. Psychol., *36*, 65-90, 1945.
1128. VanderMeer, A. W., and Cogswell, J.: Instructional Effect of the Film, "How to Operate the Army 16mm Sound Motion Picture Set." *Human Engineering Report SDC 269-7-29.* Special Devices Center, 1952.
1129. Vanek, M., and Cratty, B. J.: Ideomotor training of the athlete. In *Psychology and the Superior Athlete.* New York, The Macmillan Co., 1969, Chapter 5.
1130. Vanek, M., and Cratty, B. J.: *Psychology and the Superior Athlete.* Toronto, Canada, The Macmillan Co., 1970.
1131. Van Tilborg, P. W.: The retention of mental and finger maze habits. J. Exp. Psychol., *19*, 334-341, 1936.
1132. Vernon, M. D.: *A Further Study of Visual Perception.* New York, Cambridge University Press, 1954.
1133. Vernon, M. D.: *Human Motivation.* Cambridge, England, University Press, 1971.
1134. Vernon, P. E.: *Personality Tests and Assessments.* London, Methune, 1963.
1135. Vernon, P. E.: *The Structure of Human Abilities.* London, Methune, 1953.
1135a. Vickers, V., Poynyz, L., and Baum, M.: The brace scale used with young children. Res. Quart., *13*, 299-304, 1942.
1136. Vincent, W. J.: Transfer effects between motor skills judged similar in perceptual components. Res. Quart., *32*, 380-388, 1968.
1137. Von Neumann, J.: *The Computer and the Brain.* New Haven, Conn., Yale University Press, 1958.
1138. Walk, R. D., and Gibson, E. J.: A comparative and analytic study of visual depth perception. Psychol. Monogr., *75*, 15, 519, 1961.
1138a. Walker, R. N.: Body-build and behavior in young children. Body-build and nursery school teacher's ratings. Monogr. Soc. Res. Child Develop., *3*, 27, 84, 1952.
1139. Walker, R. N.: Measuring masculinity and femininity by children's game choices. Child Develop., *35*, 961-971, 1964.
1140. Wallace, M., and Robin, A.: Temporal experience. Psychol. Bull., *57*, 213-236, 1960.
1141. Wallach, H.: The role of head movements and vestibular and visual cues in sound localization. J. Exp. Psychol., *27*, 339-368, 1940.
1142. Walsh, M.: Prediction of motor skill attainment from early learning. Percept. Motor Skills, *17*, 263-266, 1963.
1143. Wang, T. L.: Influence of tuition in the acquisition of skill. Psychol. Monogr., *34*, 154, 1925.
1144. Wapner, S., and Heinz, W.: *Perceptual Development, An Investigation Within the Framework of Sensory-tonic Field Theory.* Worcester, Mass., Clark University Press, 1957.

17

1145. Wapner, S., Werner, H., and Chandler, K. A.: Experiments on sensory tonic field theory of perception. I. Effect of extraneous stimulation on the visual perception of verticality. J. Exp. Psychol., *42*, 341-343, 1951.

1146. Warden, C. J.: The distribution of practice in animal learning. Comp. Psychol. Monogr., *1*, 2, 1923.

1147. Warden, C. J.: The relative economy of various modes of attack in the mastery of a stylus maze. J. Exp. Psychol., *7*, 243-275, 1924.

1148. Wardweel, E.: Children's Reactions to Being Watched during Success and Failure. Unpublished doctoral thesis, Cornell University, Ithaca, N.Y., 1960.

1149. Washburn, S. L.: The new physical anthropology. *Transactions of the New York Academy of Sciences,* Series 2, v. XIII, No. 7, 298-304, 1966.

1150. Washburn, W. C.: The effects of physique and intra-family tension on self-concepts in adolescent males. J. Consult. Psychol., *26*, 460-466, 1962.

1151. Wassenaar, G. M. C.: The effect of general anxiety as an index of lability on the performance of various psychomotor tasks. J. Gen. Psychol., *71*, 351-357, 1964.

1152. Waterland, J. C.: The Effect of Mental Practice Combined with Kinesthetic Perception When the Practice Precedes Each Overt Performance of a Motor Skill. Unpublished master's thesis, University of Wisconsin, Madison, Wisconsin, 1956.

1153. Waterland, J. C., and Hellenbrandt, F. A.: Involuntary patterning associated with willed movement performed against progressively increasing resistance. Amer. J. Phys. Med., *43*, 13-30, 1964.

1154. Waters, R. H., and Poole, G. B.: The relative retention values of stylus and mental habits. J. Exp. Psychol., *16*, 429-434, 1933.

1155. Watkins, D. L.: Motion pictures as an aid in correcting baseball batting faults. Res. Quart., *34*, 228-233, 1963.

1156. Watson, J. B.: Experimental studies on the growth of emotions. Pediat. Sem., *32*, 328-348, 1925.

1157. Weatherly, D.: Self-perceived rate of physical maturation and personality in late adolescence. Child Develop., *35*, 1197-1210, 1964.

1158. Webb, W. W.: Massed versus distributed practice in pursuit-rotor learning. J. Gen. Psychol., *8*, 272-278, 1933.

1159. Weber, A. O.: Estimation of time. Psychol. Bull., *30*, 233-252, 1933.

1160. Weber, C. O.: The properties of space and time in kinesthetic field of force. Amer. J. Psychol., *38*, 597-606, 1927.

1161. Weber, C. O., and Dallenbach, K. M.: Properties of space in kinesthetic fields of force. Amer. J. Psychol., *41*, 95-105, 1929.

1162. Weber, M. E.: Development of a Conceptual Model of Human Movement from Endocrine and Perceptual Theory with Analysis of the Effect of Aberrations on Movement. Doctoral dissertation, University of California, Los Angeles, Calif., 1960.

1163. Wechsler, D., and Hartogs, R.: The clinical measurement of anxiety. Psychiat. Quart., *19*, 618, 1945.

1164. Weinberg, D. R., Guy, D. E., and Tupper, R. W.: Variation of past feedback interval in simple motor learning. J. Exp. Psychol., *67*, 98-99, 1964.

1165. Weiner, B.: The experimental study of achievement motivation. Bulletin, National Association of Secondary-School Principals, No. 323, December, 1967.

1166. Weinstein, C.: Tactile sensitivity of the phalanges. Percept. Motor Skills, *14*, 351-354, 1962.

1167. Weinstein, S., Sersen, E. A., Fisher, L., and Weisinger, M.: Is reference necessary for visual adaptation? Percept. Motor Skills, *18*, 641-648, 1964.

1168. Weissman, A.: Retrograde amnesia effect of supramaximal electroconvulsive shock on one-trial acquisition in rats. J. Comp. Physiol. Psychol., *57*, 248-250, 1964.

1169. Weitzman, B.: A figural after-effect produced by a phenomenal dichotomy in a uniform contour. J. Exp. Psychol., *66*, 195-200, 1963.

1170. Weitzenhoffer, A. M.: *Hypnotism, An Objective Study in Suggestibility.* New York, John Wiley & Sons, Inc., 1964.
1171. Welch, M.: Prediction of motor skill attainment from early learning. Percept. Motor Skills, *17*, 263-266, 1963.
1172. Welch, M., and Henry, F. M.: Individual differences in various parameters of motor learning. J. Motor Behav., *3*, 78-85, 1971.
1173. Welford, A. T.: *Aging and Human Skill.* New York, Oxford University Press, 1958.
1174. Welford, A. T.: *Skill and Age, An Experimental Approach.* New York, The Nuffield Foundation, Oxford University Press, 1951.
1175. Welford, A. T.: Stress and achievement. Aust. J. Psychol., *17*, 1-11, 1965.
1176. Welker, W. I.: Effects of age and experience on play and exploration of young chimpanzees. J. Comp. Physiol. Psychol., *49*, 223-234, 1956.
1177. Welker, W. I.: Some determinants of play and exploration in chimpanzees. J. Comp. Physiol. Psychol., *49*, 84-90, 1956.
1178. Wells, W. R.: Expectancy versus performance in hypnosis. J. Gen. Psychol., *35*, 99-119, 1947.
1179. Wenger, M. A.: An attempt to appraise individual differences in level of muscular tension. J. Exp. Psychol., *32*, 213-225, 1943.
1180. Wenger, M. A.: Muscular processes and personality. Child Develop., *9*, 261-276, 1938.
1181. Wenger, M. A., Jones, F. N., and Jones, M. H.: *Physiological Psychology.* New York, Holt, Rinehart & Winston, 1956.
1182. Werner, H.: Motion and motion perception: a study on vicarious functioning. J. Psychol., *19*, 317-327, 1945.
1183. Werner, H., and Wapner, W.: Sensory-tonic field theory of perception. J. Personality, *18*, 88-107, 1949.
1184. Werner, H., and Wapner, W.: Toward a general theory of perception. Psychol. Rev., *59*, 324-338, 1952.
1185. Werner, H., Wapner, W., and Chandler, K. A.: Experiments on sensory-tonic field theory of perception. II. Effect of supported and unsupported tilt of body on the visual perception of verticality. J. Exp. Psychol., *42*, 346-350, 1951.
1186. Wertheimer, M.: Untersuchungen zur Lehre von der Gestalt, II. Psychol. Forsch., *4*, 301-350, 1923.
1187. Wertheimer, M., and Leventhal, C. M.: Permanent satiation phenomena with kinesthetic figural after-effects. J. Exp. Psychol., *55*, 255-257, 1958.
1188. Weybrew, B. B.: Accuracy of time estimation and muscular tension. Percept. Motor Skills, *17*, 118, 1963.
1189. Weymouth, F. W.: Visual acuity of children. In *Vision of Children*, M. J. Hirsch and R. E. Wick (Eds.). Philadelphia, Chilton, 1963.
1190. Weyner, N., and Zeaman, D.: Team and individual performances on a motor learning task. J. Gen. Psychol., *55*, 127-142, 1956.
1191. White, B. L., and Held, R.: Plasticity of Sensorimotor Development in the Human Infant. Paper presented at the American Association for the Advancement of Science, Cleveland, Ohio, 1963.
1192. Whitley, G.: The Effect of Mental Rehearsal on the Acquisition of Motor Skill. Unpublished dissertation for diploma in education, University of Manchester, Manchester, England, 1962.
1193. Whiting, H. T. A.: *Acquiring Ball Skill: A Psychological Interpretation.* London, G. Bell and Sons, Ltd., 1969.
1194. Whiting, H. T. A.: Training in a continuous ball throwing and catching task. Ergonomics, *11*, 375-382, 1968.
1195. Whiting, H. T. A., Alderson, G. J. K., Cocup, D., Hutt, J. W. R., and Renfrew, T. P.: Level of Illumination and Performance in a Simulated Table-Tennis Task. Unpublished paper, Physical Education Department, University of Leeds, Leeds, England, 1971.

1196. Whiting, H. T. A., Cormack, W., and Hirst, F.: The Effect of Warm-up on the Visual Acuity of Squash Players. Unpublished paper, Physical Education Department, University of Leeds, Leeds, England, 1968.

1197. Whiting, H. T. A., and Hutt, J. W. R.: An Analysis of Perceptual Judgments of Ball Flights in Terms of Personality and Ability in a Simulated Table-Tennis Task. Unpublished paper, Physical Education Department, University of Leeds, Leeds, England, 1971.

1198. Whitley, J. D.: Effects of practice distribution on learning a fine motor task. Res. Quart., *41*, 576-583, 1970.

1199. Widdop, J.: Effects of motor training on trainable retardates. Unpublished manuscript, Department of Physical Education, McDonald College, McGill University, Canada, 1963.

1200. Wiebe, V. R.: A Factor Analysis of Tests of Kinesthesis. Doctoral dissertation, University of Iowa, Iowa City, Iowa, 1956.

1201. Wieg, E. L.: Bilateral transfer in the motor learning of young children and adults. Child Develop., *3*, 247-267, 1932.

1202. Wiener, N.: *Cybernetics,* 2nd ed. New York, MIT Press, 1961.

1203. Wiest, W. M., Porter, L. W., and Grisselli, E. E.: Individual proficiency and team performance. J. Appl. Psychol., *45*, 435-440, 1961.

1204. Wild, M. R.: The behavior pattern of throwing and some observations concerning its course of development in children. Res. Quart., *9*, 20-24, 1938.

1205. Wilson, M. F.: The Relative Effect of Mental Practice and Physical Practice in Learning the Tennis Forehand and Backhand Drives. Doctoral dissertation, State University of Iowa, Ames, Iowa, 1960.

1206. Wilkinson, D., and Adrian, P.: Visual-motor control loop: a linear system? J. Exp. Psychol., *89*, 250-257, 1971.

1207. Williams, G. W.: The effect of hypnosis on muscular fatigue. J. Abnorm. Soc. Psychol., *24*, 318-329, 1929.

1208. Williams, H.: Neurological concepts and perceptual-motor behavior. In *New Perspectives of Man in Action,* R. C. Brown and B. J. Cratty (Eds.). Engle-Cliffs, N.J., Prentice-Hall, Inc., 1969.

1209. Willington, A. M., and Strickland, B. R.: Need for approval and simple motor performance. Percept. Motor Skills, *21*, 879, 884, 1967.

1210. Wilson, M., Wilson, W. A., Jr., and Chiang, H. M.: Formation of tactile learning sets. J. Comp. Physiol. Psychol., *56*, 732-734, 1963.

1211. Winograd, S.: Relationship of timing and vision to baseball performance. Res. Quart., *13*, 481-493, 1942.

1212. Wissler, C.: The correlation of mental and physical tests. Psychol. Rev. Monogr. Suppl. 3, 1901.

1213. Witkin, H. A.: Perception of body position and of the position of the visual field. Psychol. Monogr., *63*, 1-99, 1949.

1214. Witkin, H. A.: The nature and importance of individual differences in perception. J. Personality, *18*, 145-170, 1949.

1215. Witkin, H. A.: Perception of the upright when the force acting on the body is changed. J. Exp. Psychol., *40*, 93-106, 1950.

1216. Witkin, H. A.: Further studies of perception of the upright when the force acting on the body is changed. J. Exp. Psychol., *43*, 9-20, 1952.

1217. Witkin, H. A., and Asch, S. E.: Studies in space orientation. IV. Further experiments on perception of the upright with displaced visual fields. J. Exp. Psychol., *38*, 762-782, 1948.

1218. Wolf, S., Cardon, P. V., Shepard, E. M., and Wolff, H. G.: *Life Stress and Essential Hypertension, A Study of Circulatory Adjustments in Man.* Baltimore, The Williams & Wilkins Co., 1955.

1219. Woodruff, B., and Helson, H.: Torque: A new dimension in tactile-kinesthetic activity. Amer. J. Psychol., *78*, 271-277, 1965.

1220. Woodworth, R. S.: The accuracy of voluntary movement. Psychol. Rev. Monogr. Suppl. 3, 114, 1899.

1221. Wooldridge, D. E.: *The Machinery of the Brain.* New York, McGraw-Hill Book Company, 1963.
1222. Woodson, W. E.: *Human Engineering Guide for Equipment Design.* Berkeley, Calif., University of California Press, 1956.
1223. Woodward, P.: Experimental study of transfer of training in motor learning. J. Appl. Psychol., *27*, 12-32, 1943.
1224. Woodworth, R. S.: Accuracy of voluntary movement. Psychol. Monogr., *3*, 3, 1899.
1225. Woodworth, R. S.: *Dynamics of Behavior.* New York, Henry Holt & Co., 1958, p. 403.
1226. Woodworth, R. S.: *Experimental Psychology.* New York, Henry Holt & Co., 1938.
1227. Worthy, M.: Eye-darkness, Race, and Self-paced Athletic Performance. Paper presented at the Southeastern Psychological Association Meeting, Miami, Florida, 1971.
1228. Worthy, M., and Markle, A.: Racial differences in reactive versus self-paced sports activities. J. Personality Soc. Psychol., *16*, 439-443, 1970.
1229. Wundt, W. M.: *Physiological Psychology.* Leipzig, 1874.
1230. Wysocki, B. A., and Whitney, E.: Body image of crippled children as seen in draw-a-person test behavior. Percept. Motor Skills, *21*, 499-504, 1965.
1231. Yensen, R.: A factor influencing motor overflow. Percept. Motor Skills, *20*, 967-968, 1965.
1232. Young, O. C.: A study of kinesthesis in relation to selected movements. Res. Quart., *16*, 277-287, 1945.
1233. Young, O. G.: Rate of learning in relation to spacing of practice periods in archery and badminton. Res. Quart., *25*, 231, 1954.
1234. Young, P. T.: *Motivation and Emotion.* New York, John Wiley & Sons, Inc., 1961.
1235. Zamora, E. N., and Kaelbling, R.: Memory and electroconvulsive therapy. Amer. J. Psychiat., *64*, 122, 1965.
1236. Zarron, L. J.: Maternal deprivation: toward an empirical and conceptual evaluation. Psychol. Bull., *58*, 459-490, 1961.
1237. Zartman, E. N., and Cason, H.: The influence of an increase in muscular tension on mental efficiency. J. Exp. Psychol., *17*, 671-679, 1934.
1238. Zeaman, D., and House, B. J.: The relation of IQ and learning. In *Learning and Individual Differences.* Columbus, Ohio, Charles E. Merrill Books Co. 1967, Chapter 9.
1239. Zeaman, D., and Kaufman, H.: Individual differences and theory in a motor learning task. Psychol. Monogr., *69*, 14, 1955.
1240. Zegers, R. T.: Monocular movement—parallax thresholds as functions of field size, field position and speed of stimulus movement. J. Psychol., *26*, 477-498, 1948.
1241. Zeigarnik, B.: Ulber das Behalten von erledigten und unerledigten Handlungen. Psychol. Forsch., *9*, 1-85, 1927.
1242. Zigler, E., and Kanzer, P.: The effectiveness of two classes of reinforcers on the performance of middle and lower class children. J. Personality, *30*, 155-163, 1962.
1243. Zigler, M. J., and Barrett, R.: A further contribution to the tactual perception of form. J. Exp. Psychol., *10*, 184-192, 1927.
1244. Zipf, S. G.: Effects of probability of reward and speed requirements on human performance. J. Exp. Psychol., *65*, 106-107, 1966.
1245. Zuckerman, J. V.: Commentary Variations: Level of Verbalization, Personal Reference, and Phase Relations in Instructional Films on Perceptual-Motor Tasks. *Technical Report SDC 269-7-4.* Special Devices Center, 1949.
1246. Zuckerman, J. V.: Effects of variations in commentary upon the learning of perceptual-motor tasks from sound motion pictures. Amer. Psychol., *5*, 363-364, 1950.
1247. Zunich, M.: Child behavior and parental attitudes. J. Psychol., *62*, 41-46, **1966.**

INDEX

Apparent movement, 124
Appley, M. H., 312, 446
Approval, sex differences and, 280
Approximation of skill, 407
Archer, E. J., 383, 385, 397, 471
Archery, 365
Areal factor in movement, 182
Argyle, M., 200, 440
Arnoult, M. D., 440
Aronfreed, J., 464
Arousal, 219, 273, 436
  motivation and, 264
Arps, G. F., 158, 160, 440
Arrowwood, J., 279
Asch, S., 274, 440, 486
Ascoli, K. M., 415, 440
Ashoff, J., 440
Associative fusion, 49
Associative theories of learning, 339
Asymmetries in movement, 252
Athletes, fears of, 293
  intelligence in, 251
  nonathletes vs., perceptual differences
    in, 141
  measurement of simple and complex
    reaction times of, 26
  relaxation training and, 109
  visual perception and, 136
Athletic ability and depth perception, 140
Athletic experience, 211
Athletic performance and hand pref-
  erence, 253
Athletic skill and kinesthesis, 107
Athletics, adolescent motives and, 232
  anxiety and, 293
Atkinson, J. W., 260, 261, 440
Attention, improvement of printing skill
  and, 408
  motor performance of retardates and,
    250
  retention and, 405
Attention level and single cell learning,
  323
Attention span and kinesthetic training,
  109
Attneave, F., 440
Aubert, H., 125, 440
Audience, effect of, 275
  personality of performers and, 278
  size of, and performance, 276
Audio-visual teaching of motor skill, 154
Auditory perception and space perception,
  134
Auditory space, 135
Augmenters, 63
Ausubel, D. P., 292, 440
Autokinetic effect, 124

Bachman, J. D., 223, 440
Badminton, 362, 365
  transfer and, 398
  trial and error learning in, 147
Bahrick, H. P., 102, 441, 453
Bakan, P., 105, 441
Baker, B. L., 472
Baker, K. E., 60, 395, 441, 454
Baker, R., 385, 397
Balance, 210, 237
  anatomy of, 111
  measurement of, 367
Ball interception, development of, 73
Ball juggling, bilateral transfer and, 394
Ball skill(s), development of catching be-
    haviors in, 73
  evaluation of, 133
  knowledge of mechanical principles of,
    151
Ball tracking, evaluation of, 132
Bannister, H., 137, 441
Barber, T. X., 441
Barch, A. M., 135
Bardach, J. L., 441
Barrett, R., 113
Barsch, R., 83
Bartley, S. H., 113, 266, 441
Barton, J. W., 362, 441
Baseball and transfer of training, 396
Baseball ability and perceptual qualities,
  137
Baseball batting and visual qualities, 137
Basketball skills, 362
  mental practice and, 376
  teaching of, by films, 155
  transfer and, 387
Basmajian, J. B., 22, 40, 330, 383, 441
Basowitz, H., 290, 295, 296, 303, 312
Bass, B. M., 256, 442
Bass, I. A., 442
Bastian, H. C., 91, 441
Batson, W. H., 441
Battig, W. F., 441
Batting, kinesthetic aftereffects and, 106
  visual qualities and, 138
Baum, M., 483
Bayley, N., 441
Bayton, J. A., 269, 441
Beach, B., 271
Beach, F. A., 442
Beam, J. C., 301, 442
Beardsley, D. C., 70, 442
Bechtoldt, H. P., 108, 357, 442
Behavioral primacy theory of motivation,
  259
Beier, E. G., 443
Bell, H. M., 160, 419, 442
Bender-Gestalt test, 297

Weist, W. M., 283, 486
Weitzenhoffer, A. M., 263, 485
Weitzman, B., 484
Welch, M., 485
Welker, W. I., 274, 484
Wellman, B. L., 237, 468
Wells, W. R., 263, 485
Wenger, M. A., 180, 305, 484
Werner, H., 70, 85, 86, 442, 450, 484, 485
Wertheimer, M., 54, 70, 105, 442, 445, 485
West, C., 482
Weybrew, B. B., 485
Weymouth, F. W., 485
Weyner, N., 485
White, B. L., 74, 234, 485
Whiting, H. T. A., 88, 132, 133, 143, 485
Whitley, G., 485
Whitley J. D., 375, 459, 485
Whitney, J., 205, 365, 487
Whittaker, J., 277, 473
Whole vs. part learning, complexity and, 362
  reminiscence and, 367
  sports skills and, 362
Whole vs. part practice, 153, 361
Whyte, E. D., 297, 442
Widdop, J., 109, 486
Wieg, E. L., 382, 386, 394, 486
Wild, M. R., 147, 486
Wilkinson, D., 486
Williams, G. W., 486
Williams, H. G., 73, 100, 101, 178, 179, 180, 449
Willington, A. M., 486
Wilson, A., 480
Wilson, I., 456
Wilson, M., 486
Wilson, M. F., 486
Wilson, W. A., 376, 486
Winograd, S., 137, 486

Wissler, C., 486
Witkin, H. A., 486
Wolf, K. M., 480
Wolf, S., 295, 299, 486
Wolff, H. G., 486
Woodruff, B., 486
Woodson, W. E., 487
Woodward, P., 384, 487
Woodworth, R. S., 18, 19, 101, 259, 260, 274, 344, 382, 393, 486
Wooldridge, D. E., 335, 487
Work and rewards, 268
Work methods and motor learning, 348
Work-rest ratio, 367
Worthy, B., 244
Worthy, M., 487
Wrestling and kinesthetic acuity, 108
Wrist-finger speed, 209
Writing, history of research in, 19
Wundt, W. M., 19, 49, 53, 98, 487
Wylie, R. C., 385, 441
Wysocki, B. A., 487

Yates, E. M., 396, 464
Yensen, R., 487
Young, O. C., 365, 487
Young, P. T., 256, 274, 487
Yuwiler, A., 335, 451

Zaffy, D. J., 463
Zamora, E. N., 487
Zarron, L. J., 487
Zartman, N., 306, 487
Zavala, A., 454
Zeaman, D., 250, 336, 462, 485, 487
Zegers, R. T., 128, 487
Zeigarnik, B., 423, 487
Zigler, E., 113, 487
Zipf, S. G., 487
Zubin, J., 465
Zuckerman, J. V., 487
Zunich, M., 487